THE CAUCASUS AND THE OIL

The German-Soviet War in the Caucasus 1942/43

by Wilhelm Tieke
Translated by Joseph G. Welsh

J.J. Fedorowicz Publishing

THE CAUCASUS AND THE OIL
The German-Soviet War in the Caucasus 1942/43

By Wilhelm Tieke
An English translation by Joseph G. Welsh

Copyright 1995 by
J.J. Fedorowicz Publishing

Originally Published in German as
Der Kaukasus und das Öl
Der Deutsch-sowjetische Krieg in Kaukasien 1942/43
by
Munin Verlag Gmbh, Osnabrück

Published by
J.J. Fedorowicz Publishing Inc.
106 Browning Blvd.
Winnipeg, Manitoba
Canada R3K 0L7
(204) 837-6080

Printed in USA
ISBN 0-921991-23-1

Typesetting by George R. Bradford

Printed and Bound by
Publishers Press

PUBLISHER'S ACKNOWLEDGEMENTS

We wish to thank the following individuals who have contributed to the publishing of this book.
Joseph Welsh – Translation
Susan Bradford – Proof Reading

We also wish to thank you the reader for purchasing this book, and all those of you who have purchased our other books, and have written us with your kind words of praise and encouragement. It gives us impetus to continue to publish translations of the best German books and specially commissioned books, as you can see by the additional books which are in preparation for publication in the near future. Other titles are either being negotiated or seriously contemplated, many as a result of your helpful proposals. Such proposals have also motivated us to pursue the start of a serious military art print series, focusing on the Waffen-SS and German armor. More on these in the near future, further suggestions are always welcome.

John Fedorowicz & Michael Olive

Books published by J.J. Fedorowicz Publishing
THE LEIBSTANDARTE (1 SS Panzer Division) volumes I, II, III and IV/1
EUROPEAN VOLUNTEERS (5 SS Panzer Division)
DAS REICH I (2 SS Panzer Division)
THE HISTORY OF PANZERKORPS GROSSDEUTSCHLAND I
OTTO WEIDINGER
OTTO KUMM
MANHAY, THE ARDENNES; CHRISTMAS 1944
ARMOR BATTLES OF THE WAFFEN-SS 1943-45
TIGER: THE HISTORY OF A LEGENDARY WEAPON 1942-45
HITLER MOVES EAST
TIGERS IN THE MUD
PANZER ACES
FOOTSTEPS OF THE HUNTER
HISTORY OF THE 12 SS PANZERDIVISION HITLERJUGEND
GRENADIERS (Kurt Meyer)
FIELD UNIFORMS OF THE GERMAN ARMY PANZER FORCES IN WW2
TIGERS IN COMBAT I
INFANTERIE ACES
FREINEUX AND LAMORMENIL – THE ARDENNES
THE CAUCASUS AND THE OIL

In preparation for publication in 1995
HISTORY OF THE PANZERKORPS HERMAN GORING
PANZER LEHR DIVISION (An Officer's Memoirs)
EAST FRONT DRAMA 1944
THE HISTORY OF PANZERKORPS GROSSDEUTSCHLAND 2
DAS REICH II
LUFTWAFFE ACES

J.J. Fedorowicz Publishing Inc.

SPECIAL THANKS

A very special thank you to our 2 friends; Jost Schneider
for securing the English rights, and Adrian Bowden for
securing the translation. Cheers!

CONTENTS

Involved in the Campaign in the Caucasus 1942/43 were:

Command Staffs:
Heeresgruppe A
Panzerarmee-Oberkommando 1
Panzerarmee-Oberkommando 4
Armeeoberkommado 17

Corps Staffs:
V. Armeekorps
LII. Armeekorps
XXXXIV. Jägerkorps
XXXXIX. Gebirgskorps
III. Panzerkorps
XXXX. Panzerkorps
LVII. Panzerkorps
Korpsstab Förster (with LVII. Pz.K.)

Large Formations:
3. Panzerdivision
13. Panzerdivision
23. Panzerdivision
16. Infanteriedivision (mot.)
5. SS-PzGrenadier Division WIKING
97. Jägerdivision
101. Jägerdivision
1. Gebirgsdivision
4. Gebirgsdivision
Korps Felmy
9.Infanteriedivision
46. Infanteriedivision
50. Infanteriedivision
73. Infanteriedivision
79. Infanteriedivision
98. Infanteriedivision
111. Infanteriedivision
125. Infanteriedivision
198. Infanteriedivision
298. Infanteriedivision
370. Infanteriedivision
153. Infanteriedivision

Smaller Formations:
Schweres Werferregiment 1
Weferregiment 52 and 54
Sicherungsregiment 4
Sturmgeschützbrigaden
    190, 191, 203, 210 and 249
Schwere Heeresartillerie-Abteilung
    731, 732 and 617
Kosakenregiment von Jungschulz

Allied Forces:
Rumänisches Kavalleriekorps with:
5., 6., and 9. Kavalleriedivision
2. and 3. rumänische Gebirgsdivision
10. and 19. rumänische Infanteriedivision
Schnelle slowakische Division

Luftwaffe:
Luftflotte 4
VIII. Fliegerkorps
IV. Fliegerkorps
I. Fliegerkorps
15. Flakdivision
9. Flakdivision
5. Luftwaffenfelddivision

Marines:
Kommandostab Admiral Schwarzes Meer
Seekommander Kaukasus
    (Hafenkommandanten, Geleitführer,
    Marine-Artillerie)

Naval Forces:
30. I-Bootflottille
3. and 30. Rämbootflottille
3. Art.-Trägerflottille
1., 3., 5., and 7. Landungsflottille
1. and 11. Schnellbootflottille
30. and 31. Geleitflottille
1. and 23. U-Jagdflottille

CAUCASUS, LAND AND PEOPLE

The Caucasus consists of a 500,000 square kilometer area (the Bundesrepublic of Germany = 240,000 square kilometers) between the Black and Caspian Seas. It is articulated by the Caucasus Mountain Range - in the north the Ziscaucasus, in the south the Transcaucasus.

The greatest portion of the northern foreground belongs to the enormous Russian Socialist Federated Soviet Republic.

The Transcaucasus consists of the three Socialist Soviet Republics of Azerbaidzan, with its capital Baku, Armenia, with its capital Erivan, and Georgia, with its capital Tiflis, officially Tblissi.

Geographically, the Caucasus belongs to Asia. The boundary is the Manych River and, in the south, the Turkish-Iranian border.

The Ziscaucasus has a European character. The western portion is crossed by the 907 kilometer long Kuban, which gives the fruitful Kuban region its name. The Kuban has hydrology facilities at some locations and flows into the Sea of Azov. Its wide delta is impressed with numerous lagoons and reeded moors. The Kuban has numerous tributaries. The most important city on the Kuban is Krasnodar.

The eastern portion of the Ziscaucasus is crossed by the major Kuma and Terek Rivers, which both flow into the Caspian Sea. The most important of these two is the 590 kilometer long Terek with its numerous tributaries.

The Manych Valley and Kalmuck Steppes, both in the eastern foreground of the Ziscaucasus, have a dry steppe climate. Streams and rivers mostly dry up in mid-summer or loose their current. The water courses then turn into a series of salt lakes and pools. Drinking water is scarce. The many deep wells give forth unpalatable water. The settlements are few and far in between.

The Caucasus Mountain Range is 1100 kilometers long and 100 to 200 kilometers wide. It stretches through the Caucasus. The Caucasus are folded mountains from the Tertiary period and are similar to the Alps. Their highest points are the 5633 meter high Elbrus and the 5043 meter high Kasbek.

In Russian Geography the Caucasus is subdivided as follows:

a) Western Caucasus with the sub-groups:

aa) Ponti Caucasus in the west, from Cape Anapa up to the 2853 meter high Fishty. A 220 kilometer long forested mountain range. This portion was designated as the Forested Caucasus in German military terminology.

bb) Abkhasi Caucasus in the east. The wildest and most beautiful part of all of the Caucasus, from Fishty up to the Chiper-Asau Pass, with the 4040 meter high Dombai-Ulgen and a length of 220 kilometers. This portion was designated as the High Caucasus, along with Elbrus, in German military terminology.

b) Central Caucasus from Chiper-Asau Pass (3267 meters) up to Krestovy Pass (Georgian Army Road, 2381 meters) with the 5198 meter high Dykhtau and a length of 190 kilometers.

Elbrus forms a volcanic mass isolated to the north from the main chain, which is generally accepted as being sub-ordered to the Central Caucasus.

c) East Caucasus from the 2381 meter high Krestovy Pass up to the descent into the Caspian Sea. The high point is the 4506 meter high Kchomis-Chala. It is 480 kilometers long.

The Transcaucasus is the southern foreground of the mountains with the main rivers of Rion in the west and Kura in the east.

The under-developed transport system resulted in the fact that ancient peoples maintained their native ways in the Caucasus. They can be divided into a southern group, with the Georgians, Migrelians and Swans. The northwestern group consists of the Abkhasians and Cherkessians and the northeastern group of the Arvans, Dargua, Ingush, Laks, Lesghier, Chechen, Uds and others.

Caucasia, in particular the Caucasus and Transcaucasus, is rich in mineral resources of all types. Oil production here totals 90% of the oil production in the Soviet Union. Besides the important Baku area (the center of the oil production region) the north Caucasian oil fields in Grosny/Malgobek, Maikop and Kievskoe are also important. In some places, the oil is pumped directly into the consuming provinces by long pipelines.

Introduction

After a stormy summer campaign and a costly and crisis-rich winter, the German Eastern Army stood with its allies on a 2800 kilometer long front from Murmansk on the Arctic Ocean down to Taganrog on the Sea of Azov during spring of 1942. Up to this point in time, the Soviets and the Germans had suffered considerable losses in men and equipment. However, the Soviet armies were unable to decisively tear open the German front in cooperation with their ally "Winter" and administer Hitler and his armies a defeat before Moscow, causing a subsequent withdrawal across the snow-covered terrain of the Soviet Union to the west, as the regiments of Tsarist Russia did to the "Grand Armee" of Napoleon I during the winter of 1812/13.

The German divisions had lost much valuable equipment, which could only be slowly replaced by increasing the output of the German war industries. The German Eastern Army had survived its first great crisis and was preparing to return to offensive operations. With the spring, the first transports arrived behind the front with new tanks and weapons. Train after train removed the panzer and motorized formations from their winter positions for refitting in the interior, replacing them with newly deployed or reformed infantry formations.

In the meantime, the German General Staff worked out plans which were to force the Soviet Union to its knees. The main effort was to lie in the south of the Eastern Front. The Soviet armies between the Don and Caucasus were to be destroyed and Germany would be prepared to take on its more far-reaching objectives after occupying the Kuban region and the Caucasian oil fields. Often the panzer and motorized forces could not be committed because of the shortage of fuel. Therefore, the opportunities for mobile warfare could not be fully exploited. This caused Hitler and his closest advisors to become concerned with the decisive "oil" factor. The oil, Caucasian oil, was a dream of Hitler's. He saw oil as being the key to success. All of his thoughts and plans revolved around oil. The German war objectives for summer 1942 were established in Directive Nr 41 from 5 April 1942. By holding Army Groups North and Center back, the main effort would be shifted to Army Group South. The great operational plan was outlined according to an analysis of German and Soviet forces. After the completion of peripheral operations and the capture of Sevastopol, the Kuban region and the Caucasus were established as the objectives, beginning from Voronezh and continuing to the south. The plan foresaw the advance of the 2nd Army and the 4th Panzer Army out of the Kursk area toward Voronezh; further advance of the 4th Panzer Army, to which the 6th Army was to be attached, to the southeast along the upper Don up to the Kalach area; the advance of the 17th Army and elements of the 1st Panzer Army out of the Rostov area and north along the lower Don to the east toward Kalach; formation of a small pocket west of the Oskol and on the Donets. The extended northern flank on the upper Don was to be secured by allied armies. The Soviet divisions of the South Front were to be destroyed in this pocket along the Don. The concentrated attack to the south into the Caucasus would ensue during the second phase of the operation.

The attack of the northern flank of Army Group South began in the direction of Voronezh on 28 June. The battle for the important communication center tied up considerable forces from the 4th Panzer Army. Luck and misfortune often changed by the hour. Hitler and von Bock were repeatedly faced with the question: would Voronezh be captured or not! Therefore, "Operation Blau" was already in disarray.

Additional offensive operations were conducted in sequence, however, there was little profit gained from the "small" pocket. The underestimation of the enemy led to failure and resulted in "drips" instead of "floods". On 7 July, Army Group South was divided into Army Group A (Feldmarschall List) and Army Group B (Feldmarschall von Bock).

In the meantime, the battle for Voronezh continued. Strong Russian formations tied up considerable elements of the 4th Panzer Army, which had to begin its attack to the southeast. The northern arm of the pincer was set in motion too late; this loss of time allowed Timoshenko's armies to withdraw to the east. After an argument between Hitler and the commander of Army Group B (formerly South), Feldmarschall von Bock, it was finally set in motion. Army Group B was taken over by Generaloberst Weichs.

The operational plan was changed an 13 July. The lead elements of Panzerarmee Hoth, which was located north of Millerovo and was to advance along the Don up to Kalach, were diverted to the south, in order to fix as many of the Russian divisions withdrawing from the Rostov area as possible. Only General- oberst Paulus' 6th Army continued to advance further to the east. In spite of this, the pocket formed in the Donets bend remained empty. The Soviet formations in front of the southern pincer (1st Panzer Army and elements of the 17th Army) were able to withdraw en masse. Hitler believed that the few formations destroyed represented the majority of the Soviet South Front divisions. However, the STAVKA, the Soviet High Command, had foiled the German offensive plans. Prominent Soviet marshals and English and American advisors were finally able to convince Stalin to abandon his "Halt-Stand-Die Strategy" and pay more attention to mobile warfare. If this necessarily led to great terrain losses, it did maintain Soviet combat strengths, since the main Soviet forces were evacuated from the German pockets before they were cut off.

Hitler followed these events from "Wehrwolf" Headquarters in the Vinnitsa forest. After the initial success he believed that the Russians were finished and he diverted seven combat capable divisions to Leningrad and France. On 23 July Hitler dictated Directive Nr. 45:

"1. The next mission of Army Group A is to encircle and destroy the enemy forces now fleeing across the Don in the area south and southeast of Rostov. In addition, strong mobile forces are to be dispatched to the southwest toward Tikhorets out of the bridgeheads that have been established in the Konstantinovskaya - Zymlyanskaya area. Infantry, jäger [light infantry] and mountain divisions are to be committed across the Don in the Rostov area.

The mission remains to sever the Tikhorets - Stalingrad rail line with advanced elements..."

And then, under numbers 2 and 3 of the Directive, followed the mission statement for Army Group A under Feldmarschall List:

"2. After the destruction of the enemy force groupings south of the Don, the most important mission of Army Group A is to capture the entire eastern coast of the Black Sea, denying the enemy the use of the Black Sea Fleet and the Black Sea harbors... With an additional battle group, which will be composed of all of the remaining mountain and jäger divisions, the crossing of the Kuban will be forced and the high ground near Maikop and Armavir will be captured...

"3. At the same time, a battle group, consisting of mobile formations, is to capture the Grosny area and dispatch a force to block the Ossetian and Georgian Army Road in the mountain passes. During the advance along the Caspian Sea, the Baku area is to be captured... The army group can count upon the later commitment of the Italian Alpine Corps.

These operations of Army Group A are designated with the cover name "Edelweiss".

"4. To Army Group B falls - as ordered - the mission of establishing a Don defense, destroying the force groupings in the Stalingrad area, capturing the city itself and blocking the land bridge between the Volga and Don.

In connection with this, mobile forces will be committed along the Volga with the mission of advancing as far as Astrakhan and blocking the main arm of the Volga there.

These operations of Army Group B are designated with the cover name "Fischreiher"..."

Directive 45 arrived at the headquarters of Feldmarschall List in Stalino on 25 July.

4

Feldmarschall List was born in Oberkirchberg in Württemburg in 1880. He began his soldier's career as a Fahnenjunker [officer candidate] in 1898. He served as a 1st Generalstabsoffizier [Operations Officer] during the First World War. List began the Second World War as a Generaloberst and a commander. He was the commander of an army during the French and Balkan Campaigns. After the termination of combat on Crete, Feldmarschall List became Wehrmachtsbefehlshaber Southeast and, after a short stint as a commander in the Scandinavian area, he finally became commander of Army Group A.

When, during the course of Operation "Edelweiss", the insufficiency of the force to fulfill the far-ranging mission was realized, he disapproved of the operation across the Western Caucasus. In addition, he later said: "My conscience and my soldiers would not allow me."

Feldmarschall List, an experienced soldier and army commander, doubted that the majority of the Soviet armies of the South Front were destroyed. Instead, he believed that they were scattered as indicated by the reports on the enemy situation from German intelligence. He regretted the lack of a concentrated main effort and disagreed with the dissipation of German forces by the widely separated objectives. He did not understand why the Italian Alpine Corps was following the 6th Army, when it could have been better utilized in assisting him in achieving his far-ranging objective. For the first time in the Eastern Campaign, his army group had a genuine mountain mission to master, which he had to conduct with two German and one Rumanian mountain division. However, the jäger divisions of Generaloberst Ruoff's 17th Army were not equipped nor trained for commitment in the mountains. The forcing of the mountains and passes finally proved to be an impossible mission for his few mountain units, while an entire Italian mountain corps was fighting on the Volga-Don plain.

The oil and the Caucasus were the determining factors. There was another. With one blow, the Allied transports through Iran (Persia) would be blocked. On 25 August 1941 two British and three Soviet divisions entered this country and conquered it after a four-day battle. On 30 August 1941, as Harry Hopkins met with Stalin as Roosevelt's representative, they agreed that, in addition to the Arctic Sea route, two transport routes would be established through Iran. British Prime Minister Churchill legitimized this step by stating: "In war, law means nothing." After the two transport routes were thrown open through Iran, supplies began flowing into the Soviet Union. In 1942, 705,529 tons were transported, 29.9% of total deliveries. In 1943, these increased to 1,606,979 tons or 33.5%. Next to obtaining the oil fields, the main objective of the German leadership during Operation "Edelweiss" was to stop this flow of material.

Plagued with doubts, the German army commanders ordered the attack. Operation "Edelwiess" was initiated. The German soldiers put all of their effort into the operation. The first Russian winter was forgotten. In front of them lay the objective, the Caucasus.

THE CAUCASUS

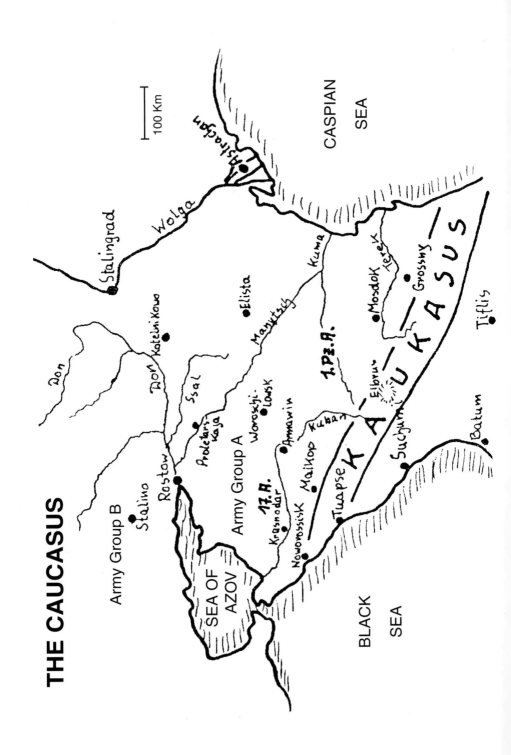

ROSTOV, GATEWAY TO THE CAUCASUS

73rd and 298th ID breakthrough - Nocturnal assembly in the anti-tank trenches in front of Sultan-Saly - "Adler an alle!" - Panzergruppe "Wiking" - Oberleutnant von Gaza's company captures the bridge - Kradschützenbataillon 43 and "Brandenburger" on the Bataisk Causeway

After the German attack formations of Army Group B reached the Millerovo area on the Don downstream from Voronezh, the Donets front set in movement. The phased German offensive plan now called for the attack of the two southern armies, the 1st Panzer Army and the 17th Army. According to this plan, strong panzer formations from the 1st Panzer Army were to attack along the lower course of the Don, join up with the panzer divisions of the 4th Panzer Army in the area south of Millerovo and encircle the forces of the Soviet Donets Front.

However, due to the barrier posed by the Donets, Don and Sal Rivers, the deployment was only half completed. As a result only one army pincer was able to move through the large elements of the 51st and 37th Soviet Armies to the east and south. On 13 July Hitler intervened and ordered the 1st Panzer Army to drive its formations, which were already located on the Donets north of Rostov, to the south, in order to help open the river crossings near Rostov. After the first week of the attack, the extensive plan had already began to come undone. The Russians, who were to be encircled in the great Don bend, had withdrawn behind the Don. Only rear guards stood and fought, utilizing the river as a barrier.

On 20 July the 4th Panzer Army (coming from the north) established bridgeheads across the Don near Zymlyanskaya and Konstantinovskaya with the 23rd Panzer Division and 29th ID (Mot.), while, on the same day, the 1st Panzer Army crossed the Donets with the 14th and 22nd Panzer Divisions on the inner flanks and drove on to the south toward Rostov. Therefore, the time for a frontal attack on Rostov had arrived.

The attack organization of the 17th Army, which was advancing on Rostov, was as follows: east of Taganrog near Sambeck the V Army Corps with the 73rd and 125th ID, to the rear was echeloned the LVII Panzer Corps with SS Division "Wiking" and 13th Panzer Division; north of the city was the III Panzer Corps with the 14th and 22nd Panzer Divisions. On 20 July the XXXXIX Mountain Corps headquarters was transferred into the Sambeck area where they took command over the formations of the V Army Corps. The 4th Mountain Division was deployed in second echelon in the Taganrog area.

The Soviet leadership was aware of the German attack plans (the offensive plan fell into their hands when a Fieseler-Storch was shot down with the 1st Generalstabsoffizier of the 23rd Panzer Division on board) and they had already foiled the German plans near Voronezh, which led to the delay of the entire remainder of the attack. At the beginning of July the commander of the Russian forces in the south, Marshal Timoshenko, ordered his troop commanders not to allow any more formations to be encircled. The stubborn holding and dying, which the Soviet leadership practiced during the first year in Russia, was now replaced by more flexible combat operations, which took the vastness of the region into consideration.

On the basis of the overall situation, the main forces of the South Front under Lieutenant General Malinovski evacuated Rostov and the region to the north and established a defense south of the river. Rostov, which had been transformed into a strong defensive bastion during months of hard work, was defended by only a few good formations.

Army Order Nr. 79 from Armeegruppe Ruoff gave the starting point for the attack on Rostov:

Armeegruppe Ruoff   A.Gef.St., 20/7/1942

Operations Section Nr. 2855/42 Secret.

Armeegruppe Order

1) Enemy situation remains unchanged. A withdrawal toward Rostov and toward the South Front up to the sea is expected at any time.

2) Lead attack elements of the 1st Panzer Army are advancing from Vladimirskaya toward Proletarskaya. The Bronitskiy bridgehead has been considerably expanded.

3) The Armeegruppe is to attack early on 21 July with Gruppe Kirchner to capture Rostov and continue the pursuit with the remaining forces.

4) Missions:

a) Gruppe Kirchner is to attack on 21 July in accordance with the special message from 19 July, Armeegruppe Ruoff, Ia/Nr. 2854/42 Secret. The attack is to begin at 0400 hours.

The advance of the 4th Mountain Division across the former 125th ID sector is now in question, due to the rapid advance of the 125th ID. The decision will be made by the Armeegruppe.

b) Gruppe Wetzel is to advance its left flank in order to cover the northern flank of Gruppe Kirchner. Otherwise, it is to advance along the Kuibyshev - Rostov road.

The 2nd Rumanian Mountain Division is to advance only as far as Novaya Nadezhda for the time being. The 4th Mountain Division has priority of march.

c) The 8th Italian Army is to finish clearing its area as soon as possible and regroup for deployment to the northeast. In addition, it is to dispatch one infantry division through Ivanovka - Asarovka into the Uspenka area on the evening of 21 July.

The march in this area will be regulated by the LII Army Corps headquarters.

d) The LII Army Corps mission remains unchanged.

The XI Army Corps is to deploy the 76th ID toward the western edge of Voroshilovgrad at the start on the evening of 21 July.

e) Gruppe von Schwedler is to continue the pursuit up to Eastern Sverdlovsk. It then is to be made available to the OKH [Army High Command]. The deployment route in the direction of Kamensk is to be reconnoitered.

f) The 3rd Rumanian Army mission remains unchanged. In accordance with the arrival of its formations, it is to take charge of the establishment of coastal defenses in the direction of Rostov.

5. Boundary lines:

a) Between Gruppe Wetzel and the LII Army Corps command: Platovo Knayasevskiy west - Lyatinskiy east - Generalskoe east.

b) Between LII Army Corps command and 1st Panzer Army: Biryukovo east.

6) Luftwaffe support mission remains unchanged. There is to be direct cooperation between IV Air Corps and Gruppe Kirchner.

7) Reconnaissance and air defense missions remain unchanged, the emphasis is on Gruppe Kirchner.

8) At 21 July at 0900 hours the Armeegruppe will be at Chistyakovo. The XXXXIX Mountain Corps evacuates all shelters assigned to the Armeegruppe no later than 21 July at 1200 hours.

The Commander
signed Ruoff

The attack on Rostov is recreated very accurately according to the records of Gruppe Ruoff. The daily report from 20 July at 2035 hours notes:

"On the right sector of the 298th ID is lively artillery destructive fire. 73rd ID: fire and detonations in front of the division sector indicates that the enemy is preparing to withdraw.

No report from 125th ID.

298th, 73rd and 125th Infantry Divisions taken over by the XXXXIX Mountain Corps."

In the morning report from 21 July 1942:

"298th and 73rd Infantry Divisions launched the attack at 0400 hours as ordered. 298th ID advancing against weak enemy resistance toward the hills east of Sambeck. 73rd ID reached the hills northwest of Sauzhenaya after an effective stuka attack."

What lays behind these sober descriptions? - At 0330 hours, the batteries of the 73rd and 298th Infantry Divisions battered the Soviet positions. Then the engineers assaulted. Wire obstacles and mine barriers were removed. The weak defenders were thrown back. The first gap was opened.

Rostov was surrounded by three defensive lines. A girdle of bunkers, antitank trenches and barriers within the city blocked all streets. The depth of the defensive field was approximately 40 kilometers, that of the bunker line was 25 kilometers.

The battalions of the 73rd and 298th Infantry Divisions advanced gradually along the Taganrog - Rostov road. During the afternoon the 13th Panzer

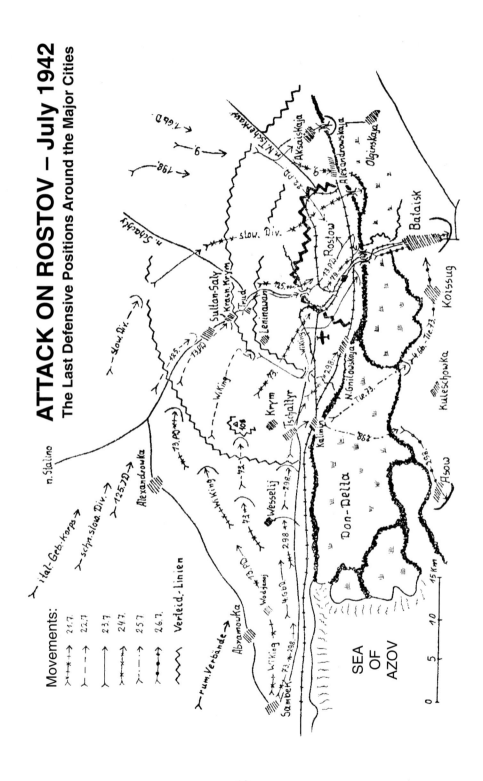

Division advanced through the gap and supported the 73rd ID with its tanks during the battle for the hills west of Vesseliy. However, the tanks then veered off in order to move to the north and reach the assigned assembly area between Aleksandrovka and Sultan Saly.

Behind the 13th Panzer Division advanced Pz.KGr. [Armored Battle Group] "Wiking", which was also subordinated to the 73rd ID. SS Division "Wiking" was only half assembled at this time. The formations under Oberführer Gille consisted of Pz.Abt., I/"Germania", I and II/"Nordland", III/5 SS AR, 12 Bttr.SS AR 5, as well as one engineer company and elements of Flakabteilung [Air Defense Battery] "Wiking". The main body of the division awaited trucks in the Uspenskaya area.

The showpiece of the "Wiking" was the newly organized Stubaf. [Sturmbannführer] Mühlenkamp Panzer Battalion, formerly commander of the Reconnaissance Battalion of the SS Division "Das Reich". In spite of considerable physical damage suffered in a short period of time, it developed into a unit with very high combat capability. The battalion, which was to go to "Das Reich", went to "Wiking", because it was capable of being committed at an earlier time. The soldiers of this new battalion were mainly combat veterans. They were retrained as tankers.

Pz.KGr. "Wiking" fought with the enemy rear guard all afternoon. When Stubaf. Mühlenkamp entered a T-shaped Balka (terrain incision) with his tanks, four sheepdogs suddenly chased his tanks. These were the so-called mine-dogs, which were directed at the sound of vehicles and carried explosives on their backs. The fuse detonated the explosives at the slightest touch. This signified death and destruction for both parties. At the last moment, Mühlenkamp's tank guns fired and killed the dog attacking the tank next to him, which was driven by Ustuf. [Untersturmführer] Nikolussi-Leck.

At another location, a tank ran over a mine. A track and the oil pan were torn through and the tank driver was wounded. These were two incidents that were new to the tankers of "Wiking". At nightfall, Pz.KGr. "Wiking" took up a hasty defense on the steppes in front of the first anti-tank trenches.

In the meantime, the 13th Panzer Division also advanced further to the north. At 1600 hours a tank trench east of Hill 119.5 was crossed by elements of the 4th Panzer Regiment. Balkas and field positions could not stop the momentum of the attack group. Then it became dark. The battle group of the 13th Panzer Division continued to roll to the north in order to reach the assigned assembly area east of Aleksandrovka, toward the apex of the Tusselov bend. Oberst Olbrich, commander of the 4th Panzer Regiment and leader of the forward-most battle group, ordered a halt when he believed he had reached the assembly area. Generalleutnant Herr, commander of the 13th Panzer Division came forward. The officers conferred. A study of the terrain and the map revealed that they had reached the assembly area. The commanders ordered the 13th Panzer Division to establish a hasty defense. During the night, officers of the 13th Panzer Division and "Wiking" discussed the attack for the following day.

The 13th Panzer Division also was combat ready with two panzer battalions, three [infantry] battalions and elements of supporting weapons. Its showpiece was the re-equipped I/66 Armored Battalion.

Its organization:

Battalion staff and communications platoon in SPW [armored infantry vehicle]. Three panzergrenadier companies to each troop, mounted on SPW. Each company had three panzergrenadier platoons with 3.7 cm anti-tank guns mounted on SPW. Each platoon had three SPW with one machine-gun each. Moreover, each panzergrenadier company had one heavy platoon with two SPW equipped with 7.5 cm cannon, two SPW with 8 cm mortars and two SPW with one heavy machine-gun platoon or one heavy machine-gun group and one each panzergrenadier engineer platoon in four SPW.

This organization and armament demonstrated the extremely high firepower and mobility of a SPW battalion.

In the daily report from Armeegruppe Ruoff, we read under 21 July 2015 hours:

"...298th ID in Vesseliy and south of there. 73rd ID on Hills 107.6 and 116.9. The forward-most battle group of "Wiking" is also there."

During the night of 22 July preparations were made for the attack on the following morning.

After a quiet night, the battalions of the 73rd and 298th Infantry Divisions attacked at 0400 hours as planned. At 1400 hours the 298th ID reached the anti-tank trenches 7 kilometers east of Vesseliy with two regiments and bogged down there in strong defensive fire. After renewing the attack, they threw the enemy forces out of the anti-tank trench positions at Chaltyr.

At 0800 hours General von Bünau's 73rd ID had already bogged down east of the intersection north of Vesseliy in heavy defensive fire. At 1245 hours they resumed the attack and penetrated into the anti-tank trenches. The attack bogged down near Hill 108 in front of strong bunker positions.

The records of the commander of the panzer battalion, Stubaf. Mühlenkamp, explain the attack along the "Wiking" axis on 22 July as follows:

"The attack order, which the battalion received from the division commander, Generalmajor der Waffen SS Steiner, paid particular attention to the threat on the right flank. Here, the enemy had strongly fortified concrete works with gun bunkers. The division attack order noted that the attack would only succeed if this threat was removed. Artillery and Luftwaffe support was also assigned."

Mühlenkamp described the terrain and his plans:

"The terrain was wide, undulating, typical tank terrain with trench and barbed wire obstacles. We had demolition commandos from the assault engineers who were to breach these wire obstacles. Artillery Battalion Schlamelcher was to be subordinated to us. The battalion was not to be deployed in position if we believed that enemy resistance would require a stronger type of artillery."

The threat to the right flank, which Mühlenkamp referred to in his report, was the high ground near Vesseliy, around which fought the 73rd ID.

What was happening in the meantime in the 13th Panzer Division area of operations?

The hasty defense set up by this division during the night had dispersed on the morning of 22 July. During the advance of the forward-most elements, a Russian group was captured which had the mission of bringing in some prisoners. Therefore, friend and foe alike were in the dark as to the location, strength and intent of their enemy.

After a short time, the first group of the 13th Panzer Division stood at a wire obstacle, 40 meters behind it was the first anti-tank trench. Now it was clear to the officers that the nocturnal assembly area was already in full view of the enemy. Events then occurred in rapid succession.

By dawn the engineer platoon of the I/66 cut a lane through the wire obstacle and reached the anti-tank trench. The enemy initiated defensive fire. The engineer platoon penetrated into the strong point and fell under concentrated fire. Major Brux, commander of the I/66 Pz.Gren.Rgt, moved forward and was shot out of his SPW two times. In the meantime, the engineers were filling in the anti-tank trenches. A strong enemy bunker, which stood directly on the anti-tank trench, was knocked out of action by explosives fastened to poles. The SPW battalion and tanks from the 4th Panzer Regiment arrived in support. Then the way was opened!

At 0925 hours the first tanks and SPW rolled through the filled-in anti-tank trenches. The 13th Panzer Division gradually reorganized for combat. During the attack, enemy positions were overran, withdrawing enemy infantry were overtaken and destroyed. The first prisoners were sent to the rear. Enemy batteries were taken by surprise.

The beginning of the attack was delayed in the "Wiking" area of operations. Then the first stuka attack was finally conducted on the strong fortifications on the right flank. Bombs and dust limited visibility. Mühlenkamp now believed the time had come. He attacked without waiting for the order from the division. His radio burst into operation. Over the ether came the order: "Adler an alle! [Eagle to all] Unlimber cannon - start engines - close hatches - clear for combat!" The battalion advanced in a wedge; Hstuf. [Hauptsturmführer] Schnabel's first panzer company was in the lead, followed by Ostuf. [Obersturmführer] Flügel's 2nd and elements of the 3rd (heavy) company. The main body, fully equipped with Pz. IV (7.5 cm cannon) waited.

They halted in front of the first anti-tank trenches. Engineers advanced under the cover of tank fire. One engineer gives a lively account of what followed:

"The lead elements of the panzer battalion reached the anti-tank trenches and the tanks deployed along the trenches in order to give the engineers covering fire. Oscha. [Oberscharführer] Holzinger's engineer group slalomed between the tanks to the front. They cautiously negotiated a mine field and burst into the depth. The first charges were placed onto the walls of the trenches. They were detonated! The trench walls fell into each other. In the meantime, one of the grenadier companies from I/"Germania" arrived. They crossed the trench and secured the other side. A Luftwaffe construction unit towed tree trunks forward. They were utilized to fortify the crossing. In the meantime, engineers removed mines from the opposite side and designated a lane. Then the first tanks rolled across the newly-created crossing. The way for Pz.KGr. "Wiking" was open!"

Mühlenkamp's panzer battalion advanced toward Leninavan, followed by the I/"Germania" under Stubaf. Dieckmann. Mortal danger lay in ambush. Soviet flame-thrower obstacles were crossed.

The "Wiking" attack bogged down west of Trud at a fortified line on either side of Krasniy Krim. Two companies of the I/"Germania" attacked. However, the resistance from the hill was too strong. The attack was called off until the attack of the left neighboring division, the 13th Panzer Division, came on line.

The 13th Panzer Division continued to gain ground. It was a magnificent sight: Tanks, SPW, motorized infantry and armored artillery! Suddenly an electronically fused mine zig-zagged for 250 meters through the forward-most battle group without causing any damage. In the evening twilight, two columns of enemy rocket launchers appeared. The order was given: "Forward march - pursue!" The rocket launchers took up positions and fired a salvo into the German battle group: the shells destroyed two SPW. A portion of the truck mounted rocket launchers were rammed by the armored vehicles of the 13th Panzer Division. The rest raced in the direction of Rostov. As instructed, the 13th Panzer Division set up a hasty defense in the vicinity of Trud. During the night, the 4th Armored Engineer Battalion constructed a crossing over the anti-tank trenches south of Trud. The advance of the 13th Panzer Division, as well as that of "Wiking", continued over it. The second belt of anti-tank trenches was overcome. Pz.KGr. "Wiking", which was also called Gruppe Gille after its leader, set up a hasty defense west of Leninavan.

The daily report of Armeegruppe Ruoff from 22 July at 2300 hours notes:

"298th ID threw the enemy back southeast of Vesseliy toward the Chaltyr anti-tank trench positions. 73rd ID, after fierce combat, has expanded the penetration position on the anti-tank trenches and is advancing on Hill 108.4. 125th ID has reached Sultan Saly with its forward-most regiment. 13th Panzer Division, after breaking through the 1st anti-tank trench positions, threw the enemy back northwest of Sultan Saly and, after breaking through the 2nd positions, its lead elements have reached Trud. "Wiking" is echeloned on the right to the rear, its lead panzer elements reached the area 5 kilometers south of Sultan Saly (west of Leninavan) at 1700 hours."

The German Luftwaffe provided excellent support for the attack during the entire day. Not one target was overlooked. Heavy attacks were already launched against Rostov. The cooperation between the ground troops and Luftwaffe, guided by the air liaison officer (known as Flivo for short) was exceptional.

On 22 July the other corps advanced against Rostov as instructed. Gruppe Wetzel with the 198th ID and the Mobile Slovak Division reached the Bolshie Saly area. On the left was von Mackensen's III Panzer Corps with the 14th and 22nd Panzer Divisions. Therefore, the ring was closed around

Rostov. The Soviet defenders of Rostov could now only withdraw across the Don to the south if the lead elements of the 4th Panzer Army remained in the Don/Sal/Manych area.

During the night of 23 July preparations were again made for the attack on the following day. Supply columns caught up. In the "Wiking" area of operations the tank drivers fetched water from a creek in enemy territory, so that they could refill with cool water. The next morning they learned that they faced a new enemy line of resistance.

On 23 July the battle for the city began. In the north, the 22nd Panzer Division penetrated into the outskirts with the 204th Panzer Regiment, while the 14th Panzer Division penetrated toward Novo-Cherkask. To the right of the 22nd Panzer Division, the fast Slovak Division, under General Turanec, overcame the first and second defensive belts, gained additional ground, and penetrated into the northern outskirts of the city.

The main effort of the attack lay in the LVII Panzer Corps area of operations. On either side of the Sultan Saly - Rostov road, the 13th Panzer Division launched its Battle Groups Olbrich and Crisolli (commander of the panzergrenadier brigade) to attack the city at 0540 hours. Combat reconnaissance elements advanced during the early morning up to the factories on the hill. Soon Battle Group Olbrich stood with the I/93 Pz.Gren. Rgt. on the right and the I/66 Pz.Gren.Rgt. on the left on the bridges from Kommolomny, where they were opposed by heavy defensive fire coming from the Temernik sector. The I/4 Pz.Rgt. closed ranks. The II/13 Pz.AR and a subordinate air defense battery took up positions and engaged recognizable targets. The forward-most elements were able to capture this most important bridge with a small, but capable assault troop. The explosives were removed, the bridge was repaired. The 3/66 Pz.Gren.Rgt and the 43rd Kradschützen Battalion established a bridgehead.

The I/66 and I/93 advanced from this base, reached the southern edge of the city and passed through the factory district. One after the other the companies disappeared into the rugged, steep terrain on either side of the main road in front of the railroad embankment. Wheeled vehicles were unable to follow. Radio communications were lost. Now the messengers went into action.

At 1020 hours the panzergrenadier battalion was in the stream area. There was less resistance there. However, the attackers ran into heavy defensive fire coming out of the residential quarter on the very edge of the city. The "Eight-Eight" battery was brought forward. The enemy anti-tank guns and even their heavy weapons were successfully engaged from open firing positions. Then it was time for the assault.

At 1050 hours Oberleutnant von Gaza assaulted the road bridge with his 2/66 Pz.Gren.Rgt. The attack was executed quickly, making the utmost of surprise. The prepared explosives were not detonated. Then the engineers arrived. The Magdeburger 4th Engineer Battalion repaired the bridge and reinforced it. Oberleutnant von Gaza was later awarded the Knight's Cross for this decisive commitment.

Under the protection of the established bridgehead the motor infantry of the 43rd Kradschützen Battalion attacked and, together with the tanks of the 4th

Panzer Regiment and the panzergrenadiers of the I/66, as well as the 3/93, partially mounted, partially dismounted, gradually gained ground to the south, breaking the enemy's resistance and removing blockades and barriers.

All of the soldiers were seized with attack fever. Above all, the major objectives were the bridges over the Don. While the combat elements of the 13th Panzer Division drove toward the Don in deeply echeloned columns behind the lead elements, enemy resistance revived on the side roads. However, like a ship, the division gradually widened its breach.

The Kradschützen drove forward, the hussars of the motorcycle, they traversed the city and reached the Don in the afternoon. They were the first to stand before the river. In the confusion of the harbor installations they had advanced too far to the east. The road bridge lay further to the southwest. Elements of the group drove toward the bridge. A Feldwebel from the 43rd Kradschützen Battalion was able to confiscate a passing barge and secure the crossing of equipment.

At 1600 hours the forward-most elements of the 13th Panzer Division stood on the important bridges to Bataisk. Both were blown. While the northern quarter of the bridges were cleared, Hauptmann Dankwort's engineers from the 4th Engineer Battalion had already begun repairing the blown road bridge. By the next morning the bridge was passable for men and light vehicles. Shortly before the Germans arrived, the Soviet "Commander of the South Front" left the city.

Rostov was burning from end to end. In the center of the city the battle still raged. The forward-most regiment of the 125th ID, which was following through Sultan Saly, was subordinated to the 13th Panzer Division.

What was happening in the SS Division "Wiking" area of operations in the meantime?

At the time of the 13th Panzer Division attack the Panzer Battalion and I/"Germania" were halted in front of Leninavan. By 1100 hours the tanks and panzergrendiers of "Wiking" were fighting for fiercely defended hill positions west of Leninavan. Stubaf. Dieckmann sent a company of his I/"Germania" against the hill positions. However, they still ran into strong defenses. In this situation, Dieckmann's radioman received a report from a German reconnaissance pilot: "3rd defensive line in the northeast is completely occupied. In the south, east of Chaltyr, it is still unoccupied. A road bridge across the 3rd anti-tank trench belt is still intact on the Chaltyr - Rostov road."

In the meantime, Mühlenkamp's tanks probed the anti-tank trench positions near Leninavan to the south. These positions were supported by a stream, whose banks were steep. At almost the same time as Dieckmann received his pilot report, Mühlenkamp observed how a Soviet motorized battery arrived from the Chaltyr road and took up positions behind the 3rd defensive line. Immediately, elements of the "Wiking" panzer battalion placed this battery under fire.

In the meantime, Dieckmann was also reacting. It was clear to him that the southern portion of the 3rd defensive line was still not occupied by the

Soviets; the formations assigned here were still fighting near Chaltyr and Krym. After a short radio message to Mühlenkamp, his battalion attacked with several tanks parallel to the 3rd defensive line to the south and captured the wooden bridge over the stream. This clever action, which ran counter to all of the rules of warfare, put the Soviet forces near Chaltyr and Krym into a difficult situation.

The main body of Pz.KGr. "Wiking" followed through this breach and advanced against the city. At 1400 hours the Panzer Battalion, the I/"Germania" and the III/5 SS AR, as well as one engineer company from the division, reached the rail line north of the airfield. There they halted. Combat reconnaissance was dispatched.

In the meantime, the resistance near Trud and Leninavan was also broken. Two battalions of the "Nordland" Regiment occupied Leninavan without a fight.

While Generalleutnant Herr's 13th Panzer Division was penetrating into the city from the north, Pz.KGr. "Wiking" also resumed its attack, after evaluating the combat reconnaissance. The Rostov airfield was enveloped in a grey cloud of smoke, which was left behind by the tanks. During a halt Hstuf. Schnabel, 1st Panzer Company commander, was wounded. At 1500 hours the first "Wiking" tanks stood on the southwestern edge of the city. An anti-tank trench and numerous houses incorporated into the defense had to be overcome.

First of all, a crossing had to be created over the last anti-tank trenches. A portion of the crews dismounted under the cover of fire from tank and machine-guns and blew up the walls with 3 kilogram explosives they carried with them. Then the first tanks rolled.

The advance of the tanks soon came to an end. The majority of the streets were blocked by barricades and walls. Stubaf. Mühlenkamp examined the terrain from one of the barricades. The railroad bridge was blown, the road bridge could not be observed.

At 1500 hours I/"Germania" was fighting in the southwestern portion of the city. The panzer battalion was in support, but the possibilities were limited. Here, as by the 13th Panzer Division, the attacks were directed at the Don bridges. The railroad station was reached north of the railroad bridge and contact was established with the 13th Panzer Division. At 1515 hours Hstuf. Bühler, commander of the 12th Battery of the "Wiking" Artillery Regiment, was located in the residential sector in the southwestern portion of the city. He surveyed the terrain from a hill. In front of Bühler was complete chaos. Soviet columns were jamming up on the road bridge to Bataisk. After a short conversation with Stubaf. Schlamelcher, the III/AR "Wiking" took up firing positions on the edge of the city, in the vicinity of the airfield.

Bühler directed the fire of the batteries from this ideal observation point. The German shells slammed into the enemy columns on the road bridge to Bataisk. Then the middle portion of the road bridge flew into the air. Before the explosion, Bühler saw German soldiers; they were the lead elements of the 13th Panzer Division. As the artillery fire grew silent, Hstuf. Bühler recognized enemy movement west of Rostov. The Soviet groups were fleeing on boats and ferries across the Don delta. Some were placed under fire.

23 July 1942 brought the German offensive forces complete success. The raid of the 2/66 Pz.Gren.Rgt under Oberleutnant von Gaza, the rapid advance of the 43rd Kradschützen Battalion under Oberstleutnant Stolz to the Don and the cleverly lead attack of Pz.KGr. "Wiking" on the bridge and the unoccupied defensive stretch between Chaltyr and Rostov all proved to be outstanding. German losses were low. For example, "Wiking" lost three dead, two severely wounded and nine lightly wounded.

Lieutenant General Malinovski was able to withdraw the main body of his "South Front" across the Don in time. However, his rear guard forces defended the city very skillfully utilizing all of the defensive possibilities at their disposal.

During the night of 24 July there were still skirmishes with NKVD troops, stragglers and partisans in the center of the city. The NKVD building was fiercely defended. The German forces went into a hasty defense in order to await the morning.

At 2200 hours, the 43rd Kradschützen Battalion began the crossing of the Don, at first in rubber dinghies and two barges, which were obtained by a Feldwebel. Then Russian ferries, which were anchored on the other side, were also utilized. Leutnant Eberlein and 28 volunteers from his 1/43 Kradschützen Btl. were the first to reach the other side, where they established a small bridgehead. Additional forces from the 43rd Kradschützen Battalion followed and advanced in the direction of Bataisk. Then Hauptmann Grabert crossed with his 8 Kp./Lehrrgt. z.b.V. "Brandenburg" ["Brandenburg" Special Purpose Training Regiment]. The first and second embankment bridges were captured intact.

From April to June 1942 the II Battalion of the "Brandenburg" Special Purpose Training Regiment trained for commitment in the Caucasus in the Tiraspol area. On 12 July the 8th Company was ordered to capture the 6000 meter long bridge embankment across the Don delta between Rostov and Bataisk. The company advanced to Taganrog in order to prepare for the difficult mission.

In the early morning of 24 July combat flared up again. The post office quarter was quickly cleared. Again heavy combat occurred around the NKVD building. At midday the I/66 Pz.Gren.Rgt., with tanks from the 22nd Panzer Division which had arrived from the north, stormed the NKVD block. Other units from the 22nd Panzer Division, which were fighting under Oberst Rodt, took the southern portion of the city, Aleksandrovskaya and Aksaiskaya. The 14th Panzer Division took Novo-Cherkask.

On the embankment to Bataisk, the "Brandenburger", Kradschützen and men of the 1/66 Pz.Gren.Rgt., as well as the 1st and 2/93 Pz.Gren.Rgt., advanced in the direction of Bataisk. During the early morning approximately 150 Russians, including several officers and commissars, tried to cross the railroad bridge over the Don and fight their way to Bataisk. They passed the 43rd Kradschützen Battalion command post, where they were dispersed and partially captured.

The following picture was presented in the "Wiking" area of operations:

Observation and air reconnaissance revealed that the Soviet forces, which had defended Chaltyr and Krym against the attack of the the XXXIX Mountain Corps on 23 July, were withdrawing through Kalinin to the south across the Don delta. The III/SS AR "Wiking" redeployed to the sand dunes near Nizhne-Gnilovskaya and placed the withdrawing Russians under fire. Disregarding the division order to wait, Stubaf. Mühlenkamp's Panzer Battalion "Wiking" attacked along the northern arm of the Don to the north-west and intersected the enemy retreat in the Kalinin area. Much equipment was abandoned by the fleeing Russians. This panzer attack created a 15 kilometer wide base on the northern bank of the Don. The last resistance in Chaltyr and Krym collapsed. Elements of the 73rd ID, as well as the 298th ID, could now advance to the east and occupy the entire Kalinin - Nizhne-Gnilovskaya river sector. For this decisive action, Stubaf. Mühlenkamp was awarded the Knight's Cross. On 24 July, the batteries of the 73rd and 298th ID advanced into the area.

While combat was raging on the river sector, the 125th ID was ordered to eliminate the numerous nests of resistance in the city of Rostov. On 23 July Generalleutnant Schneckenburger's Schwabian 12th ID followed the panzer formations after a strenuous march under the blistering sun on the Stalino - Rostov road and made it to the edge of the city with its lead elements. The majority of the division was in Sultan Saly. On 24 July the division began the clearing of the Don metropolis. And it was not easy! Throughout, the streets were blocked by bunkers and obstacles. Torn up roads and vehicle barricades, mine fields, cheval de frise and walled up building entrances made it difficult for the Schwabian grenadiers. Oberst Reinhardt's 421st Grenadier Regiment advanced along the main streets. Reinhardt divided his regiment into two groups; the I and III Battalions, in each were three assault companies. In addition to heavy machine-guns and an anti-tank gun, there was also a light infantry gun. The companies that advanced along the larger streets were reinforced with a light field howitzer. They advanced slowly. As Major Ortlieb's I and Hauptmann Winzen's III Battalions reached the assigned sector, they were followed by the II/421. All civilians were led to assembly points, since the assault groups had to secure the rear. A fierce battle flared up on the main road to the Don. Smoke from the burning houses limited visibility. The 421st opened fire. A light field howitzer was brought up and utilized in direct fire. There were similar developments on the secondary roads. There infantry guns fired at the nests of resistance. In the old portion of the city and in the harbor quarter it was even worse. Leaking gasses and a tangle of storage sheds hindered the systematic advance. Tanks from the 13th Panzer Division supported the Schwabian grenadiers.

On 24 July 1942 the German Wehrmacht Report noted: "In a special report, troops of the Army, Waffen SS and Slovak formations, supported by the Luftwaffe, have broken through the strongly fortified and deeply echeloned defensive positions at Rostov along the entire front and, after fierce combat, have captured the important communications and harbor center."

The morning report of Armeegruppe Ruoff on 24 July stated:

"The Mobile Slovak Division is fighting its way through mined streets and crossing to the southern bank of the Don in rubber dinghies.

The 9th ID threw the enemy out of the Ordshonikidze positions and captured Aleksandrovskaya.

The 43rd Kradschützen Battalion advanced to within 400 meters of Bataisk. The 170th Grenadier Regiment (73rd ID) and the 420th Grenadier Regiment (125th ID) have been crossing into the bridgehead since 1700 hours.

The 125th ID is still fighting in the inner city.

The 4th Mountain Division, 298th ID and 186th Grenadier Regiment (73rd ID) are already closing on the Sinyavka - Khopry - Kalinin - Nizhne-Gnilovskaya area."

The locations of the divisions were given in the daily report as follows:

"4th Mountain Division: Khopry - Sinyavka; 298th ID: Nizhne-Gnilovskaya - Kalinin; uncommitted elements of the 13th Panzer Division: southwest Rostov; uncommitted elements of "Wiking": northwestern portion of Rostov; 73rd ID with subordinated elements of the 13th Panzer Division and "Wiking": north of Bataisk and the southern portion of Rostov; 125th ID: central Rostov; Mobile Slovak Division: southern bank of the Don/eastern portion of Rostov; 9th ID with subordinate elements of the 198th ID: Aleksandrovskaya - Ordshonikidze; main body of the 198th ID: Bolshekrepinskaya; 2nd Rumanian Mountain Division is in march."

According to this daily report, the 73rd ID had taken command in the bridgehead; there were also elements of "Wiking" and the 13th Panzer Division subordinated to it. They were located at the bridge positions in Rostov.

During the night of 25 July at 0230 hours Hauptmann Grabert established a bridgehead across the last bridge embankment to Bataisk with his "Brandenburgers". The withdrawing Soviets finally stood their ground. Hand-grenades were flung in both directions at close range. The 8/"Brandenburg" was organized into two half-companies, each further divided into two einsatzgruppen. Moreover, they were equipped with light machine-guns, heavy machine-guns, mortars and anti-tank weapons. They were a mixture of infantrymen and engineers.

By dawn the 8/"Brandenburg" was ready to attack the last bridge. The attack began at 0400 hours. The "Brandenburgers" were met by a murderous defensive fire. However, they were able to establish a small bridgehead. The bridge ran over the last arm of the Don.

The Soviets were still not beaten. One machine-gun fell after the other. Ammunition was in short supply. The reserve platoon waded through the water and the swamp under enemy fire in order to transport new ammunition. The German forces further to the rear had to repulse enemy attacks from the swamps. Therefore, they could not support the far-extended "Brandenburgers". Contact with them was lost.

This was not all! The "Brandenburgers" were also attacked as they fought bitterly in their small bridgehead in front of Bataisk. The situation was tenuous! Again the "Brandenburgers" paid a high toll in blood. Hauptmann

Grabert suffered a head wound, but he continued to fight. Stabarzt Dr. Weber swam across the arm of the Don and treated the wounded. For 24 hours the brave "Brandenburgers" held out in the last bridgehead in front of Bataisk.

In the meantime, almost 40 batteries of the divisions of Armeegruppe Ruoff were deployed on the northern bank of the Don in positions. They relieved the assault troops with effective fire on Bataisk and Koissug. Stukas dropped their bombs in rolling attacks.

General Konrad's XXXXIX Mountain Corps was ordered to establish a bridgehead across the arm of the Don near Kalinin (regardless of developments in Rostov) and to reach the Azov - Koissug sector. We read about this development in the report from Armeegruppe Ruoff:

"Morning report from 25/7/42:

170th Grenadier Regiment (73rd ID) has established a bridgehead near Koissug today.

420th and 421st Grenadier Regiments with additional elements of the 13th Panzer Division are advancing from the north toward the Don and crossing into the bridgehead.

Daily report (evening) from 25/7/42:

298th ID reached Kumshenskiy with the 525th Grenadier Regiment.

The 73rd ID has dispatched combat capable reconnaissance from Koissug to the southwestern portion of Bataisk.

Tanks available:

13th Panzer Division: 15 Pz. II, 43 Pz. III(l), 35 Pz. III, 9 Pz. IV, 7 large command vehicles.

"Wiking": 6 Pz. II, 12 Pz. III(k), 22 Pz. III (l), 4 Pz. IV(k), 6 heavy anti-tank guns (R-Sfl)."

In all, on 25 July, the 13th Panzer Division had 109 operational tanks of various models. The III/4 Pz.Rgt. was still awaiting the arrival of its tanks. In the "Wiking" area of operations there were 34 tanks and six self-propelled weapons. The 3rd (Heavy) Company was also still not equipped with tanks.

At this time, the situation appeared to be somewhat improved by the foothold of the 73rd ID in Koissug. Therefore, Bataisk was now threatened from the west.

The 26th of July was again a very hot day. During the morning hours Koissug was completely taken by the 170th Grenadier Regiment of the 73rd ID. The anticipated counterattack was repulsed.

At 0655 hours the 525th Grenadier Regiment (298th ID) reported to the Armeegruppe: "Bridgehead established near Ust-Koissug."

At the same time, the commander of the XXXXIX Mountain Corps, General Konrad, was in Taganrog organizing the Luftwaffe support on Bataisk with Generaloberst von Richthofen. Rolling stuka attacks were to cover Bataisk. 40 batteries were to join in the battle from the northern bank of the Don.

By midday of 26 July the brave "Brandenburgers" were provided cover on the last bridge. Losses were considerable. Then reinforcements finally arrived.

General Konrad and the commander of the 125th ID, Generalleutnant Schneckenburger, went forward. They discussed the last assault. Again an attack of 36 stuka Ju 87's rocked the last resistance. Then the companies of the II/420 Gren.Rgt (125th ID) advanced and penetrated into the northern edge of Bataisk after breaking the tenacious resistance. This was at 1500 hours. In the evening report from Armeegruppe Ruoff the continuation of the attack was described:

"2100 hours: 125th and 73rd ID and 43rd Kradschützen Battalion threw the enemy out of Bataisk after overcoming bitter resistance. Generalleutnant Schneckenburger participated in the assault in the front line and distinguished himself."

While Bataisk was being assaulted, a battalion of the 170th Grenadier Regiment (73rd ID) advanced from Koissug to Bataisk. Therefore, the Soviet defenders were pinned from two sides.

West of Bataisk, the 298th ID also gained additional ground on this day. At 1500 hours the II/520 Gren.Rgt. advanced from Ust-Koissug toward the high ground 5 kilometers southwest of Koissug. The Armeegruppe evening report noted:

"298th ID attacking Kuleshovka through Kolusaevo."

With the fall of Bataisk, the gate to the Caucasus stood completely open. Outstanding was the brave combat of the "Brandenburgers", who, in the truest sense of the words, were sacrificed for a bridge. On one of the last bridge columns lay Hauptmann Siegfried Grabert. 200 meters in front of him lay Leutnant Hiller. Both had been killed. The losses of the 8/"Brandenburg" totaled: 17 dead, 16 missing, of which the majority drowned, and 54 wounded. Once more, the legendary "Brandenburgers" had led the way for the other troops. The "Brandenburg" Regiment originated from small beginnings at Brandenburg on the Havel. Its tactical symbol was the red Markischen eagle.

And what happened on 26 July in the other combat sectors on the lower Don? In the eastern portion of Rostov the 9th ID relieved the 22nd Panzer Division. The 198th ID advanced into the Aksaiskaya bridgehead, which was also established by the 22nd Panzer Division.

On 27 July Olginskaya was captured by the 36th Grenadier Regiment (9th ID) and the 198th ID. Therefore, a second reliable crossing over the Don was established in the vicinity of Rostov. The XXXXIX Mountain Corps reported the following numbers to Armeegruppe Ruoff for the time period from 20 - 27 July: 10,837 prisoners, 11 tanks, 101 guns, 50 anti-tank guns, as well as other supply goods were captured.

In the meantime, engineers constructed a ponton bridge across the Don in Rostov. The command structure was reorganized. All German army corps received their objectives for future assignment. The time to breakout of the narrow Rostov area and advance across the wide area to the south was approaching.

ATTACK OUT OF THE BATAISK BRIDGEHEAD

The XXXXIX Mountain Corps breaches the pass - Attack of the Kuban Cossacks - Supply across the Sea of Azov - Dobrenika is reached - The LVII Panzer Corps veers off to the east

Directive Nr. 45 pointed out: "...the mission remains to sever the Tikhorets - Stalingrad rail line with the advanced forces..."

The next mission for the XXXXIX Mountain Corps was to fulfill the above order. The next objective was the Kagalnik sector with the Kushchevskaya communications center.

On 27 July the XXXXIX Mountain Corps set out to reach the Kagalnik sector with the 4th Mountain Division on the right and the 73rd ID on the left. The 298th ID followed in second echelon along the coast.

After forcing the river barrier, the Soviet formations also began to move. The slow-moving foot formations infiltrated to the south in order to avoid being overtaken by the mobile German formations. Rear guards equipped with modern American weapons and vehicles, as well as the 17th Kuban Cossack Cavalry Corps (abbreviated: 17th KKKK), met the German troops in the Kagalnik sector.

On the morning of 27 July the French regiment of the 73rd ID, under General von Bünau, and the regiments of the Württemburg - Bavarian 4th Mountain Division, under General Eglseer, attacked. In the blistering sun they moved to the south and, in the evening, they reached the Kagalnik sector, which was defended by the 17th KKKK and rear guards from the 56th Soviet Army. It was similar near Aksaiskaya. Here the 198th ID forced the bridgehead open. The 198th and 9th ID joined the attack to the south. They passed through Olginskaya and Khomutovskaya.

The ponton bridge was completed at this time. Bridging engineers from the 17th Army accomplished the work quickly. The 4th Armored Engineer Battalion reinforced it. Therefore, the tanks from the 13th Panzer Division were able to roll over it without any trouble.

In the meantime, the 13th Panzer Division and "Wiking" prepared to breakout. The commander of Pz.KGr. "Wiking", Oberführer Gille, issued the order at 1000 hours. At 1640 hours they were ordered to be in march readiness at 1900 hours.

The "Wiking" march order was as follows:

"1st Group: SS Pz.Abt 5, one company of Panzerjäger, I/"Germania", SS Fla.Abt. 5, one engineer company, one light artillery battalion.

2nd Group: I/"Nordland", one mixed artillery battalion/"Wiking".

3rd Group: II/"Nordland" and 10/SS AR/"Wiking".

I and II/"Nordland" were brought up to the city. Because the deployment was delayed, the battalions were brought up into the vicinity of the airfield.

The 13th Panzer Division was the first formation to set in march on 28 July. The river crossing was conducted slowly. "Wiking" did not begin crossing until 1530 hours, after being march ready since 0400 hours.

On 28 July the 73rd ID and the 4th Mountain Division bogged down in the Kagalnik sector. The 198th ID reached the Kagalnik west of Kagalnitskaya.

In the meantime, the 13th Panzer Division veered sharply to the east from Bataisk and was located near Orlovka by evening.

"Wiking" moved through Selenoe and veered off from there sharply to the south. They passed through Kamyshesakha without a fight. However, the first contact with Russian rear guards was made on a tributary of the Kagalnik, south of this town. The river was crossed and the men established a hasty defense for the night. The Soviet Kagalnik - Manych line was torn by the deployment of the 13th Panzer Division and "Wiking". The 56th Soviet Army, which was located in the Kagalnitskaya area, turned its eastern flank toward the south.

On 28 July, due to the splitting up of the Soviet formations and in order to improve troop command and control, the South Front (formerly from Rostov to the north) and the North Caucasus Front (formerly the Taman Peninsula and the coast of the Sea of Azov) were combined under the latter's designation under the command of Marshal Budenny and subdivided into the "Don Group" (Voroshilovsk) and "Coastal Group" (Krasnodar). Marshal Budenny ordered a counterattack during the night in order to close the Kagalnik - Manych gap. This endeavor was undertaken during the night of 29 July. At 0330 hours superior enemy forces attacked the forward-most "Wiking" circular defense, which was able to hold, but only with much trouble. The "Wiking" elements further to the rear came to assist. The 5th SS Panzer Battalion and the I/"Nordland" attacked. At 0830 hours the enemy was thrown back.

The 13th Panzer Division overcame enemy resistance near Orlovka and Andronov. The 4th Panzer Regiment attacked the Verkhniy Khoruliy defenses a little later and, as the enemy also withdrew from there, the LVII Panzer Corps ordered: "Immediate pursuit!" The enemy withdrew in disorder in the direction of Salsk.

Between 1200 - 1330 hours "Wiking" again made contact with enemy rear guard elements. Again Mühlenkamp's tanks swarmed and attacked together with the panzergrenadiers. Mechetinskaya fell. In pursuit of the enemy, "Wiking" reached Yegorlykskaya and secured it during the evening of 29 July. Many Red Army soldiers surrendered there. The commissars and Politruks fled. Tactical reconnaissance revealed: Zelina and Sredniy Yegorlyk were occupied by the enemy.

To the right of "Wiking" the 198th ID also repulsed heavy enemy counterattacks. By midday the 305th Grenadier Regiment was opposed by strong enemy forces in the Kagalnitskaya bridgehead, which secured the withdrawal of their formations. Then the resistance slackened. The 198th ID continued to advance.

The 4th Mountain Division and 73rd ID broke the resistance on the Kagalnik on this day and captured the hills to the south. On the army's right flank the 298th ID conquered Kuleshovka on 28 July with the 525th Grenadier Regiment, then Peshkovo and Pavlovka on 29 July with the 526th Grenadier Regiment.

After penetrating the Kagalnik sector, the German attack again arrived at a river. Vast columns were still pressing on the Don crossings at Rostov and

Aksaiskaya. The 17th Army had just crossed the first half of its formations to the southern bank of the Don. A summary of movement across the Don bridge near Rostov shows:

"31/7/1942: Slovak Mobile Division
1/8:   Armeegruppe Ruoff Headquarters
2/8:   2nd Rumanian Division
3/8:   1st Mountain Division
4/8:   Rumanian Cavalry Corps."

The 30th of July was another blistering day. The march groups set in movement at daybreak. Long trails of dust marked the march route. The objectives for this day: SS "Wiking" was to advance on Sredniy Yegorlyk, 16th ID (Mot.) toward Salsk, 13th Panzer Division was to establish a bridgehead south of Gigant - Zelina.

The 13th Panzer Division captured Gigant and Zelina against enemy resistance. At midday the division received a new mission: "Screen from Zelina to Salsk with a strong left flank." By nightfall, Battle Group von Raczeck stood directly west of Salsk.

At 0630 hours "Wiking" also broke out and reached the Sredniy Yegorlyk area. Both flanks were unsecured. At 1500 hours I/"Nordland" and III/5 SS-AR pulled back to Yegorlykskaya, in order to secure to the west. There the different march capabilities between "Wiking", as a motorized formation, and the 198th ID, as a foot formation, became noticeable on the "Wiking" open flank.

On 30 July the 198th ID probed the advance detachment and 305th Grenadier Regiment through additional Soviet blocking positions and reached the Kugoi - Yeya sector during the evening.

To the right of the 198th ID the 125th and 73rd ID, the 4th Mountain Division and the 298th ID also advanced to the Yeya - Kugoi - Yeya sector. However, there they came to a standstill. The 17th KKKK decisively defended this sector with the 15th and 13th Cavalry Divisions and partisan units.

How did the situation then develop in this sector? – On 30 July the Mountain Reconnaissance Battalion reached the Yeya west of Kushchevskaya as the lead element of the 4th Mountain Division. The 94th Mountain Reconnaissance Battalion bogged down at an intact bridge, which was placed under enemy fire, and awaited the arrival of the 91st Gebirgsjäger Regiment. The subsequent attack of this regiment bogged down in the defensive fire of the Kuban Cossacks. In the meantime, the 13th Gebirgsjäger Regiment was able to establish a bridgehead near Leninsky. Then all of the forces of the 4th Mountain Division and all of the batteries of the 94th Mountain Artillery Regiment were committed there in order to expand the bridgehead. However, they did not succeed. The squadrons of the 17th KKKK prevented the German advance from reaching the dominant southern bank.

They did not succeed near Leninsky. However, the 73rd and 125th ID established a strong bridgehead near Kushchevskaya. The stepping-stone

ATTACK OUT OF THE BATAISK BRIDGEHEAD

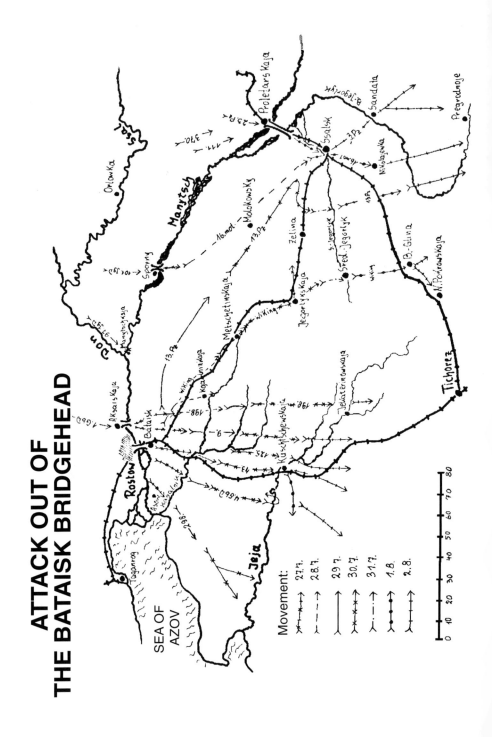

needed to overcome the river barrier was achieved!

Armeegruppe Order Nr. 89, Armeegruppe Ruoff, from 30 July 1942 stated:

"...until it achieves complete mobility, the 298th ID will continue to provide coastal protection for the Don estuary - Krugloe... M-Boot-Flotille Loeper Taganrog, which is directly subordinated to the Armeegruppe, will clear the Don delta in cooperation with the XXXXIX Mountain Corps, later the 3rd Rumanian Army, and then secure supply by sea Taganrog - Rostov."

In another order it stated:

"298th ID is subordinated to the I Rumanian Army Corps as of 1/8/42, 2000 hours."

Therefore, the course was set for the 298th ID. On 30 July the division occupied Golovatovka and Saimon without enemy resistance.

On 31 July combat continued in the Kushchevskaya bridgehead. The 13th Cavalry Division surrounded the German bridgehead and frustrated the German advance by counterattacking.

On 1 August the 91st Gebirgsjäger Regiment was also transferred into the bridgehead. And again the enemy attacked! On this day it went easier. Had the main body of the 13th Cavalry Division withdrawn?

The 91st Gebirgsjäger Regiment penetrated to the west in order to fix the enemy south of the river. Because Cossack squadrons attacked, supported by tanks, the flank attack of the 91st was battered to pieces.

On 2 August elements of the 298th ID moved further west across the river. They were also attacked. Losses occurred in the confusion.

The fierce defensive combat conducted by the 17th Kuban Cossack Cavalry Corps did, indeed, delay the German advance. However, it could not prevent it. The foot formations from the 17th Army marched through the Kushchevskaya communications center further to the south. On the left flank the motorized formations of the 1st Panzer Army gained quite a bit of ground and drove for the Kuban.

On 2 and 3 August General Konrad's XXXXIX Mountain Corps was engaged in combat with enemy rear guard elements. Then the western flank of the 17th Army also reached the Kisslyakovskaya - Dobrenika Hills. There was enough room to deploy freely. The German divisions were reassigned to new army corps depending upon their situation and mission. After some initial confusion in the bottleneck, clear-cut command and control was restored.

The advance of German panzer and motorized formations so far to the south compelled the commander of the North Caucasus Front, Marshal Budenny, to decide, on 3 August, to withdraw the main body of his western forces over the Kuban. A portion of the "Don Group" (eastern flank) was transferred into the Kuma - Malka area in order to construct a new defense. Budenny surrendered a great deal of terrain. The operations of the mobile German formations only left him with the hope that his troops would be able to stop them at the mountains and then be able to compel them to transition to the defensive. Budenny would be right in the end!

One could not fail to notice a certain amount of panic in the Soviet leadership. A naval relief operation had no influence on the advance of the German troops in the Caucasus. On 2 August the commander of the Soviet Cruiser Brigade, Rear Admiral Basistiy, put to sea with the cruiser "Molotov", the flotilla leader "Kharkov" and some smaller craft. They ended up in Feodosia Bay on the night of 3 August. On the return they were attacked by German combat aircraft and the Italian Motor Torpedo Boat 573. The "Molotov" was hit by a torpedo.

On 4 August the Germans began their supply effort on the Sea of Azov.

SPRING-BOARD TO ASIA

Inaccurate maps - Hauptmann Häberlein's 1/156 Pz.Gren.Rgt. in Asia - Oberfeldwebel Bunzel's raid fails - Landing in the swamp - 3rd Panzergrenadier Regiment captures Proletarskaya - Oberleutnant Tank and his men - The 3/39 Pz.Pi.Btl. builds the bridges

On 26 July Bataisk was captured by formations from Armeegruppe Ruoff. The gateway to the Caucasus was open. On the same day the 16th ID (Mot.) and Division "Grossdeutschland" were re-subordinated to the III Panzer Corps. General von Mackensen's former divisions, the 14th and 22nd Panzer Divisions, were marching on Stalingrad. However, the "GD" ["Grossdeutschland"] was also reorganized after reaching the Manych. Therefore, it was clear that the 16th ID (Mot.) was to be committed in the Caucasus.

Generalleutnant Siegfried Henrici's Westphalian 16th ID (Mot.) was ordered to force the crossing of the Manych in the Sporny area. Henrici and his Ia, Major von Kienle, decided, after studying the map, to cross the division at two locations on either side of Sporny. According to the map there were trails and paths leading across the marshy Manych Valley. Because they would be avoiding the main road near Sporny, the division leadership hoped that they would only run into weak resistance. The most favorable position appeared to be near Novosselevka because several trails led to the Manych from there. The 165th Kradschützen Battalion and the 60th Panzergrenadier Regiment were committed toward Novosselevka. To the west the 156th Panzergrenadier Regiment was to establish a bridgehead near Svoboda. The 116th Panzer Battalion was initially to be committed on the Manych embankment near Sporny, after the pincer attack was launched by the 60th and 156th Panzergrenadier Regiments.

Just as the division was set to go, a "Fieseler Storch" landed and a Luftwaffe officer gave Generalleutnant Henrici new air reconnaissance. The results of the latest air reconnaissance compelled the leadership to change their attack plans. The reconnaissance showed a long dam embankment with a sluice on a bridge near Sporny. Underneath the dam the Manych was channelized, above it, however, was a large reservoir.

The main effort was then shifted to the 156th Panzergrenadier Regiment, whose battalions were to advance against little enemy resistance with the objective of establishing a bridgehead near Svoboda as quickly as possible. The 60th Panzergrenadier Regiment was to remain back.

On the evening of 26 July Hauptmann Häberlein's 1st Company was the first unit from the 156th Panzergrenadier Regiment to reach the Manych. Häberlein and the commander of the 675th Engineer Battalion, Major Muschner, agreed: cross immediately!

A suitable spot was quickly found. The attached engineers brought up assault boats and rafts. The 1/156 crossed the 50 meter wide Manych Canal and established a bridgehead. Only isolated mortar fire harassed the German maneuver. While it was still nighttime the engineers built a bridge across the

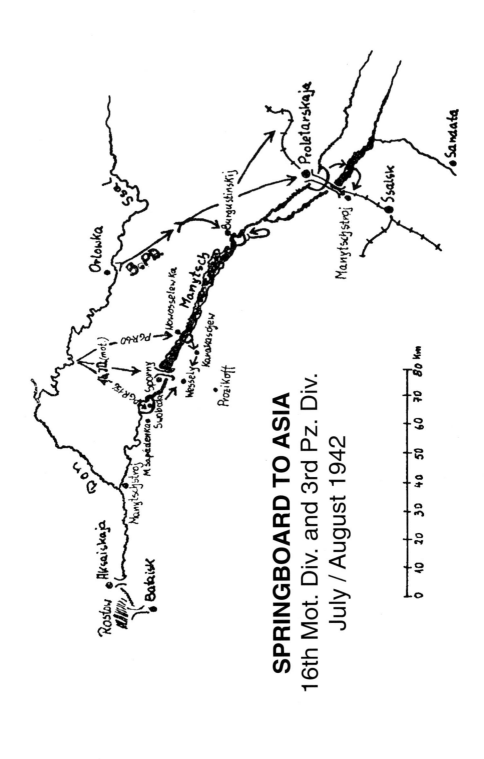

SPRINGBOARD TO ASIA
16th Mot. Div. and 3rd Pz. Div.
July / August 1942

Manych Canal.

The 3/Kradschützen Btl. 165 reached the Manych near Novosselevka as the lead element of the left flank of the division. They were immediately followed by their engineer elements. While the 2/146 AR and 6/60 AR provided cover, 13 assault boats rushed the men of the 3/165 Kradschützen Btl. across the 2 kilometer wide reservoir. Reconnaissance was quickly dispatched from the hastily established bridgehead. They discovered large enemy columns on all roads leading to the south. Budenny was withdrawing his main force from Bataisk.

The reconnaissance elements from the panzer company of the 165th Kradschützen Battalion watched over the long eastern flank. In the center of the two attack columns advanced the 116th Panzer Battalion.

The division order correspondingly read:

"The panzer battalion will quickly capture the high ground north of Sporny in the central sector of the division and obtain suitable observation positions for the artillery. Panzer and infantry assault elements will quickly capture the reservoir dam. At the same time, a company in assault boats will be committed from the east to the southern end of the reservoir dam. It must prevent the setting of explosives. At the same time, the 156th Panzergrenadier Regiment will advance from the Svoboda bridgehead to the south toward Vessely and establish a bridgehead at the head of the dam."

The objective was to be achieved from three sides simultaneously.

By early morning Major von der Schulenbürg's 116th Panzer Battalion was prepared to attack the hills north of Sporny. It was supported by two batteries of heavy field howitzers and one mortar battery. Panzers march! The heavy fire strikes by the artillery onto the high ground and Sporny led the panzer attack. Major Hammon, commander of the III/146 AR, and his adjutant rode with the tanks and directed the fire. Hill 29.6 north of the reservoir dam was captured. The 3/156 Pz.Gren.Rgt. provided covering infantry. The artillery forward observers advanced.

Again the tanks rolled. However, they were then showered with artillery fire from Sporny and south of the dam. At 0600 hours the panzer attack was broken off. The tanks rolled back to the cover of the reverse slope. Time passed. The Russians were forewarned. Only a major attack could achieve any success.

Oberfeldwebel Bunzel arrived with his platoon. The four Panzer IIIs of the 3/116 Pz.Abt. rolled at high speed toward the reservoir dam with mounted engineers. They fired, moved and communicated. The air defense guns were abandoned by their crews on the southern slope. Bunzel's platoon rolled on. Soon the dam was within their grasp, then the bright summer day was shaken by a powerful detonation. The southern part of the dam blew into the air right in front of Bunzel's nose. A flood raced through the breech, widening it. Bunzel's platoon had to turn about.

The powerful flood brought disaster to the combat bridge near Svoboda, on which the 156th Panzergrenadier Regiment was crossing into the bridgehead. Soon the bridge was washed out. The terrain was changed into a great sea by the mass of water. Major Schmal's I/156 was surrounded by water. Contact with the regiment was lost. Under these circumstances an enemy attack was launched out of Malaya Sapadenka. It was repulsed by the battalion with the support of the batteries, which were located on the northern bank.

The attack of Bunzel's platoon on the reservoir dam from the north was conducted simultaneously with an assault boat attack by the 2/165 Kradschützen Btl. 165. At 1000 hours 13 assault boats raced out of the Novosselevka area across the wide reservoir. In the lead boat were the commander of the 2nd Company, Leutnant Meyer, and the engineers. The other boats followed in a column. The motors screamed across the water. Only their heads were visible from outside of the boats. The mission read:

"Land on the southern end of the dam and prevent it from being blown!"

When the small fleet landed, the dam flew into the air. In spite of this, the 2/165 Kradschützen Btl. landed and established a small bridgehead in the vicinity of the southern dam access road. A little later a counterattack occurred. It could only be repulsed with difficulty. Ammunition was in short supply. In this critical situation the company was instructed over the radio to break contact with the enemy at 1200 hours. They returned in the assault boats. The company landed on the northern end of the demolition site.

In the meantime, the enemy was destroyed near Sporny. The 165th Kradschützen Battalion took up the security on the northern bank. The engineers constructed bridge ferries on the right flank of the division. The water was still streaming out of the reservoir. Two meter high waves made driving the ferries difficult.

After the blowing of the dam, the division ordered the 60th Panzergrenadier Regiment to cross elements over the wide reservoir in order to attack strongly fortified Vesseliy from the east on the following day. At the same time, the 156th Panzergrenadier Regiment was to attack from the west. Artillery was brought up into the Sporny river bend in order to achieve as great a range as possible.

The III/60 Pz.Gren.Rgt. was assigned the mission of conducting an outflanking attack from the east. The battalion commander, Hauptmann Fischer, was given a free hand. Fischer selected the crossing in the Novosselevka area, because no enemy resistance was anticipated there.

By the fall of darkness engineer equipment had been brought up to the bank and the construction of ferries was begun. The battalion approached and deployed for the crossing. At 2200 hours the first ferry was complete. Two others still had to be constructed.

It was a clear night with a full moon. The first group boarded the ferry. It was guided by an assault boat. The diagonal trip was estimated at 3 kilometers. They waited anxiously! Finally the ferry returned.

Hauptmann Fischer, his adjutant, Oberleutnant Risse and the battalion courier accompanied the second batch in the tug boat. The first question Hauptmann Fischer directed at the assault boat driver was: "Can you again find the location where you dropped off the first group?" The answer: "Of course, if it is still clear!"

However, it was not clear! The second group did not find the initial landing spot. They called out in low voices. Nothing. They set up a beacon position to guide them back. The battalion commander and adjutant joined the search for the first group. It soon was clear what caused the problem: small shrubbery made orientation difficult. There were marshes and more marshes. It was impossible to move. Each group had to overcome the terrain on its own. Finally, the first group reached a flat meadow. There was a light morning fog.

Hauptmann Fischer assembled his battalion, although minus the heavy infantry weapons and anti-tank guns. Only a pair of heavy machine-guns and a B-Krad [side-car], the friend of the Caucasus, provided fire and mobility.

In the meantime, they studied the data supplied by reconnaissance. It was reported that the town of Karakashev, which lay 2 kilometers to the south-west, was occupied by the enemy. There was heavy traffic on all roads. It was unnecessary to point out that the battalion would soon be discovered.

On 28 July at 1000 hours the battalion edged closer to Karakashev with a detached forward flank in order to establish a pincer attack. 500 meters in front of the town, Hauptmann Fischer ordered: "Battalion Halt! Stand still, don't move!" However, he took the side-car into the town.

Halt! Bewildered faces. The side-car replied. The uselessness of any resistance was indicated by the Hauptmann, when he nodded toward the entire battalion behind him. The Red Army soldiers were free to withdraw. However, they had to lay down their weapons. The civilians urged the Red Army soldiers on. Then a wild flight ensued. By 1100 hours the III/ 60 Pz.Gren.Rgt. had the town well in hand, along with a great number of weapons (including heavy weapons) which were utilized by the battalion during their further attack toward the hills south of Vesseliy.

In the meantime, the Svoboda bridgehead had also been reinforced. By midday the III/156 infiltrated in small groups through the small, still water-free, pass southeast of Svoboda. The I/156 expanded the bridgehead to the west and threw the enemy out of Malaya Sapadenka. During the afternoon the II/156 also reached the southern bank of the Manych. Therefore, the pre-requisite for the attack on Vesseliy was established.

The attack of the 156th Panzergrenadier Regiment gained ground to the south. The 4th Battery of the 146th Artillery Regiment was the only division element in position on the southern bank. The battery chief, Oberleutnant Hompel, directed the fire for the entire II Battalion. The fire was well placed for the attacking grenadiers. They fired on all enemy movement. Entire columns of retreating groups were placed under artillery fire. Krasniy Kut was captured. At 1700 hours the II/156 attacked Vesseliy. Oberst Eisermann, the commander of the 156th Panzergrenadier Regiment, entered Vesseliy with the first assault company. At the same time the III/60 attacked the hills directly south of the town. Then they could begin bridging operations.

During the night of 28-29 July the 165th Kradschützen Battalion crossed the river at both crossing sites and assembled south of Vesseliy. The II/156 occupied the high ground positions directly north of Protsikov, which were evacuated by the enemy.

On 29 July a stormy deployment from the Bataisk bridgehead bottleneck began. The SS "Wiking" and 13th Panzer Divisions first attacked to the east, and then veered off to the south.

On this morning the 3/165 Kradschützen Btl. set out to the south from Vesseliy. Attacking past Protsikov, the company reached the Khomutetz area, where they ran into a stronger enemy force and bogged down.

A unified German attack front existed had already existed by the evening of 19 July. 20 kilometers south of Vesseliy the 13th Panzer Division reached the Adranov - Kusnetsovka area. And another 20 kilometers to the south of there stood "Wiking".

The combat bridge was finished at midnight on 31 July, after experiencing great difficulties. It was a masterpiece of the division engineering. The double anchored bridge was 92 meters long. And the sign "Asia - Europe" told all crossing soldiers to where they were marching. The 16th ID (Mot.) immediately began crossing its wheeled vehicles over the bridge. The tanks had to be crossed on ferries.

On 31 July the division set out in pursuit of the enemy in three march groups. The objective was Salsk. Several times Soviet rear guard elements were encountered and fought. On 1 August the 16th ID (Mot.) was located near Mikhailovka. Advance groups and scouts from the 165th Kradschützen Battalion probed further and made contact with the 13th Panzer Division, which was in the Gigant - Salsk area.

On 23 July the 3rd Panzer Division reached the Sal near Orlovskaya, as the lead element of the XXXX Panzer Corps, and captured an undamaged river bridge. A bridgehead was established. However, it was three days before the division was prepared to attack any further because enemy forces had to first be repulsed between the Sal and the Don.

On 26 July at 0400 hours, as enemy forces were still withdrawing, Battle Groups von Liebenstein and Westhoven set out in march to the south. This new march direction set the course for the XXXX Panzer Corps. On this day the march groups reached the Duddenovskaya and Gantshukov area. Further to the west the 16th ID (Mot.) drove toward the Manych.

On 29 July, as the 16th ID (Mot.) established a bridgehead near Vesseliy, the 3rd Panzer Division was also able to advance further. They were delayed by a shortage of fuel. One battle group reached the Donskoy - Gudronov area east of Proletarskaya and blew the rail line to Stalingrad. Several platoons pulled off to the east, capturing additional rolling stock. By 1500 hours the western battle group was located in front of Proletarskaya. A stuka attack was conducted against the city. Behind the detonating bombs Oberstleutnant Zimmermann's 3rd Panzergrenadier Regiment assaulted into the city.

South of the city were two arms of the Manych, which were bridged by one road and one railroad crossing. In between was meadow-land leading off to a dam. At the front of the assaulting 3rd Panzergrenadier Regiment advanced a platoon of the "Brandenburgers", which had the mission of capturing the dam crossing. The raid on the second portion of the dam failed due to the vigilance of the Soviet bridge guards. Only the leader of the "Brandenburgers", a Leutnant, was able to take the northern sluice house and hold out there until reinforcement arrived. The southern portion of the dam, right on the southern arm of the Manych, was blown by the Soviets in two places.

General Breith and his 1st Generalstabsoffizier, Major Pomtov, had previously considered crossing at two places.

As Oberstleutnant Zimmermann's 3rd Panzergrenadier Regiment stood before Proletarskaya, the 2./3 Kradschützen Btl. crossed the 1200 meter wide Manych near Burgustinskiy. The II/394 Pz.Gren.Rgt. advanced up to the termination point; the 5th Company crossed and the Kradschützen followed. The bridgehead was established. The 2./3 Kradschützen Btl. advanced to the south. However, it ran into enemy forces in the next town and had to return.

After the raid on the dam south of Proletarskaya failed, the division intended to reinforce the Burgustinskiy bridgehead and attack from there to the southeast in order to open the crossing near Manychstroy. Artillery and engineer columns were also brought forward!

On 31 July the Burgustinskiy bridgehead was reinforced. Ferries brought over the first vehicles. However, when it was time for the heavy vehicles to go on, the water level sunk rapidly. The ferries ran aground. The blowing of the dam near Sporny on 27 July made itself felt. The reservoir drained. On the same day the 16th ID (Mot.) completed its crossing 40 kilometers to the northwest.

In the meantime, the great panzer raid to the south was launched from out of the Rostov bridgehead. The XXXX Panzer Corps was to be included. Time was of the essence!

With considerable difficulty, the 3./39 Pz.Pi.Btl. was able to repair the damaged road bridge across the first arm of the Manych with a K-Strecke [prefabricated bridge section]. The road and railroad ran parallel to each other on an embankment across the almost 8 kilometer wide piece of terrain between the two arms of the river. Damaged portions of the embankment were made trafficable with sandbags and railroad ties. Leutnant Möwis from the 3./39 Pz.Pi. reconnoitered three additional crossing sites over the southern arm of the Manych. All were in the vicinity of the sluice.

During the night of 1 August crossing operations over the southern arm of the Manych increased. Because Manychstroy, at the end of the crossing, was defended by strong enemy forces, an attack was launched across the damaged section of the embankment, as well as an envelopment attack. The 3 Kradschützen Battalion was committed frontally. The II/3 Pz.Gren.Rgt. was assembled for the envelopment attack, which necessitated a crossing of the Manych.

At exactly midnight a heavy artillery fire strike was initiated against the enemy positions on the southern portion of the dam and on Manychstroy. While the shells flew to the other side, engineers from the 39th Rathenow Engineer Battalion launched their assault boats into the water. The 6./3 Pz.Gren.Rgt., led by Oberleutnant Tank, jumped into the boats. Engineers from the 39th Engineer Battalion and the engineer platoon from 3 Kradschützen Battalion took up their posts! The assault boats raced to the southern bank. Oberleutnant Tank's men jumped out of the boats on top of the enemy infantrymen. They fought hand-to-hand. The company was all alone. The men held on shoulder to shoulder.

The second wave did not cross as smoothly. Russian artillery fired. Two assault boats sank. The men of the 3rd and 7th Companies, which were combined under Oberleutnant Vormann, were thrown overboard.

The third wave did not make it. Soviet artillery of all calibers hammered away at them. The Germans were still unable to direct any artillery fire because all of the forward observers were killed. Finally, Leutnant Buchmann, forward observer from the 9./75 Pz.AR, was able to advance on foot and establish communications. Soon the 9th Battery was firing. Then the others followed. They brought some relief.

NKVD troops and elements of the Soviet 19th Rifle Division were defending. The battle see-sawed. Major Böhm, the commander of the II/3 Pz.Gren.Rgt, and his adjutant were killed. The 26 year-old Leutnant Tank took command and rallied the exhausted assault troops. With "Hurrahs" one river bank position after the other was captured. The panzergrenadiers advanced on Manychstroy step by step. When the ammunition was exhausted they fought with empty weapons. They did not make it to the Manychstroy dam.

In the meantime, the 3 Kradschützen Battalion was relieved by the "Brandenburg" platoon on the reservoir dam. However, the advance of the Kradschützen was frustrated by enemy forces on the southern bank.

Artillery fire! A concentrated fire strike suppressed the enemy. Then Oberleutnant Mesiter assaulted across the dam with his 3./3 Kradschützen Btl. The enemy nests were removed from the southern bank.

The II/3 Pz.Gren.Rgt. also gained ground. Kradschützen and panzergrenadiers shook hands on the eastern edge of Manychstroy. The II/3 Pz.Gren.Rgt suffered 36 dead. Oberleutnant Tank was awarded the Knight's Cross.

Indeed, the bridgehead was established. However, artillery fire was still coming down on the bridgehead near Manychstroy. In spite of this, the commander of the 3rd Schützenbrigade, Oberst Westhoven, urged immediate bridge construction. At 0915 hours Oberleutnant Brandt's 3./39 Pz.Pi.Btl. placed the first support, at 1115 hours the last. The two large damaged sections were bridged by a double 20 ton prefabricated bridge with a total length of 29.30 meters. In the meantime, other engineers improved the marshy access and constructed a corduroy road. At 1800 hours the first vehicles rolled over the bridge embankment. An enemy counterattack was repulsed. The Berlin - Brandenburger 3rd Panzer Division had established the crossing to Asia for the XXXX Panzer Corps.

On 1 August 1942 the XXXX Panzer Corps was removed from the 4th Panzer Army and subordinated to the 1st Panzer Army.

Elements of the 13th Panzer Division and the 16th ID (Mot.) already were located 18 kilometers south of Manychstroy, in Salsk. The entire panzer assault to the south could begin.

PANZER ASSAULT TO THE SOUTH

Belaya Glina - Budenny withdraws his troops - Major Brux and his SPW battalion - Advance Detachment Pape assaults Voroshilovsk - 13th Panzer Division and "Wiking" reach the Kuban - The fake NKVD people from Maikop - Penetration into the Caucasus Forest)

With the opening of the Manych crossing between Proletarskaya and Salsk, General Geyr von Schweppenburg's XXXX Panzer Corps gained freedom of maneuver. The XXXX Panzer Corps, which had formerly fought under Hoth's 4th Panzer Army, came under the command of the 1st Panzer Army after they crossed the Manych.

On 30 July the lead elements of the 13th Panzer Division reached the western edge of Salsk. Another battle group occupied Zelina and Gigant and established a small bridgehead over the Sredniy Yegorlyk to the south.

On 31 July "Wiking" and the 13th Panzer Division had to slow down in order to allow the 16th ID (Mot.) and XXXX Panzer Corps to catch up and, secondly, to await supplies. The Soviets continued to try to stop the German formations and extract their own units, which had been bypassed, by counterattacking. A large gap appeared between the German attack formations and the supply effort, which was caused by the bottleneck on the bridges in Rostov and Aksaiskaya. At this time, "Wiking" approached Sredniy Yegorlyk and had to repulse an enemy attack in the strength of three battalions during the following night. On this day the 13th Panzer Division, which was located east of "Wiking", had to overcome great terrain difficulties in the river valley of the Sredniy Yegorlyk. The lead elements of the 16th ID (Mot.) also approached Salsk on this day.

On 1 August the 3rd Panzer Division crossed the Manych. During the night of 2 August Advance Detachment Pape, advancing along the Manychstroy - Salsk rail line, reached the city of Salsk.

With the meeting of the panzer formations from the III and XXXX Panzer Corps the prerequisite for the panzer assault to the south was achieved. The reorganization placed the 3rd and 23rd Panzer Divisions under the XXXX Panzer Corps command, the 13th Panzer Division and 16th ID (Mot.) under the III Panzer Corps and "Wiking" and the Mobile Slovak Division under LVII Panzer Corps.

During the late afternoon of 1 August, while Generalmajor Breith's 3rd Panzer Division was creating the prerequisites for an attack on the following day by crossing its formations over the Manych, the 16th ID (Mot.) advanced the 165th Kradschützen Battalion and 156th Panzergrenadier Regiment up to the Rassypnaya River and established a bridgehead near Rassypnoe. To the west, the 13th Panzer Division also reached the river and established a bridgehead near Rasvilnoe. Battle Group Brux faced fierce combat around the town itself.

On 1 August Pz.KGr "Wiking", which was led by Oberführer Gille, participated in a great battle. During the early morning the security had repulsed an enemy attack in Sredniy Yegorlyk. The significance of this was that they had to contend with combat capable rear guard elements. Marshal Budenny, striving to lead his troops behind the Kuban and Kuma river barriers and into the mountains, formed rear guards with reliable and combat capable units, which were equipped with American vehicles and weapons. They fought deftly in an attempt to protect the slow foot formations from being pursued by the German motorized formations. On 1 August "Wiking" ran into one of these units, which forced it to, at the very least, deploy and, therefore, put the breaks on the advance. On the morning of 1 August the panzer battalion and advance battalion of "Wiking" made preparations to breakout in order to secure the further advance to the south. The next objective was Belaya Glina, a small market place on the Salsk - Tikhorets rail line and a junction of the important road communications in all directions.

At the rooster's crowing the panzer soldiers and grenadiers were again on their feet. The tents were quickly pulled down and loaded onto the vehicles. Time was of the essence. The dew on the grass moistened their boots, which had not seen a brush for some time. It looked like it would be a beautiful summer day so the necessary preparations were made in good humor. Drivers filled their vehicles and checked tires and water. On days when the column was rolling there was no time to do this. The infantrymen checked their weapons and equipment and loaded on the vehicles. Breakfast was mainly eaten on the vehicles.

The lead elements drove on. In the lead was the "Wiking" Panzer Battalion. Following was the advance battalion. The other companies wove into the march formation. Although the day was young the heat and dust already paralyzed the brain and limbs. The men dozed on the vehicles. The heat shimmered across the landscape. A long trail of dust marked the march route. Men and equipment were soon covered in a thick coating of dust.

At every halt the view presented by the terrain was much different than in Germany. The soldiers missed the green trees, forests and meadows, towns with tiled roofs, the solid streets with rows of trees. An endless golden-brown sea of grain stretched before them. The wind made it wave. The grain was overripe.

Again a halt! The column closed ranks and was fired upon from out of a grain field. Stubaf. Schlamelcher, commander of the III/5 SS AR, was severely wounded in the head. The lead company dismounted. The area was combed. A group of prisoners was led off to the rear.

The tanks drove on. The tracks rattled and beat their way through the dust. The hatches were open. The heat in the tanks was unbearable. The heads of the tank commanders stuck out of the turrets. Their eyes searched the terrain. Around their necks hung the throat microphones. Forty tanks shook the golden-yellow land.

At midday reconnaissance elements from the reconnaissance battalion gathered from all directions. The result of the reconnaissance: "Belaya Glina is occupied by the enemy!"

Situation briefing. Messengers make their way to the companies. Radios crackle. Oberführer Gille assembles his force. An envelopment group supported by tanks was to cut off the enemy's retreat route from the west. The

I/"Nordland" continued the assigned frontal attack. On the flanks were scout cars and motorcycles from the reconnaissance battalion. Up to this point in time Division "Wiking" had three infantry battalions available. The II/"Germania" was closing ranks. The "Westland" Regiment and a battalion each from "Germania" and "Nordland" were still awaiting new vehicles on the Mius.

The panzer battalion under the leadership of Stubaf. Mühlenkamp started of. The lead battalion followed. They continued in march formation up to Hill 108.8 north of Belaya Glina. Then they halted! They were fired upon. They deployed for the attack!

The leading group veered off to the east with tanks and the I/"Nordland". They deployed, then turned slightly to the south. The formation rolled cautiously toward the town. In the meantime, the envelopment group was already located to the southwest behind the town. The Russians were already withdrawing. Only the rear guard still held.

The tanks advanced against the town frontally, widely dispersed, contrasting with the yellow grain fields as green flecks. The companies dismounted in the grain field. Only the driver's compartments and the tank turrets stuck up out from the grain. Cautiously the tanks approached the eastern edge. Cannon and machine-guns spoke out. The panzergrenadiers advanced against the town under the cover of the tank cannon.

Each company had a street objective. Isolated resistance was broken. Red Army soldiers surrendered. At 1700 hours Belaya Glina was in the hands of "Wiking". The majority of the enemy rear guard, including a high-level headquarters, was able to withdraw to the south in time. Several American trucks were abandoned by the Soviets in the town and in its immediate vicinity. The 4th Platoon of 3./"Nordland" brought in three American Fords. They found the vehicles 2 kilometers southeast of the town. They had become stuck in the marsh and abandoned. Mileage reading: 4000 kilometers. Only the ignition cables were disconnected. The vehicles were running again in a short time. With only 4000 kilometers on them they had essentially been transported directly from Iran to the Caucasus. The officers from "Wiking" wanted to send a "thank you" note to Roosevelt for equipping them with American vehicles. Hstuf. Bühler took command of the battalion in place of the wounded commander of III/AR "Wiking".

Pz.KGr. "Wiking" covered approximately 25 march kilometers per day. During the night of 2 August SS "Wiking" secured itself in a great half circle around Belaya Glina. This jump to the west broke contact completely with the 198th ID, which was advancing to the west. On 2 August a reconnaissance platoon from the 3./"Nordland" was already looking to make contact with the 198th ID at 0300 hours. Because the Reconnaissance Battalion had to perform other missions, a grenadier company had to help out. The reconnaissance element under Uscha. Brocks consisted of one B-Krad and the group vehicle. In front of the B-Krad Rttf. [Rottenführer] Bender led a reconnaissance element from the former 17th Company. Uscha. Brocks rode in the side-car and his partner was an infantryman with a machine-pistol. The group followed in another vehicle within sight. Two machine-guns were temporarily mounted on the vehicle. They rode non-stop to the next town. Two Panjewagens [Russian horse-drawn carts] were dispatched to the German lines.

After approximately 15 kilometers, Reconnaissance Element Brocks came upon an enemy column in company strength. One anti-tank gun and one artillery gun passed by. Brocks did not take long to make his decision. Attack! His machine-pistol rattled. The machine-guns spoke out from the trucks. The enemy column fled into the cornfield. They were taken completely by surprise. 30 Russians were killed. The 7.62 cm anti-tank gun was attached to the "Klöckner Deutz". The gun was destroyed. Reconnaissance Element Brocks returned to the battalion after reaching the assigned line. They did not make contact with the 198th ID. The infantry division lagged further behind.

On 2 August, a Sunday, the lead elements of the XXXX Panzer Corps were ready to march and again meet up with the 3rd Panzer Division. Supply problems were becoming particularly noticeable within this corps: fuel shortages had become chronic. Often fuel had to be pooled together in order to advance only one panzer division. Because of this, "oil" became a magic word to the divisions. They hoped to find sufficient fuel near Maikop and Grosny.

At 0230 hours Advance Detachment Pape was advancing along the rail line to Salsk. An additional battle group followed. Soon Salsk lay behind them. The 3rd Panzer Division drove through Sandata and Iku Tuktum in two march columns to the south.

The vast land shimmered in the sun. The blue sky beckoned the German reconnaissance pilots early in the morning. Long dust columns stretched off to the south under them. The terrain was empty in front of the lead German panzer elements. Marshal Budenny had withdrawn his 56th Army into the Krasnodar area, while the 18th Army remained deeply echeloned in the Tikhorets area. The 12th Army was already near Armavir and in the Kuban bend. While the main body of the 37th Army withdrew toward Nevinnomyskaya, rear forces from this army held the area around Voroshilovsk (Stavropol). The eastern flank of the North Caucasus Front had already withdrawn toward the Kuma and the Terek. The vastness made unified command and control difficult. Each divisional commander had to make his own decisions. Only the overall march objective was staked out.

General Breith's 3rd Panzer Division drove toward the south in two march groups as the eastern march formation. This division advanced into a sector that was already partially steppe. There were wide stretches of terrain with steppe grass and only occasional sprinkles of green. Near Salsk there were large herds of horses. They were magnificent animals. Budenny was a breeder of this magnificent race. In other locations there were large herds of cattle and sheep. There were huge chicken farms where thousands of animals covered the steppes like fields of snow. Old draw-wells were surrounded by thirsty animals, by cattle, sheep, horses and camels. Camels, the unpretentious ships of the desert, were also at home there. The residents, old, established Kalmucks and Caucasians, were divided into many tribes. They were friendly and treated the Germans as liberators. They rebelled against Russian domination and defended their freedom with some success. On the evening of 2 August the lead elements of the 3rd Panzer Division were located in and around Pregrodnoe. It was similar with the III Panzer Corps. On 2 August they made a big jump to the south and, during the evening, the 13th Panzer Division and the 16th ID (Mot.) stood in the Novo Aleksandrovka sector in the Voroshilovsk - Krapotkin area. The I/61 Flak-Rgt. was attached to the 13th Panzer Division for air defense.

Pursue, gain ground! Without any regard for the threatened flanks. Occupied villages were bypassed and starved out. All of the divisions were ordered to attack to the south!

And, on 2 August, the 13th Panzer Division attacked to the south after crossing the Rassypnaya sector. They had not run into any enemy tanks for some time, there were more rocket launchers than tanks. Oberfeldwebel Schellhorn, Headquarters Company anti-tank platoon leader from the 66th Panzergrenadier Regiment, had destroyed numerous enemy tanks during his first year in Russia with his 3.7 anti-tank gun. The Russian T-34 tanks had to be hit directly in the exhaust because the shells had no effect anywhere else. The Oberfeldwebel was being frustrated by the rocket launchers, which were christened the "Stalin Organ". Schellhorn respected the capability of the truck-mounted rocket launchers. However, he had noticed that after firing a salvo, the Russians would re-load before they redeployed. That's what gave him his idea.

A concentrated rocket salvo crashed against the Germans. Schellhorn's 5 cm anti-tank gun platoon burst into the launching position. The enemy rocket launchers were being reloaded. Schellhorn drove into firing range. The Soviets fired another salvo. However, it went over the heads of the Germans. Then Schellhorn's anti-tank guns were ready to fire and they fired on the battery. From that hour on the 13th Panzer Division was left alone by the "Stalin Organs". Oberfeldwebel Schellhorn received the Knight's Cross for his clever commitment.

On the evening of 2 August the 13th Panzer Division stood on the Uspenskaya hills 90 kilometers southwest of Salsk. However, the march was still not completed. Advance Detachment Brux was formed. It was issued all of the fuel reserve. The detachment reached the Novo Marevskiy hills 20 kilometers away. The 43rd Kradschützen Battalion advanced to within 10 kilometers south of Navolokonskiy. During the night both battle groups established hasty defenses where they stood. The division's plan for 3 August was to occupy the bridge near Armavir and establish a bridgehead.

On 3 August at 0300 hours March Group Crisolli met up with Advance Detachment Brux. The left battle group (von Raczeck) followed at 0445 hours because the fuel convoy arrived late.

Battle Group Crisolli attacked near Karmelinovskaya. Battle Group von Raczeck attacked near Pobeda into strong enemy resistance. Tanks and the I/66 overran enemy batteries in open firing positions. The I/66 attacked mounted in SPW. Fire and movement was conducted in the classic style. The marshy stream sector was no obstacle. Move, shoot. They bypassed large corn and wheat fields. The lead panzer elements were aided by concentrated air support. Any enemy force noted by the tankers was engaged. Four to six bomber, two to four interceptors and other fighters and reconnaissance aircraft were in the air at any one time. At 1300 hours Battle Group Crisolli broke through the Gorkaya sector with the reinforced I/66 near Zerkovniy. The fleeing enemy columns were pursued.

The powerful engagement continued! Aircraft dropped smoke signals showing the ground troops the way, reported enemy concentrations and pointed out the best march routes if the ground reconnaissance could not keep pace. Things were going well! There was a short fire-fight. An enemy tank platoon fired and moved away. However, they continued to advance.

Southeast of Privolny the terrain steepened to 223 meters elevation as it approached the mountain range between Yegorlyk and the Kuban. Visibility between the two attack groups was two kilometers.

Suddenly, the tanks stood in the middle of a Russian defensive line. The positions were well camouflaged and could not be made out from the small observation slits. However, the SPW companies had already reached it. Oberleutnant Riemann fought with the men from his 3./66, moving between the tanks on the battlefield. The battlefield soon merged with the well- camouflaged Russian positions, which were engaged by the SPW's. Another SPW company destroyed an enemy battery in a sun-flower field, which was pointed out by pilots. The battle degenerated into many small battles, and, while the tanks continued to advance, the last resistance was broken in their rear by the panzergrenadiers. The entire attack armada, however, continued to advance.

Suddenly the lead elements stood in the hills east of the Kuban. 10 kilometers away to the south stood Armavir. No enemy forces were discovered on this side of the river. Below in the valley near Prochnokopskaya lay the Kuban bridge, to which all eyes were directed.

Tanks march! The lead tanks rolled at full speed toward the bridge. Major Brux followed with his I/66 Battalion Staff and the 3./66. However, shortly before the entrance to the bridge they were fired upon. An enemy motorized battalion had been left behind. A fierce battle ensued. Group Brux was too weak. Then the electrically fused bridge was blown. Additional elements assembled and tried to cross the river. However, this was impossible in the heavy enemy fire. Several attempts to cross failed, resulting in heavy losses. For the time being, contact could not be established with the few tanks on the other side. The six cut-off German tanks established a hasty defense on the western bridge access.

In the meantime, the Germans observed the deployment of additional Russian formations on the Kuban. German artillery was brought forward to engage the enemy movement.

During the night, the first panzergrenadiers moved through the ruins of the destroyed bridge and crossed to the western bank in rubber boats. The grenadiers ran to the bridge in their stocking feet because their footsteps were audible and would have unleashed enemy machine-gun fire. In this manner, three companies of the I/66 and one company each from the 43rd

Kradschützen Battalion and the 93rd Panzer Regiment crossed the river during the night. The following radio message arrived from the 1st Panzer Army command:

"The Kuban has been crossed. Thanks to the admirable soldiers and their spirited leadership. -

signed von Kleist."

On 4 August the expansion of the small bridgehead was frustrated by the fierce enemy defense and enemy counter strikes. Major Brux, commander of the units located in the bridgehead, ordered the formation of a solid main combat line.

Generalleutnant Herr realized that they could advance no further. His new plan foresaw an additional crossing during the following night, approximately 1.5 kilometers from the present bridge position. Then the two bridgeheads were to be combined.

A new group was formed under Oberstleutnant Stolz. At 2300 hours Battle Group Stolz crossed the river further to the south. There was little resistance. The new bridgehead was immediately expanded with all available companies and work was begun on a combined K and ponton bridge. On 5 August at 0130 hours heavy weapons were already being crossed on 4 ton ferries. At 0435 hours the first elements of the 16th ID (Mot.) arrived, which were also subordinated to Oberstleutnant Stolz. It was the 60th Panzergrenadier Regiment, which promptly established contact with the northern bridgehead. On 5 August at 1000 hours the Magdeburger 4th Armored Engineer battalion completed the 24 ton bridge. The march could continue!

On 2 August "Wiking", as the link between the mobile divisions in the east and the slower foot formations in the west, made only a small jump of 15 kilometers. For the time being, the objective of the right neighboring divisions was the important railroad center of Tikhorets, which was captured three days later.

To avoid ambushes from enemy unit stragglers, "Wiking" conducted its march in two march groups. Each night they established hasty defenses. Each day a panzer platoon remained behind with the panzer battalion's maintenance platoon repairing damaged vehicles. In some cases, even grenadier companies would stay behind. Such groups would await the arrival of the supply column and accompany them forward. Thus the convoys were always secured. Nevertheless, on 1 August, "Wiking" lost five tankers in an ambush.

On 2 August "Wiking" dispatched a battle group toward Novo Pokrovskoe (15 kilometers south of Belaya Glina), while the main body remained in Belaya Glina and advanced later.

On the morning of 3 August the Kommodore of a group from the 500th Interceptor Squadron, Major Diering, landed his twin engine Ju-88 near Nizhnaya Dimitreievskaya in order to discuss the attack plan with the ground troop commanders. Generalmajor der Waffen SS Felix Steiner, who had taken command of the refitted Division "Wiking" (whose battle group was led by Oberführer Gille) precisely explained the plan for crossing the Kuban. A study of the terrain offered two favorable locations for crossing, one near Krapotkin, one near Grigoripolnskaya. The corps order pointed to Krapotkin,

PANZER ASSAULT TO THE SOUTH

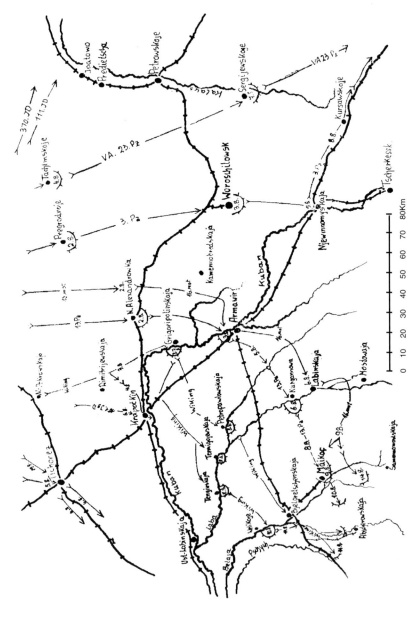

so that the deployment of the foot formations would also have a suitable bridge. Stubaf. Mühlenkamp believed otherwise. He wanted to probe the river from the Kuban bend to the south for suitable positions because he anticipated the greatest resistance near Krapotkin. Steiner was convinced.

The tanks of "Wiking" advanced, followed by the "Germania" Regiment and the I and II/5 SS AR. The deep flanks were covered by reconnaissance elements from the Reconnaissance Battalion.

There was constantly an aircraft from the interceptor squadron in the air, guiding the lead panzer elements. Generaloberst von Richthoven, commander of the 4th Luftflotte, experienced the best cooperation between the ground and the air formations during the Caucasus commitment. Such cooperation would not be possible again due to the later shortage of aircraft. Only in the summer of 1943, during the battle of Kursk, would this type of coordination reach similar perfection. In retrospect, Stubaf. Mühlenkamp described the cooperation with the Luftwaffe:

"Cooperation with the 500th Interceptor Squadron was excellent. Every day by dawn our pilots from the interceptor squadron contacted us. They talked with us over the radio or dropped messages and requested we assign them suitable landing zones, which could be designated with light markers. The Kommodore, Major Diering, landed on the unfamiliar terrain brilliantly. After a short greeting, the day's combat plans were discussed.

The pilots provided reconnaissance and weapon support. They searched for possible crossing sites. Without this help, we would have been required to spend many hours conducting ground reconnaissance. They would circle their aircraft over the crossing sites. With this help, we were able to move promptly to the sites. In addition they also reported on strongly defended sectors and offered us bypass possibilities. They joined in the ground battle with on-board weapons and fragmentation bombs or suppressed enemy forces. In all, the cooperation was ideal."

This cooperation climaxed on the 3rd of August. Below rolled tanks and mounted infantry, artillery and engineers, and in the air observers surveyed the vast plains. On this day, the advance was not impeded by Russian rear guard elements. Hstuf. Dorr, a company commander in I/"Germania", entered the following in his diary for 3/8/1942:

"Dimitrievskaya/Grigoripolnskaya: There has never been a German soldier here between the Caspian and Black Seas. The dreary steppe is interspersed with good stretches of land. There were heavy rain showers. Have to put up with heat and dust. Reached the Kuban at 1130 hours in a rapid advance. Briefings at division headquarters. Then the decision: Attack Grigoripolnskaya, where a bridge is available. Russians fleeing. We pursued them. Crossed the Kuban in rafts. Raids. It is a beautiful success for the I/"Germania".

The major events that Hstuf. Dorr only briefly sketched included other factors that he could not have known of. At midday the lead elements of the Division "Wiking" stood in the Kuban bend. Up to this point in time, the second march group, Battle Group "Nordland", had been following to Dimitrievskaya. During discussions with the senior leadership staffs the decision was made to attack with the main force of "Wiking" to the southeast in order to cover the long western flank of the 13th Panzer Division, which was already extended far to the south.

In the meantime, at 1430 hours, "Nordland" was attacked by approximately 30 Russian aircraft in the vicinity of Dimitrievskaya. At this time a "Fieseler Storch" and a Ju-88, located in a field, were set ablaze.

While the I/"Germania" was establishing a small bridgehead during the evening hours near Grigoripolnskaya, the "Nordland" Regiment had two battalions, a panzer company and the III/5 SS AR reach the Kuban bend. The battle group under Oberführer von Scholz took a break during the night in the area of the town of Vorovskoi. A little later the order for the next day arrived. It said:

"Battle Group von Scholz is to take Krapotkin and occupy the road bridge over the Kuban south of the city!"

Now we will follow the route of the XXXX Panzer Corps, which advanced on the eastern flank: On 3 August the corps had committed only one panzer division because of a fuel shortage. While the main body of the 23rd Panzer Division awaited fuel in Proletarskaya and Salsk, the 3rd Panzer Division made the great jump to Voroshilovsk (Stavropol). From the starting point at Pregrodnoe up to Voroshilovsk it is 100 kilometers in a straight line. How did they cope?

On the morning of 3 August the advance detachment under Major Pape left the town of Besopassnoe. The objective was Donskoe. The weak resistance was overcome. A transport train, laden with tanks and guns, was captured under steam at the Pelegiada railroad station.

The main force of the 3rd Panzer Division, organized into Battle Group von Liebenstein, reached Besopassnoe at 0830 hours. A weak advance detachment of the 23rd Panzer Division, which was supplied with fuel, attacked to the east as they took responsibility for security to the east.

In the meantime, Major Pape's advance detachment continued to advance and, at 1345 hours, its lead element stood in front of Voroshilovsk. It was a beautiful sight: On the other side of a wide valley, Voroshilovsk lay on a flat hill, surrounded by apricot and plum orchards. Everywhere there were traces of German air attacks. On the roads there were overturned vehicles and heavy weapons. Freight trains were still burning on open stretches of track. The IV German Air Corps had done a good job there. Enemy movement was discerned, it was the 37th Soviet Army in retreat. Major Pape did not reflect long on the situation.

"It was now or never! - The confusion had to be exploited!"

The engines burst into action. The I battalion of the 6th Panzer Regiment and the 3rd Kradschützen Battalion set in movement.

"Attack!" Tanks and Kradschützen roared through the valley, reached the edge of the city and plowed through the streets. Soviets were fleeing everywhere. Wherever resistance flared up, it was silenced. Many positions were destroyed by air bombardment. There were dead bodies and abandoned equipment everywhere. The stores were plundered. Hauptmann Rohrbeck plowed through to the airfield with his I Battalion of the 6th Panzer Regiment and secured a fuel dump. The 3rd Kradschützen Battalion captured a grain silo with 25,000 quintals of wheat.

The panzer attack by the 3rd Panzer Division broke like a summer storm over the city of 90,000. Even after the airfield was captured, Soviet aircraft still tried to land there. Eight aircraft were shot down, seven by air defense fire and one four-engine aircraft with infantry weapons. At 1550 hours Voroshilovsk was solidly in German hands. Additional forces from the 3rd Panzer Division closed ranks.

On 4 August the 3rd Panzer Division remained in Voroshilovsk. Battle Group von Liebenstein took up security.

Without concern for the lengthened supply routes and the extreme shortage of fuel, elements of the 23rd Panzer Division, which were organized into Battle Group Burmeister, set out again on 4 August and captured Tuguluk. The fuel shortage again forced a halt. Only small groups reconnoitered on the long eastern flank.

Now we return to the Kuban! On 3 August the I/"Germania" was able to establish a bridgehead near Grigoripolnskaya. However, the corps also had to establish a Kuban crossing near Krapotkin for the following foot formations. This mission fell to Battle Group von Scholz.

Battle Group von Scholz broke out of the Vorovskoi area on 4 August at 0600 hours. They were guided by reconnaissance elements from the reconnaissance battalion. They were followed by a panzer company and a panzergrenadier company. Behind them at a distance were: 1st Panzer Company, Regimental Headquarters, I/"Nordland", one panzerjäger company, one anti-aircraft platoon, III/5 SS AR, II/"Nordland" and another anti-aircraft platoon.

They moved to the west along the Nizhnaya Aleksandrovka - Krapotkin rail line. The advance detachment drove the Soviet security forces out of Kavkaskaya. At 1000 hours the main body reached the town. Halt! The panzergrenadiers utilized the halt; they supplied themselves with apricots. The numerous apricot orchards offered over-ripened fruit. In the meantime, the reconnaissance results arrived.

Oberführer von Scholz committed his battle group accordingly: One battalion from the east, one from the northeast, the reconnaissance battalion in a flanking attack from the west, two panzer companies in the assigned main effort, the III/5 SS AR followed behind the first echelon.

"Panzers - forward march!" The MTW [personnel transport vehicles] followed the tanks with mounted infantry. All were widely dispersed.

The II Battalion attacked the northeastern edge of the city into strong enemy resistance. A long Russian column was advancing. They met it before they reached the bridge. Dismounted, the battalion gained ground only slowly. When von Scholz received the report on the approximate 1000 man column, he knew that only a rapid advance would succeed. I/"Nordland", which advanced adjacent to the river from the east, had to hit the Russian column in the flank.

Fritz von Scholz mounted all available groups onto the tanks and directed them to Krapotkin. The Soviets panicked. They fled toward the Kuban crossing. The "Wiking" tanks plowed through the streets of the city with the mounted grenadiers. Many of the Soviets were forced into the side streets, where they were taken prisoner. Three to four German tanks rolled along the street toward the bridge. Shortly before the lead tanks reached the bridge it was blown into the air. There were two powerful explosions. Portions of the bridge rained down like hail. Two trains burned in the vicinity. The time was 1120 hours.

During the attack on Krapotkin, the 3/"Nordland" advanced a pair of tanks along the river toward the city. Krapotkin and the entire Kuban valley could be surveyed from the dominant northern bank. There, fully laden trains steamed one behind the other in the direction of Krasnodar and Armavir, shortly before the bridge was blown. A profitable target! The 7th Battery, which was following the 3rd Company, took up positions on the dominant northern bank. The guns were ready to fire in a moments notice. Then the tubes burst forth! A wagon with ammunition was hit. This blocked the withdrawal route in the direction of Armavir. The ammunition blew into the air like fireworks. The 7th Battery shot up several freight trains.

Krapotkin was cleared of enemy elements. Security was arranged. On the next day, the advance detachment of the 101st Jäger Division advanced into Krapotkin and took over the security arrangements. The "Nordland" Regiment was to follow the division to Grigoripolnskaya.

The 13th Panzer Division and the "Wiking" engaged in heavy fighting in the Kuban bridgeheads on 4 August. For the time being, we will remain with the SS "Wiking". Hstuf. Dorr wrote in his diary:

"4/8/42 Grigoripolnskaya: The enemy attempted to throw us back to the opposite bank during the night. The combat was fierce, but we held. I took over command in the bridgehead. However, we would not succeed with only the battalion (I/"Germania"). We were ordered to hold the bridgehead at all costs. We established another small bridgehead. The 7th Company arrived as reserve. A difficult night."

In this sober recollection of Hstuf. Dorr the combat of I/"Germania" is only illuminated in outline fashion. Stubaf. Jörchel's II/"Germania" joined in the battle with one company - the Seventh. "Wiking" engineers made preparations for operating ferries and, therefore, established the prerequisite for constructing a bridge. The mathematical calculations of the engineers had to be increased, because the tables available - which were based on the fastest German river, the Isar - were of no use there. The current was very strong at this location. During the course of the crossing Russian aircraft attacked. Bombs fell and on-board weapons hammered throughout day. However, the "Wiking" air defenses provided some support.

When Dorr wrote: "...we were ordered to hold the bridgehead at all costs...", he meant that the highest German headquarters saw this bridgehead as the prerequisite for an attack to the west, which would unhinge the entire

Kuban defense. Therefore, this offered the possibility of pinning the Soviet divisions, which stood before the German foot formations of the V Army Corps, in front of the mountains and destroying large Soviet formations. Something that had not been able to accomplish previously. However, the Soviet leadership recognized this threat and frustrated it with the bitter encirclement of the bridgehead near Grigoripolnskaya.

Hstuf. Dorr's diary had this to say about 5 August:

"Bridgehead Grigoripolnskaya: From 0200 - 0250 hours and from 0400 - 0500 hours enemy attacks were repulsed. 1st Company is holding feverishly. The crossing site is under fire. 3rd Company attacked at 0815 hours. The attack was successful. The Russians pulled back a little. The enemy is fighting fiercely. 5th Company and I/5 SS AR finally arrive at 1200 hours. Another attack was launched at 1500 hours and it established a large bridgehead. The good observation position in the church is again in our hands."

The diary explained how the Russians attempted to penetrate into the 13th Panzer Division and "Wiking" bridgehead, or at least surround it, in order to allow their divisions in the west to withdraw. The foot formations of the V German Army Corps were a three-day's march behind. This was a battle to gain time! If the bridgehead was to fulfill its mission as a spring-board, then it had to be expanded to accommodate the deployment of infantry weapons and artillery. Then the bridge-building process could begin. If tanks and heavy weapons could not be crossed to the opposite bank, then the bridgehead was worthless. Expansion and encirclement were the decisive factors in the struggle between friend and foe. Hstuf. Hans Dorr, commander of 4/"Germania" and commandant in the Grigoripolnskaya bridgehead indicated this decisive factor in his diary with the words "attack and defense". On the evening of 5 August, as Dorr made his last entries, his battle group had been in the bridgehead for 50 hours. These 50 hours were passed as follows: a company was crossed in rubber rafts and a small bridgehead was established. Combat was often hand-to-hand. Additional reinforcements arrived by rubber raft and small ferries. The bridgehead was expanded. Artillery supported and suppressed enemy heavy weapons. Engineers prepared for bridging operations. Anti-aircraft elements provided protection for the air space. Large ferries were prepared and crossed anti-tank guns, infantry guns and light field howitzers. Then additional infantry was crossed, which expanded the bridgehead. There were enemy counterattacks. Bridges were constructed. Larger formations were crossed.

On 5 August II/"Germania" had two companies across. The bridgehead was bursting at the seams. The 2./5 SS Pi. received some welcome reinforcement on this day. The corps engineer battalion arrived. The construction of the combat bridge was begun. However, all indications were that the Soviets were not giving up the encirclement. In the meantime, the "Wiking" Artillery Regiment had completely assembled: three light field howitzer battalions, one heavy field howitzer battalion, one 10.5 cm cannon battery. In addition there was corps artillery: one 10.5 cm cannon battery, two 10,5 cm howitzer battalions and one 21 cm mortar battalion. There was also one rocket launcher battalion with 15 and 28 cm rockets. A powerful fire force.

On 6 August the fierce combat continued in the Grigoripolnskaya bridge-head. Heavy Soviet artillery strikes worked on the "Wiking" artillery positions. The crossing attempt was discovered right away and placed under fire by the enemy. Soon it was clear that the Russian batteries had to be engaged by the German ones. All were located systematically. Then their secret came to light! Two Soviet artillery officers were directing fire from the church steeple in Grigoripolnskaya. The German request for them to surrender was met with pistol shots. No quarter was given. The Soviet officers were killed. Several air attacks were flown against the crossing site on this day. The "Nordland" Regiment advanced elements which figured in the collapse of enemy resistance on 7 August.

Before we describe the "Wiking" attack out of the Grigoripolnskaya bridgehead, we must first relate the events on the eastern flank.

On 5 August the 3rd Panzer Division was again ready to march into Voroshilovsk. The shortage of fuel again would not allow the XXXX Panzer Corps to move in force. The 23rd Panzer Division had to wait, dispatching only small groups to reconnoiter to the east. On 5 August Battle Group von Liebenstein was in movement in the 3rd Panzer Division area of operations.

Von Liebenstein's advance detachment broke out at 0300 hours. It was led by Oberleutnant Graf von Kageneck's 4./6 Pz.Rgt., followed by the 3 Kradschützen Battalion, I/75 Pz. AR, 39 Armored Engineer Battalion, 10./AR 70 and a supply convoy. They passed through Barssukovskaya in the direction of Nevinnomyskaya. The terrain increased in elevation. There were curves and serpentines like in the Thueringer Wald. In spite of this, they maintained high speed. At times, the tank engines could not maintain the high speeds and they had to be towed with difficulty through the mountains or be left behind. When the lead elements had closed upon Nevinnomyskaya, there were still six tanks operational.

They made a short halt for observation. The dominant western bank of the Kuban was well constructed and heavily occupied. Again Major Pape faced a similar situation as he did before Voroshilovsk, and again he made the decision to attack!

The panzers led. The kradschützen were in between. An enemy battery was overrun, then the road to the city was open. They all advanced very quickly. The resistance at the railroad station was broken and a loaded freight train was captured. The Armavir - Georgievsk rail line was severed. Two tanks were left for security. The other four plowed further through the city, crossed the 150 meter long Kuban bridge and established a bridgehead with the 2./3 Kradschützen Btl. By evening additional elements of the division had arrived to reinforce the advance detachment. The Kuban was crossed at a third location, in the foothills of the Caucasus.

Nevinnomyskaya was of particular importance. There, the important west - east railroad connection was made for shipping oil from Grosny to Rostov. And there began the Zukhum Army Road, the access point for contact with the Transcaucasus.

With the reaching of the foothills, the Soviet forces in the western and eastern Caucasus were separated from each other. Reconnaissance elements from the 3rd Panzer Division reconnoitered in all directions during the following days and established that numerous Soviet march groups were moving into the Kuban Valley to the south. Without fuel, the 3rd Panzer Division had to limit itself to guarding the gateway to the high mountain passes; it could not pursue.

The panzer assault of the XXXX Panzer Corps to the south had come to an end after reaching Nevinnomyskaya. A new phase began: the battle of the 1st Panzer Army in the eastern Caucasus! At first, the commander, Generaloberst von Kleist, had only the XXXX Panzer Corps and the LII Army Corps (which still lagged far behind) available for this mission. The III Panzer Corps was fighting near Maikop and probed further to the south with the LVII Panzer Corps. How was it going there?

On 3 August the 13th Panzer Division was able to establish a small bridgehead north of Armavir. During the night of 5 August a second smaller bridgehead was established 1.5 kilometers to the south. They were merged together during the course of the afternoon. Therefore, the groundwork was laid:

1. to make possible an attack on Armavir by the following 16th ID (Mot.) and

2. for the creation of a spring board for additional large-scale operations.

On the morning of 5 August a solid tank bridge stood in spite of the lack of technical equipment. The panzer and panzergrenadier companies then streamed across the bridge. Anti-tank trenches were overcome, additional enemy positions were overran. Maikop was within reach!

At this time the commander of the 13th Panzer Division issued the following order of the day:

"...to all commanders! - The rapid accomplishment of the division's assigned mission (capture of Maikop) will have a decisive effect upon the war. All of the officers and non-commissioned officers in the division must realize this. During the pursuit, towns will be avoided whenever possible. Crossings and fords will be reconnoitered and captured well in advance. - Forward! - signed Herr."

While the 13th Panzer Division advanced on Maikop, the 16th ID (Mot.) crossed the 13th Panzer Division combat bridge and attacked the city of Armavir with the 60th Panzergrenadier Regiment. On 5 August immediately after crossing the 80 meter wide Kuban, the 60th Panzergrenadier Regiment turned to attack the city of 150,000. Oberst Vial organized his regiment as follows: on the right, I Battalion, on the left II Battalion, III Battalion in reserve.

The I Battalion advanced well at first in open terrain. However, it bogged down at an anti-tank trench position. The II Battalion had it even more difficult as it had to advance through thick orchard terrain and dodge sniper fire from anti-tank trenches, which were difficult to eliminate. The battalion commander, Major Lindner, and his staff advanced with the II Battalion and the reserve company. A costly battle ensued for 50 - 100 meters. Behind Major Lindner lay 8-10 dead from his battalion. Lindner fired without stopping. Tears of frustration ran down his powder-blackened face. Lindner's battalion was stuck.

Then the III/60, which had just crossed the Kuban, was ordered to support the II Battalion. Hauptmann Fischer's III Battalion inserted itself into the almost two kilometer wide gap between the two other battalions in order to frontally assault the anti-tank trenches. This was risky! After an assault over almost open terrain, the 10th Company of Oberstleutnant Maah penetrated into the anti-tank trenches. The 9th and 11th Companies followed. The Soviets fled. Fischer's battalion pursued. They fought a see-saw battle through the cornfield. A row of trees was captured in an assault. Advance Detachment Kusenberg attacked with the panzergrenadiers. They took cover in the still warm Russian trenches. Then the shells of the I/146 AR pursued the fleeing Russians into the city. An assault element was on the heels of the enemy. After two hours white headlights appeared. The vehicles of the III/60 had caught up and the panzergrenadiers mounted them. More white headlights appeared in the city. Hauptmann Fischer ordered "march!" and his battalion burst into the city. By evening Armavir had fallen. During their retreat, the Soviets had abandoned much combat equipment and 50 aircraft to the Germans.

At this time Oberstabarzt Dr. Mühling was located with the 66th (Mot.) Field Hospital (16th ID Mot.) in Khleborab on the division deployment route. Through various statements from local inhabitants and prisoners Dr. Mühling learned that there was a senior Soviet headquarters in the neighborhood where important documents were buried in a trunk. After several fruitless attempts to find the trunk, Dr. Mühling would still not give up. On 8 August his efforts were rewarded. Several trunks were dug up and sent to the Division Ic in farmers' carts.

The analysis of the material revealed that Dr. Mühling had discovered a treasure, namely:

a) for the troops: good maps of the Caucasus region up to Tuapse.

b) for the leadership: an assessment of the Caucasus region between Maikop and Tuapse, with missions of the assigned defensive strong points.

c) for the OKW: espionage material about Turkey that could be used as groundwork for instigating a war between the Soviet Union and Turkey, along with plans for fortifications works in construction on the Soviet - Turkish border.

We will take this opportunity to say something about the maps that the German troop leaders had available: without exception, they were old maps from Tsarist times with German overprinting. The maps did not agree with actual terrain conditions. There was an overall shortage of maps. Thus, for example, the commander of the "Wiking" Panzer Battalion had a map of the Caucasus that originated from a school in Rostov. However, it was still better than the old maps that were issued.

On 6 August the 13th Panzer Division established a bridgehead over the

Laba near Kurgannaya. Generalleutnant Henrici's 16th ID (Mot.) reached the Laba on this day near Labinskaya. All bridges were destroyed. Engineers from the 13th Panzer Division constructed a corduroy road over the marshy river region. Bridges and fords were utilized as light reconnaissance forces from the 13th Panzer Division advanced further toward Maikop on the afternoon of 8 August.

On 7 August the 16th ID (Mot.) fought for the crossing in Labinskaya. The 165th Kradschützen Battalion penetrated into the eastern quarter of the city. The 156th Panzergrenadier Regiment was in second echelon to the right. The attack was supported by the 203rd Assault Gun Brigade and the III/146 AR. 14 aircraft were captured on the edge of the city. The kradschützen advanced to the Laba River. However, they could not go any further. The German attack collapsed.

At 1100 hours the 116th Panzer Battalion and the I/156 Pz.Gren.Rgt. advanced to the south up to Vladimirskaya in order to cross a ford that was supposed to be there and attack into the rear of the enemy opposing the 165th Kradschützen Battalion. However, all attempts to find the ford failed. At this time Generalleutnant Henrici received the latest air photos available from a "Fieseler Storch". Again (as by Manych) they held surprises: The pictures showed a new railroad crossing over the Laba in the direction of the mountains, which was not indicated on the maps. Generalleutnant Henrici ordered the engineer battalion and the majority of the 156th Panzergrenadier Regiment to set out for it, along with the Heeres air defense.

There actually was a new railroad and an almost completed solid wooden railroad bridge near the town of Sassovskaya. The tracks were already completely laid. The crossing was suitable for wheeled vehicles. Next to this bridge stood a 1.5 meter wide workers' bridge across which the men and motorcycles could move. However, the best part was that on the near side of the river there were eight railroad cars with ties that the engineer battalion only had to nail down. Stalin had thought of everything.

In the meantime the 165th Kradschützen Battalion was relieved by the following 60th Panzergrenadier Regiment near Labinskaya. It advanced to the bridge position. Under the protection of the established bridgehead, the 675th Engineer Battalion (Mot.) completed the railroad crossing for wheeled vehicles. The 203rd Assault Gun Brigade and the 116th Panzer Battalion completed the crossing south of the bridge over a ford they discovered.

On 8 August the 13th Panzer Division and the 16th ID (Mot.) prepared for their attack on Maikop. The SS "Wiking" Division was available, as it advanced from the Kuban bridgehead at Grigoripolnskaya to the Laba.

During the night of 7 August the 24 ton bridge was completed. The "Wiking" Panzer Battalion arrived at 0500 hours. A stuka attack, which was requested by the division, wore down the resistance of the defenders and struck at the enemy batteries. At 0530 hours the panzer battalion and the bridgehead troops from the "Germania" Regiment set out to widen the bridgehead. The panzer battalion stopped. Engineers led the way and constructed a corduroy road over the marsh. In the meantime, Battle Group "Nordland" crossed the bridge. At 0700 hours the deployment continued.

The march order: panzer battalion, 5./"Nordland", rest of II/"Nordland", III/5 SS AR and I/"Nordland". In second echelon followed the "Germania" Regiment with the other elements of the division.

They stopped in front of Olginskoe. Enemy movement required tank fire. A pair of tank shells were fired and the Russian rear guard fled. The tanks plowed on further, passing abandoned enemy batteries.

At first the German attack was directed to the northwest, along the Armavir - Krapotkin rail line. Along the entire stretch of approximately 30 kilometers, Russian transport trains were jammed up, having been shot up by the Luftwaffe or the "Wiking" Artillery Regiment's 7th Battery. All of the trains were laden with army goods and were to be withdrawn to Armavir. However, the 13th Panzer Division had already established a bridgehead there. "Wiking" rolled up to the area south of Krapotkin. There was no longer evidence of the Soviet Kuban defense. The 101st Jäger Division was, therefore, able to establish a crossing of the Kuban near Krapotkin.

The division separated into two groups near Gulkeviche (south of Krapotkin). Air reconnaissance reported that the crossings over the Laba River near Termigoevskaya and to the south were still intact and were being utilized by fleeing enemy formations. Generalmajor der Waffen SS Felix Steiner, the reliable and successful commander of the "Wiking" Volunteer Division, knew immediately how to treat the air reports. He ordered:

"Panzer Battalion and `Nordland' to advance on Termigoevskaya! - Battle Group `Germania' to advance on Petropavlovskaya! - Both battle groups are to capture the Laba bridges!"

This was a clear order! Panzer and panzergrenadier companies moved out. The land was sun-drenched. It was 42 degrees in the shade. Long columns of dust ran off to the southwest. An enemy blocking position was overrun by the tanks. The "Nordland" Regiment advanced mounted on the vehicles. The sun had reached its zenith. Evening approached. Darkness finally stopped the German advance.

"Halt - engines off - last break!"

This order gradually stemmed the droning of the engines. Close-in security was set up, and reconnaissance elements were sent toward Termigoevskaya. Silence, a sinister silence spread.

Soon, the reconnaissance elements returned and reported: "Termigoevskaya is full of withdrawing Russians. There is no organized defense."

Regimental commander Fritz von Scholz, known for his quick and precise decisions, reacted immediately and discussed his attack plan with the commander of I/"Nordland":

"Polewacz, one of your companies will immediately attack Termigoevskaya and capture the Laba bridge south of the town in a rapid advance. Then your battalion will clear the city itself, when the lead elements reach the bridge. Who will you assign for the raid on the bridge?"

"Hstuf. Bluhm and his Third Company!"

The dice were cast. Hstuf. Bluhm, the oldest company commander in I/"Nordland" would acquit himself well. In the meantime, midnight had come and gone. While I/"Nordland" prepared for the night attack, II Battalion secured the panzer battalion on the northern chain of hills. 3./"Nordland" made preparations for the raid on the bridge.

Hstuf. Bluhm made the situation and mission known to his platoon leaders. The order to the individual platoons followed. Hstuf. Bluhm warned: "The town is occupied by the enemy. It is unnecessary to ensure that contact be maintained!"

The platoon leaders dispersed and assembled their men. The men were already awake. Here and there were whispers. Weapons were being readied. They gathered into groups and waited.

The engineers led the way. The platoons followed; each on their own assigned street. Noiselessly the men marched through the night. Equipment clattered, leather straps creaked softly. In the east a milky haze announced the new day, for many their last. The first houses appeared as large dark blocks. Their eyes strained searching through the darkness, trying to make out enemy posts. - None! - They moved like thieves among the houses among the shadows of the night. Everything was still quiet. Would they be able to achieve surprise?

"Psst - psst!" All movement froze.

The rattle of a machine-gun broke the ghostly stillness. Machine-pistols nattered in between. Detonations thudded. Then hand-grenades.

The dark shadows jumped up. "Forward, forward to the bridge!" The thumping of the heartbeat was ignored, adrenalin was flowing. The lungs gasped for air. An intersection was overcome that was covered by enemy machine-guns. "Medic!" A wounded soldier was dragged from the zone of fire. Others jumped forward.

Weapons were also firing ahead at the river. A thunderous explosion overwhelmed the noise of combat. Where was the bridge...? One could not think anymore. Sleepy, half-dressed Russians hastened out of the buildings. Shots ricocheted. However, one could not deal with the unessential, only with what was coming next.

"Forward to the bridge!" came the inspiring words. The men staggered down a slope. River sand crunched under their boots. The 4th Platoon messenger stumbled behind his platoon leader, Oscha. Busse, and lay down in a ground depression, exhausted.

The night turned grey. The eyes began to recognize more and more. Before them the Laba River lay like a bright band. On the left the bank was covered in reeds. On the far side of the river was a forest from which machine-gun fire was forcing the Third to keep their heads down behind the sand dunes. The bridge was blown. Destroyed blocks of wood fell into the water.

The Third dispersed, taking cover in the sand dunes. However, the objective was the bridgehead.

On the left, a group of Russians emerged from the reeds. They were looking for the bridge. Instead they found Germans. One of the Russians fell, the others hurried back into the reeds.

After overcoming the seconds of panic, the Third pulled itself together. The men ran from dune to dune in short jumps. Schütze [machine-gun team] II found Schütze I. Uscha. Freiwald's heavy machine-gun group worked its way to the bank in heavy defensive fire. Uscha. Krüger's heavy machine-gun crew took up position near the bridge site and joined the fire fight. Krüger's machine-gun hammered out in long bursts. Suddenly Rttf. Petersen, a Dane, fell backward. The machine-gun grew silent. Schütze II and Schütze III pulled the dead Petersen away. Then Krüger's machine-gun burst into life again.

Uscha. Lanfhoff's heavy machine-gun crew also took up position near the bridge site. Schütze II, Rttf. Johannsen, and Schütze II, Rttf. Nielsen, a Norwegian, lay behind their machine-guns and fired. The shells disappeared into the opposing forest. There, where the flashes of muzzles appeared. One could only fire at the bursts of light. However, the enemy fire was decreasing noticeably.

Platoon Leader Busse jumped forward. His messenger followed him. An enemy machine-gun swept around. They took cover behind a dune. In front of the courier ran Schütze II and other machine-gun groups. The Russian fire swept back. Carsten Rassmussen fell.

"Medic!" The medic quickly arrived. He carried Rassmussen on his back. Red foam was coming from his mouth and nose. A shudder, a shake, and Rassmussen was dead.

The platoon leader called to the left. The messenger passed on the order. Then Uscha. Schulze's mortar group joined in. Somewhere to the rear, one could hear the thud of the launch. Unterscharführer Schuetz' and Leitner's crews worked in precision. Oscha. Ludescheidt's and Stuscha. Noack's light platoons were interspersed within the heavy platoon.

Soon there was daylight. There, on the far bank, the brave men from the engineer platoon could be made out. They were assaulting the last Russians on the other side of the bridge. However, they still could not prevent the enemy from blowing up the bridge. They were compressed into a narrow area, they fought desperately.

The Laba River was about 30 meters wide. The bridge was only a pile of wood. Guns and equipment lay in the water. Only the gun tubes and command turrets rose out of the water. And on the bank there were overturned milk cans and wagons, as well as an ambulance.

The defensive fire decreased. Engineers advanced toward the bridge in order to create a temporary lane. The first attempt failed with losses. The German fire again raged furiously. And again the engineers advanced quickly. They were able to create a temporary lane across the ruined bridge, two planks wide.

Then the men of the Third assaulted across the river. They fanned out firing and pursued the withdrawing enemy. A small bridgehead was established. "Halt - entrench!"

The bridgehead stabilized. Trees and thick underbrush complicated visibility. The Russians were still firing back. The enemy infantry fire slackened off at midday, the artillery fire in the evening.

As it grew dark "Old Fritz", as Regiment Commander von Scholz was called by his men, appeared in the bridgehead and was satisfied with the crossing and road conditions. At nightfall Hstuf. Bluhm and his 3rd Company returned to the opposite bank over the small planks, in single file.

While the "Nordland" Regiment fought near Termigoevskaya, Battle Group "Germania" also established a crossing near Petropavlovskaya on the night of 8 August, under the able leadership of Staf. Wagner. After a bridge was also prematurely blown here, "Germania" was able to establish a bridgehead across a ford. Both bridgeheads were placed under fire by the Soviets on 8 August. In the meantime, additional reconnaissance revealed that a ford existed further down river and that a Laba bridge was intact near Tenginskaya. The "Wiking" Panzer Battalion, which was closest, was immediately committed. Mühlenkamp's tanks rolled during the morning hours of 8 August. At 1000 hours the panzer battalion established a bridgehead near Tenginskaya. Companies from the "Nordland" Regiment caught up. On this day von Mackensen's III Panzer Corps already stood before the gates of Maikop. In connection with this, one operation must be illuminated.

With the attack on Maikop, one of the most daring operations in the history of the war was conducted. A small band of German soldiers in NKVD uniforms infiltrated into Maikop with the mission of preventing the destruction of the oil storage tanks and refineries. Again oil was the key word. What occurred?

Leutnant Baron Folkersam, a Baltic German and descendant of an admiral who had died in German service, organized and trained a special commando in Allenstein, East Prussia. It consisted of 62 Baltic and Sudeten Germans who spoke Russian. Their intensive training was to bear fruit.

During the night of 2 August, as the 13th Panzer Division stood in the Kuban region near Novo Aleksandrovskaya, Baron Folkersam assembled his bogus NKVD people in front of a Kuban village which was occupied by Soviet stragglers of various nationalities.

After the airwaves were surveyed by radio intercept units, the bogus NKVD unit suddenly appeared in the village. From where they came, no one could say. However, they were there. Baron Folkersam had his people assemble the Red Army soldiers and he began his speech: "Soldiers of the glorious Red Army! The fascists have still not won. Our great Stalin has decoyed the Germans into the Caucasus only to destroy them..."

A Cossack laughed out loud, one of the NKVD men drove him in front of the speaker.

"Defeatist" raged Folkersam.

"Will you liquidate me?"

"Later!" answered Folkersam and continued: "You must be thankful that you appeared here before the deserters. Nevertheless, I must make an example. Cossacks to the right! Ukrainians to the fore! - Lets go, move it!"

After the people were sorted, Folkersam ordered: "Drive the Cossacks to the north. I will be right behind you!"

The detachment started moving. The night swallowed them up. A Cossack

Ataman was quickly found that was taken into their confidence. When the Cossacks were marched to the German lines, frenzied fire simulated their execution. In the same manner, the others were also separated. Only the Russians remained behind.

Leutnant Folkersam, now Major Trukhin, assembled his bogus NKVD people, mounted them on Russian vehicles and rode with the Russians in the direction of Maikop. Soon they came upon jammed roads and could only move slowly.

On the bridge near Armavir there were real NKVD people (2 August). They were regulating traffic and directing arriving units. The bogus NKVD Major got out of his vehicle, went up to the real NKVD Colonel and reported:

"Comrade Colonel..."

"Are you finally here? We have been waiting for you! Who are you anyway?"

"Major Trukhin from the Shadow Brigade. We are coming from Stalingrad with a special mission..."

"I don't need you here. Clear the street!" Thus ended the conversation with the nervous NKVD Colonel.

The bogus NKVD Major Trukhin attached his column onto another. They headed for Maikop, directly for NKVD Headquarters.

An officer came down the staircase opposite him, one he had met in the steppe village. The liquidation of the Cossacks had already been reported to headquarters. One could not have wished for a better introduction. A little later, an NKVD General shook the bogus Trukhin by the hand and assigned him and his men quarters in a neighboring building.

Folkersam set up a watch and discussed the next mission with his people. Individual groups had to reconnoiter the oil reservoirs and refineries and work out plans to prevent them from being blown up. Folkersam himself wanted to drive to the front in order to prevent bloodshed during the German attack, which was not to occur before 8 August. During a drinking-bout that evening the NKVD General invited the bogus NKVD Major along on an inspection of the front the next day. A stroke of luck.

They inspected the positions on the following day. Trukhin was able to convince the General of several points; a large concentration of guns at one position was broken up and the guns were distributed throughout the front. Folkersam knew that the main strike of the German attack was going in here.

By 7 August the reconnaissance of the objective was also conducted and the plan completed. In the meantime, the 13th Panzer Division and the 16th ID (Mot.) stood before Maikop. Chaos already reigned in the city. Convoys and headquarters were withdrawing in the direction of the mountains. The bogus NKVD men understood their mission. Folkersam took a small element to the front. At the last minute the defense had again been reinforced where the German main strike was anticipated.

Then things occurred rapidly. During the afternoon of 8 August the lead elements of the 13th Panzer Division were located before Maikop.

Folkersam's people temporarily knocked out the central communications of the Soviet front with explosives. The Russians did not realize that these were not German shells, but three of Folkersam's men. Therefore, communications were dead.

At the same time, an element from the bogus NKVD unit occupied the telegraph office in the city. All queries were answered: "The city has been evacuated. The telegraph office is ceasing operations!" This caused still more confusion. No unit let this opportunity slip by. They all fled to the mountains.

There were great problems involved with preventing the blowing up of the important oil reservoirs which covered a large area. The bogus NKVD people did not succeed throughout in convincing the watchmen to leave. In the suburb of Makde refineries were blown and oil reservoirs were set ablaze.

During the night of 9 August the 13th Panzer Division crossed the Laba River. After a small engagement, three assault groups from the 13th Panzer Division made their way to Maikop at 1500 hours.

The first assault group of nine SPW of the I/66 from Battle Group Crisolli stood on the hills near Kalmy Kov, to the northeast of the city. Maikop lay in the distance in a valley. Russian columns continued to flee into Maikop. Clouds of dust covered the entire valley. However, the SPW were still alone. The main body of the battle group lagged behind because of a collapsed bridge. General Herr, who accompanied the lead elements, pressured for the continued advance.

The priority was given to Kalmy Kov and Glaga. A ford was discovered. In the meantime, other elements showed up. The newly subordinated II/"Brandenburg", as well as the tanks of Battle Group von Raczeck, arrived.

Herr issued new orders. The I/66, moving as left flank security, was to become involved in a forest battle, which would be broken off on order of the division commander. The SPW Battalion Brux received new orders:

"I/66 Pz.Gren.Rgt. will advance through Maikop and capture the river bridge near Maikop!"

The plan was put into action at 1300 hours. In the lead a "Brandenburger" platoon rode in four Russian trucks with Leutnants Prohaska and Säuberlich. In the first truck there was a Russian speaking Leutnant. The rest of the men were distributed throughout the remaining trucks. The lead platoon of I/66 was Leutnant Otte's platoon from the 3rd Company. A battery from the 13th Armored Artillery Regiment accompanied them.

The northeastern access to Maikop reflected the shimmering sunlight. There were still numerous enemy columns closing on Maikop from the north and the east. The "Brandenburger" platoon rushed off and turned into the city. The SPW followed. No heads were visible.

The "Brandenburgers" in Russian uniforms advanced slowly into the city. They were halted by a Soviet general and questioned as to their mission. The "Brandenburger" leutnant answered: "I am under orders to reinforce the bridge defenders with my people!" The general said, "pass!"

The "Brandenburgers" found the bridge intact. However, when they reached the bridge the mounted platoon was fired on.

"Dismount!" The platoon attacked the bridge defenders yelling "Hurrah!". They captured the bridge and established a small bridgehead. Leutnant Prohaska was killed in hand-to-hand combat. Leutnant Säuberlich took command. The "Brandenburgers" were pressured from all sides, but they held until reinforcements arrived.

In the meantime, Major Brux and his battalion reached the right access road. The SPWs burst into the city. Shots were fired from the moving SPWs and hand-grenades were thrown. A Soviet guard-post was still located in front of a headquarters building. They were civilians with arm bands and shouldered weapons.

Platoon Otte closed ranks quickly, dismounted and assaulted across the river. The SPWs cleared the streets and drove for cover. Then the next group was to follow. However, the bridge was already under heavy mortar fire.

Major Brux ordered the 2nd Company to conduct an outflanking maneuver. The men waded through chest-high water, but they made it to the opposite bank and prevented the Russians from being reinforced with flanking fire.

When Major Brux and his adjutant ran across the bridge, the hand-to-hand combat was already decided in the battalion's favor. After a short struggle, two engineers seized the explosives out of the hands of two Russian soldiers and flung them into the river. Then the first tanks arrived. A direct hit by a mortar round landed on the panzer leader's tank. Six officers were killed, including Oberleutnant Schmid, commander of the 1/66 Pz.Gren.Rgt. The wounded included Major Montfort, commander of the I/4 Pz.Rgt., and Oberleutnant Palm, adjutant of the I/66 Pz.Gren.Rgt.

The enemy tried to penetrate the small bridgehead with hastily assembled troops. Platoon Otte and the "Brandenburgers" repulsed all attacks, at times with bayonets. An enemy anti-aircraft gun, which was well entrenched behind a sand dune, was causing trouble at the crossing. Major Brux knew that this gun had to be eliminated. He did not wait long to ask a Feldwebel and a man from the 3/66 to stalk forward and put the anti-aircraft gun out of commission. Then they could see to opening the bridge. A Panzer IV from the I/4 Pz.Rgt., which was located in front of the bridge, was instructed to shove the enemy truck, which was blocking the bridge, off into the water. The tank pushed the truck in front of it like it was a bull-dozer. It pushed it off into a road-side trench. The bridge was open. Tanks from the I Battalion rolled over it and expanded the bridgehead. The defense was reorganized on a side road in an orchard.

In the meantime, Battle Group von Raczeck had reached the Maikop train station and prepared for an attack on the next day. By 1850 hours all enemy forces had been thrown out and the city quarter was cleared.

The enemy held on to the western portion of the city and defended tenaciously. Battle Group Stolz ran into tenacious resistance on the northwestern access to Maikop and had to withdraw 3 kilometers from the western edge by nightfall.

The night passed relatively quietly in the bridgehead and in the occupied portion of Maikop. On the other hand, the division's rear area elements and the advance detachment of the "Mineral-oil Brigade" were attacked along the march route by enemy stragglers. Advance Detachment Laad (Mineral-oil Brigade) suffered considerable losses. The Mineral-oil Brigade had the mission of immediately exploiting the oil fields and the refineries. When Maikop was in hand the chronic fuel shortage was supposed to be eliminated. However, the Germans were greatly disappointed: They learned that the oil fields were not located near Maikop, but much further into the mountains. The Mineral-oil Brigade was organized under the leadership of Generalmajor Homburg.

On 10 August the struggle for Maikop continued. While Battle Group Crisolli held the established bridgehead and expanded it, Battle Group von Raczeck again attacked out of the railroad station area in order to reach the southern bridge over a ford. This attack was covered on the right flank by Battle Group Stolz (43rd Kradschützen Battalion). In spite of artillery support, by 1500 hours, Battle Group von Raczeck was unable to advance any further against the tenacious enemy resistance.

The Belaba bridgehead was again expanded with panzer support. Major Brux was wounded during this operation. Hauptmann Büschleb assumed command of the SPW Battalion. The clearing of the city of enemy elements continued.

During the evening a special report was broadcast on German radio about the capture of Maikop. According to the broadcast, Generalmajor Herr was awarded the Oak Leaves to the Knight's Cross. The commitment of the Altmärkischen-Anhalt 13th Panzer Division was lauded by this recognition.

During the early morning of 11 August the right flank of the bridgehead was expanded by an attack. The II/66 Pz.Gren.Rgt. advanced to the ford in the Kudshipps sector. However, it bogged down in impassable terrain and strong enemy defensive fire. During the evening at 2100 hours an outflanking attack was conducted which resulted in the capture of the Maikop - Tuapse road bridge. The explosives were removed by German engineers at the very last moment. The bridge was intact.

In the meantime, the 43rd Kradschützen Battalion reconnoitered to the south. All of the bridges were blown in the vicinity of Tulskaya. The kradschützen made contact with the 16th ID (Mot.) near Abadsekhskaya. Now we will follow the route of the 16th ID (Mot.) during the attack on Maikop!

On 9 August the main body of this division crossed the Laba River over the railroad bridge near Sassovskaya. While elements of the 156th Panzergrenadier Regiment captured Labinskaya, the 116th Panzer Battalion and Major Brede's kradschützen from the 165th Kradschützen Battalion advanced against the southern edge of Maikop. At 1630 hours the lead elements stood near Danilov, 9 kilometers southeast of Maikop. At 1700 hours contact was established with the 13th Panzer Division, which was also driving on Maikop.

In the meantime, fierce combat with enemy columns striving to make it to Maikop developed to the rear of the lead elements. The 3rd Battery of the 151st Artillery Regiment was placed under particular pressure by an attacking enemy group. Oberleutnant Remy's battery fired from a distance of 300 meters into the attackers. Finally, the crisis was mastered by a kradschützen platoon. At another location, Major Hammon, commander of the III/146 AR, was the driving force for overcoming a crisis. He had one battery from the 203rd Assault Gun Brigade. The battery commander was killed. Hammon continued to fight with the assault guns. Three enemy tanks were destroyed. At 1630 hours Hammon reported to the division: "Deployment route open. Contact established with the 156th Panzergrenadier Regiment."

The concentrated attack of the battle group of the 156th Panzergrenadier Regiment out of Yarolau, and the 3/116 Pz.Abt., elements of the 203rd Assault Gun Brigade and the 165th Kradschützen Battalion out of Kushorskyay, frustrated the breakthrough of the 45th Soviet Rifle Brigade, which tried to escape into the Caucasus Forest to the south under pressure from the 13th Panzer Division. Only elements of this brigade achieved a breakthrough. The majority of the equipment, including almost 400 American vehicles, was captured. All of the vehicles had very little milage on them, an indication of increased Allied material assistance.

On 12 August Major Brede's battle group (165th Kradschützen Battalion with reinforcement) was committed out of the 13th Panzer Division's Maikop bridgehead in order to advance toward Khadyshenskaya through Apsherovskaya. However, the attack failed due to the enemy's tenacious defense in the impassable mountain terrain. During this operation, the brave and reliable commander of the 165th Kradschützen Battalion, Major Brede, was severely wounded.

On this day other elements of the 16th ID (Mot.) advanced through Tulskaya up to Abadsekhskaya.

That is how the combat of the III Panzer Corps developed in the Maikop area. Now we will return to the advance of the LVII Panzer Corps, which was able to conduct a crossing of the Laba River on 8 August near Tenginskaya:

After deploying additional forces in the Tenginskaya bridgehead, SS "Wiking" (with Battle Group "Nordland" led by the panzer battalion) set out toward the Belaba sector in the Belorechenskaya area on 10 August. Belorechenskaya had special significance due to railroad and road connections supporting the transport of oil to Tuapse. Important bridges were located there.

Battle Group "Nordland" advanced from Tenginskaya to the southwest. The sun was blistering. Major Diering's interceptors flew air patrols in front of the lead panzer elements. Behind the tanks Hstuf. Bluhm's 3/"Nordland" followed as the lead company. The I/"Nordland" was the lead battalion. At 1300 hours the Panzer battalion reached the Belaba River south of Velikoe after a 30 kilometer march. Air reconnaissance discovered that this sector was only weakly occupied. The Belorechenskaya sector was stronger. Generalmajor Steiner's attention was directed toward the intact crossing near Belorechenskaya. His plan was to advance a battle group north of the town across the Belaba and attack it to the south, thereby out-maneuvering the Belorechenskaya barrier from the rear.

While Battle Group "Germania" slowly advanced with the main forces of "Wiking" from Petropavlovskaya across the many tributaries of the Laba River directly on Belorechenskaya, where the Soviets expected the main strike, Stubaf. Mühlenkamp's Panzer Battalion drove toward the river on a wide front south of Velikoe. The concentrated forces of the panzer armada stopped at the river dunes and threateningly aimed their cannon and machine-guns. Nothing stirred on the other side. Protected by the tank cannon, the 3/"Nordland" dismounted and crossed the river.

There were thickets along the bank and further to the right there was a wide oak copse. The platoons of the company waded through the chest-deep, 40 meter wide, rapidly flowing mountain river, widely dispersed. They went in pairs in order to be able to support one another in the rapid current. They held their weapons high above their heads.

There was movement on the other side. Three tank shells were fired. Then all was quiet again. The 3rd Company reached the opposite bank and established a bridgehead, which, during the evening, was expanded to the right into the oak copse. A single engine enemy aircraft took off right in front of the 3rd Company and vanished into the evening twilight. In the meantime, the "Wiking" reconnaissance battalion had captured Velikoe, while covering the northern flank. During the night I/"Nordland" and elements of the panzer battalion crossed at a reconnoitered ford. The main body of "Wiking" and the lead elements of the following Mobile Slovak Division advanced up to Giaginskaya. While the Soviets expected the main strike to come from Giaginskaya, Mühlenkamp's tanks and Polewacz's grenadiers penetrated into the back door of the Russian defenses at Belorechenskaya.

During that night a reconnaissance platoon was dispatched to the south to make contact with the 13th Panzer Division near Maikop. Because the "Wiking" reconnaissance battalion was not fully combat capable at this time (as with the "Westland" Regiment and a battalion each from "Germania" and "Nordland", elements would follow later after being equipped with vehicles and weapons), battalion reconnaissance elements had to assist. Uscha. Röge, a platoon leader from the 4th Platoon, 1./"Nordland", reported:

"One evening, in the Caucasus Forest, I received orders to establish contact with the 13th Panzer Division with a reconnaissance element. During the race to Maikop, a large gap had opened between "Wiking" and the 13th Panzer Division. We were to go meet them. The distance was about 30 kilometers. Because I did not have the faintest notion of how to lead a reconnaissance element, I took along two motorcycles with side cars. Our side car driver came from the old 15/"Nordland", so he had some experience with motorcycles.

We left at 2300 hours, after surrendering our pay books to the company, making good progress in the moonlight. We came upon the first intersection after travelling 10 kilometers. Enemy formations were fleeing on the intersecting road. We approached cautiously and waited for a gap. We crossed at 0100 hours and continued on our way. After another 5 kilometers we ran into the same problem. There was another intersection. Again we waited for a gap in the march columns and crossed. However, the hunting fever was reborn in the former 15/"Nordlander". Halt! He set up the machine-gun and, as a large group of Russians reached the intersection, the machine-gun spit 600 shells into them. They fled screaming. Then he mounted the waiting vehicle and continued on to Maikop.

We started to worry. We had to make contact with the security elements from the 13th Panzer Division soon. We drove, stopped, waited. There, Germans! White headlights! The reconnaissance element advanced to be recognized.

We were summoned to Generalleutnant Herr, who gave us a friendly greeting in his command post. We briefed him on our march route and observations on the large situation map.

In the meantime, solid contact was established with the 13th Panzer Division and we drove back to our company."

The commitment of Reconnaissance Element Röge cleared up the enemy movement between the divisions. It became the model for many similar reconnaissance operations.

During the early morning of 11 August the rest of the tanks from the "Wiking" Panzer Battalion crossed the ford south of Velikoe. During the night the "Wiking" radio station intercepted a radio message from the 17th Kuban Cossack Cavalry Corps. It instructed the squadrons of the corps to assemble in the area northwest of Belorechenskaya in order to attack the bridgehead which had been established near Velikoe. However, "Wiking" proved to be faster!

The panzer battalion, with the I/"Nordland" mounted on the tanks, cleverly attacked to the southeast between Belaya and the forest line toward Pshekhskaya, destroyed the Russian cavalry assembly area and captured the town against fierce resistance. Riderless cavalry horses were running all over the terrain.

While the panzer battalion conducted the attack into the enemy's rear with the mounted I/"Nordland", the main body of "Wiking" advanced on the Giaginskaya road toward Belorechenskaya. At 0600 hours Russian march columns were still being engaged throughout and the crossing over the Belaba River was captured. 5 kilometers northeast of the town a Russian march column ran directly into the tubes of III/5 SS AR. Stubaf. Engelhardt from the "Nordland" staff was the first to recognize the enemy formation and ordered the battalion to fire. The Russians quickly surrendered: one senior lieutenant, four senior NCOs and 400 Red Army soldiers, as well as four nurses. All were completely exhausted.

During the morning hours "Wiking" attacked Belorechenskaya frontally. Soldiers from the 7th/"Brandenburg" led dressed in Russian overcoats, riding in Russian vehicles and carrying Russian weapons. Acting as if they were in terrified flight, the 7/"Brandenburg" yelled: "Tanks, tanks..." to the last Soviet defensive positions in Belorechenskaya. This caused the Soviets to panic. Horse drawn batteries stampeded to the rear. Motorized batteries followed at high speed. Soviet officers and commissars, who tried to direct the fleeing troops into defensive positions, were shouted down and seized by the panic.

The "Brandenburgers" raced across the road bridge near Belorechenskaya and prevented it from being blown up. Some of them probed further. A Soviet artillery battalion, which had wanted to take up positions behind the Belaya, was fired on from the vehicles and dispersed. Then the "Brandenburgers" reached the railroad bridge south of Belorechenskaya. They threw off their Russian overcoats and held the bridge.

A little later the main body of "Wiking" was located in Belorechenskaya and reinforced the "Brandenburgers".

The commitment of the II/Btl.Rgt. z.b.V. "Brandenburg" played an important part in leading the way for the troops of Army Group A. The 8/"Brandenburg" was under Hauptmann Grabert near Rostov. This company lost its second commander, Oberleutnant Zülch, as well as Leutnant Prohaska, Feldwebel Schink, Gefreiter Perunter and three other "Brandenburgers" at the Maikop bridgehead.

The "Brandenburgers", "Wiking" Panzer Battalion and I/"Nordland" met in Pshekhskaya. On 11 August 1942 "Wiking" forced open the gate to the Caucasus.

Generalfeldmarschall List, 1st Commander of
Army Group A (Causasus).

Generaloberst von Kleist (Generalfeldmarschall
from autumn 42) Commander of the 1st Panzer
Army and later commander of Army Group A
(after Generalfeldmarschall List).

ation briefing in the Führer Headquarters on 17/3/1943. From left to right: GFM von Manstein, Commander of
rmy Group "Don", Generaloberst Ruoff, Commander of the 17th Army, Adolf Hitler, General Zeitzler, Army
Chief of the General Staff, half covered the Commander of Army Group A, GFM von Kleist.

General von Mackensen, Commander of the III Panzer Corps and later Commander of the 1st Panzer Army.

"Wiking" kradschützen troops awaiting commitment orders.

Attack on the 1st defensive line at Rostov. Engineers blow a lane through a wire obstacle.

Combat bridge
across the Don
in Rostov.

The battle was fierce,
medics bandage the
wounded.

Panzergrenadiers
of the 13th Panzer
Division after the
battle for the city
of Rostov.

The Manych Dam near Sporny. Here the 16th I.D. (Mot.) entered into Asian territory.

"Wiking" attack on B... Glina.

German tank on the Kuban.

...nks of the "Wiking" ...nzer Battalion cross ...e Belaya River near ...likoe and establish a ...dgehead with 'Nordland".

...rning oil fields in the ...ckground near Maikop.

...rial view of the peaks ...he high Caucasus.

After the battle near Lineinaya, Stubaf. Collani, commander of the Finnish Volunteer Battalion, reports to Oberführer von Scholz, commander of the "Nordland" Regiment.

Focke-Wulf 189 close reconnaissance aircraft.

The Elbrus House at 4200 meter elevation.

the cockpit of a Focke-
ulf 189.

neral der Flieger Pflugbeil,
mmander of the IV Air
rps, greets Feldwebel
umann, a successful close
connaissance pilot.

uptmann Lang,
affelkapitaen of a reconnais-
ice staffel and Stubaf.
ichel, Ia of Division
/iking" and later
/estland" Regiment com-
nder, killed on 28/2/1943.

Aerial view of Elbrus with the east and west peaks

General der Gebirgstruppe H. Lanz, commander of the 1st Mountain Division, and Major Piloty, commander of the IV/79 Geb.Art.R

Gebirgsjägers climbing Elbrus. The Ushba in the background.

SOUTH OF MAIKOP AND ON THE TUAPSE ROAD

The XXXXIV Jäger Corps advances - Each division holds its pass - Tuapse is the objective - Advance of Battalion Langesee into rear of the enemy - Fierce combat at Oplepek - In the Neftegorsk and Kura-Zize oil fields

During a situation briefing in Kurchevskaya on 10 August 1942, when the subsequent commitment of the formations was still unclear, the commander of the XXXXIX Mountain Corps, General Konrad, proposed to the commander of Army Group A, Feldmarshall List:

1. Immediately attack with the SS Division "Wiking" behind the enemy through the mountains toward Tuapse in order to capture the important rail and road crossing (Goich Pass) and as much of the coastal road as possible and create some room for the following forces.

2. Quickly bring up the Alpine Corps, which was still lagging far behind.

3. Reinforce "Wiking" with strong mountain forces before the enemy could construct a strong defense.

In retrospect, Konrad's assessment promised success. However, the situation developed differently. Already the lack of suitable forces was making itself felt. Too large an objective with too few forces!

The decisive failure, however, is to be found in the senior German leadership, which assigned each division "their own" pass. If one did his military-geographical homework, one would realize the risk this posed. Just as difficult to understand was why German mountain formations were not committed here. A study conducted by the Fulpmes Mountain School described all of these mountain passes and assigned them numbers. Nr. 1 was the Novorossisk coastal road along the Black Sea up to Batum. Nr. 2 was the Maikop - Tuapse road, Nr. 3 was the Maikop - Kurdshinskaya - Tuby Pass and Nr. 4 the Maikop - Dakhovskaya - Adler road. The description summarized Russian geographic literature, some of which originated during Tsarist times.

We read about Nr. 2, Maikop - Tuapse: "Approximately 190 kilometers. In good condition, maintained in repair. Average descent up to Tuapse. At some locations the decline is over 10 degrees. Good cover. Few curves until Apsherovskaya Station. Filling stations 9 kilometers southwest of Maikop and in Apsherovskaya. There are many curves approximately 90 kilometers southwest of Maikop. Construction material available (forest).

Nr. 3: Tuby Pass (approximately 26,000 meters). Essentially passable by draft animals.

Nr. 4: According to two prisoner of war statements, construction began on a secret military road from Maikop to Ertos - Sadok in 1938. The road passes through the mountains by way of several tunnels."

So much for the descriptions worked out by the Fulpmes Mountain School. Only the information on the Maikop - Tuapse road was of any use. The routes through numbers 3 and 4 entailed great risk. The descriptions said next to nothing. Nevertheless, General de Gebirgstruppen Angeli's XXXXIV Jäger Corps was to lead the way in order to advance to the Black Sea through the Caucasus Forest or the Ponti Caucasus.

On 11 August "Wiking" gained entry into the mountain forests with the capture of Belorechenskaya.

While "Nordland" was committed to secure the area west of Pshekhaya, Battle Group "Germania" crossed the intact bridges and, on the afternoon of 11 August, was advancing behind the panzer battalion on a forest trail along the Pshekha toward Kubanskaya. The terrain there was already characterized by mountain forests, narrow valleys, gorges, winding roads that did not justify the commitment of a panzergrenadier division. It was certainly not tank terrain. In spite of this, the corps demanded the rapid advance of "Wiking" with the initial objective: Khadyshenskaya and the oil fields in the Neftegorsk - Neftyanaya area. Oil specialists were already following on foot in order to make the oil usable in German engines.

On 12 August "Wiking" captured Kubanskaya and advanced with I/"Germania" along the Apsherovskaya road, while Stubaf. Jörchel's II/"Germania" veered off toward Tverskaya and attacked into strong enemy forces. These were quickly suppressed with support from Oberst Rossmann's corps mortar battalion and a rocket launcher battalion. On the evening of 12 August the Pshish was reached near Tverskaya. The "Nordland" Regiment relieved II/"Germania" in security, so that they could return across the Kubanskaya, and I/"Germania" followed in the direction of Apsherovskaya. In effect, "Wiking" was widely dispersed on an impenetrable mountain front and had to await the arrival of additional formations. Throughout there was still combat with splintered Soviet forces that had become isolated.

On 12 August the "Westland" Regiment and the III Battalion of "Nordland", which came from the Mius positions, reached the division. A welcome enrichment of combat forces! Now "Wiking" had seven infantry battalions available. The "Westland" Regiment had become a mobile regiment, with two battalions of five companies each. Now only III/"Germania" was missing. It would close with the division from out of the Amvrosievka area during the last days of August.

On 12 August "Wiking" drove toward Khadyshenskaya and Apsherovskaya in two attack columns, one in the Pshish Valley and another in the Pshekha Valley. At this time, a battle group from the 16th ID (Mot.) was committed on route Nr. 2 toward Khadyshenskaya from out of the Maikop bridgehead.

The day before, Battle Group Brede (165th Kradschützen Battalion reinforced with the 4/146 AR and 203rd Assault Gun Brigade) received the following order directly from III Panzer Corps:

"Advance Detachment Brede will set out from the Maikop bridgehead early on 12 August, in cooperation with the 13th Panzer Division, in order to advance through Apsherovskaya toward Khadyshenskaya. SS "Wiking" will advance from Belorechenskaya toward Khadyshenskaya. Secondary columns of the 16th ID (Mot.) will be committed from Abadsekhskaya through Shirvanskaya toward Khadyshenskaya."

At 2300 hours the 13th Panzer Division reported that the bridge over the Kurdship was in German hands and the route for the attack was open.

During the morning hours of 12 August Battle Group Brede (commander of the 165th Kradschützen Battalion) attacked, after they were reinforced by the III/146 AR. The attack was well coordinated with the 13th Panzer Division. Immediately after the beginning of the attack, Major Brede was advised of the re-evaluation of the defensive strong points by the 16th ID (Mot.) Ic. This was based on the analysis of the Russian documents unearthed by Oberstabarzt Dr. Mühling.

At first, the attack of Battle Group Brede made progress. Then the access to the Neftyanaya oil center led through a narrow mountain gorge. Against tenacious defensive nests, which were well constructed in the rocks with gun emplacements, the supposed surprise attack of battle Group Brede bogged down suffering considerable losses. Major Brede was severely wounded. The command of the battle group passed to the commander of the III/146 AR, Major Hammon. However, all attempts to advance failed. The attack was suspended on order of the III Panzer Corps.

During the following day, in spite of the difficult terrain, the 16th ID (Mot.) penetrated into the vicinity of the Neftyanaya oil region with the 60th Panzergrenadier Regiment and up to Abadsekhskaya with one regiment and some attached units. The 16th ID (Mot.) waited in this area for the 97th Jäger Division to catch up. From there, the 16th ID (Mot.) and the 13th Panzer Division would be transferred to the Eastern Caucasus in mid-August.

And how was it going with "Wiking"?

The III/"Nordland" combat diary noted under 13 August 1942:

"0700 hours. Reached Komsomolskaya. Command post secured. "Westland" Regiment subordinated. Strong enemy artillery and mortar fire. 2nd Company commanders, Hstuf. Schnabel and Ostuf. Hilker, killed by artillery fire. - 1620 hours. Battalion continued to march toward Tverskaya and secured the town with I/"Nordland". 46 prisoners taken."

On 14 August the "Nordland" Regiment continued attacking to the south as the western attack group and captured Kabardinskaya. The lead elements stopped shortly before Muk. Oil fields and important installations were burning there.

I/"Germania" reached the area directly north of Apsherovskaya in the Pshekha Valley. II/"Germania" under Stubaf. Jörchel cleared out the mountain area between the two "Wiking" attack groups and then advanced into the Apsherovskaya area. The "Wiking" stood directly on the important Maikop - Tuapse road at two locations. However, it became obvious that they would have to wait for the XXXXIV Jäger Corps to catch up.

The 101st and 97th Jäger Divisions were a two-day march behind. The Schwäbian and Bavarian jägers were making an unheard-of march effort through the dust and heat.

Generalmajor Diestel's 101st Jäger Division reached Tenginskaya on 11 August. On the following day it continued its march. Northwest of Giaginskaya, on the western bank of the Belaya, they had to break off their march and throw back a 600 man strong enemy group. On 14 August the 229th Jäger Regiment reached Kubanskaya and the 228th Jäger Regiment Tverskaya the "Wiking" attack axis.

SOUTHWARD FROM MAIKOP
and on the
Tuapse Road

Gorjatschi - kljutsch

498.JD

Schn.-slow.Div.

Pschisch

Belorei.henskaja

Pschechskaja

Chanskaja

Guriskaja

Bielaja

Lineinaja

Twerskaja

Kubanskaja

Maikop

Kura Zize

101.Jg.D

Katoralinskaja

Pschicha

Wiking

Tulskaja

Asjaltewaja

Muk

Apscheronskaja

Kurdship

Abadsechskaja

Qadyschenskaja

Neltjanaja

Kamenamostny

Travalewa

Neltegorsk

Siewer. Kaja

Schaumjan

Geiman
1010

Gunaj
1078

Nishegorodskaja

Ssamurssaja

Dachowskaja

97.Jg.D

Indjuk

Goitsch

Oplepek
1010

18.8

Kurdshipski

1036

Rosjet

Tuby
1479

Zize

Alexejewskoje

Route #1

Route #2

2065

2237

97.3gD

Tuapse

Route #3

BLACK
SEA

Lasarowskoje

Route #4

Assault of the
XXXXIV. Jäger Corps
toward Tuapse and Adler
August / September 1942

Route #1

Adler

– – – →   Route of 97.Jg.Div.

+ + + →   Route of 101.Jg.Div.

Oil Wells   Main Points of Attack

0 5 10 15 20 25 30 35 40 km

By this time Generalleutnant Rupp's 97th Bavarian Jäger Division had also marched through Armavir into the Maikop area in order to relieve the 13th Panzer Division and the 16th ID (Mot.). The 204th Jäger Regiment reached Maikop on 13 August; the 207th Jäger Regiment reached Banalov - Kuzhorskaya.

The two divisions of the XXXXIV Jäger Corps reached their departure positions. Corps Order Nr. 108 contained the phrase: "To advance to the Black Sea coast", which stated the intent of the attack. It also said:

"XXXXIV Jäger Corps will attack out of the Belorechenskaya - Maikop area, through a line Kabardinskaya - Khadyshenskaya - Samurskatya and reach the Tuapse - Adler coastal sector."

The Baden - Württemburg 101st Jäger Division was ordered to advance through Khadyshenskaya directly to the road and rail connections and then through the Goich Pass toward Tuapse.

On 15 August the 101st Jäger Division arrived and advanced the 229th Jäger Regiment through Kubanskaya, through the "Germania" Regiment's security line, toward Apsherovskaya. The town was captured at 1500 hours, after fierce combat. The 228th Jäger Regiment advanced up to the "Nordland" security line and occupied the oil region west of Kura - Zize on this day.

However, the long flanks of the attack columns were still only tentatively secured. They were constantly in contact with enemy stragglers in their rear. On 14 August elements of the II/"Nordland" became involved in a heavy fire-fight near Guriskaya with Soviet elements trying to breakthrough to the south. In general, the western flank was in considerable danger because the Fast Slovak Division could only advance slowly in the mountainous terrain. This division was advancing west of "Wiking".

On 16 August the enemy forces were to be attacked northwest of the Pshish on a line Tverskaya - Khadyshenskaya. The official notation in the III/"Nordland" Combat Diary on 16 August:

"0330 hours: Deployment from Muk. - 0710 hours: The panzer battalion set out with the 9th Company. - 0725 hours: 10th Company advanced. 1030 hours: Lineinaya captured. Mopping up completed. Dead: Ostuf. Reus and two Uschas. Seven men wounded. - 1130 hours: 11th Company advanced and fought its way through the forest toward Lineinaya. - 1500 hours: Ustuf. Lüttgens killed during the battle. - Captured: two 4.7 cm anti-tank guns, two 7.62 cm guns, five light mortars, machine-pistols, horses, two trucks, 34 prisoners. - 1700 hours: Company commander situation briefing. Air report: 100 vehicles fleeing to the southwest."

The commander of the "Wiking" Panzer Battalion, Stubaf. Mühlenkamp, had the following to say about the attack on Lineinaya:

"After a combat march there suddenly appeared before us a clearing in the middle of the forest. On the western edge of the clearing lay Lineinaya. My tanks were moving in combat formation toward Lineinaya. Between the tanks were Finnish volunteers. The Finns kept up with the tanks by double-timing. This had already been an extraordinary effort. Our attack broke over the enemy positions in Lineinaya like a thunder-storm. The Finns did not hold back. Often they jumped on the enemy soldiers wielding their Finnish daggers."

The attack of the panzer battalion and the III/"Nordland" on Lineinaya was a page of glory in the history of the Finnish Volunteer Battalion of the Waffen SS, which was recently incorporated into the well-respected "Nordland" Regiment as the III Battalion by redesignating its companies from 1-4 to 9-12. The Finnish volunteer companies continued the glorious tradition of the 27th Jäger Battalion from the First World War. At that time, Finnish volunteers fought on the German side and then against the "Red October Revolution" for the independence of their country and the dissolution of Russia. During the Finnish - Russian War of 1940, German, Swedish and Danish students fought illegally on the Finnish side against the Soviets. In 1941 the first wave of Finnish volunteers joined the war against Russia in a formation of the "Nordland" Regiment, in the so-called Finnish Platoons (the 3rd Platoon of each company). The Finnish volunteers were well respected. However, they always suffered heavy losses. In the autumn of 1941, because of high losses, the III/"Nordland" was disbanded and distributed among other battalions. In the meantime, the "Finnish Volunteer Battalion of the Waffen SS" (2nd wave) arrived at the front and was sent to the "Nordland" Regiment as a completely national formation with limited German leadership. It was finally re-organized into the III Battalion.

The Finns, at times laying flat on the tanks, conducted themselves bravely during the combat near Lineinaya. The 17th Kuban Cossack Cavalry Corps had to give up its plan to attack out of the Lineinaya area into the flanks of the German advance and, instead, had to fight its way through a narrow valley forest to the south. On the basis of its efforts while covering the withdrawal of the Soviet main force from the Yeya sector up to the area west of Maikop, the 17th KKKK was redesignated as the 4th Kuban Cossack Guards Cavalry Corps. The two cavalry divisions were redesignated accordingly.

The attack operations of SS Division "Wiking" came to an end with the combat near Lineinaya. The XXXXIV Jäger Corps continued to attack through the Caucasus Forest. The III Panzer Corps left the area in mid-August and marched to the east. "Wiking" was committed to securing an extended 70 kilometer line, since the jäger divisions, which were limited to their attack objectives, were not in a position to secure the large, impenetrable forest.

The western flank was secured by the "Nordland" Regiment in the Asfaltovaya area. The "Germania" Regiment secured the area south of Apsherovskaya and the "Westland" Regiment secured the Samurskaya - Dakhovskaya area. Volunteers from the Netherlands, Belgium and Luxembourg were organized into the "Westland" Regiment.

Now for the attack of the XXXXIV Jäger Corps: We have already been made aware of the large objective assigned by Corps Order Nr. 108. The 97th Jäger Division was assigned the following mission:

"97th Jäger Division will attack out of the Maikop area through Samurskaya - Dakhovskaya and reach the coastal road between Laserovskoe and Adler by advancing through Khakuch (Tuby Pass/Route Nr. 3) and Krasnaya Polnaya (Route Nr. 4). In addition, the division will advance along the roads leading to the south and reach the Samurskaya - Dakhovskaya area. It is to arrive there on 14 August. The mission of the forces committed on the Maikop - Neftegorsk road will be to clear the way for the advance of elements from the 101st Jäger Division through Kubanskaya toward Apsherovskaya."

In addition to the combat missions, they also had to conduct route reconnaissance, especially since the available maps were inaccurate. The 97th Jäger Division was to try to accomplish both missions simultaneously. The reinforced advance detachment (97th Wheeled Battalion) advanced through Abadsekhskaya toward Dakhovskaya as Group Jordan. Advance Detachment Jordan was followed by the reinforced 207th Jäger Regiment under Oberst Otte. Battle Group Otte also advanced on the road to Dakhovskaya and was the left attack group of the 97th Jäger Division.

The right (western) march group was the reinforced 204th Jäger Battalion under Oberstleutnant Nobis. Battle Group Nobis followed the Maikop - Apsherovskaya road and reached the Neftyanaya area with its left flank at Samurskaya.

On the evening of 16 August 1942 the situation was as follows:

Battle Group Nobis: I/204 reached Neftegorsk through Shirvanskaya at 1500 hours and destroyed an enemy column there. It advanced further toward Neftyanaya and approached to within 3 kilometers of Neftyanaya by 1600 hours. II/204 reached Shirvanskaya at 1300 hours and took up security. III/204 set out from Shirvanskaya, reached the edge of Samurskaya at 1600 hours after facing tenacious resistance and captured the city after a fierce battle. German losses: 3 dead, 7 wounded.

Battle Group Otte: Two companies of I/207 surprised and destroyed a Soviet force of 300 men in Kurdshipskiy. One anti-tank gun, several field kitchens and 15 trucks were captured. The main body of the battalion was 2 kilometers northwest of Tennelosskoe. A squadron of the 97th Reconnaissance Battalion and some engineers removed numerous tree barriers on the Dakhovskaya - Alekseevskoe road and advanced to within 6 kilometers of Alekseevskoe. The rest of the 97th Reconnaissance Battalion and the III/207 were in Dakhovskaya. II/207 was in Kamennomostskaya. The Wallonien Battalion was in Abadsekhskaya.

After reaching this line, the jäger regiments of the 97th Jäger Division were deep in the Caucasus Forest. Numerous tree obstacles had to be removed from Maikop. The weak resistance led to the assumption that the enemy was no longer in a position to organize its exhausted formations and commit them to the defense. This assumption would be a serious mistake. On 16 August the XXXXIV Jäger Corps believed that they had the key to the success of the advance in the 97th Jäger Division sector, which they expressed in an order of the day:

"I pay tribute to the 97th Jäger Division. During a three-day battle it broke through the enemy's defenses in the western Caucasus. In unfavorable terrain, after a great march effort and under unfamiliar combat conditions it suppressed a tenaciously defending enemy. - signed De Angelis."

On 18 August the I/204 captured Neftyanaya. The oil fields there were in German hands. On the left flank of Battle Group Nobis the III/204 pursued the enemy from Samurkaya into the Pshekha Valley and defeated a stronger enemy group 4 kilometers north of Rozhet. Eleven 15 cm guns, three 7.62 cm, one 7.5 cm, three light anti-tank guns and 15 tractors were captured.

On 18 August, while the lead elements of the 97th Jäger Division were already located far to the south, fierce combat erupted near Shirvanskaya. A raid was conducted on the division command post in this area. Generalleutnant Rupp deployed all available forces there. The Soviets were systematically encircled. The hastily organized Battle Group Bichler (engineer commander) advanced to attack from all sides. The Wallonien Battalion, which consisted of Belgian volunteers and was led by Major Lucien Lippert, a Belgian Colonial Officer, particularly distinguished itself. The Wallonien Battalion fought as a formation of the 97th Jäger Division.

The Soviet defense increased in strength. Organization was restored to their defenses. This became noticeable a day after the victorious combat by the III/204 near Rozhet. Far extended, it [III/204] was attacked by superior Soviet forces in the Pshekha Valley. The Bavarian jägers defended the gate to the Tuby Pass not far from the "Wofstor" Pass. They were engaged by Soviet heavy weapons from Oplepek Mountain in their rear, while also being threatened with encirclement. The III/204 called for help over the radio. However, the division could not help because it was too widely dispersed. Finally Generalleutnant Rupp ordered: "III/204 withdraw to Samurskaya!" The guns, which were captured the day before could only be partially destroyed. The battalion's light infantry guns were lost. The III/204 fought its way back to the north with numerous wounded and was met by German security at the confluence of the Zitze into the Pshekha. The first attack on the Tuby Pass had failed.

In the meantime, Battle Group Otte advanced to the south into the Kurdships and Belaya Valleys. On 20 August the I/207 captured the Belorechenskaya Pass south of Kurdshipskiy, but it had to return to the north a day later due to strong enemy pressure. New security was set up near Kurdshipskiy.

During the following days Battle Group Nobis fought in the area south of the Khadyshenskaya - Samurskaya road. The fighting occurred around the mountain mass of the 1010 meter high Oplepek, which the Soviets had decided to defend. The Oplepek dominated the entrance to the Tuby Pass like a soldier on guard. The 204th Jäger Regiment split up into numerous groups since the enemy was deployed throughout the mountain forests. The corps hoped to renew the stalled attack through the Tuby Pass.

After the first attack on the pass, which ended in the defeat of the III/204, Generalleutnant Rupp decided to open the Tuby Pass from the east with elements of the battle group located near Kurdshipskiy, especially since it was clear that Battle Group Otte had run up against difficulties crossing to the Black Sea region on Route Nr. 4. The pass indicated on the map was not even fit for a donkey to traverse. Battle Group Otte now lay in an extended, strong-point-style, security line in the mountains.

Rupp's plan was based on the following: a frontal attack into the Pshekha Valley; an outflanking attack by one battalion from the east. In this way, the defense of the Tuby Pass would be overcome.

Battalion Langesee was designated as the outflanking group. Hauptmann Langesee was one of the most trusted and reliable officers in the 97th Jäger Division. His battalion was augmented with the 1 Geb.Bttr./AR 81. Combat reconnaissance was to be conducted by the division's only Cossack squadron, which was made up of various nationalities. The squadron was led by a German Hauptmann. Equipment and uniforms were half German and half Russian.

Major von Ernsthausen, who was without a job because of the dispersal of his mountain gun battalion, replied to a question posed by his adjutant: "It won't be long. We will join in with the Langesee operation."

How right Ernsthausen was would soon become clear to his adjutant. Shortly after Battle Group Langesee broke through, the Cossacks dispersed to the four winds. They soon returned with prisoners. They had destroyed an entire Soviet security battalion.

After a fatiguing march through the lovely Zitze Valley, Battle Group Langesee passed Forest House I and reached Forest House II at midday and rested there. The horses and the Cossack squadron remained behind. The rest began the ascent into the almost virgin forest, which was designated on the map as a "Protected Natural Area". This area was uninhabited and formed the boundary between the forested and high Caucasus.

The battalion wound through the thick forest like an indian war party. They were followed by the draft animal column [mountain artillery]. They climbed higher, becoming more and more separated from the lead elements and flank security. In front of the draft animal column and the forsaken 1 Geb.Bttr./AR 81 an engineer platoon cleared the way with axes and pickaxes. Often decayed forest trees blocked the way. Not a word was spoken. Everyone drank in the beauty of the mountains.

By evening they had passed point 1479 and Oberleutnant Mayer's draft animal group was led to a suitable bivouac site. In the meantime, Hauptmann Langesee set up circular security for his companies. The draft animals were unloaded. Cooking fires were prohibited. They all lived from tin cans.

After a refreshing mountain night morale was good. One jäger, inspired by the natural beauty, burst into song: "Wer hat dich du schoener Wald..." He was quickly silenced. Only absolute silence would protect them from being discovered. The jägers could be silenced, but the animals could not. For every sound in the early morning the silent forest gives back a thousand echoes.

"We have been betrayed!" said Major von Ernsthausen and he went to Hauptmann Langesee's tent to brief him on the situation.

On this day, Battle Group Langesee found itself 12 kilometers in the rear of the main Soviet defense. In the early morning an officers' reconnaissance was conducted to reconnoiter the prospective battlefield on the only Russian withdrawal route, far to the rear of Tuby. An artillery officer was attached to this reconnaissance element to survey suitable firing positions for the mountain battery. The jäger platoon, which had provided flank security in the Zitze Valley on the previous day, had not yet reported. Hauptmann Langesee tried to reach the flank platoon and officers' reconnaissance by radio; in vain.

In the meantime, it had become midday. The division radioed that the frontal attack in the Pshekha Valley against the Tuby Pass had not advanced. Battalion Langesee had to wait.

Hauptmann Langesee was concerned: "It would have been better if we could have attacked right away. Because we were not allowed to, we would probably be attacked ourselves. I ordered all tents to be struck and all jägers into position."

"And I ordered the draft animals harnessed. They would be able to leave quickly", explained Major von Ernsthausen. All of the participants understood that the operation, which began as an excursion, could end as a catastrophe.

Shortly after 1400 hours an order arrived over the radio: "The division attack has failed. Battle Group Langesee is to return immediately."

The reconnaissance element had not yet returned. However, several shots indicated that it could not be far away. Judging from the scattered fire the enemy must be pursuing.

Major von Ernsthausen set the draft animal column in motion. Suddenly there was machine-gun and mortar fire, Langesee's security had made contact with the enemy.

Hauptmann Langesee did not waste a moment: "Please, Herr Major, return immediately with the draft animals and be sure to make it to Forest House II by this evening. I will try to hold out here for awhile in order to cover your withdrawal and await the arrival of the reconnaissance element."

"I understand - draft animal column, march!"

Major von Ernsthausen took up the lead. Another officer took up the rear. For flank security there were only gun crews available. Five artillerymen secured the long, defenseless column on the parallel saddle to the Pshekha Valley. Heavy firing from their direction indicated that the five artillerymen had made contact with the enemy. It did not quiet down until evening.

On the way back the draft animal column ran into the flank security platoon from the previous day. This was welcome reinforcement. Nevertheless, Forest House II still had to be reached before darkness. The Cossack squadron waited there.

The draft animal column broke camp at 1430 hours. It was a five-hour march to Forest House II. After each two hours of marching the heavily packed mules were supposed to be given a half hour rest. The march was almost all downhill which made even more demands on the animals. Von Ernsthausen, an experienced mountain artilleryman who had already served in the First World War as a young mountain artilleryman on the Alpine front, considered all the facts. He had to make a five hour march without pause.

After three hours of marching a request came from the rear: "We need to rest!"

Von Ernsthausen refused. When the route crossed a small stream he allowed the animals to drink in groups and then prodded them on their way. All of the rules concerning the treatment of draft animals had to be discarded since the march would be the difference between life or death. Finally, by nightfall, the draft animal column reached Forest House II where it was met by the Cossack security. However, none of the five artillerymen, who covered the column on the Pshekha flank, ever returned. They sacrificed themselves to save the draft animal column.

Major von Ernsthausen ordered them to dismount and gather the guns. Two hours later Hauptmann Langesee and his battalion had also arrived. They were able to wait for the officers' reconnaissance party and fight a delaying battle.

In the meantime, Battle Group Nobis fought in the Oplepek area, which they finally captured. The Soviets launched a strong counterattack. The Oplepek was the "watchman" over the Pshekha Valley. It dominated the entrance to the Tuby Pass. Around it flared up heavy combat. Battalion Abbt defended the mountain mass on an extended front. However, they were thrown back in costly combat. Almost all of the wounded fell into Soviet hands.

We will now follow the commitment of the 101st Jäger Division:

Attacking from the "Wiking" base, the 229th Jäger Regiment captured Apsherovskaya at 1500 hours on 15 August. To the right, the II/228 Jg.Rgt. captured the Kura - Zitze oil region.

On 16 August the 229th Jäger Regiment advanced elements to the west toward Khadyshenskaya, creating some breathing space for the 228th Jäger Regiment. Elements of the 229th Jäger Regiment reached Traveleva. The III/228 unsuccessfully attacked the Khadyshenskaya railroad station against strong enemy defenses. During the evening the majority of the 229th Jäger Regiment was in Khadyshenskaya. Then it secured against Neftyanaya.

17 August was spent making attack preparations against the Khadyshenskaya railroad station. This group of buildings lay at the entrance to the mountain pass to Tuapse. Generalmajor Diestel and his Ia, Major Ludendorf, understood the importance of the attack that had to be made by their 101st Jäger Division.

The attack began on 18 August. However, the plan fell apart at the Khadyshenskaya railroad station. The attack of the 101st Jäger Division stalled at the tunnel. The commander of the "Black Sea Group", General I. Y. Petrov, had deployed his best division in this area on the previous day because the key to the pass lay there. The Soviet 32nd Guards Rifle Division made the Württemburgers of the 101st Jäger Division pay for every meter of ground. Even the outflanking attack failed. The III/228, which was in the Kura - Zitze area, was reinforced and was to attack in this direction from the west. The I/228 conducted reconnaissance out of the Travaleva area up to Geman Mountain. Further to the east the 500th Special Purpose Battalion established contact with the 97th Jäger Division. The entire day was taken up with the battle around the tunnel and the Khadyshenskaya railroad station. Two German air attacks and almost the entire division artillery, as well as the subordinate I/60 AR and elements of the 617 Mortar Battalion, battered the mountain. However, the attack of the 101st Jäger Division bogged down at this mountain.

The commander of the XXXXIV Jäger Corps ordered the attack to be suspended because, up to that point in time (as has already been described) the 97th Jäger Division made very little progress against the Tuby Pass. In the 101st Jäger Division sector, elements of "Wiking" relieved the trailing flank of the 101st Jäger Division. On 19 August a reconnaissance element from III/"Nordland" established contact in Abshanskaya with the 20th Infantry Regiment of the Fast Slovak Division, which was slowly attacking to close ranks.

After the 97th Jäger Division could go no further against the Tuby Pass and Oplepek, it was regrouped. The attempt to cross the mountains using routes Nr. 3 and 4 was abandoned. The XXXXIV Jäger Corps concentrated on the Maikop - Tuapse road. By 28 August the following forces were in readiness: The LVII Panzer Corps with the 198th and elements of the 125th Infantry Divisions, the Fast Slovak Division and the "Nordland" Regiment west of Khadyshenskaya. On the road the XXXXIV Jäger Corps with the 101st and 97th Jäger Divisions and the "Germania" Regiment provided security. The "Westland" Regiment was further to the east.

On the morning of 28 August artillery and air pounded the tunnel. Generalmajor Diestel committed the 229th Jäger Regiment from the northwest across Hills 519.6 and 374.2 and the 228th Jäger Regiment from the southern portion of the town of Khadyshenskaya across Hill 350.3. The day's objective for both of the attacking groups was Hill 134.4. The tunnel and Khadyshenskaya were to be captured in a pincer operation. Hill 134.4 on the rail - road - river passage directly northeast of Kurinskiy was the decisive point.

Soon after the attack began they discovered that neither air nor artillery bombardment could shake the Soviets from their positions. While the 229th Jäger Regiment slowly fought its way from the northwest, the 228th Jäger Regiment and 500th Battalion tried to approach the objective by outflanking it from the southeast; Paparotniy was captured in a see-saw battle. In the northwest the I/229 captured Hill 374.2 and advanced weak forces up to the road.

The combat diary of the 101st Jäger Division reported on the completely new style of combat in the primeval forested region in its entry for 28 August 1942:

"In all of the battalions the reduced combat strength (the jäger companies were down to a combat strength of 50 men) as well as the considerable difficulties encountered in the primeval forested region with its thick underbrush have become very noticeable. Numerous gorges, which are often not indicated on the maps, make the terrain impassible for vehicles and, at times, even for draft animals..."

On 29 August Major Liebmann's II/228 captured Hill 350.3. The prerequisite for the attack into the valley toward the rail - road - river passage near Hill 134.4 was achieved. However, the Soviets deployed new reinforcements. Fierce combat raged all day around 350.3, where the 500th Battalion and III/228 were also involved. During the evening the crisis near 350.3 was still not overcome. Would the Russians be able to reinforce their defensive forces during the night?

On 30 August fierce combat also flared up in the 229th Jäger Regiment sector between 519.6 and 374.2; it would last all day. The enemy was also able to reinforce there. The 229th Jäger Regiment advanced no further.

To the south, in the II/228 area of operations, the situation was similar to that at Hill 350.3. There the Soviets were also able to repulse every advance by the German jägers. They encircled the II/228. All relief attempts by other elements of the division failed. Finally, the division had to issue the following radio order: "II/228 will fight its way back to its departure area." With its last ounce of strength, carrying its wounded, the battalion reached the intermediate security line near Paparotniy during the night. On 31 August Major Liebmann reported to the division commander that the II/228 had returned. The attack was suspended and some of the battalions were withdrawn to more suitable positions. The first attack on Tuapse had failed.

Later the jäger divisions advanced further toward the Tuapse road. I/"Nordland" advanced from Kabardinskaya to Asfaltovaya. The II/"Nordland" was committed on the right in order to maintain contact with the Slovaks. III/"Nordland" took over security around Kabardinskaya where the regiment command post was established. The "Wiking" Division staff redeployed to Apsherovskaya. On 7 and 8 August the "Germania" Regiment relieved elements of the 97th Jäger Division in the Neftyanaya - Neftegorsk area. The 97th Jäger Division advanced further on the Tuapse road, into the Travaleva area, which first had to be cleared of enemy forces. Again the Wallonien Battalion distinguished itself as it captured a hill south of Travaleva in a spirited attack. The left sector of the 97th Jäger Division, the Kamennomostkaya area, was taken over by the "Westland" Regiment. All units were ordered into the defensive.

The front could only be secured with a line of strong-points. The defenders were more numerous at the strong points. Supplies had to be brought forward in convoys because they were constantly being ambushed in the un-surveyable mountain forests. Tanks could no longer make it through the narrow valleys. Units in strength, often in company size, had to maintain daily contact because individual motorcycle reconnaissance elements in squad strength were being overrun.

The war in the Caucasus Forest was insidious. It required the officers and men to completely rethink the way they had done things. The following report gives one an idea of what this meant:

"I/"Nordland" is located on a ridge near the town of Asfaltovaya providing security. Asfaltovaya rises up from the valley to the mountain crest. West of the town there is an oil field. The pipeline was blown by the Soviets. The drill-hole was packed with explosives. The black-brown oil now seeps out of the ground and flows in little rivulets into the valley. Asfaltovaya is a typical mountain village surrounded by mountains and forests. The battalion defense is located near the last houses on the ridge.

The 3rd Company occupies the left sector. The mountain ridge falls off considerably to the south, and from the valley it rises to the next mountain ridge. The distance to the next mountain ridge is approximately 1400 meters, and there sit the Russians. The descending slope is only partially covered with shrubbery up to the valley floor. The ascending crest to the Russian lines is thickly forested. Only on the left sector is there a large clearing, where a Kolkhoz is located.

These widely separated positions are probed daily by friendly and enemy reconnaissance elements. Each morning a reconnaissance patrol from 3/"Nordland" sets out to clarify the enemy situation and report on any changes. The Soviets are building bunkers and [fortified] positions, they are erecting a defense. The artillery forward observers place the Russian activities under fire according to the reconnaissance results. Perfect observation is impossible, due to the forest. Because of this, the returning reconnaissance element leaders can only give the forward observers approximate information. They then fire a smoke shell, make corrections, until they eventually can fire for effect.

One morning, the 3rd Company reconnaissance patrol walked into an ambush. They were able to return only with difficulty. The results: one man severely wounded, two lightly wounded. They were brought back after a difficult struggle with a Russian reconnaissance patrol.

Hauptsturmführer Bluhm, commander of the 3rd Company, made reconnaissance comparisons. Daily reconnaissance revealed that the kolkhoz in no-man's land was visited by the Russians every night to obtain water and for cooking. The adjacent melon field was obviously empty. One morning a German engineer force mined the entrances to the kolkhoz buildings. Four heavy machine-guns from the 4th Platoon, which were mounted on the Asfaltovaya mountain crest, were directed at the buildings and adjusted for elevation and wind. In this manner they could be directed at the same exact point during the night and provide effective fire.

During the following night vigilance was high in the German positions. There was an explosion near the kolkhoz at midnight. That was the signal! All four machine-guns let loose. Tracer bullets flew to the other side (the heavy machine-guns were set up to fire one tracer round every fifteen rounds), providing a brief flicker in the night sky.

Nobody could guess at the results. On the next morning the reconnaissance element found traces of blood in several locations."

This report only gives a small glimpse into the pitiless combat that took place in the Caucasus Forest. Thus, for example, a motorcycle reconnaissance element from the "Nordland" Regiment fell into a trap and was wiped out in a narrow valley passage. Only two men were able to escape into the bushes and survive. A reconnaissance element, which was immediately dispatched afterwards in combat strength, could only find destroyed side cars and the dead.

Another time a reconnaissance element from the I/"Nordland" was sent to make contact with the 101st Jäger Division. The reconnaissance element, which was led by an Ustuf., was fired upon and did not make it through. Stubaf. Polewacz remembered Uscha. Stock from the 2nd Company. Uscha. Stock, who was born in the Tirol, was summoned to the battalion command post, where the regimental commander, Oberführer von Scholz, was also present. After Polewacz clarified the mission and situation he asked Stock:

"Unterscharführer Stock, are you capable of this mission?"

"Jawohl Sturmbannführer, but only if I have a free hand. My reconnaissance element must be equipped with machine pistols. Besides handgrenades, nothing else. All heavy equipment, even the equipment belts, must be left behind. The men must wear gym shoes. We must be light and mobile!"

Scholz and Polewacz agreed to these requests. And so, a reconnaissance element departed looking as though it were going to a sporting event. Stock advanced as if he were back in his homeland. His men followed. The reconnaissance element made contact with the neighboring 101st Jäger Division and returned to the battalion without incident.

Stock already wore the Iron Cross I. He was promoted to Oberscharführer and led such groups for a long period of time.

This report cannot end without making reference to the German Luftwaffe which continued to support the ground troops. Here the 77th Stuka Squadron must be singled out for rocking the enemy with its attacks.

In August and September 1942 the Reconnaissance Staffel 3/(H) 14 Pz. was located on the Maikop airfield. The staffel was led by Oberleutnant Lang. The 3rd Staffel of the 14th Reconnaissance Group was equipped with FW 189's. The "Pz." behind the group number signified that it was equipped to cooperate with panzer formations. The FW 189 was a double fuselage aircraft from the Focke - Wulf works and was particularly suitable for reconnaissance flights with its large observation cockpit. One could follow the entire advance into the Caucasus in Oberleutnant Lang's log book. In the flight book are listed meetings at LVII Panzer Corps where the staffel captains were flown:

"28/7/1942 Taganrog
01/8/1942 Yegorlykskaya
04/8/1942 Belaya Glina
05/8/1942 Ilinskaya
12/8/1942 Alekseevskiy
16/8/1942 Belvechenskaya
21-27/8/1942 Karbardinskaya
27/8/1942 Apsherovskaya to SS Division "Wiking"."

Besides two additional air formations, which were located on Maikop airfield, the 2nd Company of the 32nd Air Communications Regiment must also be mentioned. It maintained all communications between the higher Luftwaffe command posts and the ground troops.

The first attempt of the XXXXIV Jäger Corps to break through to Tuapse with the 101st and 97th Jäger Divisions had failed. Impassable, un-surveyable terrain and an enemy, who had withdrawn into the mountains rather than be taken prisoner and who was led by the energetic requirements of the STAVKA (which had renewed its defensive orientation), had frustrated the German operations.

Before a new attack was launched on the Maikop - Tuapse road toward the Black Sea coast the units had to be reinforced. The OKW did not relent on their established objectives in the Caucasus. Again too much was required of too few troops. The 13th Panzer Division and the 16th ID (Mot.) had already left the Western Caucasus in order to advance the attack in the Eastern Caucasus. SS Division "Wiking" would follow. The high mountain front was weak, but the disengaged troops were to conduct a new attack on Tuapse. Generaloberst von Kleist's 1st Panzer Army was, as before, to carry out the attack through the Grosny oil fields up to the Caspian Sea. In addition, Generaloberst Hoth's 4th Panzer Army was to be made available later. However, Stalingrad and Operation "Fischreiher" tied this army to the Volga. The pinning of Army Group B and the 4th Panzer Army at Stalingrad would have increasing significance.

KRASNODAR, NOVOROSSISK AND THE TAMAN PENINSULA

On the Krasnodar bridges - III/308 versus the 30th Irkutsk Rifle Division - The V Army Corps attacks toward Novorossisk - Ic reports from the 46th ID - Landungsoperation "Blücher" - "Brandenburgers" destroy the roads in the enemy's rear - "The sea, the sea!"

By 2 August the attack of the 17th German Army was gaining ground only slowly in the Yeya sector due to the tenacious resistance of the 17th Kuban Cossack Cavalry Corps. On 2 and 3 August, during a delaying battle with enemy rear guard elements, the Kislyakovskaya - Dobrenika foothills were captured.

Marshal Budenny, commander of the Transcaucasus Front, withdrew his 17th KKKK into the Maikop area. While his 18th Army was still deployed in the Tikhorets area, he assembled his 56th Army in the Krasnodar area.

General Konrad's XXXXIX Mountain Corps, which consisted of the 298th ID, 4th Mountain Division, 73rd ID and, since 1 August the 9th ID, gained a lot of ground to the south during the next few days. The advance detachments of the divisions led the way. they were mobilized by trucks freed-up from supply columns.

To the left of the XXXXIX Mountain Corps advanced General Wetzel's Army Corps with the 125th and 198th Infantry Divisions. Next to the V Army Corps was General Kirchner's LVII Panzer Corps with "Wiking" in the lead already far advanced to the south. SS Division "Wiking" and the Fast Slovak Division belonged to the LVII Panzer Corps. The XXXXIV Jäger Corps, with the 97th and 101st Jäger Divisions, followed behind the LVII Panzer Corps.

By 5 August advanced forces of Konrad's division reached the Chelbas sector. At several locations important bridges were taken without a fight.

On 5 August the 125th and 198th Infantry Divisions entered Tikhoretskaya. Fierce enemy resistance was broken. Both divisions immediately attacked further toward Tikhorets, the important railroad center. Three tank platoons were shot up by advancing air defense troops with their 8.8 cm guns. Then the way was open.

On this day new orders were received by the XXXXIX Mountain Corps command, which set their further course:

"The XXXXIX Corps is to deploy the 4th Mountain Division to the southeast in the direction of Cherkesk. The V Army Corps is to immediately take command of the 73rd and 9th Infantry Divisions. The advance detachment of the 1st Mountain Division will return to the 1st Mountain Division after the capture of Timoshevskaya..."

The XXXXIX Mountain Corps deployed into its assigned commitment area to assault the high mountain passes of the Caucasus. At this time the 3rd Panzer Division took Nevinnomyskaya and the XXXXIX Mountain Corps conquered the entrance-way to the high Caucasus. The mountain divisions began the race to the mountains. The advance detachments reached them a day later.

The V Army Corps now operated on the western flank of the 17th Army.

The next objective was the capital of the Kuban Cossacks, which in 1942 was the city of Krasnodar consisting of 200,000 residents.

On 6 August elements of the 101st Jäger Division marched into Krapotkin, which was captured by Battle Group von Scholz ("Wiking"). The 97th Jäger Division also reached the Kuban bend. Both jäger divisions, which were equipped according to custom, were re-equipped for the upcoming mountain warfare. We hear from Major von Ernsthausen, commander of the I/81 AR:

"My I Battalion was re-equipped with thirty-six 7.5 cm mountain guns in a village in the Kuban Valley. They had arrived in a truck column. We took up our new guns and gave up our howitzers and horses. The battalion had to be re-equipped in four days. The draft harnesses did not fit because they came from various captured stockpiles. However, they were modified and made to fit by the efforts of the saddlers and blacksmiths."

To the right of the XXXXIV Jäger Corps, which followed the LVII Panzer Corps, the 198th ID advanced along the Kuban through Ust - Labinskaya toward Krasnodar. On 8 August the advance detachment attacked into strong enemy forces in front of Vasyurinskaya. Additional divisional elements were brought up. One battery of the I/4 Flak-Rgt. and elements of the 235th Artillery Regiment pounded the village, which was captured by the 198th ID in the evening after fierce house-to-house combat. Vasyurinskaya, just north of the confluence of the Belaya into the Kuban, was the last Soviet bulwark before Krasnodar. At this time, 50 kilometers further to the east, the lead elements of Division "Wiking" stood near Tenginskaya.

In the meantime, General Wetzel's V Army Corps assembled for a concentrated attack on Krasnodar. On 8 August the advance detachment of the 9th ID under Oberst Scheürpflug was the first to reach the outskirts of Krasnodar. The French 73rd ID was in the northwest, in the north was the Hessian 9th ID with the 116th, 36th and 57th Regiments, and in the northeast and east were the Württemberg 125th and 198th Infantry Divisions.

The attack on Krasnodar began on 9 August. The city was the largest industrial center in the Western Caucasus. It contained machine construction, tobacco, leather, textile and chemical industries. It lay directly north of the Kuban.

The battle for Krasnodar began early in the morning. Covering forces from the 56th Army fought in the approaches to the city to try to gain time. Soviet columns were still fleeing across the Kuban bridges to the south. Important supply facilities, including oil tanks, were either transported by the Soviets or set afire. On 9 August German radio news reported: "Krasnodar has been captured by our troops today...". However, that was only half of the story. The eastern suburb of Pashkovskaya was tenaciously defended by the Soviets. There were still many Soviet columns crossing into the bridgehead. During the night the 308th Grenadier Regiment (198th ID) conducted a forced march in order to attack the Pashkovskaya bridgehead and capture the Russian pontoon bridge. At midday preparations were complete. An assault element from the 7/308 under Leutnant Witsch was able to penetrate into the Soviet defense on the eastern edge of Pashkovskaya and, in spite of fierce counterattacks, was able to hold. At the same time elements of the 125th ID attacked from the north into Pashkovskaya. At 1700 hours additional elements of the 308th Grenadier Regiment were pushed into the penetration area. Oberst Schulz, commander of the 308th Grenadier Regiment, led the attack in the front line. The III/308 was committed to a flanking attack. It penetrated almost to the pontoon bridge, but was stopped by a strong counterattack and had to organize a hasty defense.

On 11 August combat again flared up around the bridge. At midday Major Ortlieb and his I/421 (125th ID) approached the bridge to within attacking distance. Hauptmann Sätzler's 2nd Company made the last jump, during which the company commander was killed. When the German lead elements approached to within twenty meters of the entrance to the bridge, it was blown. The bridge whistled into the air. The Russian vehicles that were still on it fell into the water. In the meantime, Pashkovskaya was captured by the 198th ID. Leutnant Witsch and Oberst Schulz were awarded the Knight's Cross. During the evening the 125th Infantry Division relieved the 198th Infantry Division in Pashkovskaya. The latter advanced further to the east in order to cross the Kuban at the Pshish confluence.

In the meantime, the coastal lanes were also cleared by German and Rumanian formations. On 8 August Rumanian cavalry formations, with the support of a battalion of the 298th ID and a heavy artillery battalion, captured the small coastal city of Jeisk.

On 11 August the Rumanian Cavalry Corps had reached the following areas:

5th Cav Div: Bridgehead on the western bank of the Slavyanskaya

6th Cav Div: Krasno Armaiskaya

9th Cav Div: Marching from Aleksandrovskaya to the south.

On 12 August the 298th ID was the only German division subordinate to the 3rd Rumanian Army.

On 13 August the German liaison staff to the 3rd Rumanian Army (commander: Rittmeister von Moltke) reported to the 17th Army command: "The harbor of Primorsko Akhtarskaya was cleared of enemy remnants (20 prisoners) without resistance during the evening of 12 August. All installations were destroyed. The 5th and 9th Rumanian Cavalry Divisions are following."

By 14 August all of the divisions of the V Army Corps located on the Kuban had achieved the prerequisites for crossing the river on a wide front; in the west near Yelisavetinskaya was the 73rd ID, in Krasnodar was the 9th ID, south of Pashkovskaya was the 125th ID and near Lenina on the Pshish confluence was the 198th ID.

On 14 August the 73rd ID forced a crossing near Yelisavetinskaya with the 170th Grenadier Regiment. This bridgehead was still surrounded. Heavy Soviet air attacks were conducted throughout the day. A day later, things grew easier. The 213th Grenadier Regiment arrived. The commander of the Kuban crossing, Oberst Hitzfeld, was severely wounded during an air attack. The 213th Grenadier Regiment was taken over by Oberstleutnant Marbach.

Things were not much better on 14 August in the 125th ID area of operations. Major Ortlieb, commander of the I/421, reconnoitered the area dressed

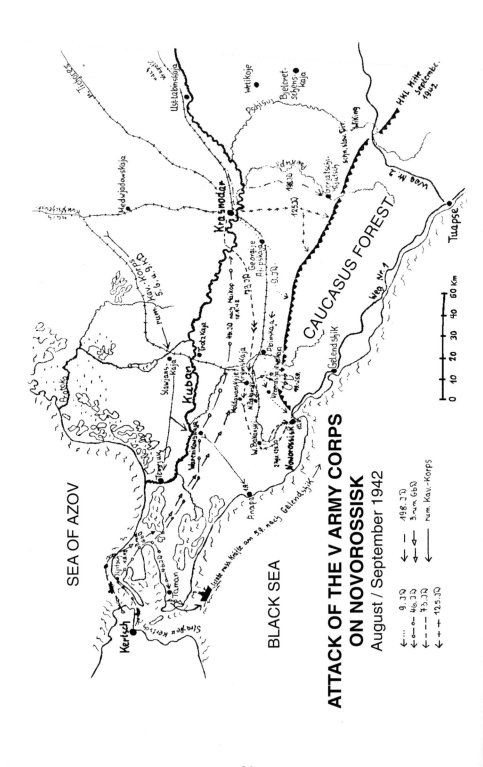

SEA OF AZOV

BLACK SEA

CAUCASUS FOREST

ATTACK OF THE V ARMY CORPS ON NOVOROSSISK

August / September 1942

0 10 20 30 40 60 Km

86

as a peasant woman. By early morning barrage fire had been initiated and they jumped into the rubber boats. Simultaneously, pontoons were brought to the water and work was begun on a pontoon bridge. The 421st Grenadier Regiment expanded the bridgehead. However, Russian air attacks hindered the building of the bridge. Pontoons were hit and sank into the water.

On the left flank of the V Army Corps (198th ID) an attack was also launched to establish bridgeheads on 14 August. At 0320 hours the division artillery initiated its barrage fire. At 0330 hours the first assault groups got into their rubber boats. There was heavy enemy fire. A rubber raft from the engineer assault element took a direct hit, exploded and threw everyone about. Other rafts had to return with many wounded. After five minutes the first crews gained a foothold and held out in the shrubbery on the southern bank of the Kuban. Additional groups followed. At 1000 hours two partial bridgeheads near Edepsukai were combined into one strong one. During the evening of 14 August four battalions of the 198th ID had crossed with their heavy weapons and a battery of light field howitzers, as well as the wheeled squadron.

The Soviet river defence was broken. The V Army Corps penetrated with its main force to the west. The next objective was Novorossisk, an important harbor and industrial center on the Black Sea and a departure point for the Tuapse - Sukhum - Batum - Turkish border Black Sea route.

The Black Sea route had special significance for the German conduct of the war because it connected all of the important Black Sea harbors of the Soviet Navy. With the occupation of all of the harbors the Soviet Black Sea Fleet would lose its bases. Moreover, this route was an important connection to the Near East. The Novorossisk Black Sea coastal road up to the Turkish border was in the military - geographical description under Nr. 1. Except for the Novorossisk - Tuapse section, which runs along the rocky coast, Road Nr. 1 was passable. Every bridge and every narrow pass was noted. So were the detours and withdrawal possibilities.

While the German attack forces approached Novorossisk, furious activity was taking place in the harbor. The first large-scale air attack on Novorossisk occurred on 2 July 1942. Hauptmann Heise's I/100 KG. destroyed the wreck of the Soviet flotilla leader "Tashkent" and sunk the Soviet destroyer "Bditelniy". The training cruiser "Komintern" was damaged.

On 7 August the cruiser "Krasniy Krym" and the destroyer "Nezamozhnik" evacuated 2895 men and 100 tons of equipment and, from 9 to 11 August, an additional 2000 men from Novorossisk to Batumi.

German patrol boats were committed against these ships. On 10 August S-102, under Kapitänleutnant Töniges, sunk a Soviet steamer near Tuapse and, on 11 August, that same boat, along with S-28 (Kptlt. Künzel), conducted an unsuccessful attack on a tanker between Novorossisk and Tuapse.

On 12-13 August the cruiser "Krasniy Krym" and destroyer "Nezamozhnik" evacuated a regiment of the 32nd Guards Rifle Division from Novorossisk to Batumi. On 16-17 August Soviet ships again evacuated 1850 men and 60 tons of equipment on the same route.

On 31 August S-102 (Kptlt. Töniges) sunk a tanker and S-28 (Kptlt.

Künzel) sunk the Soviet freighter "Zan-Tomp" (1988 BRT) off the coast of Novorossisk.

Now we return to the ground operations: On 18 August the right flank of the V Army Corps, the 73rd ID, reached the Krymskaya railroad station at the Krasnodar - Rostov rail junction during an attack to the southwest with the 73rd Reconnaissance Battalion. On 19 August the 213th Grenadier Regiment advanced as security on the northwestern flank of the 73rd ID through difficult forested terrain up to the area north of Krasny. It established a bridgehead across the Abin with the support of the II/173 AR and the 1/173 Pi.Btl. On 20 August the attack moved further into the Mievskoe area. On 21 August the 213th Grenadier Regiment, as right flank security for the 73rd ID, reached the hill line east of Shkolniy, advancing along the Krymskaya - Moldavavskoe road, and sent out reconnaissance against Moldavanskoe. On 22 August Moldavanskoe was taken against weak enemy resistance and the dominant heights in this area were occupied. There the attack came temporarily to an end.

In the meantime, the 9th ID and the other elements of the 73rd ID attacked further to the southwest through Kholmskaya - Abinskaya, while constantly setting out flank security against the Caucasus Forest. When the attack on Novorossisk on the valley road through Nizhnaya Bakanskaya and Neberdzhaevskaya failed due to heavy enemy resistance, the V Army Corps decided to shift the main effort of the attack to the west and committed two regiments of the 125th ID on the right of the 73rd ID for the breakthrough into the mountains.

What was happening in the meantime on the eastern flank of the V Army Corps? On 16 August, two days after the establishment of the Kuban bridgehead near Edepsukai, the 305th Grenadier Regiment captured an undamaged suspension bridge over the Psekups after a running battle. Strong Soviet rear guard forces were encircled and destroyed near Gatlukai with the support of the 125th ID, which was advancing on the Krasnodar - Saratovskaya road. During the evening Saratovskaya was captured by the 305th Grenadier Regiment. The 308th Grenadier Regiment and the majority of the 235th Artillery Regiment followed at double-time.

After all elements of the 198th ID caught up and contact was established with the left neighbor, the Fast Slovak Division arrived in Chernomorskaya. It attacked with a small detachment of the I/326 against Klyuchevaya. However, the attack bogged down in front of the town after overcoming several defensive blocking positions. Even reinforcements could not break the Soviet defense. The defense did not collapse until the III/305 outflanked it from the southeast; then Klyuchevaya was captured. However, the majority of the enemy forces escaped into the mountains.

On 20 August at 1400 hours the 198th ID attacked Goryachiy Klyuch. Following a good preparation by heavy weapons the II/305 and I/326 took the town. The Soviets withdrew into the forest located to the south and placed the town under heavy artillery fire.

In the meantime, it was determined that the attack on Novorossisk required the commitment of stronger forces. The Germans regrouped. The 198th ID had to take over the 125th ID sector, and received the 420th Grenadier Regiment (125th ID) under Oberst Zimmermann. Generalmajor Buck's 198th ID was assigned a new mission: "Attack into the Psekups Valley to the south. Establish contact in the Fanagoriyskoe area with the Fast Slovak Division, which is also advancing to the south." This operation had to be conducted in concert with the advance of the XXXXIV Jäger Corps on Tuapse, which was described in the last chapter. The 198th ID also received a far-reaching objective with the essential lengthening of the front and, therefore, had to make heavier demands on the front formations. It was soon realized that the assigned objectives could not be achieved there, and in the XXXXIV Jäger Corps area of operations, with the available forces.

On 22 August the I/326 and III/305 were involved in heavy fighting at the river fork southwest of Goryachiy Klyuch. The advance to establish contact with the Fast Slovak Division bogged down at the oil tank hill, which was occupied by strong enemy formations. This hill was a threat to the "Stalin Road" and was a junction between Goryachiy Klyuch and Saratovskaya. The contact established with Slovak Regiment Nr. 20, which was bogged down in heavy fighting near "Winterhuette", was again broken.

The I/305 and the I/326 fought on the right flank of the 198th ID, in the vicinity of Hill 349.5 east of Pyatigorskaya. They were opposed by the 30th Irkutsk Rifle Division which had previously demonstrated its steadfastness. On Hill 349.5 lay the Russian Dsilunov and Piruschak machine-gun positions. Their commander, Captain Bedashvili, was located at another position. The first attack on this hill failed in front of these positions. They were captured by the Germans on another day after see-saw combat.

On 24 August the 198th ID was removed from the V Army Corps and subordinated to the LVII Panzer Corps, which stood on the so-called "Stalin Road" between Goryachiy Klyuch and Khadyshenskaya with the 198th ID, the Fast Slovak Division and SS Division "Wiking".

At this time the Soviets conducted a strong counterattack out of the mountains against Oberst Zimmermann's 420th Grenadier Regiment. The 305th Grenadier Regiment had to cease clearing the Kaverse Valley and to repulse a strong enemy counterattack.

On 25 August the 198th ID resumed the attack in the Psekups Valley with the 308th Grenadier Regiment. During the morning Hauptmann Niess and his III/308 crossed the Psekups and established themselves on the eastern slope of Lysaya Mountain (451.2 meters). A supporting attack against the western slope of Lysaya Mountain from Hill 349.5 failed due to the defense of the 30th Irkutsk Rifle Division. The III/308 was encircled on the eastern slope.

The attempt to attack further to the south indicated that the 198th ID was too weak to hold the Pyatigorskaya sector and simultaneously attack into the Psekups Valley. On 29 August the following corps order arrived:

"The corps will suspend the attack and will order the transition to the defense on the present line."

At the same time it realized that the XXXXIV Jäger Corps could not continue its attack on Tuapse. The same applied to the right flank near

Novorossisk. It was necessary to regroup.

Between 29 August and 3 September the 198th ID fought around the dominant heights southeast of Pyatigorskaya. The Soviets made it pay for every meter of ground it won. Battalion Niess was committed twice and was twice encircled. The III/308 fought a hopeless battle on the eastern portion of Lysaya Mountain. It was ordered to hold the position by the highest authority. The dead Russians in front of the German position slowly decayed and soon gave off an odor that no one could stand. And every day the sun burned down from the heavens. Hauptmann Niess ordered the many wounded assembled in a circle. They could not be treated properly. On 30 August a battle group broke through to the encircled troops. The wounded were evacuated and supplies and ammunition were brought in. Then the Soviets attacked again and once more they closed the ring. Hauptmann Niess and his brave men from the III/308 held out until 3 September. They finally had to fight their way out of the encirclement to positions northeast of the Psekups. Up to that time heavy combat also continued around Hill 349.5.

On 6 September the commander of the 198th ID, Generalmajor Buck, was killed. His Ia, Major Buhl, and his driver, Feldwebel Glockenbach, were also lost to a Soviet ambush on the Klyuchevskaya - Saratovskaya road. The division was loyal to its commander, who in his quiet, Schwäbian way earned their trust which allowed him to successfully lead the division.

The 198th ID reinforced its positions and adapted to the mountain war by utilizing draft animal convoys. The draft animal leaders were recruited prisoners of war; the so-called Hiwis.

In order to resume the attack on Novorossisk it was necessary to deploy reinforcements and regroup. The 125th ID gave up two regiments for the attack on Novorossisk. The Rumanian Cavalry Corps advanced across the Protoka toward Temryuk. The 19th Rumanian ID and additional Rumanian forces penetrated into the mountain forest front south of Abinskaya - Smolenskaya. The 46th ID and the 3rd Rumanian Mountain Division stood at "parade rest" on the Kerch Peninsula in order to cross the Kerch road at the proper moment and join in the fight on the Taman Peninsula.

Developments on the Taman Peninsula were recorded in the pages of the enemy intelligence reports from the Ic of the 46th ID. On 3 August 1942 Enemy Intelligence Report Nr. 32/42 noted the following:

"Enemy situation/enemy on the Taman Peninsula: The commander of the North Caucasus [Front] forces has been located in Krasnodar since 26 July. His subordinates include, among others, the 47th Army in Temryuk, whose subordinate elements are occupying the Taman Peninsula. The 276th and 105th Rifle Regiments of the 77th Mountain Division are established in the north. The division headquarters is located in Akhtanisovskaya. The 80th and 85th Guards Regiments and the 32nd Division are located in the northern portion of the peninsula. Moreover, the 5th Parachute Brigade is located in Temryuk and the 6th and 212th Parachute Brigades are in Karchanskaya. In addition, the 47th Army command is still in radio contact with the 103rd Infantry Brigade and the 2nd Motorized Brigade. The 77th Mountain Division was defeated on the Kerch Peninsula in May 1942 and could only rescue remnant units by transporting them to the Taman Peninsula. After refitting, the division today has a strength of 8,000 - 10,000 men, but they are not completely equipped. Elements of the 65th Air defense regiment are located on Kosa Tusla Island. Little can be discerned about the regrouping of the forces on the Taman Peninsula in association with the rapid advance of German troops from Rostov to the south from either prisoner statements and agent reports or ground and air reconnaissance. The enemy is showing little replacement associated movement in company strength on the Taman, Bugas road and in platoon strength near Sapoozhskaya, near Gavrilenkov and in the northern portion of Kosa Tusla. The positions on Kosa Tusla were extended to the southwestern tip of the peninsula and some were constructed near Kordon, Cape Litvina and on the Gadyuchiy - Kut Peninsula. Explosions east of Kordon, in the region of 103.4 and south of Taman may be associated with the construction of positions in depth.

Supply traffic on all roads has not changed.

Artillery activity has increased conspicuously in past weeks. A total of 19 batteries fired 1400 rounds in the past week, of which 340 were fired at batteries approximately 1.5 kilometers west of Taman and 253 rounds fell on Kharlotte, directly south of Saparozhskaya. Fire has mainly been directed on the coastal strip between Kamysh Burun and Kerch and between Kapkany and Kayak, as well as on German artillery firing positions on the eastern tip of the peninsula.

Movement in Kerch harbor is being observed and engaged by the enemy.

Air activity also increased considerably immediately after the German fighters left and reached its climax between 27 - 29 July. Daily bombing attacks have occurred, but they have been mostly at night.

For example, during the nights of 28 and 29 July 110 high explosive and incendiary bombs were dropped. The bombing raids have been directed at the coastal strip between Kolonka and Ossovniy, on Baksy, Adzhim Ushkay, Kerch, Ak Burnu and on the Bagranovo area, Karterles, Kerch west railroad station.

Shipping has reflected no essential changes. The only observation is that boats appear in the vicinity of Kosa Tusla Island during the evening and on the southeastern tip off Anker. These are destined for the supply of the island defenders.

In conclusion it must be said that a large-scale landing attempt on the Kerch Peninsula cannot be anticipated. However, the enemy is still anticipating a landing on the Taman Peninsula.

> for the Division Commander
> The First Generalstabsoffizier:
> signed Pinski"

The enemy situation in Intelligence Report Nr. 32/42 revealed a strong massing of Soviet forces to protect the Taman Peninsula and, therefore, to protect the western flank of the Novorossisk defenses. However, in the Enemy Intelligence Report from 21 August 1942 the Ic of the 46th ID presents the following picture (extracts):

"...The enemy situation on the Taman Peninsula is governed by developments in the Kuban region. The enemy has done everything possible to construct a new defensive front on a line Kurchanskaya - Krymskaya in order to protect the harbor of Novorossisk, which has great significance for them, and to hold open the withdrawal route to the southeast. The Rumanian right flank today stands east of Kurchanskaya in contact with a fiercely defending enemy force east of Temryuk.

Under these circumstances, intelligence indicates that the 32nd ID, which is still, as of now, seated in Taman as confirmed by the location of the 80th Guards Regiment, will be displacing to another defensive front ... In the meantime, the fall of Krymskaya resulted in a penetration of this front. According to additional intelligence, the 77th Mountain Division has taken over the defense of the entire Taman Peninsula. Fishermen fleeing from Temryuk say that there are few Red Army soldiers there. Instead there is only naval infantry available to protect the city. Industry and all installations of value are planned for destruction. Moreover, on 12 August the following craft were noted in the harbor of Temryuk: 2 sub chasers ..., 3 motor torpedo boats, 2 cranes, 1 ice breaker ... On 21 August artillery boats fired on the lead Rumanian attack elements near Kurchanskaya. These ships were looking for a way to break through to the Kerch Strait because there is no other way out for them.

In summary it can be said that in numbers and in heavy weapons the defenders of the Taman Peninsula are not as strong as they were 10 days ago..."

On 24 August 1942 Enemy Intelligence Report Nr. 35/42 noted:

"... According to the latest intelligence, yesterday afternoon German troops attacked Temryuk and advanced 4 kilometers through Kurchanskaya to the northwest ... On the basis of the latest report, the 77th Mountain Division has also withdrawn from Akhtanisovskaya and has been established on the Krymskaya - Kurchanskaya front. According to Rumanian information, the following are still located in the Taman Peninsula area: The 14th Naval Infantry Battalion in Taman, the 3rd Company of the 1st Naval Infantry Battalion in Temryuk. The earlier referenced 5th, 6th and 212th Parachute Brigades have now been discovered in front of Army Group B ... Smoke has been observed at several locations, confirming the planned destruction of all war related installations..."

Enemy Intelligence Report Nr. 36/42 from 28 August 1942:

"... After elements of the 3rd Rumanian Army had taken the city of Temryuk in fierce house to house fighting on 25 August they advanced further up to the Peresypskoe confluence without running into any enemy resistance worth mentioning. They stopped there ... In the meantime, the capture of Temryuk has also been reported ... Near Troitskoe there are two Rumanian divisions crossing the Kuban to the south in order to make contact with German troops located in and south of Krymskaya ... Many medium sized and small ships and boats have been located near Cape Pekly ... We expect those ships remaining in the Sea of Azov to be brought through the Kerch

Strait under cover of darkness."

"46th ID/Abt. Ic   Div.Gef.Std., 31/8/1942
Enemy Intelligence Report Nr.37/42«)0»

1) Enemy Situation

a) Enemy forces on the Taman Peninsula:

There has not been a great change in the enemy situation. The 14th Naval Infantry Battalion, which was formerly located in Taman, has, in the meantime, arrived on the Novorossisk front. Kosa Tushla is occupied by the enemy. During the night of 31 August German reconnaissance elements observed renewed enemy efforts at laying mines and wire obstacles. Kosa Tusla is also still occupied by the enemy.

b) Artillery activity is again lively

Shipping between the Black Sea and Taman Bay has again become brisk. Several ships have been observed entering Taman Bay from Cape Tusla. On 29 August two ships (40 meters long) tried to move out of Taman Bay into the Kerch Strait; they were effectively engaged by German artillery. The larger of the two returned in the direction of Taman. The other stopped and was set afire by anti-aircraft guns on 30 August.

Road traffic is again brisk.

As before, searchlight activity remains brisk.

The overall picture reveals that enemy activity has increased during the past few days. Kosa Tusla is again occupied.

2) Situation in the Caucasus

a) Rumanian formations crossing the Kuban from the north captured Varenikovskaya and Gostagaevskaya and advanced on Anapa. On 28 August friendly troops from Krymskaya captured the hills 5 kilometers east of Natukhaevskaya.

b) Friendly troops from Khadyshenskaya attacked out of the Pshish Valley. The road from Tuapse was defended tenaciously by the enemy with the support of a tank platoon on the rail stretch within the same valley. There was an enemy counterattack in the upper Pshekha Valley, 50 kilometers northeast of Tuapse.

c) There are friendly troops in the Malaya Laba Valley 6 kilometers south of Burniy. In the Bolshaya Laba Valley, the advance has already passed through the Adsapsh Pass into the Bsyb Valley and further to the southeast toward the pass (4 kilometers west of the Dou Pass), which leads into the Babadnaya - Gumista Valley in the direction of Sukhum.

d) The city of Mosdok has been taken in the Terek area. There are strong enemy field positions on the southern bank of the Terek. Further to the west, a German attack out of the northwest from Isherskaya and Naurskaya has still not reached the rail line due to tenacious resistance. In this sector, the enemy has committed the 9th Army, which consists mainly of Armenians, Azherbeidzhanis and other Caucasians.

e) The advance in the direction of the Caspian Sea has reached Terekli - Mekteb, 80 kilometers from the coast. There has essentially been no progress near Elista. Ulan - Erge, Chilgir and Yashkul are still occupied by the enemy.

The Enemy Intelligence Reports from the Ic of the 46th ID show the development on the extreme right flank of the 17th German Army. Rumanian formations slowly advanced from the Taman Peninsula against Novorossisk. The 46th ID (General Haccius), which was badly battered during combat in the Crimea, as well as the 3rd Rumanian Mountain Division, quietly anticipated the developments on the Taman Peninsula in order to make the jump across the sea passage at the right moment.

In the meantime, the regrouping and preparation for the assault on Novorossisk had been completed. The right attack flank of the 73rd ID was reinforced by the 419th and 421st Regiments of the 125th ID.

On 28 August the 213th (73rd ID) and 419th (125th ID) Regiments attacked the mountains northwest of Nizhnaya Bakanskaya with the support of the 249th Assault Gun Brigade and blocked the Nizhnaya Bakanskaya - Grecheskoe road. Dobrovolcheskiy was captured in the evening.

From 29 to 31 August the attack of the 73rd ID advanced along the road to Nizhnaya Bakanskaya. The western flank of the division passed through the "Kaninkhenzukht" mountain group into the area north of Verkhnaya Bakanskaya. On the eastern flank, on the other hand, there was fierce fighting with forces of the 47th Soviet Army. The majority of the 73rd ID, which followed along the Krymskaya - Verkhnaya Bakanskaya valley road, was stopped by the 77th Soviet Mountain Division on 2 September 1942 in the narrow forested valley east of Nizhnaya Bakanskaya. An attempt to detour around the enemy to the south across the hills near Nizhnaya Bakanskaya failed. The 213th Grenadier Regiment, which had advanced far to the west, was committed to a flanking attack to the west through Verkhnaya Bakanskaya in order to advance to the southeast on Novorossisk. The regiment entered the narrow gorge north of the rail line and disappeared into the thickly forested area. The division nervously awaited the outcome of the operation. Then, in the afternoon hours, the voice of the regimental commander, Oberstleutnant Marbach, resounded over the loudspeaker: "The sea, the sea!" The 213th Grenadier Regiment was able to take the hills north of Verkhnaya Bakanskaya and dominate the towns in the valley with its weapons. The Black Sea could be seen from these hills. Therefore, the withdrawal route to Novorossisk of the enemy located in front of the division was also cut off and they would be forced to withdraw through the gorges to the south. The 213th Grenadier Regiment had created the prerequisite for the further attack on Novorossisk.

A day previously, advance forces of the Rumanian Cavalry Corps, which was advancing from Gostaevskaya, reached the Black Sea coast near Anapa. The counterattack of the 83rd Naval Infantry Brigade, supported by shipboard artillery, was repulsed. The ring around Novorossisk was closed from the northwest.

The 9th ID captured Neberdzhaevskaya and approached the city from the northwest.

With the conquest of Anapa by the 9th ID on 31 August the withdrawal route of the majority of the Soviets from the Taman Peninsula was eliminated. The Rumanian 5th and 6th Cavalry Divisions penetrated into the peninsula from the east. From 2 to 5 September Soviet war and transport ships (including the escort "Storm" and the artillery boats "Rostov-Don" and "Oktyabr") evacuated the majority of the army and naval infantry formations from the southern coast of the Taman Peninsula to Novorossisk under the command of the Chief of the Azov Flotilla, Rear Admiral Gorskov. During the nights of 2, 3 and 5 September Kapitänleutnant Christiansen's 1st German Motor Torpedo Boat Flotilla attacked the loading docks with S-102, (Kptlt. Töniges), S-28 (Kptlt. Künzel), S-27 (Kptlt. Büchtling) and S-72 (Oblt. z. See Schneider) and reported 19 successes. S-27 was sunk by friendly fire.

From 3 to 6 September the 73rd and the 9th ID continued to advance on Novorossisk. The 73rd ID, with the 213th Grenadier Regiment on the right and the 170th Grenadier Regiment on the left, captured Hills 445.9, 418.2 and 531.3 with the support of the 249th Assault Gun Brigade. For the first time the grenadiers of the 73rd ID had an overwhelming view of the city and the harbor of Novorossisk from Hill 445.9. The great sea fortress on the Eastern Black Sea coast lay at their feet like a model toy. The city of 95,000 accommodated a large coal industry, shipyards, a fishing industry and cement works. It was the departure point of the long coastal road that led through Tuapse, Sukhum and Batumi up to the Turkish border. Novorossisk was the key to the Transcaucasus. If Novorossisk was taken, the Soviet Black Sea Fleet's naval base would also fall. The utopian goal of advancing along the coastal road to Asia Minor and coordinating combat operations with Rommel's Afrika Korps was at hand.

The 77th Soviet Mountain Division and the 14th, 142nd, 83rd and 2nd Naval Infantry Brigades under the leadership of Rear Admiral Kholostnyakov defended the city. In spite of the support of the Soviet war ships, the flotilla leader "Kharkov" (Captain Melnikov) and the destroyer "Zoobratsitelniy" (Captain Vorkov), the V German Army Corps penetrated into the city.

On 6 September the 213th Grenadier Regiment attacked the road pass near 337.1 and to the south. After fierce combat, the mountain positions north of the rail line were taken and the road pass blocked. During the late afternoon the 213th and 186th Grenadier Regiments approached the Mefodievski city quarter. Oberleutnant Ziegler penetrated into the first blocks of houses with his I/186. The other battalions of the 186th and 213th Regiments followed and expanded the penetration into the city. From 7 through 10 September the fighting around the city of Novorossisk had stopped. On 10 September the German Wehrmacht reported:

"Novorossisk is in the hands of German troops..."

Along with the attack of the V Army Corps on Novorossisk, one of the most clever commitments of the "Brandenburgers" must be described. How did this come about?

In the summer of 1942, on the basis of numerous suggestions, a coastal jäger company was created under the cover name "Light Engineer Company, Regiment Brandenburg". Besides Russian speaking Germans it enlisted numerous Caucasian volunteers. The first time the company saw action was to protect the crossing maneuver of the German and Rumanian troops (to be described later) across the Straits of Kerch. The company was equipped with machine-guns, two light anti-aircraft guns and two 8 cm mortars. In addition, it had two large assault boats and one engineer landing boat available.

After the formations of the V Army Corps had approached the city of Novorossisk at the end of August, one platoon of the "Coastal Jäger Company/Brandenburg" was committed on the only Soviet road connection between Gelendshik and Novorossisk, its mission was to blow it up and, therefore, severe Russian supply lines. The majority of the coastal road ran along the hills on the coast.

While German bombers flew along the coast toward Gelendshik during the night and bombarded the harbor installations, two assault boats with a rein-forced "Brandenburger" platoon raced around Cape Penai and silently put in at the landing bay at Uferkies. Everything had been calculated to the smallest detail. While a weak guard was left with the boats, the "Brandenburgers" began to climb. Halfway up the rocky coast the walls of the coastal road became silhouetted against the brightening sky. An advance mine squad marked the way. Behind them the panting, heavily laden "Brandenburgers" followed. A Russian convoy of 11 trucks passed by. The "Brandenburgers" jumped for cover. They studied the nature of the road. Placing a blocking mine-field here would not be suitable. They set up security. Soon they found a suitable site. The engineers readied the explosives. Suddenly a low voice sounded: "Attention!"

A Russian truck came around a curve and its headlights fixed on a bundle laying in the road; an engineer had left his sack of explosives in his haste to take cover. The truck stopped. An officer got out. One of the men in Russian uniform had to go into action. He walked up to the vehicle and apologized, removing the sack from the road. The real Russian asked: "What are you doing here?" - "Guarding the road!" was the reply. However, the Soviet lieu-tenant was suspicious. He quickly drew his pistol and shot the "Brandenburger" dead before he could react and seek cover with his com-rades. The other "Brandenburgers" silently assaulted the Russian officer. The driver started the truck and pulled away. However, he did not get far. He was hit by a machine-gun round. The vehicle pitched over an embankment. Soon a column of 15 vehicles arrived. There was nothing left to hide. A machine-gun was placed on the road. Shots were fired into the advancing column. The guards jumped off the trucks and were swallowed up by the darkness. While the "Brandenburgers" frightened away a portion of the escort, engineers set the explosives. When they realized that one of the trucks was loaded with explosives they drove it up to the detonation site.

The first "Brandenburgers" were already descending the mountain when the engineer Feldwebel finished.

"Attention, detonation!" the call pierced the night.

Then the mountain was rocked by a powerful explosion. A little later the assault boats with the "Brandenburgers" returned to the German occupied coast.

On the next day air reconnaissance discovered a kilometer long traffic jam on the blown portion of the road.

While the regiments of the 73rd, 125th and 9th ID fought around Novorossisk on 1 September, forces from the 46th ID and the 3rd Rumanian Mountain Division crossed the Kerch Strait. The crossing was conducted under the cover name "Operation Bluecher".

During the night of 2 September the 46th ID landed on the northwestern side of the Taman Peninsula with 24 naval ferries from Kapitänleutnant Giele's 1st Landing Flotilla, siebelfähren and engineer landing and assault boats. The landing operation was covered by the 3rd Minesweeper Flotilla under Korvettenkapitän Hölzerkopf and the Luftwaffe. The landing was carried out in the Ilich area.

The 3rd Rumanian Mountain Division followed and landed near Veseliy. The landing was not opposed by the enemy.

On 2 September the crossing was completed. Then it was the time of the landing engineers and the light marine forces. The crossing was conducted in assault boats, siebelfähren and ferries in perfect time. Landing bridges were constructed near Ilich and on Kosa Chushka. They were later expanded to accept greater capacities. The landing of the 46th ID and the 3rd Rumanian Mountain Division was still more or less improvised. On 3 September 1942 Oberstleutnant Czech, Ib of the 46th ID, noted in his diary: "Supply through Ilich is moving slowly."

According to Russian sources, on 3 and 4 September elements of the Soviet naval infantry fought on the Taman Peninsula against the 46th ID. On 4 September the 46th ID occupied the city of Taman. A day later the last Soviet forces shipped out near Cape Zhelesny Rog and were taken to Gelendshik. On 4 September Czech's diary noted: "Taman taken. Supplies moving through there. The 46th ID will remain in Taman from 6 - 17 September."

On 8 September 1942 Oberstleutnant Czech, Ib of the 46th ID and responsible for supply, noted in his diary: "Decision made. We are going to the Caucasus." On 18 September the 46th ID marched through Starotitarovskaya, Varenikovskaya, Anastasievskaya, Krasnodar, Belorechenskaya into the area south of Maikop. It was to be committed during the second attack attempt on Tuapse on the left flank of the Lanz Mountain Division.

The 3rd Rumanian Mountain Division marched into the area south of Krymskaya.

On 10 September 1942 the commander of the V Army Corps, General Wetzel, was able to report the capture of the city of Novorossisk. However, the coastal road to Tuapse was still not opened.

At the beginning of September the Soviet North Caucasus Front was redesignated as the "Black Sea Group" and the Transcaucasus Front was reorganized. A tightened command and control structure resulted. The Soviet 47th Army, which defended Novorossisk, had dug into the industrial area on the eastern edge of the city and defended the access to the Black Sea coastal road.

During the Soviet reorganization and the energetic demands of the STAVKA for defense, additional troops were deployed, those that had previously been withdrawn by the enemy. From 8 - 11 September 1942 the cruiser "Krasniy Krym", flotilla leader "Kharkov", escort "Storm" and the destroyers "Zoobrazitelniy" and "Zeleznyakov" transported elements of the 137th and 145th Rifle Regiments and the 3rd Naval Infantry Brigade with equipment from Poti to Tuapse and Gelendskih.

From 12 - 24 September the regiments of the 73rd ID fought around the access to the coastal road. Adamovichka Balka, the "Proletariate" and "Red October" cement factories, the electric power station, the "Stalin" and "Kino" building complexes are names that soaked up the sweat and blood of the brave 213th and 170th Regiments. Each building, each factory was fiercely fought over in see-saw combat. The 173rd and 658th engineer battalions were bloodied there and the assault guns of the 249th Assault Gun Brigade conducted their most difficult attacks. The staff officers of the V Army Corps in Marchanskaya directed their efforts and plans there. From there the reports of the regiments went to the division operations section in Verkhnaya Bakanskaya. All of their hopes and efforts were in vain. On 24 September the "Stalin" building complex was taken. The bloodied 170th and 213th Regiments bogged down in front of the "C-Rippe" complex. The Soviet formations held onto the eastern bank of Zemess Bay and blocked the entrance to the coastal road. The front stagnated.

Then the newly-arrived Rumanian 3rd Mountain Division attempted to break through to the coastal road in the mountain forest region east of Novorossisk from out of the Abinskaya - Usun assembly area and open the way to Tuapse. This attack was conducted simultaneously with the second attack on Tuapse, on the Maikop - Goich Pass - Tuapse road.

On 19 September the Rumanians attacked and pushed the exhausted 216th Soviet Rifle Division back. On 22 September they drove a 6 kilometer deep wedge into the Soviet defenses. On 25 September a Soviet naval battalion conducted a flanking attack into the penetration and encircled the forward-most elements of the Rumanian 3rd Mountain Division. The Rumanians suffered heavy losses in men and equipment. The Soviet counterattack was stopped at the old positions. Then this front also stagnated.

From 14 - 30 October the regiments of the 73rd ID again attacked the Soviet positions on Zemess Bay. No one expected to break through to the coastal road anymore. The attack only resulted in an improvement of the German lines. Fortified winter positions had to be constructed before the outbreak of winter. The "C-Rippe" and other building complexes were taken. The Germans and Russians struggled over every meter of ground in attacks and counterattacks, exhausting themselves. At the end of this battle the remnants of the 213th Grenadier Regiment were combined into two infantry companies and two machine-gun companies. It was similar with the other regiments. This was the last attempt to open the Black Sea road to Tuapse.

ASSAULT ON THE MOUNTAIN PASSES

Race to the mountains - Kampfgruppe von Hirschfeld captures the Klukhor Pass - Assault on the summit of Elbrus - 30 kilometers from the Black Sea - "Are there no aircraft for supply?" - Defense on the main ridge

On 28 July 1942, immediately after the fall of Rostov, the commander of Army Group A, Feldmarschall List, visited the XXXXIX Mountain Corps command post and expressed his thanks to the commander, General Konrad, for his efforts around Rostov.

At the command post, which was a public house in Rostov, General Konrad learned of the future commitment of the XXXXIX Mountain Corps. "The 17th Army will be overextended during the offensive in the Caucasus", said List and, after a short pause, he asked: "Where does the corps think the XXXXIX Mountain Corps should be committed?"

Konrad: "Through Maikop!"

List: "The mountain corps will probably attack through the mountain passes west of Elbrus in the direction of Sukhum with two divisions in order to open the way to the coast into the Transcaucasus for the forces of the 17th Army advancing through Tuapse!"

During the discussion the OKW plan was revealed to General Konrad in general terms. Nevertheless, the plan would be changed several times because of developments in the situation.

The overall mission, however, was clear! The mountain corps staff immediately started planning. On hand was the study of the Fulpmes Mountain School: "The Mountain Passes of the Caucasus", which set forth three decisive factors:

1. There were only 8 weeks left until winter broke out in the mountain passes. At the end of September heavy snowfall puts an end to mountain crossings.

2. The only large road and rail crossings lead through the Caucasus Forest to Tuapse and from there to the Caucasus road and Sukhum.

3. The crossings through the mountain passes were inaccurately described; the descriptions of the important crossings and the Sukhum Army Road were also unreliable, they were actually narrow and only passable for small carts.

The most important crossing, the Sukhum Army Road, was described in the military - geographic work as follows:

"Sukhum Army Road. From the edge of Kartenord to Kurort Teberda (156 kilometers), passable for vehicles. From here another 34 kilometers is passable only for carts. - 8a - through the Dombai - Ulgen Pass (3007 meters) as 7 (glaciated, not even passable for draft animals) - 8b - through Klukhor Pass (2816 meters) - Ashara. Up to the mountain passes is a 13 kilometer long mule track with serpentine curves. The mountain passes are covered with small fields of snow. In summer, the shepherds drive their herds through the pass. It is passable for draft animals. After crossing the mountain pass, the way to Ashara is passable for carts. (Russ. 40) Passable by carts. Difficult.

(G. 41) A road through the pass began construction in 1936 and has since been completed. (G 41) - 9 - through neighboring pass (2867 meters). Passable for draft animals, difficult. The mountain pass is snow covered."

Examination of the study and the maps made it clear that only mountain elements could be committed in the high mountains. The mobile elements of the corps, heavy artillery, tank destroyer and supply columns, had to follow along the coastal road after the crossing to Tuapse was achieved.

In the meantime, the panzer and motorized formations attacked out of the bridgeheads on the Don and Manych to the south. The gebirgsjägers marched behind them. They were still 500 kilometers from the mountains. However, with each step, the mountain soldiers came closer to their element and were seized with mountain fever.

On 5 August the 1st Mountain Division ordered the creation of a high mountain company to scale Elbrus, to which the XXXXIX Mountain Corps later added a detail under Hauptmann Gämmerler with six men from the 4th Mountain Division. Both divisions were to participate in the scaling effort. The scaling of Elbrus would require the efforts of experienced men, those who had already conquered the peaks of the Himalayas. In the meantime, Hauptmann Groth, the leader of this operation, accompanied the long-range air reconnaissance from the IV Air Corps to the mountain and reconnoitered a march route to the top.

Men were divided over the value of the Elbrus operation. It did have some tactical value, since the mountain and the Elbrus House could be an important strong point. The Elbrus House offered shelter for a battalion and dominated the crossing from the Kuban into the Baksan Valley. Had they recognized its significance in time, it could have been utilized to roll over the Russian positions in the Ordzhonikidze area and the access to the pass in the Transcaucasus area from the rear, which could not be taken frontally. Of even greater significance was the dominance of Elbrus over the crossing from the Kuban into the Baksan Valley through the linkage of the Khotyu-Tau, Khassan - Khoi - Syurulgen, Asau and Chiper - Asau passes.

Soviet lines of communication were severed by the strikes of the German panzer divisions. The 46th Army from the Trans- caucasus Front was forced away from the mountain passes west of Elbrus and withdrew in disarray into the mountains. Meanwhile, the German mobile divisions had closed on the foothills of the mountains and awaited the arrival of the mountain and jäger divisions. The hour of the gebirgsjäger had arrived!

The second briefing for the commander of the XXXXIX Mountain Corps was ordered by Feldmarshall List on 10 August near Kurchevskaya. It was essentially the same as the one that occurred on 28 July in Rostov. To this point in time, the 1st and 4th Mountain Divisions, as well as the 2nd Rumanian Mountain Division, were located in the Kuban bend. In second echelon the Italian Alpine Corps followed through Rostov with three divisions, which were destined for commitment in the Caucasus. In light of this concentration of mountain units, all participating officers anticipated the immediate conquest of the mountains. However, it turned out otherwise!

Various plans circulated in the higher headquarters regarding the conquest of the passes and the crossings into the Trans- caucasus. This was because the overall situation changed daily and new decisions were always required. The 1st Panzer Army command wanted to attack the majority of the mountain divisions through Ordzhonikidze and the Georgian Army Road toward Tiflis and only block the western passes. However, Generaloberst von Kleist had his own plan; which took into consideration their limited means and fostered a reasonable establishment of strong points. It was turned down by OKW.

On 12 August the order arrived from OKW:

The XXXXIX Mountain Corps will again be subordinated to the 17th Army (it was previously subordinate to the 1st Panzer Army). The 2nd Rumanian Mountain Division will be subordinated to the 1st Panzer Army. The 1st and 4th Mountain Divisions, as well as B/F 121 Long Range Reconnaissance Staffel, will go to the XXXXIX Mountain Corps."

The mountain corps had a clear mission: the conquest of the passes in the eastern portion and in the center of the Caucasus and in the Elbrus area. However, the gebirgsjäger regiments still lagged far behind.

General Konrad set the following mission for his mountain divisions:

4th Mountain Division on the right to capture the passes in the area of the Bolshaya Laba. On the right adjacent to the XXXXIV Jäger Corps. The 1st Mountain Division on the left to capture the passes in the Teberda and Kuban area. One battalion of the 1st Mountain Division is to secure the lcft flank against the Baksan Valley and the Elbrus crossings.

Besides the advance detachments of the two mountain divisions, the regiments also formed independent advance detachments. The trucks were unloaded and the necessities were carried by the gebirgsjägers and draft animals. The race to the mountains began. Soon the advance detachments reached the edge of the mountains.

The 1st Mountain Division was assigned the Sukhum Army Road, which ran into the coastal road in the southern half of the Kodor Valley 16 kilometers southeast of Sukhum; the 4th Mountain Division was assigned the unsuitable crossing through the Bolshaya Laba Valley in the area traversed by the Bsyb, which flowed 64 kilometers northwest of Sukhum into the Black Sea.

On 10 August 1942, Advance Detachment Lawall (54th Mountain Reconnaissance Battalion with 4 squadrons, 1 platoon of the 44th Panzerjäger Battalion, one platoon of the 54th Mountain Engineer Battalion, Gruppe von Hirschfeld, Gruppe Groth) reached the edge of the foothills near Nevinnomyskaya and crossed the security lines of the XXXX Panzer Corps. On 5 August the city was captured by the 3rd Panzer Division. For five days the Soviet troops withdrew into the mountains.

On 11 August Advance Detachment Lawall reached Cherkessk and captured the undamaged bridge.

The von Hirschfeld Gebirgsjäger Battalion, which consisted of the two best companies from the 98th and 99th Gebirgs- jäger Regiments and escort weapons, advanced further to the south on the Sukhum Army Road. The town at the Teberda - Kuban river fork directly north of Mikoyan Shakhar was captured in spite of considerable enemy resistance. The enemy suffered considerable casualties. Mikoyan Shakhar was a significant industrial settlement.

With the capture of Mikoyan Shakhar the 1st Mountain Division conquered the springboard to the mountain passes. Subsequent objectives were set forth in the division order from 12 August 1942 (secret), which contained the phrase "for the advance through the Caucasus to the Black Sea". It said:

"...1st Mountain Division will assemble in area 117 - 118 (Kardonikskaya - Cherkessk) and attack through 123 - 128 (Klukhor - Dongus - Orun Pass) to the Black Sea ... Advance Detachment Lawall, reinforced with the von Hirschfeld half battalion and Alpine Company Groth, will destroy enemy forces in area 117 - 119, occupy Passes 123, 125 and hold them open for the division ... See annex for special mission to be conducted by Alpine Company Groth ... 98th and 99th Gebirgsjäger Regiments will each advance a reinforced battalion with the regimental staff in truck columns under the command of Major Hofmann against 119 (Mikoyan Shakhar)...

a) 98th Gebirgsjäger Regiment: will advance in cooperation with the advance company of Half Battalion Hauptmann von Hirschfeld (6/Geb.Jg.Rgt. 98) and occupy Pass 123 (on March Route Picker) and reconnoiter 22...

b) 99th Gebirgsjäger Regiment: will occupy the pass in cooperation with the advance company of Half Battalion von Hirschfeld (13/Geb.Jg.Rgt. 98) and Alpine Company Hauptmann Groth on March Route Kress) and reconnoiter 64...

Contact is to be maintained between 22 and 64 through 71..."

After the capture of Mikoyan Shakhar, Gruppe von Hirschfeld remained on the heels of the enemy. On 14 August it fought an "isolated pocket battle" to occupy the town of Teberda, during which 23 guns, including seven heavy guns, numerous mortars and machine-guns, two tanks, 96 trucks and 180 combat vehicles were captured. During the late afternoon Gruppe von Hirschfeld established a small bridgehead across the river, repaired the bridge and created the prerequisite for further advance.

During the evening, the commander rode to Teberda. He met von Hirschfeld on the bridge.

"Speed is decisive, von Hirschfeld, for the Klukhor Pass also!" said the General.

"That is my forte, Herr General!" replied the 30 year-old mountain officer.

On 15 August Gruppe von Hirschfeld advanced further. The real mountain fighting began south of Teberda. The worsening mountain routes were becoming more and more hemmed in by pine forests and mighty peaks until they finally turned into trails. The enemy rear guard elements took cover behind trees and shrubs as they fought their way back. Twice the Gebirgsjägers had to wade through icy mountain streams. Leutnant Harras, commander of the lead platoon, was killed. Several times enemy blockades were bypassed. The Klukhor drew the German Gebirgsjägers like a magnet. The companies marched widely dispersed, followed by the draft animal columns. The lead elements approached the Klukhor at a logging camp on foot.

On 16 August, after conducting terrain reconnaissance and setting up security at the Dombai - Ulgen Pass, they continued. However, they determined that the pass could not be taken frontally.

Major von Hirschfeld, a superior tactician, deceived the enemy in front by committing a flanking group unbeknownst to the enemy and threw them back to the Klukhor. Listen to the leader of the flanking group, Oberleutnant Neuhauser:

"Two battle groups were formed, one under the leadership of Hauptmann Pössinger, the other under my leadership. Both battle groups consisted of a high-mountain platoon, without climbing equipment, one jäger platoon, one heavy machine-gun platoon and one heavy mortar platoon. Each group had a special mission. While Pössinger persisted in front, I swung my battle group wide to the right in order to throw the enemy from their positions in the pass from the rear. We had often practiced this tactic in the Kranzberg near Mittenwald. We marched and climbed for three hours, it was our biggest effort since being transferred to the Caucasus. On the back slope of a mountain there was a flat depression, which appeared suitable for allowing us to reach our objective without being noticed by the enemy. At the upper third, we turned off to the left. However, we had to cross a wide snow field where we were fired on by the enemy. We had to step back and swing out further! The same thing happened again at a second mountain. Then I led my already exhausted battle group - they all had a great burden to bear, back packs and weapons - on a reconnaissance of the terrain. From behind a boulder came two Russians with their hands raised; a security post. I reached the crest of the ridge and caught a glimpse of the enemy in the valley. The enemy was located approximately 500 meters from us on the opposite slope. At approximately the same distance on a valley floor enemy groups were sitting around a camp fire cooking and eating. The pass was strongly defended. The following jäger groups were immediately committed along the crest of the ridge. My mission was to occupy positions that I deemed suitable for conducting a surprise attack on the encamped enemy. The machine-guns, mortars and rifles began firing into the enemy; the effect was frightening. The overall impression was that the Russians had very little security deployed.

At 1400 hours, I myself reported back as a messenger to Hauptmann von Hirschfeld to tell him we achieved the objective and report my observations. I was ordered to attack the enemy from the rear. I was to use light signals only if the situation became desperate. Pössinger would attack the pass frontally, while we provided fire support. After a two and a half hour climb, I was back with my battle group. However, there was now a new situation: the enemy withdrew in two groups which provided mutual fire support. While the frontal group under Hauptmann Pössinger attacked and quickly overran the enemy security posts, we fired at the withdrawing Russians. The pass was ours! Night fell. We were so tired that even the rocky cliffs did not keep us from falling into a deep sleep."

During the evening of 17 August 1942, the 2816 meter high Klukhor Pass was assaulted. The summit of the Sukhum Army Road was in German hands. While the Neuhauser Outflanking Group took two days rest, the battle group under Hauptmann Pössinger stayed on the rocks.

On this day, the group under Hauptmann Groth, consisting of his old 13/99 Geb.Jg.Rgt. under Oberleutnant Hierholzer and the high-mountain company of the 1st Mountain Division, which was under his direct control, worked its way east of Group von Hirschfeld through the Kuban Valley up to the 3546 meter Khotyu - Tau Pass at the western foot of Elbrus. Groth was not hindered by any enemy blocking positions, but there were blown bridges, steep rocks and impassable gravel slopes.

At approximately the 3000 meter point the 20 man lead group bivouacked under the wild southwestern precipice of Mount Elbrus on the edge of the Ullu - Kam Glacier. The draft animal group lagged behind with the weapons, ammunition and supplies; the lead group had to await their arrival. Groth dispatched an eight man group under the communications officer, Oberleutnant Schneider, just before midnight with the mission of reconnoitering the condition and capacities of shelters in the Elbrus area. The only available maps, which were 1:100,000 maps developed by the Military Geographic Department from Russian 1:84,000 maps, indicated three shelters in the Elbrus area: the 4045 meter high western hut on the southwestern crest of the mountain, a 4100 meter high hut on the endless glacier south of the eastern peak and the 4690 meter high Gastukhova hut on the southern foot of the eastern peak.

There was neither a western hut nor a Gastukhova hut, but there was a tourist hotel at the 4200 meter point. It was a modern structure, with aluminum paneling, central heating and electric lights. Moreover, it had a chart of Elbrus that indicated that there were plywood shelters at the 5300 meter point between the eastern and western peaks. Near the hotel were grouped several plywood huts around a solidly constructed meteorological station.

Equipped with his own deficient maps, and in complete darkness as to the state of affairs, Hauptmann Groth left with a small force at 0300 hours (17 August) so that the results of the reconnaissance could be obtained from Scout Troop Schneider as soon as possible. The rest of his small force was ordered to follow as soon as the draft animal column arrived.

By dawn Hauptmann Groth and his men stood on the Khotyu - Tau Pass (3546 meters). They had a clear view of the majestic peaks of the central Caucasus from Hshba across the Dyshtau up to Koshtantau. In front of them lay the 17 kilometer glacier, stretching from Asau, Gara - Bashis, Terskol and Dzhika - Ugon - Kes. Groth couldn't believe his eyes. As he surveyed this trackless vast ice wasteland he spied a metal hut on a rocky cliff about 6 kilometers away. There was no trace of Reconnaissance Element Schneider. They did not leave any tracks on the hard ice during the night. Groth was convinced that Schneider and his people had seen the apparently uninhabited building and occupied it. He left orders on the pass for the main body to follow.

As the sun rose, the ice became softer and the snow deeper. By midday each step became torture. The shimmering objective slowly grew nearer.

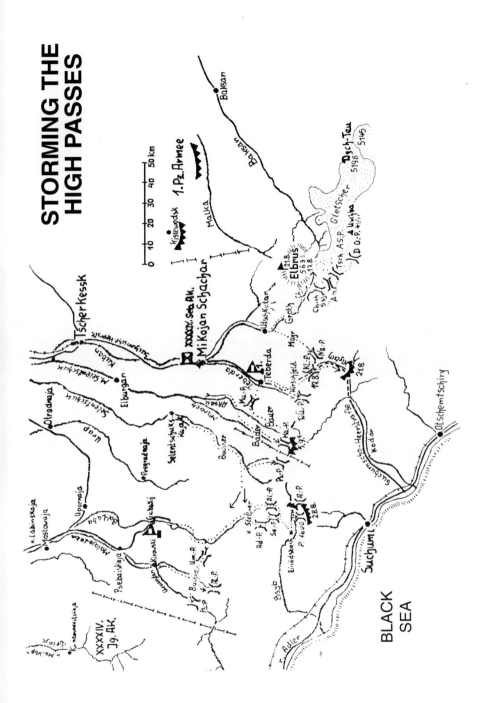

STORMING THE
HIGH PASSES

Then they saw it: welcoming smoke was rising! That could only be Schneider with his people!

In the meantime, the following had come to pass: during the night and the early morning hours Schneider had reached the building and had realized in time that it was occupied by the enemy. Therefore, Reconnaissance Element Schneider avoided the position. Bergführer Schwarz remained behind to warn his Schwäbian compatriots.

Groth reflected: Attack? - This was idiotic. Bypass? - senseless in front of the mouths of the Russian machine-guns.

He summoned his trusty messenger, Steiner from Munich, and took a white handkerchief from his backpack. Waving it with the courage of the desperate, he stomped through the bottomless snow toward the first Russian double machine-gun post. While he was being led to a group of officers, who had their command post in the meteorological station, he noticed an old experienced mountain infantry company commander, whose high- mountain Kirghitz platoons occupied and defended the complex. The success of the Hauptmann's mission depended on his ability to convince the leader of the Russian force that it was surrounded on all sides by a superior enemy force and that he was sent as a negotiator to allow them to withdraw in order to prevent bloodshed.

The incredible happened. After talking it over with various civilians, the meteorologists and his staff, it was agreed that the majority of the Russians would leave for the Baksan Valley with their weapons and essential staff. Four slant-eyed soldiers were left behind with a whispered mission, which the Hauptmann did not hear. It turned out that all four were friendly peasants from the vegetable paradise around Osh and Fesgana. They entertained Groth with cakes and tea from the kitchen of the meteorological station. That sealed their friendship. They laid their weapons down. Steiner and Schwarz were summoned. Steiner took the Reich battle flag from his field blouse and Schwarz raised it on the flagpole over the meteorological station, which was the signal for victory.

The valuable strong point was in German hands without one shot being fired. During the evening, the advance troops trickled in. Defenses were established that night. The anticipated counterattack did not occur.

Hauptmann Gämmerler arrived with the main force. The Elbrus House offered 150 beds in 40 rooms; in addition there was food and other supplies. After setting up the necessary security, the alpinists of the 1st and 4th Mountain Divisions rested on the following day in order to gather strength for the assault on the peak. There was no longer a trace of the approximate 45 Russian defenders of Elbrus House and the weather station. They had descended into the Baksan Valley on the previous day.

On 19 and 20 August there were snow storms. In spite of these, the men conducted a route march up to the 5000 meter point in order to get accustomed to the thin air. An attempt on 19 August came up short. On the evening of 20 August the categorical order from the commander of the 1st Mountain Division arrived over the radio to climb the Elbrus peak. While 21 August promised to be a suitable day, it turned out otherwise.

During the night an even wilder storm raged around the house. The assault on the peak was begun at 0300 hours. The early morning light proved to be pale and unfavorable. There was a snowstorm; visibility was zero. In spite of this, they advanced; there were six roped parties of three men each, including four from the 4th Mountain Division. A weak group was left behind to secure Elbrus House. They still had to anticipate an enemy counterattack.

At 0600 hours the Throne of the Gods was covered in a thick mist. Again there was a strong snowstorm. The Elbrus chart indicated there was a small shelter at 5319 meters where the climbers could stop for rest. Should they turn back?

Iron will and the great unknown drove them further. Each step to the top became more difficult in the thin air. The pelting of the ice crystals cut the faces of the men like knives. At 1100 hours Oberfeldwebel Kümmerle jammed the flag pole with the German battle flag into the icy peak. The Edelweiss standard of the 1st Mountain Division and the Enzian standard of the 4th Mountain Division were planted next to it. The climbers shook hands.

They descended cautiously. The battle flag was already tattered from the storm during the descent, it appeared that the Gods resented the intrusion into their 5633 meter high empire. The majestic Elbrus peak vanished from the view of the climbers.

At the very same time (1130 hours) a Russian high-mountain company composed of Pamirs under the leadership of a Russian alpinist was at the 5000 meter point. They had given up their attempt to reach the Elbrus House because of the raging snow storm.

In order to effectively secure the eastern flank of the XXXXIX Mountain Corps in the Elbrus area, Company Groth was given two additional battle groups. They were committed in the glacier area south of Elbrus; in particular on the Asau Pass, on the Chiper - Asau, on the Khassan - Khoi Syurulgen, on Khiper and on Khotyu - Tau. The Dauner and Hoerl units from the 99th Gebirgsjäger Regiment climbed into the rugged mountain world and blocked the Asau Pass.

They realized that the enemy would not cease their attempts to capture the Elbrus House. They constantly tried to approach the Elbrus House with reconnaissance in combat strength. The elite of the Russian mountain climbers participated in these operations. Captain Gusev, one of the first climbers of the 7495 meter high Stalin Peak (highest mountain in the Soviet Union), was the leader of these alpine and military operations. However, they failed due to the vigilance of the defenders of the Elbrus House (now in company strength).

The enemy attacked with air support in mid-September. They were thrown back with losses. The Elbrus House strong point proved to be impregnable, if it was purposefully defended. It remained in German hands until its defenders descended in January 1943. In late winter the Soviets repeated the German undertaking of 21 August 1942. A special unit was formed from all of the mountain troops in the Soviet Union under Gusev, Geletzkis and Gusales. They removed the Edelweiss standard of the 1st Mountain Division and the Enzian standard of the 4th Mountain Division from Elbrus' peak and raised the red banner with hammer and sickle.

At the beginning of September a German reconnaissance against the 3198 meter high Dongus - Orun Pass was repulsed by the Russians. The gebirgsjägers were situated in the middle of an overwhelming mountain world. They constantly turned their gaze to the east; there was the 4697 meter high Ushba, the Matterhorn of the Caucasus, in its majestic beauty, and further to the east was the double peaked Dych Tau just short of 5200 meters.

What was happening in the 4th Mountain Division sector at this time? - On 14 August, while the 1st Mountain Division was already standing in Teberda, the advance detachment of the 4th Mountain Division reached the town of Opornaya at the foot of the mountains by advancing through Labinskaya. Route conditions in the 4th Mountain Division sector were very poor. In spite of this the division commander, General Eglseer, an experienced Austrian mountain officer, was optimistic. He promptly committed his forces in the Bolshaya Laba Valley to advance to the south. Oberst Stettner von Grabenhofen pursued the weakened enemy with elements of his 91st Gebirgsjäger Regiment and soon reached the Gubskiy Farmstead. There they struggled with the enemy and the adversity of nature. Battle Group von Stettner continued to fight skillfully. Several times large mountain rivers had to be crossed. Bridges, footbridges and rope bridges had to be constructed. Supply was brought up with great difficulty.

In the meantime, the 2nd echelon of the 4th Mountain Division, the 13th Gebirgsjäger Regiment under Oberst Buchner, marched east of Group Stettner into the Selenchuk Valley to the south. Mother Nature and the route conditions hampered rapid advance.

Both assault groups of the 4th Mountain Division followed the courses of the rivers. Buchner ordered a battle group to advance further to the south in order to secure the Pshis and Marukh Passes directly to the left of the boundary with the 1st Mountain Division. The main force leap-frogged to the west and its lead elements met up with the lead elements of Group Stettner on 22 August south of Koshi.

The Selenchuk Valley appeared to be sufficiently secured. A corps order assigned the 4th Mountain Division a new mission: detach a regimental staff to which units arriving at the 4th Mountain Division will be subordinated. This force was to advance through the Umpyrski Pass into the Malaya Laba and Urushten Valleys and occupy the Psseashcha and Aishcha Passes, which were considered as a departure base on the right flank of the XXXXIX Mountain Corps for an advance on Adler. The German leadership hoped to gain an additional trump card with this regrouping. However, it turned out that too many trump cards had already been played. Many of the crossings over the high mountains were not crossings at all. Many of the roads noted on the maps were no more than cart trails, often they were only foot trails. In spite of these realizations, the German leadership did not veer from its military objectives. And the gebirgsjägers marched further through the impassible mountain valleys to the south with one hope in mind: behind the next group of rocks would peek the palms on the edge of the Black Sea coast at Sukhum.

After Battle Group von Hirschfeld had taken the Klukhor Pass, the following group, with the 6/98, 6/99, 2/54 and several platoons of heavy machine-guns and mortars, attacked further to the south. The II/98, under Major Salminger, followed. Arriving from Uchkulan, a battle group of the II/99 covered Hirschfeld's advance from the Nakhmar Pass. The main group still lagged behind. The majority of the 98th Gebirgsjäger Regiment followed in the Teberda Valley, trying to catch up with the lead elements. In the Kuban Valley, the 99th Gebirgsjäger Regiment, which had taken over security in the Elbrus region, followed Battle Group Mayr of Gruppe Salminger to the Nakhar Pass.

In the meantime, Oberst Kress took command in the region south of Klukhor (after Oberst Picker fell ill). The far advanced Battle Group von Hirschfeld was not harassed by the enemy, but by numerous supply problems. The lead battalion established that the Sukhum Army Road from the Klukhor Pass up to the Klych Farmstead, where the Klych and Gvandra flow together, was only a cart trail. Battle Group von Hirschfeld already had a handful of gebirgsjägers located near the Klych Farmstead on 21 August, the same day the German flag was being raised on Mount Elbrus. Soviet resistance stiffened at the Klych Farmstead. The Germans were prevented from exiting from the mountains. Intermediate sub-tropical vegetation bogged down the German Gebirgsjägers. From the south, the wind brought up the clean air from the Black Sea. It was a short 50 kilometers from the coast. Battle Group von Hirschfeld had to wait in the vicinity of their objective, until additional forces arrived which would allow them to make the last jump.

Hauptmann von Hirschfeld could not know that in the main headquarters of the military forces of the Soviet Union, in the STAVKA in Moscow, Stalin had pounded the table and ordered that further withdrawal be stopped and that the German advance be halted, at the latest, in the mountains and on the Baksan - Terek sector. He was bringing commanders to trial, publicly exposing serious lapses in leadership down to regiment commanders, and threatening serious measures if his orders were not followed in the future. He reproached the 46th Army of the Transcaucasus Front for doing too little to defend the passes. For example, the III Rifle Corps from this army had given up the passes of the Sukhum Army Road too soon. However, Stalin did not accuse himself; even though he also did not believe (as did his subordinate troop leaders) that the Germans would be able to cross the impassible mountains west of the Elbrus. Therefore, the defense had to be conducted with hastily thrown together troops as they became available at the passes.

However, STAVKA was then able to fathom the German plan, namely the opening of a route to the Black Sea coast through the Sukhum area by the XXXXIX Mountain Corps for the corps fighting in the west and then opening the way into the Transcaucasus.

In the Soviet work "The Battle for the Caucasus", the author divided the battle into several stages. On 18 August, the Russian troops began to strengthen their resistance. After reaching the Caucasus, the Soviets reinforced their defensive efforts under the leadership of the Central Committee of the Party and the High Command of the Armed Forces of the Soviet Union. Training centers for mortarmen and machine-gunners and for high-mountain staffs, as well as for the supply services, were created. The commander of the Transcaucasus Front ordered the immediate commitment of mountain troops and retrained active units into the battle to re-establish contact with cut off units. The Soviet Air Force took over a portion of the supply effort.

The fruits of these efforts were experienced by Gruppe von Hirschfeld at the Klych Farmstead. Although Oberst Kress deployed new companies, the breakout into the open plain was not achieved.

A new attempt had to be made to open the route. While Battle Group von Hirschfeld lay in front of the enemy with the reinforced III/99 Geb.Jg.Rgt., Oberst Kress committed the II/98 Geb.Jg.Rgt. to the east in an outflanking attack of the Soviet main group. However, Major Salminger's outflanking group ran into a Soviet counterattack and was splintered and thrown back. The planned combined attack of the III/99 and the II/98 did not come to pass.

The two battalions held out in the positions on the Klych Farmstead until 26 August. The pressure increased considerably. Supply was a problem, even more difficult was the evacuation of the many wounded over the cart trail. The troop surgeons Drs. Schleinzer, Beck, Höllriegel, Sebalt, von Langsdorff and Zimek and their medical personnel worked without pause and spent many a sleepless night.

Increased Soviet activity was also indicated on the right flank of the 1st Mountain Division. There, at night, they were able to infiltrate the 808th and 810th Regiments, as well as mortar and engineer units, gain access to the Marukh Pass and throw back the weak German defenders, which consisted of elements of the 13th Gebirgsjäger Regiment of the 4th Mountain Division, to the north on 25 August. At the same time, the I/98 under Major Bader was advancing to the south in the Aksau Valley. General Lanz and the corps recognized the threat to the seam between the two mountain divisions, which was represented by the penetration of at least five enemy battalions into the Marukh Pass. The majority of the 2nd High Mountain Battalion (Bauer), which had just arrived in Teberda in the 1st Mountain Division area of operations, was inserted into the Mukhinskoi Pass to the west on 26 August in order to prevent the further advance of the enemy to the north, together with the I/98 Geb.Jg.Rgt., and later to recapture the Marukh Pass. The 1st Company of the 2nd High Mountain Battalion was committed to block the Dombai - Ulgen Pass (3006 meters) in the Teberda area.

The I/98 and the 2nd High Mountain Battalion arrived in the Aksau Valley together. The I/98 turned off to the west into the Marukh Valley. Both battalions probed to the south, but the I/98 soon ran into considerable enemy resistance and bogged down. Reconnaissance revealed that the Marukh Pass was occupied by strong enemy forces.

General Lanz entrusted Oberstleutnant Eisgruber with the command of the combined battalions I/98 and 2nd High Mountain. The assault on the Marukh Pass was immediately prepared. On the 3145 meter peak, which lay between two valleys, General Lanz, Oberstleutnant Eisgruber, the battalion commanders and the forward observer of the mountain artillery met for the last attack briefing.

The cloudy afternoon of 4 September turned into a clear frosty night. The men of the 2nd High Mountain Battalion lay on the Marukh gap and secured the outstanding fire point. An icy wind swept over the gap. The majority of the 3rd and 4th Companies huddled together in snow dugouts and awaited the results of reconnaissance. Then came the report: "The route is free of enemy!" The outflanking maneuver of the two high mountain companies began.

During the frosty clear night, veering off to the east, the two companies were able to get into the rear of the enemy, since they were directing all of their attention to the I/98 to their front. The 4th Company climbed over the Marukh gap on icy steps. It finally reached its assigned departure positions on the southern wall of this glacier gap. The mountains, glacier and ridges appeared ghostly in the clear, starry night. The fields of snow shimmered in the waning moonlight. The hours-long night climb ended when they reached the assault departure area. 500 meters under them lay the Russians, who were defending the pass. They felt secure. Noises drifted up to the Germans, as the Russians were preparing for a new day.

The 3rd Company broke out at almost the same time as did the 4th and they reached their crest south of the Marukh glacier over a reconnoitered path. Heavy machine-guns were set up in suitable positions. Mortars were set up in the rear behind boulders. The forward observers from the 2nd and 8th Batteries of the 79th Mountain Artillery Regiment immediately took up their observation positions. The batteries would give effective support to the attack of Battle Group Eisgruber.

Gradually the day dawned. The Soviets on the pass below had still not noticed that the German gebirgsjägers were in their rear. The outflanking group waited quietly for the start of the attack. There was visual contact between the two high mountain companies. Then Major Bauer gave the signal. The 3rd Company opened fire. Mortar and machine-gun fire pounded into the rear of the enemy creating a fiery hell. When the Russians tried to set up a defense, the shells from seven mountain guns crashed among them.

Then the 4th Company attacked into the enemy's flank from the east. The enemy was pinned down by well-placed fire from the 3rd Company and the mountain guns. Line after line of the Russians were suppressed from the dominant firing positions. The I/98 also attacked at 1100 hours. Attacked frontally and on the eastern flank, their withdrawal obstructed in the rear, the strong defenders of the Marukh Pass had no chance. The weapons grew silent. Only a few Russians were able to break out to the west over a steep slope because this area was not completely encircled. At 1845 hours, a thunderous "Hurrah" announced that the Marukh Pass was again in German hands.

German losses totaled seven dead and eight wounded, the Soviets lost over 300 dead along with 557 prisoners. Besides numerous light infantry weapons, 19 heavy machine-guns, 13 heavy mortars, 117 anti-tank rifles and a lot of ammunition was captured.

While the 1st Mountain Division fought around the access to the Klych Valley, the main effort group of the 4th Mountain Division, under Oberst Stettner von Grabenhofen worked its way against the Adsapsh (2570 meters) and Sancharo Passes (2592 meters). When the lead elements of the 13th and 91st Gebirgsjäger Regiments met the force of the commander of the 91st Regiment then consisted of the II/13 and III/91. Oberst Buchner, who followed von Stettner in second echelon into the Selenchuk Valley with the 13th Gebirgsjäger Regiment, was shifted from the left flank of the 4th Mountain Division through the Umpurski Pass to the right flank in order to create an additional position for an attack on Adler by occupying the Pshcha and Aishcha Passes. New groupings resulted from this regrouping, which further disrupted the unity of the two gebirgsjäger regiments of the 4th Mountain Division. In two main groups, separated by over 40 kilometers, the two commanders attempted to lead their formations to victory. Buchner's objective was achieved by reaching and blocking the passes in the right division lane. Stettner's group still had the objective of Sukhum on the Black Sea. How did von Stettner attempt to achieve this goal?

On 23 August the II/13 captured the 2579 meter high Adsapsh Pass without a fight. A little later, the III/91 occupied the defended Sancharo Pass (2592 meters). The II/13 pursued the weak enemy into the Psekh Valley and, therefore, had overcome the main ridge. On 25 August the III/91 took the 2726 meter high Allistrakhu Pass and turned its main body to the west to the march route of the II/13. Both battalions drove on the Bsyb Valley.

On 26 August at 1400 hours the II/13 broke the weak enemy resistance in the northern section of the small settlement of Pshu, which was christened Einödsbach [Wilderness Creek] by Stettner's gebirgsjägers. Before they emptied into the Bsyb Valley, strong enemy forces halted the advance of the II/13. The III/91 caught up with an enemy of unknown strength and unclear status on the deep flank; further advance was temporarily suspended. The battle group set up a defense on three sides in order to let ammunition and supply catch up. Gradually reconnaissance reports arrived from elements that were far advanced and on the flanks. Prisoner of war statements corroborated these reports stating that only rear guard elements stood in front of Battle Group Stettner, in an attempt to gain time for the Soviets to construct defenses on the southern course of the mountains. After considering all of the facts, Oberst von Stettner made the decision to attack the southern passes immediately.

On the morning of 27 August the enemy withdrew from in front of Battle Group von Stettner. II/13 was immediately committed to the east into the Bsyb Valley in order to capture a bridge 8 kilometers from Einödsbach, which was an important crossing into the southern passes. II/13 again ran into strong enemy forces and bogged down. In the meantime, the III/91 had penetrated to within 4 kilometers, but the day had come to an end. On 27

August the situation near the forward-most II/13 had no longer changed.

By morning of 28 August mountain engineers created a 22 meter- long crossing over the Bsyb during a march halt by the III/91. The battalion took the opposite bank. While the majority of the battalion advanced against Pass 1600, the 13/91 advanced upstream on the southern bank of the Bsyb and opened a bridgehead for the II/13. The important river crossing to the Achavkhar Pass was in German hands. However, it was soon established that the 1389 meter high pass was strongly defended and another advance against the pass had only weak possibilities of success. Oberst von Stettner ordered the II/13 (with the 13/91) into the bridgehead in order to defend the crossing and prevent the enemy from advancing downstream.

In the meantime, the III/91 moved all of its draft animals across the footbridge. After an undisturbed one and a half hour march the route veered off to the south and Pass 1600 where it became considerably worse. Thick young growth and wild vines were interspersed among the old trees, complicating the beginning of the march. Long rocky slopes, fields of boulders and crevices complicated the last part of the march for the men and animals. The draft animals had to be constantly unloaded and rested.

At 0930 hours the lead elements came upon a Caucasian herdsman. He informed them that there were approximately 500 Russians climbing up to Pass 1600 at the same time. Every minute counted to see who would capture the pass!

The commander of the III/91, Major Grooter, who was located with the lead elements, immediately dispatched the lead platoon, which consisted of 30 gebirgsjägers from the 12th Company, to race for the pass. They left their gear behind. Further to the south the route descended in a serpentine manner through thick woods and on both sides of the trail were rock slides and deep trenches.

At 1000 hours the lead platoon reached this area and quickly prepared to defend. At 10005 hours the lead platoon fired at the first advancing Soviets, who were taken by surprise at the closeness of the range they were being fired upon. Nevertheless, they did not give up so easily. The following elements looked to see if they could outflank the lead platoon in order to get into the rear of the Germans. When additional elements of the 12/91 arrived, this attempt was given up. At 1100 hours the 12th Company of the 91st Gebirgsjäger Regiment had won the race to Pass 1600.

It was another four hours before the majority of the III/91 arrived. A pack animal had fallen into a narrow trench and blocked the slope. All of the following animals had to be unloaded, their burdens had to be dragged 90 meters before they could be re-loaded. During the evening security troops were deployed on both sides of the pass and the pass itself was strongly secured. By 30 August Gruppe von Stettner was holding an occupied position. Soviet activity increased considerably, but the crises were overcome.

In order to give the reader a better idea of the strengths, weapons and equipment involved, the organization of Battle Group von Stettner is provided. It was similar to all of the gebirgsjäger units. Naturally, the data was diluted considerably by losses.

Battle Group Stettner consisted of:

1. Regiment staff with a communications platoon, surgeon and medical group, 3 high-mountain scout squads and one engineer platoon from the 1/94 Geb.Pi.Btl.

2. III/91 Geb.Jg.Rgt. consisted of:

Headquarters company with communications platoon, engineer platoon and light infantry gun platoon (2 light infantry guns, 7.5 cm)

Heavy company with a heavy machine-gun platoon with three heavy machine-gun groups (6 heavy machine-guns each) and a mortar platoon of two mortar groups (four 8 cm mortars each)

Three jäger companies each with three platoons of four groups (12 light machine-guns), one heavy machine-gun group per company (2 heavy machine-guns)

one mortar group (two 8 cm mortars) per company

The total strength of III/91 Geb.Jg.Rgt. was 900 men and 250 pack animals, of which the combat strength was approximately 550 men.

3. II/13 Geb.Jg.Rgt. was organized like the III/91.

4. The subordinate artillery group consisted of:

Headquarters and communications platoon,

one artillery platoon from the I/94 Geb.AR with two 7.5 cm mountain guns

two artillery platoons from the II/94 Geb.AR with four 7.5 cm mountain guns.

Strength of the artillery group: 250 men and 80 pack animals.

From this summary it can be seen that a large part of the manpower and almost all of the pack animals were given over to weapons transport and ammunition supply. This contrasted with operations on flat land. Here the physical effort put out by the mountain artillery was particularly high. The mountain guns were carried in several sections by the pack animals. Ammunition, radio equipment, etc. had to be conveyed in the same manner.

And now for the supply! The supplies for Battle Group von Stettner had to be transported over a straight line distance of 60 kilometers. The 60 kilometers, as the crow flies, passed over mountain trails, large mountain streams, rock fields, mountain crests, foot trails that, at the very least, doubled the effort for every kilometer marched. Often the supply route stretches were so bad that even pack animals could not be used and their loads had to be reduced. Prisoners were mostly utilized in these cases.

After initial difficulties, supply for Battle Group von Stettner was organized and moved through six stations. The Ib, who was responsible for all of the supply for the division, directed the effort from Gubskiy. The supplies were transported into the Bolshaya Laba Valley 15 kilometers south of Gubskiy by motor vehicles. Then things became difficult. The march time for the following stretch was about four days.

The phases were: from the departure point of Roshkovo to strong point S1, the 24 kilometer stretch was traversed by horse-drawn vehicles and carts. Along this stretch, the loads had to be unloaded and carried across rope bridges.

From S 1 to S 2 the 17 kilometer stretch was covered by ox carts. Round trip was 12 hours.

From S 2 to S 3 only pack animals could be used to make the 13 kilometer long stretch. Round trip was 12 hours.

From S 3 over the Adsapsh Pass to S 4 and further on to S 5 (Einödsbach) only pack animals could be employed. The time required for this 25 kilometer stretch varied and depended upon weather and the physical capabilities of the carriers. As a rule, 5 hours were normally required for the 5 kilometer long stretch over the pass.

In Bsyb Valley the pack animals of the battalions located in the southern passes took responsibility for the supplies.

The immense effort of the supply troops can be appreciated by the reader in just this short description.

The reader can now well imagine what Gruppe von Stettner went through before it had to suspend the advance - with their objective so close at hand. They were a short 30 kilometers from the coast of the Black Sea, but they could not cover these 30 kilometers without large reinforcement. Battle Group von Stettner had to hold out. In order that the troops be quickly and sufficiently supplied, the Oberst radioed back: "Have you no aircraft for supply?"

No, the majority of them were at Stalingrad. And Hauptmann Beck's reconnaissance staffel, which was assigned to the XXXXIX Mountain Corps, was fully committed to reconnaissance and flying out the severely wounded. The situation was the same with the 1st Mountain Division.

The reason the XXXXIX Mountain Corps did not make it any further was because of the lack of forces. However, where were the Italian mountain divisions of the Alpine Corps?

General Konrad learned where they were on 21 August when he was summoned to the Führer Headquarters near Vinnitsa in order to report on the situation in the XXXXIX Mountain Corps area of operations. The Italian Alpine Corps was marching to Stalingrad!

On 2 September 1942 Feldmarshall List, Generaloberst Ruoff and General Konrad arrived in Krasnodar. At this meeting it became obvious that the advance of the XXXXIX Mountain Corps over the high mountain passes had failed due to the lack of troop reinforcement and the increase of resistance in the coastal region on the Black Sea. Any further advance with the available forces would only lead to the defeat of the mountain corps because the XXXXIV Jäger Corps' attack on Tuapse had also bogged down and they would not be available for a relief attack toward the XXXXIX Mountain Corps in the coastal strip.

In spite of this, Hitler did not give up on the idea of attacking further with the mountain corps. After a tug-of-war between the Führer Headquarters and the mountain corps, the corps proposal was finally accepted and the order was issued for transition to defense on the high ridges of the Abkhasi Caucasus.

On 31 August at 1130 hours Oberst von Stettner in the Bsyb Valley spoke with the division, which was almost 80 kilometers away, over the just completed telephone line. General Eglseer explained that the battle group had to withdraw because of supply difficulties. A new defensive line had to be occupied, for the time being, north of Bsyb at Einödsbach. The division planned on further withdrawals from the front.

This was an important decision for Battle Group von Stettner, but it was hard for them to give up the trump card from their hand. The main reason for the withdrawal can be found in the supply difficulties. The supply of the 4th Mountain Division, which required approximately 30 tons of supplies per day (of which a good portion went to Battle Group von Stettner) could not be accomplished as the weather worsened. "...Count on further withdrawals from the front." This sentence made it clear to all of the gebirgsjägers that they were on their own. They could not count on any reinforcement. It was as clear on the Bsyb as it was with their comrades from the 1st Mountain Division at the foot of Elbrus.

Von Stettner's small combat staff planned the withdrawal, which would take place on the passage of a code word. On the afternoon of 31 August the II/13 Geb.Jg.Rgt. was attacked in the Bsyb bridgehead. The enemy attack collapsed. Had the Russians caught wind of the German plans?

During the evening, severe thunderstorms arrived. The mountain rivers swelled, the trails turned into mud. At 2200 hours (it was still raining heavily) the III/91 repulsed a strong enemy attack on Pass 1600.

The withdrawal began. The III/91 left the pass on 1 September at 0400 hours, leaving the 13/91 at Pass 1600 as a rear guard. The ascent was difficult, even more difficult than the descent. They carried over 30 wounded with them. On the evening of 1 September the majority of the III/91 stood on the southern bank of the Bsyb. However, they could not cross due to the swelling of the river. The situation remained unchanged in the II/13 area of operations.

Engineers were brought forward. During the night work was begun on the repair of the bridges. By the morning of 2 September there was not one man nor one animal from Battle Group von Stettner on the other side. The III/91 set up security in a half circle around the bridging position. Additional work was performed on the bridge. At this critical point the Soviets attacked the II/13 again in the east and tried to outflank them. Elements of the III/91 attacked and threw the enemy back. At 0930 hours (2 September) the rear guard reported their withdrawal from Pass 1600.

During the late afternoon the construction of the crossing was finally complete. During the crossing, combat organization became a problem in the darkness. Pack animals constantly fell into the rising river, which was by then over 20 meters wide, or got their hooves stuck in the wooden covering. The battalion veterinarian worked untiringly with his people so that no animals were lost, but several had to be shot. At midnight the moon came out and it was a little better. Nevertheless, by morning only the III/91 was on the northern bank.

In the meantime, two additional crossings were completed. The artillery platoon then crossed. Battle Group von Stettner withdrew and occupied a new defensive line on either side of Einödsbach.

The enemy recognized the difficult situation Battle Group von Stettner was in, as demonstrated by the crossing, and probed the hastily occupied positions with assault troops. The first enemy attempt to outflank the positions was foiled. Then, however, the enemy launched an almost continuous air attack. On the evening of 5 September losses to the air attack in the Einödsbach area climbed to 16 dead and 45 wounded, as well as the loss of 106 pack animals. There was no longer any doubt: the Soviets wanted to destroy Battle Group Stettner in the Einödsbach Valley.

On 7 September the enemy pressure was so strong that von Stettner ordered the continuation of the leap-frog withdrawal at 1400 hours, without awaiting approval from division. And it was high time! Almost outflanked in the rear, Battle Group von Stettner reached the safety of the Adsapsh, Sancharo and Allistrakhu Passes on 8 September.

As in the 4th Mountain Division area of operations, Battle Group Kress of the 1st Mountain Division had to withdraw from the Klych Valley. On 27 August the von Hirschfeld and Salminger Battalions occupied a defensive position on the Elbrus Pass line.

From mid- to the end of September the Soviets increased the pressure against the defenses on the high ridges. Several forward positions had to be given up. Then, after many days of rain and fog, the mountain winter arrived. Combat operations froze in the frost and snow. Based on the weather conditions in the high mountains, the German leadership came up with a new plan:

1. The main ridges could be defended with fewer forces.

2. Therefore, half of the forces of the XXXXIX Mountain Corps could be freed up to break through to Tuapse.

3. The breakthrough would be into the Caucasus Forest, where winter would not arrive until five weeks later.

In accordance with this plan, battalions from the two mountain divisions were marched into the Caucasus Forest, so that there were practically only two gebirgsjäger regiments holding the entire corps front. The elements taken from the XXXXIX Mountain Corps were organized under General Lanz. The rest of the 1st Mountain Division, which consisted of the 99th Gebirgsjäger Regiment, the I and II/79 Geb.AR, as well as the reconnaissance and engineer battalions, was taken over by Oberst von Le Suire, General Schoerner's former Chief of Staff in Finland. There were also changes within the 4th Mountain Division. General Eglseer turned the division over to the former commander of the 99th Gebirgsjäger Regiment, Generalmajor Kress.

ACROSS THE KUMA TO BAKSAN

Pyatigorsk is captured - No further on the Baksan - Oberleutnant Pöllmann and his men - Crushing Russian air superiority

On 5 August 1942, the Berlin - Brandenburg 3rd Panzer Division reached Nevinnomyskaya at the edge of the mountains. From there, the 1st Mountain Division advanced over the passes of the main ridges further to the south.

Generaloberst von Kleist, an exceptional army commander of the Second World War, intended to attack with the majority of the panzer and motorized formations along the mountains to the east to reach the Grosny oil region and block the Georgian Army Road in the Ordzhonikidze area. He wanted to carry along the majority of his mountain divisions as part of his 1st Panzer Army and use them to penetrate into the Transcaucasus across the Georgian Army Road. However, Generaloberst von Kleist could not get his plan past the OKW. The 1st Panzer Army, which was equipped to advance along the mountains, only had the XXXX Panzer Corps with the 3rd and 23rd Panzer Divisions available. The III Panzer Corps was still in the Maikop area and the LII Army Corps was marching through the Manych bridgehead near Proletarskaya in the direction of the Kalmuck Steppes, in order to cover the deep eastern flank. However, von Kleist ordered the XXXX Panzer Corps to set out in hope that the 4th Panzer Army would soon be freed up in the Stalingrad area in order to achieve the far-ranging objectives in the eastern Caucasus together with the 1st Panzer Army.

Chronic fuel shortages forced the motorized formations to constantly stop. On 5 August, while the lead elements of the 3rd Panzer Division stood in the Nevinnomyskaya area, the 23rd Panzer Division could only push the Burmeister Advance Detachment up to Tuguluk (60 kilometers northeast of Voroshilovsk) and reach the Kalaus near Ipatovo with its right flank group, Gruppe Bachmann, on 6 August. All other elements of the division lagged far behind and (as soon as the fuel supply columns arrived) gradually followed along the 3rd Panzer Division's march route.

How insecure the Soviet stragglers made the supply routes is indicated by the following event: On 5 August the II/210 Pz.Rgt., which had just been supplied with fuel, advanced to Dmitrievskoe. In the early morning of 6 August the light column of the I/7 Flak Rgt., which was located in Biluchni, was overrun and destroyed from the west. Thus, the rollbahn was severed. At 0400 hours the tanks of the II/201 Pz.Rgt. were alerted. The 1/128 Pz.Gren.Rgt. was attached. The German tanks were rushed in the direction of Biluchni under the leadership of the First Generalstabsoffizier of the 23rd Panzer Division, Major Freyer, while a kradschützen company was detoured to the south, east of Yegorlyk. In the meantime, the Russian lead elements had advanced up to Svachintsev and cleared the breakout route to the east. The kradschützen prevented a retreat across the river to the east. Tanks with mounted infantry attacked into the enemy column and dispersed it. The tanks of the II/201 Pz.Rgt. pursued the fleeing enemy. Ten trucks from a Luftwaffe column had again fallen into enemy hands. The area was combed by forces assembled in the meantime. The breakthrough attempt by the 4th Soviet Rifle Division was frustrated. Into German hands had fallen: 2240 prisoners, 100 horses, 50 vehicles with equipment and ammunition, 23 tractors, 5 field kitchens and 36 guns of various calibers.

On 7 August the Burmeister Advance Group was finally refueled. By evening they had reached the Kalaus near Sergievskoe and established a bridgehead. Oberst Burmeister's battle group, which consisted of the staff and III/201 Pz.Rgt., II/128 Pz.Gren.Rgt., I/128 Pz.AR and engineer and anti-tank elements from the 23rd Panzer Division, had advanced to the same line as the 3rd Panzer Division. General Geyr von Schweppenburg could then launch his XXX Panzer Corps. During the evening the corps order arrived, according to which the 3rd Panzer Division was assigned Pyatigorsk and the 23rd Panzer Division Mineralnie Vody as their next objectives.

On 8 August the 3rd Panzer Division marched to the east in three march groups. Some light resistance was broken on either side of the Baku - Rostov oil pipeline. Nevertheless, each pumping station was set ablaze. The 3rd Panzer Division drove on toward its objective through the heat and dust. Security was placed out on the flanks. They had to make an unwanted stop in Soluno - Dimitrievskoe because all of the bridges across the Kursevka were blown. This wasted time. Then they moved on. The forward-most group set up a hasty defense for the night near Kangly. They had covered 180 kilometers. The soldiers from the 3rd Panzer Division saw Elbrus for the first time on this day.

Battle Group Burmeister covered 100 kilometers on this day, from Sergievskoe to 15 kilometers north of Mineralnie Vody, and, by evening, was located on Mount Kinzhal (497.1). Both divisions of the XXXX Panzer Corps stood just before their objectives.

On 9 August at 0245 hours engineers from the 3rd Panzer Division advanced to Kuma. The 39th Rathenow Engineer Battalion built two 16 ton bridges over the main branch and a tributary in a short period of time. Shortly after 0300 hours the first motorcycles crossed. Tanks and wheeled vehicles followed. The advance continued. The terrain became increasingly mountainous. There were curves and forests. The enemy's resistance stiffened more at each new hill.

Major von Cochenhausen's 3rd Kradschützen Battalion again led the way, directly followed by the I/6 Pz.Rgt. At 0730 hours they attacked Smeika. The Soviets retreated. They halted at another hill line. Artillery and anti-air-craft guns were brought up and the hill positions were placed under fire. At 1300 hours the advance detachment advanced further toward Karras. Oberst Westhoven's battle group, to which the I/394 had caught up, reached the railroad embankment between Smeika and Mineralnie Vody. They quickly assembled. Then they attacked Pyatigorsk from the north and west. The enemy was thrown from the northern portion of the city during the first attack.

The resistance stiffened in the city. When Hauptmann Rohrbeck's I/6 Pz.Rgt. closed and joined in the battle, the advance continued. A Russian 15 cm battery, which was unpleasantly effective, was destroyed by tank cannon fire. With the support of the I/6 Pz.Rgt., the 3rd Kradschützen Battalion, I/394 and 3/39 Pi.Btl. penetrated further into the city. The tenacious defenders belonged to an NKVD division, to a tank troop school and to a women's battalion.

Elements of the I/6 Pz.Rgt. attacked into the city and made it across the 60 meter long Podhumok bridge on the first try. The tanks had to retreat without infantry support. Then the first kradschützen arrived!

A second assault by the 2/3 Kradschützen Btl., supported by tanks and the 5/75 Pz.AR led to the establishment of a bridgehead on the southern bank of the Podhumok.

In the meantime, the other battle groups from the 3rd Panzer Division also advanced during the high summer heat of almost 50 degrees. Oberst von Liebenstein's battle group defeated the relief attack of a Soviet battalion near Suvorovskaya and advanced over the 100 meter wooden bridge against Pyatigorsk. At 1600 hours the battle groups of von Liebenstein and Pape reached the city and relieved Battle Group Westhoven, which was still fighting in the southern sector.

On 9 August the 23rd Panzer Division reached the Kuma river sector north of Mineralnie Vody with the Burmeister Battle Group. The river crossing to Mineralnie Vody had to be broken off due to the marshy terrain and mine obstacles. Battle Group Burmeister circled the city to the west and was subordinated to the 3rd Panzer Division.

After a restless night, the 3rd Panzer Division assaulted the southern portion of Pyatigorsk. On the afternoon of 10 August 1942 the city was completely in German hands.

With the achievement of this objective, the XXXX Panzer Corps stopped all major movement in order to allow the elements lagging behind, some of which were still on the Manych, to catch up. In order to assist these elements, they received all of the fuel assigned to the XXXX Panzer Corps. Only small operations were conducted to create a departure base for an advance along the mountains to Baksan.

On 11 August a small battle group from the 23rd Panzer Division, consisting of the 6/126 Pz.Gren.Rgt., II/128 Pz.AR and two light anti-aircraft platoons, attacked to the southeast and established a bridgehead across the Lyssogorsk, which was later reinforced by Battle Group Bachmann (128th Panzergrenadier Regiment).

On 12 August Battle Group von Liebenstein advanced up to Yessentuki and covered the southern flank in the mountains.

After the prerequisites for a continued attack along the mountains were established, the XXXX Panzer Corps again set out on 13 August with the 3rd Panzer Division on the right and the 23rd Panzer Division on the left.

The mixed Pape battle group (led by the 2/3 Kradschützen Btl.) reached the area north of Malka by 0730 hours. A subsequent attack on the town of Malka bogged down in strong enemy defensive fire. Enemy artillery fire from the mountains stopped all movement. Crossing the large Malka was impossible.

ATTACK ON THE BAKSAN-TEREK-BARRIER

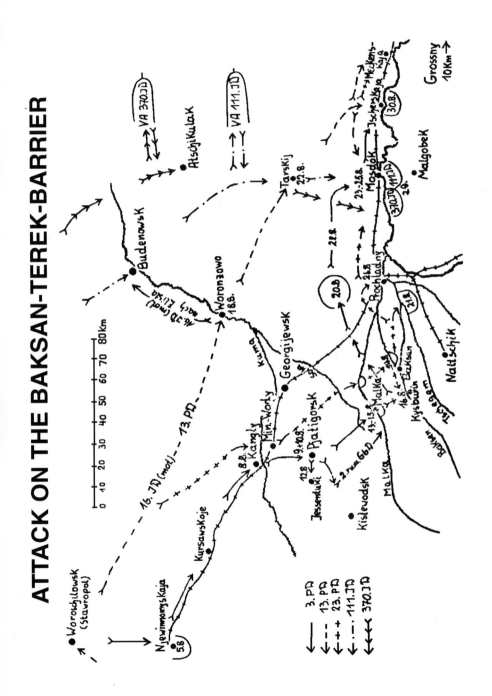

On the same day, the 23rd Panzer Division crossed the Solka against considerable enemy resistance with Battle Group Bachmann and captured Marinskaya at 1000 hours. The II/128 Pz.Gren.Rgt. advanced across the Malka and threw the Soviets out of Kuba.

On 14 August there was considerable pressure on the 3rd Panzer Division, which was advancing on the Pyatigorsk - Nalchik road. The advancing units were engaged with artillery from out of the mountains. A day later the 3rd Panzer Division crossed the Malka over a combat bridge built by the 39th Armored Engineer battalion; after that they captured the town of Malka.

On 14 August the 23rd Panzer Division assaulted Baksan. Battle Group Burmeister advanced through Tokoi and Psarisha up to Baksanenok and partially occupied the neighboring town of Kishpek. From there, Oberleutnant Pöllmann crossed the Baksan into Kishpek with eight men from the 5 and 7/128 Pz.Gren.Rgt. A small bridgehead was established. However, the nine men would later be lost.

While Oberleutnant Pöllmann and his men established themselves in the houses of southern Kishpek, the Soviets breached the Baksan dam west of Kysburun. An enormous flood of water rushed out. Gruppe Pöllmann was cut off. Several times engineer reinforcements attempted to cross the raging Baksan without success.

On 15 August the attempts to get to Gruppe Pöllmann continued. However, the raging flood foiled each attempt at a crossing. The majority of the 3rd Panzer Division crossed the Malka on this day.

The Baksan sector was very significant for the Soviets. It offered the extension of a defensive barrier which connected Ordzhonikidze, along with the important road crossing to Tiflis and the Grosny oil region, with the Terek. The Baksan - Terek barrier ended in the west at the rugged and impenetrable Baksan trench, which continued into the glacier of Mount Elbrus. After giving up the Russian defenses on the Don and Manych, Marshal Budenny withdrew reliable forces to this sector in order to stop the German attack there.

On 16 August Oberleutnant Pöllmann and his men were in a hopeless position. The flood was still raging. Attempts to cross reinforcements or withdraw the small band failed. A battle group was committed along the Baksan in order to force a crossing on the upper course. The town of Baksan was taken, but a crossing attempt near Kysburun failed in the defensive fire of the Soviets. Pöllmann and his men tried to break out to the west on their own in order to make contact with any friendly troops. However, all trace of them was soon lost. On 29 August a Russian aircraft dropped pamphlets with Pöllmann's photo and the demand to cease fighting. Therefore, it was established that Oberleutnant Pöllmann and his men were captured by the Russians.

During the afternoon of 16/8 the lead elements of the 3rd Panzer Division closed ranks with the forces of the 23rd Panzer Division in Baksan and relieved them.

On this day the second battle group of the 23rd Panzer Division (Burmeister), which had refueled in the meantime, set out from Kuba and reached the area north of Altud.

"Establish a bridgehead near Kysburun!" read the order to the 3rd Panzer Division for 17 August. An officer reconnaissance party was dispatched in order to survey the terrain. The Baksan was about 80 kilometers wide. Rocky cliffs were on the far side on which the enemy were positioned in favorable defenses. The near side was flat.

Oberst Dr. Weissenbruch and Major Pape realized the difficulty of the mission, which was to be conducted by the I/3 Pz.Gren.Rgt. Hauptmann Erdmann, I/3 Pz.Gren.Rgt., committed a reinforced assault force toward Kysburun III, which was repulsed after loosing three armored infantry vehicles and 13 wounded.

On 18 August the sky was overcast. There were heavy thunderstorms. The Baksan swirled like a witch's cauldron. In the late afternoon the division commander, Generalmajor Breith, and the commander of the XXXX Panzer Corps, General Geyr von Schweppenburg, inspected the forward-most units. They came to the conclusion, which was proposed by the 1st Panzer Army, to give up the crossing near Kysburun and turn to the east.

On this day the left group of the corps, Battle Group Burmeister, forced a crossing over the Chegem near Novo Poltovskoe. During the subsequent attack the I/128 Pz.Gren.Rgt. threw the enemy back further to the south, captured Novo Ivanovskiy and held out against several counterattacks. On 19 August the II/128 Pz.Gren.Rgt. advanced and continued the attack. The crossing over the Urvany was quickly forced and the small village of Pravurganski was occupied. The Soviet Baksan defense was broken. All counterattacks were repulsed with the support of the 128th Armored Artillery Regiment.

This success made the planned crossing of the 3rd Panzer Division near Kysburun unnecessary. The 3rd Panzer Division assembled for a new deployment in the area northeast of Prokhladny. At last Hauptmann Stein's II/394 was relieved by elements of the 2nd Rumanian Mountain Division in the Baksan area.

New possibilities for breaking through the Soviet Baksan - Terek defense were offered by the arrival of the III Panzer Corps from the western Caucasus. On the evening of 17 August the initial elements of the 13th Panzer Division were located in hills near Sablinskaya, covering the left flank of the XXXX Panzer Corps. A fuel shortage only permitted the arrival of an advance detachment of the 13th Panzer Division (III Panzer Corps), which, after a short struggle that evening, occupied the Kuma crossing near Vorontsovo - Aleksandrovskoe. On 22 August the 13th Panzer Division was again moving and reached Tarskiy with advance forces and Miropolskiy, 50 kilometers north of Mosdok, with the main body. The 16th ID (Mot.) followed to Vorontsovo and was detached from the III Panzer Corps on 25 August in order to operate as an independent combat formation to maintain contact between Army Group A and Army Group B in the Kalmuck Steppes. On 23 August the 13th Panzer Division reconnoitered up to Ishcherskaya on the Terek, where strong enemy forces were discovered.

In the meantime, on 21 August Battle Group Burmeister attacked out of the

Urvany bridgehead against Maiskiy. The attack bogged down at an anti-tank barrier and in infantry and artillery fire. The Soviets blew up a road bridge and a railroad bridge further to the south. The attack companies of the 23rd Panzer Division were withdrawn to their departure positions. For the time being, this was the last attempt to break through the Soviet defenses in the Terek - Baksan - Malka triangle.

Due to the terrain difficulties and increasing resistance, the German HKL [Main Combat Line] was withdrawn to the northern bank of the Baksan. The 3rd Panzer Division, which was assembled in the area northeast of Prokhladny, was to attack Mosdok, supported by the 23rd Panzer Division, the I and II/201 Pz.Rgt. and the 126th Panzergrenadier Regiment. The Baksan sector was being defended by the 2nd Rumanian Mountain Division and other assembled forces.

The Soviets discovered the German regrouping and reacted accordingly. The defenders of Mosdok (formerly the 4th Rifle Division) were reinforced by the 8th Guards Rifle Division. Combat positions and mine fields were erected in haste. Powerful Russian air activity harassed the deployment of the German formations. Soviet aircraft of all types, including English and American ones from Lend-Lease shipments, buzzed about the assembly area and demonstrated their crushing air superiority.

On 24 August the 13th Panzer Division, which was located north of Mosdok, was subordinated to the XXXX Panzer Division in order to simplify command and control. The III Panzer Corps command took over responsibility for Baksan where, on the following day, smaller operations were indicated; the I/99 Geb.Jg.Rgt. (1st Mountain Division) captured the town of Suyakovo on the extreme right flank, held it against a superior enemy force and screened the Baksan front against the mountains. On 26 August the commander of the 23rd Panzer Division, Generalmajor Mack, was killed along with other officers of his entourage during an inspection at the front near Novo Poltovskoe.

Battle Group Burmeister, which consisted of the staff of the 201st Panzer Regiment and the II Battalion, as well as the 126th Panzergrenadier Regiment, was temporarily committed at the Prokhladny strong point in order to then advance further to the east and establish contact with the 3rd Panzer Division. Battle Group Burmeister captured Prokhladny in a pincer attack on 26 August, left a weak security element and, a day later, followed the 3rd Panzer Division along the northern bank of the Terek.

During August, while the panzer assault moved to the south, General Ott's LII Infantry Corps marched as east flank security for Army Group A through Proletarskaya south along the Manych, through Kalaus and Kuma to the east. In burning heat, the regiments of the 111th and 370th Infantry Divisions made enormous march efforts. Finally, their dusty standards were in the steppe region of the Manych. Each oasis on the march route was surrounded by thirsty soldiers and horses. A small motorized battle group from the 370th ID was committed against Elista, but it was unable to capture the capital of the Kalmucks. When the reconnaissance battalion from the 111th ID, under Major Eitel Goll, arrived as reinforcement, Elista was captured. Elista, however, only lay on the edge of the relentless march of the LII Army Corps.

The regiments turned to the south from the Budenovsk area. The German leadership observed that an infantry corps in the vast steppe region on either side of the Manych Canal was out of place. This area was only fit for motorized divisions!

The 111th and the 370th ID then turned to the south. They marched under the burning August sun, the 50th, 70th and 117th Grenadier Regiments, the 117th Artillery Regiment and the divisional units of the 111th Infantry Division; in addition, there were the 666th, 667th and 668th Grenadier Regiments, the artillery regiment and the divisional units of the 370th Infantry Division.

On 27 August the advance elements of the LII Army Corps reached the area north of the Terek. The 111th ID, under Generalmajor Recknagel, was to establish a bridgehead near Mosdok and the 370th ID, under Generalmajor Becker, was to establish one west of there.

IN THE KALMUCK STEPPES

The 16th ID (Mot.) as the connecting link - An area as large as Belgium - Combat around the Oases - Fernspähtrupps on the Caspian Sea - Kalmuck Steppe pilots - A bridge that did not exist

After catching up to the foot formations of the 17th Army, the III Panzer Corps withdrew from the area south of Maikop and marched off to a new commitment in the east.

On 14 August 1942, the 116th Panzer Battalion rolled through Yaroslavskaya toward Mostovie and, on 17 August, was following directly behind the 13th Panzer Division. The majority of the 16th ID (Mot.) followed along the same route on 16 August. They took a day of rest in Armavir, then a 200 kilometer march on 18 August through Voroshilovsk, then on to old Stavropol near Sergievskoe.

From 18 to 25 August the 16th ID (Mot.) had to stay immobile between Voroshilovsk and Budenovsk on order of the III Panzer Corps due to a fuel shortage; indeed, it had to turn over all fuel supplies to the 13th Panzer Division so that this division could advance.

On 23 August 1942 the following army group order arrived:

"...16th ID (Mot.) is directly subordinated to Army Group B, it is to cover the area between Army Groups A and B in mobile combat operations."

The right boundary was fixed by the Manych Valley and the Kuma confluence, the left boundary was staked by the town of Yenotaevsk on the Volga. The assigned area was as large as Belgium. The divisional supply was assigned to Army Group A along a railroad route through Voroshilovsk - Petrovskoe - Divnoe. By accident, the demolition of the northern Petrovskoe - Divnoe stretch was prevented. Railroad engineers from Army Group A were to demolish this stretch and make use of the tracks elsewhere because Army Group A saw no use for a rail line running to the north.

Because of a shortage of fuel, the 16th ID (Mot.) could only dispatch a small combat-capable advance detachment on 25 August. This was the 165th Kradschützen Battalion with two accompanying batteries from the 146th Artillery Regiment, the 3/228 Pz.Jg., as well as additional platoons of escort weapons. The advance detachment reached Divnoe via Ipatovo on the evening of 25 August. During this evening a kradschützen company and the 3/228 Pz.Jg. was moved from there to Elista in order to relieve the last elements of the 370th ID.

On 26 August at 0930 hours the majority of the reinforced 165th Kradschützen Battalion (Battle Group Laroche) reached Elista, rested in order to await the arrival of the 60th Panzergrenadier Regiment, and then continued marching toward Ulan Erge. On the evening of 26 August Battle Group Laroche relieved the II/666 from the 370th ID in Ulan Erge, which immediately marched to the Terek. On the same day reconnaissance reported that Sovkhoz Dolgan (18 kilometers east of Ulan Erge) was occupied by the enemy.

On 27 August Battle Group Laroche and the following I/60 under Hauptmann Torley attacked the enemy-occupied sovkhoz. The enemy was thrown back and withdrew to the east.

On 28 August Battle Group Laroche, which was reinforced by artillery in the meantime, attacked Yashkul. The difficult attack had to be conducted under completely different conditions. In almost open terrain, Hauptmann Torley's I/60 Pz.Gren.Rgt. penetrated into Yashkul while receiving effective support from the Hammon Artillery Battalion. After a spirited night attack the I/60 finally threw the enemy out of Yashkul. The first important oasis in the Kalmuck Steppes was in German hands. Hauptmann Torley, who was already awarded the Knight's Cross, received the Oak Leaves. To honor him, the oasis was baptized the Torley Oasis.

With the penetration of the 16th ID (Mot.) into the Kalmuck Steppes, the clever combat leadership had to deal with completely new terrain conditions. The Kalmuck Steppes and the Manych Valley exhibited a steppe climate. Streams and rivers dried up or disappeared in August/September. The water courses dissolved into a chain of pools. There was a shortage of drinking water. The supply of water played the decisive role during military maneuvers.

At first the 16th ID (Mot.) only had 1:300,000 maps available. They portrayed the divisional operation area as a large white speck through which a highway was indicated in red. In reality this highway was only a dirt road. In addition, there were a few stretches of dunes which determined lateral contact and were indicated as only camel paths. Several blue specks signified salt water pools or oases. These map problems were soon eliminated. One day the division commander was presented with a good Russian 1:100,000 map by a regimental commander. General Henrici took the map to the 4th Panzer Army Map Section. In a few days the 16th ID (Mot.) had a good number of the new maps with German notations. The troops then actively participated in the search for additional maps and by November 1942 the division had a 1:100,000 map covering Astrakhan and some parts of the Volga.

The residents of this region were Kalmucks (Mongols) with Mongolian speech patterns. They were Buddhists. They originated in northwestern China and had advanced across the Volga during the Mongol invasions. The Kalmucks were nomads and wandered with their herds of cattle in constant search for new pastures. They lived in Yurts (leather tents). They were meat eaters. Characteristically (as were all Asians) they were difficult to approach at first. However, after one gained their trust, they were helpful and friendly.

During their centuries-long march to the west, the Kalmucks reached the lower Volga between 1630 and 1662, where they were settled by the Tsars in the steppes between the Volga and Manych. In 1771 they tried to wander back to Asia. A great flooding of the Volga allowed only a portion of the Kalmucks to return. The portion remaining west of the Volga continued their nomad life-style. The cities of Elista, Ulan Erge and Yashkul were Kalmuck centers. Their administration was taken over by the Russians.

Since 1920 the "Autonomous Kalmuck Republic" had existed as part of the

USSR with 220,000 inhabitants. Because of their friendliness to the Germans the "Autonomous Kalmuck Republic" was disbanded in 1943.

The Special Commissioner for the Kalmucks, Rittmeister Baron von Richthofen, described his impressions in an empirical report from "Fremde Heeres Ost", (IIz) Nr. 5/43, from 14 January 1943:

"Findings of the German military - geographic reports from 1941: `The majority of the Kalmucks continue to live as nomads in tents'; many now live in flat roofed houses made from loam... The military - geographic specifications on the Kalmuck region: `Other than cattle, the land has no economic value and poses no problem for troop movement' also does not hit the mark... The description of Elista in the military - geographic reports as an insignificant speck with 8500 residents (according to the census of 1932) is completely wrong... The difficulties in finding drinking water and food are as described in the military - geographic reports. However, there are also new oases that supply good water to Elista which somewhat alleviate the problem. The supply of water is particularly difficult in the Khalkuta area... The density of the population at the beginning of the war was 2.3 men per square kilometer and 4.6 men per square kilometer in the Elista area... Elista gives the impression of being an isolated southern Russian provincial city. In 1940 Elista had 13,614 inhabitants, as well as 60 industries..., of which, one factory produced 50 pairs of felt boots per day for the 16th ID (Mot.)... Raw materials and other economic possibilities: oil, natural gas, salt from the sea, alabaster, quartz for glass-making... cattle industry (in 1939 there were: 63,000 cattle, 775,000 sheep and goats, 7500 pigs and 4000 camels)."

Rittmeister Baron von Richthofen's study revealed the unfriendly, if not outright hostile, feelings of the Kalmucks for the Stalin regime. The good work by the Ic of the 16th ID (Mot.), Oberleutnant d. Res. Holtermann, as well as the understanding treatment they received from the entire division, resulted in the Kalmucks gradually coming over to the German camp. This was reflected in the creation of a volunteer Kalmuck squadron which cooperated with the German staffs. The constant NKVD party-led espionage and harassment activity was mostly foiled by Kalmuck units.

On 28 August a battle group from the 16th ID (Mot.) captured the important hub of Yashkul. With their penetration into the steppes, the battalions of the 60th Panzergrenadier Regiment were committed directly from the march into the wide security belt around Elista. The line was very thin and established on strong points, most of which were only in company strength with accompanying escort weapons. The 10/60 occupied Chilgir (80 kilometers north of Elista). Contact with the regiment in Elista was conducted over the intact Elista - Stalingrad telephone lines which were also still being used by the Russians.

On 29 August Battle Group Laroche advanced up to the Utta oasis and dunes and prepared for an attack. The Russians evacuated Utta during the following night and withdrew. On 30 August Utta was occupied without a fight. The 165th Kradschützen Battalion combat diary remarked about Utta: "... in Utta there were 15 clay huts and 2 oases, otherwise nothing", and under 30 August after receiving the results of long-range reconnaissance:

THE 16.(mot.) INFANTRY DIVISION
IN THE KALMUCK STEPPE

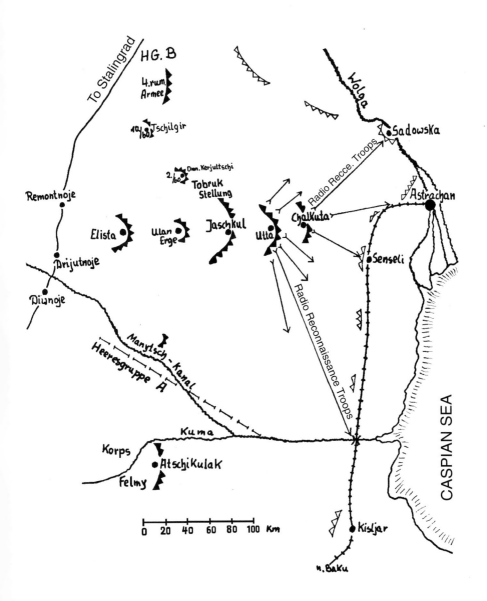

"...many positions on the Utta - Astrakhan road. 45 kilometers west of Astrakhan there are anti-tank trenches. According to prisoner of war statements, there are strong defenses around Astrakhan. Morale is poor..."

In the meantime, the 60th Panzergrenadier Regiment was able to refuel and advance through Utta into the Khalkuta area. The reinforced 60th Panzergrenadier Regiment attacked the strongly defended dunes of Khalkuta. Despite being thrown back after fierce combat, the enemy was able to establish themselves again on the high ground 5 kilometers east of Khalkuta.

Combat began around the important water station. There a single Obergefreiter carried his comrades along in a decisive assault on the last dunes. The throats of the men were parched. The sun beat down mercilessly on the dunes. Obergefreiter Kulot led his comrades in assault, and his example was effective. During the assault over the dunes the water station was captured and the enemy thrown back. Henceforth, the oasis was called the Kulot Oasis. Obergefreiter Kulot was awarded the Knight's Cross. Right after this engagement the character of the desert war changed. Water stations became the vital decisive factors. The failure to capture a water station near Khalkuta resulted in the withdrawal of battle groups of the 16th ID (Mot.) to Utta.

Khalkuta, which the Landser called Calcutta, was transformed into a fortified position during the following days. The Khalkuta positions were the eastern-most German positions. The Soviets attacked the positions several times without effect. The 60th Panzergrenadier Regiment held.

In the meantime, the 156th Panzergrenadier Regiment advanced up to Elista and was assigned several missions. Near Vodin, west of Derbety, contact was established with the Rumanians. The mission, to attack through to the Khanata - Surgan road, had to be cancelled due to superior enemy forces and changed into a blocking mission. While covering the northern flank the 7/156 was attacked by superior enemy forces near Bakhana on 30 August. The 5/156 was attacked near Sertin. Both blocking companies repulsed all enemy attacks with artillery support. The artillery had a hard time finding suitable positions in this flat terrain. The wounded were evacuated to Elista under the protection of armored cars. Orientation was only possible by compass.

In spite of repeated enemy attacks the 156th Panzergrenadier Regiment's defensive front stabilized along a line Kharnud - Mosheen - east of Zharkov. Moreover, the 2/156 was located in Chilgir and the 11/156 was in Keryulchi. The regiment received the newly organized Kalmuck squadron.

On 3 September the Ju 52s were first utilized to transport wounded and supplies over the great distance to the Elista supply point.

On 7 September a stronger enemy attack on the Khalkuta fortifications was repulsed with artillery and panzer support. In the meantime, elements of the 4th Rumanian Army took over responsibility for a portion of the northern security sector of the 16th ID (Mot.). The 156th Panzergrenadier Regiment relieved the 60th Panzergrenadier Regiment in the Khalkuta positions.

At first, Generalleutnant Henrici intended to insert his division into two or three adjacent fortified strong points and monitor the vast area from there with Reconnaissance elements. He soon realized, however, that the southern area up to the eastern Manych posed no serious threat. Corps Felmy was committed there. The northern flank and the Astrakhan area were still a threat. The 16th ID (Mot.) was committed all by itself in the steppes. A huge gap yawned 150 kilometers to the north and 200 kilometers to the south. There was the constant threat that strong enemy groups would penetrate through the strong- point line into the interior and be able to sever the supply routes.

Only once, during the night of 17-18 September, did a tactically well-led formation from the Astrakhan Non-commissioned Officer's School success-fully attack the 2/60 Pz.Gren.Rgt. strong point in the town of Keryulchi. Contentions that the Soviets rode into the strong point in German uniforms and in German trucks were not confirmed. However, the day before a Russian reconnaissance force in German uniforms and in German trucks was discovered. The raid was first made known to the 60th Panzergrenadier Regiment twelve hours later by a messenger. Nevertheless, the commitment had only limited success. The enemy withdrew to Astrakhan. The 2/60 in Keryulchi was completely destroyed. In the positions there were indications that the defenders defended themselves fiercely. The reinforced II/156 attacked together with an armored engineer company up to Khask and caught a portion of the enemy raiding party. During the battle their four trucks, including two from the 60th Panzergrenadier Regiment, were recov-ered; four anti-tank guns were captured and one gun was destroyed. During the return march, the II/156 was stopped in Ulan Erge and diverted to Utta because an attack on the Khalkuta fortifications was anticipated during the night of 20 September.

During the night of 20 September the 156th Panzergrenadier Regiment was attacked by strong enemy forces in Khalkuta. However, they had underesti-mated the German defense. Indeed, the enemy did penetrate deep into the defensive ring, but they were beaten back in a counterattack with the support of the 2nd Panzer Company. On 20 September reinforcements from the 16th ID (Mot.) arrived in Khalkuta because a repeat of the enemy attack was anticipated. However, the enemy evacuated their departure positions and withdrew. After these battles, and after the experience of the previous few weeks, Generalleutnant Henrici established his division in two fortified camps: One reinforced regiment in Khalkuta and one reinforced regiment in Utta. The towns in the interior were secured by weaker units.

Using this deployment, the 16th ID (Mot.) successfully fulfilled its mission. With the help of the population and the commitment of local Kalmuck for-mations a thick defensive net was established through which no enemy forces or partisans could infiltrate. The division communications battalion, under Hauptmann Herzer, making use of the many intact Russian telephone lines, laid a communications network and maintained it in working order. In addition, there were two communications points which were of inestimable value to the division. A non-commissioned officer maintained communica-tions with the Rumanians, who were 100 kilometers away to the north. His tactful behavior with the allies, as well as his precise reports, kept the division leadership informed as to the situation with their northern neighbor. In the south, a communications site in Adyk (100 kilometers south of Yashkul) maintained communications with the southern neighbor and, in addition, functioned as a report station for the Kalmucks.

Oberleutnant Damm, the division Flivo, wrote about the commitment of the Luftwaffe in the 16th ID (Mot.) area of operations:

"The following were committed to the division at the end of September 1942: 1 interceptor Me 110, 4 fighter Me 109s and the Nahaufklaerungsstaffel 5(H)/12 with double fuselage FW 189s at Yashkul airfield. The Utta airfield was supplied with fuel, ammunition and rations by the 1/DFS 4, a staffel of DFS 230 transport gliders towed by Hs 126s. In addition, there were ground units such as the weather troop of the 6/4 Ln.Rgt., the air couriers of the 7/38 Ln.Rgt. and a troop from the 3/38 Ln.Rgt. Air reconnaissance provided an inestimable service to the division. Often, the aircraft would join in the ground battle or engage enemy movements independently."

Tactical reconnaissance played a very big role. Other than in Africa, there was nowhere else that the German armored reconnaissance elements had such a vast operations area as in the Kalmuck Steppes. One reconnaissance mission might last three days. A combination of reconnaissance vehicles, motorcycles, light anti-aircraft guns, engineer groups and a supply troop, including a medic, were utilized during missions. It was important to carry sufficient water and fuel.

On 13 September the 16th ID (Mot.) committed four reconnaissance elements to conduct route reconnaissance. The reconnaissance elements advanced on either side of the Utta - Astrakhan road.

Reconnaissance Element Schroeder soon made contact with the enemy after breaking out east of Utta. Leutnant Schroeder was killed, Dolmetscher [Interpreter] Maresch and Feldwebel Weissmeier were wounded. The reconnaissance element broke out and returned on the next day under Leutnant Euler.

The reconnaissance element under Oberleutnant Gottlieb was located 40 kilometers in front of Astrakhan on 14 September. On 15 September it was only 25 kilometers from the Volga. It had a wide view of the river from a high sand dune. The terrain was inaccessible. Information from nomadic Kalmucks was confirmed as they drove on the Kislyar - Astrakhan rail line. The reconnaissance mission was fulfilled.

Leutnant Euler had the mission of advancing on Sadovska, reconnoitering the defensive installations there and determining whether enemy troops were crossing the Volga. On 16 September Euler and his two armored reconnaissance vehicles stood 5 kilometers in front of Sadovska. Euler established that there was a strong bridgehead position with an anti-tank trench there. When the German reconnaissance vehicles were recognized, the enemy became nervous. The reconnaissance element withdrew under enemy defensive fire. A staff officer from the 36th Machine-gun Battalion and his messenger were cut off there. Both of the Russians were taken back to Utta by the reconnaissance element.

Leutnant Schliep's long range reconnaissance element reached the Kislyar - Astrakhan railroad line on the second day. Schliep reported:

"We saw 50 to 60 civilians working on the railroad embankment. It was a single track line and both sides were framed with a sand wall. We were greeted amiably by the civilians; they were Ukrainians, old men, women and children. Suddenly smoke was visible in the south. The reconnaissance vehicles quickly drove behind a sand dune to take cover. A long freight train with two locomotives steamed by. Six shots from the reconnaissance vehicle's cannon and the locomotives blew apart. We then fired on one car after the other. They were all oil cars and they burst into flames. Finally, we moved to another position and, as we passed the railroad station, a telephone rang. Our interpreter picked it up and reported: "Stantsia Senseli, Nalchik! - Da, da Tovarish!" he protested. On the other end was the Astrakhan freight station. They wanted to know whether the oil train from Baku had passed by because there was a train coming in the opposite direction on the side track at Bassy. The interpreter told them to let the train go. However, the Astrakhan railroad attendant felt something was wrong and quickly hung up. A little later, the Senseli railroad station was blown into the air."

Reconnaissance Element Schliep tried to reconnoiter Bassy, but ran into the enemy there. The railroad attendant sounded the alarm. On 17 September Reconnaissance Element Schliep returned to Utta. The reconnaissance results confirmed that the enemy forces in the Astrakhan area were not planning any major operations at that time. The reconnaissance of the Kislyar - Astrakhan rail line, which was built by the Soviets in a very short period of time, confirmed the previous air reconnaissance.

A reconnaissance element from the 16th ID (Mot.), which was committed somewhat later, engaged an enemy column of six trucks in the steppes and brought them back to Khalkuta. In this manner a Russian field movie projector also fell into German hands.

Another reconnaissance operation was conducted on the order of the army group against a railroad bridge across the Kuma, which was indicated on the map. In order to relieve the overtaxed kradschützen battalion, this mission was conducted by a small band from the 156th Panzergrenadier Regiment. The bridge on the newly-constructed Baku - Astrakhan rail line was supposed to lay in the Kuma Estuary area about 20 kilometers west of the Caspian Sea coast. The long-range reconnaissance element was gone for four and a half days and what they found was surprising: The bridge over the Kuma did not exist! The Kuma is a desert river which only flows through to the Caspian Sea during rainy years. This was not the case in 1942.

Another reconnaissance element reported the appearance of Saigags herds, a type of antelope appearing in Russia under natural conditions.

There is still one more operation which demonstrated the good cooperation between the ground troops and the Luftwaffe. It interfered with Soviet preparations for a large-scale attack operation. At the end of October air reconnaissance reported enemy east to west movement 20 kilometers south of

Khalkuta. According to the map, this had to be in the vicinity of a water station. A small combat formation from the II/60 Pz.Gren.Rgt. was committed. However, it missed its attack objective in the steppes. The operation was repeated with the cooperation of two fighter aircraft. The fighters led the ground formation to the objective. Over 100 Soviets, who were establishing a supply point for a following enemy formation at an oasis, were surprised and, after a short battle, captured. The water station and the supply dump were blown and the area was mined.

The combat in the steppes slowly changed. The 16th ID (Mot.), which had, in the beginning, conducted far-ranging reconnaissance, had to prevent the enemy from establishing supply points with combat operations.

The Flivo, Oberleutnant Damm, reported on two additional commitments as follows:

"In the early morning of 27 October we drove with the reinforced II/60 (Major Lindner) toward the Komintern Cattle Kolkhoz to attack the enemy forces reported there. A reconnaissance aircraft and two fighters guided us. The enemy positions were so well described by the pilots through message drops and radio that Major Lindner was able to commit his formation from the march. The kolkhoz was captured after a short battle in which the aircraft also participated.

On 29 October we were operating with the reinforced II/156 (Hauptmann Böhme) in an action against the Kalinina, Lenina and Iliche Cattle Kolkhozes. From the SPW I had constant communications with the division through the air communications troops. I requested fighters, which appeared over the battlefield in a few minutes and joined in the attack. The enemy fled over the sand dunes to the east to avoid capture.

On 30 October at 0430 hours we again drove with the II/60 against the Budenovo Cattle Kolkhoz, where, on 29 October, fighters located an enemy concentration receiving reinforcement by trucks. After a short fierce battle, the enemy was thrown back. The fleeing trucks were the booty of the attacking fighters.

On 13 November we again had to ride with the II/60 to the Komintern Cattle Kolkhoz because the enemy was again trying to establish positions there. They were driven out."

On 15 November Generalleutnant Henrici was entrusted with the XXXX Panzer Corps, which was located north of the Terek. The 16th ID (Mot.) was taken over by Generalmajor Graf Gerhard von Schwerin.

In the meantime, the storm clouds gathered around Stalingrad.

On 21 November the combat diary of Army Group A noted:

"Attacks in the 4th Panzer Army and 16th ID (Mot.) areas of operations. At 0915 hours the commander of the 16th ID (Mot.), Generalmajor Graf von Schwerin, reported that the regiment located near Khalkuta would have been encircled yesterday. The encirclement was avoided during the night with the support of a second regiment (60th Panzergrenadier Regiment). Three companies were destroyed (including equipment). The Russians did not pursue. He (von Schwerin) intended to leave a rear guard in Utta, where he was located, and withdraw the main body of the division into prepared positions near Yashkul."

On 22 November the same combat diary reported:

"Information from the 16th ID (Mot.): the main body of the division is located in a half-circle east and south of Yashkul. The positions are good. The division command post is in Ulan Erge. The rear guard was forced out of Utta; the enemy has established himself 20 kilometers west of Utta. Apparently, he is operating with the 28th Guards Rifle Division, the 152nd Motorized Rifle Brigade and the 6th Heavy Tank Brigade. After defending against these forces, he (von Schwerin) wants to deploy as many forces as possible in order to attack the enemy in the north. - 1730 hours: message arrived: the 16th ID (Mot.) will be subordinated to the 4th Panzer Army. It and the 4th Rumanian will be subordinated to Generaloberst Hoth as Gruppe Hoth with the mission of holding line Yashkul - Tundutov while covering the northern flank in the Ahsai area."

With the subordination of the 16th ID (Mot.) to the 4th Panzer Army, the divisional leadership's wide-ranging operational freedom was taken away. Large movements in conjunction with orders from the 4th Panzer Army could no longer be conducted without permission. Apparently, the German High Command did not agree with the withdrawal of the 16th ID (Mot.) from Khalkuta and Utta. As far as we could tell from the reports in the combat diary of Army Group A, strong forces were already pressuring the division. Graf von Schwerin did the correct thing: he withdrew his regiments from the far-advanced camps and committed them in the so-called Tobruk positions near Yashkul. Then the value of the Tobruk positions would be demonstrated. However, it was also clear that the 16th ID (Mot.) was tied to these positions. Further developments will be described in a later section.

ATTACK ON MOSDOK AND ADVANCE TO THE EAST

Duel of armored giants - 3rd Panzer Division captures Mosdok - Major Gollob's fighters versus the crushing superiority - Across the Terek in assault boats near Isherskaya - Gruppe von Bodenhausen reaches the railroad junction 25 kilometers northeast of Grosny - The last regiment fails

After the breakthrough of the XXXX Panzer Corps through the Baksan defenses failed, the corps organized for an attack on Mosdok.

The III Group of the 52nd Jagdgeschwader under Major Gordon Gollob was assigned the air space over the XXXX Panzer Corps by the Luftwaffe. In Gollob's notes we read:

"21/8/1942: Mineralnie Vody: The 3rd Panzer Division advanced today through Apollonskaya and Sovietskaya to the east in order to establish a bridgehead across the Terek from the north near Mosdok."

On 22 August the attack forces of the XXXX Panzer Corps were located in the Edissya area, 40 kilometers north of Mosdok. In order to deceive the enemy attacks were launched to the east. On the same day the 13th Panzer Division's lead elements were near Tarskiy, 50 kilometers northwest of Isherskaya, screening the area north of the XXXX Panzer Corps. Due to a fuel shortage, the 13th Panzer Division was spread apart and unified command and control was no longer possible. Oberstleutnant Stolz conducted a combat reconnaissance with elements of his 43rd Kradschützen Battalion against the Isherskaya area in order to feint a crossing of the Terek there. Non-commissioned Officers Wrede and Schatz from the 43rd Kradschützen Battalion cleverly led their groups on a far-ranging scouting operation into the salt steppes.

General Geyr von Schweppenburg, supported by his capable Chief of Staff, Oberst Wagner, had a cunning plan: stage a feint north of the Terek to the east, then turn the main body of his formation to the south against Mosdok.

Major Gollob's notes reflect the following under 22 August 1942:

"Gonshtakova. I finally redeployed here today, after I had seen to the security with the panzer corps. It is the first time that an airfield has been chosen outside of the secured area. The field was immediately occupied and secured."

Here is the history of this exceptional element of the 52nd Jagdgeschwader: Major Gordon Gollob was entrusted with the leadership of the 52nd Jagdgeschwader on 23 July 1942. The geschwader was formerly led by Major Ihlefeld. For several days the III/JG 52 flew out of Taganrog-West, then the squadron staff and III Group was transferred to Rostov. During the continuous attack to the south by the German formations, sorties were flown in succession from airfields in Solniy, Orlovka, Sred Yegorlyk, Belaya Glina, Armavir and Mineralnie Vody.

23 August promised to be a beautiful Sunday. It had rained the day before. The battle groups of the 3rd Panzer Division were in a feverish mood, something that was noticeable before every attack. After the endless waiting for all of the vehicles to be refueled, Battle Group Westhoven was set in march

...les, the loyal four-
...ged animals of the
...irgsjäger. The Elbrus
...cier at the 4200 meter
...vation.

...der the Dombai-Ulgen
...40 meters).

...ht air defense near
...erba in the central
...ucasus.

A 7.5 cm Geb.G 36 mountain gun being brought into position.

A gebirgsjäger supply strongpoint in the cent Caucausu above the tr line.

Evening in the central Caucasus.

... endless Kalmuck
...pes. The artery of the
... ID (mot.) to Elista,
...ugh Yashkul and
... to Khalkutta.

... battle in the Kalmuck
...pes was a battle of
...r points. A drinking
...r station of the 16th
...mot.) near Yashkul.

... Kalmuck Steppes.
... 8.8 cm anti-aircraft
... of the 16th ID (mot.)
... ing position.

German tanks on the march in the Kalmuck Steppes (panzer battalion of the 16th ID [mot.]).

SS Division "Wiking" armored scout car and anti-tank gun during attack.

On the march to the south.

Gebirgsjägers in a pass position.

Multi-purpose aircraft "Fieseler Storch".

General Geyr von Schweppenburg (with overcoat), commander of the XXXX Panzer Corps; General Breith, commander of the 3rd Panzer Division; and Oberstleutnant Pape (right), commander of the 394th Panzergrenadier Regiment.

Tail section of the emergency landed Me 109 of major Gollob.

IL-2 shot down near Kurgannaya. Major Gollob's 114th victo

Mineralnie Vody air In the foreground is Me 109 of Uffz. Petermann, which w rammed by a Russia 153 and had to make emergency landing.

Road marker and sign forest.

Major Gollob, Commodore of the 52nd Fighter Squadron, achieves his 150th air victory on the Terek.

Full assault boat crosses a river.

1942.
Before Voroshilovsk.
394th Panzergrenadier
Regiment in the attack.

1942.
To the south. The 394t
Regiment in the attack

1942.
Memorial cemetery in
Isherskaya on the Tere
(August-November '4:
A gun salute for the fa
en of the 3rd Panzer
Division.

at 1000 hours. Enemy aircraft continued to be an irritation. Major Gollob's fighters did what they could. 17 Soviet aircraft were shot down by evening.

Gruppe Westhoven continued to veer to the right and Gruppe Liebenstein to the left, heading north to Mosdok. Oberleutnant Pollmann and his 6/394, which was reinforced with a panzer company as well as engineers and an infantry gun platoon, was the advance detachment of Battle Group Westhoven. Suddenly, strong defensive fire came from the hills south of Russkiy. Advance Detachment Pollmann hit the dirt and waited for the return artillery fire, which later opened up onto the nest of resistance.

At 1100 hours Oberleutnant Pollmann prepared his battle group to attack. The grenadiers broke into the enemy positions with elan. The positions were, at first, defended tenaciously and bitterly. When the first Russians fled, the Germans captured Russkiy in a subsequent attack at 1345 hours and reached the 4 meter wide Lenin Canal.

Pollmann quickly reviewed the situation; then he knew what to do. A damaged bridge lay nearby.

"Onward!" shouted Pollmann.

Tanks of the II Battalion advanced and supported the grenadiers. The first men of the 6/394 assaulted the bridge. The bridge planks groaned under their steps. Then the first men reached the opposite bank of the Lenin Canal.

Soon the entire 6/394 was across. They attacked through to the town, reached the main bridge and prevented it from being destroyed. The II/394 and II/6 Pz.Rgt. quickly followed and expanded the bridgehead.

Further to the left, the combat operations of Battle Group Liebenstein coincided with those of Battle Group Westhoven. Graf Kageneck's 4/6 Pz.Rgt. and the 6/3 Pz.Gren.Rgt. reached the hills in front of the canal as the advance detachment. A short fierce battle was also fought there. Russian defensive fire came out of the bushes and woods, but it was quickly silenced by fire from the combat vehicles. The tanks advanced further, penetrating into Grafskiy and likewise not allowing the Russians there time to blow the canal bridge.

The following main body of the I/6 Pz.Rgt. did not wait until the panzergrenadiers were finished. The panzer raid continued. At 1400 hours the I/6 Pz.Rgt. was located near Vesselovskoe and was penetrating to the southwest toward Mosdok. In a short time Battle Group von Liebenstein was located on the northeastern edge of the city. The panzergrenadiers and artillery fired on it.

Cautiously the 4/6 Pz.Rgt. continued to advance on Mosdok. Feldwebel Thevoz approached to within 300 meters of the first houses when a railroad train steamed out of the city. Thevoz directed his gun sights on the target. Suddenly a blast of fire belched from his tank.

"An armored train - open fire!" shouted the Feldwebel. The cannons of his Panzer IVs launched shells against the armored train. That was the signal!

Other tanks then joined in the battle. Armored giants faced off. Broadside to broadside the armored train fired at the vehicles of the I Battalion, and they replied. Gun powder and locomotive smoke covered the entire area until a tank shell hit the locomotive tender. At the same time, a shell hit the ammunition wagon. With a powerful crack the armored train exploded, taking its courageous fighters to death with it.

The 4th Panzer Company assembled at a cemetery with oriental grave markers. However, the halt was very short. The company then caught up with the attack of the II/6 Pz.Rgt., which was advancing against the city on the right. An enemy anti-tank obstacle was shot up. The tanks of the 2nd and 4th Companies penetrated into the city, but the defense had already been reinforced. Anti-tank weapons and mines caused losses. The tanks had to wait until the panzergrenadiers caught up.

Farther to the west, at 1600 hours, Battle Group Westhoven had also reached the edge of the city with the II/6 Pz. Rgt. After breaking through an anti-tank obstacle, the tanks of the II Battalion had to fight it out with skillful infantry. Then a second armored train rumbled from the Novo Georgievskiy station. It had to be taken on in combat by the German tanks. A battle erupted similar to that with the first armored train and was again decided in favor of the German tank cannon. When both locomotives were destroyed a third armored train suddenly appeared. Once more the tanks and and the 12.7 cm guns exchanged blows. Major Frank's II Battalion was forced to concentrate its efforts. The luck of the battle was again on the side of the Germans. An ammunition wagon blew into the air and, at the same moment, the train ran into one of its predecessors. Frank's tanks rolled forward, completed their destruction and then waited for the following panzergrenadiers. By the fall of darkness the II/394 had closed ranks and established a defense south of the rail line.

During the night the Russians reinforced their troops by deploying elements of the 6th, 8th and 10th Airborne Brigades. On the next morning the reconnaissance elements from the 3rd Panzer Division attacked into the strong enemy forces. In spite of this, the corps demanded the attack be continued. Both battle groups of the 3rd Panzer Division began clearing out the northern portion of the city. Assault units penetrated further into the city. They could not hold and had to withdraw.

In the meantime, the artillery was brought up and fired into the city. At 1330 hours (24 August) a new attack by the 1/6 Pz.Rgt. and the 6/394 Pz.Gren.Rgt was launched. It was temporarily stalled by a mine obstacle and heavy defensive fire. At the critical moment Hauptmann Rohrbeck advanced with his 1st Panzer Company and the enemy withdrew. The panzer attack was reinforced by the arrival of the II/394 and penetrated along the main road up to the large church, where the companies set up a hasty defense at night. At 2100 hours the noises of combat faded away.

The 25th of August 1942 was a beautiful summer day. The Germans prepared to attack on both sides of the large church. The artillery launched a fire strike. And then the panzergrenadiers of the II/394 attacked to the road with the support of tanks, reaching the Terek. The city of Mosdok had fallen.

The Terek lay before the men of the 3rd Panzer Division. The river flows to the east with much force. Foaming, the water rushes over rocks and sand banks. The Terek rises in the Kasbek and at first flows to the north. Near

Prokhladny it bends sharply to the east and flows through the Nogai Steppes into the Caspian Sea. The river provides a natural barrier in front of the Grosny oil region. The dominant and rocky southern and eastern banks offer excellent defensive possibilities, which the Soviets made full use of. The defense was particularly strong in the Mosdok area. Therefore, the German leadership searched for another location to breach the Terek defense. While the 3rd Panzergrenadier Regiment, led by Oberst Zimmermann, remained in Mosdok, other elements of the 3rd Panzer Division advanced further to the east along the northern bank.

Generaloberst von Kleist intended to penetrate the defensive line in the east with the 3rd, 13th and 23rd Panzer Divisions and conquer Grosny from the north. The LII Army Corps marched out of the Kalmuck Steppes; it was to be committed near Mosdok with its 111th and 370th Infantry Divisions.

On 25 August Major Gollob was at a meeting discussing the further commitment of his III/52 JG in the XXXX Panzer Corps area of operations. There were serious concerns voiced by the participating panzer leaders about the upcoming battle around the planned Mosdok bridgehead and the subsequent advance into the Grosny oil region with regard to supplying the formations with fuel and ammunition. General Geyr von Schweppenburg tasked Major Gollob to take these concerns to the superior Luftwaffe headquarters. Support from the Luftwaffe could only be promised in a small circumference because the Luftwaffe also suffered from fuel and ammunition shortages. In addition, Major Gollob wrote:

"In order to save as much fuel as possible and to be able to reach the enemy faster, I reconnoitered a departure field from Gonshtakovka on 26 August 1942 and found a suitable sized field northwest of the planned bridgehead. From there we would fly group sorties with the best results."

From Mineralnie Vody to Gonshtakovka in the direction of the future bridgehead on the Terek required a total flight time of 17 minutes with the Me 109. This included take-off and landing. The flight time required by a Ju 52 between these locations was a half an hour. The new field was located considerably closer to the bridgehead.

During the fighting around the Terek, the German Luftwaffe was to be often criticized by the Landser in the trenches. The enemy air superiority was crushing. The German fighters rarely appeared over the air space, mostly after the Soviets had left. The author of this book was himself a soldier on the Terek front and wanted to know the reasons why this was the case.

This becomes more understandable when one takes into consideration the number of operational aircraft available. It was dismaying! Like the ground troops, the German Luftwaffe was also over tasked. The strength of a group from a jagdgeschwader was supposed to be 30 aircraft. In Armavir, the III/52 JG had only half of its aircraft operational. In a letter to the author, the then Major Gollob wrote:

"...It might be of interest to you to know that on the Terek front sector there were no more than four aircraft operational at any one time. Thus, as a rule, we flew in groups. We lacked aircraft, we lacked fuel, ammunition was in short supply, therefore, we had to organize into the smallest groups possi-

ATTACK ON MOSDOK AND ADVANCE TO THE EAST

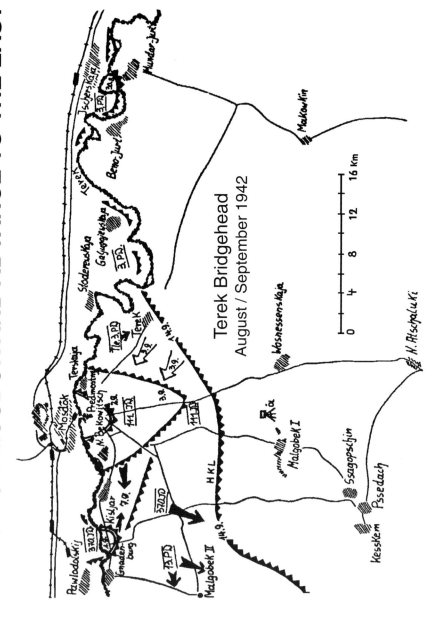

Terek Bridgehead
August / September 1942

ble in order to be able to monitor the front..."

The reader and, in particular, the former soldier, who had fought on the Terek, can now come to their own conclusions about the German Luftwaffe. The German Luftwaffe did what it could do.

On 25 August, as the 3rd Panzer Division was conquering Mosdok, the 13th Panzer Division (from this day on, subordinated to the XXXX Panzer Corps) attacked with Battle Group Stolz against the Terek, 30 kilometers east of Mosdok. Battle Group Stolz's mission read: "Reconnoiter near Meckenskaya and establish a bridgehead near Isherskaya!"

Oberstleutnant Stolz, the successful commander of the reinforced 43rd Kradschützen Battalion, led his battle group with great circumspection. While the motorcycle reconnaissance elements reconnoitered Meckenskaya, the main body reached the area north of Isherskaya at 1745 hours. Clever, successful reconnaissance, under Leutnant Rudolsch, penetrated into the northern portion of the large town and reconnoitered the weak positions of the Russian defense.

On 26 August at 0900 hours Battle Group Stolz attacked Isherskaya and captured the town at 1500 hours, after a fierce battle. The first elements of the 3rd Panzer Division closed and took over the security of Isherskaya. Battle Group Stolz was subordinated a day later to Gruppe von Bodenhausen (23rd Panzer Division), which advanced further to the east.

During the following days the regiments of the 13th Panzer Division moved into the Alpatovo - Meckenskaya area. The 3rd Panzer Division prepared to establish a bridgehead near Isherskaya. In Mosdok the 3rd Panzergrenadier Regiment was relieved by the 50th Grenadier Regiment (111th ID). The Terek defense was to be breached at four locations: near Kislyar with the 370th ID, near Mosdok with the 111th ID, near Isherskaya with the 3rd Panzer Division and near Naurskaya with the 13th Panzer Division. Fuel shortages and other problems delayed the undertaking.

On 29 August 1942 Major Gollob shot down his 150th enemy aircraft over the Terek area. During the time period from 14 to 29 August, 32 enemy aircraft had been shot down in the Mineralnie Vody - Mosdok area during 38 sorties, averaging two per day. Gollob achieved his 150th air victory during his 464th mission. On the day of the attack of the 3rd Panzer Division, the enemy was effectively eliminated with the help of the Luftwaffe. This was confirmed by the following intercepted enemy clear-text message: "Help, help, the enemy air force is completely suppressing our own air force and army!"

On 30 August the III Group of the 52nd Jagdgeschwader shot down its 1500th enemy aircraft. Hauptmann Dickfeld achieved his 120th air victory. Major Gollob had to make an emergency landing shortly after he took off on his second mission for this day. The pistons in his Me 109 froze. It was his 4571st flight and, temporarily, his last. Major Gollob was grounded and later assigned another mission.

The Berlin - Brandenburg 3rd Panzer Division was the first to attack the

Terek defenses. On 30 August 1942 at 0330 hours 75 guns and 10 mortars spat death and destruction across the river. Under the masterly direction of Oberst Ullrich, 26 German batteries fired onto the crossing sites. The crossing group under Major Pape, consisting of the 394th Panzergrenadier Regiment, elements of the 52nd Engineer Battalion and the reinforced 906th Assault Boat Kommando, waited for the order to attack.

At 0340 hours the fire preparation jumped forward. Hauptmann Baron von der Heyden-Eynsch gave his I/394 the signal to attack.

In the lead, the panzergrenadiers of the I/394 advanced to the river bank and jumped into the assault boats. The engines roared to life. The assault boats probed through the rapidly flowing river with their cargo of men to the southern bank. Just as the enemy recovered from his shock, the first wave arrived.

As the second wave hurried to the assault boats, enemy artillery and mortar fire was unleashed and covered the crossing site with a hail of shells. Baron von der Heyden-Rynsch, his adjutant and an ordnance officer, as well as other men and assault troops, died on the northern bank.

The assault boats went to and fro. The panzergrenadiers ducked down behind the sides of the boats and only their steel helmets were visible. Around them the impact of the shells boiled the water. More and more sacrifices were demanded. Oberleutnant Duerrholz, commander of the 2/394, fell wounded into the river and disappeared forever.

On the southern bank, the panzergrenadiers and engineers under Oberleutnant Eggert fanned out and advanced on their bellies. By 0530 hours all of I/394 and two companies of the 39th Armored Engineer Battalion had crossed.

The II/394 crossed in the assault boats in second echelon. Hauptmann Stein, the battalion commander, was severely wounded. However, as always in difficult situations, the courageous men found a way to master the problems. Oberleutnant Pollmann from the 6th Company brought the II/394 under his command on the opposite bank, where they expanded the bridgehead with the I/394.

Finally, the 3rd and 7th Companies of the 3rd Panzergrenadier Regiment crossed. Hauptmann Müller-Röhlich took command in the bridgehead. Of the 36 assault boats which began the assault there were only five still intact at 0700 hours. The division ordered: "Entrench and hold!" The elements that had crossed were too weak to continue to attack toward Mundar - Yurt. German losses were high. All of the forward observers who had crossed had been killed.

At midday the enemy's artillery fire increased. Swarms of Russian fighter-bombers and bombers attacked the crossing site. Major Gollob's fighters attacked the Russian air groups, but their inferior numbers could not stop the waves of Russian sorties.

In the meantime, it was established that the Isherskaya bridgehead was unsuitable for building a bridge. In spite of this, it was ordered to be held for the time being because it tied up considerable enemy forces. The artillery was deployed forward in order to be better able to defend against the repeated enemy attacks out of Mundar - Yurt.

While the battle in the Isherskaya bridgehead raged, the 13th Panzer Division was advancing to the east and preparing to establish a bridgehead near Naurskaya. Because of a fuel shortage, the regiments of the 13th Panzer Division reached the assembly area late. Naurskaya was again occupied by Russian forces that had crossed the Terek. On 1 September the 126th Panzergrenadier Regiment (23rd Panzer Division), under Oberst von Bodenhausen, recaptured Naurskaya. During the afternoon additional forces of the 13th Panzer Division had caught up. They were deployed in Naurskaya to prepare for a crossing, but this bridgehead mission was cancelled.

On 2 September the 111th ID established a bridgehead over the Terek near Mosdok. The 13th Panzer Division moved its main body out of the Naurskaya area into the area north of Mosdok.

Oberst von Bodenhausen's battle group, to which belonged the 126th Panzergrenadier Regiment (23rd Panzer Division) and 43rd Kradschützen Battalion (13th Panzer Division), advanced reconnaissance elements in combat strength north of the Terek far to the east. One group reached the railroad junction 25 kilometers northeast of Grosny and discovered the area to be weakly occupied by the enemy. An effective blocking of the railroad junction would have severed the connection through Kislyar to Astrakhan, over which Allied assistance rolled for Stalingrad. However, the German force was too weak to be able to hold out there. Once again the last regiment failed. Supply problems and the threat to the rear area, as well as numerous Russian attacks, forced Battle Group von Bodenhausen to withdraw. On 10 September it was again located near Meckenskaya and took over the security for the 3rd Panzer Division.

On 4 September, after the Mosdok bridgehead had been fortified, the Isherskaya bridgehead was given up.

THE STEPPE FRONT NORTH OF ISHERSKAYA

In the Nogai Steppes - The threatened northern flank of the 1st Panzer Army - Sondergruppe "Korps Felmy" - The steppe excursion of the Guard Cossacks

The Nogai Steppes began north of Isherskaya. They were bordered in the south by the Terek River, in the east by the Caspian Sea and in the west by the line Mosdok - Achikulak. The Kalmuck Steppes were adjacent to the north. This vast area was a water-less steppe with a desert climate.

The northern flank of the 1st Panzer Army was open in the Nogai Steppes. It was secured only by small German motorized formations in a strong point-like manner.

On 11 September, while the battle raged in the Mosdok bridgehead, strong Russian forces launched a relief attack north of the Terek and pressured the advanced Bodenhausen and Brückner battle groups. The 3rd Kradschützen Battalion and four batteries from the 75th Armored Artillery Regiment were freed-up and committed on either side of Meckenskaya.

While the X Soviet Guards Rifle Corps harassed the German forces on the river front near Meckenskaya with local attacks by the 4th, 6th and 7th Brigades, as well as the 92rd Artillery Regiment, air reconnaissance discovered enemy movement further to the north at the same time. The Soviets, who recognized the weak northern flank, wanted to destroy the German strong point with a wide outflanking maneuver.

On 13 September the II/210 Pz.Rgt. was withdrawn out of the Mosdok bridgehead and deployed to the infantry brigade of the 3rd Panzer Division, which was screening the steppe front of the XXXX Panzer Corps on a line Naurskaya - Alpatov - Lednev - Naidonovskoe under Generalmajor Westhoven. The II/210 Pz.Rgt. destroyed the enemy near Naurskaya in cooperation with the 3rd Kradschützen Battalion.

Additional movement indicating an outflanking of the XXXX Panzer Corps forced the shortening of the 80 kilometer long corps front and the withdrawal to a new HKL near Isherskaya.

The constant threat to the German northern flank resulted in Battle Group von Liebenstein being removed from the Mosdok bridgehead and committed to mobile combat operations on the steppe front.

During the night of 16 September Battle Group von Liebenstein prepared to attack north of the Lenin Canal with the 6th Panzer Regiment, II/201 Pz.Rgt. and II/75 Pz.AR, in order to destroy the enemy in front of the northern flank of Battle Group Westhoven. The commitment of Battle Group von Liebenstein led to the formation of a pocket near Shefatov, where 400 prisoners, 20 guns, 21 anti-tank guns and 13 mortars were captured.

On 17 September Battle Group von Liebenstein conducted a new attack to the east into the Ilpatovo area. The fiercely contested Hill 113 fell into German hands. The II/201 Pz.Rgt. suffered 13 casualties. The battle forced the X Soviet Guards Corps to suspend its attack to the west.

THE STEPPE FRONT NORTH OF ISHERSKAYA

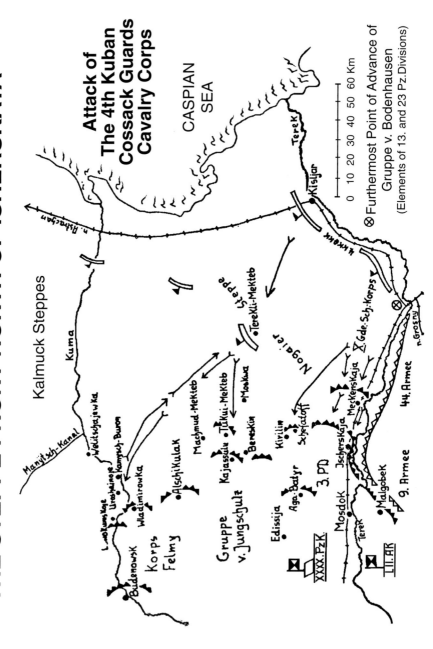

**Attack of
The 4th Kuban
Cossack Guards
Cavalry Corps**

CASPIAN
SEA

⊗ Furthermost Point of Advance of
Gruppe v. Bodenhausen
(Elements of 13. and 23 Pz.Divisions)

0 10 20 30 40 50 60 Km

Kalmuck Steppes

Kuma

n. Astrachan

Terek

Kisljar

Steppe

Terekli-Mekteb

Nogaier

Machmud-Mekteb

Tukui-Mekteb

Moskwa

Berekin

Kajassule

Alschikulak

Welitschajewka

Kampich-Buren

Urozhainoje

L. Welitschajewka

Wladimirowka

Budenowsk

Korps
Felmy

Manytsch-Kanal

Gruppe
v. Jungschult

Edissija

Aga-Batyr

3.PD

XXXX.PzK

Kirilin

Schefatoff

Meckenskaja

X Gde.Sch.Korps

44. Armee

n. Grosny

Ischerskaja

Mosdok

Terek

Malgobek

9. Armee

LII.AK

146

On 19 September the Soviets began systematic attacks on Isherskaya supported by air and artillery. Four Russian battalions crossed the Terek in improvised ferries near Beno - Yurt. The attack collapsed in the fire of the 7/394, under the leadership of Oberleutnant Schulze. Unteroffizier Königstein exploited the Russian panic and counterattacked with his group, which was followed by the entire company, and the enemy was thrown back to the river.

The see-saw battle brought neither side decisive success. The Russian attackers were exhausted. The number of defectors increased. The Caucasians made use of every opportunity to defect. On 27 September alone 14 officers and 523 men crossed over to the Germans, according to a corps report. On 5 August and 10 October Soviet attacks on the Isherskaya front failed. The German positions were rebuilt. Combat positions, shelters and mine obstacles appeared in great numbers. The general fuel shortage led to the establishment of a trucking service to the rear area. The trucks utilized were nick-named "Kurier Pape".

In the meantime, at the end of September, the 4th Kuban Cossack Guards Cavalry Corps, which was withdrawn from the Tuapse area, was launched on an outflanking maneuver around the northern flank of the XXXX Panzer Corps near Kislyar in the Nogai Steppes. The Cavalry Corps broke out during the first days of October. They marched through the arid steppe. Orientation was difficult. Cossack squadrons, guns and machine-gun wagons were spread out for many kilometers on the steppes. Camel caravans laden with ammunition, fuel, rations, horse feed and water followed. The march groups were secured by aircraft. In spite of these protective measures, the maneuver was discovered by German air reconnaissance.

In order to block the Russian maneuver on the steppe front, a mixed battle group was formed on 2 October 1942 under the commander of the 201st Panzer Regiment, Oberst Burmeister, to which was subordinated the panzer companies of Cossack Regiment von Jungschulz. This Cossack formation consisted of Caucasians and had already been tested in security and reconnaissance missions.

In the meantime, the 4th Soviet Kuban Cossack Guards Cavalry Corps advanced far to the west and occupied the small steppe settlements of Makhmut - Mekteb, Tukui - Mekteb, Bereskin, Biryulki and Moskva.

Battle Group Burmeister advanced on Biryulki and Moskva and beat two cavalry regiments back. The Cherventiy Kolkhoz was captured in pursuit. On 1 October small reconnaissance elements were located near Terekli - Mekteb, 80 kilometers from the Caspian Sea. Battle Group Burmeister was not assigned any further operations. As before the threat continued to be an outflanking maneuver in the north.

To secure the northern flank of the 1st Panzer Army the Special Purpose Corps Felmy [Korps Felmy] was inserted into the Achikulak area. To the corps - approximately 6000 men - belonged soldiers of various nationalities, specialists who were trained for commitment in the Caucasus and the Near East. Besides Caucasian, in Korps Felmy Oriental languages as well as

English and French were spoken. The corps had all branches of arms available and could operate quickly and independently like a motorized formation. General Felmy's corps was selected, after reaching the Turkish - Iranian border, to advance into the oil region of the Near East and make contact with Rommel's Afrika-Korps. Because the prerequisites for this could not be created there, Korps Felmy was committed to protect the northern flank of the 1st Panzer Army in the Achikulak area.

On 15 October elements of the 4th KKGKK penetrated into Urozhainoe. By this time Korps Felmy had already occupied a loose security line from Levokumskoe through Achikulak up to Kayassulu, from which all attacks by the Soviet Cavalry Corps were thrown back. Korps Felmy recaptured Urozhainoe. The Soviet Cavalry Corps was consumed by supply problems, water and food shortages. The Cavalry Corps was forced to return to the Terekli - Mekteb area (more because of nature than the enemy) and was reduced to protecting the Kislyar - Astrakhan rail line.

MOSDOK BRIDGEHEAD

Kompanie Waask crosses the Terek - Grenadierregiment Nr. 50 struggles over a fishing village - Armored combat on the Georgian Army Road - Crisis in the bridgehead - The bridge in a hail of bombs

On 27 August 1942 after an endless march through the sun scorched steppe, Generalmajor Recknagel's 111th Infantry Division reached the Lenin Canal north of Mosdok. A little later Generalleutnant Becker's 370th Infantry Division had also advanced to this line. Therefore, General Ott's LII Army Corps stood in the vicinity of the Terek River barrier, which had to be broken. All of the preliminary orders were already issued by the corps.

Generalmajor Recknagel advanced his forward-most regiment, the 50th Grenadier Regiment, in order to relieve the weak security of the 3rd Panzer Division in Mosdok and make preparations for building a bridge. On the afternoon of 28 August the III/50, which was located in Poltansky, relieved the security of the 3rd Panzergrenadier Regiment in Mosdok on the northern bank of the Terek. The III/117 AR followed. They were then followed by the I and II/50 Gren.Rgt. The 50th Grenadier Regiment was selected to make the first jump across the river.

In the meantime, preparations were being made for the crossing. A reconnaissance staff combined all of the reconnaissance results; according to which: the crossing would be made on the western edge of Mosdok to the southeast, directly west of the Georgian Army Road.

After instructing the unit leaders in the plan and coordinating with the supporting weapons, Oberst Röpke's 50th Grenadier Regiment was ready to cross. The operation had to be delayed 24 hours because there was still not enough engineer equipment available.

Preparations had ended on 1 September 1942 at 1800 hours. The leader of the first crossing group, Oberleutnant Maters, commander of the 3/111 Pi.Btl., had a total of seven assault boats, 38 large and 32 small rubber rafts available.

The time for the crossing was set at 0200 hours in order to surprise the enemy and make use of the moonlight. To secure surprise, the first wave would cross on small rubber rafts. The assault boats would not be used until the enemy discovered the crossing. On either side of the assigned crossing site lay two battalions of the Soviet 8th Rifle Brigade in good positions.

An impressive report on the crossing was written by Oberleutnant Waask, commander of the 11/50 Gren.Rgt., who was later killed:

"On the evening of 1 September 1942 the company was assembled in the basements of some houses on the river so that they would be protected from the Russian bombardment.

The attack was ordered to begin at 0200 hours on 2 September 1942. Only one company could be crossed at a time because of the narrow crossing site. This mission, which was to first make it to the other bank, penetrate into the approximately 1.5 kilometer long town of Predmostny (nicknamed Fischerdorf), then capture the anti-tank trench, which lay about 500 meters behind it, was assigned to the 11th Company.

Everyone knew the difficulty of the mission and that the success of the corps depended upon it.

At 0145 hours the rubber rafts were brought up to the river. The men lay next to each other silently. The attack was to begin without artillery preparation in order to secure surprise. However, all tubes were ready to join in if necessary. The 1st Platoon under the leadership of Leutnant Weber already lay in their rubber rafts on an island 30 meters distant from the near side of the river bank. The first operation went unnoticed by the enemy, but this was understandable because the little noises were swallowed up by the gurgling of the main branch of the river.

At 0200 hours the rubber rafts with the 11th Company were launched. However the first one had not yet hit the water when enemy machine-guns began to rattle from the bushes on the far side. That was the signal for the heavy weapons to open fire.

First the heavy infantry weapons under Oberleutnant Koch were committed. They fired on the area west of Fischerdorf, which was later covered in heavy artillery fire. This unsurveyable area (designated by artillery target numbers 404 and 414) offered the enemy the opportunity to attack the assault company on the right flank, but this did not happen.

After the enemy had discovered the crossing, the assault boats were brought to the water. They soon were racing across the river with their powerful motors raging.

My fear that the company, which was boarded in eight small and eight large rubber rafts, would float apart in the strong current while it was still dark was unjustified. As we had practiced a number of times, the platoons landed at the assigned locations, fought their way from both sides to the road leading to Fischerdorf, and, in tenacious house-to-house fighting, where the detonations of the hand-grenades were overwhelmed by the commands shouted by the leaders, the resistance in the first houses was broken. The crossing was solidly in the hands of the 11th Company. At 0210 hours I reported to the regiment over the radio:

`Unit Waask has landed. Enemy resistance broken. Advancing well!'

At 0308 hours the 11th Company traversed Fischerdorf and was located at the anti-tank trench."

The first decisive step was taken. However, success was not completely secured.

The artillery effort lay on the high ground on either side of Terskaya and in the river bank area west of Fischerdorf. The 117th Artillery Regiment, whose battalions were in positions on either side of the main church in Mosdok, had engaged the targets effectively. Fire direction was successful due to the brave forward observers who crossed in the first wave with the grenadiers. The 117th Artillery Regiment, under Oberst Barth, performed exceptionally well!

Other companies of the III/50 also followed in the assault boats. At 0420 hours the majority of the reinforced III/50 had reached the anti-tank trenches on the southeastern edge of Fischerdorf. There was bitter combat around the brick-works on the left flank of the battalion. The battalion commander, Hauptmann Lyhme, led the attack in the front line.

At the same time, the regimental commander, Oberst Röpke, stood at the crossing site. It was clear to him that Battalion Lyhme had to be reinforced with additional forces before daybreak, if the Germans were to beat the clock.

By early morning the I/50 began the crossing. One company crossed, then, at 0430 hours, the enemy initiated heavy counter-fire. The crossing attempt was threatened with failure. Russian artillery fired from the hills on either side of Terskaya. The Russians fired infantry weapons from the shrub- covered bank on either side of the crossing site.

Realizing the difficult situation the I/50 was in and the urgent necessity of reinforcing the III/50, the commander of the I/50, Hauptmann Nacke, jumped into the first assault boat and crossed with his men in spite of the raging enemy fire.

While the III/50 had to defend against constant enemy attacks in the brick-works area, the I/50 advanced on the left out of Fischerdorf, then penetrated to the southeast toward the anti-tank trenches and achieved a loose contact with the left flank of the III/50. Hauptmann Nacke fought at the head of his battalion. The enemy was thrown from the rock bunkers in a hand-grenade battle. In this manner, a mortar battery with 12 super-heavy launchers was taken and set up adjoining the anti-tank trenches. The surprise attack of the I/50 forced the enemy to give up the bank east of the crossing site. Withdrawing forces were engaged by German artillery. The effect of the enemy infantry weapons was removed from the northern portion of the bridgehead, but not in the south.

By 0700 hours Oberleutnant Nicklaus and his 6/50 were unable to clear the bank southwest of the crossing site. In spite of the commitment of friendly artillery the assault boats were still being fired upon. Rubber boats were sinking in the river. In order to remove this threat, Oberst Röpke ordered Major Moshammer to immediately cross his II/50 and comb the unsurveyable terrain on the western edge of Fischerdorf, which was accomplished by 0845 hours.

At this time the Soviets began their counterattack. They attacked under the leadership of courageous officers and put the 50th in a desperate situation. Oberleutnant Waask described how it appeared to the III/50, which was located in front of the anti-tank trenches:

"In the meantime, all hell had broken loose. In front of us we saw a line of hills several hundred meters away. We had to take these hills if we were to prevent the enemy from having a shot directly into the crossing site!

Nevertheless, the Soviets were now able to assemble their forces and launch a counterattack. No sooner had the faithful Unteroffizier Wieczoreck and his men attacked and captured the largest of the hills on the right of the Georgian Army Road, then the Russians counterattacked in company strength. Group Wieczoreck could not hold on. Leutnant Weber ordered his platoon into positions in the anti-tank trenches in order to give covering fire to Borgmann's platoon and Leutnant Böhm's machine-gun group and allow them to withdraw. This line was held against all enemy attacks. However, he would be denied the capture of the hills on this day."

The Soviets also defended the brick-works fiercely. The III/50 could advance no further there. It wasn't until Leutnant Buchholz, with two engineers and Gefreiter Hase from the 10th Company, courageously intervened that the nest of resistance was removed.

In the meantime, the Soviets tried to advance along the river up to the crossing site. The left flank company, 1/50, repulsed the attack from the north with much difficulty. Their losses were high. A forward observer from the 117th Artillery Regiment, Leutnant Kornitzky, filled in for the wounded commander of the 1st Company, Leutnant Kucher. He led the grenadier company with amazing flair. Likewise, the II/50 defended the southwestern road against a superior enemy force.

The enemy attacked out of the unsurveyable terrain southwest of the crossing site up to the beachhead, thus it was changed into a small bridgehead! At 0955 hours Oberst Röpke crossed the I/117 in order to cover the deep right flank of the struggling III/50. The attack of the I/117 ran into heavy defensive fire. The battalion had to take up positions on the western edge of Fischerdorf.

The western flank had stabilized with the commitment of Hauptmann Schwamberger's I/117, but not the northern flank. The I/50, which was tied up on the front, had to defend on two sides. The 1/50, which was committed on the open northern flank on the north of the bridgehead, could no longer parry the pressure on the flank with only 14 rifles and had to withdraw to the battalion command post in the brickwork area.

The II/50, which was located on the southern flank, was to advance out of the area of targets 403 and 404 to the northeast in order to cover the open river bank flank of the I/50. However, this maneuver did not succeed because the II/50 was tied down by the enemy. Thus, the the two forward battalions, the I and III/50, went from one crisis to the next. The two battalions entrenched on the rocky slope of the river and lay under the fire of the enemy hill bunker line, which was 500 to 1500 meters distant. Both battalion commanders independently came to the decision that the bunker line had to be taken.

The III/50 attacked at 1800 hours. Right from the beginning the battalion ran into a counterattack, which it repulsed. However, the attack of the III/50 also stalled. The I/50 also attacked and, by 1830 hours, captured two bunkers. With the fall of darkness the enemy reinforced their defenses. The I/50 withdrew to its departure positions.

During the night of 3 September continuous Soviet counterattacks gave no rest to the I and III/50. On the right, the I/117 established contact with both of the forward battalions of the 50th Grenadier Regiment. Therefore, three battalions of the 111th ID now stood in a half-circle around Fischerdorf.

The engineers worked feverishly on the crossing site. Under the cover of darkness ferries were put in service. The bridging equipment was prepared.

MOSDOK BRIDGEHEAD
111. INFANTRY DIVISION
September 1942

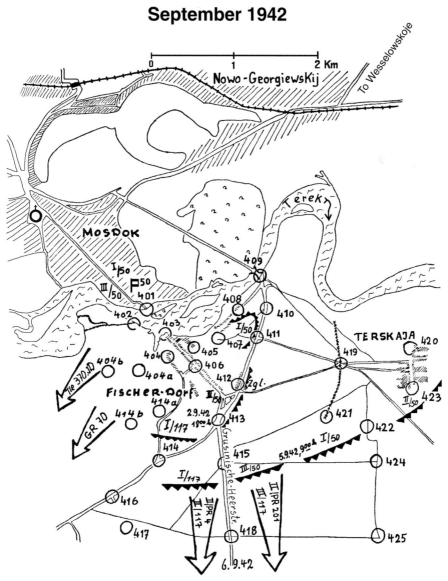

During the night the II/210 Pz.Rgt. (23rd Panzer Division), which was attached to the 111th ID on 2 September, crossed the 5th Panzer Company. Other units from the battalion followed on 3 September.

In the early morning of 3 September Hauptmann Nacke again led an attack of his I/50 against the high bunker line. In a tenacious struggle, the important hill positions, which had a view into the town of Terskaya, were captured. All counterattacks, some occurring from Terskaya, some out of the forest to the northeast, were broken up by the I/50 and the exceptional firing by the 117th Artillery Regiment.

At the same time the III/50 also attacked the high bunker line, capturing the left sector and establishing loose contact with the I/50. The right flank stalled at three strong bunkers near target point 415.

The artillery launched another fire strike into the area of target point 415. Tanks of the 5/201 Pz.Rgt. rushed forward. The I/117 followed in assault. At 0935 hours the grenadiers of the I/117 and the III/50, well supported by tanks, had also taken the operationally important high bunker line in the south.

In order to insure success on the still insecure northern flank of the I/50, the II/50 was deployed from the western edge of Fischerdorf to the north. At 1045 hours the battalion captured the northern portion of the bunker line near target point 410.

Through the cooperation of all formations and weapons, the bridgehead on the southern bank of the Terek was so expanded that the enemy no longer had any influence on the crossing site. The bridge building operation could begin. This success was a feather in the cap of the Landsberg (Warthe) Grenadier Regiment Nr. 50 and its brave officers and soldiers.

At midday the commander of the LII Army Corps, General Ott, the Chief of Staff of the III Panzer Corps, Oberstleutnant von Grevenitz, as well as the divisional commander, the Ia and the 50th Grenadier Regiment commander met at the regimental observation post in order to discuss further commitment from the area of the bridgehead.

Meanwhile, the enemy conducted continuous air attacks against the crossing and bridging site and harassed the bridging operation for the entire day. The Germans deployed additional air defense forces. While defending against an enemy attack, the rainy 3rd of September 1942 came to an end in the Mosdok bridgehead.

On 4 September at 0900 hours 23 operational tanks of the 201st Panzer Regiment (23rd Panzer Division) and the III/117 set out on the Mosdok - Voznessenkaya road in order to clear out an area for larger formations. The hilly terrain and the tenacious resistance allowed them to gain only little ground. The Soviets, who had realized the German intent, which was to (after breaking off the attack along the mountains) was to advance to the south toward Ordzhonikidze from Mosdok, feverishly constructed one defensive line after the other. On 4 September the attack of the tanks and grenadiers ran into a new anti-tank obstacle and Soviet tank units. The 201st Panzer Regiment destroyed seven T-34s without suffering any losses.

On the same day the II/50 attacked the town of Terskaya with the support of tanks and the 6 and 10/117 AR. The attack began at 1600 hours. By the fall of darkness they had reached the eastern edge of the town. On the morning of 5 September the last houses in Terskaya were cleared and a defensive line was constructed on the eastern edge. With the capture of Terskaya, the eastern flank of the bridgehead position was cleared to the necessary depth.

In the meantime, work was feverishly being conducted on the Mosdok combat bridge. After the expansion of the bridgehead, a second bridge was started near Gnadenburg. 14 bridging columns with 175 pontoon and 63 support wagons were brought to the Mosdok area. Engineers from the army and the army corps took part in this task. Soviet aircraft attacked the Mosdok bridging position constantly. In spite of this, the bridging operation was completed at 1400 hours. Vehicles and troop reinforcements could then roll.

For the time being, Generaloberst von Kleist held firmly to his plan to advance on the road to Voznessenskaya. The II/4 Pz.Rgt. and the I/13 Pz.AR were deployed from the 13th Panzer Division to the 111th ID on 5 September. All attack formations were placed under the command of Oberst Herfurth, commander of the 117th Grenadier Regiment. During the night of 6 September the German deployment was ended. The Soviets had also utilized the time to reinforce their defenses.

On 6 September at 0400 hours the attacking formations set out on the Voznessenskaya road. In the lead were: II/4 Pz.Rgt. and the II/117 Gren.Rgt. In spite of good artillery support, the attack advanced only slowly. The second echelon followed with the II/201 Pz.Rgt. and the III/117 Gren.Rgt. and was committed on the left next to the first echelon. Ground was gained only with difficulty because blocking fire from Soviet artillery, "Stalin Organs" and anti-tank guns put the brakes on the attack. Russian aircraft buzzed incessantly over the battlefield. The well-placed enemy battery positions could not be engaged by the German artillery. The German attack collapsed, after some initial success, in sweat and blood. The front froze halfway between Fischerdorf and Voznessenskaya. Heavy Soviet counterattacks were repulsed.

At the same time, incessant air attacks were conducted on the Mosdok bridge position. In spite of the reinforcement of the air defense formations, the air situation did not change much. The German fighter forces were insufficient to achieve air superiority. On 6 September the combat bridge suffered a direct hit. Seven ferries sunk. The damage was repaired relatively quickly.

While Battle Group Herfurth was engaged frontally, an enemy assembly area was discovered at 1000 hours in front of the II/50 on the northern flank of the bridgehead. It was immediately engaged by the 6/117 AR. At 1100 hours a defecting Soviet artillery officer made the following statement: "The remnants of the 10th Brigade (approximately 600 men) were assembling in the town of Terek (6 kilometers east of Terskaya) with 25 tanks in order to recapture Terskaya after an artillery strike and attack through to the bridge position with tanks in the lead."

On 6 September this enemy force caused great concern since it signified both the cutting off of Battle Group Herfurth, which was fighting so hard in the front, and the destruction of the bridgehead.

At 1130 hours the Russian attack was launched out of the town of Terek. Five enemy tanks penetrated into the defensive front of the 11/50 Gren.Rgt. directly east of the Georgian Army Road. Oberleutnant Waask and his men defended bitterly. Three tanks were destroyed in close combat; the remaining two turned back. In the II/50 sector near Terskaya, the enemy attack was parried 500 meters in front of the HKL. During this battle, Unteroffizier Kimmeritz from the 14/50 Gren.Rgt. destroyed the lead tank with his 5 cm anti-tank gun. An additional tank was destroyed by a gun from the 111th Tank Destroyer Battalion. The enemy advanced in close groups into the thickly covered Terek Valley; a rapid firing 2 cm Heeres anti-aircraft gun averted the crisis.

Oberst Herfurth, who had recognized the mortal threat to his far advanced battle group, had to finally remove his attached panzer battalions from the Voznessenskaya area in order to commit them on the left flank of the town of Terek, the source of the danger. The II/201 Pz.Rgt. and the II/4 Pz.Rgt. broke contact and veered off to the north. A bitter armored duel ensued! At 2030 hours Major Gomille's II/4 Pz.Rgt. broke contact with the enemy in the Terek area; they had destroyed 46 enemy tanks and one gun on this day and had captured 10 mortars and five vehicles.

The III/50, which had to withdraw a little during the Soviet midday attack, was again attacked in the evening. The attack collapsed. The time for a German counterattack had arrived! The III/50 attacked, supported by a rocket launcher battalion, and reached their old defensive positions. Besides the enemy's suffering high losses, 120 prisoners were captured. During the night the III/50 defended on the Army Road and the II/50 repulsed an enemy attack near Terskaya.

Things appeared gloomy for the far advanced 117th Grenadier Regiment. On 6 September the regiment had been severely bloodied. The combat strength of the III/117 totaled only 80 men. Generalmajor Recknagel faced an important decision: should he withdraw the 117th Grenadier Regiment into the general line between the 70th and 50th Grenadier Regiments? He had to! The I/117 was inserted in the gap between the 70th and 50th Grenadier Regiments. The hard hit II and III/117 were withdrawn to the anti-tank trenches directly south of Fischerdorf.

These withdrawals in no way completely relieved the pressure on the situation of the advanced attack elements. An 800 meter gap yawned on the inner flanks of the 50th Grenadier Regiment area of operations between the III/50 on the right and the I/50 on the left, which could be covered by fire during the day, but was an unknown factor during the night. And the Soviets found this gap.

On the afternoon of 7 September the Soviets attacked, with tank support, for the first time into the gap in the 50th Grenadier Regiment area of operations. Tank destroyers were brought up. The 191st Assault Gun Brigade, under Hauptmann Kapp, which had a jumping buffalo as a tactical symbol, raced forward. In cooperation with the artillery, the enemy attack was stopped. A new enemy attack on the Georgian Army Road collapsed in the fire of the tank cannon of the II/4 Pz.Rgt. and the 1/13 Pz.Jg.Abt. Forty enemy tanks were destroyed or damaged, as were another 22 Mark III and T-34s in the second wave. The 1/13 Pz.Jg.Abt. registered 22 kills alone.

On 7 September the 70th Grenadier Regiment expanded the bridgehead to the west. The small bridgehead established by the 370th ID on 1 September near Kislya merged with the one near Mosdok.

On 8 September at 0415 hours the enemy launched another strong attack on the Georgian Army Road with two fresh battalions supported by 14 tanks. This time the III/50 was thrown back. The II/4 Pz.Rgt., under Major Gomille, counterattacked and again led the III/50 back into their old positions.

At 0955 hours the Soviets repeated their attack with a fresh regiment supported by 15 tanks. The exhausted III/50 was again thrown back. Hauptmann Lyhme, who was wounded, withdrew the rest of the battalion 500 meters south of target point 415 on either side of the Georgian Army Road into a security position. Lyhme waited on the stragglers. At 1200 hours he reported to the regimental commander that the III/50 consisted of two officers, one medic, two non-commissioned officers and 38 men, with five light machine-guns and two heavy machine-guns. After repulsing three enemy attacks with two counterattacks, was no longer combat effective.

After discussions with Oberst Herfurth, Oberst Röpke made the decision that the 117th Grenadier Regiment was to take over the former sector of the III/50 and that the 50th Grenadier Regiment would establish contact with the 117th Grenadier Regiment by lengthening its right flank.

This maneuver withdrew the Mosdok bridgehead back to its departure base. Battle Group von Liebenstein (elements of the 3rd Panzer Division) were freed-up in the Isherskaya area and advanced into the Mosdok bridgehead. Elements of the 6th Panzer Regiment, II/201 Pz.Rgt. (23rd Panzer Division) and the 3rd Panzergrenadier Regiment were combined into this battle group under the command of the commander of the 6th Panzer Regiment, Oberst Baron von Liebenstein.

On 9 September the II/4 Pz.Rgt. supported an attack of the 70th Grenadier Regiment in the western portion of the bridgehead, which led to expanding the combined Mosdok - Kislyar bridgehead.

At the same time, at 0600 hours, tanks and grenadier vehicles from Battle Group von Liebenstein rushed across the Terek bridge to the south. Crossing the front of the 50th Grenadier Regiment, they penetrated in two columns to the northeast and ran into an anti-tank obstacle. While the 4th Panzer Company covered the flank, Hauptmann Rodenhauser's 1/6 Pz.Rgt. attacked the enemy frontally, destroyed eight enemy anti-tank guns and placed seven others out of commission. During a further attack through a sunflower field, several anti-tank obstacles and battery positions were destroyed. The way was open! At 1800 hours Battle Group von Liebenstein assaulted the town of Terek. In the north the bridgehead was expanded 10 kilometers. During the following night, Battle Group von Liebenstein established a hasty defense near the town of Terek.

On the morning of 10 September the enemy assembled forces supported by tanks southeast of the town. The 4/6 Pz.Rgt. had to withdraw. Artillery fire and air attacks were launched. In the afternoon the panzer companies were withdrawn and the newly formed HKL was held by the 3rd Panzergrenadier Regiment. By 12 September the front was improved by small attacks. The front in the northeast of the bridgehead was stable.

On 11 September the Soviets launched a relief attack north of the Terek. German battle groups Bodenhausen and Brückner, which were located far to the east, were being pressured in the Meckenskaya - Naurskaya area. Air reconnaissance discovered reorganization activities in the north of the steppe front. The new situation called for the removal of the panzer forces of Battle Group von Liebenstein and their transfer north of the Terek. Only Oberst Zimmermann's 3rd Panzergrenadier Regiment remained, for the time being, in the positions near the town of Terek.

While the 111th ID and elements of the 3rd Panzer Division struggled fruitlessly in the Voznessenskaya main attack direction against forces of the 9th and 44th Soviet Armies from the "Northern Group of the Transcaucasus Front" for entrance into the Alkhan - Churt Valley, the 13th Panzer Division and the 370th ID assembled in the Kislyar and Mosdok bridgeheads. They extended the unified bridgehead to the southwest. By 13 September Malgobek II and Nizhniy Kurp had fallen. From Nizhniy Kurp the new front line ran due north and reached the Terek near Khamidiya. From there a new attempt began to advance forces into the Terek bend. The Alkhan - Churt Valley and Ordzhonikidze were the objectives.

IN THE TEREK BEND

Classic night attack of the I/66 Pz.Gren.Rgt. - 32 aerial bombs on the Arik bridge were not blown - The struggle over the Caucasian "Porta" - Panzergrenadiers become mountain infantry

While the 11th ID was establishing the Mosdok bridgehead and fought to expand it, the 370th ID was also able to establish and hold a small bridgehead near Kislyar.

The 13th Panzer Division, which was committed toward Naurskaya, was recalled and re-subordinated to the LII Army Corps. At the same time, the 370th ID screened its Kislyar bridgehead from enemy forces north of the Terek, which were still located in the river towns.

On 3 September the first unit of the 13th Panzer Division, the I/66 Pz.Gren.Rgt. reinforced by the 1/13 Pz.Jg.Abt., advanced out of the 13th Panzer Division assembly area, Russkiy - Grafskiy, into an area 3 kilometers east of Pavlodolskiy. There forces from the 370th ID had tried fruitlessly for days to capture the town.

Major Brux was ordered by the LII Army Corps to take Pavlodolskiy with his I/66 and remove the flank threat to the Kislyar bridgehead. After basic reconnaissance, the attack of the I/66 began during the night of 4 September. It was completely unexpected by the Russians. By midnight assault troops of the 1st and 2nd Companies had bypassed the town and were located in the west. The 3rd Company attacked frontally from the east. In the north stood the majority of the battalion's SPWs, deployed on a wide front. They attacked at exactly midnight. Three Russian anti-tank guns were overpowered on the eastern edge. While the panzergrenadiers penetrated from the east and the west into the town, the SPWs in the north moved out and placed the northern edge under fire. The surprised enemy groups defended desperately, but the German assault overran them. Thus Pavlodolskiy was captured.

An assault element from the 3/66 attacked further to the south, crossed a footbridge to an island on the Terek and reached the ferry site connecting the island with Gnadenburg on the southern bank of the river. In the meantime, the fighting in Pavlodolskiy came to an end. Russian groups, which wanted to cross the foot bridge to the southern bank, were captured by the 3/66. After strong artillery and mortar fire was levied on the island, the assault element was withdrawn. Over 400 prisoners were captured as were numerous weapons. The 3/66 took responsibility for the security of the town. The other companies prepared for another night attack to capture the town of Novo Ossitinovskaya. After deploying similarly as in Pavlodolskiy, this town was captured by the 5 and 6/66 and reconnaissance was dispatched against the last enemy occupied town on the northern bank of the Terek. During the night of 7 September Chernoyarskaya was taken by the rest of the II/66. The northern bank of the Terek up to Prokhladny was in German hands. The three night attacks of the I/66 Pz.Gren.Rgt. brought success at the cost of few German losses. It was only possible because of exceptional leadership and disciplined troops.

In the meantime, the Mosdok and Kislyar bridgeheads were combined on 7 September. Strong enemy air attacks continued against the bridgehead and on German occupied towns. On 10 September Battle Group Gomille (13th Panzer Division) was withdrawn from the Mosdok bridgehead for refitting. At the same time, another battle group of the 13th Panzer Division stood ready in the Nizhniy Bekovich area to expand the unified Mosdok - Kislyar bridgehead to the west.

On 10 September at 1300 hours Battle Group Crisolli, consisting of the 13th Panzergrenadier Brigade staff, I and III/4 Pz.Rgt., 93rd Panzergrenadier Regiment, I/13 Pz.AR, 1/13 Pz.Jg., 3/4 Pz.Pi.Btl. with a K-Strecke and an element troop from II/"Brandenburg", attacked to the west. The intersection south of Gnadenburg was captured in spite of tenacious resistance. During the battle, the commander of the 4th Panzer Regiment, Oberst Dr. Olbrich was killed. The battle group was deployed in front of Gnadenburg during the evening and had contact with the 668th Grenadier Regiment of the 370th ID in the south.

During the early morning of 11 September Battle Group Crisolli advanced further in the fog and, at 1000 hours, captured Novo Nikolaevskiy and Gnadenburg. Rainy weather prevented the enemy from noticing the German movement. Battle Group Crisolli veered off sharply to the south and, at 1700 hours, attacked east of Kurp Malgobek II from the north. The attack was broken off 2 kilometers in front of Malgobek II at the fall of darkness. In the meantime, the 43rd Kradschützen Battalion advanced north of there up to the Kurp and secured it. The I/66, taken from the 370th ID, moved across the Kislyar bridge and was committed between the 668th Grenadier Regiment and Battle Group Crisolli. On 12 September at 0830 hours Battle Group Crisolli captured Malgobek II after fierce combat. During a subsequent attack, a small bridgehead was established over the Kurp south of the town. After that, the main attack of the 13th Panzer Division turned to the fortified bunker line over Hill 350 in the direction of Nizhniy Kurp. An enemy counterattack on the left flank was repulsed.

At 1350 hours reconnaissance forces penetrated into Nizhniy Kurp. Because the tanks were fired upon the subsequent attack on Nizhniy Kurp stalled. The 666th Grenadier Regiment (370th ID) fought its way through the bunker line and covered the left flank of the 13th Panzer Division, which prepared to attack Nizhniy Kurp with two battle groups. The attack order read:

"13th Panzer Division is to capture Nizhniy Kurp and the hills on either side. 4th Armored Engineer Battalion is to maintain the ferries across the Terek near Pavlodolskiy. A 16 ton ferry [bridge] will initiate service on the afternoon of the 13th. - Division command post: Gnadenburg, later the bridge north of Nizhniy Kurp."

It was a clear mission. And the 13th Panzer Division fulfilled it in an exemplary manner. On the morning of 13 September the two battle groups attacked and overcame numerous bunkers and field positions. The Russian Air Force tried to prevent the advance of the 13th Panzer Division with continuous air raids, but their attempt was in vain. The enemy fled. In a subse-

IN THE TEREK BEND

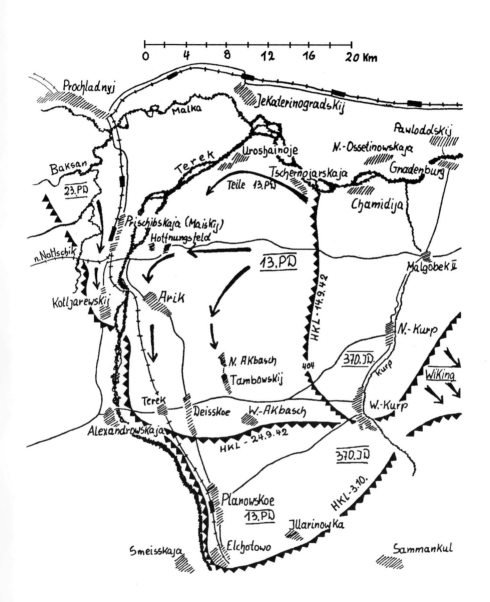

quent attack the dominant Hill 404 was captured. By the fall of darkness, the attackers approached the town of Verkhniy Kurp.

On the right flank of the 13th Panzer Division, Battle Group Stolz (43rd Kradschützen Battalion) repulsed an enemy attack against Khamidiya and dispatched combat reconnaissance to the west. On the evening of 13 September the 13th Panzer Division stood on a 13 kilometer-wide front around Verkhniy Kurp.

On 14 September the Soviets launched a strong counterattack, placing the 13th Panzer Division, which was located in a half-circle around Verkhniy Kurp, and the left flank of the adjacent 370th ID in crisis. Enemy air raids hit the front and the rear area day and night. Verkhniy Kurp had to be given up. The 13th Panzer Division's 66th Grenadier Regiment could no longer hold Hill 404 and withdrew. A Soviet penetration between the 370th and 111th ID threw the hastily formed Battle Group Montfort (elements of the II/4 Pz.Rgt.) back. On 16 September when the 16 ton bridge near Gnadenburg was completed, the attack of the newly-formed battle group under Oberst von Raczeck along the Terek to the west began. This led to the conquest of Terekskoe. On this day there was fierce defensive combat around the hills on either side of Verkhniy Kurp.

On 17 September the I/66 Pz.Gren.Rgt. recaptured Hill 404. Mounted infantry on 80 SPW's rolled out of the morning fog on a wide front and over-ran the enemy positions. Eight captured enemy guns were immediately incorporated into the German defense. 400 brand-new, never-used anti-tank rifles from a newly organized anti-tank battalion fell into German hands.

Leutnant Wendt and his platoon (4/93) distinguished themselves on 18 September in fierce defensive combat in the Verkhniy Kurp area. Hill 489 was held against 17 counterattacks.

The Soviet 151st and 275th Rifle Divisions and the newly- deployed 57th, 59th and 60th Rifle Divisions were severely battered during the day-long attack. As a result, the Soviet counterattack petered out.

In order to reduce the strength of the Soviet air superiority and better support the ground troops, an air liaison element under Oberleutnant Heimberg was attached to the 13th panzer Division. The air liaison element had direct contact with the few fighters of the 52nd Jagdgeschwader. Six Me 110s were immediately committed to the ground battle. They were assigned ground targets by Oberleutnant Heimberg. This was an attempt to improve the good cooperation between the ground elements and the Luftwaffe. In spite of this, the enemy air superiority remained oppressive because many of the German air formations were decimated due to the loss of aircraft, while others were withdrawn to Stalingrad.

On 19 September the German defense had so stabilized that the 13th Panzer Division was able to attack again. After some basic reconnaissance Generalleutnant Herr committed his battle groups to the west between Terek and the mountain chain, which ran parallel approximately 10 kilometers to the south, and ordered them to turn to the south when they reached the Terek bend. The objective was to break the Soviet mountain defense near Elkhotovo in the Valley of the Terek. On the evening of 19 September the

162

13th Panzer Division was able to report:

"Enemy in the Kolyarevskoe - Urozhainoe area destroyed by Battle Group Raczeck and some elements thrown back to the south and west. Battle Group Crisolli has taken Hill 396 with Brux (I/66) and the enemy forces there have been broken through. Strong enemy elements fleeing to the south have been effectively engaged by the 13th Armored Artillery Regiment. Enemy 151st Rifle Division is as good as destroyed. On 20/9/1942 the 13th Panzer Division destroyed the battered enemy and attacked through to the south on either side of Arik and reached a general line Terek bend - 4 kilometers south of Terek - Belog Linskiy - Verkhniy Kurp/Tambovskiy road and is defending this in connection with the high ground west of Hill 489. Anticipate strong enemy air raids. Division command post: 1.5 kilometers south of Maliy Kaberdinskiy."

At 0715 hours Battle Group von Raczeck attacked along the Terek toward Arik. An attached assault element from II/"Brandenburg" succeeded in over-powering a bridge guard post west of Arik. At 0900 hours the railroad and road bridges were in German hands. A desperate counterattack was repulsed. At 1000 hours the I/66 Pz.Gren.Rgt. penetrated into Arik, overrunning eight enemy anti-tank guns which could not register a hit on the fast moving SPWs of the battalion. The western portion of the town was taken by the II/66. Both battalions advanced further to the south during the course of the day and, at 1900 hours, captured the town of Terek.

While Battle Group von Raczeck advanced alongside the river, Battle Group Crisolli fought its way to the south on the left. After overcoming numerous obstacles and removing 260 mines, the battle group reached the Tambovskiy area and set up a hasty defense. During the night 32 bombs, each 100 kilograms, were found on the Arik bridges. Thanks to the raid of the "Brandenburgers" they were not used to destroy the bridges. The engineers had a dangerous job.

On 21 September the attack continued. The II/66 advanced from the town of Terek. The I/66 captured Daiskoe. Both battalions were prevented from advancing further by strong multiple rocket and artillery fire. An assault troop from the "Brandenburgers" drove to the Terek - Aleksandrovskaya road bridge to prevent the blowing of the bridge by the Soviets. The long western flank of the 13th Panzer Division was no longer threatened.

In the morning Battle Group Crisolli broke through the enemy defense and captured Verkhniy Akbash, where the following I/667 established a defense. The II/667 was encircled in Verkhniy Kurp. Elements of the 4th Panzer Regiment relieved the II/667 with a counterattack. A continuous line was constructed between Verkhniy Kurp and Verkhniy Akbash.

On 21 September the attack of the 13th Panzer Division came to a stand-still. An extensive mine field south of Verkhniy Akbash and deeply eche-loned enemy defensive positions north of Planovskoe forced it to make intensive preparations before resuming the attack. The breakthrough into the Elkhotovo Pass was negotiated on 21 September by the III Panzer Corps, which assumed command over the 23rd and 13th Panzer Divisions and the 370th ID. Besides the 111th ID, the LII Army Corps received the SS

Panzergrenadier Division "Wiking", which was deploying out of the western Caucasus, for the planned attack in the area south of Gnadenburg - Mosdok.

On 22 September the commander of the III Panzer Corps, General von Mackensen, visited the 13th Panzer Division in order to discuss the attack on Elkhotovo. The outcome of the discussion:

"On 24 September the III Panzer Corps will attack with the objective of breaking through the Elkhotovo Pass. The 13th Panzer Division (on the main axis) will paint an exact picture of the terrain and enemy positions from air photos, defector reports and tactical reconnaissance in order to conduct the breakthrough at the weakest point."

On 23 September preparations continued. The I/52 Werfer Rgt. was subordinated to the 13th Panzer Division. The repair companies of the 13th Panzer Division worked day and night to make the damaged tanks operational, so that the number of operational tanks reached 110. The 4th Armored Engineer Battalion neutralized numerous mines.

With the attack of the 13th Panzer Division, the 23rd Panzer Division, which, in the meantime, had assembled in the area between Malka and Terek, took up the attack to the south. On 23 September, it captured Prishipkaya (Maiskiy) and, on 24 September, Kotlyarevskiy. The long security line of the 13th Panzer Division in the Terek bend was essentially shortened.

On 25 September the 13th Panzer Division attack began. Oberst von Raczeck committed his II/66 on the right (adjacent to the Terek) and his I/66 on the left toward Planovskoe. By the fall of darkness the reinforced 7/66 crossed the small arm of the Terek, slipped past Planovskoe on the west, hid on the western edge of the town and reported by radio the occupation of the departure position. The attack of the 66th Panzergrenadier Regiment then began. While the II/66 penetrated into the northwestern portion of Planovskoe, the I/66 and the attached panzer battalion stalled in front of a mine field and an anti-tank front. Oberst von Raczeck, therefore, transferred the I/66 into the II/66 sector and both battalions broke through the enemy defenses into the town. The 7/66 played an essential role in this success, as it operated in the enemy's rear and had caused a great deal of confusion.

At the same time, the attack of Battle Group Crisolli was launched on Illarinovka. The 43rd Kradschützen Battalion led in the morning fog. Then the 93rd Panzergrenadier Regiment and 43rd Kradschützen Battalion attacked further through the bunker line and field positions, supported by the II/4 Pz.Rgt. The 3/4 Pz.Pi.Btl., together with the "Brandenburgers", distinguished themselves by defeating the strong concrete bunkers. By evening Illarinovka had fallen.

The day's combat demonstrated the limits of a panzer division. The wild hilly terrain, almost without trails, in addition to the strong enemy in well-camouflaged and well-constructed positions, would only allow an infantry advance. Tanks and vehicles could only follow in some instances. In spite of this, on 25 September the 13th Panzer Division achieved its attack objectives. On this day it lost its capable and beloved division commander,

Generalleutnant Herr, through a mine explosion and head wound. The commander of the 13th Panzer Division was taken over by Oberst Crisolli.

On 26 September there were extensive preparations for an attack on the Elkhotovo Pass. Sixteen reconnaissance elements clarified the enemy situation. Their results:

"Because of strong defensive lines a frontal attack on Elkhotovo is not possible. An attempt must be made to penetrate into the forested mountain terrain east of Elkhotovo in order to outflank the town or capture it from the eastern flank."

These short sentences do not express accurately the major difficulties that the 13th Panzer Division had to overcome in the mountainous terrain. The division tried to adjust to the mission. Gebirgsjägers were created from panzergrenadiers.

Kradschützen and panzergrenadiers paved the way through the forest up the steep slopes of Mount Seko and Hill 703. On the edge of the forest (departure point), the SPWs of the I/66 were driven to a vehicle park, which maintained constant communication with the advanced companies and took responsibility for their supply and the defense against eventual enemy attack on the edge of the forest. Mount Seko and Hill 703, five kilometers southeast of Elkhotovo, were occupied. The enemy deployed the 8, 19th, 60th and 150th Rifle Brigades in an attempt to prevent a German breakthrough into the "Caucasus Gate".

On 28 September there was an attack on Elkhotovo from the northwest. The Kharista positions (small stream valley) were broken through after fierce combat. Four German tanks were destroyed. At 1530 hours the 13th Armored Artillery Regiment conducted an artillery bombardment of Elkhotovo with 1500 rounds. The forward-most battle group drove to within 3 kilometers of Elkhotovo, but the attack stalled. The 13th Panzer Division lacked the strength to concentrate on the main effort. Its strength was frittered away on necessary flank protection.

On 29 September the flanks of the 13 Panzer Division became the target of numerous enemy attacks. In spite of this, the 93rd Panzergrenadier Regiment on the left flank penetrated into a deeply echeloned, three-terraced defensive zone south of Illarinovka and, on 30 September, gained additional ground.

The resumption of the attack on Elkhotovo, planned for 2 October, was cancelled due to morning fog.

During the night of 3 October, at 0230 hours, the planned attack by Battle Group von Raczeck on Elkhotovo began. Again the 7/66 waded a portion of the Terek, outflanked the enemy security and penetrated into the northwestern section of Elkhotovo. The enemy positions were overrun in hand-to-hand combat and a breach was created through which the 66th Panzergrenadier Regiment launched a surprise attack into Elkhotovo and conquered the city after fierce combat. At 0725 hours forces from the 66th Panzergrenadier Regiment were already blocking the railroad and road on the southern edge of the city. The Elkhotovo Pass was indeed opened, but the Germans lacked the strength for a subsequent attack to exploit the success of the breakthrough. During the battle for Elkhotovo, two well-led armored trains made their successful debut under the command of Major Kononenko. The Russian armored trains returned undamaged to Darg - Kokh.

On 3 October the 370th ID recaptured Kurp. However, the battle for the Elkhotovo Gate had also ended on this day. The achieved line was soon established as a solid HKL.

The battles of the 13th Panzer Division occurred at the same time as the attack of the SS Panzergrenadier Division "Wiking", which was just deployed to the LII Army Corps, and was to penetrate into the Alkhan - Churt Valley through the Sagopshin key point. Therefore, there was the possibility of advancing to the east through this valley toward Grosny and advancing to the south to facilitate the 13th Panzer Division breakthrough into the Elkhotovo Gate and block the Georgian Army Road near Ordzhonikidze.

However, forces were lacking. Those last necessary battalions were again missing. The divisions of Army Group A were frittered away in too many locations. The 4th Panzer Army, which long before was to reinforce the 1st Panzer Army in the fight in the east Caucasus, was not available. It was being bloodied in the battle of Stalingrad.

THE STRUGGLE FOR SAGOPSHIN AND MALGOBEK I

At the Nizhniy Kurp anti-tank trenches - Rgt. "Nordland" is pinned down - Pz.Abt. "Wiking" and "Westland" struggle for Sagopshin - Obersturmführer Flügel's panzer company in the rear of the enemy - "Germania" conquers Malgobek - Finns struggle for Hill 701

The battle in the Mosdok bridgehead soon suffered from a lack of forces. Moreover, the subordinate formations of the 13th and 23rd Panzer Divisions were organized under the III Panzer Corps in order to advance them along the Terek in the direction of Ordzhonikidze. The III Panzer Corps had to first break through the Elkhotovo Pass. The LII Army Corps was to simultaneously attack and capture Sagopshin at the entrance to the long Alkhan - Churt Valley with the SS Panzergrenadier Division "Wiking". In this manner, the dominance of the Mussakai hills would be negated and, secondly, the possibility of an advance on Grosny would be offered. There was also an additional possibility of an attack on Ordzhonikidze.

The SS Panzergrenadier Division "Wiking" was relieved in the western Caucasus, subordinated to the LII Army Corps and marched to the Terek.

On 15 September the first element of "Wiking", the III/"Nordland", was relieved in Lineinaya and Kabardinskaya by the 503rd Construction Battalion and a Cossack squadron. A day later the I and II/"Nordland" were also withdrawn from their security positions near Asfaldevaiya and assembled for the march to the Terek. The "Nordland" Regiment, as well as the III and II/SS AR 5 and "Wiking" Panzer Battalion, were marched through Maikop, Labinskaya, Armavir, Mineralnie Vody into the Pavlodolskiy area on the northern bank of the Terek between 17 and 15 September 1942. Two days later the "Westland" Regiment followed.

The "Nordland" Regiment was to be committed south of Mosdok near the 111th ID. Oberführer von Scholz reconnoitered the terrain in the 117th Grenadier Regiment sector with his adjutant, Ostuf. Mayer, and Stubaf. Engelhardt. On 22 September another order came from corps. In connection with the attack of the III Panzer Corps on Elkhotovo, the LII Army Corps was now to attack Malgobek I and Sagopshin with "Wiking". The advancing "Wiking" battalions were immediately directed into the Godinaev - Pavlodolskiy area.

Regiment Commander von Scholz reconnoitered the attack terrain east of Nizhniy Kurp with his staff officers and the commanders of the II and III/5 SS AR. On 24 September the division commander, Generalleutnant der Waffen SS Felix Steiner, his Ia, Ostbaf. Reichel and the commander of the "Wiking" Panzer Battalion, Stubaf. Mühlenkamp, took part in the final inspection of the attack terrain. The attack plan foresaw the "Nordland" Regiment attacking the mountain range on either side of the long, approximately 2 kilometer wide valley toward Sagopshin with two battalions on the left and one battalion on the right. This would facilitate the main attack of the "Wiking" Panzer Battalion with the "Westland" Panzergrenadier Regiment, into the valley toward Sagopshin. The prerequisite was the removal of enemy fire possibilities from the flanking heights on either side of the valley on Sagopshin. The "Nordland" Regiment had to accomplish this mission first.

During the night of 23-24 September the III/"Nordland" (Finnish Battalion) relieved the 666th Grenadier Regiment (370th ID) in a security position northeast of Nizhniy Kurp. On 24 and 25 September the combat diary of the III/"Nordland" noted:

"Artillery fire on Malgobek. Russian mortars and snipers firing on our positions."

On 25 September the II and III/5 SS AR moved into positions directly east of Nizhniy Kurp. The "Wiking" Panzer Battalion was moved into an assembly area and the "Nordland" command post was established on the high ground, which was cut by many balkas. At 1200 hours the last commitment briefing of all the commanders took place at the III/5 SS AR (Bühler), in which the corps artillery commander, Oberst Lukasch, participated. The attack plan was gone over in minute detail. After that I/"Nordland" set out along the southern slope of the northern mountain range toward Malgobek I. On the left, the III/"Nordland" was to eliminate the enemy fire on the hills above I/"Nordland". II/"Nordland" had the same mission south of Nizhniy Kurp, advancing on the northern slopes of the Mussakai in the direction of Kesskem.

The I and II/"Nordland" arrived in the Nizhniy Kurp sector in the evening. Both battalions advanced into the assembly areas. Rttf. Johansen reported from the 3/"Nordland":

"All day we rode through dusty field trails in the burning sun and arrived at the assembly area two hours before the beginning of the attack. However, even then we could not think of getting any sleep. The dusty weapons had to be cleaned. We could not eat. The new day was already dawning in the east. This was our signal for attack."

As it was later determined, at the same time, the Soviets wanted to attack Nizhniy Kurp with four battalions in order to relieve their hard-pressed regiments near Elkhotovo from the 13th Panzer Division. They did not notice the arrival of the "Nordland" Regiment. The start of the German attack was set for 0500 hours. The Soviet attack was set for 0530 hours.

At 0500 hours on 26 September 1942, after a short artillery fire preparation, the "Nordland" Regiment attacked toward the mountain range on either side of the long and narrow Sagopshin Valley. The Regiment had the mission of clearing the flanks for the later attack of the "Wiking" Panzer Battalion and the "Westland" Regiment. It turned out that I/"Nordland" became increasingly involved in the main effort of the battle because it ran into the four Soviet battalions which were to attack Nizhniy Kurp a half hour later. Let us listen to an eyewitness report from the 3rd Company of the "Nordland" Regiment:

"During the night of 26 September the company reached its assembly area. There wasn't much time for instructions. It was known that the

Russians were in well-constructed positions in front of Malgobek.

By early morning Hstuf. Bluhm took his platoon leaders to the ridge in order to instruct them in their attack lanes.

"Everything clear?" asked Bluhm?

"Everything is clear" answered the platoon leaders, who then returned to their platoons which were camped on the reverse slope.

Hstuf. Fritz Bluhm, the brave and circumspect commander of the 3rd Company, was to later give up the company and take command of a battalion. This attack was supposed to be his last with the company. And it would indeed be his last. He returned to his company troop leaders and said: "Don't forget hand-grenades."

The new day dawned mistily over the hills and valleys. The company was ready to attack and was organized as ordered behind the mountain ridge. Shortly before 0500 hours the artillery began its fire strike. The shells screamed over the heads of the waiting company. It was hard to believe that anyone could survive such a fire strike. However, the Russians were in well-constructed positions. They hunkered down and kept their heads low. Most of them survived in their small trenches and positions.

After the artillery fire strike the order was given to the company: "Forward - March!" The Third got up and moved toward the hill. There was little cover on the far side of the hill. Wild infantry fire slammed in between the assaulting company, which worked its way into a half-grown cornfield.

Hstuf. Bluhm was one of the first to be killed. A minute fragment of a shell took his life. Oscha. Skorpil, the heavy platoon leader, instructed his heavy machine-gun group to move out of the cornfield. Then he died without making a sound. He was shot through the heart. Rttf. Johannsen, Heavy Schütze [machine-gunner] I, was seriously wounded in the head. Rttf. Nielsen, the little Norwegian, dragged him back. Rttf. Hermsen, from Uscha. Schütz' mortar crew, received a belly wound. Ustuf. Handke, 1st Platoon leader, was seriously wounded. Sturmscharführer Noack, the 3rd Platoon leader (and the father of four children) was killed. The company suffered head wounds, chest wounds and stomach wounds. The commander was killed, two platoon leaders were killed, one platoon leader was wounded. Leaderless, the remainder lay in the cornfield on the forward slope and attempted to gain ground. The shells continued to come in from the other side. Within thirty minutes the company had suffered 40% casualties."

It was no better with the 1st Company, which was attacking on the left of the 3rd. The commander, Ostuf. Tunner, was also killed right at the beginning of the attack. The 1st Company was even battered more than the 3rd and could not advance any further.

The III/"Nordland" attacked the higher ground, with the mission of eliminating the enemy fire above the I/"Nordland". According to the combat diary of the Finnish Battalion, the attack can be reconstructed thusly: The 11th Company assembled in the 9th Company sector at night. At 0500 hours the attack began. At 0630 hours the 11th Company (on the right flank of the battalion) and the 9th Company (in the center) reached the initial attack objective. The 11th Company received heavy flanking fire from the southeast and from out of a cornfield. At 0730 hours the battalion had four dead and eight wounded. The 10th Company, which was on the left flank of the battalion, fell under increasingly heavier artillery and machine-gun fire.

The 11th and 9th Companies advanced further. The attack was directed to the southeast in order to fix the enemy forces in front of the I Battalion in the northern flank. The attack of the III/"Nordland" was supported by all of the battalion's heavy weapons. Each Russian position had to be taken individually. By 0830 hours the battalion's losses increased to nine dead (including the Finn Ostuf. Hannus) and 30 wounded. At 0845 hours they could advance no further. The 11th Company, which was on the main axis, entrenched.

The regimental commander, Oberführer von Scholz, rushed from one battalion to another, to the artillery and then back to the battalions. It was hopeless! The I Battalion had already suffered heavy losses and could advance no further. The III Battalion was also pinned down. Only the II Battalion, advancing on the northern slope of the Mussakai, was gaining any ground. The division urged it to press on the attack because the second phase of the attack, the main effort by the panzer battalion and the "Westland" Regiment, was about to begin. It was soon established that the German artillery was in no position to support the attack of the I and III/"Nordland" effectively because the batteries were in unsuitable firing positions in the cover offered by the balkas near Nizhniy Kurp.

They made another attempt to restart the stalled attack of the I Battalion. Stubaf. Polewacz ordered the artillery to fire on targets in the valley behind the anti-tank trenches; the so-called "Wurst". Ostuf. Bergfeld's 13th Company was firing their heavy infantry guns with good results from out of the II Battalion sector (northern slope of the Mussakai) into the flanks of the enemy strong points in the attack lane of the I Battalion, an area which could not be engaged by the artillery. Ostuf. Körner, the regimental ordonnanzoffizier, rushed to the front in order to take command of the 3rd Company. On the way he was wounded. Ustuf. Spörle took command of the 1st Company, but he was also wounded. And the division continued to press for the elimination of the enemy flanks, so that the panzer battalion and the "Westland" Regiment could attack.

Ostuf. Thöny, the battalion adjutant, rushed forward and took command of the 3rd Company. Stubaf. Polewacz stirred the leaderless 1st Company to attack. The heavy infantry guns of the 13th/"Nordland" fired with excellent effect into the attack lane of the I Battalion. They were finally able to advance!

Ostuf. Thörny roused the 3rd Company to attack. The company listened to him and stormed the hill on which the enemy lay.

"Hurrah..."

The hill was taken step by step. Enemy trenches and foxholes were cleared with hand-grenades. The Third reached the initial attack objective. The men took a breather on the captured hill, sweating and gasping for breath. So did the 1st Company on the left.

At the same time I/"Nordland" resumed its attack, III/"Nordland" also resumed theirs. At 1130 hours the 11th Company was reinforced with light infantry guns, anti-tank guns, heavy machine-guns and mortars. Then they attacked the second hill. There was strong flanking fire from the southeast. Platoon leader Ustaf. Müller was severely wounded. Each meter of ground required the selfless commitment of the men. At 1700 hours the 11th Company bogged down in front of the hill. Weakened by losses, it was no longer in a position to take the high ground or hold the area it had already captured. At 1745 hours the battalion commander, Stubaf. Collani, had to withdraw the 11th Company back to the first hill. III/"Nordland" had suffered 25 dead and 54 wounded, of which the majority were from the 11th Company.

The attack of II/"Nordland" on the southern flank of the division gained more ground. The battalion, under the leadership of Stubaf. Stoffers, drove toward the hill and created the possibility for an attack on the anti-tank trenches.

II/"Westland" and the panzer battalion followed the attack of the "Nordland" Regiment into the valley at 0700 hours. On 26 September at 0930 hours the "Wiking" Panzer Battalion, reinforced by the 3/5 SS Pz.Jg.Abt. and escorted by the 3/5 SS Pi.Btl., moved up to the anti-tank trenches east of Nizhniy Kurp. Engineer troops made it to the anti-tank trenches and blew the walls. The II/"Westland" was to secure the bridgehead over the anti-tank trenches with infantry. Under heavy enemy fire, the engineers created a crossing over the anti-tank trenches on the edge of the northern hill range by blowing the rocky walls. Russian artillery was firing out of all tubes. The heavy caliber 17.2 cm guns were causing heavy losses everywhere.

Ostuf. Flügel, commander of the 2/Pz.Abt. "Wiking", wrote:

"It was the custom in the panzer battalion that the lead panzer company would be the Pz IVs of the 3rd Company. During the attack on 26 September on the anti-tank trenches at Nizhniy Kurp, Hstuf. Schnabel, commander of the 1st Company, had a birthday wish. He wished to lead with his company. All of the documents, such as air photos and terrain maps, were given to Hstuf. Schnabel. I took up another attack position with my platoon, just in case the 1st Company needed the help."

At 1000 hours Hstuf. Schnabel's first tanks rolled up to the anti-tank trenches. The lead tank with the 2nd platoon leader, Ustuf. Kollotzschy, took a direct hit and blocked the access. The entire crew was dead. The engineers widened the access and the tanks rolled again. Then two tanks were lost to mines. Ostuf. Flügel's 2nd Company was under heavy artillery fire for almost four hours. Soviet fighter-bombers constantly buzzed the battlefield.

At 1445 hours five tanks from the 1st Company were still rolling east. 15 minutes later the 2nd Company also advanced. The tanks broke through the enemy infantry lines behind the anti-tank trenches. The II/"Westland" followed. 26 September would go down in the battalion's pay book as a day of hand-to-hand combat.

On the morning of 26 September "Wiking" received a radio message from the commander of the 1st Panzer Army, which briefly underlined the day's objective:

"To the commander of "Wiking".

The entire army is watching your division. You have the mission of advancing the army's attack toward Grosny. I expect to be with your lead attack elements this evening at 1800 hours near Sagopshin.

signed von Kleist."

At 1600 hours Hstuf. Schnabel's 1st Company, with five tanks in the lead, was located halfway to Sagopshin. By the fall of darkness the Russians cut off the lead panzer element from the following battalion. Fog was forming. The forward-most five tanks of the 1st Panzer Company established a hasty defense. Within the hasty defense, one of the tanks was still set afire by a Molotov-cocktail.

At the same time Ostuf. Flügel's 2nd Company was rolling behind the 1st. It was followed by the 3/Pz.Jg. (Sfl) of Hstuf. Höck. Ground was gained on the right and left in the balkas. then strong artillery fire was levied from the southern slope onto the main body. In order to get out of the range of the heavy caliber weapons, Stubaf. Mühlenkamp ordered the attack to the south into the deadly mouths of the guns. Ostuf. Flügel describes this maneuver:

"My company rolled in spread formation over the hills into the valley and was to veer off toward Sagopshin, but it could not because the steppe grass was burning in many locations. Then we took artillery fire from the southern slope and from Malgobek and Sagopshin. We attacked into a Russian defensive line near Sagopshin. A great drama was being played out there. I could follow it all over my company radio, although I was also in a difficult situation. Mines were thrown in front of our tanks. The Russians climbed onto our tanks and threw hand-grenades into the hatches. We had to keep watch over each other and fire our machine-guns. A 7.62 cm anti-tank gun was put out of commission. Ostuf. Wörmer was wounded in the head, Ustuf. Perthes was killed. By the fall of darkness we rolled behind a small earthen wall and established a hasty defense in a cornfield. We were all alone. "Westland" could not follow because there was still Russian infantry between us."

On the evening of 26 September the battalions of the "Nordland" Regiment were located approximately 6 kilometers deep in the Russian defensive field. The anti-tank groups in the valley were still deeply echeloned. Generaloberst von Kleist's demand to be in Sagopshin on the evening of 26 September could not be met.

On 27 September the panzer battalion caught up with the hasty defense of the five tanks from the 1st Company. During the night a platoon from the 2nd Panzer Company attacked into the open southern flank of the Russian tank security and destroyed it. During the battle it was established that an entire enemy battalion was inserted there. What were the Russians up to?

On this day the battalions of the "Nordland" Regiment advanced on either side of the valley to the chain of hills. The "Wiking" Panzer Battalion remained the entire day widely dispersed taking cover behind a rise. The II/"Westland" fought its way through the Russian infantry and caught up with the panzer battalion. Again the main attack in the valley was to take place when the enemy flanking fire from the hills was eliminated. However, "Nordland" could advance no further. The corps shifted the main effort into the valley, without concern for the threatened flanks.

At 1500 hours General Steiner asked Oberführer von Scholz for a plan to continue the attack. Stubaf. Engelhardt, a constant companion of the "Nordland" Regiment commander and a former Danish General Staff officer, proposed two plans to the division leadership which had been worked out with von Scholz. One saw an attack on Malgobek in the III/"Nordland" sector, the other on the southern hills toward Kesskem. Under no circumstances did they suggest an attack in the valley. However, the LII Army Corps had another idea. They would force a breakthrough in the valley. This was also the plan of the army, which had still hoped for a collaboration with the attack of the III Panzer Corps toward Elkhotovo. Fritz von Scholz, whose regiment was assigned the attack into the valley, believed that if the attack in the valley failed, his regiment would be lost. He believed that the enemy flanking fire from the surrounding hills had to first be eliminated before the attack could be made on Sagopshin. Even the commanders of the forward deployed panzer battle groups agreed to this. However, the corps persisted. It was necessary for "Nordland" to attempt a night attack to advance.

27 September saw only small ground gains. Fierce enemy artillery fire from Sagopshin and Malgobek covered the German attack formations during the entire day. In the late afternoon I/"Westland" arrived on the battlefield from the western Caucasus and was committed behind the panzer battalion. It was immediately hit with heavy artillery fire and suffered heavy losses. The arrival of the "Westland" Regiment changed the attack orders for the "Nordland" Regiment. The regiment attacked in its previous attack lanes. The 70th Grenadier Regiment prepared to attack Malgobek.

On 28 September the attack on Sagopshin was repeated. Stubaf. Mühlenkamp, whose panzer battalion was pinned down on 27 September by fierce enemy fire, requested from the division commander the elimination of the enemy flanking fire from the surrounding hills as a prerequisite for the new attack. The commander of the 5th SS Artillery Regiment, Oberführer Gille, believed he could do this with the battalions of his regiment. Anti-aircraft forces were brought up, in case enemy air raids were conducted on the assembly areas and local shelters during the first day of the attack. During the day fighters and fighter-bombers joined in the ground battle. For the first time the Soviets used phosphorus. The air superiority was crushing. The open steppe grass and corn fields offered no cover from the aircraft. And the III/52 JG, which had only four Me 109's operational, was in no position to impose its dominance over the entire Terek area.

The night of 28 September saw the "Wiking" Panzer Battalion in a large cornfield. Tanks and self-propelled weapons set up a large hasty defense.

ATTACK ON SSAGOPSCHIN AND MALGOBEK
September / October 1942

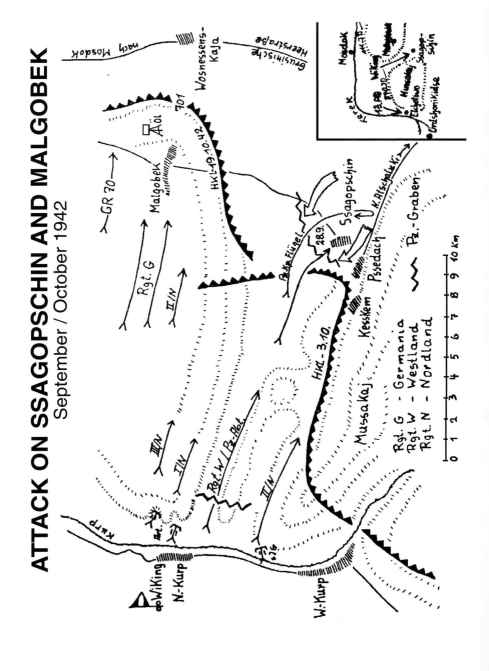

Rgt. G – Germania
Rgt. W – Westland
Rgt. N – Nordland

0 1 2 3 4 5 6 7 8 9 10 Km

Russian artillery fired into it. The "Westland" Regiment suffered its first losses.

The attack plan foresaw: 1/Pz.Abt. "Wiking" conducting a frontal attack on Sagopshin with the main body of the "Westland" Regiment; 2/Pz.Abt. "Wiking" reaching the Sagopshin - Nizhniy Achaluki road in the rear of Sagopshin by bypassing it to the north, blocking it and, depending on the situation, attacking Sagopshin from the rear.

The start of the attack was moved up on the suggestion of the commander of the "Wiking" Panzer Battalion in order to make use of the daily morning fog and eliminate the advantage of the T-34's effective range. The German PZ III and IV were inferior in this aspect.

It began in the dew of 28 September. The panzer attack advanced in the cover of the fog. The 1/Pz.Abt. "Wiking" led, followed by the lead company of "Westland", under Hstuf. Harry Willer. I/"Westland" was on the right, II /"Westland" was on the left. In the morning fog the initial Sagopshin positions and one anti-tank trench were overran. "Westland" caught up. Mühlenkamp's tanks continued to roll to the east in order to hit Sagopshin frontally and outflank it with the 2nd Company.

I and II/"Westland" bit into the frontal attack on Sagopshin. The commander of the lead company, Hstuf. Willer, was killed. Then the fog cover lifted. A murderous fire slammed into the panzer battle group and the "Westland" Regiment from all sides. Stubaf. Mühlenkamp realized that the majority of his panzer battalion was located in a Russian defensive position between Malgobek I and Sagopshin. Ostuf. Flügel's 2nd Panzer Company was attacking around the left. Heavy artillery fire was coming from the Malgobek hills. The panzer battalion was driving more toward the north into the deadly corner of the hill range.

In the meantime, the "Westland" Regiment had to withdraw from a Soviet tank attack between Sagopshin and Kesskem shortly before penetrating into Sagopshin. Again it was obvious that the terraced town would not be taken on the first attempt. The "Wiking" Panzer Battalion, fighting in the middle of the Russian Sagopshin defensive positions, was hit by a superior enemy armored force in the southern flank. A bitter panzer battle ensued. Over 80 T-34s and Mark IIIs rolled against the 40 "Wiking" tanks. The air shook from the thunder of tank cannon. Soon damaged tanks were rushing hither and thither.

The commander of the "Wiking" Panzer Battalion, Stubaf. Mühlenkamp, reports:

"Earlier than anticipated, at 0700 hours, the sun broke through; the fog was suddenly washed away. We were in the middle of the Russian defensive positions, between long rifle trenches and defensive nests, which were all well occupied. Through the hatch opening, I looked into the trenches which we were overrunning. The enemy was firing machine-guns and machine pistols into our hatches and optical slits, throwing hand-grenades. On a wide front at about 800 meters distance on our right numerous T-34 tanks were offering to duel. The first shot hit right behind my turret, the engine blew up, the turret lifted up slightly (it weighted 13 tons), the backrest from my seat was destroyed. I was thrown forward over the gun and yelled "abandon ship!" About 60 shells were on board, 6000 rounds of machine-gun ammunition. Under the seat there were 30 hand-grenades for close combat and in the turret were 30 rounds of light ammunition, in addition to two full fuel tanks! It would explode at any second...

Then there was another hit on the frontal hatch. My tank driver Fritz Kröbsch collapsed, blood streamed from his head. A third round hit the turret from the right rear. The heavy hatch fell into the combat compartment and hit my radioman Heinze, who also services the on-board machine-gun, on the right arm. All of this happened in seconds. I pushed the driver and radioman through the emergency exit hatch and dragged them a few meters from the tank. Then my gunner showed up, in the command tank this is always the battalion communications officer, Ustuf. Köntrop. Just before I was hit, I had looked out of the turret and realized that we were in the middle of a Russian position. With pistol in hand, I jumped into a Russian trench to make sure it was clear. Then we brought in the wounded. I saw that we were surrounded by the Russian T-34s, which were engaging the panzer battalion and elements of the "Westland" Regiment. This Russian tank element was well commanded. Approximately 100 meters behind us suddenly appeared a T-34 and it was directing its machine-gun at us. Köntrop cried out, an entire burst hit him in the right leg. I picked Köntrop up and dragged him into the Russian trench. The trench, which had been recently occupied by Russians, was empty. Then I dragged the severely wounded tank driver Kröbsch and the radioman Heinze into the trench. On my instructions, the loader had taken the on-board machine-gun and secured the wounded comrades. I wanted to go to find help and get back to my tank because Köntrop grabbed me with his last ounce of strength and told me that he was near his end. Shortly after that he was dead. Köntrop was a fearless young officer, a Berliner. I reached my tank. The wounded and dead from my crew were brought in.

Ostuf. Flügel was on the left, passing behind Sagopshin, and had run into enemy tanks there. On my right, the 1st Company had come to a standstill. Several tanks had been hit so hard that the turrets were damaged and the cannon could not be moved. Hstuf. Schnabel from the 1st Company and Hstuf. Darges from the 3rd Company had also been shot up."

The attack of the 2/Pz.Abt. "Wiking", which was to bypass Sagopshin, was described by the company commander, Ostuf. Flügel, as follows:

"I led the outflanking attack on Sagopshin with my reinforced company, which was equipped with the newly deployed Pz IV, 7.5 cm long barrel. Ustuf. Schicker, Büscher and Schuhmacher from the 3rd Company joined the party. Stubaf. Köller's Wespen Battalion, in particular the 3rd Company of the "Wiking" Tank Destroyer Battalion under Hstuf. Höck, supported us with their 7.62 self-propelled weapons during the attack on the left flank against Malgobek. The valley was mined in our attack direction. By chance, just before the attack, the Russians had cleared a wide lane through the mines. We advanced through this lane. We were echeloned with the 3rd

Platoon of Ustuf. Nicolussi-Leck in the lead. The other two platoons screened against the hills."

This is supplemented by a report from Sturmmann Werner Neumann from the 2/Pz.Abt, followed by Ostuf. Flügel's. Both reports were written directly after the battle. Whether Neumann is still alive, is not known. Neumann wrote:

"28 September 1942. Darkness withdrew before the light of the new day. Thick fog covered the land around us and restricted vision to 20 meters. The engines were cranked up, we moved. Shapes were visible in the grey of the fog. A company of the "Westland" Regiment arrived and mounted the tanks. "Panzers march!" We attacked. We traversed a wide lane in a mine-field. In a short time the optics and view finders were covered in mist. Thick water drops from the fog hung from them and complicated visibility. Eyes were strained to search the fog. In vain! The mounted infantry had to be doubly attentive in order to eliminate an ambush. Our tanks moved through the fog like ghostly spirits.

Suddenly, the fog thinned. Here and there we could see up to 100 meters. Then, suddenly, visibility was clear. Sunlight streamed down. We were advancing quickly.

"Attention! Enemy tanks at 3 o'clock, 1500 meters in a depression!" I heard these words come over the radio, even though I did not have earphones on. It was our first meeting with enemy tanks, everyone was tense. Then commands began coming in from the commanders. I got the armored shells ready. In the meantime, I found the time to take a quick glance out of the side portal. In the depression to the right in front of us at the announced distance were approximately 25 enemy tanks. They were moving toward us at great speed.

Suddenly a shell shrieked over us. Was it anti-tank or tank? We advanced quickly. "Attention! 1 o'clock, 400 meters, enemy tanks!" More tanks! I quickly shoved my armor shells into the tube. Several tanks had already opened fire. It was a tank duel! Our tank was recognized by the enemy. "Open fire!" The first armor shell left the tube. Tense seconds passed. Next to us a tank blew up. There was fire on either side of us. "A hit" yelled our commander. "Again!" When I glanced out of the slit, I saw two Soviet tanks at 2 o'clock, 200 meters. They were at the edge of a sunflower field. We continued to fire. Then our commander called: "231 is burning!" We saw the crew of Ustuf. Nicolussi-Leck, the platoon leader, abandon ship. Then I saw the column of smoke indicating that another enemy tank was hit.

Over the radio I heard a fourth enemy tank was hit. We were very glad, but this was not the last hit."

Ostuf Flügel wrote:

"After a short time, we were rushing into the attack against the enemy tanks. We were locked so close in combat that the decks of the tanks scraped against each other. Next to me rode Ustuf. Nicolussi-Leck and he took a round in the engine compartment at short range from the side. The tank ignited. Nico abandoned ship.

Through the slit we did not notice anyone following us. The Wespen (self-propelled anti-tank guns) were not following. "Westland" dismounted. Artillery fire opened on us from Malgobek."

Neumann wrote about the continuation of the attack:

"Our company commander utilized the enemy's confusion. We attacked further into the valley. At the beginning of the tank battle, the infantry had to dismount and fight in small groups behind us. We quickly gained ground and came upon anti-tank gun fire and bazooka fire at the anti-tank trenches. This was a dried up river bed, which was hastily prepared as an anti-tank trench. Crossing it was difficult. Oscha. Bachschuster was killed by a shell fragment. The remaining tanks crossed.

In the meantime, we had skirted Sagopshin. Now we turned to the right in order to advance on our attack objective, the Sagopshin - Nizhniy Achaluki road. Immediately the lead platoon (Ustuf. Scheel) came in contact with additional enemy tanks, which were located on the road. After a short time, several of them were burning. We reached the road and they blocked it. The Russians were taken completely by surprise. We were very proud of the number of hits: there were six T-34s and five English Mark IIIs. Two additional T-34s were disabled.

Later we found out that we had attacked into the lead elements of a second tank unit. It had been assembled as a reserve. Our attack had separated the two tank formations. In order to take account of the tanks, the company commander advanced a platoon on the left side of the road. However, anti-tank fire suddenly erupted there. After some time, the platoon leader reported the destruction of two 7.62 anti-tank guns. The platoon was now being fired on by two enemy tanks, but they could not reach us with the 5 cm cannon at that distance. The 2nd Company formed a large half-circle with elements of the 3rd Company.

Soon loud sounds of combat came from Sagopshin. The order to camouflage the tanks from enemy air attack was given. 18 Russian bombers appeared, but they did not attack us. Instead they dropped their bombs on Sagopshin. Had the "Westland" Regiment taken the city? We began to fight our way toward Sagopshin. We hoped that our infantry and self-propelled weapons would soon catch up and secure the territory we captured.

Unexpectedly, anti-tank fire passed over us. They still did not achieve any hits. The two T-34s half way up the hill in front of us opened fire, but they still could not reach us with their cannon. Suddenly, the ground was churned up in front of us. Heavy caliber Russian shells were exploding around us. We had to roll back in order to change our position, but the artillery fire followed us. This was a 17.2 cm battery, which had caught us in direct fire. It was nerve wracking to be in a tank, to hear the fire and wait for the explosion. Up to then, the Russian batteries must have assumed that we were friendly tanks.

At midday, the company commander decided to roll us into the anti-tank trenches in order to escape from the effective range of the enemy artillery fire. Carrying out this order turned out to be difficult because, as the first tank drove up the position, the enemy immediately laid fire on it. However, all of the tanks made it in. We were covered in the trenches up to our turrets. Then, for the first time, we could unlatch and take a breath of fresh air. We camouflaged our vehicles and cleared away the damage, while the machine-gunners took up security. The commander went from vehicle to vehicle and asked after the wounded.

I glanced at my watch, it was 1600 hours. We had been in the trenches for an hour. Our command tank maintained radio communications with the battalion and the division. Our infantry was advancing. However, because of strong resistance, they were doing so only slowly. Thus we awaited the fall of darkness.

The day ended slowly as twilight set in. We had our hand weapons at the ready. There, noises! The sound of the firing of a machine-pistol grew nearer. Russians. We were ordered to take cover. 17 Russians were coming toward us.After a little while the order was given to move out of the anti-tank trenches in platoons and to form a vehicle defense in the open terrain. We mounted, withdrew from the anti-tank trenches and established a circular defense."

Ostuf. Flügel continues:

"During the night the Russians feverishly tried to establish connections. We took prisoners. We were short of water. Ten Russians were released to fetch water from Sagopshin. They came back with the water and an additional 20 prisoners.

I decided to send Ustuf. Schumacher back with the damaged tanks and the wounded and to report to the battalion. It did not seem possible to hold out for the next day, because we were low on fuel and ammunition. I was able to speak with General Steiner with the last of the transmission energy. He promised me that he would infiltrate infantry through the gap in the minefield, but no one ever showed up."

These are the reports on the advance of the 2/Pz.Abt. "Wiking". However, what was happening in front of Sagopshin on 28 September?

After being knocked out, Stubaf. Mühlenkamp jumped into another tank. Slowly, order returned to the battalion, which had withdrawn approximately one kilometer after the tank duel. Of the 40 tanks, with which the battalion entered the battle, a third were knocked out or damaged in some other way.

In the 3/5 SS Pz.Jg.Abt. (Sfl) area things were no better. The company commander, Hstuf. Höck, was shot up and had to crawl back with 14 fragments in his ankle.

In the afternoon, when the enemy flank attack was launched from Kesskem, Engineer Battle Group Schäfer advanced and repulsed the attack. The "Westland" Regiment was bloodied the worst on this day. When the fog lifted it was located in a Russian defensive field in front of Sagopshin and was hit with a murderous artillery fire from the hills on either side. Moreover, Russian aircraft dropped their bombs. Some additional notes from Rttf. Stöckle:

"We made it to the town on the first attempt. We took the first trenches with heavy losses. Enemy tanks were in front of us, and the enemy fired on us with Stalin Organs as we redeployed."

The attempt of the I/"Westland" to bypass on the right, to penetrate between Sagopshin and Kesskem into the Sagopshin defenses, failed with heavy losses. There the enemy batteries also fired on any movement in the valley from the surrounding hills.

Stubaf. Mühlenkamp wrote further:

"I had no sooner reorganized my panzer formation (the Russian T-34s were no longer advancing) when I was again hit in another tank. It was approximately 0900 hours when my tank was hit in the right side. The round went through the combat compartment and into the buttocks of the gunner on the left. In the afternoon at 1500 hours I was in another tank, the third for this day.

When I later arrived at the I/"Westland" command post, I saw that the battalion commander, Stubaf. von Hadeln, was completely distracted by the loss of order in his battalion. There were several piles of arms and legs torn off by the heavy caliber Russian artillery. I will never forget that picture of horror! At first I had the impression that von Hadeln had lost his composure. Then he hung onto his men and was again a thoughtful and solicitous superior."

In the meantime, the "Westland" Regiment was withdrawn two kilometers to the west and found the necessary protection in a ground depression. Throughout the night the regiment constructed defensive positions in the valley depression in front of Sagopshin. The "Wiking" Panzer Battalion conducted several attacks to the east. Aircraft continuously bombarded during the construction of the German HKL. As night fell, the battlefield finally became quiet.

28 September was the bloodiest day in the history of the "Westland" Regiment. The attack, which began with such hope, was literally torn apart by the Russian artillery. The well-meaning attack plans were soon upset by the new situation. Moreover, the Soviets were attacking with two strong tank formations along the Mussakai Ridge to the west, south of the "Wiking" Panzer Battalion, which was located in the valley. They wanted to block the anti-tank trenches near Nizhniy Kurp, deep in the rear of the far-advanced Germans and, thereby, destroy them. The "Wiking" Panzer Battalion, which entered the battle on 28 September with 40 tanks (if one includes the self-propelled weapons from the 3/5 SS Pz.Jg.Abt., there were 50) had to fight a panzer battle with an enemy consisting of almost double the number of tanks. The panzer battle was in no way planned nor desired, but turned out to be a meeting engagement that developed out of the situation.

Much has been discussed about the pros and cons of the attack into the Sagopshin Valley and it seems impossible to find an appropriate opinion. It was obvious that there were strong differences of opinion between the division leadership and the army corps and that the attack was called for over the head of division commander Steiner. Tactically speaking, the attack in the valley was an impossibility because of the lack of clarification about the enemy situation and, above all, the threat from the flanks. This is agreed on by all of the surviving soldiers and officers of "Wiking". However, if one views the attack of "Wiking" in the Sagopshin Valley in conjunction with the attack of the 13th Panzer Division on Elkhotovo, which occurred simultaneously, then there was the possibility of negating the threatening Mussakai Ridge, which acted as a watchman, blocking the further advance of the III Panzer Corps toward Ordzhonikidze and the LII Army Corps toward Grosny. This had to be taken into consideration! Especially since it was believed that the attack of the "Nordland" Regiment on the ridge line would gain ground quickly and eliminate the threat on the flanks. In fact, the "Nordland" Regiment had Malgobek as their attack objective for the first day. A chain of unfortunate circumstances, including the lack of forces, tipped the scales of victory in favor of the enemy. And how often this is the case!

On 28 September the II and the III/"Nordland" followed their old attack lanes into the valley and were able to capture several hills. I/"Nordland" was temporarily reinforced by the arrival of convoys. The many dead were buried in the anti-tank trenches near Nizhniy Kurp.

On the evening of 28 September Oberführer von Scholz was named the sector commander in the Sagopshin Valley. Obersturmbannführer Geissler, the commander of the "Westland," therefore, came under his command. Geissler's method of leadership was controversial. It was said that Obersturmbannführer Geissler led from behind and, therefore, things got out of hand. On the other hand, Fritz von Scholz practiced another form of leadership: he led from the front. He had to see everything with his own eyes in order to make decisions on the spot. Fritz von Scholz, who as a young officer in the Austrian Army during the First World War was awarded the highest Austrian award for bravery, would never request his soldiers to do anything that he had not already done. This gave him the undying trust and love of his subordinates. During the time period from 29 September to 15 October, Oberführer von Scholz remained sector commander in the valley as the battalions changed. Up to 3 October the LII Army Corps command persisted: there would be an attack in the valley.

Now we will hear the report of Sturmann Neumann, who was in a hasty defense with the 2/Pz.Abt. "Wiking" northeast of Sagopshin:

"It was 0400 hours in the morning. The outposts heard engine and tank noises. The commander was awakened. Without a doubt they were Russian tanks. We strained to determine their route. They were moving into our rear in order to cut off our retreat.

Immediately our commander summoned the platoon leaders. He ordered: "Prepare to march!" Since midnight the command tank no longer had any radio contact with the battalion; the transmission batteries were used up. Thus, the commander decided to break out. "Panzers march!" The outlines of the tanks in front of us could only weakly be made out. We drove in a column, two Panzer IIIs and one Panzer IV. 100 meters after the first one left we met the first enemy tank, a Kv I with its cannon aimed at us. Ustuf. Buscher's Pz IV fired. He made a direct hit at 35 meters distance with the long-barreled cannon. The turret on the Kv I lifted and the tank rocked back. Now all hell broke loose! No one could pick out a target in the heavy fog and shoot. Therefore, there was only one thing left for us to do: we left at great speed. Our driver did all he could to follow the tank in front of us, so that he would not loose him in the fog. We broke through the enemy block. Since we were in a column, we only had to battle one of these tanks in the block. Then we reached our infantry lines.

We had anticipated that it would be a lot easier. However, we then noticed that the battle had followed us. Unfortunately, we suffered wounded in tank 212, where an anti-tank rifle made a direct hit at close distance, penetrated the armor and wounded the loader in the foot."

On 29 September Oberführer von Scholz took command of the "Wiking" forces in the Sagopshin Valley. The corps was pressuring for the attack. Now was the time for improvisation! The early morning hours were spent working out the attack plan. This was solid general staff work. I/"Nordland" was brought forward. It was to lead the attack with II/"Westland". II/"Nordland" was to advance on the right on the slope against Kesskem and one company of III/"Nordland" was to follow the attack on the Malgobek Ridge. Then the battalions were assembled in their areas. At 1430 hours the attack began. At 1530 hours the artillery fire shifted with the assaulting infantry, which now stalled in the flanking fire from the north and south. At Oberführer von Scholz' observation post, Stubaf. Engelhardt requested the commander of the 5th SS Artillery Regiment to shift the artillery fire back 400 meters and then to advance it 100 meters in five minutes. The "Wiking" Artillery Regiment had already fired a great deal of ammunition and now only had a reserve left that had to be maintained in case of a Russian counterattack.

The II/"Westland" had heavy losses. The battalion commander, Stubaf. Steinert, was wounded. The battalion was taken over by Hstuf. Bäuerle, who continued the attack. At 1700 hours the attack battalions II/"Westland" and I/"Nordland" captured the Russian positions 800 meters west of Sagopshin. However, they could go no further. Heavy flanking fire pinned the attackers down. During the following night, von Scholz' command post was redeployed.

III/"Nordland", which had taken the northern ridge sector over from I/"Nordland", had to give up one company to the left neighboring 70th Grenadier Regiment (111th ID) to resume the attack. However, while the 10th Company was moving into the assembly area, it suffered heavy casualties. The order was repeated: Assemble during the night and attack with the 70th Grenadier Regiment on 30 September 1942. This order was rescinded while they were occupying the assembly area.

On 30 September I/"Nordland" and II/"Westland" attempted to penetrate out of their positions on the edge of Sagopshin into the terraced defenses of Sagopshin. Without success!

At 1700 hours Oberführers von Scholz and Gille, as well as Ostubaf.

Geissler, drove to the division in order to protest the senseless attack with the insufficient support. General Steiner, who had already expressed his feelings against the attack in the valley, again lodged a complaint with the LII Army Corps command. However, the corps persisted: attack Sagopshin. Another attempt was to be made to capture Sagopshin after regrouping.

At 2000 hours there was a new order: during the night, III/"Nordland" would take over the front of the battered II/"Westland". Then III and I /"Nordland" were to attack and the two battalions of "Westland" were to follow on the northern and southern hills and eliminate the flanking fire.

At 2000 hours the 9/"Nordland" was relieved on the Malgobek Ridge by the 70th Grenadier Regiment and advanced to within 3 kilometers northwest of Sagopshin. At 2100 hours 10 and 11/"Nordland" followed.

The attack for 1 October was well prepared. Because of the enemy flanking fire, the beginning of the attack was again shifted to take advantage of the morning fog. Each company formed an assault troop, for a total of six, which were to pave the way for the following companies.

On 1 October 1942 at 0415 hours the assault troops set out. They consisted of the best people in the companies led by the bravest junior leaders. Each assault troop was followed by a heavy machine-gun crew. Everything was well though out. Everyone knew their route and their target. The attack was built around the morning fog, which should cover the wide valley until almost noon.

On the right, the assault troops of I/"Nordland" worked their way forward. They were brave men - Germans, Danes and Norwegians. On the left were the Finns of the III Battalion. Behind them, the companies were ready to leap.

The same question was on everyone's lips: "would this finally succeed?"

However, it appeared that everything was stacked against the companies. Right in front of the enemy positions, 50 meters in front of Sagopshin, the fog lifted earlier than usual and the sun shone through brightly. Then all hell broke loose. Hand-to-hand combat erupted. Defensive fire was set loose. From the hills screamed the rounds of the heavy batteries. The assault troops, the path-makers for the companies, were far advanced and pinned to the ground. Any movement called forth a hellish fire. The assault element leader of the Third, the brave Uscha. Brock, was killed. His men lay in a half-circle around him. It was similar with the other assault elements. Oberführer von Scholz ordered a retreat to approximately one kilometer west of Sagopshin, where the terrain finally offered some protection. Most of the assault elements had to endure heavy artillery fire for the entire day. When night fell they were able to withdraw. Fritz von Scholz was up all night trying to construct a new HKL 3 kilometers west of Sagopshin. Even the two "Westland" battalions were withdrawn there. In this manner they established a continuous stable front, which ran through the valley. The 1/5 SS Pi. again advanced into the old positions in order to stop the pursuing enemy on 2 October and permit the construction of the new positions.

On 2 October it remained relatively quiet. At 1000 hours Oberführer von Scholz was summoned to the division command post in order to receive new instructions. Von Scholz decisively refused to conduct further attacks on Sagopshin until sufficient air and artillery support could be provided. As a prerequisite, Oberführer von Scholz requested: the elimination of the flanking fire. He proposed attacking with the II/"Nordland", which had suffered least, onto the ridge south of the valley (Mussakai), if there was to be any attack at all. General Steiner endorsed this plan. However, it would be 4 October, at the earliest, before the I/5 SS AR arrived from the Western Caucasus, so it appeared that the two battalions of division artillery would be too weak to eliminate the flanking fire and support an immediate attack.

And again the corps pressed for an attack! At 1930 hours the division order arrived to attack with the II/"Nordland" on the Mussakai Ridge on 3 October.

The night was spent in making attack preparations. Stubaf. Stoffers and Stubaf. Mühlenkamp, who both had set up their command posts on the high ground south of the valley, agreed that the panzer battalion would turn over four tanks to II/"Nordland" for the attack.

Early in the morning of 3 October the attack of II/"Nordland" began. At 0800 hours Stoffer's battalion captured a hill approximately 800 meters north of Kesskem (and 1500 meters west of Sagopshin) in a spirited attack supported by four tanks. Elements of the 57th Soviet Brigade were either thrown back or captured. Guns and heavy infantry weapons were destroyed or captured. The Soviets had conducted flanking fire on all of the German attacks on Sagopshin from this hill.

At the same time, the 1/5 SS Pi., under Ostuf. Wanhöfer, which was all alone in the positions in front of Sagopshin, repulsed the Soviets as they were withdrawing into the new German defensive line.

Hard words were passed between the LII Army Corps command and the division leadership. "Wiking" had not taken Sagopshin, and General Ott demanded Steiner come up with a new plan for the continuation of the attack on Grosny. Steiner indicated that Malgobek was the key. In fact, without taking this dominant town the HKL in the valley could not be held for long. The commander replied: "In the morning your 'Germania' Regiment arrives from the Western Caucasus. It will take Malgobek!" The main effort was now shifted from Sagopshin to Malgobek.

On 3 October the first company of the "Germania" Regiment arrived. With them was the I/5 SS AR. By 5 October the I and II/"Germania" were assembled in their assembly areas on the ridge-line west of Malgobek.

The commander of the "Wiking" Panzer battalion wrote:

"The panzer battalion, which was withdrawn into the valley (most of the tanks were in repair), was deployed for the attack on Malgobek. It was a difficult operation on mountain trails and bare terrain. Only individual tanks could be committed at any one time, just like assault guns. This was against all of the leadership principles of a panzer formation."

On 4 October Staf. Wagner assembled all of the unit commanders in his regimental observation post in order to discuss the attack with them. Organization for the attack: on the right I, on the left II/"Germania". To the right of I/"Germania" was the II/"Nordland", which was relieved on the southern front of the division by the "Wiking" Reconnaissance Battalion, which had, likewise, just arrived from the Western Caucasus. On the left next to II/"Germania" was to be the 70th Grenadier Regiment (111th ID). The 1/Pz.Abt. "Wiking" was to support the attack.

On 5 October at 0500 hours the attack of the "Germania" Regiment on Malgobek began. There was approximately 6 kilometers of mountain terrain laying in front of the elongated city. Enemy blocking positions were overcome. The 1st Company of the "Wiking" Panzer Battalion assisted the grenadiers. Each balka had to be fought for individually. In some places, the grenadiers were mounted on the tanks. On the right next to Stubaf. Dieckmann's I/"Germania" followed the II/"Nordland", screening the attack against Sagopshin. On the left of Stubaf. Jörchel's II/"Germania" closed the 70th Grenadier Regiment under Oberst Tronnier. During a situation briefing, seven officers from the panzer battalion were killed or wounded by 17.2 cm caliber Russian artillery fire. The radio station was knocked off the air by the Russians. The commander of the 1/Pz.Abt. "Wiking", Hsruf. Schnabel, was killed. The 1st Panzer Company had no officers left; it was led by Company Truppführer Grosskopf, who was later awarded the Knight's Cross in the "Wiking" Panzer Regiment.

At 1100 hours the "Germania Regiment" stood 500 meters in front of Malgobek and waited on an arranged stuka attack. 20 minutes later 20 stukas flew in from the west and dropped their bombs on the Malgobek target area.

The grenadiers resumed their advance. Russian artillery again fired. The firing was coming from Sagopshin. Oil storage tanks burned, black - brown smoke filled the city. There was heavy infantry fighting everywhere. However, the resistance gradually decreased. At 1400 hours Malgobek-West had fallen. The companies changed over to defense. It was obvious that the elongated city, which consisted of several sections, could not be taken in one effort.

Hstuf. Hans Dorr, commander of the 4/"Germania", noted in his diary that the first day of the attack of the "Germania" Regiment had cost 33 dead and nearly 200 wounded. It was clear to the divisional leadership that the "Germania" Regiment had to be reinforced because its III Battalion had still not arrived from the Western Caucasus, due to a delay in their being relieved. The southern front between Kesskem and Nizhniy Kurp was stretched thinner and the III/"Nordland" was, thereby, freed-up.

On 6 October the attack was continued in the morning fog. The two assault battalions slowly advanced and, by midday, Malgobek- East had fallen. The companies advanced about a kilometer through the eastern edge and went on to the defense. At 1500 hours the large Malgobek-East oil reservoir was in German hands. The Malgobek oil region produced good aviation fuel.

While the assault companies were entrenching, the flank forces tightened up. On the southern flank, the II/"Nordland" repulsed a counterattack supported by tanks. On the northern flank the 70th Grenadier Regiment closed ranks.

The Soviets recognized the great threat and quickly shifted their reserves out of the Sagopshin and Elkhotovo areas into the Voznessenskaya area in order to stop the "Wiking" attack.

On 7 October at 0230 hours the III/"Nordland" was removed from the positions in front of Kesskem. The positions were taken over by the I/"Nordland". At 1300 hours the III/"Nordland" prepared to attack in the Malgobek-East area. On this day the "Germania" Regiment attempted to advance further in the direction of Voznessenskaya (on the Georgian Army Road). The terrain there increased in elevation. Every hill had to be contested. The companies of the "Germania" Regiment took two to three hills. However, the front then stiffened and the exhausted forces could gain little or no additional ground.

On 7 October the 1st Panzer Company was relieved by Ostuf. Flügel's 2nd Company. The 1st Company was taken over by Ustuf. Nicolussi-Leck. Ustuf. Weise, the technical officer of the panzer battalion, brought all of the damaged tanks to the maintenance company for repair. On 10 October the 1st Company had 10 tanks available.

On 8 October I/"Germania" captured a dominant hill on the right sector. Further attacks on "Dieckmann's Hill" failed. The Finnish Battalion was inserted on the right. Their combat diary noted:

"8 October 1942, 0900 hours: Battalion attacked. 11th Company on the left flank captured a dominant hill in spirited attack. The right flank of the battalion received strong flanking fire out of a cornfield (out of the southeast). Counterattack by 4 enemy tanks did not stop the advance of the 9th and 10th Companies. Before twilight, the companies were on line and entrenched. 3 men dead, 23 wounded, including the commander of the 10th Company."

During the night the Finnish Battalion was again pulled back and assembled 2 kilometers east of Malgobek for an assault on dominant Hill 701. This hill lay between Malgobek and Voznessenskaya. From there one could influence the Georgian Army Road. Both sides placed great significance on this hill. This and the Voznessenskaya defenses were the last bulwarks in front of the Grosny oil region, which lay approximately 60 kilometers further to the east; the ardently desired objective of the German troops.

While I/"Germania" fought around the so-called "Dieckmann's Hill" and the neighboring hills, and II/"Germania", with elements of the 70th

Grenadier Regiment had to partake in the 111th ID attack to the east, the Finnish Battalion, on 9 October, was committed for the first time on Hill 701, which lay between the two attack wedges. Hill 701 lay in front of the attack on Voznessenskaya. If the attack on Grosny was to succeed, then Hill 701 must first fall.

10 and 11/"Nordland" were combined under Ostuf. Mühlinghaus. At 0700 hours (9 October) preparations were completed. Sturmbannführer Sollani briefed the company commanders. At 0900 hours reconnaissance elements returned with four wounded. Ustuf. Poyanletho, a Forest Meister from Finland, reported the results of the reconnaissance; is was not encouraging: First a 300 meter long forward slope without any cover had to be overcome, then the ascent to Hill 701 began, which was strongly occupied by the enemy. Moreover, there was flanking fire from both sides, which well covered the long forward slope. At midday Collani reported to the "Germania" Regiment that an attack could be made only with heavy losses. The flanking fire must first be eliminated. The regiment agreed. A strong fire-strike by the artillery concentrated on "Dieckmann's Hill".

At 1350 hours the artillery fired smoke. Then the battalion attacked with two companies. After they had assaulted for 300 meters, the Soviets recognized the attack and fired blocking fire with mortars, artillery and tanks. They could not get through this wall of fire. The regiment ordered: "go over to the defense and entrench!" Losses: 3 dead, 24 wounded.

During the night they returned to their old assembly area.

III/"Nordland" received 24 engineers from the 70th Grenadier Regiment with the mission of blowing up bunkers and tanks during the next attack. At 0855 hours the Russians placed a strong artillery fire strike on the assembly area; during this, two officers and nine men were lost. Reconnaissance results: six enemy tanks on "Dieckmann's Hill" and two on Hill 701. The Soviets anticipated the new attack. Their artillery fired nervously. At 0945 hours the forward observers from the 1/5 SS AR and 607th Artillery Regiment were killed by a direct hit. In spite of this, the Finnish Battalion attacked at 0950 hours, but again they did not get far. At 1000 hours the fresh Soviet 9th Rifle Brigade counterattacked from the east and southeast, supported by twelve tanks. The situation grew serious. II/"Germania" received the main weight of the attack on the northern flank. At 1645 hours the battle finally petered out. They were able to hold a continuous front. Finnish Battalion losses: 4 dead, 24 wounded, of which 5 were officers.

The days of 11 to 14 October were characterized by tenacious defensive combat. The initiative had switched over to the Soviets. The German battalions, which were formed into a crescent around Hill 701, dissipated. The 1st Company of the "Wiking" Panzer Battalion again relieved the 2nd Company and supported the defensive combat of the grenadiers. During these four days III/"Nordland" suffered another seven dead and 17 wounded. The balance sheets for I and II/"Germania" showed similar numbers. The companies were only at platoon strength.

Finally Hstuf. Hack's III/"Germania" arrived from the Western Caucasus. It approximately offset the combined losses of the I and II Battalions. The "Germania" Regiment, therefore, did not gain in combat strength. The III Battalion was inserted by companies on the long northern flank next to the 111th ID.

In order to advance the right flank of the 111th ID, the II/4 Pz.Rgt. (13th Panzer Division) was set in march to the 111th ID on 11 October. On 14 October at 0400 hours the battalion attacked with the 111th ID. With tanks leading, Hill 478.9 was captured against heavy enemy resistance. The attack stalled at Hill 390.9 to the north. On the right, contact was established with "Germania", which was able to take a neighboring hill in a spirited attack. The II/4 Pz.Rgt. had destroyed three Mark III tanks. German losses: one officer dead, two wounded. The total of eleven tanks lost through enemy action or because of technical damage shows the effect of the stress placed on the equipment in the mountainous terrain.

In the meantime, the 9th Rifle Brigade had to pay a high price near Hill 701 in front of the German positions. The time had arrived for a German counterattack. They regrouped during the night of 15 October. The 1/Pz.Abt. also prepared.

On 15 October the attack was launched with two main effort groups. Battalions Dieckmann and Nickel (70th Grenadier Regiment) with the 9/"Germania", supported by four rocket launcher batteries and four assault guns from the 191st Assault Gun Brigade and an engineer company from the 70th Grenadier Regiment attacked Hills 694 and 701 at 0700 hours. The attack stalled in enemy defensive fire after gaining little ground. In order to eliminate flanking fire from a Kolkhoz, the Finnish Battalion was committed at 1625 hours. At 1730 hours 9/"Nordland" was pinned on the flank. An outflanking maneuver was indicated. Ostuf. Pallesche ordered: "9th Company will fight its way back to the departure area!" The attack cost the Finnish Battalion another 13 dead and 16 wounded. Similar losses were registered by Battalions Dieckmann and Nickel.

On 16 October five tanks from the 1/Pz.Abt. "Wiking" advanced to support the attack of the III/"Nordland" on Hill 701. This time they were to attack without artillery fire preparation.

At 1730 hours, an unusual attack time, the battalion and the tanks advanced at great speed, which panicked the enemy and did not allow him time to establish his defense. This attack was reminiscent of the spirited attack on Lineinaya. At 1800 hours (after a half hour) Hill 701 was in the hands of the Finns. An enemy counterattack was repulsed from the hill. 80 prisoners were taken, five anti-tank guns and numerous infantry weapons were captured. The battalion suffered two dead and 16 wounded.

On the right the I and on the left the II/"Germania" captured the flanking hills and caught up. Hill 701 was fought over for seven days until it was finally captured by the Finnish Battalion. However, the Soviets would still not leave it alone.

On 17 October 1942 the combat diary of III/"Nordland" reported:

"0300 hours: A courier was dispatched to gather 25 men from the supply services as replacements.

0500 hours: Stronger enemy attack on Hill 701. Thick fog (visibility 30 meters) made it possible for the enemy to approach to within a small distance.

0515 hours: Company commanders of the 9th Company (Ostuf. Pallesche) and 11th Company (Ostuf. Mühlinghaus) severely wounded (both died from their wounds), Company Truppführer, Uscha. Sahlmann, dead. Forward observer from the 11/5 SS AR wounded; no contact with the forward observer 3/5 SS AR. The equipment was operated by a Fernsprechunterführer, who could also direct blocking fire. Ustuf. Ertel took command of the 9th Company. Hand-grenade battle.

0700 hours: The Russians have worked their way up to within 20 meters. Two enemy tanks counterattacked.

0730 hours: Friendly infantry gun and mortar fire stops the enemy right in front of the friendly positions. The hand-grenade battle continues.

0735 hours: 25 replacements temporarily filled the gaps.

0800 hours: Russian attack collapsed in a hand-grenade battle.

1400 hours: Russians again attacked with 300 men.

1402 hours: Blocking fire directed. Four enemy tanks in support.

1430 hours: Five enemy tanks counterattacked, two are disabled.

1445 hours: Strong infantry, mortar and anti-tank fire on the positions.

1515 hours: Commissars driving the Russians forward.

1635 hours: Hill 701, which was taken yesterday, remains in our possession with the fortified positions and bunkers, in spite of strong enemy attacks. 22 prisoners taken from the 337th Rifle Division (1127th and 1129th Regiments). Both regiments have attacked over the course of the past few days. Friendly losses: 11 dead and 36 wounded."

After a relatively quiet 18 October the combat flared up on 19 October again. Again from the combat diary of III/"Nordland":

"1200 hours: Enemy attacked in strength of 300 to 400 men.

1203 hours: Blocking fire directed.

1235 hours: On the left flank the enemy approached to within 50 meters and then stalled.

1250 hours: Forward observer from 5/5 SS AR dead. AVK directing fire.

1310 hours: Three friendly tanks counterattacked twice.

1330 hours: The enemy attack stalled 100 meters in front of the friendly HKL.

1535 hours: The Russians attacked again.

1615 hours: The hand-grenade battle is decided. The enemy suffered great loss. All attacks have collapsed. Hill 701 solidly in our hands. 19 prisoners.

2215 hours: The battalion is relieved by I/"Germania".

The Soviets tried for two days to retake Hill 701, but I/"Germania" repulsed all attacks. The few tanks from the "Wiking" Panzer Battalion had to be committed repeatedly. The "Wiking" Panzer Battalion had already established its winter quarters in Malgobek. The maintenance section of the panzer battalion worked untiringly, under Werkmeister Weise, to restore the damaged tanks.

Reciprocal relief was conducted throughout the division sector. Positions were improved and blocking positions/obstacles were erected. The troops organized for winter. The "Wiking" sector ran from the left neighbor, the 111th ID, north of Malgobek I, through the hills, including Hill 701, then swung back in a gentle bend to the southwest, crossed the valley approximately 4 kilometers west of Sagopshin and on the northern slope of the Mussakai to within approximately 4 kilometers east of Verkhniy Kurp, where it made contact with the 370th ID.

On 20 October 1942 General der Waffen SS Steiner was summoned to the 1st Panzer Army at Pyatigorsk in order to report to Generaloberst von Kleist and the visiting Army Chief of the General Staff, General Zeitzler. Steiner made it perfectly clear that he could not advance out of the Malgobek area with the forces available. He made sure that they understood that the area gained was paid for by high sacrifice. He refused to conduct any further attacks because he felt responsible to the Finnish people for the well-being of the Finnish Volunteer Battalion of the Waffen SS (III/"Nordland"). None of the participants could deny Steiner's arguments, and the tempest finally subsided.

A day later, on 21 October 1942, there was a regrouping for new operations. The III Panzer Corps was again to undertake the attempt to breakthrough the Russian front in the Baksan - Terek triangle and advance on Ordzhonikidze. The 13th and 23rd Panzer Divisions were also assembled. The 13th Panzer Division was withdrawn from the Elkhotovo - Verkhniy Akbash sector from 21 to 23 October and assembled in the Arik area. The 370th ID took over this division's sector, as they inserted their formations to the west. "Wiking" extended its front and took over the sector on either side of Verkhniy Kurp from the 370th ID.

During the attack of the III Panzer Corps, the Soviets were forced to weaken their front in the great Terek bend in order to deploy reserves to the front near Ordzhonikidze. Offensive combat ended in the Malgobek area, the front solidified.

At that time personnel changes were made in the SS Panzergrenadier Division "Wiking". The "Westland" Regiment was taken over by Stubaf. Polewacz; his former I/"Nordland" was taken by Stubaf. Lohmann. Oberführer Fritz von Scholz moved to the northern sector of the Eastern Front and took over the Latvian Brigade. The new regimental commander for "Nordland" was Ostubaf. Jörchel. II/"Germania" was taken over by Hstuf. May.

DEFENSE IN THE HIGH MOUNTAINS
The mountain winter arrives - Combat on Elbrus - The highest gun positions of the Second World War - Everything must be transported to the mountains - The valor of the surgeons and medics

In mid-September the winter began in the high mountains. Inevitably, all offensive operations came to a halt. The defense could essentially be conducted with fewer forces, if they were concentrated on the passes and crossings. This actually corresponded to the XXXXIX Mountain Corps withdrawing to the main ridges. The forces freed-up were deployed in the direction of Maikop for a second attack on Tuapse. The freed-up battalions of the 1st and 4th Mountain Divisions were organized under General Lanz into a divisional formation bearing his name.

Division Lanz was committed to the left of the XXXXIV Jäger Corps in the Caucasus Forest, where the winter arrived eight weeks later.

Each mountain division left one gebirgsjäger regiment on the 180 kilometer-long high mountain front. As winter continued the defensive forces in the high mountains were reduced even further. The defensive forces in the high mountains were organized under Oberst von Le Suire.

The gebirgsjäger positions on the high mountain front were located in the mountains at elevations between 2000 and 4000 meters. The tree line was at 1800 meters. The northern side of the mountains fell off steeply, the southern side more gradually. The defensive zone consisted of battlements, ridges, boulders, glaciers and fields of rubble. The highest German mountain positions were: on Kara-Kaya (3893 meters), on Aksaut (3908 meters), on Amanaus Pass on Belaya-Kaya (3919 meters), on Dombai-Ulgen (4040 meters), on Bu-Ulgen (3915 meters) and on Nakhar Pass with the Gvandra (3988 meters). Elbrus House and the Elbrus peak remained in German hands. Near the house, at 4300 meters, were the highest positions in German military history. Asau-Bashi at approximately 3800 meters held the record for the second highest artillery position in German military history (the highest was during the First World War: on the Königsspitze in the southern Tirol).

On 27 and 28 September 1942 one of the most unusual battles of the Second World War occurred in the Elbrus area at 4000 meters. Major Hans Mayr, the sector commander, reports:

"27 September 1942, command post, Elbrus sector: At 1700 hours the daily reports from strong points "Storch", "Traktorenweg", "Krugosor", "Felskop", "Chiper-Asau", "Asau Pass" and "Khotyu-Tau Pass" arrived. It was derived from almost all of the reports that the enemy probed out of the Baksam Valley at several locations and had been driven back by defensive fire. An enemy attack was evident. Therefore, listening posts were deployed.

Twilight set in the high Caucasus with a seldom seen play of colors over the mountains, the eastern and western peaks of Elbrus, Dongus-Orun and Ushba. The last bit of sunlight reflected off the snow fields in glittering colors.

At 2100 hours an enemy artillery barrage was suddenly launched on the

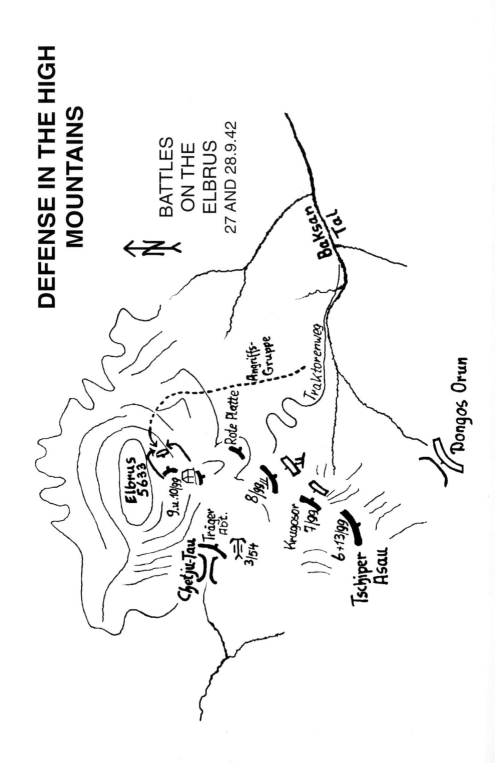

DEFENSE IN THE HIGH MOUNTAINS

N

BATTLES
ON THE
ELBRUS
27 AND 28.9.42

German positions, not sparing the command post in the meteorological building in the upper half of Elbrus House. Alerts were sounded in all of the positions and strong points. On "Traktorenweg", on the "Rotten Platte" and near "Krugosor", the enemy moved up his heavy infantry weapons to the German positions under the protection of the barrage. However, the advance stalled in the defensive fire of the German mortars and machine-guns. It did not appear likely that the enemy would infiltrate between the cracks in the Asau glacier during the night.

Several times the enemy concentrated fire on individual strong points, but the infantry attacks did not take place. We ceased firing in order to save ammunition. At 2300 hours the enemy fire leveled off and finally ceased completely. I could get no rest. What was the significance of the fire?

At 0400 hours, in the morning twilight, heavy machine-guns rattled on "Storchennest", the highest security post on the eastern slope of Elbrus at approximately 4800 meters. Alert! The unthinkable had happened. During the night the enemy infiltrated from the north through the breaks in the glacier and was attempting to roll over our positions at the Elbrus House. All reserves took up position! The enemy attack disappeared into a glacial depression 200 meters in front of strong point "Storchennest", it could no longer be engaged by our infantry weapons. Our Type 36 mountain cannon could not be committed because of the proximity. Our light machine-gun platoon was in position near the meteorological station, but only one gun was operational and even this one missed with the first rounds because of recoil damage. In the meantime, the Russians were firing mortars. They had to have a good observer located somewhere; the fire was well-placed. They were also not sparing ammunition. We now committed our mortars.

Rifle fire flared up again. The Soviets advanced from the depression on a wide front. They were difficult to make out in their camouflaged clothing and in the twilight. Finally it was daylight. In order to spare ammunition we ceased firing and committed longer ranged rounds. Wherever a head appeared over a rock, a shot was fired from our side. We estimated the enemy to be at company strength. We were unsure of his intent, especially since quiet reigned at all other strong points and the enemy still had not committed his artillery from the Baksan Valley and the Dongus-Orun.

At 0500 hours a German assault squad was located in the enemy's rear; they had worked their way around over ice, crevices and fissures. An attack on the enemy occupied snow depression could only lead to great sacrifice, so it was not conducted. The assault troop was assigned the mission to interfere with the withdrawal of the enemy. A Hiwi in our service was assigned the mission of crawling as close as possible to the Russian positions and induce them to defect. However, he had little success. The Hiwi returned with three wounded Soviets. Their interrogation revealed that an approximately 100 man-strng enemy group, led by a Senior Lieutenant and a commissar was attempting to climb the mountain. 20 men had already fallen and another 20 were wounded.

A second assault squad advanced against the enemy occupied snow depression. Again the Hiwi asked the Soviets to give up. Our mortars again fired into the depression. Then the two assault squads attacked. 57 Russians were captured. Their leader, a senior lieutenant, was a mountain guide on Elbrus. He was shot by the commissar and wounded. The commissar committed suicide during the German attack, after he had realized the hopelessness of the battle.

The enemy group had the mission of recapturing the Elbrus House. They had been climbing the eastern Elbrus peak from the north for three nights and had hidden in depressions during the daytime. Their armament consisted of automatic weapons. The attack on the Elbrus House was to have occurred on 27 September at 2300 hours, but unforeseen difficulties encountered during the negotiation of a glacier fissure had so delayed the deployment that the attack could not begin until 28 September at 0400 hours.

In the afternoon Russian aircraft overflew the German positions. Perhaps they were looking for their comrades. The German flag still waved over the meteorological station."

After many damp, foggy and rainy days, the first half of October was sunny and clear. On 13 October the frost and snowfall arrived. After five days the snow cover was 80 cm deep on the passes. At the end of October the snow depth increased to two meters. Snow storms and new snowfall piled up the snow to four meters in some places. And that was still not all! Dark clouds swept in from the Black Sea with high humidity, covering the ridges and valleys with white flakes.

With the arrival of winter there were difficulties that could be overcome only with the help of all of the soldiers in the high mountain front. This was true for both sides.

The first solid winter positions sprung up around passes. The entire defense was constructed around main strong points, which were tied together by smaller positions. A continuous mountain front, as in the First World War, was not possible. First there were nests and small combat positions, which were established in the rocks and were later expanded. Some were covered with tents for shelter. Later they were mounted on the stone walls to create more room. The artillery observers also set up their observation posts. Most of the time the heavy weapons were set up in the forward-most line in order to be able to place all of the surrounding area under fire from the dominant position. Often the positions were selected so that they could trip rocky avalanches. They could also be tripped by heavy machine-gun and mortar fire. At these elevations wood is a rarity, the tree line was much lower. Heated shelters had to be created because of the increasing cold. 20-30 man block huts were constructed. The block huts were constructed in sections in the forest camps by the engineers and moved to the mountain positions, where they were assembled. One hut would require approximately 400 loads.

From this description it can be seen that everything the gebirgsjäger needed to live or fight had to be transported: rations and ammunition, stoves and fuel. In many cases, pack animals could no longer be utilized; only the men could do it.

The mountain engineers were the right-hand men of the gebirgsjägers, they had to construct paths and footbridges, block huts, stoves and sleds. In addition, in the beginning, they had to construct the positions; in many cases, small connecting paths had to be blasted in the rock.

The radiomen had no less important a job. One of the most important prerequisites for a successful defense in the mountains is a well-functioning radio net. Often flag signals, light signals and megaphones were also used.

Surgeons and medics are seldom mentioned in military history books, even though they provide a particularly important service. While combat at the front threatens life with destruction, the surgeons and medics fight for the lives of the wounded. Any monument erected to these men would be too small. Listen to the testimony of one of the wounded, Gefreiter Zech, from the 4th Mountain Division:

"At the end of September combat in the Urushten and Malaya Laba Valleys flared up again (on the right flank of the 4th Mountain Division). The Russians had forced back our weak security to the north and attempted to isolate the 4th Mountain Division with the capture of the Umpyrski Pass. Elements of the 91st Gebirgsjäger Regiment, the 94th Mountain Reconnaissance Battalion and the 94th Feldersatz [Field Replacement] Battalion were committed to the counterattack in order to throw the Russians back across the Pseshcha and Aishcha Passes. We were able to throw the enemy back, but the passes remained in his hands. The battle lasted from 1 to 10 October 1942.

On 8 October I was wounded in the Urushten Pass. Between 1700 and 1800 hours I was hit in the right upper thigh. I temporarily bandaged myself. Then my comrades carried me back from the rocky position. I was ultimately transported on a small mountain trail for three hours, where there was still no sign of trees. I received a tetanus shot at a block hut. On the next day, at 0700 hours, a larger transport of 14 wounded was organized. Russian prisoners with two German escorts carried us on makeshift stretchers made from branches and canvass for 15 hours through strong point "Weberhütte" (between Urushten and Malaya Laba Valleys) to M 1 (main first aid station in the Malaya Laba Valley). There, in the light of a carbide lamp, my right leg was amputated. A day later, a "Fieseler Storch" arrived, but it could not land. At midday on 11 October I was carried with six other comrades on a seven hour march to strong point U (approximately 7 kilometers north in the Malaya Laba Valley). On the next day, after a 10 hour march (10 kilometers), we made it just shy of strong point M (Kirovskiy, at the confluence of the Urushten into the Malaya Laba), where ambulances waited at the beginning of a road at the fall of darkness. They brought us to the field hospital."

When Gefreiter Zech was wounded, the mountain winter had begun in the Urushten Valley. The treatment of the wounded and their evacuation became more difficult as winter progressed. By then akyas and ski sleds were being used.

Deployed in the high mountain front from east to west (Gruppe von Le Suire) at the end of December were: 99th Gebirgsjäger Regiment (minus I/99, that was committed in the 1st Panzer Army area of operations), the 94th Feldersatz Battalion, the 2nd High Mountain Battalion, 94th Mountain

Reconnaissance Battalion, I/79 Geb.AR and II/94 Geb.AR.

The gebirgsjägers of these units not only fought against the enemy, they also had to struggle against the forces of nature.

SECOND ATTACK ON TUAPSE

The season presses on - Mount Tunnel falls - The stuka as flying mountain artillery - Shaumyan - The struggle for the Oplepek - Blood and sweat soak the Semashcho - The great horse extermination

At the beginning of September the forward-most forces of the XXXXIX Mountain Corps pulled back to the passes on the main ridge line in order to defend there. Combat bogged down in the frost and snow. Based on the weather situation, the German leadership came up with a new plan:

1. The main ridge line can be defended with fewer forces.

2. Half of the forces of the XXXXIX Mountain Corps can, therefore, be freed-up to attack through to Tuapse.

3. The breakthrough would be through the Caucasus Forest, where winter would not arrive for another eight weeks.

By the end of September the assigned objective was not achieved. The XXXXIX Mountain Corps had to go over to the defense in the high Caucasus. The XXXXIV Jäger Corps was left on the road to Tuapse in the Caucasus Forest. It was no better on the right flank of the 17th Army. And time marched on! The mountain winter had already made its entrance in the high passes.

Because of the lack of forces the leap over the mountains had to fail. Hitler passed the blame onto others. The commander of Army Group A, Feldmarschall List, had to go, because he refused to operate any further with so few forces. And the Italian Alpine Corps, which was assigned for commitment in the Caucasus, was marching on Stalingrad.

Now they were to again attack Tuapse with strong forces. For this purpose Division "Lanz" was formed from the 1st and 4th Mountain Divisions. It was to set out on the left flank, after the XXXXIV Jäger Corps moved up.

On 14 September the commander of the XXXXIX Mountain Corps was summoned to Vinnitsa in order to discuss the new plans. Hitler asked General Konrad: "When can you attack south of Maikop on the left flank of the XXXXIV Jäger Corps?"

General Konrad knew that his freed-up forces were deploying from the mountain front and replied: "Approximately on 1 October!"

"That seems too late to me. I think more like 25 September!"

During the following days the march groups of Division "Lanz" approached the city of Maikop. The French 46th ID marched from the Crimea and relieved elements of "Wiking" and the 97th Jäger Division in the area south of Apsherovskaya and in the Pshekha Valley. The 97th Jäger Division advanced on the Tuapse Pass road. The LVII Panzer Corps deployed west of the pass, while the 198th ID concentrated its attack forces in the area south of Goryachiy - Klyuch. Elements of the 125th ID, which were adjacent to the west, were also brought up. The Fast Slovak Division, which secured the link on the Asfaltevaya - Goryachiy - Klyuch road, was to join in the attack.

After they took up their assembly areas, the organization reflected the following:

1. On the right (west): LVII Panzer Corps with elements of the 125th ID, 198th ID and Fast Slovak Division. This battle group was to cover the right attack flank and join in the attack of the XXXXIV Jäger Corps.

2. Center: XXXXIV Jäger Corps with the 101st Jäger Division on the right and the 97th Jäger Division on the left. This corps would fight on both sides of the road to Tuapse.

3. Left (east): XXXXIX Mountain Corps with Mountain Division "Lanz" and the 46th ID. While the 46th ID protected the left flank, Mountain Division "Lanz" was to advance out of the Neftyanaya area across Mount Gunaiy toward Goich and Indyuk and open the coastal road by a flanking attack. We will forestall the description of the attack and examine the mission of the Mountain Division "Lanz", which was organized for combat on 27 September 1942.

How utopian the mission of Division "Lanz" was, in view of the unbelievably difficult forested terrain and the extreme difficulty of supply, is indicated by the following combat organization:

98th Mountain Jäger Rgt with I, II and III/98

13th Mountain Jäger Rgt with II and III/13

79th Mountain AR with II and III/79 and I/94 Geb.AR

Gruppe Winkler with the 54th Feldersatz Bn

Gruppe Sommer with IV/79 Geb.AR and IV/94 Geb.AR

48th Heeres Engineer Bn (Herzog)

During the course of the coming weeks these forces were often joined by resubordinated battalions of the 46th ID and the III/114 AR.

With this meager force a frontal sector of at least 25 kilometers (Goich to Oplepek), at times as wide as 32 kilometers (Shaumyan to Oplepek), was to be attacked through an impassible forest and then held in defense.

The experienced will immediately be skeptical as to this operation's chances of success. The negative experience in the Caucasus would lead one to be very pessimistic.

The German regrouping did not remain a secret. The double fuselage "Focke-Wulf" reconnoitered the enemy situation every day.

On the Russian side, the "Black Sea Group of the Transcaucasus Front" under the commander General I. Petrov increased its defensive efforts. The 18th Army, in the anticipated main axis, and the 56th Army, near Goryachiy - Klyuch, prepared reserves. In the meantime, the defeatist attitude and war-weariness were overcome by the rigorous intervention of the STAVKA and the Central Committee of the Communist Party and the entire defense in the Caucasus was reorganized. Numerous new formations were marched in. The key lay on the road to Tuapse. Both sides concentrated all of their efforts there.

On 23 September at 0900 hours the great autumn offensive against Tuapse began under the cover-name "Attika". The left flank regiment of the 125th ID (Generalleutnant Schneckenburger), the 419th Grenadier Regiment with the subordinate I/326 of the 198th ID, captured the dominant, 451 meter high Mount Lyssaya south of Goryachiy - Klyuch, after an intensive artillery and air preparation, and, therefore, created the prerequisite for an attack into the Psekups Valley to the south in the direction of Shaumyan.

On 24 September the attack battalions of the Baden- Württemberg 198th ID set out from the area south of Goryachiy - Klyuch as the main striking force. By evening the 308th and 305th Regiments had reached the ridge line on either side of Osunavo and thrown back the enemy.

The divisional commander, Generalmajor Müller, assigned the 198th ID a clear mission for 25 September:

"308th Grenadier Regiment on the right, 305th Grenadier Regiment in the center and the 326th Grenadier Regiment on the left will attack to the Popova Ridge and capture the town of Besymyannoe. The 419th Grenadier Regiment will advance into the Psekups Valley."

The regiments quickly reached the foot of the Popova Ridge, but the enemy defense then stiffened. A battle flared up in the thick forested terrain, man against man. Assault guns supported the attack, but the terrain obstacles were insurmountable. During the evening the 308th and 305th Regiments stood on the Popova Ridge. The left flank regiment, the 326th, stalled in front of the dominant Hill 514.2. The hill was the key to the attack objective, Besymyannoe.

On 26 September the attack continued. German fighter-bombers were guided into the combat area by artillery smoke shells and the Flivo. The forest was bombed and strafed by on-board weapons. The 395th Soviet Rifle Division defended in well camouflaged bunkers and went over to a counter-attack at one location. On 27 and 28 September the battle for Hill 514.2 was decided; it was finally captured. From the area south of Kutayskaya advanced the Fast Slovak Division, whose II/20 made contact with the 198th ID, which, in the meantime, had fought its way toward the village of Khatyps.

On 29 September Battle Group Fasel (198th ID) attacked Besymyannoe. The battle group consisted of three assault guns, one engineer company and one tank destroyer company. The attack was conducted in conjunction with the 419th Grenadier Regiment of the 125th ID. Only the 11/235 AR could support the attack from its firing positions south of Goryachiy - Klyuch. An artilleryman reported in the History of the 198th ID:

"From our tree on the Popova Ridge we could pick out the 308th, as they worked their way from the northwest to the protection of the Psekups cliffs. Gruppe Fasel moved its anti-tank guns up. The infantry groups halted. Heavy machine-guns were set up in position on the slope. Then the infantrymen swung over the slope and assaulted the town. There the Russians were trying to bring the Maxim machine-gun into position. The battle began and it appeared that it would stall in the Russian defensive fire, as the other attacks had. Then the Russians were engaged in the east by the 421st Grenadier Regiment and thrown into confusion. In the meantime, our heavy field howitzer was ready to fire. Was the fire order accurate? An error in calculation would send the shell into the middle of our own troops or onto the observation post. - "Second gun, fire!" - Hearts raced. After 40 seconds the first shell shrieked over our heads into the valley. - "Attention, detonation!" - There was fire, dust and smoke in the southern portion of the town. - "Down 100 meters! Entire battery four groups!" - Soon there was a wall of fire. Our grenadiers made use of the enemy's confusion and assaulted. Additional salvoes slammed in and completely broke their resistance. The Russians ran back, our shells followed them. By evening, Besymyannoe was in our hands."

On 30 September Mount Fonari had to fall, as it threatened the conquered town from the flank. At 1130 hours Stukas attacked Mount Fonari. Fighter-bombers attacked targets designated by smoke. The lead elements of the 305th Grenadier Regiment set markers. The 326th Grenadier Regiment worked its way from the northeast. Mount Fonari was a bubbling volcano. At 1435 hours the 326th Grenadier Regiment reported: "Mount Fonari is in our hands!"

On the same day the 308th Grenadier Regiment attacked out of the Besymyannoe area into the Psekups Valley, captured Hill 326.4 and, in the evening, the town of Fanagoriskoe. Elements of Heeres artillery and the division artillery followed and took up positions in the Besymyannoe area.

1 October was noted for heavy counterattacks. The regiments of the 198th ID went over to the defense. The 421st Grenadier Regiment closed ranks at Fanagoriskoe. So much for the course of the attack of the LVII Panzer Corps.

Now we will turn to the XXXXIV Jäger Corps on the road to Tuapse:

The Baden-Württemberg 101st Jäger Division was located in the Khadyshenskaya area at the beginning of the attack. It was reinforced with the 72nd Grenadier Regiment of the 46th ID.

The Bavarian 97th Jäger Division, which was relieved in the area south of Neftegorsk by Mountain Division "Lanz", was located further to the west. Both divisions were to advance while maintaining close contact and remaining adjacent to the road. The attack of the XXXXIV Jäger Corps began on 25 September after an artillery and air preparation.

The 101st Jäger Division, which attacked with the 229th Regiment (including the 500th Training Battalion), 72nd Grenadier Regiment (46th ID) and out from the Paparotniy frontal salient with the 228th Jäger Regiment, first had to capture the dominant Mount Tunnel and the entrance to the long railroad tunnel west of Khadyshenskaya. The already half- encircled bastion of Mount Tunnel was defended by the 32nd Guards Rifle Division. General Petrov, commander of the "Black Sea Group", was not let down by the 32nd Guards Rifle Division. The soldiers of this elite Soviet formation fought like the devil. The German attack did not achieve any success there. Generalmajor Diestel reorganized and threw the 228th Jäger Regiment around to the north in order to capture Mount Tunnel with both regiments. The 228th Jäger Regiment marched for the entire night from the left to the right flank. The left flank in the Paporotniy area was covered by Gruppe von Amsberg (reconnaissance battalion, Turkish Battalion and engineer training battalion). The main effort also now lay to the west of the Tuapse road.

On 26 September the battalions resumed the attack. The 72nd Grenadier Regiment took several bunkers on the southern exit of the railroad tunnel and gradually advanced to the south. At 1000 hours the 229th Jäger Regiment attacked after a strong artillery fire preparation, penetrated into the Soviet defenses after costly combat and fought around Hill 519.6. The 228th Jäger Regiment followed into the same area. Combat in the 72nd Grenadier Regiment area of operations lasted all day. They were effectively supported by the I/4 Flak-Rgt. and the 3/210 Stu.Geschtz.Brig. The 32nd Soviet Guards Rifle Division made the Germans pay dearly for each meter of ground.

Things were different in the 97th Jäger Division area of operations. They attacked on 26 September with the 207th Jäger Regiment on the right (adjacent to the 101st Jäger Division) and the 204th Jäger Regiment on the left. After breaking through several forest and bunker positions, the 204th Jäger Regiment captured the 704 meter high Mount Lyssaya after a fierce battle and against the resistance of the 236th Rifle Division.

The combat report from the 204th Jäger Regiment describes the fierce combat around this mountain on the following day:

"In the early morning of 27 September the enemy, who had reorganized during the night, counterattacked, firing out of all tubes and yelling "Hurrah!" The available engineer assault troop from the 2/97 Pi.Btl. was thrown against the enemy and brought the attack to a halt. However, the enemy immediately launched an attack under the leadership of a commissar with shouts of "Hurrah!" The remaining elements of the III/204, which had been brought forward in the meantime, were immediately committed against the counterattack and the enemy was thrown back in hand-to-hand combat. Then the enemy launched another counterattack and so, for a third time in a row, a counter-counterattack was conducted from the positions. The "Hurrahs" of the entire III/204 mixed with the "Hurrahs" of the Russians, the detonations of the hand-grenades and the firing of machine-pistols. The combat around the mountain was the bitterest yet experienced by the regiment. Losses were high, but by the end of the attack the positions were still in our hands."

On 29 September the initial attack momentum of the 97th Jäger Division was used up. Too many requirements were placed on the troops. Above all, forces had to be diverted to secure on both sides of Mount Lyssaya. A strong enemy bunker line ran throughout, which, for the time being, frustrated the breakthrough to the south.

On 27 September at 1100 hours, in the 101st Jäger Division sector, the 2/500 z.b.V. launched a spirited attack into the Soviet main defensive line southeast of 519.6 and reached the Minerya trench. Immediately the breakthrough was widened by elements of the 228th and 229th Regiments. At the same time, the 72nd Grenadier Regiment (46th ID) fought its way through to the Khadyshenskaya railroad station between the rail line and the road.

During the morning of 28 September the 229th Jäger Regiment, which was fighting on the right flank, broke through additional defensive lines, but it stalled in front of the village of Kurinskiy. Leutnant Kult had more success with his 3/228. In a spirited attack the company captured a hill directly north of Kurinskiy, which dominated the road to Tuapse. On 29 September the counterattacks of the 32nd Guards Rifle Division increased. Advantages were gained during the counter-counterattacks. The 72nd Grenadier Regiment captured Pervomaiskiy, near the Khadyshenskaya railroad station. 30 September was characterized by fierce defensive combat. Concentrated artillery fire from four battalions was conducted on Russian held positions south of the Khadyshenskaya railroad station in order to destroy enemy assembly areas. On 1 October the situation did not change very much. Both sides were exhausted. Reconnaissance was conducted and positions were probed. Even the artillery fire of the 85th Artillery Regiment on the Kurinskiy area was ended on this day.

The 3/88 Pi.Btl. (mot.) under Oberleutnant Krauss also fought as part of the 72nd Grenadier Regiment. Oberleutnant Krauss had played a big part in the struggle against and the removal of the numerous bunkers. He skillfully led a flame-thrower assault troop against the numerous forest bunkers and, most of the time, he had a flame-thrower on his own back. Because of this commitment Krauss was recognized by the German Army.

Right after discovering the German attack on the road to Tuapse the Soviet leadership deployed additional reserves. From 28 - 30 September the destroyer "Nezamozhnik" and the escort "Storm" transported over 8000 men of the 408th Rifle Division from Poti to Tuapse.

The first phase of Operation "Attika" took shape in the XXXXIX Mountain Corps area of operations as follows:

Coming from Maikop, Division "Lanz" advanced into the Neftegorsk area, where the 98th Mountain Jäger Regiment took over the former positions of the 97th Jäger Division. The mission of the division formed from elements of the 1st and 4th Mountain Divisions read: Attack out of the Neftyanaya area across Mount Gunai toward Goich. The 46th ID followed on the left flank and covered the advance near Maratuk.

On 27 September Division "Lanz" attacked in the following combat order: on the right with objective Nr.1, Mount Geiman, Major Reisinger's 1st High Mountain Battalion. On the left with objective Nr. 1, Mount Gunai, the 98th Mountain Jäger Regiment under Oberstleutnant Salminger. To the left of Salminger was the 13th Gebirgsjäger Regiment under Oberst Buchner with Oberst Auer's subordinate 42nd Grenadier Regiment (46th ID). On the left flank securing near Mount Oplepek and around Samurskaya were Groups Winkler and Eisgruber.

The attack of Division "Lanz" began on 27 September. A day later the French 46th ID (General Haccius) arrived on the left flank.

The combat region was an almost trackless, uninhabited forested area with subtropical vegetation. Elevations over 1000 meters and numerous stream valleys favored the Russian defenders. The South German and Austrian troops of Division "Lanz" fought their way through bunker lines and obstacles, effectively supported by Oberst Sommer's artillery group. On 29 September Mount Gunai (1078 meters) fell to the 98th Mountain Jäger Regiment. A little later the 1st High Mountain Battalion conquered the 1060 meter high Geiman against fierce resistance. At the same time, Battle Group Buchner (13th Mountain Jäger Regiment) advanced into the source region of the Gunaika. This deep flanking attack threatened the Soviet defenses on the Tuapse road near Kurinskiy. If Division "Lanz" succeeded in advancing to the west into the Gunaika Valley, then the Soviet forces in front of the XXXXIV Jäger Corps would be threatened in the rear. However, the resistance also increased considerably in the "Lanz" sector. It became ever more difficult to advance German artillery into the narrow mountain valleys.

The attack formations fought their way through the natural mountain and forest obstacles with difficulty; the enemy defended skillfully. The artillery, which they brought with them, and the heavy artillery, which Gruppe Winkler advanced on the left flank, only seldom found targets to engage. Often the deep valleys and the air cover did not allow them to be employed.

In this case another weapon had to be substituted. It was provided by the I Gruppe of the 77th Stuka Wing (Major Orthofer), which was located in Belorechenskaya, 60 kilometers from the combat area. For a lively description of this "flying artillery" we read in the diary of Stuka Pilot Jung:

"While flying back we heard target instructions for our staffel being passed by "Kommissar". "Kommissar", that was the cover name of the Kommodore of the I/77 Stuka Geschwader, Major Orthofer, called "Ali" by his men for short, had the sharp eyes of a hawk and was a master of the Ju 87. He circled for hours over the combat area without fighter support, penetrated deep through the thick forests and searched out targets, which he then turned over to the staffel.

Other than a few passes, there were only some mule tracks which led off into the forest. Deployment, concentration and redeployment of artillery was a problem in this terrain. It was completely unsuitable for tanks. Therefore, the stuka had to take over the missions of the heavy weapons.

For us pilots it was difficult to find targets. We could only recognize the friendly lines by colored cloths or light signals which were raised out of the thickets. We had to constantly change the color of the recognition signals because the Russians would use them to their own benefit. The Soviet nests of resistance often lay directly in front of the friendly positions. The use of "flying reconnaissance troops" and "flying command posts" were the tactical solutions to these targeting problems.

Unassuming mule trails often had strategic significance in the mountain forests. Often a well-placed bomb would block movement in the forests for several hours. The Russians were constantly improving their single tracked rail stretches. We hunted for an armored train for three days that consistently hid in a tunnel until it came out on the tracks. The lead German troops were only four railroad stations distant from Tuapse.

The Russians had established several anti-aircraft regiments near Tuapse in order to escort supplies to the threatened front from the sea. Whenever a transport arrived our squadron was given a maritime mission. The flight to Tuapse included the anti-aircraft hell of Novorossisk.

The anti-aircraft rounds exploded among the white clouds. The pier lay 3000 meters below us. In the vicinity was a 5000 ton tanker, around which was a ring of anti-aircraft and coastal boats. We probed through this fire screen for the vertical attack. Altitude, speed and wind direction all had to be taken into consideration. The aircraft would pull away at 600 meters. The pilot would use all of the tricks he knew to avoid the anti-aircraft fire. On the flight out the batteries in the mountains above the harbor would also fire at us.

Then the battle with the Russian fighters began. 500 meters behind me appeared a Soviet fighter, he was in an ideal firing position. My radioman drove him off with the machine-gun. Then another fighter angled in from the right, but the radioman drove him off too. A Yak 3 with a red Soviet star whistled by us, passing within 10 meters. I went into a steep climbing curve; a round slammed into the tail unit. At the last light of the day, we landed in Belorechenskaya."

This report from a stuka pilot indicates the difficulties confronted by the pilots. Stukagruppe Orthofer, which had to support the attack on Tuapse alone, did so as long as weather conditions permitted. They were too weak to help throughout.

After regrouping and assembling all available units, the 101st Jäger Division launched the 228th, 72nd and 229th Regiments into the attack. On 3 October the elongated town of Kurinskiy was captured. The division was again exhausted and had to take a breather. So did the opposing 32nd Guards Rifle Division.

The 198th ID fought in the area around Fanagoriskoe for additional advantage. On 3 October the regiments were tied up with the mopping up of the area because the Soviets were a constant threat to the lines of communication in the deep western flank. The security front of the following 125th ID was already over-extended. They could no longer oversee the deep western flank.

On 4 October the situation on the western flank was cleared up, but the Soviets also kept this in mind. III/308 was encircled by the 255th Naval Infantry Brigade on Hill 326, 3 kilometers northeast of Fanagoriskoe. They were able to breakout to Fanagoriskoe with their last ounce of strength. The critical situation in the 326.4 - Fanagoriskoe - Mount Fanori area lasted until 10 October. Then the counterattack of the 395th Soviet Rifle Division grew weary.

How was the left flank of the attack going?

On 4 October Gruppe Winkler (54th Feldersatz Battalion, 1/79 Geb.AR,

1/86 Pz.Jg.Abt.) captured the mountain village of Maratuki after an attack out of the Neftyanaya area. A day later the 46th ID captured the 1010 meter high Oplepek. Still further to the east elements of the 97th Regiment blocked the lower Pshekh Valley.

Gruppe Auer (III/72, I and III/42) fought its way through the mountains to the west in order to maintain contact with Division "Lanz". In the course of this advance Gruppe Auer and elements of Gruppe Buchner fought all day around the small village of Kotlovina.

On 13 October the Soviets counterattacked against the left flank of the XXXXIX Mountain Corps in order to relieve their troops on the Tuapse road. In an outflanking attack they were able to push back the II/97 Gren.Rgt., which was securing the Pshekh Valley, and recapture the dominant Oplepek. A hill located to the south was held by Leutnant Scholtes and engineers from the 2/88 Pi.Btl. against a day-long enemy attack, until it could be later incorporated into the defensive line. From then on the hill was known as "Scholtes Hill".

After a pause, the jäger regiments of the 101st Jäger Division and the subordinated 72nd Grenadier Regiment set out again on 13 October. After a strong artillery and air preparation the 228th and 229th Regiments advanced in assault to a line 327.3 - 166.4.

At the same time the 97th Jäger Division attacked. Oberstleutnant Nobis' battle group reached the Pshekh Valley with the II/204 and 97th Reconnaissance Battalion, after overcoming numerous bunker lines, and established contact with the 101st Jäger Division. At the same time Oberstleutnant Otte's battle group advanced into the Shubinka Valley to the southwest and, after a Stuka bombardment, took the forested hill south of the Shubinka and, by evening, the small town of Navaginski.

During the evening Corps Order Nr. 123 arrived at the division headquarters of the 101st and 97th Jäger Divisions: "On 14 October the 101st Jäger Division will continue the successful attack with its main body along the Pshekh across Hill 527 toward Navaginski. Enemy influence on the Kurinskiy basin is to be eliminated. Some forces will support the attack of Battle Group Nobis by attacking out of the northwest against Hill 356.3. The division will determine the start of the attack."

On 14 October the struggle for the Pshekh bend began. While the 72nd Grenadier Regiment covered the northwestern flank in the Kura Valley region, the 229th Jäger Regiment, under Major Schury, advanced on Hill 527. The 228th Jäger Regiment, under the leadership of Oberstleutnant Schratz, veered off to the west into the Pshekh bend and, in cooperation with Battle Group Nobis, took Hill 356.3, which lay in the Pshekh bend 6 kilometers south of Kurinskiy.

On 15 October the further attack of the XXXXIV Jäger Corps failed against the tenacious Soviet defense. The corps also had to stop because its right flank was insufficiently protected; the LVII Panzer Corps had to first catch up.

During the night of 13 October the 308th Grenadier Regiment was relieved by elements of the 125th ID in the Fanagoriskoe area and prepared to attack the ridge line north of Khatyps with the 326th Grenadier Regiment.

On 14 October at 0500 hours German artillery fire was committed; at 0600 hours so were Stukas. The hills north of Khatyps shook as if hit by a powerful hammer. The infantry attack gained ground; the 326th Grenadier regiment veered off to the west, the 308th Grenadier Regiment to the east in order to bypass the hill positions. A bitter struggle ensued. A relief attack by the II/20 IR (Slovak) created some breathing space. In the I/326 area of operations the battalion commander, Hauptmann Scherg, fell heavily wounded. Major Grassmann's II/326 advanced. However, Grassmann was also wounded and the attack threatened to stall. Grassmann bandaged himself, rushed back to the front and rallied the attack again. After a new Slovak relief attack, the 326th captured the northwestern portion of the Khatyps ridge. The 308th Grenadier Regiment, which was attacking to the southeast, destroyed the headquarters of the Soviet 714th Rifle Regiment, which then dispersed leaderless. The Fast Slovak Division advanced up to Hill 225.8, 3 kilometers east of Khatyps. The Soviet 714th and 726th Regiments were completely wiped out.

The attack of the 198th ID continued on 15 and 16 October. Adjacent to the Psekups Valley, by evening of 17 October, the 308th Grenadier Regiment fought through the wild mountain forest and against the fierce enemy resistance to the foot of Hill 614.4, the western corner-stone of the Kochkanova ridge. The 326th Grenadier Regiment followed and covered the long eastern flank against Tri Duba (Three Oaks). In the meantime, the 305th Grenadier Regiment was freed-up by elements of the 125th ID near Fanagoriskoe. The 235th Engineer Battalion had already repaired the supply route up to Khatyps and secured it against enemy stragglers.

A day-long, bitter battle flared up around the Kochkanova ridge. This was a threat to the German attack on Tuapse in its western flank.

In the meantime, Division "Lanz" advanced further to the west in order to pin the Soviet defense, which fronted the XXXXIV Jäger Corps in the Mount Sedlo - Elissavetpolskiy Pass sector, in the rear. On 15 October the road-railroad intersection 2 kilometers south of Shaumyan was opened. The report of the XXXXIX Mountain Corps described the difficulty of the battle:

"In 19 days of battle in the trackless mountain forests Division "Lanz" attacked through 98 bunker groups, taking 1083 combat positions. In this manner the battle group of the 98th Mountain Jäger Regiment attacked 36 kilometers deep into the 1000 meter high mountain forest, the battle group of the 13th Mountain Jäger Regiment 40 kilometers deep. As a result of the bitter resistance on the extremely difficult terrain German losses were high. Remaining on the battlefield [dead] were: 5 officers, 384 non-commissioned officers and men. 53 officers and 1417 non-commissioned officers and men were wounded."

On 16 October the 1st High Mountain Battalion (Reisinger) reached the last hill directly east of Shaumyan. Battle Group Otte was coming from the north and Battle Group Nobis was coming from the south. All forces were located in a half-circle around Shaumyan. The elongated town lay in a beautiful valley. The Russians had evacuated the town and the Germans also did not bring

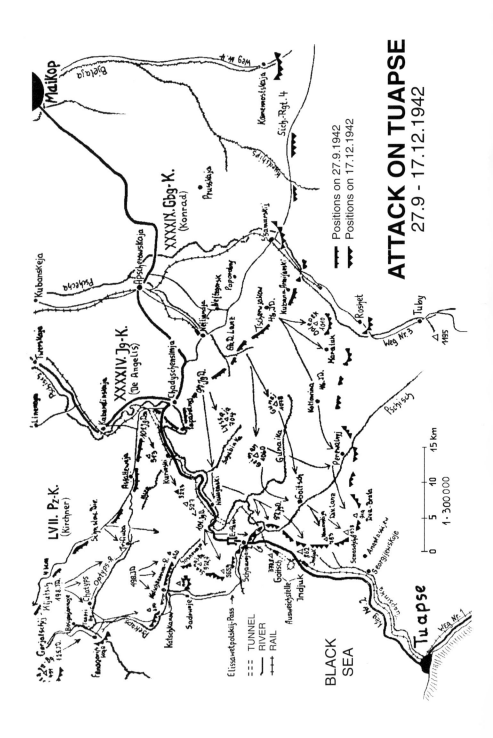

ATTACK ON TUAPSE
27.9 - 17.12.1942

Positions on 27.9.1942
Positions on 17.12.1942

TUNNEL
RIVER
RAIL

BLACK
SEA

1 : 300 000

0   5   10   15 km

up large forces because the Shaumyan Valley was dominated by Russian artillery, their observers had an excellent view from Mount Indyuk, which lay 7 kilometers to the south. Forces of the 97th Jäger Division soon followed into the front north of the Pshekh Valley in order to free-up the Reisinger High Mountain Battalion and elements of the 98th Mountain Jäger Regiment located there. Lanz needed these forces for the upcoming attack on the last ridges in front of Tuapse. Because the road in the Pshekh Valley was still being blocked by an enemy group north of Shaumyan, supplies for Division "Lanz" had to be run across Mount Gunai into the Gunaika Valley. This was an indescribable burden on the supply and for the evacuation of the wounded! The heavy weapons also had to be deployed through such efforts.

Oberst Sommer, the Arko [artillery commander] of Division "Lanz", had his concerns. Several guns made it to Kotlavina. The [type] 36 mountain guns were advancing over difficult mountain trails. Division "Lanz" was preparing for the attack into the upper Pshekh Valley and on the last ridges in front of Tuapse.

In the meantime, the fierce combat on the western flank continued. Even though the Soviets north of Shaumyan had to fight on three sides, they did not give in. They defended tenaciously against the 198th Infantry and 101st Jäger Divisions. The grenadier regiments of the 198th ID struggled over the Kochkanova ridge. On 18 October it began to rain. The routes turned into morasses. Supply and artillery could only follow with great effort. For a conventional infantry division, like the 198th, the unusual mountain combat required imagination and improvisation from the officers and men.

The 326th took Hill 614.4 on the western portion of the Kochkanova ridge and, therefore, had a view into the town of Kochkanov and the upper Psekups Valley. The 305th Grenadier Regiment fought around Hill 620 without success. The remnants of the Soviet 417th, 723rd and 726th Rifle Regiments defended there, they were organized under new leadership. As the attack of the 101st Jäger Division progressed and threatened the Soviets in their eastern flank, they evacuated Hill 620.8, which was then immediately occupied by elements of the 305th Grenadier Regiment. During the following days, both sides probed with reconnaissance and harassment.

On 24 October the 101st Jäger Division, adjacent on the left, fought in the Hill 565.4 (Mount Sedlo) area. The 500th Battalion, which had taken the 772.4 meter high Mount Sarai on the day before, assisting the 198th ID on the eastern portion of the Kochkanova ridge, captured Hill 490 a little bit further to the south on 24 October. The III/229 captured Hill 565.4 and the II/229 took Hill 475.8 to the east. Therefore, the Soviet defense on the Elissavetpolskiy Pass was slowly being outmaneuvered. The 228th Jäger Regiment advanced into the area south of Shaumyan and prepared to attack to the south in order to follow the attack of Gruppe Lanz.

On 25 October the Soviets attacked the extended western flank of the 101st Jäger Division. The 500th Battalion could no longer hold out on Hill 470.9 and withdrew to the north. Two companies of this battalion lost their way during the night and experienced an adventure fighting their way back to friendly lines. In the south, the III/229 was encircled near Hill 565.4 (Mount Sedlo). By radio request, the high mountain platoon of the 101st Jäger Division was to reinforce the III/229 and, simultaneously, bring ammunition and rations. The leader of the high mountain platoon, Oberleutnant Dannemann, wrote the following about the indescribable efforts of the men and animals: "The route led through difficult terrain in the middle of the Russian lines. The ascent through the Tuk Valley to the 229th Regiment command post during the night with heavily laden animals was troublesome. Three times animals fell into trenches; we thought that was that, but five minutes later, the animal would stand again. It is unbelievable what a Russian horse can go through. For eight days they ate nothing but foliage and bark, then they had to carry such loads through the mountains...

We saddled up and made the ascent on two routes. Finally arriving at the regiment, I left behind a portion of the load. At 0100 hours I received the latest information from the regimental commander, Major Schury. Then we were on our way again! The terrain was extremely difficult. Below in the valley, 300 meters under us, lay the Russian supply troops and kitchens; above us were the Russian outposts. The rocky slope was cut by at least a dozen deep trenches. After 20 minutes we ran into a Russian outpost, which we suppressed. Then all of our attention was concentrated on the terrain. The primeval-like forest, the numerous decayed and rotting trees, the steep trenches all made the highest demands on the men and animals. In addition, we had weapons and ammunition and heavy packs. The Russian pack animal driver (a prisoner volunteer) behaved excellently. We crossed Russian supply routes twice. After an eight hour march past Mount Sedlo we reached the area south of Hill 565.4. After dividing the platoon into three groups we advanced to the top. Two of the outflanking groups made contact with the enemy. I took a group to the top and had a good view into the enemy positions north of 565.4 and drew a diagram. From the orientation of the Russian positions I could figure out the location of the encircled battalion. While moving to the west we fell under a Russian mortar attack. We suffered killed and wounded. We were in a nasty situation. In the meantime, the Russians were advancing on all sides. While advancing to the west our lead force ran into a bunker line, which could not be overcome. After one bunker was destroyed the only thing we could do was retreat. We withdrew with Gruppe Heyd as rear guard, which allowed us to break contact with the enemy. This time we smuggled ourselves a little higher on the mountain in order to avoid the threatening trenches, but we soon had to move in deeper because the Russians had also occupied the upper portion. Additionally, on the last part of the route, we had to cross several trenches, a very difficult operation, during which two pack animals fell and were left behind because we were being pursued by a Russian reconnaissance element. In this difficult terrain it was impossible to lead the pack animals after dark. They were left behind with Unterfeldwebel Dlaska and under the protection of Gruppe Heyd. With the rest of the platoon and the severely wounded Obergefreiter Rizzol I made it to the German lines. Eight men came toward us from the German positions. They took Rizzol, who had closed his eyes forever on the way up. On the next morning our pack animal group reached the friendly positions."

The crisis continued in the seam between the 198th ID and 101st Jäger Division. There was fierce combat there. There was still the threat of a Russian attack into the long western flank of the XXXXIV Jäger Corps.

There was also fierce combat around the Kochkanova ridge. The LVII Panzer Corps had to direct all available batteries to support there if the ridge was to fall. Several of the guns were moved up with much difficulty. They were conventional cannon and howitzers. In addition, the majority of the 235th Artillery Regiment, the I/77 AR, elements of the 704th Artillery Regiment, the I/844 AR and one battery of the Artillery Training Regiment were brought forward. Necessary communications were established between the LVII Panzer Corps and the XXXXIV Jäger Corps across Sadovoe. There was also an attack to the south! However, the Soviet leadership played their trump in Sadovoe.

Both sides planned on clearing the Kochkanova ridge area on 26 October. While the regiments of the 198th ID prepared to attack to the south, north of Kochkanova, the Soviet 83rd and 86th Marine Brigades assembled to the south.

On the morning of 26 October German fighter-bombers and Stukas buzzed over the mountain and attacked the concentrations of artillery. The Soviet assembly areas were plagued with hefty artillery strikes. The Soviets could not advance for the time being.

The German attack went off as planned. After initial ground gains the battalions of the 198th ID stalled in front of strong bunker positions. The Russians launched a counterattack, which was repulsed. fierce combat continued until late into the afternoon. Losses were high on both sides. The 326th Grenadier Regiment had a combat strength of only 200 men.

There was also heavy fighting on 27 October. By evening the regiments of the 198th ID had taken back the initiative. Artillery was brought up. Because the Fast Slovak Division hung far back the Slovaks were left out of the operation. The 421st Grenadier Regiment (125th ID), under Oberst Reinhardt, was subordinated to the 198th ID. This was a regiment that had contributed decisively in the battle for Rostov. Direct contact was to be established with the XXXXIV Jäger Corps (101st Jäger DIvision) by the attack of the 198th ID to the south. The immediate objective was the town of Sadovoe, located 5 kilometers to the south of Kochkanov.

On 29 October a Soviet counterattack was repulsed. On 30 October the attack regiments were in their departure positions. It was raining. The clouds hung low over the valleys. The Luftwaffe could not support them. The artillery was "blind". The start of the attack was delayed until 0930 hours.

At 0940 hours 15 Stukas from the 77th Wing took off, in addition to 12 fighter-bombers and 12 double fuselage aircraft. They engaged the Soviets in the Sosnovaya trench. In spite of this the infantry attack stalled because the activities could not be overseen. In spite of repeated Luftwaffe sorties they could advance no further. Only the III/305 was able to advance into the area south of Kochkanov (3 kilometers south of Hill 620.8) by evening and establish themselves there in a bunker line.

On 31 October the bitter struggle continued. The German attack battalions were constantly coming upon new bunker lines. The trenches made an outflanking maneuver impossible. The Russian forces held out in the gaps. They made it to the entrance of the Sosnovaya trench. They gradually advanced to the south. After six days, on 5 November, the 421st Grenadier Regiment captured the important Hill 415, from where contact could be established with the 101st Jäger Division.

On 20 October the reorganization of Division "Lanz" for the attack on the upper Pshekh Valley and the Semashcho ridge was completed. On 21 October the attack into the Pshekh Valley was begun in the pouring rain. Perevalny and Goich fell into the hands of Battle Groups Buchner (II and III/13 Geb.Jg.Rgt., 54th Feldersatz Battalion) on the right, Lawall (I, II and III/98 Geb.Jg.Rgt., I/42 Gren.Rgt.) in the center and Auer (III/72 Gren.Rgt., and III/42 Gren.Rgt.) on the left. One battalion headquarters and 1800 of the Russian defenders were captured.

On 22 October Hauptmann Siebeck and his men conquered the 1038 meter high Semashcho, the last natural bulwark in front of Tuapse, 22 kilometers as the crow flies from the sea coast. Siebeck was carried from the peak seriously wounded. Most of his men were sacrificed to the furious Russian counterattack. During the following weeks, up to 13 December, the mountain changed hands many times.

On 23 October Battle Group Lawall fought through to Semashcho. The I/98 and III/98 reached the dominant mountain in an assault. In the last light of the day the Black Sea and the city of Tuapse with its harbor lay in front of the German gebirgsjägers. Again the hope was raised that after all of the heavy fighting the objective of Tuapse would still be reached. Battle Group Buchner reached Hill 783 on the right flank with the II/13 Geb.Jg.Rgt.

On 24 and 25 October Hauptmann Werner and his II/98 Geb.Jg.Rgt. fought out of the Perelavny area toward the Semashcho ridge, but he could not reach the southern bulwark of the ridge, the 919 meter high double peaked Dva-Brata (Two Brothers).

Battle Group Auer caught up with the attack of the II/98 and advanced its security line through Perelavny and into the upper Pshekh Valley to the south.

On the same day (25 October), the 46th ID attacked Oplepek, which had been recaptured by the Soviets on 13 October. The mountain was won back in a pincer attack by elements of the 72nd and 97th Grenadier Regiments. Thus, once again, the dominant bastion in the Pshekh Valley was in German hands.

All successes were won with great sacrifice. The German companies had melted away and had an average combat strength of 30 men. Numerous pack animals and draft horses could not hold up under the unbelievable demands and were destroyed. The objective, just before their eyes, could not be reached with the available forces. The divisions that were to be quickly freed-up near Stalingrad to reinforce the Caucasus were being bloodied in front of the city on the Volga. Thus, the glorious combat of the German gebirgsjäger, jäger and infantry divisions on the road to Tuapse appeared to be a tragedy of immense proportions. There were just not enough forces! Two to three fresh divisions, a pair of regiments and the objective could have been taken.

On 27 October a command meeting took place at 17th Army in Krasnodar. Generaloberst Ruoff listened to the proposals of his commanders. General Kirchner, commander of the LVII Panzer Corps, proposed establishing his corps in the mountains. Further ground gains could not be made.

General de Angelis reported that his XXXXIV Jäger Corps, which only had two divisions available, had lost considerable combat strength and his improvised pack animal formations could not guarantee sufficient supply.

General Konrad informed them that his XXXXIX Mountain Corps could not continue the attack alone, especially since they had suffered considerable losses and lacked sufficient supply. The situation was clear. The officers and soldiers had achieved the impossible, but there were limits to what else they could accomplish, and they reached their limit!

And how about the other side?

From 20 to 23 October the Soviet cruisers "Krasniy Krim", "Krasniy Kavkaz", the flotilla leader "Kharkov" and the destroyers "Soobrazitelniy" and "Bespostsadniy" transported the 8th, 9th and 10th Guards Rifle Brigades from Poti to Tuapse. This was a total of 12,600 men with 50 guns, 65 mortars and 100 tons of ammunition.

The Soviet deep interior had good supply lines from which troops could be moved like chess pieces. Despite this, their last defensive positions in front of Tuapse were battered. The commander of the "Black Sea Group of the Transcaucasus Front", General Petrov, was replaced by General Cherevichenko, who immediately instituted new measures and mobilized all reserves. Soon the XI Guards Rifle Corps (8th, 9th and 10th Guards Rifle Brigades) and the 165th and 2nd Rifle Divisions were assembled in the Pshekh Valley around the Goich rail point. The Armenian 408th Rifle Division was inserted in the Mount Indyuk area and the 107th Rifle Brigade was deployed east of the Goich Pass.

On 28 October the 101st Jäger Division undertook an attack attempt against the Goich Pass. The 228th Jäger Regiment (Oberstleutnant Schratz) attacked out of the Shaumyan area to the south. During this time, the 229th Jäger Regiment repulsed an enemy attack into the western flank toward the Elissavetpolskiy Pass. On 29 October Oberstleutnant Schratz and his jägers captured Hill 388.3; some elements fought their way to the northern foot of Hill 379.8. At this time the 97th Jäger Division was located on the railroad and road intersection 5 kilometers south of Shaumyan.

The Soviet attempt to pin the 101st Jäger Division on the western flank on 29 and 30 October failed. The attack of Gruppe Schratz, which was located in front of the Goich Pass, had to be suspended and the group was withdrawn to the departure positions.

In the meantime, a bitter battle raged around the Semashcho ridge. The Soviets tried to break through the thin front of the German gebirgsjägers from three sides with strong counterattacks. Frontal attacks were repulsed, but the Soviets soon discovered a weak position. Flanking attacks tried to cut off Battle Groups Buchner (right) and Lawall (left) from their lines of communications. The 13th Gebirgsjäger Regiment advanced up to 800 meters toward the 98th Gebirgsjäger Regiment, but even the 48th Heeres Engineer Battalion (Herzog) could not close the gap from the north. The transfer of the left flank of Battle Group Buchner made the right flank too thin and it could only be held in a strong-point manner. The Soviets found these gaps. Oberst Buchner's two right battalions were gradually encircled, but they held out.

It was no better on Lawall's left flank; the II/98 was being attacked from three sides, but they held out southeast of Hill 919 (Dva Brata). All attempts by this battalion to take Hill 919 failed. The Soviets were constantly deploying new forces from Anastassievka, particularly to the Hill 919 front. The Germans watched artillery being brought up before their very eyes, without concern of being destroyed. The German artillery could not reach them, and there was little to spare from the German Luftwaffe; they were flying against Stalingrad.

The II/98 Geb.Jg.Rgt., which was formerly led by Major von Hirschfeld and, while under his leadership, took Goich, was led by Major Werner. Major von Hirschfeld was summoned to the Führer Headquarters after capturing Goich in the upper Pshekh Valley and was awarded the Oak Leaves to the Knight's Cross. He remained there as a liaison officer until autumn of 1943 and then returned to Greece to command the 98th Gebirgsjäger Regiment after Salminger's death. Later von Hirschfeld took command of a Schwabian division.

Strong enemy forces also attacked in the Battle Group Auer area of operations. The 9th Guards Cavalry Division tried to attack through from Perevalny to the north without success. Oberst Auer concentrated all of his forces and held out.

The extent of the struggle to make the final jump to the objective was described by General Lanz on 29 October in short military sentences as follows:

"The overall situation on the Semashcho ridge worsened from hour to hour. During the afternoon I brought up my last reserves, the engineers, removing them from their work on the roads to support the front. Even supply troops and staffs are now facing the enemy. I now have no other reserves available and must place my trust in my troops that they will hold the present positions. Combat strength is reduced hourly, now the companies consist of about 40 men. The loss of officers, now over 100, is particularly serious. In complete understanding of my responsibility and the significance of the contested territory, I must report that I can only guarantee the holding of the ridge under continuous enemy attack for a short time. In addition, were bad weather to set in, the front must be withdrawn. For the next few days of this battle, I am filled with concern not only for holding the positions, but for the condition of the division."

How much good sense and feeling for his gebirgsjägers he expressed in this report to the XXXXIX Mountain Corps!

The combat diary of Army Group A noted under 3 November 1942: "IV Air Corps supports the struggling forces before Tuapse." And under considerations it noted: "...The 73rd ID is being replaced by a Luftwaffe Field Division and will be committed to the attack on Tuapse." It further noted: "...additional battalions from Gruppe Kress will be taken from the high mountain front and sent to the Tuapse area..."

These notes demonstrate the weakness of the German forces. However, no fresh divisions were available. The battle continued on the Semashcho ridge. The enemy was able to advance elements of the 9th and 10th Guards Rifle Brigades between the 13th and 98th Gebirgsjäger Regiments across the ridge to Goich. They were finally stopped shortly before the 98th Gebirgsjäger Regiment command post. Oberstleutnant Lawall mastered the critical situation by hastily gathering all of his radiomen and staff soldiers. The combat in the rear of the Semashcho front continued until 17 November, when the last enemy groups were wiped out. The encirclement of the German Semashcho group was avoided. For this commitment Oberstleutnant Lawall received the Knight's Cross.

In order to reinforce the thin front the western flank had to advance continuously. The 97th Jäger Division advanced up to Mount Indyuk. On the eastern flank, the 46th ID advanced its reconnaissance battalion to Gruppe Lanz. From the high mountain front came the I/13 Geb.Jg.Rgt. and engineer battalion. All available artillery was deployed to the front and concentrated.

The weak jäger regiments could only thinly occupy the front. The artillery had to help and be in position to dominate the enemy's approach routes. The prerequisite here was observation posts, which had to be manned by good marksmen.

Major von Ernsthausen, battalion commander in the 81st Artillery Regiment of the 97th Jäger Division, was assigned as the forward observer commander on the Pshekh southeast of Shaumyan. All batteries in this sector fell under his command. The heavy batteries were located in the area of the confluence of the Gunaika into the Pshekh. The 1st and 2nd Mountain Batteries of the 81st Artillery Regiment, which were equipped with the collapsible [type] 36 Mountain Gun, were able to be deployed on the hills north of the Pshekh. A decisive section of the route in the southern Pshekh bend was in Russian hands. Because of this, supplies for Gruppe Lanz had to be transported with difficulty across the mountain. This portion of the Pshekh promised to be tenaciously defended by the Soviets. All of the attacks of the 97th Jäger Division in this terrain sector failed. The Russians continued to deploy reinforcements there. A penetration by the enemy from there into the upper Pshekh Valley would threaten Gruppe Lanz in the rear.

The combat see-sawed all day around this sector of the Pshekh. The Wallonien Battalion under Major Lucien Lippert and the reconnaissance battalion and the engineer battalions from the 97th Jäger Division fought like the devil. The mission of the artillery was to hold this threatened Pshekh sector. Major von Ernsthausen visited this sector and determined that the depth of the Pshekh Valley could not be observed from all sides of the thin HKL.

Leutnant von Leeb, a nephew of Generalfeldmarshall von Leeb, searched for a suitable observation post from where the entire valley would be visible. And he found it - toward the valley between the fronts.

Major von Ernsthausen, Leutnant von Leeb and Oberfeldwebel Ludwig left to occupy the observation post. They clambered up the slope and crept like indians, jumping from one group of bushes to the next, from one block of boulders to the next, until they reached the site that was previously reconnoitered by Leutnant von Leeb. The effort was worth it. They could observe the entire Pshekh Valley. There were Russian shelters all over, traffic was being regulated. They could make out the faces of the Russians through the binoculars. Major von Ernsthausen had already made his plans: "early tomorrow we will both lay wire to here!" he told Oberfeldwebel Ludwig.

The artillery could now fire into the enemy positions with so much more effectiveness that it was a constant threat to the western flank on the Indyuk.

Major von Ernsthausen became the "observer on target". The enemy lay only several hundred meters in front of him. The German shells shrieked directly over the observation post. The [type] 21 mortars and the 7.5 cm mountain guns fired where the field howitzers could not reach. Thus the artillery was mutually supportive!

In the meantime, the Russian attacks on the western flank were increased. A serious crisis developed at the seam between the 198th ID and 101st Jäger Divisions northwest of Shaumyan. The Soviets did not give up on their plan to attack deep into the western flank in order to hit the German attack groups facing Tuapse in the rear. During the night of 6 November a heavy fire strike began on the 421st Grenadier Regiment, which was located on Hill 415 as a breakwater south of the Kochkanova ridge. This was the only blocking position held by the regiments of the 198th ID. Soon it was obvious that the Soviets wanted to recapture Hill 415 in order to mount a further attack against the western flank of the 101st Jäger Division and the Elissavetpolskiy Pass. On 6 November the Soviets hit the positions of the 421st Grenadier Regiment. The battle lasted several days. Oberst Reinhardt's battle group repulsed attacks from three sides with the support of the I/421, I/419 and III/419. Oberst Reinhardt was the soul of the resistance. He did not leave his post even after being wounded. The climax occurred on 12 November. At 1000 hours Oberst Reinhardt reported to the 198th ID: "Enemy has penetrated into gaps in unknown strength. I/419 being attacked in the rear. Request permission to withdraw the battle group."

Generalmajor Müller, commander of the 198th ID, did not delay very long. It had to be done! The corps engineer battalion and elements of the division were committed to facilitate the withdrawal of Battle Group Reinhardt; by evening they had taken up positions on the Kochkanova front.

It began to rain at the beginning of November. The mountain terrain was turned to grey from the low hanging clouds. Small streams became flowing rivers. The loamy ground was changed into a sticky mush. Supply became a problem and, in some places, ceased to exist. Feverishly the repair companies and supply elements worked under the leadership of Hauptmann Baron von Eyb to clear the tunnel near Navaginskaya so that it could be used again. The rain interfered with all large combat operations.

From 26 to 29 November the Russians conducted another attack on the Semashcho positions. From 1 to 10 December the Soviet cruiser "Krasniy Krym", the destroyers "Nezamozhnik" and "Bespostsadniy" and Minesweeper 9 transported a Soviet mountain infantry division from Batumi to Tuapse. The arriving battalions were immediately deployed on the front. By this point in time the light German surface naval forces were no longer in any position to interfere with the enemy unloading efforts in Tuapse harbor. The last German attack occurred on 24 October with four motor torpedo boats of Kptl. Christiansen's 1st Motor-Torpedo Boat Flotilla on a Soviet transport formation; two torpedoes detonated on the pier and one ran up on land.

It continued to rain!

On 28 November the only Pshekh bridge in the upper river valley was washed away by the rising flood waters. Nine battalions on the Semashcho ridge depended on it for communications. The engineers worked without stopping to erect a new bridge.

On 1 December Gruppe Lanz reported to XXXXIX Mountain Corps:

"Situation on Semashcho ridge serious. According to enemy activity and prisoner statements, anticipate an enemy attack with new forces in both flanks. The troops are exhausted. 60 horses are lost daily. Rising waters in the Pshekh prevent supply. Ammunition available for only 2 to 3 days, rations for only one day; no feed for the horses. Evacuation of the wounded not possible. Occupation of the Pshekh positions, as long as the rising waters allow, indispensible because, otherwise, troops will be lost. Supply through the Gunaika Valley tied up due to high water. Supply is only at one-third of the requirement. Immediate commitment of several aircraft necessary, otherwise troops will be without rations in two days."

The poor health status of the soldiers comes through in a report from the division surgeon on 23 November:

"Food supplies have considerably diminished. 50% have stomach and intestinal viruses from eating food cold (impossible to light fires). Clothing is wet, often completely torn. Only capable of defense."

In view of these circumstances, General Konrad, the commander of the XXXXIX Mountain Corps, wanted to give up the bridgehead to the water line, but first he needed permission from higher headquarters to do so. He immediately sent a secret correspondence:

"From XXXXIX Mountain Corps commander to Gruppe Lanz!

Gruppe Lanz is to immediately reconnoiter positions north of Pshekh..."

The army group tried to facilitate matters in another way. On 2 December Army Group A ordered:

"German Luftwaffe will conduct temporary air supply of XXXXIV Jäger Corps and XXXXIX Mountain Corps at the expense of reconnaissance."

The combat diary of Army Group A gives information on the air supply as follows: "7 December 1942: A total of 18,700 men and 600 pack animals in the area south of Gunaika. Continuous air supply questionable. At 1815 hours the 1st Generalstabsoffizier of the 17th Army reported that the Luftwaffe had flown 17.5 tons of rations, 6.5 tons of horse feed and 3.5 tons of engineer equipment into the Pshekh bridgehead in 61 sorties.

8 December 1942: Because of the weather situation only 8 tons of goods were flown into the Pshekh bridgehead by 38 sorties." In actuality, air supply remained a "drop in the bucket". Many times the drop zone lay within range of enemy weapons and only a portion of the supplies could be recovered. The Russians got the rest. Much was lost to enemy fire and the mud.

Lanz repeated the alarming reports daily:

"Troops are on half-rations. The outbreak of the cold weather has increased the cases of consumption. There have been 14 deaths from exhaustion in the past seven days. Linen is literally rotting on their bodies. Infections are the result. The death of the horses continues. The 98th Gebirgsjäger Regiment will have lost its horses within ten days. The wounded lay in the main first aid station in wet tents, often for many days. Their evacuation by "Storch" has been cancelled because of weather conditions. Artillery ammunition has not been delivered. Help from the Luftwaffe is dubious; a third of the goods are lost. The weather alternates between snow and rain, the temperatures range between 5 degrees and minus 5 degrees."

The list of suffering went on and on. However, Hitler still refused to approve the evacuation of the Semashcho ridge.

General Lanz reported to the XXXXIX Mountain Corps on 14 December 1942: "Fate is running its course. Relief (withdrawal of the front), which is anticipated from hour to hour, never comes. Without positive evidence, I have the impression that the reports from the division and corps are not getting to the right place. What my brave men have suffered in the past weeks has surpassed all relevance. One can only stand before these soldiers with thankfulness and wonder, as they shoulder every burden..."

As it was with Division "Lanz" it was also with the 97th ID and 101st Jäger Division and on the right flank in the 198th and 125th Infantry Division areas of operations. In spite of the poor weather the Soviets continued to launch their unsuccessful attacks against the deep flanks. Mount Sarai and Mount Sedlo, Tuk Valley, the hills northwest of Shaumyan and Shaumyan itself kept turning up in combat reports. In the 198th ID area of operations there was fierce combat on the Kochkanova ridge, on the "Russian Head" and in the positions south of Kochkanov. The 68th and 255th Marine Brigades continued to crash against these positions. And it continued to rain, and the streams turned to flowing rivers. Ten horses, one wagon and four men from the 3/235 AR were washed away by the flood of the otherwise "tame" Khatyps.

And it was no better on the eastern flank: There the 46th ID also faced the weather, powerless to do anything about it. This division covered the eastern flank of the attack wedge and maintained contact with the 4th Security Regiment and the Platov Cossack Battalion. The 46th ID, a conventional infantry division, quickly became a mountain formation. Pack animal drivers were enlisted from the prisoners. Two columns of 200 pack animals each were created. The pack animal drivers were Russian, the column leaders were German. Prisoners of war were conversant in the native methods of driving and equipping pack animals. The Ib, Oberstleutnant Czech supplied the battle groups of his division near Perevalny, Maratuk, on the Oplepek and near Sanurskiy with these Russian supply columns.

In spite of the poor weather the Russians continued to attack. As before the Pshekh block and the Indyuk front were threatened. The battalions of the 97th Jäger Division could prevent penetration only with difficulty. A division order from 5 December gives only a small idea of what was being played out there:

"In days of fierce combat, Battle Group Nobis (204th Jäger Regiment) and the left flank of Battle Group Otte (207th Jäger Regiment) have repulsed fierce enemy attacks. On 4 December 1942 Oberstleutnant Nobis, with the 7/"Brandenburg" and small elements of the 207th Jäger Regiment, the 1/97 Pi.Btl., his regimental staff and elements of the Headquarters Company, attacked and defeated a 400 to 500 man strong enemy attack group, suffering heavy losses..."

Nobis discovered the enemy group at the break of day. In a decisive operation he arrived before the enemy attack. The plucky Nobis, a former Austrian mountain officer, who spent only four months as a Major before being promoted to Oberstleutnant and who was promoted to Oberst after this commitment, left the battlefield severely wounded. Major Malter took command of the 204th Jäger Regiment.

The units of the 97th Jäger Division advanced further toward the Indyuk. On 14 December the 204th Jäger Regiment stood opposite the Indyuk, maintaining contact with Division "Lanz" on the left. By early morning the Russians were in the German HKL. Battalion Abbt was battered. Hauptmann Abbt and an element of his jägers fought their way through to Division "Lanz". A penetration was also achieved further to the south. Oberleutnant Widmer stood between these two penetration forces with 40 jägers. Fortunately, there was a forward observer in his area and the wire obstacles were not penetrated. Battle Group Widmer held out the entire day. In spite of well-directed artillery they could not remove the penetration. They spent a sleepless night.

On 15 December Major Malter organized a small group of 30 men, including 12 from the 7/"Brandenburg", under a Hauptmann. These were the last

12 members of the special company that had captured the Belorechenskaya bridges for "Wiking" in August. After a short preparation they were to launch a counterattack because the Soviets continued to attack. They were repulsed.

"We are going to attack now, but this time with artillery support!" said Major Malter. They quickly made contact with the forward observer, Major von Ernsthausen.

"When can you begin the fire preparation?" asked Malter.

"1300 hours!"

"How long will the barrage last?"

"A quarter of an hour!"

"Then I will attack at 1315 hours!"

After a good artillery preparation, the jägers and "Brandenburgers" assaulted. The enemy was thrown back and contact was reestablished with the encircled Battle Group Widmer.

When Major von Ernsthausen looked up Major Malter in his bunker after the battle, he lay wounded on his stretcher. His white head bandage was covered in blood. A shell fragment in his ear caused him much pain.

"You should go to the hospital, Malter!"

"No, I'll remain with the troops. As long as you are here, how do you assess the situation?"

"Untenable, if we are not reinforced soon!"

Major von Ernsthausen was correct. But reinforcement was out of the question. The constant alarming reports from the Semashcho ridge and the energetic requests from corps and army were finally heard. The order to evacuate arrived - finally - almost too late.

During the night of 16-17 December 1942 the battalions broke contact with the enemy and withdrew through the Pshekh Valley. A new HKL was occupied on the hills north of the river, which was constantly reinforced and improved. The noticeable decrease in enemy activity and considerable improvement in the supply of the troops soon brought relief.

27 years prior to the day of the evacuation of the Semashcho positions, 16 December, General Ludendorff wrote: "Missed opportunities in this war cause damage to the Fatherland. I am not a bitter malcontent, but a German, who with sorrow sees how the strength of the people was wasted because fate was lacking to seize the fortunes of war."

"... the strength of the people was wasted..." this was especially true for the attack on Tuapse.

During the combat around the Semashcho ridge from 21 October to 16 December 1942 Gruppe "Lanz" lost: 823 dead, 2412 wounded and 199 missing. Division "Lanz", which started the attack with battalions at almost full combat strength, registered the following losses:

Losses of Division "Lanz" from 27 September to 31 December 1942:

	Officers	NCO's	Men
killed:	35	164	1267
missing:	1	7	182
wounded:	128	472	4009
Evacuated Ill:	68	111	1426
	232	754	6884

Replacements from 27 September to 31 December 1942:

18	174	2619

Losses of animals during this period of time:

killed:	996
died from illness:	251
died from exhaustion:	2979
	4226

Similar losses, which do not stand in relation to the terrain conquered, were also registered in the other divisions. This is easy to say in retrospect. They had all hoped to achieve the assigned objective, and they died with this hope.

cm rocket battery in
ng position.

ket salvo shortly after
g.

onation of a rocket
o, 32 cm incendiary
ls. The last German
nations crossed over
e Kerch Peninsula
er the cover of such a
of fire.

3rd Panzer Division. At a regimental command post in Isherskay on the Terek in autumn 1942. From left to right Major Cochenhausen (battalion commander) Oberstleutnant Pape (394th Panzergrenadier Regiment commander) Hauptmann Müller-Röhlich (commander of II/394 Pz.Gren.Rgt.).

Panzergrenadiers in the Caucasus.

Heavy German guns firing.

Rocky Terek banks near Khamidiya with a combat bridge over the river.

Battlefield near Malgobek and Sagopshin. "Wiking" combat vehicles at anti-tank trenches near Nizhniy Kurp.

General Recknagel, commander of the 111th ID and Oberst Herforth, commander of the 117th Grenadier Regiment, during the combat on the Terek.

Personal hygiene in the trenches in front of Sagopshin. Mortar positions of the 3/"Nordland".

A group of Finnish volunteers after heavy combat near Malgobek

A Russian armored train destroyed by the 13th Panzer Division near Ardon on the Terek.

manian Machine-gun
ops.

ack on Nalchik.
man assault guns and
nanian gebirgsjägers.

avalry patrol of a
sack squadron from
erst von Jungschulz'
le group.

Waffen SS. The platoon leader.

Temporary bridge across a mountain river in the western Caucasus.

General Haccius, commander of the 46th ID (center), with officers of his staff.

...saks from the Terek
...on.

...ssing a mountain river.

...ng a German mortar.
...ck in the Caucasus
...est.

Attack toward Tuapse through the Caucasus Forest.

Evening in the forest front before Tuapse. The Black Sea shimmers behind the hills.

The attack on Tuapse stalls during the November muddy period.

98th Gebirgsjäger Regiment takes Senashcho after a day long struggle. Oberstleutnant Sawall (left) and Oberleutnant Rall discuss further combat operations.

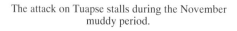

THE BATTLE NEAR NALCHIK
AND THE ADVANCE TO THE GEORGIAN ARMY ROAD

Nalchik falls - German bombs render the 37th Soviet Army leaderless - The armored trains from Arden - The advance to Ordzhonikidze with "blinders" - The 13th Panzer Division in the Gisel pocket - Stalin on the front - True Waffenbrüderschaft

On 19 October 1942, when, as already indicated, the attack of the LII Army Corps in the Terek bend brought no operational success, the commander of the III Panzer Corps was given the task of working out an attack plan on Nalchik. Generaloberst von Kleist wanted to resurrect his old plan, an advance along the mountains toward Ordzhonikidze and the blocking of the Georgian Army Road.

General von Mackensen, supported by his capable Chief of Staff, Oberstleutnant von Grevenitz, submitted an operation plan that was sanctioned by the 1st Panzer Army. According to this plan von Mackensen wanted to attack Nalchik frontally across the Baksan with the subordinate 2nd Rumanian Mountain Division, while the main attack was to take place a day later with the 13th and 23rd Panzer Divisions breaking out of the Maiskoe - Kotlyaevskiy area on the eastern flank in order to outflank and capture Nalchik.

As heavy combat raged in the great Terek bend in September and October the Baksan front solidified, since both sides continued to throw in forces. The 23rd Panzer Division earlier had to give up its powerful formations to the LII Army Corps and XXXX Panzer Corps; now they were again concentrated in the Kotlyarevskiy area. The 13th Panzer Division was withdrawn from its positions near Elkhotovo and Illareinovka and assembled in the Arik area. The 370th ID moved further to the west and took over the 13th Panzer Division's positions. One portion of the 370th ID sector was taken over by the SS Division "Wiking".

The re-groupings went smoothly. The III Panzer Corps displaced according to the new mission. The 2nd Rumanian Mountain Division with the I/99 Geb.Jg.Rgt. (1st Mountain Division) formed "Attack Group West", which assembled around the town of Baksan. The 13th and 23rd Panzer Divisions formed "Attack Group East" and assembled in the Arik - Kotlyarevskiy area. The area between these two attack groups was secured by weak forces, which were concentrated under "Security Sector Center". The commander of "Security Sector Center" was the commander of the 52nd Rocket Launcher Regiment, Oberstleutnant Emsmann.

On the morning of 25 October the attack of "Attack Group West" was launched out of the Baksan area. Once again German combat aircraft were concentrated in great numbers and bombarded the enemy positions. The gebirgsjägers of the I/99 under Major Kopp led the attack, which had reached its objective of the day, Chegen I, by midday.

The surprising German success was explained by the Russians in their Caucasus book as follows: "Numerous German bombers joined in the battle.

A headquarters of the 37th Army, which was located south of Nalchik in Dolinskoe, was bombed and lost all communications with its units. Therefore, the army was leaderless."

On the morning of 26 October 1942 "Attack Group East" attacked. The 23rd Panzer Division set out on the left near Kotlyarevskiy in the waning moon light and captured the city of Argudan. Therefore, the Nalchik - Ordzhonikidze road was blocked. Then the 23rd Panzer Division advanced to the south toward Stariy Lessken with Battle Group Brückner, Battle Group Burmeister veered off to the east and captured the village of Osrek with the II/201 Pz.Rgt.

There the headquarters of the 257th Soviet Rifle Division and numerous supply formations were defeated. Under the screen of their southern flank, Battle Group Burmeister penetrated to the north and attacked in the rear the enemy forces located in Aleksandrovskaya. The frontal attack of the 128th Panzergrenadier Regiment continued north of Aleksandrovskaya. Platoon against platoon, the nests of resistance were removed and, a day later, Aleksandrovskaya was completely in the hands of the 23rd Panzer Division. Enemy elements breaking out to the east fell under the fire of the 370th ID.

The 13th Panzer Division attacked out of the area west of Kotlyarevskiy adjacent to the 23rd Panzer Division at 0440 hours with Battle Group von Hake. Mine-fields and anti-tank barricades delayed the attack. The advance did not pick up speed until midday, after a stuka attack made some room. They soon reached Nizhniy Cherek. Oberst von Hake, commander of the 4th Panzer Regiment, then released his second panzer echelon, which advanced the attack to Stariy Cherek. Heavy enemy batteries there were overrun and captured. A commando of the II/"Brandenburg" probed ahead in order to capture the Cherek bridge in a raid, but the bridge was blown by the Soviets. The 13th Panzer Division, which was to detach some elements to the north toward Nalchik, stood before the river without a crossing. Soon they found a ford and the advance continued on toward Urban. A little later the 4th Armored Engineer Battalion made the Stariy Cherek bridge trafficable with a K-Strecke.

In the meantime, Battle Group Scholz, which was echeloned on the left behind Battle Group von Hake, also reached Stariy Cherek, after overcoming heavy resistance near the Kotlyarevskiy sheep farm and numerous mine-fields. By evening, it advanced to Pssyganssu without coming upon any resistance worth noting.

On 26 October the 2nd Rumanian Mountain Division and the I/99 Geb.Jg.Rgt. penetrated into the northern portion of the city of Nalchik. Tenacious and costly combat occurred around each street objective, it would last for several days.

The decision was already made on 26 October with the capture of Argudan; the deep defensive field of the Soviets between Baksan and Cherek was out-maneuvered. The Russian history notes: "The main attack was directed toward the Nalchik - Chikola - Digora - Alagir road. In this manner the Nalchik defense was broken from the rear and collapsed. The troops of the

37th Army withdrew. The reasons for the failure can be found in insufficient combat reconnaissance (the tank concentrations near Kotlyarevskiy were appraised to be only a diversion for the Soviet troops before the upcoming battle) and the loss of command and control in the 37th Army."

The Russian self-criticism serves to point out how a well prepared and well concealed operation will confuse the enemy and reduce friendly casualties. General von Mackensen and Generaloberst von Kleist had not counted on such success, as they were to later admit.

On 27 October the 23rd Panzer Division's left flank reached Stariy Urukh and Stariy Lessken. The 13th Panzer Division compressed the Nalchik pocket in cooperation with the Rumanians. The majority of "Security Sector Center" came in from the north to participate. The commander of the 43rd Kradschützen Battalion, Major Crüznacher, was killed near Vladimirskaya. The dissipated forces of the 13th Panzer Division were repeatedly attacked by groups of enemy stragglers, which tried to breakout to the southeast. Battle Group Scholz (93rd Panzergrenadier Regiment) advanced from Pssyganssu to Anshiger and blocked the mountain flank.

On 28 October elements of the 13th Panzer Division participated in the mopping up of Nalchik. By evening the capital of the "Soviet Republics of the Karbardin and Balkars" was in German hands. On the next day the German Wehrmacht reported: "Rumanian mountain troops in conjunction with German gebirgsjägers attacked the strongly fortified and tenaciously defended city of Nalchik west of the Terek. The enemy forces encircled in the northeast were either wiped out in combat or captured. Therefore, within four days, several Soviet divisions were defeated, 7000 prisoners were taken, and 66 guns and tanks, as well as numerous other war equipment was either captured or destroyed."

On 28 October Battle Group Scholz penetrated further into the mountains and captured Zhemgala.

On 28 October the 23rd Panzer Division entered the second phase of the operation. After the Soviet forces were defeated in their main defensive field the pursuit began. The new objective was: the Georgian and Ossetian Army Road! Battle Group Brückner set out from Stariy Lessken, captured Lessken, crossed an 800 meter high pass, captured Khasnidon in the evening and established a bridgehead across the Urukh, which was held against heavy enemy counterattacks. After Battle Group Brückner had established a departure base, the attack of Battle Group Burmeister from Stariy Urukh toward Urukh was broken off because of heavy enemy resistance and Battle Group Burmeister was transferred into the Khasnidon area. To the 23rd Panzer Division were subordinated: elements of the 66th Panzergrenadier Regiment and the 52nd Rocket Launcher Regiment and, for screening the mountain flank, the 10th Rumanian Mountain Infantry Battalion.

At this time the following order arrived at "Security Sector Center":

"The Commander　　　　Command Post, 28 October 1942
of the III Panzer Corps
To Security Sector Center

Security Sector Center will be disbanded tomorrow, its units will be put to new use. The elements of the sector under the leadership of the commander of the 52nd Rocket Launcher Regiment have played an essential role in the successful termination of "the Battle of Nalchik".

I express my thanks to the participating battalions, the 73rd Engineer Battalion, the 8th Technical Battalion and the 22nd and 23rd Feldzüg Battalions, as well as the III/52 Werfer Rgt. and the Corps Cossack Company. The three non-combatant battalions have fulfilled their combat assignments.

I will review proposals for the awarding of the Iron Cross.

     signed von Mackensen
     General der Kavallerie"

On 29 October the 23rd Panzer Division expanded its small bridgehead near Khasnidon and advanced against heavy enemy resistance toward Chikola. The 13th Panzer Division, which was relieved by the 2nd Rumanian Mountain Division in the Cherek Valley, closed on the left with Battle Group von Hake as the first formation making it into the Urukh sector near Nuru - Urukh and formed a fire front to the east with its tanks in the hills. The subordinate I/128 Pz.Gren.Rgt. rolled forward, advanced over the weak wooden bridge into the steep river valley under the cover of the fire and established a bridgehead. The 4th Armored Engineer Battalion reinforced the wooden bridge. During the night the 13th Panzer Division was regrouped for an attack toward Digora within a few hours. This is only possible with a well-led and disciplined troop.

On 30 October the 23rd Panzer Division captured the tenaciously defended village of Chikola and reached the high ground to the east. The 13th Panzer Division had difficulty in the marshy Urukh Valley after making the crossing. By evening it overcame the terrain problems and created the prerequisite for an attack on the next day.

On 31 October both panzer divisions of the III Panzer Corps were ready for a combined attack. The mission for the 23rd Panzer Division, which was located on the mountain side (right) read:

"Attack through Digora toward Alagir and block the Ossetian Army Road." For the 13th Panzer Division, which was advancing on the left, the mission read: "Attack through Ardon - Arkhonskaya toward Ordzhonikidze."

The 23rd Panzer Division broke through numerous enemy positions with Battle Group Burmeister, which was reinforced with the II/201 Pz.Rgt., which had just caught up, crossed the Dur - Dur sector west of Digora and, by evening, advanced on the village.

The 13th Panzer Division, which was advancing on the left, eliminated a dangerous anti-tank front 6 kilometers west of Digora and turned to the north, bypassing Digora, toward Ardon. The lead elements stopped in view of the Darg Kokh - Alagir rail line, in order to allow additional forces to catch up. The attack plan foresaw: II/4 Pz.Rgt. and 43rd Kradschützen Battalion making a frontal attack from the west. The majority of Battle Group von Hake would bypass to the north to attack from the east.

The 13th Panzer Division attacked! After gaining several hundred meters the attack stalled in heavy enemy fire. Reconnaissance and observation revealed that the Soviets faced the 13th Panzer Division with three armored trains, 10-15 tanks of various types and strong infantry forces. Oberst von Hake dispatched his first tanks into the battle. The I/4 Pz.Rgt. concentrated fire on the first armored train, it was immediately set ablaze; the guns fell off and the ammunition exploded. The armored train continued to move several hundred meters then stalled on the tracks. Six of the enemy tanks attacking from the southeast were shot up by the II/4 Pz.Rgt., the rest withdrew. The second armored train blew up in flames under the fire of the II/4 Pz.Rgt. and the 1/13 Pz.Jg.Btl. The infantry penetrated into the western edge of Ardon covered by the 43rd Kradschützen Battalion and established themselves. The I/4 Pz.Rgt. and the I/66 Pz.Gren.Rgt. gained additional ground in the north. Two tanks trying to breakout to the north were destroyed there. By the fall of darkness the I/4 Pz.Rgt. and the I/66 reached the northwestern edge of Ardon, but they could do no more because of the darkness. In the meantime additional forces of the 13th Panzer Division were needed to cover the long northern flank. The 13th Panzerjäger Battalion and elements of the II/"Brandenburg" were ordered to capture the rail and road bridge near Darg Kokh in a raid. On the evening of 31 October 1942 the following message was received by the two panzer divisions:

"III Panzer Corps - The crossing of my two panzer divisions over the steep Urukh demonstrates a first class tactical and technical effort. Clever operations and superb engineer work have made this success possible. It has provided the precondition for the pursuit, which has gained ground today. - Ordzhonikidze remains our objective!

signed von Mackensen."

Indeed, von Mackensen could hope that the objective of Ordzhonikidze, which had alluded them for so long, would finally be reached.

On a sunny 1 November Digora, which was abandoned by the Russians that night, was occupied. The I/126 Pz.Gren.Rgt. under Hauptmann Bucher advanced in a clever attack up to Ardon, removed the explosives from the bridge and secured a bridgehead for the 23rd Panzer Division. Then the 23rd Panzer Division turned to the south and captured the city of Alagir, against fierce resistance, in a pincer attack. The Rumanian mountain infantry followed on the long mountain flank and relieved the security forces of the 23rd Panzer Division.

The 13th Panzer Division, which stood in front of Ardon, attacked through the city, which was evacuated by the enemy during the night. The city was immediately placed under heavy enemy artillery fire. While security forces were being diverted to the north, Battle Group von Hake attacked through several enemy field positions with "blinders" on [translator's note: looking

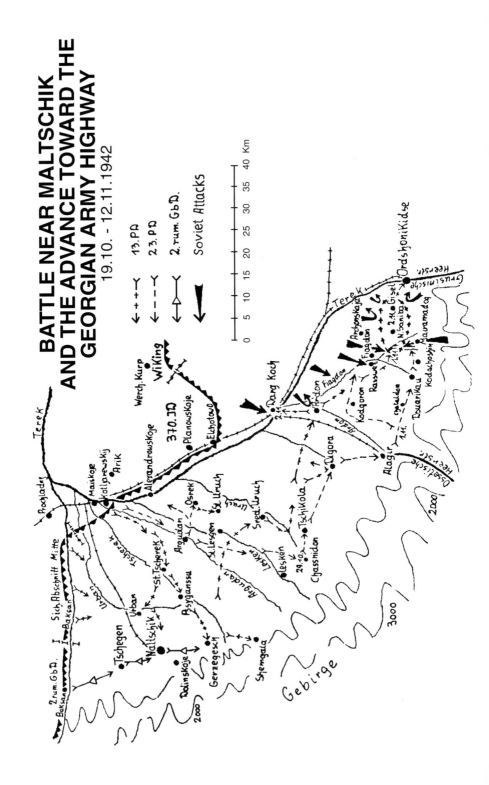

BATTLE NEAR MALTSCHIK
AND THE ADVANCE TOWARD THE
GEORGIAN ARMY HIGHWAY
19.10. - 12.11.1942

13.PD
23.PD
2.rum.GbD.
Soviet Attacks

0 5 10 15 20 25 30 35 40 Km

forward, disregarding flanks, as a horse with "blinders"] and, thereby, crossed numerous small water courses and some difficult terrain. Oberst von Hake, the clever and successful commander of the 4th Panzer Regiment and 13th Panzer Division Battle Group commander, mastered the successful advance maneuver in cooperation with his subordinate commanders, Major Brux, Major Ratzel and Hauptmann Kuklik. Von Hake spared his battle group long drawn out combat in towns by outflanking them and outmaneuvering the Soviet defenses.

In a spirited attack Battle Group von Hake advanced west of the Fiagdon to the southeast in the hope of finding a ford to cross to the opposite bank. He thought he had found the spot south of the village of Fiagdon, but the Soviet defenses there were also very strong.

While approaching the enemy positions running in front of the Fiagdon, heavy anti-tank and mortar fire was committed from the town of Fiagdon located to the east. In this situation, only speed would achieve success! Without cover, Hauptmann Niedick's III/4 Pz.Rgt. advanced into the fire and was the first formation to cross the wide, but shallow, mountain river. Major Brux followed with his tried and true SPW battalion and the tankers and panzergrenadiers soon broke into the well- camouflaged and strong enemy field positions. The following I/13 Pz.AR (self-propelled) moved into position and engaged recognized targets with fire. The penetration into the tenacious defensive positions was a feather in the troop's hat. The panzer crews, which were bravely led in groups, and the individual fighters determined the outcome of the battle. While the tanks attacked through the panzergrenadiers dismounted from their SPW's and fought in the enemy positions.

During the evening of 1 November Battle Group von Hake established a strong bridgehead south of the villages of Fiagdon and Rassvet. As the next reinforcements, the 43rd Kradschützen Battalion and the II/66 with the subordinated I/4 Pz.Rgt. fought their way into the Fiagdon bridgehead. Battle Group Scholz with the 93rd Panzergrenadier Regiment and the II/4 Pz.Rgt. could not close with the bridgehead due to great terrain problems.

With extended open flanks and a strong threat from the villages of Rassvet and Fiagdon it was difficult to expand the clever attack of Battle Group von Hake into the outer defensive ring of Ordzhonikidze for a decisive success. During the night supply vehicles were advanced to the bridgehead. The efforts made by the drivers and supply troops would appear in few military histories. However, these men, who had to deal with weather and terrain problems and fight in enemy infested sectors, were the nameless ones who helped decide the battles. The same goes for the medical service. Surgeons and medics, the Samaritans who fought for the lives of their wounded comrades, who performed their duty quietly in the shadows, deserve special thanks.

On 2 November at 0500 hours "Operation Darg Kokh" began. As already explained, a group from the 13th Panzerjäger Battalion, under Hauptmann Barth, and the 5/"Brandenburg", under the leadership of the II/"Brandenburg", Major Jakobi, were committed to the Northwest after the capture of Ardon in order to capture the railroad and road bridge near Darg Kokh in a raid and, if necessary, block against a Russian flank attack.

After a careful preparation, Gruppe Barth-Jakobi captured the railroad bridge in a raid. The enemy, who was at first surprised, assembled and launched a counterattack. The Germans on the railroad bridge were systematically placed under fire. Heavy Russian artillery, which was positioned to fire to the north, turned their guns to the east and participated in the battle. A German stuka attack gave only little relief. The 370th ID, which was to attack out of its positions near Elkhotovo to the south in order to reach the bridge on the eastern bank of the Terek, did not leave its positions. Therefore, the few elements on the railroad bridge were forced to withdraw, but the railroad bridge could still be covered by machine-gun fire. During the following night, however, the Russians blew a portion of the railroad bridge. Officers who were killed during "Operation Darg Kokh" included Leutnant Freye from the panzerjägers and Major Jakobi and Leutnant Reinicke from the "Brandenburgers". Later the Soviets would continue to attack from this area in order to bring down the German defenses which had, in the meantime, been established between Terek, Fiagdon and the mountains.

On 2 November Battle Group von Hake also continued its attack. During the night the 43rd Kradschützen Battalion, II/66 Pz.Gren.Rgt. and I/4 Pz.Rgt. closed ranks. The divisional commander, Oberst Dr. Kühn, and his Ia, Oberstleutnant Kraemer, reached the lead elements with the reinforcements. By early morning the I/66 attacked dismounted. After penetrating the security the panzergrenadier companies reached the village of Nizhnaya Saniba, advancing through poor terrain over Hill 604.1, but without coming upon any notable resistance. The battalion regrouped and, after leaving Nizhnaya Saniba, took heavy defensive fire from Gisel. After crossing the wet Gisel sector, the first elements of the I/66 penetrated into the northern portion of Gisel. A bitter battle ensued for the town. The 66th achieved a foothold in Gisel. All of the companies of the I/66 followed. Because the enemy situation to the north was unclear, strong security was set out oriented in that direction.

Enemy tanks with escorting infantry rolled toward Gisel from the north. The tanks drove through the security and reached Gisel. The enemy's escorting infantry was repulsed. A similar combined enemy attack was launched on Gisel from the south. The situation was serious. The I/66 was encircled in Gisel. Combat grew fierce. Each house was fought for. However, the combat tested panzergrenadiers did not loose their nerve for one moment. Finally tanks and SPW arrived, having found a way across the difficult terrain, and soon all of the enemy tanks in Gisel were destroyed. At midday Gisel was completely occupied by the Germans.

By 1300 hours the vehicles were refueled, ammunition was resupplied and the formation was organized again. Then the attack continued toward Ordzhonikidze. The Russian defensive fire considerably increased with anti-tank, artillery and rocket launchers. Rolling air attacks covered the lead attack elements with bombs. New phosphorus bombs rained down inflicting horrible burns on the skin. In spite of it all Battle Group von Hake penetrated into the Ordzhonikidze defensive belt. As soon as the German panzer forces formed for a new attack the Soviets again attacked into their rear from north and south of Gisel, forcing the lead German elements to stop. By evening, when the II/66 was able to close on Gisel, the German attack wedge was better stabilized. The assault group from Battle Group von Hake established a hasty defense at the fall of darkness near Point 632.6, 2.5 kilometers in front of the northwestern edge of Ordzhonikidze. Battle Group Scholz (93rd Panzergrenadier Regiment) advanced through many terrain obstacles, maintaining a constant defense against enemy flanking attacks, and made it to Nizhnaya Saniba. A I/66 freight train with ammunition and fuel made it through enemy and terrain obstacles to the advanced I/66.

On 2 November the 23rd Panzer Division also advanced further to the east. While Battle Group Brückner secured near Alagir, Battle Group Burmeister captured Khataldon against weak resistance, attacked across an undamaged Fiagdon bridge and reached the road fork to the east bypassing the village of Dzuarikau

On 3 November the dramatic battle for Ordzhonikidze began. This city was formerly known as Vladikavkaz; it was the gate to the Georgian Army Road, a pass over the high mountains possible by even heavy vehicles. In order to estimate the significance of this pass the military-geographic work of the Fulpmes High Mountain School interpreted prisoner statements, descriptions and interrogations of natives, Russian literature and agent reports. All of the mountain crossings were camouflaged with numbers. Under number 17 we read: "Ordzhonikidze through Krestoviy Pass - Tiflis (Georgian Army Road. 214 kilometers): With the exception of January and February, because snow blocks the pass, suitable for transport of vehicles of all types.

Ordzhonikidze - Kazbek sector: Road runs into the Daryalsker Gorge. West of the road there is a rocky mountain extending 3-5 kilometers. There is no turn-around on the entire stretch. No natural camouflage. Radii of the curves average 10-100 meters. There are many hairpin turns. In some places there is only one-way traffic. There is snow drifting in winter. There are telegraph poles with 12 lines along the stretch. There are no possibilities for landing.

Kazbek - Ananuri sector: No two-way traffic possible. Radii of the curves average 5-10 meters. The pass is blocked in January and February. There is insufficient camouflage, especially in front of the pass. There are telephone and telegraph poles with 6-8 lines. There are landing possibilities between Kazbek and Passanauri..

Ananuri - Kuptiantkari sector: No lateral movement possible. Radii of the curves average 50-100 meters. There is a landing possibility 2 kilometers north of Kupriantkari.

Kupriantkari to the southern edge of the map: Only limited turn-around areas available. Shrubs and forest are on either side of the road.

The following garrisons are located on the Georgian Army Road: Distance from Ordzhonikidze:

12.0 km opposite Balta station
73.5 km 8 km south of Koba, Baidar Garrison

75.8 km mountain pass (2388 meters)
82.5 km near town of Kumlis-Zikhe
131.7 km 14 km south of Passanauri."

Under Nr. 14 the study had the following to say about the Georgian Army Road, which began near Alagir:

"Salugardan - Alagir through Mamisson Pass (2829 meters) - Kutaissi (Ossetian Army Road): The pass is free of snow from June to the end of September. The road is possible by carts. Mountain troops have to tow small combat vehicles. Essentially passable by all-terrain vehicles. The road can be easily blocked at many locations, gorges and bridges."

Add to this military-geographic description another short historical extract:

The Georgian Army Road has had great significance since ancient times. Here ran an important route of the Turkish Empire, which once encompassed all of the Caucasus. Many of the mountain people were followers of the Prophet Mohammed. When the Turkish Empire fell, the Russians penetrated into the Caucasus, threw the mountain people into camps and christianized them. Its incorporation into Russia occurred in 1801. After the area was christianized a great cross was erected on the mountain pass, from which the pass was named.

From this description it can be seen that the Georgian Army Road was the only passible crossing in the eastern portion of the mountains. In retrospect it is understandable why von Kleist wanted to put the majority of the German gebirgsjägers there, to block the unsuitable crossings. Von Kleist had his objective within reach. However, besides his III Panzer Corps, he only had the I/99 Geb.Jg.Rgt. available under his clever and mountain experienced Major Kopp. A German gebirgsjäger battalion and General Dumitrache's 2nd Rumanian Mountain Division, which lagged behind the German mountain divisions in equipment and training, had to achieve this important mission.

First they had to push open the door to Ordzhonikidze. In addition, on 3 November 1942 the 13th Panzer Division was also committed. The I/99 Geb.Jg.Rgt. with a battery of the 203rd Assault Gun Battalion and a company of the 627th Engineer Battalion were subordinated to the division. They had the mission of penetrating to the Georgian Army Road after the city fell.

Supply problems delayed the commitment of the 13th Panzer Division. Then it attacked! With the II/66 on the left, the II/93 on the right and the I/66 echeloned to the rear on the left the battalions worked their way over the highlands to within 2 kilometers of the western edge of the city. Rolling air attacks by the 4th Soviet Air Army and heavy artillery blocking fire caused considerable losses. The weather made air support from distant bases impossible. The I and II/4 Pz.Rgt. advanced laterally to within 800 meters southeast of Gisel and supported the advance of the panzergrenadiers. The III/4 Pz.Rgt. covered the ever threatened northern flank with the 43rd Kradschützen Battalion. The II/66 fought its way up to the anti-tank trenches at the airfield. The II/93 closed on the same line at 1445 hours. The I/66 followed slowly in second echelon. A fierce battle began in the Ordzhonikidze defensive zone. At the fall of darkness 15 bunkers were destroyed and two successive anti-tank trenches were overcome.

In the meantime a dramatic battle was being played out behind the forward battalions. Newly deployed enemy elements attacked into the thin flank cover from the north. A company of the 93rd Panzergrenadier Regiment and a company of the 43rd Kradschützen Battalion had held out near the town of Fiagdon since early morning by committing all of their forces. This location appeared to be a tender spot. Realizing this, von Mackensen diverted the lead elements of the 23rd Panzer Division, Battle Group Burmeister, from Dzuarikau to the north in order to reinforce the flank security of the 13th Panzer Division. A subsequent attack by Battle Group Burmeister on Arkhonskaya stalled in enemy fire. The strong enemy occupied town of Fiagdon dominated the 13th Panzer Division supply route and the ford with heavy fire.

At the same time the long supply route near Ardonski was severed by the enemy. The weakened 128th Panzergrenadier Regiment was deployed there from the Alagir area and committed, but its attack stalled. Meanwhile, the 126th Panzergrenadier Regiment, which was left in the 23rd Panzer Division bridgehead, repulsed a Soviet relief attack near Dzuarikau. The 23rd Panzer Division, therefore, was split apart and had the mission of mopping up the rear of the 13th Panzer Division, as it was fighting near Ordzhonikidze. The losses of the 13th Panzer Division on 3 November totaled: 67 killed, 159 wounded and 6 missing.

During the early morning of 4 November Battle Group von Hake continued its attack, eliminated several enemy bunkers and assaulted enemy field positions that lay one behind the other. Hauptmann Steinberg and his II/93 Pz.Gren.Rgt. reached the radio station at 1130 hours and, an hour later, a large industrial area. The airfield was covered by infantry weapons. On this day ground gains totaled 600 meters. The division leadership informed the corps that further advance would not be possible until the threatening flanking fire on the supply route on both sides of Nizhnaya Saniba - Gisel was removed and reinforcements were deployed. 13th Panzer Division losses for 4 November 1942: 14 killed, 88 wounded. 70 tanks were operational.

The 23rd Panzer Division (General von Boineburg-Lengsfeld) tried to remove the threat in the Fiagdon flank. Battle Group Burmeister suffered considerable casualties during an attack on the town of Fiagdon. The II/201 Pz.Rgt. had only ten tanks left, which were distributed to other battalions.

The supply services and staffs were combed for replacements to fill the gaps in the combat formations. Von Mackensen's corps had no reserves left. Together the two divisions had a front of 40 kilometers to hold.

On the third day of the battle the Soviets had overcome their initial shock in the foreground of Ordzhonikidze. They tenaciously hung on to their defense, which consisted of numerous field positions, bunker lines, anti-tank trenches and anti-tank gun and mine obstacles. On the third day of the battle for Ordzhonikidze Generallissimo Stalin was to visit the city and exhort them to reorganize the defense. Stalin, the Georgian, would leave no stone unturned to prevent the Germans from penetrating his former homeland. The door to Georgia was made impregnable; tanks were thrown into the battle right from the factory. Allied shipments to Ordzhonikidze were increased. Reserves for a new counterattack were taken from the Malgobek and Grosny areas and thrown into Ordzhonikidze. With each passing hour the enemy resistance increased in Ordzhonikidze.

In spite of all of this the 13th Panzer Division attacked again on 5 November. The brave I/99 Geb.Jg.Rgt. fought at the edge of the mountains through numerous obstacles and advanced through the most difficult terrain and knocked out 15 bunkers from a deeply echeloned bunker line. They went over to the defense near Sayatdshiaa Balka. Contact was established with the 93rd Panzergrenadier Regiment, which was fighting in the left rear. Forces from the I/99 Geb.Jg.Rgt. occupied Hill 1035 during the night.

To the north the 93rd Panzergrenadier Regiment and the II/66, supported by several tanks, captured a tenaciously defended Kolkhoz and advanced to a dominant ridge line on the northwestern edge of the city.

The 4th Armored Engineer Battalion was in heavy combat near Nogir, to the north of the city. The battalion, which had lost its fearless commander, Hauptmann Dankwort, near Fiagdon, was now led by Hauptmann Baranek.

On the left next to the engineers fought the 43rd Kradschützen Battalion on the Arkhanskaya - Gisel road. It was constantly attacked by the enemy Air Force. Two enemy armored trains from the Tulatov - Ordzhonikidze stretch joined in the battle. This was also detected by Battle Group Burmeister, which could not advance in the Rassvet - Fiagdon area west of the 43rd Kradschützen Battalion.

On 5 November the 13th Panzer Division could only achieve small ground gains. It was stalled on the western and northwestern edge of the city, while the northern flank security was extended to the Nogir area (8 kilometers north of the city). On this day a radio message intercepted by the I/99 Geb.Jg.Rgt. confirmed the rumor that Stalin was in the city.

It was already clear that the III Panzer Corps had to be supported by a relief attack. Of interest is the notation in the Army Group A combat diary on 5 November 1942: "In the LII Army Corps area of operations, "Wiking" improved the positions near Malgobek by a surprise attack..." and under considerations was noted: "... relieve "Wiking" with the 50th ID and advance it through the Elkhotovo pass or through Voznessenskaya to the south."

In fact, such a relief attack would have helped the 13th Panzer Division, especially since the Soviets would also have to denude their front before the LII Army Corps. However, the Russians were quicker and they dictated events.

On 6 November the Soviet counter-strike began in front of Ordzhonikidze. A reinforced brigade each, supported by numerous tanks, broke out of the narrow area from the north and south, behind the 13th Panzer Division, which was standing in front of Ordzhonikidze. The dark November day prefaced the destruction of the 13th Panzer Division. The Russians broke through from the north and the south between them and the elements of the 23rd Panzer Division, which were fighting near Rassvet. At the same time a second attack occurred out of the Mairamadag Valley to the north, which pushed back the forces of the 23rd Panzer Division and the 2nd Rumanian Mountain Division toward the Dzuarikau bridgehead. In this situation the 13th Panzer Division had to withdraw its forward-most elements from Ordzhonikidze and establish them in a new defense near Gisel. The 43rd Kradschützen Battalion and the 4th Armored Engineer Battalion had held out for some time on the northern flank when they were threatened by 15 enemy tanks. The rapidly deployed II/4 Pz.Rgt. destroyed 10 of them. The III/4 Pz.Rgt., which was located further to the left, pushed the enemy breakthrough forces to the west, then attacked into their flank; another 9 tanks were destroyed. Enemy elements broke through to the 13th Panzer Division supply route and destroyed vehicles and entire convoys. The 13th Panzer Division was cut off.

It was similar in the south. There an enemy attack ran into the Wiedling Alert Battalion, which had taken up positions during the night near 576.3 (north of Mairamadag). The battalion, which was composed of supply troops and staff members, was surprised and fought its way to Dzuarikau. Much of the 13th Panzer Division supply was destroyed by enemy tanks and infantry.

The 23rd Panzer Division, which had some forces located in the Dzuarikau bridgehead and others near Rassvet and Fiagdon in order to hold open the road to the 13th Panzer Division, was bloodied in this punishing battle. The battalions averaged a combat strength of only 80 men.

On 7 November the crisis worsened even more. Enemy forces penetrated into the weakly occupied Ardon; they were thrown back at great effort. The Darg Kokh - Ardon sector was secured half-way to Fiagdon by a hastily thrown together battle group under Oberst Kampfhenkel (Arko 3). Battle Group Illig (10 tanks from the 201st Panzer Regiment and two Rumanian battalions) attacked out of the Dzuarikau area to the east and was able to establish contact with the southern flank of the 13th Panzer Division. There was no change on the northern flank of the encirclement front.

The 13th Panzer Division lay in a half-circle around Gisel and repulsed bitter enemy attacks. The division was organized into Sectors "Nord" (43rd Kradschützen Battalion), "Mitte" (4th Armored Engineer Battalion) and "Süd" (Battle Group Scholz with the 93rd Panzergrenadier Regiment). Battle Group von Hake with the 66th Panzergrenadier Regiment was to open the way to the west. It was in combat with enemy tanks 4 kilometers west of Nizhnaya Saniba. By evening it was able to fight its way to the ford near Dzuarikau and make contact with the 23rd Panzer Division elements located there. However, the overall situation was not improved.

How attentively the senior German leadership followed the battle taking place before Ordzhonikidze was indicated in the daily telegrams. On 7 November at 2300 hours the Army Chief of the General Staff pointed out to the Chief of Staff of Army Group A that the 3rd Panzer Division must remain as active as possible in order to pin the enemy and simulate an attack. This was good advice, but no more than that! The 3rd Panzer Division, which was on the Army Group A northern flank, had enough problems watching over and holding its own front.

On the morning of 8 November the new division commander, General von der Chevallerie, arrived at the 13th Panzer Division command post near Nizhnaya Saniba in a tank. The Soviets were reinforcing on all sectors and entrenching in front of the 13th Panzer Division. In front of Sector "Nord" eight attacking enemy tanks were destroyed. The I/4 Pz.Rgt. (Major Montfort) had to intervene on this sector several times because heavy attacks were repeated. Contact with the 23rd Panzer Division was also sought, but it was not established. During the evening the I/4 Pz.Rgt. broke out to the west in order to guide a freight train near Khataldon with rations, ammunition and medicine into the pocket. In the main first aid point at Nizhnaya Saniba were 400 severely wounded, who could not be evacuated. During the evening the division reported to the corps that the defensive line on the eastern edge of Gisel could not be held much longer.

On 9 November 1942 under "Sector" in the Army Group A combat diary was noted: "... the attack wedge against Ordzhonikidze is withdrawing and a new main effort is being established near Malgobek; including the 13th Panzer Division, 50th and 111th ID and SS Division "Wiking"."

This was hurrying things! On this day General von Mackensen had already issued the order to withdraw the 13th Panzer Division. While the 4th panzer Regiment was ready, it withdrew into three sector groups to the eastern edge of Gisel. The I/4 Pz.Rgt. returned with supplies into the pocket. All wheeled vehicles had to be left behind due to the weather and the supplies were loaded in and onto the tanks.

The important ford across the marshy and steep Mairamadag and Solanaya Valleys, which had become increasingly bottomless from the bad weather, still lay under the effective fire of heavy enemy weapons. There, at this ford, the last phase of the drama before Ordzhonikidze would be played out.

As the dramatic developments unfolded before Ordzhonikidze, the 50th ID, which was severely battered in the Crimea and then sent to protect the coast and be refitted, was prepared for commitment in the Caucasus. The security of the Crimea was taken over by the 5th Luftwaffe Field Division. On 27 October the commander of the 50th ID, Generalmajor Schmidt, was oriented on the situation by the XXXXII Army Corps. On 31 October the units of the 50th ID reached Kerch and immediately crossed. Their subsequent march objective was: Krasnodar. In the meantime the 50th ID was subordinated to the LII Army Corps. The first regiment, the 122nd Grenadier Regiment, was flown from Krasnodar to Armavir and then further transported by rail. It arrived in Pavlodolskiy on 11 November 1942 and relieved the SS Division "Wiking" platoon by platoon in the Malgobek sector. "Wiking" had already freed-up battalions on its front and replaced them with alert units.

II/"Nordland" was the first formation of "Wiking" to arrive in the 23rd Panzer Division area of operations through Kotlyarevskiy - Stariy Urukh - Ardon - Alagir on 10 November and was immediately committed to relieve the 13th Panzer Division. On 11 November the I and II/"Germania" arrived and were also committed to relieve the 13th Panzer Division at 2000 hours.

Also on 10 November the 23rd Panzer Division made a fruitless attempt to expand its narrow foothold. Moreover, elements of the 4th Panzer Regiment were assembled. Strong enemy attacks, supported by tanks, flared up along the entire 13th Panzer Division defensive front. With great sacrifice, the three sector groups prevented matters from turning into chaos. During the evening the defensive front of the 13th Panzer Division was in a half-circle around Nizhnaya Saniba. In the meantime all wheeled vehicles were prepared for the breakout. The division order read:

"... all transportable vehicles, weapons and equipment are to be taken. Everything else is to be destroyed..."

On the afternoon of 10 November General von Mackensen conducted a briefing with the commander of the II/"Nordland", Stubaf. Stoffers, and other staff officers. Also attending were the liaison officer from the II/"Nordland", Ustuf. Kallmann, as well as the assault group commander, Oscha. Karl Orf from the 7/"Nordland". They decided to attack with an assault troop opposite the breakout attack of the 13th Panzer Division to remove the wounded.

At 1500 hours the mostly empty vehicles of the 13th Panzer Division set out to break out to the west. Leading were the vehicles with the severely wounded under the command of Oberst Dr. Kühn. The lightly wounded were moved on foot and in vehicles. The columns approached the ford in good order. In the meantime Battle Group von Hake cleared the area east of the ford and pushed the Soviets back to the north. The columns marched further; tanks were in the lead, followed by Oberst Dr. Kühn with the wounded and then the other vehicles. They crossed the ford. On the opposite side, the I/4 Pz.Rgt. passed through the security to the old 13th Panzer Division march route. Anxious minutes passed in no-mans land, then Oberst Dr. Kühn at the head of the wounded ran into Assault Troop Orf from the 7/"Nordland". They made it! Under the protection of the II/"Nordland", the 13th Panzer Division columns fled to the west. At 2300 hours, after the majority of the vehicles with the wounded had passed the ford, the division headquarters also withdrew from Nizhnaya Saniba.

The vehicles rolled across the ford to freedom during the entire night. However, with the dawn of the new day (11 November 1942), enemy fire engaged the ford. Anti-tank guns, anti-tank rifles and mortars fired from dominant positions. Vehicles were hit and blocked the ford. Twenty tanks from the 4th Panzer Regiment and infantry weapons were committed against the Russian fire front without success. The Soviets dominated the activities on the ford from good positions. Tracked vehicles tried to re-open the ford without success. Vehicle losses increased rapidly. Under these circumstances the division commander stopped the operation in order to await the fall of darkness and search for a new ford.

On 11 November 1942 the difficult decision was made to break out with all of the forces of the 13th Panzer Division remaining in the east, even if the numerous vehicles had to be destroyed, especially since a new tank attack was anticipated from the Mairamadag Gorge. The southern portion of the foothold had become extremely shaky. That a catastrophe did not occur here was thanks to the commander of the "Wiking" Panzer Battalion, Stubaf. Mühlenkamp. It was his battalion that marched through Ardon - Alagir. The assembly of enemy tank forces was discovered in the Dzuarikau bridgehead. Mühlenkamp, the old, experienced panzer leader, was able to figure out what was happening there. By chance he noticed the unloading of a Luftwaffe anti-aircraft battalion while he was passing through Alagir. After a short discussion with the commander of the 23rd Panzer Division, General von Boineburg-Lengsfeld, Mühlenkamp received permission to deploy the Luftwaffe anti-aircraft battalion. The eighty-eights moved into position. Not a minute too soon, 20 enemy tanks were already rolling out of the Mairamadag Valley in the direction of Nizhnaya Saniba. The eighty-eights destroyed the enemy tank attack.

By the fall of darkness the three defensive sectors of the 13th Panzer Division withdrew. In spite of the dramatic circumstances everything went like clockwork. At 1630 hours Sector "Mitte" evacuated its positions under the cover of a weak rear guard. Sector "Süd" followed. "Süd" and "Mitte" joined to breakthrough into Nizhnaya Saniba. The wounded were in the center. The enemy resistance was broken, but the new ford presented another obstacle. It was next to an extremely marshy area that could not be crossed by wheeled vehicles. Many vehicles had to be abandoned there; they were disabled. These included almost all of the vehicles and rocket launchers of the II/52 Werfer Rgt.

The 43rd Kradschützen Battalion (Sector "Nord"), which was the last to withdraw with the rear guard, broke contact unnoticed by the enemy at 1800 hours, found a new ford, across which most of the vehicles passed, and made contact with friendly troops.

The majority of the 13th Panzer Division, including all of the wounded, was able to withdraw into the temporary positions established by the initial elements of "Wiking" (I and II/"Germania", II/"Nordland", the panzer battalion and elements of the "Wiking" Panzerjäger Battalion) because of concise leadership.

On the early morning of 12 November the Soviets realized that the Gisel - Nizhnaya Saniba pocket was empty. The 13th Panzer Division, which was to open the door to the Georgian Army Road, was not destroyed. Indeed, many of its vehicles were left behind, but its combat morale was not shaken. No one gave up, no one lost their head. It must also be noted that not a single wounded soldier was left behind. The sacrifice was high, but they performed their soldierly duty well.

The loss balance sheet for the III Panzer Corps and the Soviets for the time period 19 October to 12 November 1941, the period of the entire operation from Baksan to Ordzhonikidze, was given by von Mackensen in his book, "From the Bug to the Caucasus", as follows:

Enemy losses: 16,100 killed; 188 tanks and 4 armored trains destroyed. 249 guns and 881 heavy infantry weapons captured. Friendly losses: 1,275 killed, 273 missing, 5008 wounded.

The combat diary of Army Group A offered: 507 killed, 1918 wounded, 82 missing.

According to the Army Group A Diary, 13th Panzer Division vehicle losses for the same time period were:

26/10 - 11/11/1942: 45 tanks, 592 trucks.

On the night of 11-12/11 (breakthrough: 18 tanks and 496 trucks.

A German panzer division had a full strength of about 150 tanks (three battalions). In the reports from the 13th Panzer Division we read under 1 November 1942: 119 operational tanks. 4 November 1942: 70 operational tanks. 17 November 1942: 32 operational tanks.

On the other hand, we have Russian sources. "The Battle for the Caucasus" resulted in: "...140 damaged tanks, 70 guns, 91 mortars, 4 rocket launchers, 84 machine-guns and 2350 trucks were captured. In the Gisel area, the Germans left more than 5000 dead."

The 23rd Panzer Division is often reproached for not energetically pursuing the removal of the crisis on the northern flank of the 13th Panzer Division. Calculations show that they were in no position to do so. At the end of October the 23rd Panzer Division was located on the right, on the mountain flank, and had a bridgehead near Dzuarikau over the Fiagdon. Its security groups were delayed in being relieved by the Rumanians. On 1 November the 13th Panzer Division made it to Gisel and, at the same time, crises developed near the villages of Rassvet and Fiagdon, which necessitated the diversion of considerable forces from the 23rd Panzer Division. Thus, the combat strength of the 23rd Panzer Division was dispersed.

Nevertheless, the fortunate retreat from Gisel would have been questionable without the commitment of the hastily deployed SS Division "Wiking". Once again the true Waffenbrüderschaft between the "Wiking" and the 13th Panzer Division, which had already been cemented during the first year of the war in Russia in the III Panzer Corps, bore fruit.

DEFENSE ON THE MOUNTAIN FLANKS

Ardon, hard fought for cornerstone - Tanks iron out a penetration - The III Panzer Corps withdraws - Christmas celebration with tank fire - Finns and Romanians block the Kossolkun Valley

During the night of 12 November the withdrawing 13th Panzer Division moved behind a blocking line which was formed by the 23rd Panzer Division and "Wiking". The new HKL ran through the Dzuarikau bridgehead - Rassvet - Fiagdon River - east of Ardon and made contact with the LII Army Corps near Elkhotovo. The new defensive line was thin at first because "Wiking" was only slowly being relieved by the 50th ID. All available units were brought up to reinforce the defensive line; including Oberstleutnant Emsmann's 52nd Werfer Regiment Headquarters, the I and II/52 Werfer Rgt. and elements of the 1st Werfer Regiment which had taken over the artillery defense in the Rassvet sector. The responsibility for this sector lay in the hands of the 23rd Panzer Division commander, General Baron von Boineburg-Lengsfeld, and his Ia, Oberstleutnant Freyer.

In the meantime the 13th Panzer Division assembled in the Alagir area to refit its formations. For several companies, this was to be only a short break. Since the III Panzer Corps had no reserves left, the 13th Panzer Division could not complete the refitting of its battalions. At this time Major Brux took over the 43rd Kradschützen Battalion; his I/66 Pz.Gren.Rgt. was taken over by the former commander of the 2/66, Hauptmann von Gaza. On 13 November the battalion was subordinated to the Arko 3 and set in march to Kadgoron. The Arko 3 was securing the lower Fiagdon with weak forces. Ardon, the cornerstone of the Rassvet - Dzuarikau frontal salient, was already indicated as the main effort of an upcoming battle. The newly reorganized elements of the 13th Panzer Division were transferred to this area as they became ready; so much for their respite.

Right after the battle near Gisel the commander of the "Transcaucasus Front" was summoned to STAVKA. New plans were coordinated. On 14 November the 1st Generalstabsoffizier of Army Group A notified the 1st Generalstabsoffizier of the 1st Panzer Army that the Hitschold Luftwaffe formation (stukas and fighters) had to be deployed to the Stalingrad area.

On 13 and 14 November Russian formations attacked the front of the 23rd Panzer Division at several locations and were repulsed. In the meantime additional elements of "Wiking" advanced to take over the Dzuarikau sector from the 23rd Panzer Division.

On 15 November General von der Chevallerie took over the Arko 3 front and inserted the 13th Panzer Division into the front on either side of Ardon as reinforcement.

On 16 November the Soviets tried to breakthrough the German HKL at their old Rassvet deployment point. A report describes the commitment of the "Wiking" Panzer Battalion and a smaller panzer group from the 23rd Panzer Division as follows: "The "Wiking" Panzer Battalion has the following mission: The enemy is penetrating into the HKL north of Rassvet with strong forces, including tanks, anti-tank guns and anti-aircraft guns. The panzer battalion has to restore the old HKL with two companies. They are to attack from the south, from Mount Rassvet, where the enemy is also trying to penetrate. The mission of the tanks is to support the weak German infantry. Tanks of the 23rd Panzer Division will also attack here from the north and later join up with the "Wiking" Panzer Battalion."

At 1000 hours the panzer companies left the assembly area. They advanced over extremely unfavorable terrain which offered the enemy every opportunity for defense, but the German tanks forced their way into the forward slope positions of the enemy. The enemy recognized his advantage and occupied favorable positions with his tanks. Soon the tanks faced each other, both sides ready to attack, each side anticipating that the other would advance first into his guns. A direct attack of the German tanks was not conducted because it would have resulted in heavy losses. During the evening the situation reflected the following: Approximately 26 enemy tanks, effectively supported by strong artillery, anti-tank guns and anti-aircraft guns, faced the German tanks.

During the early morning of 17 November the artillery duel began. There were low-lying clouds and visibility was poor. The tanks of the 23rd Panzer Division attacked from the northwest toward the "Wiking" tanks and inserted themselves to their left. They were widely dispersed and camouflaged with oak leaves. Both commanders discussed the situation. A direct attack would lead to heavy casualties; a flanking maneuver was not possible due to the terrain. They would try to create a gap in the enemy's positions with a barrage. In order to increase the effectiveness of this barrage, all of the tanks would quickly advance under its cover and join in the barrage with their own cannon.

It came to a bitter shoot-out between German and enemy tanks, in which enemy anti-tank and anti-aircraft guns played a part. Tracer rounds flitted here and there. However, the "cat and mouse" game came to an end on this day. At 1500 hours the falling darkness hindered visibility. The artillery duel surged to a crescendo then ebbed in the darkness. Then they had to wait to see if the enemy would redeploy under the cover of darkness.

At 0300 hours, a half-hour before dawn, the second artillery battle began, first with isolated shots, then with mounting concentrations. The Germans discovered that the enemy tanks had withdrawn a little. This gave the German tanks an opportunity to attack. It was initiated with heavy artillery fire. The German tanks advanced into the smoke of the artillery rounds. The attack was played out in the command tanks of the two commanders as follows:

The 3rd Company, whose code name began with B, reported over radio at 0835 hours, approximately 5 minutes after the attack began, that the German artillery attack on the enemy had been effective and requested a second barrage. 0837 hours: B receives strong tank, anti-tank and anti-aircraft fire from the right.

0838 hours: W, the 2nd Company, which was advancing on the right of B, reports: Reached gravel pit. A platoon is advancing on the right.

0839 hours: W reports: A T-34 is in flames. W requests artillery fire on enemy battery which is firing on the company from the right.

0850 hours: W reports: Enemy tanks have withdrawn across the stream (Fiagdon) and are establishing a strong fire front on the other side. Request artillery on Town N. (Norton) because we are in their direct line of fire.

0900 hours: W reports: Friendly infantry is advancing from left to right and is making contact with us. - Query from the commander to W: Where do you want artillery fire? On assembled tanks or on positions in the town further to the left? W to commander: Please fire on the tanks.

0920 hours: Commander queries Platoon E (reconnaissance platoon): What is the situation in your area? - E to commander: Supporting the attack to the north. Strong incoming artillery and air defense fire.

0930 hours: E to commander: Enemy infantry penetrating into village. Holding R. (Rassvet) with friendly infantry.

0945 hours: Commander to panzerjägers: Panzerjägers advance to my line. Commander to my command post.

1000 hours: W to commander: Urgently request strong artillery fire on tanks. Tanks located to the left of the command post in the white houses.

1010 hours: B to W: Pass it on! Enemy tanks are advancing to the left in a counterattack.

1020 hours: W to commander: Enemy attacking with 12 tanks on the right flank. Request artillery fire on the northern edge of R. Order to panzerjägers: Advance another 300 meters. Order to artillery: Concentrate fire on assigned target.

1022 hours: W to commander: Enemy tanks moving from right to left and are trying to reach the gravel pit again.

1023 hours: E (Reconnaissance Platoon) attacks the enemy tanks from behind.

1024 hours: Order to artillery: Increase fire.

1025 hours: To artillery: Fire on the right flank. Order to W and B: Stay on the reverse slope and let the enemy roll by you.

1026 hours: Order to the tanks still in the assembly area: Advance on the right flank immediately and take up flank security.

1030 hours: B to commander: Urgently request artillery fire on the depression in front of me.

1041 hours: W to commander: Second wave of enemy tanks, at least 10 tanks, coming out of the cornfield.

The enemy artillery fire was not as strong as the German. One German tank, which withdrew to repair some small damage, took back wounded infantrymen. The artillery fire roared in between the tattering of the machine-gun fire. Stalin Organs fired and set off long curtains of dirt and smoke.

1110 hours: W to B: Look further to the right. An enemy tank is trying to slip around and attack you in the flank.

1113 hours: W to commander: Heavy enemy infantry movement in front of me. The enemy has an anti-tank gun.

A tank from the 23rd Panzer Division came back with a wounded tank crew. It stopped next to the medical tank. The wounded were laid in a small depression. The tank provided cover. A surgeon and some medical personnel helped the wounded.

1130 hours: W to commander: Ten enemy tanks crossing the stream in a new attack.

1131 hours: Commander to W: Where do you want the artillery fire?

1132 hours: B to commander: Four enemy tanks attacking to the gravel pit; they have at least a battalion of infantry with them. Fire artillery over the fire-fight.

1137 hours: W to commander: The artillery fire is ok.

1139 hours: W to commander: The artillery fire is very precise. The fire is very effective. B to commander: Enemy infantry attacking out of the right from village N. They are about two companies strong. Four T-34's are coming from the same direction.

1151 hours: E to commander: Enemy attack on northern edge of R. repulsed. Tanks and friendly infantry again in their old positions.

1157 hours: W and B to commander: Enemy attack has stopped. Infantry again in their old positions.

1158 hours: Report to division: Old HKL re-established. Proposal: Disperse infantry between the tanks and mine the front of the HKL.

The mission of the panzer battalion was accomplished. The artillery continued firing on both sides. Tanks and panzerjägers were widely dispersed along the defensive front in case they were needed. In the late afternoon the enemy again tried to break through with tanks. After a short but fierce fire-fight this attack was also repulsed. Two additional enemy tanks were burning, five were rendered inoperable. The panzerjägers reported several destroyed and several damaged tanks.

According to a report from Uscha. Eckert the cooperation between the various branches of arms was significant. However, he also pointed out the cooperation between the leaders and their subordinates.

On 19 November Division "Wiking" was subordinated to the III Panzer Corps. It took over the right flank of the corps front. On 24 November the last elements of the SS Division "Wiking" arrived and, therefore, the withdrawal of the 23rd Panzer Division began at the same time. The 23rd was marched to Prokhladny in order to be deployed by rail to the 4th Panzer Army near Kotelnikovo for its relief attack on Stalingrad.

From 18 to 23 November there were several successful attacks against the front of the 13th Panzer Division near Ardon. Further attempts to penetrate the German defense on the southern Dzuarikau cornerstone failed in the time period from 27 to 30 November because of the steadfastness of the "Germania" Regiment. There were many incidents on the mountain front; the Romanian officers continued to leave their posts during the night. This was soon noted by the Russians, who then committed their assault troops. The energetic attacks of Hstuf. Pförtner from the "Germania" Regiment finally halted these drives and forced the Romanian officers to remain in their positions. Later the Romanian companies were committed in conjunction with German ones.

At this time the drama at Stalingrad was revealed. Slowly the Soviets also gained operational freedom in the Caucasus. Hitler, who had taken "remote-control" of Army Group A from Feldmarschall List, was incapable of doing anything with it. The commander of the 1st Panzer Army, Generaloberst von Kleist, was named the new commander of Army Group A, with its headquarters in Voroshilovsk (Stavropl). The 1st Panzer Army was taken over by General von Mackensen and the III Panzer Corps by Generalleutnant der Waffen SS Felix Steiner.

On 25 November 1942 the Soviets began a new strike against the III Panzer Corps which stood in the frontal salient on the Fiagdon. The Soviet objective was to break through the German defenses in the 13th Panzer Division sector near Ardon and reach Alagir in a subsequent attack. A second attack was to occur out of the Chikola Valley and gain ground to the north.

Battlegroups of the 13th Panzer Division located near Ardon at the confluence of the Fiagdon and Terek were rocked by barrage fire. Penetrations were ironed out by counterattack. Enemy aircraft joined the battle and paralyzed German troop movement. On the evening of 25 November the 13th Panzer Division was still standing in its positions; it lost no ground.

After weak attacks on 26 November, the Soviets resumed heavier strikes on 27 November. The German HKL was penetrated at several locations under the massive commitment of artillery, tanks and fresh brigades. The few operational tanks of the 4th Panzer Regiment chased from one corner of the front to another with infantry forces organized in commitment groups. At Ardon the 93rd Panzergrenadier Regiment under Major Brux defended desperately. The dairy changed hands several times. The Magdeburg 4th Panzerjäger Battalion struggled around Hill 381.7 and lost its commander, Hauptmann Graul, during a counterattack. Hauptmann Littau took command of the battalion. The 66th Panzergrenadier Regiment and the 43rd Kradsch^349tzen Battalion defended in the Fiagdon bridgehead south of Ardon. The latter finally had to be withdrawn from the front due to heavy casualties. 30 enemy tanks were destroyed in an armored counterattack. The losses of the 13th Panzer Division totaled: 30 killed, 168 wounded and 33 missing.

The morale of the troops, which had had no rest since Gisel, was still excellent. Since the 13th Panzer Division had no reserves available, II/"Westland", the "Wiking" Panzer Battalion, the 203rd Assault Gun Brigade and a battery each of SS air defense and artillery were deployed.

After a frost and a light snow fall on 28 November the sun came out again. The Soviets resumed their attack on the 13th Panzer Division sector. An enemy attack supported by tanks was repulsed near Kodgoron and beaten back by reserves. An enemy battalion broke through the German defense at Hill 435.9, but it was then so weakened by artillery that it had to withdraw that night.

At 1515 hours II/"Westland" was committed against a breakthrough position southeast of Ardon. In spite of tenacious defense the old HKL was regained by the fall of darkness. The bitter combat around the northern cornerstone of the Fiagdon frontal sack [pocket] continued on 29 November. Again the penetrating enemy was thrown back on the right division flank near Kodgoron by Battle Group Polster and II/"Westland"; seven enemy tanks were destroyed.

On 30 November the Soviet attack ceased. After two days of quiet the enemy resumed his attack in the 13th Panzer Division area of operations. Again bitter combat raged, which was described in a combat report from the 93rd Panzergrenadier Regiment: "In 14 days of defensive combat the enemy conducted a total of 67 attacks against the regiment. Of these 4 were in regimental strength, 58 were in battalion strength, the rest were at the strength of two companies.

The enemy's combat objective was Ardon and the Ardon - Alagir road. The X Soviet Guards Rifle Corps (deployed from Isherskaya), with the 5th, 6th and 7th Brigades and the 140th Tank Brigade of 50 tanks, conducted the attack with the support of artillery and mortars. During the battle the enemy amplified his attack with elements of the 319th Rifle Division (1336 Rifle Regiment), the 389th Rifle Division (1277th, 1279th, 545th Rifle regiments) and the 52nd Tank Brigade.

The width of the regimental sector, the unfavorable terrain and the weakness of the regiment, caused by heavy casualties resulted in their battalions attacking into platoon sectors of the regiment.

The enemy achieved 15 penetrations into the HKL and six breakthroughs into the depth of the HKF [Main Battle Field]. To eliminate them the battalions conducted 18 counterattacks, the regiment 15, some supported by tanks and assault guns. After the termination of combat on 8 December the HKL was solidly in German hands. Losses in dead, wounded and missing: 661 men..."

It was similar with other battle groups of the 13th Panzer Division. The division had an average of 30 operational tanks, some of which had to be handed over to the corps reserve so that only three to four commitment groups could be reinforced with four to five tanks. It was the same with The "Wiking" Panzer Battalion.

While the 13th Panzer Division faced heavy defensive combat on its northern flank, it was relatively quiet in the "Wiking" area of operations in the center and on the southern flank. After the "Germania" Regiment had repulsed a large enemy attack in the Dzuarikau area at mid-month, the "Wiking" front was only attacked at times in battalion strength. The defense was strengthened by the intensive construction of positions.

On the long mountain flank the Romanian mountain infantry closed ranks with the German combat formations. To secure the northwestern mountain access, Gruppe "Bergmann", consisting of three to four Turk battalions, was

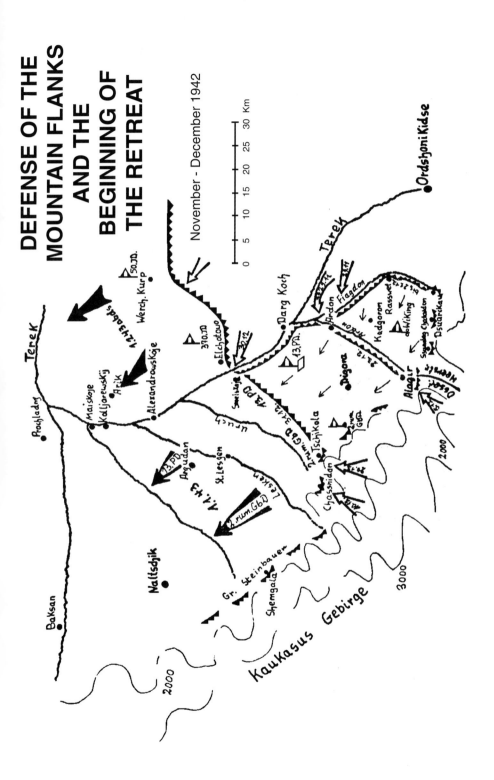

DEFENSE OF THE
MOUNTAIN FLANKS
AND THE
BEGINNING OF
THE RETREAT

November - December 1942

0 5 10 15 20 25 30 Km

deployed; so was Battle Group Steinbauer, which consisted of Georgians. Under 2 November the Army Group A combat diary reads: "A command position from Gruppe Steinbauer advanced to northeast of Lashkuta over difficult terrain. - 19 November 1942: Nizhniy Baksan in the Baksan Valley is occupied by Gruppe Steinbauer. The molybdenum, tungsten and platinum works there were found destroyed."

There is more written in the situation reports about Gruppe Steinbauer later on.

It did not stay quiet on the long mountain flank. There were small groups, no more than battalion strength, attacking the security of the III Panzer Corps. The main defense and attack efforts naturally lay at the entrances and exits to the high mountain valleys. Two of the most threatened points were Alagir on the Ardon and at the beginning of the Ossetian Army Road and Chikola further west in the Urukh Valley.

On 4 December the Soviets attacked Chikola from out of the mountains. Weak security from elements of the 52nd and 54th Rocket Launcher Regiments were pushed back or outflanked. The sector commander, Oberstleutnant Emsmann, requested reinforcements. The III/"Nordland" (Finns), which was located in Digora as a reserve, was alerted and marched to Chikola. In a spirited attack, supported by the launcher batteries, the Finns pushed the attackers back. 13 officers and 246 men were captured. The 295th Soviet Rifle Division attacked with two weak regiments with the mission of capturing Chikola and attacking through to Darg Kokh. The old Soviet plan to cut off the III Panzer Corps on the Fiagdon was still being pursued.

A day later, on 5 December, the Russians attacked in the Ardon - Zrau Valley. There I/99 Geb.Jg.Rgt. blocked the Ossetian Army Road. In the forested mountain terrain the 351st Rifle Division, which was filled with young members of the Communist Youth [Komsomol], gained ground. The gebirgsjäger strong point was lost. A well prepared counterattack by the gebirgsjägers, which was supported by a platoon of the 5th SS Engineer Battalion and artillery from elements of the 1st Heavy Rocket Launcher Regiment and the II/Rum.Geb.Haub.Abt [Howitzer], returned the old positions into German hands on 8 December. Major Kopp held onto the extremely important sector with his headquarters company, his three jäger companies and his heavy companies.

On 10 December III/"Nordland" was again transferred to a shaky front. The companies were committed as "corset rods" in the sector of the 2nd Rumanian Mountain Division between Khasnidon and Toldsgun. The Romanian element in Khasdon was subordinated to the 9th Company under Ustuf. Ertel. During the next few days the enemy probed the German front for a weak spot.

On 15 December the Russians attacked with two battalions against "Wiking" in the Norton area and were thrown back. Two enemy tanks were destroyed.

In the meantime the situation climaxed at Stalingrad. The relief attack of the 4th Panzer Army stalled 60 kilometers in front of the Stalingrad pocket. The Soviets launched new counterattacks; the race for the cut-off at Rostov began. The 4th Panzer Army had to fight a delaying withdrawal battle. The situation in the eastern Caucasus was overshadowed by the events in the Don bend and near Kotelnikovo. Division "Wiking" was freed up and deployed to General Hoth's panzer army.

The front of the III Panzer Corps, which was extended far toward Ordzhonikidze, had to be withdrawn first. The I and II/"Nordland" began on the evening of 21 December and withdrew several kilometers from the middle sector of "Wiking" in order to hold an intermediate position on 22 December. On 23 December both battalions rolled through Alagir, Digora, Chikola toward Prokhladny, where Stubaf. Lohmann's I/"Nordland" became the first "Wiking" unit to load up on rail transports for Stalingrad on 24 December.

On 22 December 1942, it was similar on the right sector in the "Germania" Regiment area of operations. Ostuf. Wanhofer, who defended the Suadag strong point with his company from the 5th SS Engineer Battalion south of the Alagir - Dzuarikau road and was subordinated to the "Germania" Regiment, reported his impressions: "All of the commanders and strong point commandants were assembled in the "Germania" Regiment command post. After a brief greeting the regimental commander opened discussions with a grave countenance. He began with a summary of the situation near Stalingrad and on the entire southern front. He passed over the local situation and he made known the decision of the senior leadership to withdraw the elements in the Fiagdon pocket. After a three day withdrawal the division was to be withdrawn and committed in another sector. He had no doubt that the most difficult days of this campaign lay ahead. Because of the developments near Stalingrad the Caucasus were also in danger of being cut off. Moreover, winter could set in any day. Motorized movement would be utilized to the greatest extent.

'Begin the withdrawal this evening at 1800 hours.'

These words flashed through the attending officers like an electric shock. The units had to be ready to march and break contact with the enemy within several hours.

After the company commanders returned, preparations for the withdrawal were begun in the strong points. During the early afternoon the supply columns were set in march to Alagir, while the combat vehicles drove up the back roads leading to the rollbahn. With the fall of darkness everything was march ready; the security, which was left in the positions, waited for the order to withdraw. The engineers were not to leave their positions until the last infantry units had passed by, then they were to follow as the rear guard.

Then they stood at the road fork and waited for the train. It was a clear starry night. In the direction of the abandoned houses, which were swallowed up by the darkness, as were the mountains laying behind them with their glittering fields of snow, towered the majestic Kazbek. The next day was Christmas Eve. The engineers remaining in the shelters of Suadag would be glad to take advantage of a few Christmas-like hours."

On the morning of 23 December 1942 "Wiking" stood along the Ardon River in a shortened line. The A and B intermediate positions were occupied without enemy harassment and were later given up.

On 24 December 1942 the "Caesar Positions" were held throughout the day. While security was left behind, "Wiking" and the 13th Panzer Division marched into the "Vierov Positions". The "Wiking" Panzer Battalion formed the rear guard. The commander of the 2nd Panzer Company, Ostuf. Flügel, reported: "We arrived in the new positions. We were invited by Stubaf. Mühlenkamp to a small Christmas celebration at his command post. It was a single family house; a small Christmas Tree was already set up. Stubaf. Mühlenkamp gave a short Christmas speech; then tank shells came crashing through the roof. Everybody ran out! My company went out on security. Nothing else happened that night. We rode to a reconnoitered reverse slope position. On the morning of 25 December 1942 the Soviets literally rode to their destruction. We destroyed 14 T-34s in several minutes. Henceforth we were left alone by the Soviet tanks."

While the German formations withdrew from the frontal salient, combat sprung up again on the long mountain flank. Under 24 December 1942 the combat diary of the III/"Nordland" noted: "0445 hours: Enemy attacked out of the Bolshoi Kossulkun Valley with a strength of 1 - 2 battalions east of the 11th Company and ran into a minefield on the left boundary. At 0930 hours and 1300 hours other enemy attacks were repulsed by the I/875 and 70th Fallschirmjägers."

By 29 December this sector was the focus of fierce combat. The Soviets continued to try to tear into the mountain flank and interfere with the German withdrawal. The Finns of the III/"Nordland" and the Romanian mountain infantry participated in the success.

After all of the units of the SS Panzer Grenadier Division "Wiking" were loaded in Prokhladny and Soldatskaya and transported to the 4th Panzer Army, the III Panzer Corps stood with the III/"Nordland" and the 2nd Romanian Mountain Division on the right and the 13th Panzer Division on the left in a 25 kilometer wide front from Chikola to Elkhotovo, where the corps made contact with the LII Army Corps.

THE WITHDRAWAL CASTS ITS SHADOW

The northern flank storm center - Stalin orders: Pin the 1st Panzer Army on the Terek - "Syangenwalde" and "Kusselhöhe" near Verkhniy Kurp - General Ott assembles his division commanders in Gnadenburg

The German withdrawal from the Eastern Caucasus was inevitable. Hitler long fought against it, but developments in the overall situation gave him no other choice. After the Russians overcame their low point, they turned the war around. And Stalin wanted more than just Stalingrad. Army Group A, which stood far to the southeast, was ripe for destruction, if the door to Rostov could be slammed shut.

Stalin's plan would only be successful if the 1st Panzer Army was held up at the Terek for as long as possible through offensive operations. Therefore, he ordered the "Northern Group of the Transcaucasus Front" to commit as many elements as possible there.

The steppe front continued to be an unknown factor. There were two more German advances to mention, which were to hinder the deployment of the Russians. On 8 November Hauptmann von Rohrbeck and his II/6 Pz.Rgt. advanced through Artashikov to Staro Bukharov and defeated a resting cavalry regiment there. Ten infantry guns, eight anti-tank guns and numerous bazookas were destroyed and 365 prisoners were captured. On 17 November the II/6 Pz.Rgt. undertook a new advance on Alpatovo, during which Hauptmann Rohrbeck died and nine German combat vehicles were lost.

On 30 November, in the XXXX Panzer Corps sector, which had in the meantime been taken over by Generalleutnant Henrici, an attack was launched by the 44th Soviet Army 12 kilometers north of Isherskaya into the von Jungschulz Cavalry Group sector. The Caucasian volunteers halted the attack. Also, Battle Group Munzel (Oberst Munzel became commander of the 6th Panzer Regiment, after General von Liebenstein went to Africa) and the 3rd Kradschützen Battalion participated in repulsing the enemy. During this battle the 2/6 Pz.Rgt. under Oberleutnant Fiehl shot up twelve type "Stuart" enemy tanks with the guns of the subordinate 543rd Panzerjäger Battalion. On the next day superior infantry forces were dispersed by concentrated artillery fire. After stronger fire forces were assembled, the hotly contested Hill 113 was evacuated and the security on either side of Sporny was withdrawn.

Hauptmann Volcken and his 7/6 Pz.Rgt. were dispatched on an outflanking maneuver to the north. During a rest stop Volcken observed the deployment of an enemy brigade. His panzer company was not discovered. He gave a short command: "Panzers march!" The engines of the Panzer IIIs and IVs roared to life. They attacked into the enemy column; a rifle brigade fled leaderless back into the steppes. Three T-34s were destroyed. Russian losses in men and equipment were great. For the clever attack Hauptmann Volcken was awarded the Knight's Cross.

There was no longer any contact with Oberst von Jungschulz' battle group. A battle group under Major Stockmann was thrown against the 12th Guards

Cavalry Division, which was moving to the west through Aga Batyr. The 3rd Panzergrenadier Regiment captured Aga Batyr, relieved von Jungschulz' formation and defeated the 259th Cavalry Regiment.

The attack also involved Corps Group Felmy. There the BF 110 Nahaufklärungsstaffel joined in the defensive battle with bombs and onboard weapons. Less successful was the defensive battle of Battle Group Munzel near Dydymkin. The counterattacks could not throw the Soviets back.

The Soviets deployed new formations into the Aga Batyr sector. An attack out of the steppes hit the I/3 Pz.Gren.Rgt. particularly hard; the commander, Hauptmann Erdmann, was killed and six SPWs were lost.

In view of the constant threat to the northern flank of the 3rd Panzer Division, the new division commander, Generalmajor Westhoven, withdrew the HKL (cover name Schlieffen). On 9 December Isherskaya and the salient were given up and a new HKL was occupied along the line Stoderevskaya - Krivonossov. Soon the Soviets were pressing against the new positions.

Under 10 December the combat diary of Army Group A noted: "Because the Luftwaffe is committed with Army Group Don, only Nahaufklärungsgeschwader 1 was available to attack the vehicle concentration near Alpatovo."

On 12 December Battle Group Munzel advanced in a relief attack into the steppes and ran into a group of ten T-34s and ten additional tanks of another type. Eight German tanks were lost during the battle. Hauptmann Volcken, the youngest Knight's Cross winner in the 6th Panzer Regiment, met a soldier's death. The panzer battle group withdrew under the protection of the fire of the accompanying artillery.

On 14 December Leutnant Noack and his 1/6 Pz.Rgt. were thrown against an enemy outflanking group; six enemy tanks were shot up.

On 21 December 1942, after a pause, the Soviets resumed their attack near Dovlatin. A day later they tore through the German front near Tomasov with the support of 20 tanks. The Soviets were pushed back by a counterattack and the front was again closed. On 23 December there was another enemy attack against Tomasov, which was repulsed by the 3rd Kradschützen Battalion. Even Major Steinbrecher's 52nd Engineer Battalion repulsed a regimental attack.

Christmas Eve was also active. Artillery on both sides fired repeated firestrikes. Oberfeldwebel Lesch from the 6/3 Pz.Gren.Rgt. penetrated 6 kilometers behind Russian lines with two comrades and three Cossacks, observed the deployment of a Russian regiment and captured two Russian officers.

On 25 December 1942 thirty T-34s and American type tanks attacked the I/394 Pz.Gren.Rgt. on the southern flank. The attack collapsed in massive defensive fire. As 20 enemy tanks burned, the accompanying infantry withdrew. During the month of December the XXXX Panzer Corps captured 8037 prisoners. 1037 Soviet soldiers crossed over to the Germans. 68 tanks, 27 armored scout cars, 34 guns, 74 anti-tank guns, 223 mortars, 286 anti-tank rifles and 225 machine-guns were either destroyed or captured. The

Eberswalder 75th Armored Artillery Regiment fired 17,978 shells from 1 September to 31 December 1942.

As with the XXXX Panzer Corps it was similar in the LII Army Corps area of operations, as the Soviets harassed them with both small and large combat operations by the 9th Army. The main point of harassment was the 50th ID frontal sector near Verkhniy Kurp. The forested mountain terrain was very suitable for harassment attacks.

First some background on the deployment and commitment of the 50th ID. The division gathered its personnel from Pomerania and Ostbrandenburg and was commanded by Generalmajor Friedrich Schmidt.

The 50th ID was severely battered during the battle for Sevastopol and was assigned coastal duty on the Kerch Peninsula while it re-established its combat strength. When the crisis in the Eastern Caucasus developed the 50th ID was deployed to the 1st Panzer Army. From 31 October to 24 November 1942 the units crossed the Kerch Strait. They were then transported by rail to Krasnodar. The 122nd Grenadier Regiment was the first regiment to be flown from Krasnodar to Armavir to relieve SS Division "Wiking" because of the events near Gisel. On 11 November the regiments gradually arrived on the Terek and took over the "Wiking" positions between Malgobek I and Verkhniy Kurp. Because of the overburdened rail lines the 50th ID did not completely deploy in the new German sector until 14 December 1942. Luckily, enemy forces were limited here because they had committed all of their reserves near Ordzhonikidze. In mid-December the units were reorganized and the defenders of the division front were disposed as follows: On the right was the 121st Grenadier Regiment from the southern edge of Verkhniy Kurp to the stream area. The 123rd Grenadier Regiment was in the irregular positions in the valley. On the left was the 122nd Grenadier Regiment on either side of Malgobek.

During the last days of November the 50th ID front was not very quiet. In the Malgobek sector several enemy assault elements tried in vain to penetrate into the positions of the 122nd [Regiment] during the night of 1 January. At the beginning of December there was rain and sleet, as temperatures seldom dropped below zero.

On the morning of 7 December outposts from the III/121 discovered that the enemy had been committed on the "Kusselhöhe" during the night. This hill offered excellent observation far into the interior of the German deployment.

On 12 December, under the cover name "Fuchsjagd [Fox Hunt]", an operation was undertaken to throw the Soviets back. Engineer groups from the neighboring divisions participated because the 50th ID had to give up its 71st Engineer Battalion to Stalingrad. Sixteen enemy bunkers were blown and 26 prisoners were captured. German losses totaled: 10 killed, 10 wounded and 8 missing. A Soviet counterattack was repulsed.

On 13 December enemy pressure increased; the 176th Rifle Division was newly deployed. During the night of 15 December the "Kusselhöhe" was again occupied by the enemy.

On 16 December at 0700 hours a heavy artillery attack initiated the anticipated Soviet attack, which was soon expanded to the entire front of the 121st Grenadier Regiment in the Verkhniy Kurp sector, and even involved the III/123. At 1000 hours the front flared up along a breadth of six kilometers. While the center held, an enemy regiment each was able to penetrate into the HKL on the left and right flanks of the regimental sector. The "Stangenhöhe" on the right flank was recaptured in a counterattack by the 1/121 and defended. In the stream area, the front was broken through along a 2 kilometer width and contact with the neighboring regiment was severed. Both regiments turned their flanks inward and blocked the penetration. A counterattack did, indeed, bring the enemy attack to a halt, but they could not regain the old HKL. During the night reserves were deployed from the army corps, which contained the penetration in a half-circle.

On 17 December, enemy advances on the HKL and the "Stangenhöhe" were repulsed. Reserves tried without success to eliminate the penetration to Lake Am. When one examined the reserves, it became very clear that the LII Army Corps was at the end of its rope. The reserves were from a wheeled vehicle repair company. Generalmajor Schmidt transferred his command post to Nizhniy Kurp and reorganized. The rear area elements and staffs were combed for replacements. The corps also dispatched its last reserves.

On 18 December a Soviet regiment renewed the attack out of the penetration area on the "Stangenwald". I/121 Gren.Rgt. held. The I and II/150 AR supported the hard-pressed grenadiers with effective fire. At 1000 hours the attack on the "Stangenhöhe" was defeated.

Then both artillery battalions laid concentrated fire on the penetration area south of Lake Am. A subsequent counterattack threw the Soviets back. By evening half of the lost HKL was again in German hands. On 19 December the enemy-occupied HKL west of the stream was also recaptured in a counterattack.

During the night and the morning hours of 20 December the Soviets deployed new reserves. Foggy weather favored this movement. German artillery could not interfere. The Soviets attacked six times and were repulsed. Of the participating 317th, 176th and 89th Rifle Divisions, the latter was so battered that is was lost for some time.

Also on 21 December, repeated enemy attacks on either side of the "Stangenhöhe" stalled without success. Generalmajor Schmidt felt it was time to recapture the 400 meters of the HKL along the stream sector still occupied by the enemy. After deploying the 2/191 Stu.Gesch.Brig., the 2/370 Pi.Btl. and the Pyatigorsk Alert Battalion, Operation "Frithjof" was launched on 24 December. Battle groups from the 123rd Grenadier Regiment, elements of the 150th Wheeled Battalion and assault guns recaptured the old HKL after a two hour battle.

On 28 December the German counterattack on the "Stangenhöhe", which had been occupied by the enemy for twelve days, led to a complete success after a strong artillery and rocket launcher preparation.

Verkhniy Kurp and "Stangenhöhe" were the targets of a Soviet attack on 29 December, which, however, was repulsed well in front of the HKL. The 50th

ID held out in its positions.

In the combat diary of the 50th ID we read: "From 16 to 30 December 1942 the division repulsed 71 enemy attacks in one regimental sector (121st Grenadier Regiment) alone; three of them were in brigade to division strength." German losses were considerable; 22 officers and 651 non-commissioned officers and grenadiers were killed or wounded.

On 29 December Generalmajor Friedrich Schmidt was summoned to Gnadenburg. The commander of the 111th ID, Generalmajor Recknagel, and the commander of the 370th ID, Generalmajor Becker, were already there in a poor farmhouse. General Ott briefed them on the overall situation with a serious face. There was no doubt that the hardest part of the commitment lay ahead. For the first time the word retreat cracked like a whip. The word which many had wanted to voice, but could not, was now a fact. The great retreat to the Terek began!

THE WITHDRAWAL TO THE TEREK BEGINS

"Hochwasserverhütung" - The bridges at Soldatsko-Aleksandrovskoe - "The march route is the HKL!" - Gruppe von Le Suire leaves the mountain passes - Order: "Increase the march tempo!"

The objectives of the Soviet shock armies on the Don front were already obvious. After Stalingrad, Stalin's objective was Rostov on the lower Don. Hitler had to also order the withdrawal of his 1st Panzer Army; a decision he delayed for some time. However, the German withdrawal in the Solka - Kuma sector had to be completed first.

As General Ott was briefing his division commanders on the upcoming withdrawal, there were also briefings in the headquarters of the III and XXXX Panzer Corps. Generalleutnant der Waffen SS Steiner and Generalleutnant Henrici (former commander of the 16th ID (Mot.) and, since 15 November 1942, commander of the XXXX Panzer Corps) also gave their briefings with serious faces.

Heavy activity dominated in the headquarters of the 1st Panzer Army in Pyatigorsk. The German retreat was laid out. The corps staffs developed the plans for the divisions, the divisions for their regiments. Besides withdrawing the troops, the equipment also had to be taken into consideration.

As in all of the divisions, there was much activity on the night of 30 December 1942 in the headquarters of the 50th ID in Khamidiya. Major Stephanus worked out the withdrawal plan based on the instructions of the LII Army Corps. Generalmajor Schmidt and his staff officers faced the coming days with much trepidation. How would the troops take the withdrawal? Would they be able to put up with the efforts of the high march tempo on the muddy roads during the phased movements? Would they be able to construct new positions in a short period of time and repulse the enemy? There were questions upon questions!

On New Years Eve the companies of the 50th ID were notified of the forthcoming withdrawal, which ran under the division cover name of "Hochwasserverhütung [Flood Prevention]". The soldiers did not realize that the term "Hochwasserverhütung" had so much relevance to their fate.

The withdrawal preparations could not be kept secret from the Russians. The Russian countermeasures, which were being prepared feverishly, were described in the Russian Caucasus work: "While counter-strikes were conducted at the edge of the mountains, an offensive was also to be initiated against the northern flank of the Germans on the Terek. Moreover, elements of the 44th Army were prepared with cavalry and strong artillery and tank support. The Germans were to be pushed back to the line Achikulak - Stoderovskaya under the weight of the Soviet attack."

In the headquarters of the XXXX Panzer Corps there was not only concern over the withdrawal, but also for an upcoming Russian attack. Generalleutnant Henrici and his chief of Staff, Oberst Carl Wagner, reviewed all of the facts. There was the threat that the Soviets would be able to interfere with the upcoming withdrawal. A premature withdrawal could upset the entire 1st Panzer Army retreat plan. Thus the hours passed slowly, too slowly. On 29 December the withdrawal order arrived at Generalmajor Westhoven's 3rd Panzer Division. The phased withdrawal of the XXXX Panzer Corps began on New Year's night. A day later the LII Army Corps and the III Panzer Corps would join in.

In the 3rd Panzer Division sector several Russian officers were captured with important documents in their possession by the I/394 Pz.Gren.Rgt. They revealed that a Soviet attack was planned on 1 January 1943 with 120 tanks. Even the assembly area was noted on a map. Immediately artillery and a rocket launcher battery were committed against the target area. At exactly midnight on 1 January 1943 the 75th Armored Artillery Regiment and the rocket launcher battery opened a concentrated fire onto the assembly area. The rounds came in without pause; the long trails of the rockets simulated a bloody New Year's fireworks display, which was soon joined in the enemy positions by grenadiers with machine-gun and rifle fire.

Thick fog covered the steppes as New Year's morning dawned. During the night the German outposts heard the rattling of vehicles on the enemy side. They then nervously awaited New Year's Day. The ground shook with a detonation. The powerful enemy strikes rained like hail against the German positions on the northern flank. The soldiers of the 3rd Panzergrenadier Regiment and the panzer crews of the 6th Panzer Regiment ducked their heads. They couldn't look up. In between the detonations of the shells the rattling of many tanks could be heard.

Soviet tank and rifle formations tore through the front between the 3rd Panzer Division and Battle Group von Jungschulz to the north and attacked through to the west. Light air defense positions were overran. Oberleutnant Fiehl's 2/6 Pz.Rgt. fired into the attackers without stopping. Knight's Cross winner, Oberfeldwebel Blaich, saw 62 Russian tanks coming at him after the fog lifted. The situation was completely confused.

Russian tanks stood before the command post of the I/394 Pz.Gren.Rgt., which was located to the south. Infantry followed in masses. 400 Russians penetrated into one company area. Oberfeldwebel Steinführer counterattacked with his platoon and recaptured the old positions. The Russians fell under the fire of their own artillery on a bare slope.

In front of the I/394, Russian motorized and horse-drawn formations were wedged into a depression. After the fog lifted they were engaged by the 75th Armored Artillery Regiment. One of the guns worked its way into the vicinity of the battalion command post and aimed direct fire into the Soviets.

It was similar in the 3rd Panzergrenadier Regiment area of operations to the north. The positions there were also overran. An enemy attack hit the 7th Company. However, as always in such situations, there can be found courageous men to take up the battle. There it was Oberfeldwebel Kruse, commander of the 7th Company, who assembled his company and led them in a counterattack. In mortal combat the panzergrenadiers threw themselves at the Soviets, destroyed Russian tanks with close combat weapons and pushed the infantry back. For this feat of arms Oberfeldwebel Kruse became the

245th soldier to be awarded the Oak Leaves to the Knight's Cross.

In light of this situation, Generalmajor Westhoven ordered the withdrawal of his northern flank a day earlier than planned. In the late afternoon the 3rd Panzergrenadier Regiment withdrew to previously prepared positions.

In the LII Army Corps sector the front remained quiet. There the combat tested regiments of the 111th, 50th and 370th ID prepared for the withdrawal. All superfluous supply staffs and artillery units were already on the march. For one last time the grenadiers set their gaze on the vast mountainous terrain, which already had a steppe character in the 111th and 50th ID areas of operations, but still resembled a forested mountain area in the 370th ID area. Malgobek, Nizhniy Kurp, Verkhniy Kurp, Illarinovka and Elkhotovo, names that had appeared constantly in the Wehrmacht reports, would never again be mentioned.

From the town of Terek on the Terek, opposite the positions of the 3rd Panzer Division near Stoderevskaya, up to the other end of the great Terek near Elkhotovo, where the right flank of the LII Army Corps met the 13th Panzer Division, little unrest was perceived by the regiments of the 111th, 50th and 370th ID. They entrusted everything to their leadership staffs. And the staffs knew that they could also count on their regiments. Then the first phase of the withdrawal began.

On 1 January it was still quiet on the front of the 50th ID. In fact, the enemy had pulled back. During the night of 2 January 1943 the regiments withdrew from their positions on the great Terek bend in order to occupy the initial intermediate positions in the interior of the Terek bend near Mosdok and Gnadenburg and from Khamydiya to Arik. Only the rearguards remained behind.

Each soldier knew that the rearguard required the utmost concentration from him. The rearguard leaders were the bravest and most circumspect officers and non-commissioned officers, capable of conducting independent operations. We read a description by a soldier from the rearguard of the 50th ID, which had to cover the withdrawal of German formations at that time:

"After the companies withdrew, a ghostly stillness lay over the trenches which we had occupied for six long weeks. Several men walked through the abandoned positions with their fingers on the triggers of their machine-pistols. The enemy was already approaching the trenches. The endless night passed without event. Undisturbed, and as planned, the main body of the trench troops reached the "Augsburger Line". At midday on 2 January two enemy battalions followed us to Malgobek II. We slowly withdrew. A powerful reconnaissance patrol against Khamydiya was repulsed by the 122nd."

In the III Panzer Corps area of operations on the mountain flank, the weapons had been silent since Gisel. As before, the Soviets tried to pin the right flank of the 1st Panzer Army from out of the mountains.

On 24 December 1942 the Russians attacked out of the Bolshoi Kossolkun Valley and were repulsed. Additional attempts were repulsed by the Finnish companies of the III/"Nordland" and Romanian mountain infantry during the next few days. Toldsgun, Lesskem, Sindsikau, Khasnidon again appeared in the Finnish and Romanian combat reports. This front was also the commitment area of the rocket launcher batteries, which supported the trench fighters with their fire. Often they themselves became trench fighters; 15 and 28 cm rocket launcher batteries often formed the HKL.

Gruppe Emsmann defended near Surkh Digora; they were the main defense for the I/99 Geb.Jg.Rgt. On 27 December Major Kopp and his gebirgsjägers recaptured Surkh Digora. A day later there was again fierce fighting there as the Russians were supported by 20 tanks.

On 29 December 1942 Oberstleutnant Emsmann wrote in his diary:

"Enemy attack on Surkh Digora and Chikola repulsed. 1600 hours: Penetration in the 7th Romanian Mountain Infantry Battalion area. Two rocket launchers were lost. After two hours the situation was restored. Engineers and construction troops left Chikola.

30 December 1942: Commander, General Steiner, and Romanian General Dimitrachu visited my command post. During the evening the order to evacuate the headquarters of the 52nd Rocket Launcher Regiment and Gruppe Winkler (heavy rocket launchers) arrived.

31 December 1942: Deployment to Marenskaya. Rear area services to Essentuki. Fuel supply quite a problem; sufficient for moving a portion only to Nalchik.

1 January 1943: Reached Nalchik. Demolition begun. Ration stores removed.

3 January 1943: Regiment immobile due to the lack of fuel."

In the combat diary of the III/"Nordland" the beginning of the withdrawal was described as follows:

"31 December: Order to Withdraw issued.

1 January 1943, 0200 hours: Battalion begins withdrawal starting with the left flank to a line Bery Kessyn and field positions 3 kilometers to the northwest. 9th Company returned to the battalion (Company Ertel was used as a corset rod in the Romanian Marci unit). - 0700 hours: Enemy noticed the withdrawal. - 0745 hours: Enemy concentration (600 men) in Toldsgun placed under fire. - 1300 hours: Russian scouts in strength of 20 men shot up on the right sector (8 dead). - 1600 hours: Battalion again broke contact with the enemy as ordered. - 2020 hours: Battalion marched from Lessken through Argudan and Nalchik to Baksan (80 kilometers)."

The Finnish Motorized Waffen SS Freiwilligen Battalion followed Division "Wiking" in march through Pyatigorsk, Voroshilovsk and Salsk into the Manych area, where "Wiking" was placed opposite the Soviet attack on Rostov as part of the 4th Panzer Army.

Another critical area for the III Panzer Corps at the end of the year was at the seam with the LII Army Corps near Elkhotovo. There on the Caucasian "Porta" were the battalions of the 13th Panzer Division, as well as the II/"Brandenburg" and the subordinate II/667 Gren.Rgt. (370th ID), which were blocking the Russians from the eastern route through Smeiskaya - Aleksandrovskaya. Bitter combat was still raging there. The German companies had to pay the price for holding so that the great withdrawal could go as planned. The 731st Heavy Heeres Artillery Battalion (Mot.), which had so often supported the III Panzer Corps in attacks and defenses in the past, again participated there.

On 30 December 1942 at 0900 hours Generalleutnant Steiner was at the command post of the 13th Panzer Division in Urukh and gave the following orientation: "The III Panzer Corps will give up the area around Nalchik and withdraw in phases to the northwest. The main responsibility for the withdrawal will be born by the 13th Panzer Division. The advance of the enemy out of the Elkhotovo Pass will receive particular attention under these circumstances. The enemy must be stopped there until the main body of the corps can withdraw from the difficult mountain terrain. All unnecessary rear area elements and units are to be withdrawn immediately. Because the corps is assigned one road (Nalchik - Pyatigorsk), strict march discipline will be necessary."

On this day the Soviets entered Smeiskaya. Again the 13th Panzer Division threw together all of its reserves and recaptured the village.

On 31 December 1942 the II/"Brandenburg" ran into heavy fighting while withdrawing to Smeiskaya. Again the Soviets penetrated into the village and blocked the withdrawal route. In a last desperate attempt the village of Smeiskaya was freed by German companies, which then marched off to the north.

Therefore, the entire 1st Panzer Army was on the move. The troops withdrew in phases to fortified lines. The march tempo was brisk; the Solka - Kuma sector had to be reached quickly. The withdrawal was to come to an end there and winter positions were to be established. Or so Hitler believed. However, the commanders did not think so; the withdrawal would continue!

The withdrawal of the 1st Panzer Army was complicated by difficult terrain. While the XXXX Panzer Corps and the 111th ID were withdrawing on the flat steppes, the 50th and 370th ID and the III Panzer Corps had to contend with the marshy terrain of the Terek bend and the foothills of the Caucasus.

The 3rd Panzer Division was organized into three march groups: A tracked formation under Oberstleutnant Schmidt-Ott, a foot formation under Oberst Zimmermann and a motorized formation under Oberstleutnant Pape.

On 2 January 1943 the southern flank of the 3rd Panzer Division broke contact. The movement was coordinated with that of the 111th ID. Important war industries were blown up in Mosdok. On the early morning of 3 January the rear guard left Mosdok. On the same day Soviet troops under Generals Khomenko and Melnik crossed the Terek and entered Mosdok.

The ice, slush and mud required extreme effort from the men and animals. The motors of the vehicles were overtaxed. It was the same with the pursuing Russians. By 3 January the "Augsburger Line" was occupied. On 4 January the 1st Panzer Army was in the "Stuttgart Line". On 5 January they were in the "Heidelberg Line". On 6 January they were to reach the "Mainz Line" and on 7 January the "Potsdam Line". The "Potsdam or Solka - Kuma Line" was the first recovery line. The river course was to make the positions easier to hold. Was this line with a frozen river course still an obstacle in winter?

Every day the German divisions overcame icy and muddy roads with great effort. Because of such difficulties, on the morning of 6 January, the 50th ID, which was supposed to be occupying the "Mainz Line", was dispersed on a wide front of 36 kilometers breadth and 25 kilometers depth. The enemy was pursuing with tanks at several locations. All ticklish situations were mastered with the help of the 525th Panzerjäger Battalion and two batteries of the 24th Anti-aircraft Regiment. All elements of the 50th ID reached the new blocking position.

It was similar with the 111th ID. There the Russians reached a portion of the "Mainz Line" before the Germans could occupy it. They were thrown back out with the support of the tanks of the 3rd Panzer Division and the integrity of the "Mainz Line" was restored.

7 January was a black day in the history of the 50th ID. On this day they were to have reached the "Potsdam Line". In the morning fog strong Soviet forces with supporting tanks broke through toward Novo Sredny between the I and II/122 Gren.Rgt. and surprised the weak III/122 Gren.Rgt., which was located in reserve. Then the enemy forces turned on the two battalions. The radio messages of the 122nd Grenadier Regiment sent to the division on 7 January 1943 illuminate the destruction of this regiment:

0820 hours: More than 30 enemy tanks attacking against Novo Sredny.

0840 hours: Tanks in Madkugorin. Assault guns and anti-tank guns committed.

0920 hours: Enemy, at least 1 tank and 1 rifle brigade, pursuing through Kurgany.

1018 hours: Russians breaking through near Madkugorin out of the east with tanks. Regiment holding a line Kommayak - Novo Sredny - Hill 275. Subordinate II/121 committed.

1120 hours: Request permission to withdraw at 1230 hours.

1125 hours: Have fired up all artillery and anti-tank guns. Have ordered artillery to withdraw. Grothe.

1210 hours: In the pincers, position untenable.

That was the last message from the 122nd Grenadier Regiment, but what was going on behind the abrupt radio traffic?

A Soviet tank wedge was brought to a stop at the positions of the reinforced I/122 near Kommayak by German anti-tank guns. At the same time an enemy tank attack between the I and II/122 broke through to Novo Sredny. The morning fog favored the attackers and surprised Leutnant Utecht's III/122, which was in quarters. Chaos resulted! 30 tanks with accompanying infantry encircled individual groups which had no antitank defenses nor close combat weapons. 4/150 AR could only engage a few of the tanks. The staff surgeon, Dr. Becker, treated the numerous wounded, until he was also hit by a tank shell. At 1230 hours the regimental command post, which lay further to the rear, was also threatened with encirclement. Oberst Grothe ordered an immediate withdrawal to the "Potsdam Line". Hauptmann Gnädig's II/122, which was committed in the south, made contact with the 123rd Regiment. The battle group located on the right near Kommayak defended throughout the day and was finally encircled. During the night the majority of the I/122 fought its way to the "Potsdam Line". During this battle the commander of the I/122, Hauptmann Schmidt, was killed.

On this day the right flank of the 50th ID also suffered a serious crisis. There the III/123 had to prematurely give up the Orlovka - Avantgart area. The I/123 held near Novo Pavlovskaya. During the evening the 123rd Grenadier Regiment was attacked from three sides. Major Melzer ordered his regiment to withdraw.

In spite of all of the crises, the 50th ID occupied the Solka - Kuma Line on the morning of 8 January. Because the front was so extended, the HKL could only be defended in a strongpoint manner. To the 111th ID yawned a 3 kilometer wide gap that was later closed by elements of the 3rd Panzer Division.

On 8 January the 3rd Panzer Division stood with all of its elements in the Kuma sector. Up to this point in time all of the defective vehicles were brought along; now the division ordered: "All vehicles in tow that cannot be repaired as soon as possible with the means on hand are to be destroyed!" And the great destruction began!

Major Musculus, commander of the 111th ID Panzerjäger Battalion, stood before the Kuma sector with his battle group. His mission was to hold open the Kuma bridges near Soldatsko - Aleksandrovskoe. The 111th Panzerjäger Battalion had survived the difficult combat on the Terek without many losses. The remnants of the regimental panzerjäger companies were organized into the battalion. The panzerjäger battalion was the only fully motorized formation in the 111th ID. Therefore it was assigned rear guard missions. Such a mission had to be fulfilled in front of the Kuma bridges. German vehicles were still rolling across the bridges; the Soviet lead elements were right behind them.

In between Letrovskiy and the Kuma, Oberstleutnant Piedmont established an anti-tank obstacle with the 2/111 Pz.Jg.Abt. in the middle of the marshy region of the Solkazu River. In the second line a battery from the 117th Artillery Regiment was directly on the road to Soldatsko - Aleksandrovskoe. It was the 6th of January 1943.

Shortly before darkness a weak cavalry squadron attacked from the south and was shot up.

Then the second wave showed up! However, Gruppe Piedmont also shot this one up.

Then the third attack was launched! This one was also stopped with the last of the ammunition. Individual riders continued to press against the defending anti-tank guns, but they were too few to overcome the Germans.

The fourth attack did not take place! The men took a breather as darkness fell and the ammunition stocks were replenished.

On the far side of the Solka stood the 1/111 Pz.Jg.Abt. holding the town of Mikhailovskiy. The Russians attacked from the east; the panzerjäger company was encircled. By the fall of darkness the company opened a lane and withdrew to Soldatsko - Aleksandrovskoe.

In the early morning of 9 January Oberleutnant Klümpel stood on the upper Kuma bridge with a platoon of his 1/111 Pz.Jg.Abt., which had the mission of holding the bridge open for those who followed and blowing it up on the approach of enemy tanks. The terrain was suitable for defense. A deeply cut river bed and a road embankment had to be overcome. A 3.7 cm anti-tank gun was set up in front of the bridge; two others were placed behind the bridge.

In the meantime engineers from the regimental engineer platoon of the 50th Grenadier Regiment prepared the bridge for demolition. Unteroffizier Ebel was the demolition troop leader.

The rear guard passed over the bridge, but stragglers were still coming. Oberleutnant Buchholz, who commanded the engineers and the security of the 50th Grenadier Regiment, waited. Then a vehicle came barreling down on the bridge. Right behind it was the first T-34. Buchholz debated: blow it up or wait?

The T 34 stopped 300 meters in front of the bridge. Then it fired. The forward-most anti-tank gun remained silent; there was nothing it could do against the T-34. Enemy infantry accumulated. Oberleutnant Buchholz gave the order to blow it up. Anti-tank guns, machine-guns and rifles fired at the tank. Unteroffizier Ebel sprung to the bridge and fused the explosives. There was a detonation! A powerful column of smoke stood over the bridge. However, as it lifted, everyone gasped - the bridge was still standing. Recognizing their chance, the Russian infantry advanced behind the protection of the tank.

Seconds passed! Ebel had to go to the bridge again. He knew the demolition plan. He knew where each explosive was located. He also knew that one of the fuses did not take. Under the protection of his comrades fire, he made it to the bridge again, found the fused explosive, fidgeted with it, put it back and threw himself flat on the embankment. At the same instant the air shook, the ground vibrated from a powerful detonation and debris sprinkled to the ground from out of an enormous column of smoke. The enemy stood before the destroyed bridge. Ebel received the Knight's Cross.

The withdrawal was supposed to end at the Solka - Kuma sector, but Hitler had to bury his hopes of attacking out of this sector in the spring. The Soviets were dictating events. The company agitators hammered new slogans at their soldiers. During the defense they yelled: "Not one step backward!" and then they yelled out the new combat slogan: "Defeat and destroy the fascist German interlocutors with decisive attacks!"

Plainly speaking, it appeared that the German formations would not be able to stop there. Without stopping to rest, the rear area services and supply units continued the withdrawal. Fleeing local inhabitants joined them. All of the roads leading to the northwest were overloaded.

The great withdrawal reached a crisis! The security of the gebirgsjägers was withdrawn from the mountain ridges. The high mountain defense, which blocked the few passes still usable in the winter, went with Oberst von Le Suire's group (II and III/99 Geb.Jg.Rgt., 94th Feldersatz Battalion, 2nd High Mountain Battalion, 94th Mountain Reconnaissance Battalion, I/79 Geb.AR and II/94 Geb.AR), together with elements of the 1st and 4th Mountain Divisions. On 4 January 1943, Gruppe von Le Suire left the high passes at Khotyu Tau, Klukhor, Dombai Ulgen and Marukh. A difficult march through the deeply cut high mountain valleys began for the gebirgsjäaegers. The mountain guns had to be dragged for wide stretches, then they had to be moved by sled and, finally, by pack animal. The majestic Elbrus was left behind. Following the river courses, Gruppe von Le Suire joined in the withdrawal of the 1st Panzer Army. It had to fight its way through north of Cherkessk.

And the withdrawal of the 1st Panzer Army continued. The regiments marched in silence; lead elements occupied the new lines; rear guards remained in the old positions. The staffs observed the rhythm of the withdrawal with concern. They had to motivate their formations to speed up. And the grenadiers marched and marched, in spite of their weariness.

The blowing of the Kuma bridges near Soldatsko - Aleksandrovskoe did not hold the Russians up for long. On the same day (9 January) the 111th ID was hit in the flanks. The neighboring division came to its assistance.

On the Solka sector, Major Bärenfänger's III/123 prevented the Russians from advancing toward Georgievsk. In the north, the II/394 Pz.Gren.Rgt. quickly constructed a blocking position near the Kuma railroad station, through which the 50th Grenadier Regiment withdrew.

During the night of 10 January 1943 the Kuma was crossed at several locations. The continued holding by the German formations was senseless. During the same night the 50th ID withdrew to the Podkuma sector and was met there by the 13th Panzer Division. For the 50th ID the march continued through Georgievsk, Podgornaya to Aleksandriskaya.

During the same night the weak security of the 13th Panzer Division was pushed back or outflanked on the Podkuma and the Soviets continued to march on Georgievsk. A stronger formation advanced against Mineralnie Vody, another against Obilnoe. The withdrawal route of the 50th ID and 13th Panzer Division was threatened. The Russian Caucasus book, "The Battle for the Caucasus", reports:
"During the battle for Georgievsk, the fascists tried to withdraw their main force to Mineralnie Vody. In order to frustrate this withdrawal from Georgievsk and Pyatigorsk to Mineralnie Vody, a tank battalion under the leadership of Captain Petrov and additional rifle companies advanced on 11 January at 1000 hours as the lead element of Lieutenant Colonel Filippov's combat group crossed the Kuma to the eastern edge of Mineralnie Vody and then further to the railroad station, where two military trains stood. First the two locomotives were set afire. Another four trains coming from Georgievsk were blocked and had to halt. Two other trains with tanks and ammunition were intercepted in front of the Mineralnie Vody station. In the meantime the Germans were withdrawing out of the Vorontsovo, Aleksandrovskoe and Georgievsk areas. They tried to break through to Mineralnie Vody at any price and committed 30 tanks and an infantry regiment. During the evening of 11 January Mineralnie Vody remained in our hands. After that our troops dispersed the enemy near Kangly."
In actuality the 13th Panzer Division was often in crisis on the edge of the mountains. They were the main force of the III Panzer Corps advancing on the Nalchik - Pyatigorsk - Mineralnie Vody road. The 13th Panzer Division had to go back to help the 2nd Romanian Mountain Division.

WITHDRAWAL FROM
THE CAUCASUS
1943

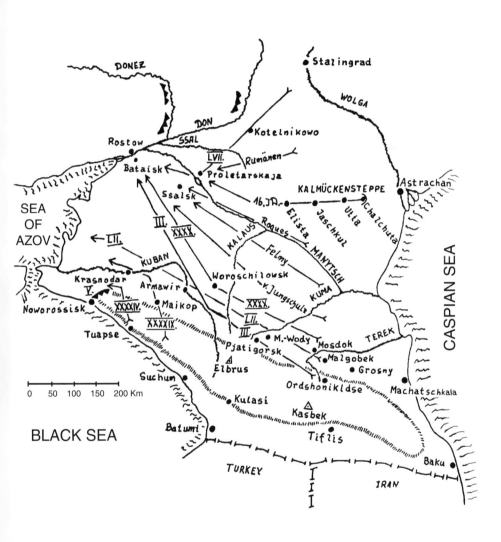

DONEZ

Stalingrad

WOLGA

DON

SSAL

Rostow

Kotelnikowo

LVII. Rumänen

Bataisk

Proletarskaja

Astrachan

Ssalsk

16.JD. Elista MANYTSCH Ichalchuta

KALMÜCKENSTEPPE

Jaschkul

Ulla

SEA
OF
AZOV

III.

XXXV.

LII.

KALAUS

Roques

Felmy

KUBAN

Woroschilowsk

Krasnodar

Armawir

v.Jungschulz

KUMA

V.

XXXX.

XXXXIV.

Maikop

LII.

Noworossisk

XXXXIX.

III.

M.-Wody

Mosdok

TEREK

Tuapse

Pjatigorsk

Malgobek

Grosny

Elbrus

Ordshonikidse

Machatschkala

CASPIAN SEA

Suchum

0   50 100 150 200 Km

Kulasi

Kasbek

BLACK SEA

Batumi

Tiflis

Baku

TURKEY

IRAN

265

The attack of Battle Group Filippov, described in Soviet literature, also effected the 50th ID. On 10 January the 50th ID gave up the Solka sector. The last security elements of the 13th Panzer Division still held out on the Podkuma sector. During the night the 50th ID marched through Georgievsk to Aleksandriskaya and rested there. However, the rest was a short one. In the meantime the Russian Battle Group Filippov was threatening the march route to Mineralnie Vody.

The 50th ID, resting in Aleksandriskaya, was alerted! The exhausted companies were difficult to rouse to combat. Finally the division was prepared to deploy. The exhausting night march evolved into a murderous day march. The good roads to Mineralnie Vody could no longer be used. Generalmajor Friedrich Schmidt was determined to withdraw his division to the "Mittenwald Line" no matter the opposition. Each minute was precious! He issued the following short, but precise, order: "The 50th ID will withdraw to the `Mittenwald Line'. During an attack by enemy tanks, positions will immediately be taken up along the march route. Infantry will cover, then artillery. The march route is the HKL!"

Schmidt slowly led in his jeep, monitoring the route. His division followed behind him in combat formation. The feeling of fatigue had left, the exhaustion of the night march was gone, the iron will for self-preservation was stronger. After an exhausting march on washed out roads, the 50th ID reached their 15 kilometer wide sector on the "Mittenwald Line" between the 13th Panzer Division and the 111th ID on the evening of 11 January.

On 11 January the last German rear guards left the Podkuma sector. Again long march formations moved on all of the roads to the northwest. The next objective was the Kalaus sector, which was to be reached in several intermediate stages. The course of the river was an obstacle, but only where it was defended. As was shown in the Solka - Kuma sector, this could not be taken for granted. Friend and foe raced to get the good roads to facilitate their advance. And the good roads ran in an approximately 60 kilometer wide strip along the northern edge of the mountains to the northwest. The Russian Caucasus work was critical:

"The main effort of the northern group of the Transcaucasus Front was concentrated along the Prokhladny - Mineralnie Vody - Nevinnomyskaya railroad line, which was incorrect if the enemy was to be forced out of the foothills instead of being forced into them. The main effort should have been shifted to the northern flank. A combined cavalry and tank group was formed to outflank the northern flank and cut off the withdrawal route.

The advance was complicated by destroyed bridges and roads, as well as by the loss of contact between the staffs and troops, while the Germans had intact road and communications networks available. Thus, the staff of the "Northern Group" completely lost contact with the cavalry - tank corps operating on the northern flank."

The main responsibility of the delaying German defense lay with the mobile units of the 3rd and 13th Panzer Divisions. They were supported in their far-ranging mission by small motorized formations from the infantry divisions. The northern flank of the 1st Panzer Army was covered by the mobile Cossack squadrons of Cavalry Group von Jungschulz, which operated independently in the road-poor peripheral region of the steppes.

On 11 January the 3rd Panzer Division had several crises to master during this mission. Strong enemy forces were pressuring their Vorontsovo - Salbya - Aleksandrovskoe withdrawal route. Generalmajor Westhoven had to commit an attack from the withdrawal in order to relieve the slower 111th ID marching on foot. The last tanks of the 6th Panzer Regiment and the II/394 Pz.Gren.Rgt. launched the relief attack. It ended up in a tank duel. The enemy was stopped.

At the same time Hauptmann Rode and his I/394 held out near Sablya and met the hard-pressed and already outflanked 50th Grenadier Regiment of Oberst Friemel.

On 12 January the Soviets were pressuring the "Mittenwald Line". During the night of 13 January 1943 the formations marched into the "Garmisch Line". Winter had finally arrived; entrenching could no longer be considered!

Constantly being pressured by Russian tank and cavalry formations, the withdrawal continued without pause. The I/394 was cut off from the withdrawal route east of Srieevskoe. The subordinate assault guns fought back in the winter moonlight, destroyed four of eight Russian tanks and opened the way.

On 13 January the pursuing Soviets again stumbled on the seam between the 50th and 111th ID. An enemy cavalry regiment advanced through the gap to the west. When it turned to the south to pin the 50th ID, Generalmajor Schmidt ordered the withdrawal to the "Kalaus Line". Russian cavalry harassed the withdrawing companies. A fierce maneuver battle developed. Again the march route became a wandering HKL. A snow storm finally separated the combatants, but it also severely hindered the march. This was the last night for many of the horses and trucks.

By 18 January the icy snowstorm continued unabated. The Russian cavalry formations repeated their outflanking maneuver against the northern flank of the 50th ID, but the III/121 Gren.Rgt. frustrated this attempt.

In the cold and the snow the German divisions of the 1st Panzer Army continued to move to the northwest. On the southern flank marched the regiments of the 2nd Romanian Mountain Division, the 13th Panzer Division, the 370th ID and the 50th ID. Their objective was Armavir on the Kuban. They met the gebirgsjägers of Gruppe von Le Suire coming out of the high Caucasus near Nevinnomyskaya.

On the northern flank marched the 3rd Panzer Division and the 111th ID; their objective was Voroshilovsk. Kavalleriegruppe von Jungschulz operated on the open northern flank.

The "Kalaus Line" was held until 18 January. On 18 and 19 January the withdrawal resumed. The snow storms ceased. Temperatures reached minus 30 degrees. The Russian formations again made contact. Artillery, that had no means of transport, was destroyed. Vehicles, which could go no further, were set afire. The withdrawal route was littered with memorials of the defeat. Hitler, who at first wanted to direct the entire 1st Panzer Army into the Kuban bridgehead, ordered on 22 January that some elements and then, on 24 January the entire 1st Panzer Army be directed to Rostov in support of the hard-pressed Army Group Don. However, this order would also be changed and the LII Army Corps would be diverted to the Kuban bridgehead with the 50th and 370th ID.

In the meantime things were already overcome by events on the Don front. Hoth's 4th Panzer Army could only hold on the Sal and Manych with difficulty and the Soviet 51st and 2 Guards Armies advancing on Rostov were gradually making headway.

On the basis of this strained situation the comments of the commander of the 52nd Rocket Launcher Regiment are understandable: "20 January 1943: The march tempo has been ordered increased because the basic situation has changed."

The battalions of the 52nd and 54th Rocket Launcher Regiments, as well as the 1st Heavy Rocket Launcher Regiment, had proven themselves in numerous commitments in the offensive and defensive efforts of Army Group A. They operated like motorized units, most of them assigned by battery to rear guards, on the shaky front positions. The 5/1 Werfer Rgt. fought in the rear guard of the 50th ID. As their fuel ran out, they fired their last rounds, blew up the launchers and vehicles and withdrew with the grenadiers.

On 20 January the 1st Panzer Army stood on either side of Voroshilovsk. The history of the 50th ID tells us more about the withdrawal: "20 January 1943: The division reached the Kuban bend northwest of Tatarski (50 kilometers southeast of Armavir). The rear guard is in contact with the enemy. The corps order drove the exhausted companies further: `New situation compels increased march effort. The new HKL on the `Krems Line' is to be reached on 21 January.' The march continued; 50 kilometers with short rest stops. The `Krems Line' was not to be occupied for long. On 22 January the 50th ID occupied the new positions east and south of Armavir. The Russians launched a strong attack on the III/123 Gren. Rgt. The battalion had to be withdrawn to the southern edge of Armavir. Enemy forces infiltrated through the thin lines into Armavir. The corps issued a withdrawal order to a line located 12 kilometers northwest of the city. Elements of the 50th ID fought their way through Armavir at night. On 24 January they reached the interim positions. On 26 January the crossing to the north near Krapotkin was completed."

In the meantime the course was set for the 111th ID, 3rd Panzer Division and the von Jungschulz Cossack Regiment. Under the leadership of the XXXX Panzer Corps they passed through Rostov to Army Group "Don" (von Manstein). They were preceded by the III Panzer Corps. The LII Army Corps veered off across the great Kuban bend to the southwest and established the large Kuban bridgehead on the northern flank adjacent to the Sea of Azov.

While the mobile formations of the 3rd Panzer Division provided cover the regiments of the 111th ID continued to march without pause. The exertions of the grenadiers were unimaginable. Blown vehicles and destroyed equipment, burned out ration stores and euthanized horses littered the routes. By the time they reached Rostov the 3rd Panzer Division had lost over half of its trucks and tanks.

With what difficulties the repair units fought for each truck and each tank is expressed in the following report from Unteroffizier Kraatz's crew, Gefrieters Sternberg, Satte and Kullrich, from the 2/6 Pz.Rgt., which had only two Panzer IVs left:

"We had to drive to the rear area because of a damaged fuel pump. The snow was knee deep. The temperature was minus 20 degrees. The tank treads looked like polished chrome. The road was icy. The tank skidded. The crew jumped out. The tank landed in a frozen trench. We tried to back it out. The ice broke. The Panzer IV sunk deeper. The water was already coming through the floor plates. The motor stalled!

Then it was night. Long columns passed by; they were becoming ever thinner. We were freezing from the cold. Should we blow it up or wait for the repair team, that was the question? Then a message came over the radio: "Hold on - we're coming!"

We were all alone. There were engine sounds - were they ours or Russians? It was Technical Inspector Bärwinkel with two 18 ton prime movers.

"He told us: "There was no question of blowing it up!" Each prime mover had a Panzer III in tow. One of the prime movers used a Panzer III as a block. They righted our Panzer IV by turning it over twice. Water, ice and oil covered the inside of our tank. We took our places and followed the prime movers back to the regiment."

On the morning of 23 January the XXXX Panzer Corps stood in the Tikhorets area. On the morning of 24 January a battlegroup under Hauptmann Müller-Röhlich reached Nesamaevskaya, from where they conducted reconnaissance to all sides. Elements of the battlegroup advanced up to Plosskaya and destroyed a Russian tank element consisting of two tanks.

On 24 January the "Northern Group of the Transcaucasus Front" was regrouped. The new army group was assigned the mission of reaching Tikhorets, as well as the Primorsko and Akhtarsk harbors on the Sea of Azov. The advance forces of the 3rd Panzer Division withdrew to the Yeya sector near Borosovskiy using mobile combat tactics. All bridges were blown. On 26 January Oberst Zimmermann was entrusted with command in the Yeya sector. The Yeya sector was reinforced with the deployment of the 802nd Caucasian Battalion and additional elements of the 3rd Panzer Division. Solid contact was established with the LVII Panzer Corps, which was withdrawing from Salsk.

On 28 January the 802nd Caucasian Battalion gave up Kalnibolotskaya to heavy enemy pressure. In order to prevent their being cut off, an additional battle group had to be committed. Nesamaevskaya became the focal point held by the elements of the 3rd Panzer Division against the superior enemy force.

East of Irinovka lay the next defensive line of the 3rd Panzer Division. Soon the pursuing cavalry was crashing against this line. The few operational tanks of the 3rd Panzer Division conducted a relief attack and established contact in Rossoshinskiy with the 11th Panzer Division, which had beat back a threatening attack wedge of the 2nd Soviet Guards Tank Army out of the Manychkaya bridgehead. This occurred 3 kilometers in front of the Bataisk bridges at a point in time when the LVII Panzer Corps was still located far to the east in the Proletarskaya bridgehead.

At the end of January the 3rd Panzer Division had a front 100 kilometers wide, which could only be occupied with strong points in a half-circle around Bataisk. The 3rd Panzer Division rear area service units, which, according to the initial plan, were to have been directed to the 1st Panzer Army in the Kuban bridgehead, were already located there and had to be diverted across a 60 kilometer long ice road over the Sea of Azov into the Taganrog area. The last rearguard elements from the 3rd Panzer Division crossed the Don bridges near Bataisk on the night of 3 February. The division had fought its way back for almost 700 kilometers in a short four weeks.

"Operation Edelweiss" had ended for the 3rd Panzer Division. On 6 February 1943 the 111th ID was the last formation to reach the Bataisk bridges.

AND AGAIN TO ROSTOV

The LVII Panzer Corps fights for time - In the ice desert between the Manych and Sal - The Simovniki breakwater - Krasnoe Znamya - Proletarskaya bridgehead - The 16th ID (Mot.) drives toward Sporny - The Soviet Manychkaya bridgehead is crushed

On 27 November 1942 Generalfeldmarschall von Manstein took command of the newly-created Army Group "Don", with which he was to master the crisis near Stalingrad where the 6th Army under Generaloberst Paulus was encircled. Von Manstein had temporarily constructed a defensive front on the Chir. The 4th Panzer Army fought to the Myshkova and established a bridgehead 70 kilometers from the southern portion of the Stalingrad pocket.

Stalin no longer wanted to destroy only the 6th Army. He wanted to destroy the entire southern flank of the German Eastern Front, including the Caucasus group. While seven Soviet armies surrounded Stalingrad with an iron ring, three armies attacked the frontal sector of the 8th Italian Army on the upper Don and broke through. The lead Soviet tank elements were directed at Rostov.

In this situation von Manstein had to commit the 6th Panzer Division from Hoth's group to block the breakthrough in the Italian area because he had no other formations available. This meant that Generaloberst Hoth had to make the relief attack on Stalingrad with only two exhausted panzer divisions, the 17th and the 23rd. And there was still more. Soon Hoth was opposed by strong enemy forces. Both panzer divisions were pushed back and, when the Romanians, who were securing to the south, fled from weak enemy pressure, the southern flank was opened. The Soviet 51st and 28th Armies attacked into this gap, while the 2nd Guards Army attacked into the Kotelnikovo area and was directed into the area between the lower Don and the Sal toward Rostov.

Stalin wanted to capture Rostov with three armies from the north and three from the south. The attack from the north was parried, but Hoth's 4th Panzer Army remained at the focus of the great race. It had the mission of fighting a delaying battle in order to keep the Rostov gap open for the German Caucasus troops.

The battles of the 16th ID (Mot.) must be described in connection with this, since it stood alone in the Utta - Elista area. The division was the mobile link between Army Groups A and B; the connection between Stalingrad and the Caucasus.

On 21 November 1942 the commander of the 16th ID (Mot.), Generalmajor Graf Gerhard von Schwerin, informed Army Group A that his regiment in Khalkhuta was almost encircled, but it had avoided the encirclement during the course of the night. The Russians did not succeed. He (von Schwerin) planned to leave a rearguard in Utta (from where he was speaking) and withdraw the main body of the division to prepared positions near Yashkul. This news indicated that not only was Corps Felmy in trouble in the Kuma Valley on the northern flank of Army Group A east of Budenovsk, but there were storm clouds gathering in the 16th ID (Mot.) area of operations also.

A day later von Schwerin informed Army Group A that his division had to occupy new positions in a half-circle around Yashkul. The divisional command post was located in Ulan - Erge. The rear guard was withdrawn from Utta and reestablished 20 kilometers to the west. It appeared that it was operating against the 38th Guards Rifle Division, the 152nd Motorized Rifle Brigade and the 6th Tank Brigade.

On 26 November the 1st Generalstabsoffizier of the 16th ID (Mot.), Oberstleutnant von Kienle, informed Army Group A that the enemy had attacked the division positions near Oling with strong forces on the previous day. Penetrations were eliminated with counterattacks.

On 9 December 1942 the 16th ID (Mot.) stood unchallenged in its positions near Yashkul. According to defector statements, the enemy was awaiting the deployment of another tank brigade with which to take Yashkul.

When the encirclement of Stalingrad was completed in the second half of November 1942, all available German formations were directed to Army Group B. This meant that there would be no operational reserve. Under 27 November 1942 the combat diary of Army Group A noted:

"Deploying to the 4th Panzer Division in Salsk:

Oberst von Pannwitz' headquarters

23rd Panzer Division (with 67 operational tanks)

LVII Panzer Corps command

Special Panzer Formation (23 tanks, originally slated for the 13th Panzer Division)

203rd Assault Gun Battalion

Anti-aircraft Artillery and Luftwaffe units organized under the 15th Luftwaffe Field Division

To the 16th ID (Mot.)

Naval alert formation

Alert formation organized from the headquarters of Army Group A (110 men)."

So what did they have for formations? Oberst von Pannwitz with the local national Cossack squadrons; the 23rd Panzer Division, which was battered in front of Ordzhonikidze; the LVII Panzer Corps command from the western Caucasus; a special formation that was supposed to reinforce the 13th Panzer Division; the 203rd Assault Gun Battalion, which had fought on the Terek; and finally the 15th Luftwaffe Field Division under Generalleutnant Mahnke, which was assembled in the Sals area. The alert formations going to the 16th ID (Mot.) only had a strength of two companies.

Another threatening gap was in the Manych Valley. There, on 1 December 1943 General von Roques took command with his special staff. Forces of the 15th Luftwaffe Field Division were subordinated to him, among others. The battlegroup took up defenses in the Divnoe - Driyutnoe sector. On 18 December Generalleutnant Auleb took command of Battle Group von

Roques by order of Army Group A.

The relief of Stalingrad had to be given up. Hoth's panzer formations were forced onto the defensive. They had to fight for time in order to hold open the Rostov gap for the 1st Panzer Army. On the basis of this development Hitler had to finally permit the III Panzer Corps to withdraw from Ordzhonikidze. He had to do this in order to free up another division by shortening the front, and to give it to Hoth.

On 20 December 1942 at 2300 hours, Army Group A was ordered by OKH to immediately withdraw the III Panzer Corps and remove the SS Panzergrenadier Division "Wiking". On 23 December the 1st Panzer Army was notified by Führer Directive that "Wiking" was to be marched at speed tempo 4 (the highest transport ptiority) to Army Group "Don".

On 24 December 1942, Christmas Eve, I/"Nordland" was the first march group to unload in Prokhladny. In train after train "Wiking" was transported by rail in the direction of Salsk. Except for III/"Nordland", which remained in the III Panzer Corps area of operations until 31 December 1942 and covered the mountain flank with the Romanians, all other "Wiking" units were transferred by the year's end.

We read of the rapid transport of the "Wiking" in the notes of Rttfhr. Blah, chief driver from 3/"Nordland":

"25 December: Krapotkin - 26 December: Salsk. Very cold, colder than in the Caucasus - 27 December: Arrived in Kuberle. Unloaded - 28 December: Motor marched through Simovniki - Remontnaya - 31 December: In the early morning a T-34 shadowed the advancing vehicles. At 1100 hours I/"Nordland" was attacked. The attack was repulsed. There was a counterattack with stuka support. The enemy skedaddled."

To this point in time as the "Wiking" was being transported so quickly into the LVII Panzer Corps defenses near Kotelnikovo, the 16th ID (Mot.) reported on 27 December 1942 strong infantry and vehicle traffic moving to the west from Astrakhan in the direction of Utta. It had to count on being attacked.

A day later the Romanians fled from the Sagista sector, opening a gap between the 16th ID (Mot.) and the 4th Panzer Army. Because the LVII Panzer Corps was tied up with heavy enemy attacks it could not intervene in the Romanian area of operations. In the evening report on 28 December the 16th ID (Mot.), which was located near Yashkul, noted that Russian assault groups were advancing on Remontnoe and Divnoe. They were paving the way for an outflanking of the northern flank of the 1st Panzer Army. Hitler had to order the withdrawal of the 1st Panzer Army from Terek. The 16th ID (Mot.) was instructed to hold its positions as long as possible and then withdraw in the direction of Elista.

The combat diary of Army Group A describes the further movement of the 16th ID (Mot.):

"29 December 1942: 16th ID (Mot.) repulsed a fierce attack in the Ulan - Erge area. They were attempting to outflank. The threat remains. No further contact with the 4th Panzer Army."

There is still the threat that in the following days strong enemy forces will advance against Troitskoe in order to then turn to the south against Elista. Then the 16th ID withdrawal route would be blocked.

30 December 1942: 16th ID (Mot.) reported the advance of a 15 kilometer long march column from Ulan - Erge to the west. In the lead are 12 companies with strong tank support which will attack Elista.

31 December 1942: The column continued to advance on Elista to where the 16th ID (Mot.) is withdrawing.

Gruppe Auleb reported that the Manych was frozen and trafficable. III Soviet Guards Motorized Corps is advancing out of the Savetnoe area. II/6 Pol.Rgt [Polish] was transferred from the Kuma Valley into the Divnoe area. At 1510 hours the 16th ID (Mot.) reported that his forces can no longer hold Elista.

At 1605 hours Generalleutnant Auleb ordered the 16th ID (Mot.) to fight its way to Driyutnoe."

On 31 December 1942 at 1745 hours Army Group "Don" briefed Army Group A on the constant enemy pressure in the Kotelnikovo - Simovniki area. There the enemy had already advanced into the area south of Zymlyanskaya."

If one realized that Zymlyanskaya lay approximately 10 kilometers west of the confluence of the Chir into the Don, then one would also realize that the northern flank of the 4th Panzer Army was already outflanked. There the 2nd Guards Army, with the III Guards Tank Corps in the lead, advanced between the Don and the Sal in the direction of Rostov. Hoth's 4th Panzer Army consisted practically only of the LVII Panzer Corps and the newly subordinated 16th ID. He could no longer count on the Romanian corps which belonged to his army. Thus, General Kirchner's LVII Panzer Corps stood alone with the difficult mission of holding, holding and holding some more, so that the 1st Panzer Army, which was withdrawing from the eastern Caucasus, would reach the Rostov gap in time.

And what did General Kirchner have available? On 31 December 1942, in the Kotelnikovo area, the 17th Panzer Division was on the left and the 23rd Panzer Division was on the right. Both divisions were there fighting back to Remontnaya. The enemy pressure was strong. In this situation the first elements of the "Wiking" arrived in the corps area of operations. On 31 December I/"Nordland" conducted a relief attack from Remontnaya to the southeast in order to help the 23rd Panzer Division.

Under 1 January 1943 the combat diary of the LVII Panzer Corps noted:

"At year's end the corps conducted a withdrawal operation behind the Maloe Kuberle on either side of Simovniki up to its confluence into the Sal with the 23rd and 17th Panzer Divisions, as well as the 156th Panzergrenadier Regiment (16th ID), because of the threatened outflanking from the deep eastern flank..."

In the meantime the regiments of the "Wiking" arrived. The "Germania" Regiment was first subordinated to the 17th Panzer Division and occupied positions around Stoyanovskiy, while the "Westland" Regiment assembled in Simovniki 10 kilometers to the south.

On New Year's Eve the first "Wiking" tank transports were halted shortly before reaching the Kuberle railroad station. North of the transport trains march columns made their way to the west. The "Wiking" tankers believed that they were Russians. Stubaf. Mühlenkamp and his officers wanted to be unloaded at an open stretch of track, but the technical officer, Ostuf. Weisse, told them this would cause equipment damage and lead to the loss of tanks. In the meantime reconnaissance elements returned with news: "They are fleeing Rumanians!" The transports continued to roll and, on 1 January, unloaded in Kuberle. After additional transports arrived, the "Wiking" Panzer Battalion rolled in the afternoon and, after a night march, reached Simovniki on the morning of 2 January 1943.

At this time Simovniki was a sensitive point. There was no solid defense. Russian formations had already penetrated into some portions of the town. The crisis had to be eliminated if the town was to become part of the Maloe Kuberle defense. Simovniki became a LVII Panzer Corps defensive point on the following day. While I/"Nordland" still fought its way back into the Remontnaya area, the "Westland" Regiment set up a defense in Simovniki. The commander of II/"Westland", Hstuf. Ziemssen, reported:

"On 30 December 1942 the II/"Westland" unloaded in Simovniki (two transports). Romanian personnel without weapons, without officers, without order were fleeing to the rear. There was no friendly HKL here. Hoth's army headquarters withdrew from Simovniki on the previous day and only the Ic was still there so he could instruct the arriving elements of "Wiking". He pointed out that we must count upon the arrival of Soviet lead tank elements at any time. The arriving "Westland" elements were directed into the defense, but they could not construct a unified HKL with the few forces available. The I/5 SS AR and a mixed Luftwaffe air defense battalion were subordinated to the regiment."

I/"Nordland", which was still located in the foreground, was withdrawn and subordinated to the "Westland" Regiment in Simovniki. On 31 December I/"Nordland" conducted a relief attack to the southwest. With the support of artillery and stukas, the attack gained ground through the airfield and pushed the Soviets back. An abandoned German rations dump was again in German hands and, this time, evacuated. Among the Russian supplies the grenadiers of I/"Nordland" found a lot of American products. The packages of meat carried the logo of the American meat company, Mayer.

Throughout New Year's Eve Russian tanks rattled toward Simovniki with accompanying infantry. During the night and in the early morning a fierce battle developed. The Wanhöfer Engineer Company and a company Feldwebel with his rear services personnel, which were subordinated to the "Westland" Regiment, destroyed the tanks with close combat weapons, while the grenadiers repulsed the infantry attack in the foreground.

On New Year's Day the I and II/"Nordland" repulsed a hefty enemy attack, but the Russians started occupying some sections of the town.

"2 January 1943: 'Westland' repulsed penetrating enemy forces from

Simovniki and defended exceptionally well...", thus stated the combat diary of the LVII Panzer Corps. On this day the panzer battalion also joined in the battle near Simovniki. During the next few days the destroyed advance troops in Simovniki were followed by five Russian division or brigade formations. In deeply echeloned, up to 3 kilometer wide waves the Soviets crashed against them several times a day and were always repulsed. Playing a big part there were the reinforced companies of the "Westland" Regiment, which were armed with captured weapons, the Wanhöfer Engineer Company, the I/5 SS AR, as well as the Luftwaffe air defense battalion. The "Wiking" Panzer Battalion helped to hold and stabilize the front by counterattacking. During one counterattack to the south, the 2/Pz.Abt. "Wiking" captured five new German Panzer IIIs with the long barrel and heated combat compartment, which were abandoned by the 23rd Panzer Division. The tanks were given back to the 23rd Panzer Division on the order of the division commander, Oberführer Gille.

We find the following passage in the combat diary of the LVII Panzer Corps: "3 January 1943: Enemy forces that penetrated into Simovniki have been thrown back - 6 January 1943: Enemy pressure persists near and north of Simovniki..."

The defense of Simovniki on the important rail and road connection with Proletarskaya was a feather in the cap of the "Westland" Regiment, as it gained valuable time for the LVII Panzer Corps in costly combat.

While the "Westland" Regiment was in and around Simovniki Generalleutnant von Senger und Etterlin's 17th Panzer Division had all it could handle with the attack on the northern flank of the corps. The area was free of troops and the division had to constantly parry enemy outflanking attacks in mobile combat. On 3 January the 17th Panzer Division reported that the enemy must be counted on to reinforce and advance toward Proletarskaya. The 17th Panzer Division received the heavy 503rd Panzer Battalion (Tiger). Immediately, an engineer company was dispatched to occupy the bridge in Martinovskaya in order to prevent Russian forces from crossing the Sal there from the north into the rear of the LVII Panzer Corps. By 5 January, the situation on the northern flank of the corps had worsened considerably. The 17th Panzer Division was powerless in facing the ever-increasing enemy formations, especially since they only had a strongpoint type of defense in which there were huge gaps.

There was a similar situation on the south of the corps front. There the 16th ID (Mot.) was fighting its way cleverly to the LVII Panzer Corps. Gruppe Auleb, which was located in the south, withdrew to Salsk. The 23rd Panzer Division, on the right flank of the corps, was exposed to considerable Soviet pressure.

On 7 January the 2/Pz.Abt. "Wiking" was committed to a counterattack in the 17th Panzer Division area of operations. On this day General Kirchner wanted to withdraw his corps front to Bolshoe Kuberle. An impressive picture of the combat, weather and orientation difficulties was given to us in a report by the commander of the 2nd Panzer Company of "Wiking", Ostuf.

Flügel: "On the morning of 7 January 1943 I set out with my company and some mounted engineers in order to conduct a counterattack against lead Russian tank elements. I was trying to outflank the enemy tanks with my company and hit them in the flank. The maneuver succeeded; we shot up several enemy tanks and anti-tank guns. The Russians withdrew.

At 1600 hours darkness fell and we had no further opportunity to establish contact with the 17th Panzer Division. Unfortunately, we also had wounded. Since we had also lost contact with our battalion, we broke contact with the enemy and drove in two columns, with cannon and machine-guns aimed in all directions, to the west toward the steppe. Orientation was almost impossible. After a short distance we drove past a Russian camp where Russians were sitting around a fire trying to warm themselves against the cold.

From the orientation of the camp I determined where the 17th Panzer Division must lie. We continued in that direction. At 2000 hours my company was located between the 17th Panzer Division and the pursuing Russians (in the meantime, General Kirchner had ordered the withdrawal of his corps to the Bolshoe Kuberle sector). The 17th Panzer Division rearguard and the pursuing Russian tanks were firing at each other. It was difficult for us to make contact with the friendly formations because we could be fired upon as an enemy.

We withdrew from the vicinity of the combatants and, in a short time, came upon a frozen stream and some nearby houses. We noticed some movement, but was it friendly people or Russians? My first tanks approached the houses; we could not determine whether the headlights were yellow Russian or white German. In the next moment engines were started up near the houses and tanks were heard moving. Then my unit took some fire. I ordered: "Drive back to the stream bed and wait!" I could not be heard over the firing. Then I ordered a strict cease fire. We approached the group of houses on foot in order to see who was there, but they had left in the meantime.

We continued to drive. Our withdrawal became a problem because of a lack of fuel. However, because of the cold, we could not stop the tank engines.

We drove in a column. I drove in the lead in order to determine from the tank tracks with what we would have to deal with. Finally, at 0500 hours, Landser jumped from their positions and yelled: "Password?", which I did not know. However, I soon was able to establish that this was the security of the 17th Panzer Division and that the tank formation that had fired on us during the night was a rear guard of the 503rd Heavy Panzer Battalion.

I drove with the company to the nearest troop surgeon and turned over my wounded. In the meantime I found out where we were and how I could find my way back to the battalion strong point. The other companies had already withdrawn. We quickly refueled and stocked up on ammunition. We had just finished supplying the tanks when Russian T-34s drove into my halted company. They fired in all directions; two of my tanks were hit. In the meantime we took up the battle. Of the five T-34s, two were hit at close range. The rest retreated. We rolled to the west at the break of day."

On 7 January the LVII Panzer Corps withdrew to Bolshoe Kuberle. On 8 January the divisions were again prepared to defend: On the northern flank was the 17th Panzer Division, in the center was the "Wiking" and on the southern flank was the 23rd Panzer Division. Already on the first day in the new positions all of the divisions faced a new crisis. On the northern flank, which bent back in a bow, the 63rd Panzergrenadier Regiment (17th Panzer Division) had to counter constant enemy attempts to outflank it from the north with mobile combat operations. In the "Wiking" sector, enemy lead elements were advancing through the gaps in the front toward Orlovka. At 0740 hours the "Wiking" was ordered by corps to destroy the penetrating enemy forces in Orlovka. This mission fell to the "Germania" Regiment, which was still on the move. This regiment was directed to establish a defense southeast of Orlovka, maintaining loose contact with the 23rd Panzer Division. The "Westland" Regiment occupied Orlovka. North of there, in Kammenaya Balka, lay elements of the "Nordland" Regiment.

On 8 January the 16th ID (Mot.) ran into the security of the 23rd Panzer Division and was channeled through to Proletarskaya. The division had to fight its way north of the Manych and then had to parry constant outflanking attempts by the 28th Soviet Army by withdrawing in a leap-frog manner.

However, on this 8 January 1943, a new report startled General Kirchner. At 0915 hours the 4th Panzer Army informed the LVII Panzer Corps that two reinforced enemy companies had crossed the Manych dam near Sporny and occupied Vesseliy on the southern bank. This dam was crossed at the same location and in the same direction by the 16th ID (Mot.) as the lead element of the III Panzer Corps at the end of July, when they were advancing on the Caucasus. This time lead Soviet elements were located there in the rear of the LVII Panzer Corps. To complete the misfortune, the lead elements of the Soviet III Guards Tank Corps established a bridgehead across the Don near Manychkaya, 30 kilometers east of Rostov. Stalin's longed- for objective was near. And the majority of the 1st Panzer Army was still far away in the Caucasus; its divisions were urged to make haste.

However, the troops in the snowy mountains did not hear of the threatening danger. They were too busy fighting the enemy and the cold. They could only see a short distance, to their next intermediate objective. They knew that they had to hold out in order to prevent great harm. And they persevered and struggled against the superior enemy. Often life and death struggles took place around a bit of warmth; winning signified life, while, in this winter wasteland and in the icy cold, losing could mean death.

The Bolshoe Kuberle line was only held for 24 hours. Because of the outflanking in the north a bridgehead had to be quickly occupied around Proletarskaya. Ostuf. Flügel reported on the withdrawal from the Bolshoe Kuberle sector: "During the withdrawal from Bolshoe Kuberle the `Wiking' Panzer Battalion had the mission of covering the withdrawal of the units. In a driving snow storm I and my 2/Pz.Abt. "Wiking", which was reinforced with three Panzer IVs from the 3rd Company, had the mission of holding off the Russians until new positions could be occupied by the division. It was a cursed night! The tanks could not get a grip on the snow drifted routes. My tank stripped a gear during a sideways slide. We could not leave it, especially since it had the only radio contact with the battalion. One of the company tanks towed the command tank. The pursuing enemy continued to close in. The snow storm intensified. The lane through the minefield for my company still lay at some distance. I only had a map section to orient by. Then the towing tank slipped down a balka. I was in it, giving instructions when, it turned over. I was bounced about and finally thrown out of the turret in front of the towed tank. Luckily, the towed tank came to a stop. I was bruised and fractured. I turned over the company to Ustuf. Büscher. Then I was evacuated in a 1 ton prime mover. On the way we fell under fire and two of the crewmen were wounded, but I was able to guide the prime mover through the minefield. The following company also accomplished its mission and returned."

The 1st Panzer Company under Stubaf. Schneider had a similar mission.

On 10 January 1943 the "Wiking" stood in the Kundryucheskiy - Sundova line. On the northern flank of the corps, elements of the 17th Panzer Division were encircled in Novo Nikolaevskiy and then liberated. The 17th Panzer Division was diverted by radio message to the southwest toward Proletarskaya.

On 11 January Staf. Wagner's "Germania" Regiment repulsed a strong enemy attack near Kundryucheskiy. A day later Stubaf. Lohmann and his I/"Nordland" fought to occupy the village of Kammennaya Balka. South of there, the "Westland" Regiment threw back a hefty enemy attack on Orlovskaya.

Under 12 and 13 January the combat diary of the LVII Panzer Corps noted:

"Lively enemy offensive activity in front of the 17th Panzer Division and 'Wiking'. 0845 hours: 'Wiking' reports that the enemy was penetrating into Zhuravlev on the left flank, but was driven back.

1545 hours: During the battle for Orlovka, Stubaf. Polewacz, commander of 'Westland' Regiment, and Stubaf. Baron von Hadeln, commander of I/'Westland', were killed. Gap between 'Wiking' and the 23rd Panzer Division cannot be monitored, to say nothing of closing it.

13 January 1943: Enemy situation: It appears that strong enemy groups will also outflank the southern flank of the LVII Panzer Corps due to their crossing the Manych.

0940 hours: 503rd Heavy Panzer Battalion and 60th Panzergrenadier Regiment (16th ID) assembling in Yekaterinovka in order to block the enemy forces crossing the Manych."

On 11 January the 16th ID (Mot.) was committed on the left next to the 17th Panzer Division in order to prevent the outflanking of the northern flank of the corps and to close on the Proletarskaya bridgehead. The division would remain in this area until 14 January.

From 13 to 15 January Division "Wiking" was at the focal point of the combat. The regiments were inserted into the front. Ostubaf. Jörchel's "Nordland" Regiment was in the north making contact with the 17th Panzer

Division; the II Battalion was in Grakov and the I Battalion was in Krasnoe Znamya. The III Battalion arrived directly in Proletarskaya from the Caucasus.

In the center was Ostubaf. Reichel's (former Ia of "Wiking") "Westland" Regiment, with a battalion in Donskoi and one in Renichanskiy. On the southern flank of the "Wiking" was the "Germania" Regiment around the Romanov farmstead.

On 14 January 1943 heavy combat raged in the "Wiking" sector. Under this day Blah's diary noted:

"Icy snow storms. Russians attacked with tanks. Our I/'Nordland' suffered heavy losses. During the evening Russians were thrown back in a counterattack out of Krasnoe Znamya, which they had already captured. Tanks have shot up many houses."

What was happening there will be explained later.

On 14 January "Westland" and "Germania" repulsed enemy attacks which were conducted with superior forces, but Soviet forces advanced in the direction of Proletarskaya into the gap between the "Wiking" and the 23rd Panzer Division in the "Germania" Regiment area. At 1405 hours the 23rd Panzer Division reported to the LVII Panzer Corps: "... a captured order indicates that the German forces near Sovkhoz I are to be destroyed and Proletarskaya is to be encircled."

Under 15 January 1943 in the combat diary of the LVII Panzer Corps one reads: "Main effort on the southern flank of the corps - 1020 hours: Krasnoe Znamya attacked - 1030 hours: 23rd Panzer Division withdrawn to protect the land bridge between the Manych and Lake (salt) Kosinka - `Wiking' occupies a narrow bridgehead around Proletarskaya. 17th Panzer Division was withdrawn and committed to protect the withdrawal route east of Salsk."

Now we read the accounts of front soldiers. The defensive battle of the I/"Nordland" in Krasnoe Znamya will represent all of the companies and battalions in this combat area. The battalion commander, Stubaf. Lohmann, wrote: "During the withdrawal battle in January 1943 the strongpoint defense was influenced by the weather. The dominant terrain played a large role; it was important to include housing, which offered protection from the cold, in the defensive plan.

Thus, on 13 January 1943 I/'Nordland' arrived in Krasnoe Znamya during the course of the withdrawal battle. Combat posts in platoon strength were placed in depressions, which lay in front of the long and narrow town.

I had not counted upon immediate contact with the enemy. As commander of I/'Nordland' I ordered the companies to exchange their weapons with the Waffenmeister. A light snow was falling. The day seemed like it would pass without incident."

Oberscharführer Stock reported: "Early on 14 January 1943 I was ordered by the battalion commander to relieve a platoon of another company, which had established a forward strongpoint approximately 2 kilometers northeast of the village, with my platoon from the 2nd Company. I was assigned a heavy machine-gun and a mortar group as reinforcement. Our vehicles brought us to the strongpoint which was established on a hillock. After turning it over, the relieved platoon returned with the vehicles. We established a circular defense. We had contact with the battalion over a field telephone.

At midday Soviet infantry in white camouflage appeared about 500 meters north of us crossing a slight rise in the direction of Krasnoe Znamya. We reported the observation to the battalion and were ordered to remain quiet and wait.

In the meantime there were sounds of combat coming from Krasnoe Znamya. More Russian infantry appeared. I was ordered by the battalion commander to take three infantry groups to Krasnoe Znamya and leave the two heavy groups in the strongpoint. The group leaders were: Uscha. Krueger from Danzig, Rttfhr. Lühr from Norddeutschland and Rttfhr. Matzen from Denmark. The platoon troop leader was Uscha. Roth. The heavy machine-gun group was led by Uscha. Bleise and the mortars by a Dutch Rottenführer.

We moved in column to the left behind the slope. On the slight rise, from which the village could be seen, was a row of shrubs and a path leading to the village. As soon as I decided to open fire on the Soviets, who were fighting on the eastern edge, six T-34s moved in from the right along the row of shrubs. They stopped in front of us and fired on the village. I gave the signal to remain completely quiet. After a while the tanks drove off in the direction of the village. We went back to the strongpoint. I reported over the telephone and was ordered to wait and call the battalion command post every half hour. However, when I next called there was no contact."

Sturmbannführer Lohmann: "Suddenly, from the side where no enemy forces were anticipated, Russian tanks appeared between the command post and the battalion's security. The companies took up their defensive positions as quickly as they could. Approximately one dozen tanks advanced on the road to the town, firing as they moved. The Russian infantry, which accompanied the tanks, was repulsed.

I still had telephone contact with the regiment and reported the situation and requested immediate support from anti-tank weapons, tanks or assault guns. The regimental commander, Ostubaf. Jörchel, did not appear to believe my alarming report. While speaking, a tank rolled directly at my command post. In order to back up my request I yelled into the telephone: 'Obersturmbannführer, what you now hear is a Russian tank that is passing right by my house!' I opened a small window and held the receiver outside.

Fierce combat developed. The tanks drove back and forth and shot up almost all of the houses, and they covered each other so well that they could not be approached. We were slowly pushed back. I was determined to hold at least the hill on which the command post lay because behind it lay the troop first aid station where there were still many wounded. They could not be transported and were still being treated by troop surgeon Dr. Spitzy and his medics. Even the medical people grabbed their weapons. The enemy attack

281

encompassed two-thirds of the town. We were able to lay a temporary mine-field around the battalion command post hill."

After receiving the report from Krasnoe Znamya, support measures were prepared for I/"Nordland". Under 14 January the combat diary of III/"Nordland" noted: "The battalion was alerted in Donskoe. 1435 hours: Regiment ordered one company to be marched to the I Battalion in Krasnoe Znamya. 1505 hours: 11th Company left and will be subordinated to the I Battalion. The enemy has occupied two-thirds of the town with 8 tanks and 400 men. 1615 hours: 11th Company and I Battalion threw the enemy out of the village in a counterattack. The enemy lost 200 killed. Losses of 11th Company: 2 killed, 13 wounded."

The enemy attacked again, since the houses offered warmth for the coming cold night. Again, the infantry penetrated into the village with the support of tanks. Unterscharführer Schmidt, Gruppenführer of the 6/"Nordland" report-ed: "On 13 January the 6th Company had occupied shelters in Grakov. We were alerted on the afternoon of 14 January! Hstuf. Treuker, our company commander, informed us of the situation and our mission. The Russians had penetrated into the I Battalion area. The II Battalion had to launch a counter-attack with two companies and throw the Russians out of Krasnoe Znamya.

Two companies of the II Battalion launched the attack. When we were half way up a small hill we saw the elongated town of Krasnoe Znamya. We took infantry fire. The attack was suspended; the companies took cover behind the slope.

Shortly after that I was summoned to the battalion commander, Stubaf. Krügel, and ordered to take my squad toward Krasnoe Znamya and deter-mine whether the I Battalion was still holding out in Krasnoe Znamya. My squad and I got underway. Before us lay the elongated village. There were noises of combat coming from the right third of the village. We headed in that direction. We reached the town and ran into men from the I Battalion. I was briefed on the situation in the battalion command post by the comman-der. Then I returned with my men and reported to Stubaf. Krügel.

At twilight, widely dispersed, the two companies moved toward Krasnoe Znamya and waited there for further orders. Then the order arrived for the counterattack: At exactly 2400 hours a white light was flashed, the signal for the attack. We assaulted firing and yelling `Hurrah!' The Russians were so surprised that they could not offer any serious resistance. It all happened so quickly that we did not have the time to search the houses. We fired a few rounds at the windows and doors and then moved on to the next block. A number of Russians surrendered and were led off to the rear with hand sig-nals and 'Davai, Davai! [Move, Move!]' The tanks tried to join in the battle, but they could not in the dark. When one was destroyed, the rest withdrew. We quickly advanced and soon saw the end of the village in the light of a burning house. However, there stood three T-34s at a wide intersection. With their fire, they prevented us from advancing any further. A reserve platoon was committed on the flank from the garden side and cleared out the last houses. Then the tanks and infantrymen withdrew. The I Battalion took over the security at the edge of the village and the companies of the II Battalion marched back to Grabov while it was still nighttime."

Sturmbannführer Lohmann: "If we could not get the T-34s off of our heels with anti-tank weapons, then it was clear that a withdrawal, taking along our many wounded, would be very difficult.

On the morning of 15 January the combat again see-sawed. Again we were pushed back. At midday a report came in from a balka behind us that an assault gun Hauptmann was awaiting instructions. He was with four assault guns in a depression behind the town. The tactical emblem of the assault guns was the elephant (203rd Assault Gun Brigade). I went forward with the Hauptmann, whose name escapes me now, briefed him on the situation and pointed out the T-34s to him. Then we made our counterattack plan. I was also able to gather our outpost platoons, which we had heard nothing from for the past 24 hours. Then the counterattack was launched with the support of the assault guns."

Untersturmführer Ertel, commander of the 9/"Nordland", reported on the counterattack: "On the morning of 15 January I was ordered to drive to Krasnoe Znamya with my Ninth and conduct a counterattack with assault guns. We dismounted before we got to the city. I was briefed on the situation and the attack plan by Stubaf. Lohmann. My company was still 35 men strong. We set up the counterattack so that the 2nd Platoon under Oscha. Spöck would attack on the left of the road and the 1st Platoon under Oscha. Elmgren would attack on the right. I was with the heavy machine-gun squad and the mortars near Platoon Elmgren. The attack would begin on the signal of the assault gun commander.

The attack was launched. The assault gun commander, who advanced in a jeep, led his assault guns successfully. The assault guns moved in attack formation and shot up the first T-34 without stopping. House after house was stormed in a rapid counterattack. At several locations columns of smoke designated the destruction of enemy tanks. After a half hour we reached the edge of the village. All seven of the T-34s that were originally operational on this day were destroyed. We saw the rest of the enemy flee."

The combat outpost leader, Oberscharführer Stock, reported: "We observed fires during the night in Krasnoe Znamya and waited in anticipation of the new day. On the morning of 15 January I conducted a reconnaissance with Gruppe Krueger in the direction of the village to clarify the situation. The sounds of combat grew silent and it appeared that our battalion had evacuated the village. We began to take enemy fire, so we returned to the strongpoint.

I talked it over with the squad leaders and we came to the conclusion that we would destroy the heavy weapons at the fall of darkness in order to preserve enough strength (we had gone two days without rations) to march in the direction of Proletarskaya. Then we waited for the evening.

In the early afternoon we heard strong combat noises coming from Krasnoe Znamya. Russians were fleeing over the rise they had climbed a day before. We opened fire from all barrels into the fleeing Russians. Then four tanks came over the rise with mounted infantry. Were they Russian or German? A white light was flashed. Soon an assault gun was approaching us. We quickly got onto the assault gun and were driven back to Krasnoe Znamya.

After the tension relaxed, our stomachs acted up, but we still did not get our rations right away. The battalion was exhausted; our company numbered only a handful of men. We assembled the combat strength of the battalion and had to move immediately to the edge of the village to support the guarding assault guns. In the meantime, the numerous wounded were evacuated. A new enemy attack was repulsed far from the village.

At 2000 hours we were to break contact with the enemy. We returned and assembled with the assault guns at the entrance to the town. Suddenly there was an ear splitting 'Hurrah!' The enemy was pursuing. Immediately the assault guns turned around and opened fire along the village road. We yelled 'Hurrah!' and assaulted on the left and right of the road. After a short time the Russians were again thrown back. We could now conduct our withdrawal in peace."

Finally, Sturmbannführer Lohmann wrote: "This day in Krasnoe Znamya, which played out a 'cat and mouse game' over a few huts in the white desert, would never be forgotten by those men who participated in it. Special thanks go to the assault guns for saving a hopeless situation."

On 15 January 1943, as I/"Nordland" fought in Krasnoe Znamya to be able to withdraw to Proletarskaya, the 16th ID (Mot.), which had been committed on the northern flank of the corps since 11 January 1943 to parry the outflanking attempts of the enemy, probed the Soviet Sporny - Vesseliy bridgehead. This was after it gave up the line Bakaevskaya - Novo Sradkovsky (a small land bridge between the Sal and Manych). Hauptmann Tebbe's 116th Panzer Battalion led the way, followed by the Münster 60th Panzergrenadier Regiment. They paid no attention to the enemy occupied towns. Like hunters in the wild the force rolled from the northeast into the small Soviet bridgehead and destroyed it. Platoon leader Oberfeldwebel Bunzel of the 3rd Panzer Company was the first to press onto the Sporny dam. His tanks suppressed the Russian bridge guards. Bunzel knew the terrain well enough. During the previous July, he was also the first to reach thar point, but, at that time, the bridge was blown up before his eyes.

While the following companies of the 16th ID (Mot.) cleared out the Russian bridgehead, Oberleutnant Klappich and his III/60 Pz.Gren.Rgt. probed across the bridge further to the west into the thick snow drifts, approached Samodurovka and captured the village in a surprise attack. The Chief of Staff of a Russian brigade was captured. His statements indicated that the foothold of the Cossack troops was to be destroyed from there. Bataisk lay only 30 kilometers away. There German formations crossed the saving bridges without pause.

The 16th ID (Mot.) established a defense around Sporny - Vesseliy. It blocked the enemy forces attacking from the north from the Manych crossings and held open the withdrawal route for the LVII Panzer Corps, which was still located near Proletarskaya - Salsk. The division was supported in this endeavor by the Stichnoth Armored Reconnaissance Element from the

"Wiking" Reconnaissance Battalion. Reconnaissance Element Stichnoth, which was subordinated to the 16th ID (Mot.) on order of the corps, consisted of an eight-wheeled and a four-wheeled reconnaissance car. Untersturmführer Stichnoth conducted far-ranging reconnaissance daily and gave the 16th ID (Mot.) a good picture of the enemy's movements. In this manner Oberleutnant Klappich's force held onto Samodurovka and threatened the main Russian Manychkaya bridgehead. As a result, the Soviets were forced to divert strong forces. However, this took time, time that Generalfeldmarschall von Manstein needed to take his countermeasures. On 23 January Major General Rotmistrov's III/Guards Panzer Corps, which was assembled in the Manychkaya bridgehead, was to take the Bataisk bridges. However, Manstein got there before him.

Thanks to the perseverance of the III/60 Pz.Gren.Rgt., the German counterattack was not too late. On 22 January General Balk's 11th Panzer Division (arriving from action with Armeegruppe Hollidt) crossed the bridge from Aksaiskaya. During the first assault Rotmistrov's advance detachment under Colonel Yegerov was defeated near Kolkhoz Lenin. Five T-34s and two T-70s were burning, three T-34s and one T-70 escaped to Manychkaya. The lead Russian element was defeated 4 kilometers east of Bataisk.

On 23 January the 11th Panzer Division and the 16th ID (Mot.) threw the Soviets back to the eastern edge of Manychkaya in a spirited attack, but the attack stalled there. On 25 January General Balk cut the Soviets off from their reserve in order to prevent them from regrouping. The main German attack was launched on the southern edge of Manychkaya. By evening the threatening bridgehead no longer existed. Over 600 dead Russians and 20 burned out Russian tanks lay between the houses. By 31 January the 11th Panzer Division was left in the Novo Bataisk area as the "bridge watch".

In the meantime, from 16 to 19 January 1943, the "Wiking" held out in the narrow Proletarskaya bridgehead. On 16 January a counterattack by the "Wiking" Panzer Battalion and elements of the engineer battalion at Sovkhoz Nr 1 (southeast of Proletarskaya) succeeded in throwing back the enemy forces which had penetrated into the 23rd Panzer Division area. Major Freyer, the Ia of the 23rd Panzer Division, was wounded. The last elements of the 23rd Panzer Division were relieved in Stalinsky (between the arms of the Manych) during the evening. The 23rd Panzer Division followed the 16th ID (Mot.) and secured the southern bank of the Manych.

The 17th Panzer Division was transferred to the south and secured east of Salsk along the Novo Manych - Sandata line; the 17th Kradschützen Battalion was in Varanikovskoe and the II/40 Pz.Gren.Rgt. was in Novo Yegorlyk.

On 17 and 18 January Stubaf. Schaefer's "Wiking" Engineer Battalion was attacked in Stalinsky by superior enemy forces. Several attack waves collapsed in the defensive fire of the engineers, a rocket launcher battalion and the division artillery. At the critical moment, as hand-to-hand combat raged, a group of "Wiking" tanks attacked the enemy in the flank and decided the combat.

On 17 January the "Westland" and "Germania" Regiments repulsed a heavy enemy attack in the Proletarskaya bridgehead. In the "Nordland" Regiment sector, which was located on the left flank adjacent to the Manych, things remained relatively quiet.

After the "Wiking" Engineer Battalion had repulsed repeated breakthrough attempts to the Manych dam, which was the only connection to the bridgehead, the Soviets tried again in the south. The frozen Manych, with its tributaries and the salt lake, was no longer an obstacle for infantry.

The 17th Panzer Division secured the southern bank of the Manych, on the Novo Manych - Sandata line, with a thin line of strongpoints. The Soviets stumbled onto a gap there. General Gerassimenko, commander of the 28th Soviet Army (from Army Group "South Front"), ordered his 99th Rifle Brigade to cross the Manych and capture Yekaterinovka in order to cut off the "Wiking" and destroy it in a subsequent attack on Salsk.

During the evening hours of 18 January the lead element of the 99th Rifle Brigade crossed the ice on the northern edge of the 17th Panzer Division's security and penetrated unopposed into the northeastern portion of Yekaterinovka. During the night they were reinforced in order to conduct an attack against the "Wiking" withdrawal route on the morning of 19 January.

General Gerassimenko was satisfied. He believed he finally had a grip on the "Wiking", but he was wrong. The weak security of the 17th Panzer Division, which was located in Novo Manych, noticed the enemy movement. After the "Wiking" divisional commander, Oberführer Gille, received the alert report, a glance at a map was all he needed to recognize the threat represented by this enemy maneuver. He made a short telephone call to the 17th Panzer Division. This division had already been ordered to advance in front of the 23rd Panzer Division to the lower Manych in order to join in the combat around the Manychkaya bridgehead.

"We must help ourselves!" said Gille. His Ia, Stubaf. Schönfelder nodded in agreement. "Who will we assign to plug the gap?"

Schönfelder had all of the latest reports in his head and replied: "Germania' and 'Westland' have been in heavy defensive combat all day. We can only remove forces from the left flank, in the 'Nordland' area."

Gille and Schönfelder studied the situation map once more and, after a few minutes, it was all clear: "Immediately arrange to have III/'Nordland' withdrawn from the left flank. Its positions are to be taken over by another of 'Nordland's' battalions. The III/'Nordland' will be sent to Shablievka in order to attack the enemy in Yekaterinovka in the early morning."

And it went as planned. Here we read about it in the combat diary of III/"Nordland":

18/1:   1900 hours: I/"Nordland" takes over the battalion's security positions.

2130 hours: The battalion marched to Shablievka. The battalion had the mission of throwing the enemy forces, which have penetrated into the northeastern portion of Yekaterinovka, out on 19 January. The 9th Company will be left behind for local security in Shablievka.

19/1: 0605 hours: The battalion arrived in the southwestern portion of Yekaterinovka. The battalion was subordinated to the 40th Panzergrenadier Regiment, which was located in the western portion. Situation: Strong enemy forces (at least 1000 men) have occupied the eastern and northeastern portion of the village. Mortars and 7.62 cm cannon were noted.

0740 hours: The 10th and 11th Companies assembled on the southern edge of the village. On the right was the 11th Company (Ostuf. Deck) with two tanks and one assault gun, on the left was the 10th Company (Hstuf. Porsch) with two tanks, one assault gun and the forward observer of the 12th Battery.

Disposition: Stream region on the northern edge of the village is the immediate attack objective.

0900 hours: The attack began. The companies drove to the north with the right flank bent back.

0915 hours: In a spirited attack, the individual houses lying in the attack lanes were combed and the enemy security overran.

0945 hours: Enemy resistance reinforced. The 10th Company was able to confuse the enemy with its rapid attack. Each house was fought for. Handgrenade battle ensued.

1000 hours: 10th Company commander (Hstuf. Porsch) fell victim to head wound. Ostuf. Pohjanletho took over the 10th Company. Enemy strength increased steadily.

1015 hours: Enemy movement from out of a Kolkhoz 2 kilometers to the east.

1030 hours: Enemy launched a counterattack against the 10th Company with 600 men. The attack was repulsed with the enemy suffering heavy casualties. A German counterattack assaulted enemy mortar positions.

1130 hours: New enemy forces attacked the 10th and 11th Companies. Our light infantry guns and anti-tank guns fired without stopping. The forward observer from the 12th effectively placed the massed enemy under fire.

1135 hours: The remnants of the engineer platoon deployed to the 10th Company.

1215 hours: New enemy forces attacked out of the northeastern portion of the village (approximately 400 men).

1245 hours: The attack was beaten back.

1300 hours: Engineer platoon from the 40th Panzer- grenadier Regiment was committed to the left flank of the 10th Company. Additional attacks were repulsed by artillery, light infantry guns and anti-tank guns firing at close range. The enemy lost over 300 killed, 159 prisoners, including a battalion commander, the communications officer of a brigade and an engineer officer.

Booty: 2 panje wagons with radio equipment, 5 super-heavy mortars, 1 light mortar, 13 anti-tank rifles, 2 heavy machine-guns, 5 light machine-guns and many hand weapons.

German losses: 1 commander, 3 junior officers and 5 men killed, 24 wounded.

20/1: Enemy situation: The enemy deployed new forces into the northeastern portion of the village during the night.

0755 hours: 10th Company, supported by 2 tanks, attacked the northeastern portion of the village. One group fixed frontally, the rest rolled over the house positions from the west. The enemy suffered over 100 killed and 73 prisoners.

Booty: 3 super-heavy mortars, 4 bazookas, 1 anti-tank gun, 3 heavy machine-guns, 2 light machine-guns and many hand weapons, 1 field kitchen, 5 ammunition wagons and 12 wagons with equipment...

In closing it reads: "...The withdrawal route of the forces in Proletarskaya was cut off. Their intent was frustrated by the brave commitment of the III/'Nordland'."

Again the "Finnish Freiwilligen Battalion" of the Waffen SS proved its worth, paying in blood. By May 1943 255 Finns had died in the "Wiking" formation. Many succumbed to their wounds in their homeland. In summer 1943, when the battalion was disbanded and returned to its homeland at the behest of the Finnish state leader, Marshal Mannerheim, many Finns did so only grudgingly. Most of them received higher positions in the Finnish Army.

During the night of 20 January the Proletarskaya bridgehead was evacuated. While the Finnish Battalion was located in Yekaterinovka the "Westland" Regiment was occupying new positions in a half-circle around Salsk. The 17th Panzer Division marched on the Manych. The "Germania" Regiment occupied new positions on the Manych dam near Manychstroi and to the west. The I and II/"Nordland" reinforced the defenses in Yekaterinovka and Shablievka.

On 21 January the "Wiking" repulsed heavy enemy attacks. The main effort of the attacks lay near Salsk.

What about this Salsk? This name was constantly popping up! Salsk is a small city on the edge of the Manych depression. There were good railroad and road connections from there to Rostov and Tikhorets and to the north over the Manych dam and through Proletarskaya to Stalingrad. On 1 August 1942, Salsk was captured by the 3rd Panzer Division. All of the formations assembled there for the delaying battle. After the supply airfields of Tatsinskaya and Morosovskaya had fallen, the last supplies were flown from there to Stalingrad. Flight distance was 400 kilometers, the limit of the range of the Ju-52.

At that time, the security of the "Westland" Regiment was located near Salsk. On the nearby airfield were still some Me 109's from the II Gruppe of the 52nd Fighter Geschwader, which was led by Major Steinhoff. At Christmas time the gruppe was still near Simovniki providing cover for the Ju-52 supply staffels.

A new massed enemy attack against the eastern edge of Salsk forced the "Westland" Regiment back. Soviet assault troops penetrated up to the air-

WITHDRAWAL BATTLE OF THE LVII PANZER CORPS TO ROSTOV

January / February 1943

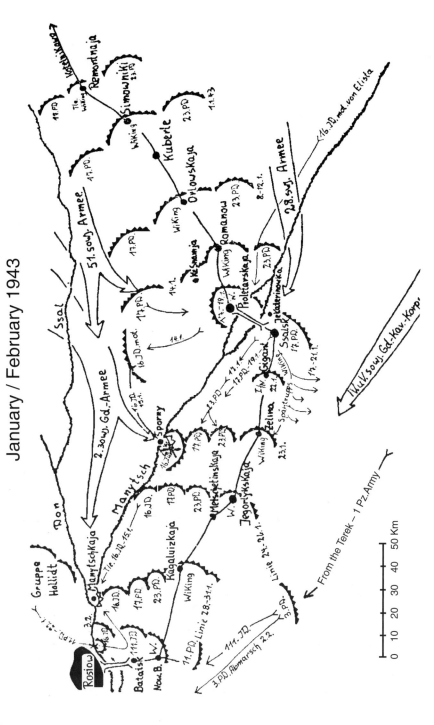

field. An armored counterattack with accompanying infantry threw the enemy from the airfield. There were only two of Steinhoff's aircraft remaining. The two Me 109s finally took off and headed to the west.

During the night of 22 January the "Wiking" withdrew. On the next morning they occupied new positions: I/"Nordland" was in Gigant, III/"Nordland" was in Zelina, II/"Nordland" was in the vicinity of Pechakovskiy, II/"Westland" had loose contact with the 23rd Panzer Division in Adronov, I/"Westland" was in Zelina. The "Germania" Regiment withdrew the furthest and constructed new defenses on both sides of Nesseliy.

On 22 January 1943 the last phase of the battle, to win time for the LVII Panzer Corps, began. Hanging back the furthest, on the Salsk - Bataisk road, was the "Wiking".

I/"Nordland" stood as a breakwater on the main road to Bataisk and was to gain time for the division to construct new defenses. By dawn I/"Nordland" arrived in Gigant. It immediately took up a defense oriented primarily to the east and the north. Gigant was a large village with sufficient houses. There were also some small factories and a large grain silo.

We now listen to the battalion commander, Stubaf. Lohmann: "It was clear to me that the Russians were doing everything they could to make our withdrawal on the main roads impossible. In the early morning I ordered the OO-2, Oscha. Schlüter, to reconnoiter the withdrawal possibilities south of the large Salsk - Zelina road with the battalion's motorcycle sidecars (equipped with light machine-guns).

Soon the enemy was probing Gigant; the northern defensive positions made the first contact with them. The enemy was approaching Gigant from the north with several tanks. An anti-tank gun was committed there. It engaged the tanks. By midday the battle for Gigant was in full swing. To the query as to when we could count on receiving the withdrawal order, the division replied that the battalion had to hold out.

When the battle for Gigant began the commander of the engineer battalion and the commander of the "Wiking" Panzer Battalion came to my command post; both thought that it would be pure luck if the battalion got out of this one. In the meantime the OO-2 returned and reported that he reconnoitered a withdrawal route and the kradschützen platoon was committed as ordered."

I/"Nordland" repulsed all of the enemy attacks, which occurred in several waves. The Russians brought up artillery and fired on the village. The center of attraction was the high grain silo in the center of the town. Bursting shells continuously bounced off of the walls without having any effect.

By 1500 hours the fierce combat around Gigant stopped. Stubaf. Lohmann observed the battle with concern. A strong Soviet outflanking group advanced north of Gigant and blocked the withdrawal route. Luckily, the terrain was passable almost everywhere. The snow was only 30 cm deep and there were drifts in just a few locations.

The battalion commander again: "Based on the new situation, I requested, over the radio, that the division block the large road near Verkhniy Khutor and allow me to withdraw from there on the main road to Zelina. The division agreed and, at the same time, gave me the order to withdraw at the fall of darkness. In the meantime the enemy forces had increased so much that we could hold out for only a short time. The company commanders could not get away, so I dictated the important withdrawal order to them word for word.

The withdrawal was organized so that the vehicles would be brought up directly behind the houses behind the HKL. The companies mounted starting on the right flank, while the company adjacent on the left provided them with fire cover. The subordinate units were formed up by the company in whose sector they were committed. The battalion headquarters filed in front of the last company.

In a hail of fire, we rolled off the line and drove to the south, then we turned to the west. Oscha. Schlüter led as navigator. At each intersection we were joined by kradschützen covering forces, who then formed the rearguard. Near Verkhniy Khutor we ran into the receiving positions constructed by III/"Nordland" and, from there, we drove on the main road to Zelina.

The battalion only had to leave behind one anti-tank gun because it could not be removed from its firing position without endangering the prime mover."

Between 1945 hours and 2130 hours I/"Nordland" passed by the receiving positions at Verkhniy Khutor. Forty minutes later III/"Nordland" gave up the reception positions and followed the I Battalion.

On Sunday, 23 January 1943, the main effort lay on the road to Rostov. After a night march in indescribable cold, the grenadiers of the I and III/"Nordland" arrived in Zelina in their vehicles. They were assigned new positions. Except for the necessary watch posts, the rest ran into the houses in order to put life back into their bodies. There was no rest for the drivers; they had to refuel the vehicles and repair small damage. The diesel engines had to run without stopping. If a motor stalled it would often not start for some time. The motor would then freeze into a block of ice. In such cases it was often simply destroyed.

At midday a motorized reconnaissance element returned from the road to Gigant and reported: "Strong enemy groups with six tanks on the march toward Zelina!"

Unterscharführer Hollinger, Gruppenführer of the 3/"Nordland", quietly listened to the report from the reconnaissance element. It was like this everyday. Dismantle in the evening, so that they could be ready to defend in new positions on the next morning.

This time Hollinger had a bad feeling. Was it because his group, which consisted of two light machine-gun units (6 men), was located by itself in the forward railroad station strong point on the eastern edge of Zelina? Behind Gruppe Hollinger lay the I/"Nordland", the III/"Nordland" was adjacent to the northwest and southwest of Zelina stood the I/"Westland" led by Hstuf. Sitter. A panzer reserve stood ready for commitment. In the defensive front around Zelina were anti-aircraft platoons from the "Wiking" Anti-aircraft

Battalion set up for ground combat.

When the first indications of an attack were recognized, the company messengers arrived with the order: "Open fire at the red light signal!"

At 1230 hours the first attack wave advanced. The terrain was flat. The dark forms stood out against the snow. Behind the first formation there were second and third waves.

Gruppe Hollinger had been ready for some time. One machine-gun was located on the road embankment; the other was on the road itself. - Still 1000 meters - 800 meters - 500 meters - 300 meters. The weapons were still silent. Such fire discipline! Especially since all of the units were well aware of the attack from the loud "Hurrah!" that was storming down on Zelina.

Finally the red light signal was flashed and then all hell broke loose. Machine-guns rattled, rifles pinged, on the right a four-barreled anti-aircraft gun bellowed. The blustering "Hurrah!" changed into a gurgling moan. The first wave wallowed in the snow; as did the second and third waves.

Three T-34s remained at a respectful distance on the road embankment. A strong enemy group wanted to outflank to the north, but it was halted in its tracks by III/"Nordland".

During the evening Gruppe Hollinger came under increasing mortar fire in the Zelina railroad station, but the cellar offered protection. A T-34 advanced in the twilight against the railroad station. Hollinger and his men were ready. However, what could they do without anti-tank weapons, especially since the T-34 was accompanied by infantry? There was only one thing to do: observe, so they could quickly react!

Suddenly the engine of the lead T-34 roared and it raced along the road embankment toward the railroad station.

"Tank - Gruppe Hollinger return to the town, behind the long building!" shouted Hollinger. The group ran for their lives, but in the middle of their run there was a loud discharge from the northern edge of the town. A tracer whooshed toward the T-34. There was a loud thud. A cloud exploded. Men were thrown through the air. That was the end!

Ustuf. Hancke shouted: "Counterattack! - Hurrah!" His platoon and Gruppe Hollinger assaulted and reoccupied the railroad station. "How were we to know that there was an eight-eight behind us?" mused Hollinger. "It brought the T-34 down with a single shot" explained Bimbo, the 2nd gunner.

Gruppe Hollinger again stood in the railroad station strong- point, but as darkness increased, the men became more nervous, especially since the weakness of the strongpoint was now known.

Tank noises from behind! Mühlenkamp's tanks advanced up to the railroad station. In the town the vehicles were already making noises; the companies were withdrawing. Gruppe Hollinger followed the tanks as the rear guard.

The combat diary of the III/"Nordland" noted under 23 January 1943:

"1945 hours: Broke contact with the enemy as ordered. Battalion marched from Zelina to Yegorlykskaya and pulled in at 2230 hours.

24 January 1943/0200 hours: Enemy tanks fired on the village. 0245 hours: Enemy tanks penetrated into the village. A security line was established against enemy infantry..."

These sentences serve as a link between two successive "Wiking" commitments. What preceded them?

Since the 17th Panzer Division was withdrawn from Salsk in order to be committed south of the 16th ID (Mot.), the southern flank of the "Wiking" had been left open. They had no contact with the 3rd Panzer Division, which was coming from the Terek. The "Wiking" Panzer Battalion was, as before, the strong backbone of the division. Trying to avoid as many losses as possible, Stubaf. Mühlenkamp committed his tanks in small groups. Because the tank was most suitable for conducting mobile combat operations, Stubaf. Mühlenkamp was obliged to take responsibility for the open southern flank. To assist him in this mission, all of the remaining armored cars from the "Wiking" Reconnaissance Battalion were organized into a reconnaissance company under Ostuf. Falke and subordinated to him.

The "Wiking" Reconnaissance Battalion had conducted far-ranging reconnaissance for the division. The Reconnaissance men were constantly underway, providing the leadership with the necessary reports for the commitment of the formations. The elements penetrated up to 60 kilometers into noman's land. During a reconnaissance expedition into the Kalmuck Steppes, Reconnaissance Element Stichnoth brought back a wounded and completely exhausted Oberfeldwebel, who had survived a crash in a Ju 52 that had flown to Stalingrad.

The reconnaissance element from the "Wiking" Reconnaissance Battalion under Ostuf. Falke advanced into the open southern flank. At the same time an enemy tank formation advanced on this flank. A reconnaissance element never lets an enemy out of its sight. Several times a day the enemy movements were reported over the radio. They were exact reports, giving strengths and march direction. And Stubaf. Mühlenkamp transposed the reports onto his map. Soon it could be seen that the lead enemy tank element would meet the division in Yegorlykskaya. The division took corresponding precautions.

Except for a rearguard group, all of the "Wiking" tanks were assembled in Yegorlykskaya on 23 January. I/"Westland" had been in the village for two days already. II/"Westland" was the next battalion to take up positions in the southern portion of the village. Then II/"Nordland" arrived and took up positions north of the rollbahn. Two companies arrived from the engineer battalion; only the Wanhöfer company was missing. I and III/"Nordland" were on their way from Zelina.

Stubaf. Mühlenkamp arrived in Yegorlykskaya with the panzer rearguard. He went to the engineer battalion command post, which was located in a house on the access road. He greeted the commander, Stubaf. Schaefer, and informed him that it was highly likely that, because of the cold, the Russians would advance to the village.

In the meantime the Soviet tanks rolled toward Yegorlykskaya. There was an indescribable traffic jam on the eastern exit; in the darkness it was impossible to untangle it. Stubaf. Lohmann was trying to guide his I/"Nordland" into the village. Behind them was still the Wanhöfer company.

Ostuf. Wanhöfer was summoned to a situation briefing. A little later all of the company commanders from the "Wiking" Engineer Battalion were hovering around a situation map in a hut on the edge of the village. Stubaf. Schaefer urgently began the briefing: "Russian tanks could appear at any time. The road is to be cleared immediately..." Schaefer got no further. At that moment a shell slammed into the roof. The candles went out. Limestone fell from the roof.

"That's the tanks - run to your companies!"

Engines fired up. In no time the traffic jam was cleared up. The vehicles took cover behind the walls of buildings. The German tanks took cover on the right and left of the main road, but they were prepared to fire in the direction of the road entrance.

On 24 January at 0200 hours the first shots were fired by the Soviet tanks. 45 minutes later six T-34s rolled into Yegorlykskaya. They were followed by weak infantry forces. As ordered, they were allowed to pass through the positions on the edge of the village. They established a hasty defense in the town square and were secured by infantry. The hastily assembled engineer troops were unable to destroy the six T-34s with close combat weapons as they entered the narrow town streets.

The defenders of Yegorlykskaya prepared themselves for a bloody dawn. Cautiously, the German tanks took up firing positions. They were individually directed into suitable positions. And so were the panzerjägers. Each German tank picked out his target. Mühlenkamp's calculated plan was being carried out.

The day finally dawned. A flare lifted the radio silence and into the headsets of the panzer commanders came the voice of the commander:

"Adler to all - free fire on assigned targets!"

The devil was set loose! In one volley 13 enemy tanks were hit. Only a few were able to escape the fire. Through the short, but loud, combat noise at the entrance to the village rolled the six T-34s from the village center in order to attack to the edge of the village. However, one after the other they were shot up.

The armored battle at Yegorlykskaya was an example of ideal cooperation and fire discipline. The great success was made possible thanks to the exemplary commitment of Ostuf. Falke's reconnaissance element.

After this bloody morning the Soviets lost their appetite for their attack on Yegorlykskaya. Demolition troops from the engineer battalion blew up the enemy tanks in the foreground and those that had not been completely destroyed in the town.

New Russian formations advanced, but they bypassed Yegorlykskaya to the north. The "Germania" Regiment was located northwest of Yegorlykskaya near Balabanov and Komuna and had lost contact with the 23rd Panzer Division to the north, which, at that point in time, was commanded by Oberst von Normann (later Generalmajor).

Yegorlykskaya was held on 24 and 25 January 1943. The Soviet main effort was shifted toward the "Germania" Regiment which ran into increasing enemy pressure near Komuna and Tishchenko. III/"Nordland" was set in march to Mechetinskaya on the morning of 25 January and took up the local security. I/"Nordland" followed in the evening; the last elements had to make a detour because the rollbahn was blocked by the Soviets. During the night of 26 January II/"Nordland" and the "Westland" Regiment also left Yegorlykskaya. "Westland", on the southern flank of the division, occupied Oktyabrskoe with one battalion at the confluence of the Yegorlyk into the Kugo - Yeya, where contact would later be made with the 3rd Panzer Division coming from the Terek. I/"Westland" occupied new positions around Mitrotanov. II/"Nordland" was located near Milayarovo/Grekhov.

On 26 January the "Germania" Regiment gave up the area around Komuna against strong enemy pressure and was inserted between the "Nordland" and "Westland" Regiments, a little to the rear. The Soviets then increased their pressure against I and III/"Nordland" in Mechetinskaya. On 27 January, at 1100 hours, a German panzer attack into the enemy rear gave the defenders of Mechetinskaya some breathing space. The enemy withdrew to the south-east. German aircraft attacked enemy concentrations throughout the day.

From 28 to 30 January "Nordland" held out in Mechetinskaya. To the south, "Germania" and "Westland" were also involved in heavy combat. Individual villages would change hands several times. German forces were cut off and then liberated. Division "Wiking" had to hold this line because the 111th ID coming from the Terek had not yet arrived.

With the arrival of the LVII Panzer Corps in Rostov, Generalmajor Graf Gerhard von Schwerin's 16th ID (Mot.), which had blocked the Sporny - Vesseliy Manych gap, was also withdrawn to the southern bank of the Manych. The attached Reconnaissance Element Stichnoth ("Wiking" Reconnaissance Battalion) covered the withdrawal with its two armored reconnaissance cars. Untersturmführer Stichnoth received a handwritten note from the divisional commander thanking the two brave reconnaissance car crews for their support of the 16th ID (Mot.).

We read of the see-saw combat in the Yegorlyksaya - Mechetinskaya area in the notes of Stubaf. Mühlenkamp, which will serve as an example for all of the front officers and commanders:

"The time was passed by the panzers as follows: During the day they fought in all directions. At night they marched toward Rostov, mostly on the side of the large road in the grim cold. Recently we experienced minus 42 degrees. We had to use a 2 liter blow-torch to warm the vehicle up before each start because the lubricants would solidify. The 450 horsepower engines had to be hand-cranked by two men. We often drove by the stars, like sailors. Yesterday I had to go into a house to re-orient myself, also in the hope of finding some warmth, because I then would have to spend the entire night standing in the turret in the minus 35 degree cold. The extreme temperature difference temporarily knocked me unconscious. The constant strain on the nerves also had something to do with this, the constant concern and responsibility for the loyal soldiers and the successful accomplishment of the assigned mission."

On 31 January 1943 General Kirchner's LVII Panzer Corps occupied a stable defensive front around the Bataisk and Aksaiskaya Don crossings: on the Don - Manych confluence stood the 16th ID (Mot.); around Selenaya Roshcha and Kanzyshevakha was the 17th Panzer Division (Generalleutnant von Senger und Etterlin); near Shukovo Tatrskiy and Don Pakhary was the 23rd Panzer Division; on the southern flank of the corps was the SS Panzergrenadier Division "Wiking" with (from north to south) "Nordland" around Sernograd, "Germania" in the farmstead on either side of the Meshetka Valley and "Westland" near Rossoshinskiy; the 3rd Panzer Division was near Zun-Zun with its southern flank on the Kugo - Yeya near Ugolnik.

In the meantime the 111th ID continued to advance. Slowly the southern flank of the LVII Panzer Corps bent back toward Bataisk. By 2 February the Kagalnik sector had been reached at several points. During the night of 3 February 1943 the last elements of the 111th ID entered the LVII Panzer Corps bridgehead. The 3rd Panzer Division crossed the ice road on the Sea of Azov and the Bataisk bridges to Army Group "Don". This division had ended the long march from the Terek to Rostov. General Kirchner could begin to withdraw his corps across the Don crossings.

On 3 February the 17th and 23rd Panzer Divisions marched across the Don. From north to south were deployed: the 16th ID (Mot.) around Olginskaya; the 111th ID near Khomutovskaya and Katachi; the "Wiking" along the line Gavrilov - lower Kagalnik - Novo Bataisk. The strongest enemy attacks were directed against the southern flank, especially since the Soviet pursuit groups from the Caucasus had, by then, joined up with the 28th Soviet Army.

The Wanhöfer company from the "Wiking" Engineer Battalion faced a particularly difficult situation during the night of 4 February. The company was located south of the Meshetka and had the mission of opening the withdrawal route to Novo Bataisk, which was already occupied by the enemy, for the withdrawing "Westland" Regiment. Ostuf. Wanhöfer wrote of the experience during the frosty night: "After withdrawing approximately 20 kilometers the column was stopped by a kradschützen security force: The housing group in front of us was occupied by Soviets. Probably cavalry! - The Russians were very careless. The kradschützen reported that there were no outposts set up at the entrance to the village.

A withdrawal was impossible for various reasons. Wanhöfer considered the situation for a short time and said: "We go forward! We will be there before they discover us. Fire only if the enemy fires first, but then fire from all weapons!"

"Forward!" After a few hundred meters, the first vehicles came upon the first group of houses in the spread-out town. Horses could be made out in the weak moonlight. Obviously a cavalry unit was spending the night there. There were no guards to be seen. As the vehicles approached, the horses became restless. Then a door opened. Light escaped from within. A figure stood in the doorway, raised a rifle to its shoulder and fired.

"Germans - Germans!"

The engineer company opened fire from the moving vehicles and, before the Russians knew what hit them, the company had burst through the village.

We traveled to the north for several hours. However, then the Kagalnik had to be crossed. And there was no bridge! Finally a suitable location was found. The ice crackled, but it held. Then the last vehicles crossed the river."

The example of the Wanhöfer company serves for many other situations. Often a difficult situation was mastered by quiet circumspection.

On 4 February there was still heavy combat in the entire "Wiking" sector. At 0430 hours the Russians attacked the 111th ID in Kasachi/Slodeiskiy and to the south into Gavrilov, where the III/"Nordland" was located. 150 Red Army soldiers broke through between two II/"Nordland" strongpoints. By dawn Ostuf. Deck counterattacked with 20 Finns and destroyed an enemy anti-tank company with three guns. At 0800 hours there was an enemy attack in the strength of 300 men, supported by seven tanks, on the right strongpoint of the 11th Company. A German anti-tank gun shot up a Mark III, but the strongpoint had to be given up. The defenders withdrew to a Kolkhoz in the northwest.

A half hour later, at 0830 hours, a group from the "Wiking" Panzer Battalion arrived and attacked the Soviets from the east. Three enemy tanks were destroyed; the rest drove off. III/"Nordland" then launched a counterattack and destroyed the enemy infantry. The battalion suffered one killed and eight wounded; the losses of the enemy were manifold. The right strongpoint was again occupied.

Two companies from the 50th Grenadier Regiment were sent to the III/"Nordland" in Gavrilov and subordinated to it. A gap yawned to the northern neighbor in Kasachi (70th Grenadier Regiment). Contact was made with the southern neighbor but the large gap to the II/"Nordland", which stood as the cornerstone at a farmstead, was not closed.

At 1330 hours the withdrawal order for III/"Nordland" arrived: "...The battalion is to withdraw at 1700 hours with the subordinate elements of the 50th Grenadier Regiment and anti-aircraft."

At 1715 hours the III/"Nordland" broke contact with the enemy and marched through Bataisk - Rostov toward Kirilov, with the 10th Company as the rear guard.

A report from 3/"Nordland", which during the night of 4 February 1943 advanced on the right flank of the regiment into the last defensive positions in Vassilevo - Shamshevo, sums things up: "After a night march the company reached the village. It wasn't really a town, just a collection of houses on both sides of the winding Kagalnik. It stretched almost as far as Novo Bataisk. It was still nighttime when the company dismounted. It could not be called a company, it was more like a reinforced platoon. We walked in the moonlight and passed the dark groups of houses until we reached the HKL. Gruppe Hollinger nestled into a house on the right flank of the regiment. The deep flowing Kagalnik turned into a narrow bend there. One machine-gun was set up in a vegetable garden, on a steep section of the bank. The other was placed to the left of the house. The left flank of "Germania" lay on the right, in a group of houses 400 meters away. We had no contact.

Having no faith in the terrain, the "dance" began in the early morning of 4 February. First the machine-gun on the rocky bank was placed under fire. The guards returned wounded. Hollinger and Schütze I jumped forward to take up the machine-gun again, but they couldn't stay there because of insufficient cover. Heavy infantry fire was coming from a group of houses. Soon an anti-tank gun chimed in. Ant-like, Russians jumped into the river bed and avoided the defensive fire.

In the meantime day had dawned. Gruppe Hollinger came under increasing fire, including mortars. The men persevered and waited for the enemy attack. However, the Russians took their time. They drove into the left company flank with three T-34s. Their cannon and machine-guns covered the company. Gruppe Hollinger (6 men) was literally shot out of its position on the river bank. In spite of the good fire support from their tanks, the infantry attack did not materialize.

At 0800 hours an order arrived: "Gruppe Hollinger will withdraw to the next group of houses!" The men withdrew one at a time. From the flank, at about 200 meters distance, the tanks fired at each man as he jumped up but all reached the next group of houses without injury.

The 13th Company had only two heavy infantry guns but they were not fired because they were located directly in the HKL and the Russians were too close. The vegetable garden would not allow the T-34s, which were 300 meters away, to be approached. The arrival of additional enemy forces intensified the situation. The enemy attack would soon take place.

A black mass of men moved out of the river bed. 3/"Nordland" fired, but it was an unequal battle. Was a withdrawal possible in this situation, especially since the company had to cross a long unprotected slope?

During the battle all of the straw roofs were set on fire. The wind was favorable. The smoke fogged up the slope. It was now or never! The heavy infantry guns were limbered. The gun groups followed. Except for a pair of men, all made it back. The company took up new positions in open terrain that evening."

Similar developments occurred in the "Germania" and "Westland" Regiment areas. On 4 February the "Wiking" Panzer Battalion had to help again. During the evening the SS Panzergrenadier Division crossed the Bataisk bridges. The last stragglers were led on foot to Rostov by Uscha. Riedel.

We read again the words of the "Wiking" Panzer Battalion commander:

"We followed the oil pipeline back to Bataisk. Our dead comrades, whom we could no longer bury, accompanied us to Rostov. In one of the tanks lay

Ustuf. Büscher, behind Flügel, the commander of the 2nd Company. He was shot in his tank, killed immediately. After a short time he was frozen stiff and it was impossible to extract him from the tank. We had to break his arm before we could remove him, but we did not want to leave him behind."

An order of the day dignified the commitment of the SS Panzergrenadier Division "Wiking":

"The Commander   Command Post, 4/2/1943
of LVII Army Corps (Mot.)

To SS Panzergrenadier Division "Wiking"

Today the SS Panzergrenadier Division "Wiking" is being removed from my panzer corps. From the first day to the last of its attachment the division proved itself in spirited attack and in tenacious defense during an unbroken, weeks-long battle under unfavorable weather conditions against a tenacious superior enemy force. His objective (breakthrough and outflanking) was not achieved thanks to the steadfastness of the division. Thus, today I witness the detachment of the brave men of the SS Panzergrenadier Division "Wiking" from my formation with a heavy heart. My thanks and my admiration go out to the leadership and the troops.

signed   Kirchner."

The appreciation of "Wiking" expressed by the commander of the LVII Panzer Corps was supplemented by a report on English radio during the night of 13 to 14 February 1943 as follows: "The fact that the German armies were able to conduct an ordered withdrawal from the Caucasus was only due to the SS Division "Wiking". However, even this division was destroyed."

Without belittling the brave commitment of the other divisions of the LVII Panzer Corps, it must be said that the "Wiking" was the mainstay of the withdrawal to Rostov. Constantly in the heat of the battle, it was committed on the main rail and road routes. It held the Proletarskaya bridgehead to the last. They were the last to give up Salsk, Gigant, Zelina and Yegorlykskaya and made it possible for the neighboring divisions to withdraw to new defensive positions.

Why was this so? The key lies in the volunteer nature and youth of this division, which had an average age of 21 years. Only a few were married. In addition, the troops were well led and well trained.

On 5 February 1943 only the 111th ID and 16th ID (Mot.) were still south of the Don. Generalmajor Recknagel's 111th ID held out in a narrow bridgehead around Bataisk until 6 February. The panzerjäger battalion and anti-aircraft troops held the embankment open until the last. However, during the night, Soviet lead elements crept over the ice of the Don tributary to defuse the explosives. Then it was high time! The rearguard crossed the embankment to Rostov. Behind them the explosives thundered in the night. However, the most important bridge was only half destroyed.

Forty-eight hours later the last German vehicles, Oberleutnant Kühne's tanks from the 16th ID (Mot.), rolled across the Don bridge near Aksaiskaya. A little later Feldwebel Wagner from the 675th Engineer Battalion blew the bridge, which was constructed by the 21st Bridge Kommando in ten days, into the air with 1.5 tons of explosives.

The 1st and 4th Panzer Armies ended their commitment south of the Don. Thanks to the delaying battle of the LVII Panzer Corps the Soviets could not penetrate to the foothold in Rostov. The planned penetration of strong Russian formations from Bataisk to Tikhorets and further to the Taman Peninsula into the rear of the 17th Army failed. If the Soviet plan had succeeded, the destruction of the 17th Army, indeed, the entire Army Group A, would have resulted. It would have been a second Stalingrad.

Felix Steiner

Oberführer Gille

Staf. Mühlenkamp

Oberführer Wagner

The harbor of Novorossisk with the c[i]ty in the background. In t[he] foreground is a ship bombed by the 77th Stuka Squadron.

German U-Boat return[s] from action in the Blac[k] Sea.
(U-23, Kptltn. Wahlen[)]

Motor-Torpedo Boat S-102 in the Kerch St[rait]

…illery barge on the …icasus coast.

…man mine-sweeper in …Kerch Strait.

…al ferries at a dock …r Kerch.

Naval ferries laying mines to protect the transport of German troops into the Kerch Strait.

A ferry during the crossing of a Romanian cavalry formation in the Kerch Strait. On the rigging is the standard of the German naval forces in the Black Sea with the slanted white cross.

Finnish volunteers during a counterattack in the Krasnoe Znamya, an original photo taken during the battle by a Finnish photographer.

THE GREAT WITHDRAWAL BREEDS FURTHER CRISIS

The "Seilbahnbewegung" begins - The Krasnodar turntable - The difficult retreat of the heavy weapons out of the muddy mountain valleys -
The XXXXIX Mountain Corps on the road - Oberst Auer's rearguard

After weeks of combat, the German attack on Tuapse became bogged down
in mud and blood. During the night of 17 December 1942 the Semashcho
front was given up and new positions were occupied north of the Pshish. The
hotly contested Mounts Semashcho, Dva Brata and Indyuk were left behind.

The front stagnated. The gebirgsjägers of the 1st and 4th Mountain
Divisions waited in new, improved positions for the gradual withdrawal of
their formations from the high Caucasus. The jägers of the 97th and 101st
Jäger Divisions waited also and the grenadiers of the 46th, 198th and 125th
ID waited for the new spring. They still did not know that they would not be
spending it there!

Their days at the front were filled with fierce combat; combat not only
against the enemy, but also against the weather and winter and to improve
their own living conditions. Thus the 46th ID put into operation their own
"factories", which, at first, produced the pack animal harnesses that were
lacking. Then these operations expanded to making wooden tiles to cover the
block huts and bunkers.

However, soon the name "Stalingrad" began to circulate in the mountain
forests. The great withdrawal to the Terek began.

In the meantime personnel changes occurred. The long-time commander of
the 1st Mountain Division, General Lanz, went on to a larger mission. In his
place arrived Generalmajor Stettner, Ritter von Grabenhofen. The 1st
Generalstabsoffizier of the 1st Mountain Division, Oberst Steets, who went
to the Finnish front, was replaced by Oberstleutnant Thilo. The leadership of
the 4th Mountain Division was turned over from General Eglseer to
Generalmajor Kress.

Due to the events at Stalingrad, the LVII Corps command (Kirchner) was
transferred to the 4th Panzer Army on 26 November 1942 and replaced by
the von Förster Führungsgruppe z.b.V. [Special Purpose Command Group].
On 20 December this headquarters was also removed for use elsewhere and
its formations (198th ID and Fast Slovak Division) were transferred to the
left neighboring XXXXIV Jäger Corps. On 23 December, the former commander of the 125th ID, Generalleutnant Schneckenburger, became commander of Army Group "Don".

On 31 December 1942, as the German withdrawal on the Terek began, the
divisions of the XXXXIV Jäger Corps and the XXXXIX Mountain Corps
received the withdrawal plan in encoded format. It foresaw the phased withdrawal out of the Caucasus Forest, where the eastern flank had to almost go
around the western flank near Goryachiy Klyuch. The rotation of the outer
flanks had to be coordinated with the arrival of the 1st Panzer Army.

In the meantime, the Soviets also became active in the western Caucasus.
At first, a main strike was to be made from Rozhet to Maikop. In preparation

engineer units constructed a 155 kilometer road and 800 meters of bridges. The strike was to go through the Tuby Pass, for which the 97th Jäger Division had fought in August, with the objective of Maikop and the subsequent objective of Tikhorets - Bataisk. Due to insurmountable difficulties the plan had to be shelved.

The new Soviet plan saw an advance across the mountains west of Goryachiy Klyuch toward the Rumanian positions. Subsequently, Krasnodar, Tikhorets and Bataisk were also to be reached. The plan was initiated, but there were also unplanned delays. All of the heavy weapons and the necessary supplies became stuck in the narrow mountain valleys.

At the end of December, the German divisions began withdrawing the heavy equipment and artillery. The 97th and 101st Jäger Divisions, as well as the 4th and 1st Mountain Divisions, adhered to a single road, the Tuapse - Khadyshenskaya - Maikop road. In the 97th and 101st Jäger Division area of operations, where artillery stood on the road to Khadyshenskaya, it went relatively well. It was more difficult withdrawing the batteries of the XXXXIX Mountain Corps. The artillery commander of this corps, the experienced Oberst Winkler, described the difficulties: "The first impression was that it would be impossible to remove the valuable artillery in the alloted time across 25 kilometers of muddy valley, over 42 fords on the Gunaika and Pshish. A normal tactical withdrawal of the artillery across the Gaiman - Gunaika - Kamm was not possible.

The few animals still available could not execute the redeployment, and motorized artillery was out of the question. Only three guns per mountain battery could make the redeployment. For the majority of the artillery and for the field kitchens, trucks, ammunition dumps and other equipment, this meant organizing phased transport with the available heavy prime movers.

The prime movers oscillated between four artillery strong- points: from Kotlovina over a pass into the lower Gunaika Valley (Point I), then to the Gunaika bend (Point II), from there into the lower Gunaika Valley (Point III) and finally across the Pshish up to the railroad embankment (Point IV). At that point there was a relatively passable road to Khadyshenskaya.

Prime movers went out of commission daily, but they were repaired thanks to the work of the I Staffel [maintenance]. In most cases two prime movers were needed to tow one gun.

A critical time was projected with alternating rain and frost and rising fords, but the objective of 15 January was achieved."

The Soviet attack preparations could not remain hidden from the German leadership. Increased partisan activity indicated that the Soviets would advance between Goryachiy Klyuch and Kholmskaya. Krasnodar, an important center for the 17th Army, was particularly threatened, as was the Krasnodar - Krymskaya road, where the German southern flank had to be moved into the Kuban bridgehead. It was projected that the XXXXIV Jäger Corps would be set in march to Krasnodar.

One also had to consider transferring the 97th Jäger Division into the Salsk area in order to parry an attack on Rostov. Notes in the combat diary of Army Group A alluded to this. Developments near Krasnodar compelled them to commit the 97th Jäger Division there.

During the night of 3 January 1943 the first companies of the 97th Jäger Division were withdrawn from their positions southeast of Shaumyan. A day later the 101st Jäger Division closed ranks. During the night of 4 January the 228th Jäger Regiment gave up the fiercely contested Shaumyan. With the continued withdrawal and the shortening of the defensive lines, more and more battalions of the XXXXIV Jäger Corps were freed-up and immediately marched through Maikop to Krasnodar. By giving up the positions south of the Sassnovaya Trench, the 198th ID had also shortened its front. On 4 January 1943, the division came under the command of the XXXXIX Mountain Corps. The left neighbor was now the 4th Mountain Division.

On 10 January Generalmajor Müller, commander of the Badden-Württemberg 198th ID, assembled his regimental commanders at the 235th Artillery Regiment headquarters in Tri Duba (Three Oaks). What he had to say to them has already been described. He also announced: Retreat! All measures would be conducted under the cover name "Seilbahnbewegung [Cable Railway Maneuver]". The intermediate positions were designated B through F.

During the night of 17 January the B line on either side of Mount Gaiman was given up and the C line, between Lyssaya and Oplepek, was occupied without trouble from the enemy.

During the night of 23 January the C line was evacuated. Again the gaze and thoughts of the soldiers wandered over the blood drenched mountains south of the Sassnovaya Trench and the summit of the Sarai, to Indyuk the watchman, and the much struggled over Goich Pass, to Semashcho, to Gaiman and Oplepek. Quickly their belongings were packed together, the last weapons were taken from the parapet; the squads, platoons and companies were then ready to march. The order "March!" was given. A light rain was falling. The companies marched to the north over the muddy paths. Only a rearguard was left behind.

However, it did not go smoothly everywhere. On Mount Lyssaya the 4th Squadron of the 1st Mountain Division Reconnaissance Battalion, which was the rearguard, suffered losses. Also, the enemy immediately pursued on the eastern flank, but he was repulsed by the 97th Grenadier Regiment.

The D line was held for a day. Then the withdrawal continued. On the left flank the 46th ID had to hold until the 1st Mountain Division withdrew through Maikop. The 4th Mountain Division reached the main road near Belorechenskaya.

The destruction of the passes complicated the enemy pursuit of the supply and artillery convoys. Khadyshenskaya, the key point on the Tuapse road, was given up on the night of 24 January. The troops marched to the E line.

There were still stores of captured ammunition in Apsheronskaya, which could no longer be transported. The 88th Engineer battalion (46th ID) was ordered to blow up the captured ammunition. Because there was no engineer officer available who was familiar with the new German fuses the adjutant,

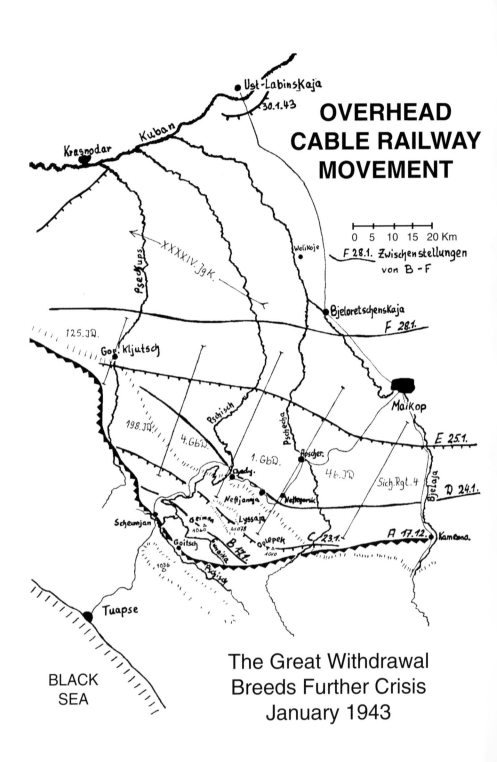

OVERHEAD CABLE RAILWAY MOVEMENT

Ust-LabinsKaja

30.1.43

Kuban

Krasnodar

Pseckups

XXXIV. Jgk.

WeliKoje

0 5 10 15 20 Km

F 28.1. Zwischenstellungen
von B - F

125. JD.

Gog. Kljutsch

Bjeloretschenskaja

F 28.1.

MaiKop

E 25.1.

198. JD.

4. GbD.

Pschisch

Pschecha

1. GbD.

Aoscher.

46. JD

Sich. Rgt. 4

Bjelaja

D 24.1.

Chady.

Neftjanaja

Lyssaja

Netfegorsk

Scheumjan

Geiman
△
1060

△ 1078

Oplepek
△
1010

C 23.1.

A 17.12.

Kamenno.

Goitsch

B 19.1.

1036

Pschisch

Tuapse

**BLACK
SEA**

The Great Withdrawal
Breeds Further Crisis
January 1943

304

Oberleutnant Neubauer, prepared the ammunition stores for destruction. On the evening of 24 January the fuses were all placed.

During the night of 25 January the Pshekh bridge on the Apsheronskaya - Maikop road was blown into the air, after the 1st Mountain Division had crossed it. The 46th ID remained behind as rearguard.

On the morning of 25 January the huge ammunition dump at Apsheronskaya blew into the air in a thunderous explosion. On this day the main German force stood on the E line, 10 kilometers south of Maikop.

In the meantime the Soviets initiated an attack near Goryachiy Klyuch. These were elements of the Soviet 9th Mountain Division, a hastily recruited formation. Only every third man was in uniform. They desperately attacked the key Hill 349.6. The III/421 Gren.Rgt., under Hauptmann Winzen, held until the elements of the 198th ID had achieved their objective, then the III/421 (125th ID) also withdrew. On 24 January the main force of the 198th ID was prepared to defend five kilometers southeast of Goryachiy Klyuch, while other forces occupied new defensive positions near the Oil Tank Hill Winter Camp (201.2), Kutais and south of Kutaiskaya.

On that day a threatening crisis occurred in the 125th ID sector. The Soviets blocked the withdrawal route at the intersection of the "Stalin Road" and the main road to Saratovskaya. The 419th Grenadier Regiment, which was still located near Goryachiy Klyuch, was cut off. Elements of the 198th ID and the 419th Grenadier Regiment assaulted the Soviet blocking position on the "Stalin Road" and fought their way back to Saratovskaya.

In the meantime, the main body of the XXXXIX Mountain Corps marched on the Maikop - Belorechenskaya road to Ust Labinskaya. Large traffic jams were finally unraveled in front of the rear guards. Ust Labinskaya was the key point for the mountain corps. Everybody flooded into there across the Kuban bridges, including the formations of the 1st Panzer Army.

On 26 January 1943, the 46th ID passed through Maikop as it had to cover the "Seilbahnbewegung". Oberst Auer and his 42nd Grenadier Regiment was the last formation of the 46th ID to arrive in Maikop and reported to the division command post. General Haccius led him immediately to the map table and explained: "Here - look at the Maikop - Belorechenskaya - Ust Labinskaya road - it crosses the Kuban here. The entire mountain corps, with all of its support troops and refugees, has to cross behind the Kuban on this single road. You are the commander of the rearguard and have responsibility for: your regiment, a gebirgsjäger battalion, which lies ready in Belorechenskaya, a wheeled battalion with three companies, a light towed artillery battalion and a heavy motorized battery.

Your mission is to secure the withdrawal of the corps, not allowing the pursuing enemy to close so that the only way to break contact is by suffering casualties. When the last German soldier has crossed the bridge at Ust Labinskaya, give the engineers the order to blow it."

Oberst Auer repeated his mission and said: "Herr General, if you were a Bavarian, I would say to you: 'Herr General, thanks loads for the suicide mission!'".

Then Auer studied the map, noted the ammunition dump points and committed them to memory. Returning to his command post, he explained the mission to his adjutants and summoned the subordinate battalion commanders for a situation briefing. Soon the mission was laid down in a clear order:

"1. There are four ammunition dumps along the march route. One officer and two non-commissioned officers will be dispatched to each dump immediately. They are to insure that the ammunition is made available to the passing rearguard artillery.

2. The light towed artillery battalion will withdraw early tomorrow morning, 27 January, to the gebirgsjäger battalion at Belorechenskaya. Both formations will occupy positions there, where they will repulse all attacks on the withdrawal route.

3. The wheeled battalion will also advance early tomorrow through Belorechenskaya to Velikoe and occupy a blocking position there.

4. The 42nd Grenadier Regiment and the heavy motorized battery will be prepared to march on 28 January at 2400 hours to the northern entrance to Maikop. The individual units will receive orders according to the development of the situation."

With a sixth sense, Oberst Auer had anticipated the upcoming commitment since, on the morning of 28 January, the Soviets were already attacking the gebirgsjäger positions near Belorechenskaya. Almost all of the attacks collapsed well in front of the German security line in the fire of the light artillery battalion. The Russians were unable to bring any artillery up through the mud. In spite of this, the Germans were still a little nervous on 28 January 1943, as the 42nd Grenadier Regiment could not leave Maikop before midnight.

However, it came off very well; better than during maneuvers. The brave men fulfilled the assigned order. As described, the 42nd Grenadier Regiment passed through Belorechenskaya at 0300 hours on 29 January. The towed artillery finally limbered and withdrew. The gebirgsjäger battalion and the wheeled battalion followed.

During the commitment, Oberst Auer had his infantry formations and the artillery take up positions at each ammunition dump. And the tubes had a great time! Four batteries and an infantry gun company fired as much ammunition as they could. When an ammunition dump was used up, they moved on to the next.

During the night of 30-31 January 1943, Oberst Auer's force crossed the Kuban and was met by German security forces. Auer briefed the waiting engineer officer. A little later the two combat bridges over the Kuban near Ust Labinskaya were blown into the air with a thunderous explosion. The rearguard mission of Gruppe Auer, which cost only a few wounded, was over. The well thought-out planning and the disciplined elements lent their support to the withdrawal of the XXXXIX Mountain Corps.

The gebirgsjäger formations from the high Caucasus and the I/99 Geb.Jg.Rgt. from the 1st Panzer Army met up with their original divisions in Ust Labinskaya.

CRISIS IN THE RUMANIAN AREA OF OPERATIONS AND SOUTH OF KRASNODAR

Soviet Plan "Mountain" - The XXXXIV Jäger Corps saves the day - "Still no report from Behle?" - Combat around Tugurgoi - Grenadierregiment 326 as rearguard in Krasnodar

On 16 January 1943 the Soviets initiated Plan "Mountain" with an attack out of the Goryachiy Klyuch area, and another further to the west, on the Rumanian positions. Krasnodar was to be reached from the south, while the Krasnodar - Novorossisk road was to be blocked against the withdrawing XXXXIV Jäger Corps.

The 125th and 198th ID frustrated the rapid advance of the Soviet 56th Army on Krasnodar. In the Royal Rumanian Cavalry Corps area of operations the Soviets were able to tear through the German front south of Severskaya and near Kalushkaya. On 17 January, the first battlegroup of the 97th Jäger Division (II and III/204 and 97th Engineer Battalion) (under Major Malter) aeeived and counterattacked and won back the old HKL.

On 18 January, additional units of the 97th Jäger Division arrived to support the Rumanians. However, on this day, a new crisis arose. The I/207 Jg.Rgt. was encircled in the southern portion of Smolenskaya. The III/207, which was committed across Hill 164.3, ran into heavy combat and could advance no further. The II/207, which was advancing on Stavropolskaya, was encircled by the 20th Mountain Rifle Division. The 61st Rifle Division and the 55th Guards Rifle Division resumed their attack out of the Kalushskaya area in order to break through the German withdrawal route toward Novo Dimitrievskaya and Georgie Afipskaya. Small combat groups (mostly staffs) were defending in Grigorievskaya and Novo Dimitrievskaya. German columns continued to move on the withdrawal route toward Kholmskaya. Soviet aircraft constantly attacked the march columns.

The 97th Jäger Division held its sector in spite of the critical situation. It held the XXXXIV Jäger Corps withdrawal route open. To reinforce the thin defense, the 36th Grenadier Regiment (9th ID), Battle Group Kohl (5th Luftwaffe Field Division) and Battle Group Busche (101st Jäger Division) were attached to the 97th Jäger Division.

A lively picture of the crisis was presented in a report from Obergefreiter Krieger from the staff of the 97th Jäger Division: "Soviet forces were infiltrating throughout the thin lines of the division in an attempt to reach the important rollbahn to Krymskaya. The division staff established a defense in Grigorievskaya and was encircled. We saw Generalleutnant Rupp in front of his house. He had his machine-pistol at the ready in his hands. Now he had to do what he had often ordered his jägers. The defenses were prepared.

The Soviets were thrown back repeatedly. The battle lasted all day. Two other villages were captured by the Soviets. Their supply line ran over a small trail. The occupied villages were departure bases for new Soviet advances. This was the critical hour! The enemy would not be thrown back with the few forces available.

The wheeled battalion was ordered to advance through the forest against the enemy's supply route, establish a hasty defense there and block the enemy's supply. Everyone knew what they had to do to prevent chaos. They set out. The great forest swallowed them up. Later a report came back: "Reached the trail!" Then the forest fell silent.

'Still no report from Behle?'

'No, still no report, Herr General!'

The hours passed slowly, too slowly. The day passed. Then a long night; then another day and still another night went by. And still no sign of Behle! However, the Soviets did not attack. Finally, on the third day, a report from Hauptmann Behle: 'The blocking commando has fulfilled its mission. The enemy supply column had fled!'

Now it was time to recapture the two villages with the remaining forces and subordinate elements from other divisions. Among the last of the enemy forces to surrender was a drunken Red Army soldier who said: "Stalingrad! Now all of the Germans are kaput. That's what our Junior Lieutenant Said!'"

The new HKL was stabilized, the movement of the XXXXIV Jäger Corps was secured.

Reference must be made to the I/204. It blocked a penetration near Akhtyrskaya - Kholmskaya in the Romanian area and repulsed heavy enemy attacks, supported by superior forces, from the main withdrawal route between 20 and 25 January 1943. The dominant Mount Lambina changed hands three times. The battalion commander, Hauptmann Abt, found his soldier's death. The decisive combat of the I/204 was recognized by the awarding of the Knight's Cross to Oberleutnant Jakob.

While the 97th Jäger Division overcame the crisis in the Romanian sector, the 125th and 198th ID, as well as the Fast Slovak Division, gradually withdrew to Krasnodar. The 101st Jäger Division followed behind the 97th Jäger Division; its formations were partially committed with the 97th Jäger Division.

In the meantime the XXXXIX Mountain Corps marched though Ust Labinskaya. The XXXXIV Jäger Corps had to halt south of Krasnodar. Therefore, it was to withdraw to the Kuban bridgehead in the south; the XXXXIX Mountain Corps to the north.

However, it did not happen this way. After the 97th Jäger Division had repulsed all of the attacks on the Krasnodar - Novorossisk road, the Soviets shifted their main effort to the Kuban crossings south of Krasnodar. On 22 January the staff of the 101st Jäger Division reached Krasnodar. Battlegroup Busche took up the securing of the southern Kuban crossings.

On the morning of 28 January the last companies of the 125th ID and 198th ID and the Slovak Division left the Kutaiskaya area. While the 125th ID continued to withdraw, the 198th ID occupied a new defensive line in the Prizepilovka area. To the left, stood the Slovak Division, adjacent to the Psekups. On this day the forward-most Soviet attack groups reached the Ganzew area through a gap between the 101st Jäger Division and the 198th ID. During a subsequent attack the Krasnodar bridges were blocked. Under

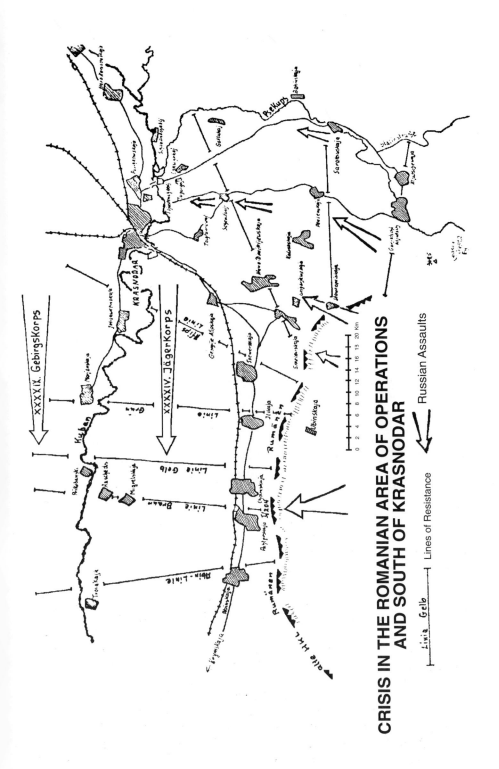

CRISIS IN THE ROMANIAN AREA OF OPERATIONS AND SOUTH OF KRASNODAR

Linie Gelb ⊢——⊣ Lines of Resistance

⬇ Russian Assaults

309

the leadership of the 101st Jäger Division staff, the Soviet attack on the Tiyustenkhably bridge was frustrated. The combat diary of the 101st Jäger Division notes:

"On 29 January the enemy attacked with the 5th and 6th Guards Rifle Brigades southeast of Shendshiy in the direction of Lakshikai. The main body of the 5th Guards Rifle Brigade appeared to have temporarily penetrated toward BP 115 through Battle Group Schury. The 6th Guards Rifle Brigade was able to reach the canal west of the Tugurgoi Forest by the evening of 29 January.

...Today (30 January) the main body followed in the morning and was able to advance up to southeast of Yablonsky. They were destroyed there. The 32nd Guards Rifle Division had conducted an attack near Lakshukai with the 82nd and 85th Regiments and suffered heavy casualties. The 101st Jäger Division had achieved a defensive success on 30 January. The unsuccessful attack of the 6th Guards Rifle Brigade, which was conducted without the support of heavy weapons (they could not bring them forward because of the ice), led to the essential destruction of this brigade. The enemy's plans to overrun Krasnodar failed."

The 419th Grenadier Regiment (125th ID) also participated decisively in this success as it recaptured Tugurgoi in a counterattack.

On 31 January the Soviets tried to advance on the Kuban bridge located further to the east near Shabanokhabl. They punished themselves in continuous attacks against the positions of the Slovaks near Shagancheriyabl. They did achieve a deep penetration. The left flank regiment of the 198th ID, the 308th Grenadier Regiment located in Gatlukai, helped the Slovak Division eliminate the penetration.

On 4 February the Soviets renewed their attack on Krasnodar with fresh forces. Battlegroup Schury lay along the main effort in the village of Zhendzhi. At 0730 hours Schury radioed: "Situation in Zhendzhi unclear. Enemy tanks in the village." However, during the following night, Battlegroup Schury gave up the hotly contested village.

On 5 February the enemy attack was expanded to include the entire 101st Jäger Division sector. Generalmajor Vogel's regiments, with the support of elements of the 9th Rumanian Cavalry Division under Colonel Negrescu, held. Eighteen enemy tanks were destroyed.

Heavy combat also developed in the area of the left neighbor, the 198th ID. There, the strongpoint defense in the towns also held and then was given up. During the retreat the Fast Slovak Division was withdrawn from the corps.

By 10 February the 198th ID and 101st Jäger Division had fought their way through the towns on the south of the river. In the early morning of 10 February the I/326 Gren.Rgt. was the last battalion to cross the Kuban near Tlyustenkhabl. After blowing up the bridge, the 326th Grenadier Regiment occupied the eastern positions in Krasnodar and secured to the east ("Main Line"). All important war installations in the city were destroyed.

The 326th Grenadier Regiment had the mission of holding Krasnodar until 11 February at 1700 hours. Then it was to leave the city over the western

Kuban crossing and seek contact with the German formations on the south side of the river.

On 11 February, the III/235 AR fired a last concentrated attack on the pursuing Soviets. At 1700 hours, the 326th Grenadier Regiment broke contact from the enemy and withdrew. The regimental commander, Oberst Keiser, crossed the Kuban bridge located in the southwest of the city with the last security elements just before the bridge was blown. The 326th Grenadier Regiment caught up with the German troops marching on the road to Severskaya.

The 56th Soviet Army was unable to decisively hinder the German withdrawal to Krasnodar with eight divisional formations and nine rifle brigades.

After Generalmajor Müller fell ill, the leadership of the 198th ID was passed to Oberst Feldmann. On 12 February Oberst (later Generalmajor) von Horn took command of the division. During the following days individual formations of the division were committed with the 97th and 101st Jäger Divisions, as well as the 5th Luftwaffe Field Division, and the 305th Grenadier Regiment was committed with the V Army Corps in Novorossisk.

WITHDRAWAL TO THE KUBAN BRIDGEHEAD

Ju 52s supply the bridgehead - The mortal combat of the I/228 Jg.Rgt. in the Ausheds - Abinskaya breakwater - Combat in the swamps and lagoons - The "Rice Road" - The 50th ID holds on the northern flank

With the establishment of the Kuban bridgehead, the German leadership hoped to use it as a departure base for a new offensive into the Caucasus.

During the withdrawal to the Kuban bridgehead, the main effort lay in the XXXXIV Jäger Corps and XXXXIX Mountain Corps areas of operations in the Ust - Labinskaya - Krasnodar frontal salient. In order to destroy the German force concentrations there, the 37th Soviet Army was committed against Krasnodar from the northeast and the 56th Army from the south. A second, larger pincer, was formed by the 58th and 9th Armies in the north and the 47th Army in the south. Both groups were to meet in the Slavyanskaya area. Therefore, the 17th German Army was to be destroyed. That was the Soviet plan, but the tenacious German defense frustrated it.

"On 22 February 1943 the Russian attack was located along a front line north of the Kuban, on a line Kalabatka - Prikubanski, and south of the Kuban, on a line Prokovski - Kholmskaya. The encirclement of the 17th Army was thus planned!" That was the analysis of the Soviet military historical writings.

During the night of 31 January 1943, the rearguard of the 46th ID crossed the combat bridges near Ust Labinskaya, which were then blown up. After the bridges were destroyed, the pursuing enemy forces were temporarily halted. Then, however, they crossed the Kuban ice to the north and south. Between Ust Labinskaya and Krasnodar battlegroups under Lieutenant Colonel Abramov and 2nd Lieutenant Gradassov had completed the crossing, but were too weak to seriously threaten the German movement.

On 1 February 1943 a meeting in Voronezhkaya between the commander of the 17th Army, Generaloberst Ruoff, and the commander of the XXXXIX Mountain Corps, General Konrad, resulted in the following decisions:

1. All damaged vehicles were to be destroyed.

2. A phased withdrawal was to be conducted into the Kuban bridgehead. Subsequent positions were to be fortified by construction battalions, which would be made available to the corps.

3. As soon as the condition of the ice permitted, the withdrawal of formations destined for the Crimea and Army Group "Don" would begin, while simultaneously reducing the size of the Kuban bridgehead.

Similar arrangements were made with the other corps of the 17th Army. All of the army corps formed reconnaissance staffs, which searched out the subsequent positions and oversaw the construction work. While the southern flank of the 17th Army remained near Novorossisk, the northern flank withdrew behind the Protoka by 25 February.

On 31 January the withdrawing German divisions took up a new defensive line and occupied it with the following formations:

Sea of Azov: The LII Army Corps with (from north to south) the 2nd Romanian Mountain Division, 50th ID and 370th ID.

North of the Kuban, on either side of Ust Labinskaya: The XXXXIX Mountain Corps with the 46th ID, 1st and 4th Mountain Divisions.

South of the Kuban: The XXXXIV Jäger Corps with the 101st and 97th Jäger Divisions, 125th and 198th ID and some Romanian formations.

Novorossisk and to the north: The V Army Corps: which would remain in its positions.

The 1st Mountain Division disbanded its reconnaissance battalion and feldersatz battalion, the transport battalion along with the veterinary and supply company, as well as the Bauer High Mountain Battalion, and used them to bring the other formations up to combat strength. Similar measures were taken in almost all of the other divisions. The first elements of the 46th and 198th ID were transported to the rear by air.

In four large phases and numerous smaller phases, the 17th Army was gradually withdrawn to the "Grosse Gotenstellung [The Position of the Great Gods]".

With the severing of the supply route through Bataisk and Rostov, supplies for the Kuban bridgehead had to be routed through the Taman Peninsula - Kerch Strait - Crimea. The supply over the Kerch Strait, which had been barely sufficient, had to be considerably increased in order to support the 17th Army. Suddenly this was not possible because the condition of the ice would not permit bridge construction. In fact, all vehicle traffic came to a halt. Then only the Luftwaffe could help! After the costly air supply of Stalingrad it had to supply the Kuban bridgehead by air. This was a glorious page in the history of the German air transport formations. We will now describe the commitment of a kampfgeschwader, which, in addition to the Ju 52 formations, also flew in air supplies:

The 200th Kampfgeschwader [KG] (FW 200/four-engined combat aircraft) under Major Willer flew air support to Stalingrad. Although Grossadmiral Dönitz needed the 200th KG in the Atlantic for long-ranged reconnaissance, it remained, for the time being, in the east and was subordinated to Transport- führer Oberst Morzik in Zaporozhe. The KG, which consisted of experienced air personnel, had the mission of flying ammunition, fuel and supplies with all available operational aircraft into the Kuban bridgehead and bringing out wounded, specialists and copper to Zaporozhe. The combat sorties planned against the Baku and Grosny oil region did not take place because of this turn of events. The commitment of the four- engined aircraft, which, during peacetime was known as the "Condor", was as follows:

4/2/43: 7 FW/200 with supplies from Zaporozhe to Krasnodar. Return flight with wounded, personnel and copper.

5/2/43 6 FW/200 with supplies to Slavyanskaya. Double sortie between Slavyanskaya and Kerch IV. Return flight to Zaporozhe. Transport mission the same as on the previous day.

6/2/43: 7 FW/200 supply flights as on the previous day. Zaporozhe to Krasnodar and Krasnodar Bagerovo (Crimea). Return flight to Zaporozhe.

7/2/43: 4 FW/200 supply flights as on the previous day.

8/2/43: 6 FW/200 with ammunition from Zaporozhe to Timashevskaya. Return flight with soldiers and wounded to Bagerovo. Supplies to Krasnodar. Return flight with copper to Zaporozhe. 2 FW/200 combat missions in night sortie.

9/2/43: 3 FW/200 round trip missions as on previous day. Zaporozhe - Krasnodar - Mariupol - Slavyanskaya - Zaporozhe. Order for transfer to Berlin - Staaken arrives.

10/2/43: 2 FW/200 missions as previous day.

11/2/43: 4 FW/200 missions as previous day.

12/2/43: 3 FW/200 missions as previous day.

Every night a sortie by one FW/200 was flown on a railroad mission.

On 13 February the last supply mission was flown by the FW/200. During the return from the Kuban bridgehead, the airfields at Krasnodar and Timashevskaya could no longer be approached.

In all, from 4 to 13 February 1943, the FW/200 KG flew 41 sorties from Zaporozhe and 35 sorties between the Crimea and the Kuban bridgehead. They flew in 116 tons of ammunition, 75.6 tons of rations, 50.4 tons of fuel and 12 tons of equipment. They flew out 830 wounded, 1057 soldiers and 55.1 tons of copper.

The good old Aunt Ju 52, as it was lovingly referred to by the Landser, was the backbone of the air supply. We now review the specifications on this reliable transport aircraft:

Junkers Ju 52/3:

Crew: 3 men
Engines: 3 BMW 132/A each 660 horsepower
Wing-span: 29.25 meters
Length: 18.90 meters
Height: 4.40 meters
Max speed: 270 km/h
Take off speed: 200 km/h
Landing speed: 100 km/h
Weight: 6510 kg
Load capacity: 4030 kg
Flight weight: 10,540 kg
Max. Altitude: 5500 meters
Max. Range: 1280 km
Armament: 3-4 MG/15

Other specifications:

Fuel 2450 liters. Take-off distance (fully laden without wind) 500 meters.

After the heavy losses suffered by the Ju 52 transport formations during the Stalingrad commitment they had to be reorganized. The newly formed transport formations available for the supply of the Kuban bridgehead were:

	Commander	Airfield
KG. z.b.V. 9	Oberst Jäckel,	Sarabus
	Hauptmann Ellerbrock	
KG. z.b.V. 102	Oberstlt. Erdmann	Sarabus
	Major Penkert	
KG. z.b.V. 50	Major Baumann	Samorsk
KG. z.b.V. 172	Major Zähr	Bagerovo
KG. z.b.V. 500	Major Beckmann	Kherson

The staging areas were all located in the Crimea. The landing zones in the bridgehead were surveyed locations on the rollbahn. The constantly changing front caused the landing zones to change. Landing zones included: Krasnodar, Temryuk, Slavyanskaya, Timashevskaya and Varenikovskaya.

The air transport formations had 40-50 aircraft each with an average of 30 aircraft operational per day. According to the combat diary of Luftflotte IV, on 5 February, these transports carried 107.7 tons of ammunition, fuel and rations. 366 wounded, 357 soldiers and 25.7 tons of equipment were flown out. From 6 to 25 February 1943 approximately the same daily averages were achieved.

On 4 February 1943 a Soviet landing was conducted west of Novorossisk. The new situation brought new difficulties. The 17th Army proposed to the OKH constructing a defensive front in the later, so-called "Kleinen Gotenkopf", especially since the enemy foothold in Novorossisk made the city and the harbor worthless.

After Hitler discussed this with the commanders of Army Groups A and Don and the 17th Army, he did not make an immediate decision. He finally notified the 17th Army on 23 March. According, Novorossisk would be included in the "Grosse Gotenkopf" for the following reasons:

1. To pin strong enemy forces and, therefore, relieve Army Group Don.

2. Considerably limit the mobility of the Soviet Black Sea Fleet.

3. Relieve the Crimean defenses.

4. It would have a favorable political effect on the Turks.

5. Hold on to the oil resources west of Krymskaya.

In the meantime, on 7 February 1943, the 3rd Landing Flotilla began supplying the bridgehead across the Kerch Strait, even though the ice conditions were still not favorable. As before, the main burden was borne by the Ju 52 transport groups.

On 11 February Krasnodar was given up by the rearguards of the 198th ID. The 10th Guards Rifle Brigade, the 40th Motorized Brigade and the 31st Rifle Division occupied the city. On this day Generalleutnant Haccius, the commander of the 46th ID, was killed by a shot through the heart north of Krasnodar, while monitoring the withdrawal of his division.

During the night of 14 February, the XXXXIV Jäger Corps withdrew to the Ubinka Positions. On 18 February, this corps stood on the "Green" Line; on 20 February on the "Yellow" Line (Eibsa Positions); on 21 February on the "Brown" Line (Akhtyr Positions); on 22 February on the Abin or Goten Positions. The withdrawal of the XXXXIX Mountain Corps north of the Kuban was accomplished in a similar manner.

On 22 February the withdrawal along the Rice Road into the "Poseidon" (P) Positions behind the Protoka began. Only by Slavyanskaya was there a smaller conduit. There began the notorious Rice Road over which the supply of the XXXXIX Mountain Corps, and a good portion of the LII Army Corps, as well as the army, had to travel. No soldier who had travelled on it would ever forget the Rice Road. On the left and right of the road embankment extended one vast field of mud. In the summer it was a fruitful rice field. This abundance from the countryside was made use of by the German divisions. The rice mills of Slavyanskaya worked day and night. Each day they produced a rich quantity of rice.

The rhythm of the withdrawal was similar in all of the numerous columns. Officers Winkler and Remold tirelessly monitored the withdrawal of the vehicles. Soviet bomber formations constantly attacked the jammed vehicles. After all of the damaged vehicles were destroyed, the withdrawal behind the Protoka was completed on 24 February. However, west of the Protoka was another story. A 50 kilometer long vehicular snake was stuck in the mud. Rainy weather set in so there was only one thing to do: Hold the Protoka Positions and wait for better weather, which would allow for the withdrawal of the vehicles.

The withdrawal did not go as smoothly on the northern flank of the 17th Army. There the Soviets attacked, one large pincer with the 58th and 9th Armies serving as their objective was to advance along the lagoons of the Sea of Azov to the south toward Slavyanskaya in order to meet up with the pincer attacking from the south and to cut off the 17th Army far from its rear area.

On 9 February, the Soviets wrenched open the extended front of the 50th ID near Novo Korssunskaya. The division had a front 24 kilometers wide as the crow flies. A penetration near Braybinskie with an accompanying bridgehead over the Beisugshek was eliminated at the cost of considerable loss. On 10 February the withdrawal over the Z Line into the B Line, which was 50 kilometers distant, began. During the night of 14 February the Russians pursued, attacking the B Line on the following morning. In see-saw combat the Pomeranian and Ostbrandenburger 50th ID repulsed all enemy attacks.

On 15 February the Soviets penetrated into the northern neighboring 2nd Romanian Mountain Division. The 50th ID helped the Romanians. In spite of this the situation remained critical. In order to reinforce the northern flank of the 17th Army, an armored battle group from the 13th Panzer Division under Oberst von Hake was deployed and committed to the fighting. Three rifle divisions and four other brigades did not get through the 50th ID sector. The Soviets shifted their main effort again to the Romanian sector. They attacked the Romanians along the lagoons of the Sea of Azov. On 26

February Battle Group von Hake and two battalions of the 50th ID had to iron out the critical situation in the Romanian area of operations, but enemy pressure had become considerably stronger. On 1 March the extreme northern flank was withdrawn behind the Protoka.

The 46th ID was withdrawn in the course of the shortening of the front; the first formations were flown from Slavyanskaya to Zaporozhe on 22 February.

On 26 February the first air transport of the 198th ID staff and grenadier regiments followed. They were flown over forest, land, lagoons and sea from Varenikovskaya to Zaporozhe. A Ju transport was attacked by Soviet light infantry and was forced to conduct an emergency landing in the lagoons near Temryuk.

From 1 to 8 March 1943, extended rainfall tied up all large-scale combat operations on the northern flank of the 17th Army. On 3 March the LII Army Corps command was withdrawn for use elsewhere. The combat formations were subordinated to the XXXXIX Mountain Corps. The units set up defenses in the Protoka sector, especially since the snow melt swelled the river into a good sized obstacle.

At this time air transport reached its peak. We include the efforts of the transport formations (Ju 52):

Day	Flown in	Flown out
26/2	192 t supplies	1622 soldiers
27/2	113 t supplies	905 soldiers
28/2	228 t supplies	1245 soldiers
	892 soldiers	
	56 t equipment	
1/3	2 relief companies	300 wounded and elements of
	32 t supplies	the 198th ID
2/3	1 relief company	350 wounded
3/3	60 t supplies	250 wounded
4/3	90 t supplies	400 wounded
5/3	250 t supplies	2000 wounded and soldiers,
	510 t supplies	187 t equipment
6/3	441 t supplies	1890 wounded and soldiers,
	120 t equipment	
7/3	430 t supplies	1080 wounded and soldiers,
	152 t equipment	
9/3	355 t equipment.	120 soldiers
	1st commitment of seaplanes	
10/3	450 t supplies	1321 wounded and soldiers,
	60 t equipment	
11/3	355 t supplies	1600 wounded and soldiers

12/3	660 t supplies	862 wounded and soldiers,
	154 t equipment	
13-18/3	Taman supply	wounded and equipment
22/3	590 t supplies	1660 soldiers, 140 t equipment
23/3	600 t supplies	
	1380 soldiers	
25/3	supplies	
28/3	150 t supplies	
	840 soldiers	
29/3	supplies	
30/3	7 t equipment,	
	50 soldiers (last flight).	

During the 50 day supply period 5418 tons of supplies were flown into the Kuban bridgehead. This was a daily average of 182 tons. The daily average for Stalingrad was 94 tons. Better weather conditions and safer and shorter flight paths made the difference.

In spring of 1943, moreover, 22 Type Do 24 seaplanes and a Ju 52/See formation was assembled in the Crimea under the leadership of the commander of the Seenotbereich (SNB) XII, Oberstleutnant Hansing, as well as:

A group of Ju 52/See, located near Kerch under Major Gude,

1. Seetransportstaffel Sevastopol, 11 Do 24 under Hauptmann Tretter,

2. Seenotstaffel Sevastopol, 11 Do 24 under Oberstleutnant Huelsmann.

Approximately 1000 tons of supplies were flown into the Kuban bridgehead from Sevastopol. The loading and unloading of the 3 ton loads was accomplished by engineers. The seaplanes landing in the Kuban were unloaded by engineer assault boats that were fitted with pontoons on either side and could carry 1.5 tons.

The skill of the transport pilots was significantly tested during the period of bad weather. When the air supply was suspended, traffic was picked up in the Kerch Strait.

During the withdrawal to the Kerch bridgehead, the XXXXIV Jäger Corps was constantly being pressured by the 56th Soviet Army. In the 101st Jäger Division area of operations, which was withdrawing south of the Kuban, 22 February was a black day. The 500th Special Purpose Battalion and the II/229 Jg.Rgt. were attacked in Migrelskaya from the east and south. The focus of the battle lay to the north in Ausheds in the I/228 Jg.Rgt. area of operations. The battalion was overrun six times by Captain Molchanov's Soviet tank battalion because it lacked anti-tank weapons. The I/228 lost all of its heavy weapons. During the battle the commander of the 3rd Company, Knight's Cross holder Oberleutnant Kult, was killed. This initial success was exploited by the Soviet commander, who committed additional tanks into the battle. The German battle- group, which consisted of the I and II/228 Jg.Rgt., the I/85 AR and the 2/101 Pi.Btl., was cut off and pushed back to the Kuban. Major Shutov's Soviet tank formations solidified the encirclement of

Oberstleutnant Schury's Germans.

On 24 February, the II/229 got caught up in Shutov's pincer and had to withdraw in heavy combat in the direction of Troitskaya. Since Troitskaya was already occupied by enemy forces, and because it was included in the "Grosse Gottenstellung", a devilish situation developed. Contact between the XXXXIX Mountain Corps and the XXXXIV Jäger Corps was lost. The XXXXIX Mountain Corps had to help. An army order reflected:

"The XXXXIX Mountain Corps will move corresponding forces west of Troitskaya across the Kuban, capture Troitskaya, attack along the rail line to the south and reestablish contact with the XXXXIV Jäger Corps."

During the night of 25 to 26 February a battlegroup under Major Eisgruber (98th Gebirgsjäger Regiment, a Heeres engineer battalion, 44th Panzerjäger Battalion and I/79 Geb.AR), after constructing a combat bridge, which was complicated by heavy ice drifts, crossed the Kuban to the south. A strong artillery group covered the commitment from the northern bank. Enemy occupied Troitskaya was quickly captured. Then a battalion attacked to the south along the railroad embankment and reestablished contact with the XXXXIV Jäger Corps about 10 kilometers south of the Kuban.

At the same time fighting erupted again in Troitskaya. In the morning, Russian infantry attacked frontally while 30 tanks from the Shutov formation, swinging to the south, penetrated into Troitskaya. The infantry was repulsed; heavy close combat developed with the penetrating tanks. Several tanks were destroyed, the rest withdrew. On 27, 28 and 29 February there was more fierce fighting near Troitskaya. However, the enemy attack, supported by tanks, collapsed in the defensive fire of Battlegroup Eisgruber. The desperate fighting by Battle Group Schury along the Kuban embankment continued. Finally, engineer elements from the 4th Mountain Division succeeded in constructing a combat bridge near Nechaevskiy and Battlegroup Schury crossed the Kuban to the north. The desperate fighting by Battlegroup Schury at least delayed the occupation of Troitskaya by strong Russian forces and led to the occupation of the Protoka Positions by the XXXXIX Mountain Corps as planned.

On 26 and 27 February, and on 1 March, Soviet assault regiments attacked Abinskaya frontally and from the northeast. Abinskaya was to be a breakwater held by the 97th Jäger Division: the hastily formed Battlegroups Höhne and Salzer advanced across the Abin to the east, splt the enemy attack forces and inflicted considerable losses on them. On 2 March the German Wehrmacht reported: "... A counterattack took place in the southern portion of the Eastern Front yesterday. A clever offensive operation by German troops on the lower Kuban battered enemy force groupings and frustrated their attack preparations."

After concentrating additional forces and bringing up strong artillery, the Soviets attacked Abinskaya again on 10 March. A German stuka attack brought some relief to the defenders. Battlegroups Otte and Malter held. Nineteen enemy air attacks were logged on this day, four aircraft were shot down. The fierce combat lasted until 13 March. By then the Russian attack

WITHDRAWAL INTO
THE KUBAN BRIDGEHEAD

31.1 – 4.4. 1943

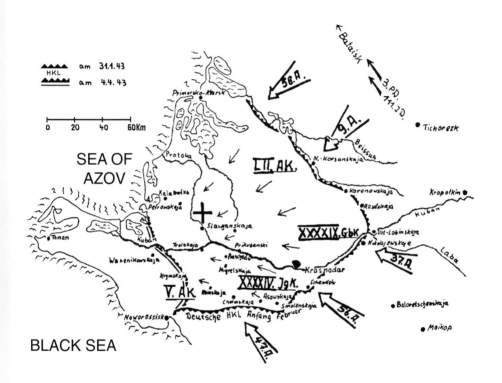

strength was broken. The 17th Army sent the following radio message:

"I express my thanks and recognition to the tried and true 97th Jäger Division for successfully repulsing strong enemy attacks on Abinskaya.

signed Ruoff, Generaloberst and Commander 17th Army"

During the night of 24 March the Abin line was evacuated and the Kuafo sector was occupied and held for 24 hours. On 25 March the 97th Jäger Division stood ready to defend in the "Grosse Gottenstellung" before Krymskaya.

In the meantime, Russian pressure on the Protoka front increased, particularly near Slavyanskaya, where the 4th Mountain Division repulsed several enemy attempts to cross.

While the German formations were withdrawing to the Protoka sector, a serious crisis developed in their rear. After the 13th Panzer Division and elements of the 50th ID had repulsed an enemy attack on the northern flank of the 17th Army, the Soviets turned further to the north and infiltrated strong forces through the still-unsecured lagoon region on the Sea of Azov to the south. They were soon discovered by German radio reconnaissance. The Germans took immediate defensive measures. A battlegroup was formed under the commander of the 1st Mountain Division, Generalmajor von Stettner, which consisted of a small staff, the 4th Security Regiment, the 42nd Grenadier Regiment, the II/98 Geb.Jg.Rgt., a corps Cossack regiment, two motorized artillery battalions and panzerjägers.

During the night of 27 February 1943, the guards at an ammunition depot 18 kilometers behind the corps command post were overwhelmed by infiltrated forces. Oberst Auer, commander of the 42nd Grenadier Regiment of the 46th ID, provides a description:

"On 25 February my regiment was the last of the division to be withdrawn from the front in order to be flown from Slavyanskaya to the Crimea on the morning of 27 February. The other divisional units had already been flown out. On 26 February my regiment made preparations for the flight. Late that evening I went over the departure times for the battalions with my battalion commanders.

Getting almost no sleep, I was rudely awakened at 0100 hours on 27 February. First the Chief of Staff showed up, then the commander of the XXXXIX Mountain Corps. They briefed me on the following situation:

"Enemy of unknown strength is advancing into the marshes and lagoons on the edge of the Sea of Azov to the south and now stands behind the corps command post, as well as to the west of Anastasievskaya. The 42nd Grenadier Regiment is to march immediately to the corps command post.'

The regiment was alerted. Since, by this time, all of the supplies had to be flown into the Kuban bridgehead, the regiment had already given up all of its ammunition. It had to be resupplied with ammunition! At 0330 hours the regiment marched off. At daybreak there was an air attack. The march was conducted over the Rice Road, on which there were 6000 stuck vehicles.

I was directed to the corps command post by the Chief of Staff:

"The enemy battalions have been harassing us for days in the unsecured lagoons. Due to ground fog, air reconnaissance was of no use. Therefore, the 1st Cossack Regiment and the 4th Security Regiment were ordered to secure in the Gorlachev - Svistelnikov area. Road conditions have delayed these deployments. Therefore, ground reconnaissance is also lacking. The local inhabitants believe that they are infantry forces with mortars and light infantry guns. The enemy is established in and around:

1. Chernoerkovskaya, where the 13th Panzer Division is trying to throw them back in counterattack at this time,

2. Shedelgub - Svistelnikov,

3. Korshevski, where he has severed our withdrawal route,

4. Otrub, from where he constantly attacks the army ammunition depot.

The intent of the corps is to attack into the flank of the enemy, cut him off from his supply line and then destroy the enemy from the rear. Gruppe von Stettner will be formed under the commander of the 1st Mountain Division. Advance your regiment to the northern edge of Anastassievskaya, then attack them toward Shedelgub.'

Until commander von Stettner arrived I utilized the time for terrain reconnaissance. I discovered:

1. That it was wide, unsurveyable and flat. Unfavorable for an attack.

2. The marshy terrain had many pools. It had a brittle ice cover.

3. Vehicles and artillery could only move along the Anastassievskaya - Svistelnikov route.

On the basis of this terrain assessment, the 42nd Grenadier Regiment received the following commitment order:

1. According to prisoner of war statements, the enemy consists of three brigades, which were specially assembled for their mission. The main body is advancing out of the Chernoerkovskaya Pass into the lagoons.

Armament: machine-guns, machine-pistols, mortars. The northern group also has infantry guns.

Mission: Close the Kalabatka - Oktyabris Pass and secure our supply.

2. The attack of the 13th Panzer Division into the Chernoerkovskaya Pass would appear to tie up additional enemy following forces.

3. The von Stettner attack group will attack tomorrow, Sunday, 28 February 1943. The 1st Cossack Regiment waits exhausted in Gorlachev and will still not be able to set out tomorrow.

The 4th Security Regiment has been able to penetrate into Svistelnikov South. Tomorrow it will clear the entire village and then attack through to the west toward the Kurka bend north of Kalabatka in order to prevent the enemy from withdrawing into the lagoons. A battalion of the 4th Security Regiment will take Korshevski.

The 42nd Grenadier Regiment will take Shedelgub with the subordinate I/115 AR and throw the enemy back into the lagoons.'

On 28 February the 42nd Grenadier Regiment left the Sheltered area with two combat strength battalions and reached the assembly area before dawn.

ATTACK OF
DIVISIONAL GROUP
von STETTNER

27.2 to 3.3. 1943

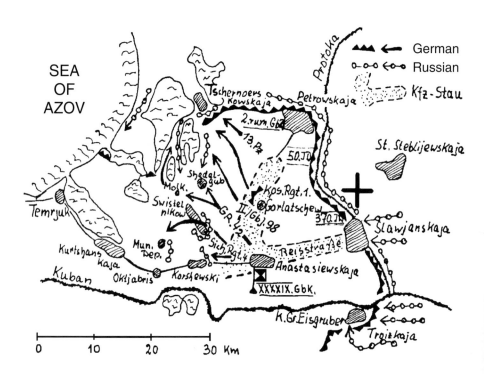

Because the northern portion of Svistlenikov was still occupied by the enemy, only the II/42 was to attack Shedelgub; the I/42 was to be on the left in second echelon screening against Svistelnikov.

The beginning of the attack was delayed because the artillery was very late in getting into position and ready to fire due to the muddy roads. However, the artillery was the only factor that could even up the numerical enemy advantage.

Thaw and rain changed the marsh region into mush. The brittle ice forced detours. The reeds provided the enemy with the best cover. We would stumble upon each other, then fight hand-to-hand.

After an artillery fire-strike, two companies advanced frontally against Shedelgub. The 150 meter wide open space in front of the village was overcome in assault. Then they initiated a fierce house-to-house battle. Finally, when a flank attack was carried out by a third company, the Soviets lost their nerve and fled into the reeds. The coming twilight prevented a pursuit. Shedelgub was taken.

Meanwhile, the 4th Security Regiment also moved against the enemy from Svistelnikov North.

An uncomfortable night followed. The majority of the 42nd Grenadier Regiment lay in the open, covered in mud and soaked to the skin. Warm rations did not show up.

On 1 March the pursuit of the enemy was resumed. At the same time contact was made with the 13th Panzer Division. What the soldiers endured at this time is indescribable. Constant rain, sodden cold rations, only individual groups were able to find shelter for a short time in ruins or stables. They were constantly fighting enemy remnants. The artillery could not follow.

On 2 March the Reisinger Battalion (1st Mountain Division) also arrived and advanced further to the north until it made contact with the 13th Panzer Division.

On 3 March the 42nd Grenadier Regiment withdrew into the Shedelgub area. A battalion and the regimental staff marched further to Varenikovskaya in order to be flown to the Crimea from there. The II Battalion was ordered to take the dairy, which was still occupied by the enemy directly north of Svistelnikov. The battalion commander, Knight's Cross winner Major Stigler, carefully prepared for the attack.

The dairy was somewhat elevated over the surrounding marsh region. It consisted of several brick buildings surrounded by rifle trenches. Machine-gun nests and anti-tank positions controlled the few access roads to the dairy.

Major Stigler decided to attack across the marsh because he anticipated less resistance there. During the night before 4 March each attack company created a crossing over the marshy terrain and prepared for the attack.

On the morning of 4 March each company was ready to spring up from the assembly area. The arranged stuka attack was conducted. The bombs hit their targets. While the smoke still lay over the dairy, a battery launched a fire-strike. Then the companies attacked. The Soviets fled. The II Battalion pursued. For the entire day friend and foe waded through swamps. There was another battle at a fishery. Again the Soviets were thrown back. Many weapons were left behind. The number of prisoners rose. It wasn't until night fell that the combatants separated.

On 5 March the 6th Company continued the pursuit through the lagoons. Heavy fog prevented the battalion from following. Hours of concern followed; there were no reports from the 6th Company.

The Sixth attacked through the lagoon and spent the night in the water with a number of prisoners. On 6 March they attacked south from Chernoerskaya toward the Reisinger Battalion and, from there, ran into the withdrawal of II/42. The Stigler Battalion remained another two days as security in the Svistelnikov area, then it withdrew to the airfield for the flight out."

Oberst Auer's report describes the defeat of the Soviet forces in the rear of the XXXXIX Mountain Corps. The difficulty of the commitment in the poor weather conditions was unimaginable. As difficult as it was in Auer's regimental area it was similar in the areas of the other participants. The 4th Security Regiment served well, even though it was not trained for this type of commitment. It is necessary to note the lack of mobility of the Soviet leadership: none of the three brigades attempted to offer the others any assistance; they simply waited until they were attacked themselves. It is also necessary to note a Soviet radio message that was intercepted by the Germans on 4 March: "Stay and freeze in the water. There is nothing we can do about it!"

After another eight days the last remnants of the Soviets in the rear of the XXXXIX Mountain Corps were wiped out. The withdrawal of the XXXXIX Mountain Corps to the Protoka was still not over; it then had to fall back in phases from the Protoka to the Kurka. The corps had to fight for its vehicles and hold out on the Protoka for 14 days. On 10 March 1943 a frost set in, then the vehicles could finally move.

On 13 March, the mountain corps withdrew its left flank. While shortening the front, the 13th Panzer Division and the 2nd Romanian Mountain Division were detached from the corps; elements of the 13th Panzer Division and the 2nd Romanian Mountain Corps and, after 21 March, also the entire 1st Mountain Division, were transported over the Kerch Strait which had, in the meantime, become free of ice, for commitment elsewhere. The 50th ID was then the left flanking division in the lagoons of the Sea of Azov.

On 18 March the 50th ID occupied the "Paula Positions" after taking up interim positions. With the outbreak of spring weather the Soviets prepared to resume their attacks. On 22 March the II/121 and the 43rd Kradschützen Battalion (13th Panzer Division) conducted a harassing attack. A little later German stukas attacked enemy concentrations in front of the northern flank of the XXXXIX Mountain Corps. They were preparing to attack into the German withdrawal.

During the night of 23 March the "Anna Positions" were occupied without any trouble. In the vast reed forest in front of the new positions, the Russians again assembled their 417th and 276th Rifle Divisions, as well as another five rifle brigades and a tank brigade.

The storm broke on 26 March! The focal point was the 123rd Grenadier Regiment area. The batteries of the 150th Artillery Regiment fired until their barrels gave out. The Soviets penetrated into the II/123 area with 40 tanks and accompanying infantry. Oberleutnant Meinhold, commander of the machine-gun company, and Feldwebel Rudolf, distinguished themselves as leaders of counterattacks and received the Knight's Cross. Of sixteen attacking tanks, fourteen were destroyed in the II/123 area of operations. Only two escaped. Then it became quiet.

During the night of 29 March, the Soviets prepared themselves again. At 0400 hours on the new day all of the battalions of the 150th Artillery Regiment fired a concentrated attack on the suspected assembly positions. At daybreak the Soviets returned the artillery fire. It was barrage fire! At 0500 hours Soviet artillery concentrated fire on the II/123 sector. At 0630 hours the artillery fire shifted back to the German artillery positions; two Soviet regiments attacked and the German artillery struck again. Two stuka attacks pinned an enemy tank concentration directly behind the attack front. The German infantry joined in. At 0930 hours the battle was decided in favor of the 50th ID.

On 30 March, the enemy undertook another attack attempt. Again the Soviet assault troops were battered by concentrated fire from infantry and artillery, supported by stukas. The tank graveyard in front of the II/123 Gren.Rgt. grew to 26 tank wrecks.

During the night of 31 March the "Anna Line" was evacuated. It had held up against 26 Soviet attacks for eight days. The enemy lost 2000 dead and 32 destroyed tanks. In the 50th ID area of operations during this time two officers and 54 non-commissioned officers and men were killed. The division also suffered 177 wounded. Besides those already mentioned, Leutnant Weiss, commander of 11/121, was praised for his commitment during the battle in an order of the day from the mountain corps on 26 March.

On 31 March the "Susanne Line", the last positions in front of the Kuban bridgehead, were occupied. At 0800 hours an enemy infantry attack occurred with the support of 10 tanks. After see-saw combat the new HKL was held. However, this was only the beginning! At 1200 hours about 3000 men set out against the center and the right flank of the 50th ID in a major attack. The artillery made the difference! The entire 150th Artillery Regiment, an artillery battalion from the neighboring 370th ID, as well as corps artillery, established a wall of fire that no one could penetrate. 1200 dead and nine destroyed tanks were left in front of the German defense. The Soviet attack strength in front of the northern flank of the 17th Army was broken.

During the night of 4 April the 50th ID withdrew into the "Kathinka Positions". The dramatic withdrawal from the Terek into the Kuban bridgehead was, therefore, over for the 50th and 370th ID. Both divisions were the lone subordinate units of the XXXXIX Mountain Corps. Preceding the 4th Mountain Division, which was withdrawn from the Krasny - Oktyabr line on

30 March, and withdrawn into the Gostagaevskaya area in order to prepare for an attack on the Myshako bridgehead near Novorossisk, the 2nd Romanian Mountain Division, the 46th ID, the 1st Mountain Division and elements of the 13th Panzer Division, which had been subordinate to the XXXXIX Mountain Corps, were all withdrawn through the Crimea to serve on other fronts. The 1st Mountain Division was committed in Greece.

THE NOVOROSSISK LANDING OPERATION

Stalin's new plan - The German naval forces in the Black Sea - Soviet landing near Osereika and in "Kleinen Land" - The secondary landing enjoys greater success - Combat in Novorossisk and on the Myshako - German U-Boats join in

On 24 January 1943, as has already been established, when the majority of the 1st German Panzer Army escaped Stalin's planned Caucasus pocket through Rostov, a secret meeting took place in the STAVKA at the Kremlin. All of the senior troop leaders from the Stalingrad and Caucasus area participated in it. Stalin fumed at his commanders that the assigned objective would not be achieved in time; the names Tikhorets, Bataisk and Rostov kept turning up. The fate of the 6th German Army in Stalingrad had already been sealed, but the 1st Panzer Army and the 17th Army were slipping out of the noose.

At this meeting Stalin developed a new plan to destroy the 17th Army in the Kuban bridgehead. The great Soviet pincer operation against the slowly establishing bridgehead was frustrated by the steadfastness of the German soldiers. Another attempt to achieve what had previously failed would be conducted in a large coordinated sea and land operation in the rear of the 17th Army.

Naval landing operations were not new to the Soviets. In 1941 they withdrew their defenders from Odessa by sea. Likewise, in 1942, the last defenders of Sevastopol, Taman, Anapa and Novorossisk were evacuated by sea.

Of interest is the study in the combat diary of Army Group A from 1 to 31 December 1942 which assumed that the Soviets were planning a landing at the beginning of December 1942 northwest of Novorossisk. It was to be coupled with the advance of the Soviet Black Sea Fleet into the western Black Sea. The referenced combat diary notes under 1 December 1942:

"Report from the commander of the Crimea: German naval forces note active radio communications between Sevastopol and Constanza. It appears to represent operations by flotilla leaders, destroyers and cruisers. These elements are in radio contact with the battle ship "Pariskaya Kommuna", as well as the light cruiser "Krasniy Krym". German naval forces advise that they may be heading toward the Romanian - Sevastopol area. Air reconnaissance has been initiated."

Enemy defectors in the 17th Army sector revealed that a landing was to occur during the night of 2 December 1942 between Anapa and Novorossisk.

At 1255 hours the commander of the Crimea reported on enemy ship movements:

1. The Luftwaffe reported a Soviet cruiser and a destroyer infiltrating southwest of Sevastopol.

2. Between 0600 and 0745 hours, one of the islands in the Danube estuary was fired on by five enemy units.

3. Radio direction finding established that the Russian battleship "Pariskaya Kommuna" was located southeast of Feodosia.

4. The Romanian Mountain Corps reported an exchange of fire between Russian and German ships 20 kilometers south of Sudak.

At 1635 hours the 1st Generalstabsoffizier from the Crimean Command reported that 7 enemy war ships (1 cruiser and 6 smaller elements) were located off Anapa. This report was immediately passed on to the 17th Army.

The "Black Sea" Admiralty had offered all available naval forces to defend against the upcoming landing attempt near Anapa. At the same time a landing attempt was also anticipated near Feodosia. The Romanian coastal forces were reinforced by weak German forces.

A day later the combat diary of Army Group A noted: "Air reconnaissance has discovered Russian naval forces withdrawing into the eastern Black Sea.

This movement of naval units was not explained in Russian military historical writings. At the same time the initial report arrived. Air and naval reconnaissance determined that the enemy ships were no longer evident.

On 20 December 1942, agents and defectors again reported an upcoming landing near Anapa. The German defense was reorganized:

1. Coastal Battle Group, consisting of the 73rd ID and the 10th Romanian ID, under the leadership of the commander of the 73rd ID.

2. Battle Group Albin, consisting of the 9th ID and the 3rd Romanian Mountain Division, under the leadership of the commander of the 9th ID.

This predicted landing at least got the attention of the German leadership and, from then on, they would always be anticipating such an operation. There was one difference, however. During the withdrawal from Odessa, Sevastopol and Taman, the Soviets were evacuating a point they held; during a landing operation, they first had to fight for the landing zone.

At the end of January 1943, the troops on the left flank of the "Black Sea Group" began to develop plan "Sea" and launch attacks against Novorossisk. The main attack was to take place against Verkhne Balanski and not toward Krymskaya, in accordance with the change in the plan. As soon as this area was reached, additional forces were to be landed in the Yuzhnaya - Osereika area, Novorossisk was to be taken, and they were to advance to the Taman Peninsula.

With the successful breakthrough attempt of the 56th Soviet Army against the XXXXIV Jäger Corps in the Abinskaya - Krymskaya area, the 47th Soviet Army was to pressure the positions of the 9th and 73rd ID northwest of Novorossisk at the end of January/beginning of February. However, the breakthrough in the direction of Verkhne Bakanskaya also did not succeed.

Although the northern pincer from Novorossisk, which was to penetrate up to the Volchi-Vorota Pass, did not pan out, Stalin still initiated his plan.

The Soviet landing operation was to be prepared immediately. Air reconnaissance created a picture of the German defenses for the leadership. Everything was planned in the smallest detail. Would they achieve surprise?

During the night of 31 January 1943 the Soviet cruiser "Voroshilov" and three destroyers fired on the German positions in the Novorossisk area. Was this a deception maneuver? Then the Soviets' radios became silent.

There was wild speculation at the German headquarters! Generaloberst Ruoff, commander of the 17th Army, did not believe there would be a landing on the frontal region and issued "Alert Level I" for the Crimea and the coast of Anapa up to Taman. He anticipated a cutting off of his army in the Kerch Strait. On 3 February 1943 at 2000 hours Major Dr. Lahmeyer, the commander of the 789th Heeres Coastal Artillery Battalion which was stationed around the Bay of Osereika, telephoned the 17th Army command in Slavyanskaya. He expressed his suspicions concerning an upcoming landing in the Bay of Osereika, which were based on an increase in enemy air and naval reconnaissance. However, what was the commander to do about it? The army command, which received many such reports, still believed, as before, in a strike against the Kerch Strait.

The commander of the 73rd ID, General von Bünau, and his artillery commander, Oberst Peslmüller, who were responsible for Novorossisk, leaned in support of the theory that the Soviets would land in the frontal region. An exercise, which lasted several days, pointed out the weakness of the defense. Moreover, guns were still being emplaced in the coastal defenses.

And the wild speculation continued!

During the night of 4 February 1943, the Soviet destroyer "Boikiy" and four sub-chasers fired on the harbor of Anapa. Four torpedo cutter cruisers were conspicuous in the Cape Zhelesny Rog area. Were they paving the way for a landing there? The German coastal batteries, which were at Alert Level I, watched.

In Glebovka, 5 kilometers north of the Bay of Osereika, Lahmeyer's staff was awakened at exactly midnight by bombs. What was going on? Bombs were falling on Osereika, Vassilevka, Borisovka and Medfodievka. At the same time, positions in the Bay of Osereika were being shelled by naval artillery. Major Lahmeyer had no further doubts. The Russians would land in the Bay of Osereika! With a breadth of two kilometers and a length of 10 kilometers, the Bay of Osereika was an ideal landing zone.

Major Lahmeyer telephoned the batteries of his battalion. The battery chief, Oberleutnant Holschermann, reported "everything is in order with the 3/789 Heeresküsten Art.Abt.!" and the forward observer, Leutnant Kreipe, reported: "Heavy naval artillery fire from the sea. Because of the darkness I can only see the muzzle flashes!" The 3rd Battery was located within the Glebovka Hills and had a good field of fire; its two 10.5 cm howitzers under Oberwachtmeister Wagner were established as reinforcement for the coastal troops.

The 2nd battery stood on a hill near Glebovka and had a good field of fire in the bay, including the Osereika Trench and the roads leading there. The battery commander, Oberleutnant Mönnich, reported: "Everything in order at 2nd Battery. No losses from bombs or naval artillery!"

The 1st Battery was located on Lake Abrau, also in an excellent firing position. The battery commander, Oberleutnant Kerler, reported: "Everything in order!"

Lahmeyer called the Romanian Captain Nicolai, who was located with the 5th Company of the 38th Romanian Infantry Regiment on the shore in front of the coastal artillery. Nicolai reported: "Several strong points have not reported. The fire of the naval artillery shredded the wire obstacles on the shore and hit the positions!"

Major Lahmeyer telephoned General von Bünau. They agreed that a landing would occur in the Bay of Osereika. The corps (informed by von Bünau) still held the opinion of the 17th Army: "If there were a landing, it would take place near Anapa or on the Kerch Strait."

The Russian ferry plan in the Bay of Osereika foresaw:

1. Effective fire by the covering group under Vice Admiral Vladimirskiy with the cruisers "Krasniy Kavkaz", "Krasniy Krym", the flotilla leader "Kharkov" and the destroyers "Besposadniy" and "Soobrazitelniy" on 4 February 1943 from 0100 to 0200 hours. In this manner the wire obstacles were to be destroyed and the acquired infantry and gun positions would be engaged.

2. At 0200 hours the first wave of marine and armored forces (1500 men) would land and establish a beachhead.

3. The main force would land before the beginning of daylight with heavy weapons and additional tanks. The covering group would steam away in order to escape out of the range of the German coastal batteries before dawn.

After the effective fire on the Bay of Osereika, the Soviets believed that the German and Romanian defenses were battered. However, except for several light Romanian batteries, they did not register any hits. All of the cannon batteries of the 789th Artillery Battalion were still intact. The battery commanders and forward observers searched the surface of the bay with night glasses. As instructed, all of the guns remained silent. Surprise was the key to the success of the German defense.

At 0200 hours the wall of fire lurched toward the land. The night was pitch black. Light signals were passed between the heavy units of the covering group. The first wave advanced: 2 destroyers, 3 artillery boats, 5 minesweepers and the 1st Cutter Division. Two large ferries approached the coast with American made tanks, types "Stuart", "Lee" and "Grant". The tension was noticeable in the landing craft of the first wave. And there was still no defense! Were the German and Romanian coastal positions destroyed by the naval artillery?

The German coastal batteries no longer had communications with the battalion; the lines were severed by the firing. However, the battery commanders knew what to do. And Captain Nicolai's Romanians who had survived the inferno, crawled out of the covered trenches and made ready their weapons. Like a ghostly finger, a search light suddenly shined on the water. There were the dark shadows of the landing flotilla. Then the silent German guns let loose!

Leutnant Kreipe continued to shine the search light from the 3rd Battery. Each time that he turned it on, Oberwachtmeister Wagner's four guns and the two 10.5 cm howitzers tossed their shells onto the landing flotilla. There were explosions. There were hits. The artillerymen worked feverishly.

In spite of this, the landing boats of the first wave continued on, and the marine infantry waded onto the land. Oberwachtmeister Wagner placed the shore under fire with his guns.

The first elements of the 83rd and 255th Marine Brigades, as well as the 165th Rifle Brigade, landed and were placed under fire by the Romanians. An armored landing ferry received a direct hit and sunk; the second one unloaded its tanks too soon. Water flowed into the exhausts, the engines sputtered. They stopped! Only a few reached the shore and joined in the battle. Other landing craft turned back. Some were forced aside and landed on the small rocky coast and were battered by the defenders there. Two cutters from the 1st Division, which were in the first wave, ran onto mines and sank.

In the meantime, the combat in the bay dissolved into numerous individual battles. Oberwachtmeister Wagner's guns and a Romanian battery were lost. Major Lahmeyer's guns maintained fire at an undiminished rate.

The Soviet communications officer in the Bay of Osereika believed that it was then time to request the main body of the landing flotilla: "Have beachhead, need reinforcements!"

The commander of the landing formation, Vice Admiral Basistiy, observed from his flag ship and waited for this signal. But it was almost an hour before the main landing fleet arrived, and then it was already daylight!

At 0415 hours, exactly as planned, Vice Admiral Vladimirskiy steamed out into the open sea with the heavy elements of his covering group. When it became light the effectiveness of the German fire increased and threw the landing fleet into confusion. Several transports were hit and sunk. At the decisive moment, the fire support of the cruisers "Krasniy Kavkaz" and "Krasniy Krym", the large destroyers and the flotilla leader "Kharkov" and the destroyers "Besposadniy" and "Soobrazitelniy", with their modern, large caliber tubes, was missing.

In addition, the Russian book: "The Battle of the Caucasus" noted:

"... However, the landing ships did not arrive on time. In the meantime dawn arrived and the German artillery fire increased so that the ships in the main landing force had to turn around without fulfilling their mission. Thus, the moment of surprise was lost."

On the German side, there was no question of being surprised. The book hid the reason for the failure; it became known later. The landing operation was preceded by a quarrel between the Army and Navy leadership. The Army leadership saw their best chance as being during the cover of night. The Navy leadership in the early morning, so that they could see somewhat. Therefore, the main landing flotilla arrived too late (apparently delayed by the Navy) and had to turn about.

In the meantime, the 1st landing wave fought its way toward the land. Soviet assault troops fought like the devil. On the morning of 4 February three American tanks stood in front of Glebovka and attacked a Romanian mortar position. The Soviets were thrown back in a counterattack. During

THE NOVOROSSISK LANDINGS
4.2. 1943

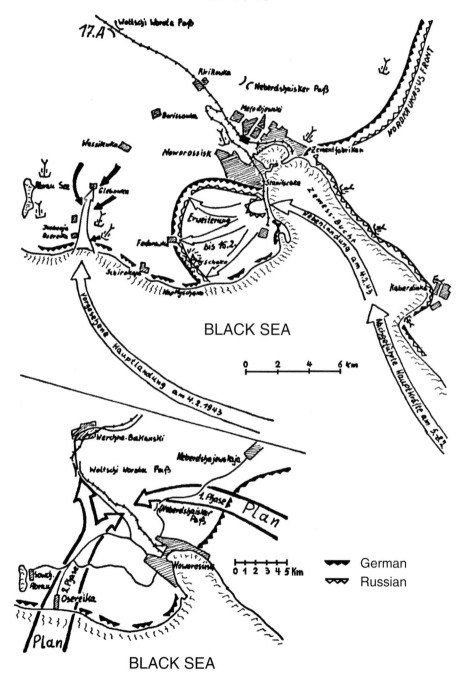

BLACK SEA

0 2 4 6 km

BLACK SEA

0 1 2 3 4 5 Km

German
Russian

334

the evening guns from the 164th Reserve Anti-aircraft Battalion and panzerjägers from the 173rd Battalion (73rd ID), under Hauptmann Gutschera, destroyed six enemy tanks which had broken through. Therefore, the attack of the 1st wave was over. In the meantime, the brave Russian marines realized that they were alone. They tried to penetrate the front individually and in groups. The 213th Grenadier Regiment, which was in positions northeast of Novorossisk, stopped several of these groups.

After the landing operation in the Bay of Osereika was discovered, the III/229 (101st Jäger Division), which was located in Krymskaya, was taken to the Novorossisk area in trucks and subordinated to the 73rd ID. The 13/229 under Leutnant Wieczorek advanced together with the Romanians on 5 February from Glebovka to the shore. They found only dead, wrecks of tanks and beached, shot-up landing craft. 620 killed and 31 shot-up US tanks were counted. There was an equipment graveyard in the shallow water. By 6 February 1943, 594 prisoners were rounded up. 1216 men were accounted for from the original 1500 from the 1st landing wave. The Black Sea was the graveyard for the rest and only a few were able to reach their own lines by land.

Simultaneous with the main landing operation in the Bay of Osereika, a smaller landing operation was being conducted by a detachment of Black Sea sailors in Stanichka, a suburb of Novorossisk. What the Soviets failed to do in the Osereika area they achieved here. Originally a deception maneuver intended to mislead the Germans, it later went down in military history as a brilliant example of a sea landing operation. The leader of this landing group was Major Kunikov, an engineer and and officer in the naval infantry.

At exactly midnight on 4 February 1943 Kunikov's Black Sea sailors were taken to Gelendshik in cutters from the 4th Coast Guard Flotilla, which was commanded by First Lieutenant Sipyadon. The small flotilla moved along the rocky coast under the cover of Russian coastal batteries to the hills of Cape Myshako. Then the Russian coastal batteries fired from the eastern side of the Bay of Zemess, laying down a good destructive fire on the target area. The coastal defense of the 10th Romanian ID collapsed. An anti-aircraft combat troop from the 164th Reserve Anti-aircraft Battalion, with two 8.8 cm guns, was located 300 meters above the harbor entrance. One of the guns perceived ship movement in the Bay of Zemess. However, because no alarm was given, it was thought to be a friendly craft. Then it was too late! The first landing group was already on the coast in the blind spot of the guns. One of the guns was destroyed by a direct hit, the second was blown up as the Russian assault troops approached. Kunikov's right cover group entered the houses in Stanichka.

The German command posts were in confusion. A landing operation near Osereika and another in the Bay of Zemess! The few reserves were committed to the most threatened positions. However, where was the Russian main effort? The 73rd ID was responsible for the defense of Novorossisk. The 186th Grenadier Regiment was located in the city with its headquarters, engineer and panzerjäger units, and the 16th and 18th Naval Harbor

Kommandanturas [local headquarters]. One of these was destined for the harbor of Tuapse.

No one in Novorossisk knew what was going on. The arriving counterattack reserves advanced to various positions and were repulsed. With the break of day the Soviet coastal batteries fired on all German movement from the eastern side of the Bay of Zemess. The Russian forward observers directed the fire onto the beachhead. The Russian batteries on the Bay of Zemess fired from dominant positions at 5 - 8 kilometer ranges, which allowed them to control all German movement.

In the meantime, the Soviets followed up their 250 man strong initial landing with a second of 600 men. They expanded the beachhead and made themselves at home in the mountainous terrain. Ignorance of the strength and mission of the Soviets made the Germans insecure. General von Bünau, as well as the corps and army, ordered a prepared attack after the first counterattack failed near Stanichka, but that would take time. And the Soviets made use of the time!

General Petrov, the commander of the Russian "Black Sea Group" who was responsible for the landing, recognized the chance the brave Kunikov detachment provided him after the failure of the landing in the Bay of Osereika. Petrov ordered the main landing group not to unload.

During the night of 5 February a regiment was committed in the Stanichka beachhead. During the second night followed the entire main landing group, which was originally assigned to the Osereika operation. On 7 February 1943 over 8000 men were on the beachhead. On 9 February there were 17,000.

And the Germans? Who could shoulder the blame for the Germans not being quick enough to take countermeasures when none of the German command posts realized the extent of the Soviet operation during the night of 4 February? And where would the necessary reserves have come from? At this point in time all of the corps were withdrawing to the Kuban bridgehead. The XXXXIV Jäger Corps was located south of Krasnodar in heavy combat and could not even give up one company. The XXXXIX Mountain Corps and the LII Army Corps had their hands full. Even the V Army Corps, which was still in positions, had to repulse heavy enemy attacks in the Neberdzhaevskaya area.

On 4 February there were only divisional reserves that could be committed in a counterattack. On 5 February the III/229 Jg.Rgt. (101st Jäger Division), which was located in Krymskaya, was transported to Novorossisk in trucks. On 7 and 8 February the 305th Grenadier Regiment (198th ID) followed.

On 8 February, when the German counterattack began, the Russian forces had an enormous superiority. The main German attack, which ran along the coast through Stanichka, and was to cut off the Russian forces in the Myshako mountain terrain from their rear area, did indeed recapture a good deal of Stanichka, but it accomplished little more. The heavy coastal batteries under the command of Lieutenant Colonel Matushenko shot up the German counterattack. Entire groups fell to the large caliber salvoes. A pair of attached assault guns from the 191st Battalion could not turn the tide. The recently reconstituted I/213, as well as Oberstleutnant de Temple's 305th Grenadier Regiment, were bloodied in costly house-to-house combat. On 7 February, the 305th Grenadier Regiment went to Novorossisk with 41 officers, 168 non-commissioned officers and 738 men. On 16 February its strength was 27/118/476. The II Battalion, which was committed in the northwest of the city, suffered the most; its combat strength was 2/5/49. On 20 February the remnants of this regiment were disbanded. The 305th Grenadier Regiment followed its infantry division to the Zaporozhe area by air.

Major Kunikov was the man of the first few hours. A political officer with the rank of a Colonel, Leonid Brezhnev, was born a laborer's son in 1906. He fired up the troops and was the leader of the political front which had been very powerful since the October Revolution. Brezhnev alternated between the mainland and the beachhead. He was constantly on the move making fiery speeches and handing out party books.

The battle for the beachhead was fought by both sides with ever increasing forces. By October Soviet forces had risen to 78,000 men. The Myshako bridgehead was not expanded with the great success initially hoped for so that it would result in the destruction of the 17th Army, but it did tie up considerable forces. The harbor of Novorossisk remained closed to both sides. Neither operational nor smaller German naval forces could use it as a base. They ran from the Anapa and Blagoveschenskaya harbors, from Taman and Kerch.

And how were the German naval forces doing?

The "Black Sea" Admiralty, Vizeadmiral Kiederitzky, was responsible for the entire Black Sea, including the Crimea and the protection of freight traffic between Sevastopol and Constanza. His forces were composed of a U-Boot-flotilla (250 ton boats), two motor-torpedo boat flotillas, two mine-sweeper flotillas, two freight flotillas, one artillery flotilla, two sub-chaser flotillas, as well as four landing flotillas. Harbor Kommandanturas were established in all harbors. The commitment of the naval forces in the Kerch Strait and on both sides of the Taman Peninsula was under the direction of the Caucasus Seekommandant. The tonnage ratio was: Soviets 300,000 BRT - Germans 100,000 BRT. The German units were collections of small craft. Motor-torpedo boats, mine-sweepers and the 30th U-Boot-Jagdflotilla formed the core. In addition, there were naval ferries, Danube steamers, barges and cutters. Therefore, the German naval force was primarily a defensive force. Fortunately, the Soviets also limited themselves (with a few exceptions) to defensive naval operations.

During the establishment of the beachhead, the 1st German Motor-Torpedo Flotilla under Kptlt. Christiansen was again committed against Russian shipping in the Bay of Zemess. The small boats often attacked enemy shipping at night and sowed the access routes with mines. By the end of February the 1st Motor-Torpedo Boat Flotilla sank the mine-sweeper T-403/Gruz and the artillery boat "Krasnaya Gruziya". A transport cutter, presumably with Leonid Brezhnev on board, was sunk by a German mine. Sailors rescued the unconscious Brezhnev.

Kptlt. Rosenbaum's 30th U-Boot-flotilla was committed against the troop transports along the Caucasus coast. The flotilla had available the following 250 ton boats; U-9, 18, 19, 20, 23 and 24, of which 2-3 were always at the wharf in the harbor of Constanza, while the remaining were committed. These small U-Boote were partially disassembled and transported by train to the Black Sea and later reassembled.

From 10 to 25 February 1943 U-Boote U-9, 19 and 24 were located in the Gelendzhik and Tuapse area. At that time the Soviet destroyers "Zeleznyakov", "Nezamozhnik", "Besposadniy" and "Soobrazitelniy" transported 8037 troops from Tuapse to Gelendzhik, in addition to other troop transports. In spite of tight convoy security U-19 (Oberleutnant zur See Gaude) sank the transport "Krasniy Profintern" (4648 BRT) on 14 February.

During the night of 22 February the flotilla leader "Kharkov" and the destroyer "Soobrazitelniy" fired on German positions in front of the Myshako beachhead.

In the meantime the supply of the 17th Army in the bridgehead by sea was in full swing. Besides the Kerch convoys, there were Convoys "Kleiner Bär" 1-99 from Feodosia to Anapa, with 2-3, later 5-6, naval ferries from the 3rd Landing Flotilla under Fregattenkapitän Strempel and, in April, elements of the 5th Landing Flotilla of Korvettenkapitän Mehler. The convoys were repeatedly attacked by Soviet submarines, but the torpedoes skimmed under the flat ferries. During an air attack against Convoy 89 (19 May) ferries 309 and 367 were sunk. An air attack sunk ferry 332 in Convoy 99 (30 May).

German U-Boote operated against Soviet supply traffic on the Caucasus coast. U-19 (Olt. z.S. Gaude) damaged a freighter and U-24 (Kptlt. Petersen) sank the tanker "Sovietskaya Neft" (8228 BRT) in the Bay of Gagry on 31 March.

During an attack of the 1st Motor-Torpedo Boat Flotilla on Tuapse and in front of the Myshako beachhead, S 26 and S 47 torpedoed a medium tanker, which was being towed to Tuapse. During the night of 31 March motor-torpedo boats S 72, 28, 47 and 102 laid a mine obstacle in front of the Myshako beachhead.

On 30 March 1943 the 4th Mountain Division was freed-up in the course of the withdrawal to the Kuban bridgehead. The division, along with the 125th and 73rd ID, and the 6th Romanian Cavalry Division, was committed against the Myshako beachhead. The elimination of the Soviet beachhead was complicated by the terrain conditions. Myshako, which was occupied by the Soviets, was to be captured by the 4th Mountain Division.

The plan foresaw the 13th Gebirgsjäger Regiment advancing elements from the west and attacking the right flank along the coast. At the same time the 91st Gebirgsjäger Regiment would be attacking frontally.

On 6 and 10 April the attack had to be postponed because of fog and rain.

On 17 April the operation was initiated under the cover name "Neptun". Clouds and fog limited the visibility of the stuka pilots. In order not to endanger their own troops, they dropped their bombs deep in the Russian interior. Numerous stuka attacks and several attacks by He 111s, as well as attacks by heavy batteries on the Bay of Zemess, did not shake the Soviets.

Assault troops of the 91st Gebirgsjäger Regiment attacked the mountain peak. The tenacious defenders struck back at the gebirgsjägers. Stuka attacks threatened their own troops. Flame-throwers spit fire. Hand-grenades thrown up the hill rolled back down against the attackers. Defensive fire came from every nook and cranny. Where were the Russians? German losses mounted and caused confusion. Generalmajor Kress ordered the attack broken off against the will of the V Army Corps.

A day later the 125th ID attacked the western portion of the beachhead, but this attack also stalled.

On 25 April the attack on the Myshako beachhead was suspended. Both sides suffered heavy casualties. Brezhnev's political work bore fruit. The men of the first few hours, Major Kunikov and Lieutenant Romanov, who landed with the first assault group, had been killed.

During Operation "Neptun" the 1st Motor-Torpedo Boat Flotilla, the 3rd Mine-sweeper Flotilla and the Italian IV Motor-Torpedo Boat Flotilla conducted night attacks against Soviet supply traffic. S 47, 51, 102, 72 and 28 sunk several small Soviet craft with torpedoes and destroyed several landing bridges. Operations were continued even after the completion of Operation "Neptun". Some heavy engagements occurred with Soviet escorts and torpedo cutters. Attacks of Soviet torpedo cutters against the harbor at Anapa had little effect. On 5 May U-9 (Olt. z.S. Schmidt-Weichert) torpedoed the Soviet tanker "Kreml" (7666 BRT).

Soviet attacks on the German Anapa - Feodosia convoys increased. During the night of 13 May the torpedo cutters TKA-115 and 125 fired on the Anapa harbor. During the following night the flotilla leader "Kharkov" and the destroyer "Boikiy" fired their guns into the Anapa harbor and, during the night of 21 May, the "Kharkov" fired on the Feodosia harbor while the destroyer "Besposadniy" fired on Aluzhta. Soviet aircraft increased the number of British mines in the Kerch Strait. During an attack against a Soviet supply convoy on 20 May, S72 and S 49 torpedoed two small craft in front of the Caucasus coast. U-9 and U-18 attacked shipping targets near Sukhum and Poti against strong defenses, without success. On 22 May Ju 87s flew several attacks on Soviet convoys in front of Gelendzhik, during which the cutter SKA-041 was sunk and the transport "International" was damaged.

During the night of 21 August, Soviet escorts "Skval" and "Storm" and four SKA cutters fired rockets onto the Anapa airfield.

In the meantime, a bitter positional war was taking place on the Myshako front. The 12 kilometer long front was continuously reinforced by both sides. The enemy was able to harass the German positions and interior from Myshako. On 24 and 28 July a well prepared attack by the 94th Gebirgsjäger Battalion (formerly a feldersatz battalion) failed to recapture the mountains and suffered heavy casualties.

After the withdrawal of the 125th ID, the Romanian 6th Cavalry Division under Colonel Teodorini, which was committed on the right flank in the Osereika coastal sector, was subordinated to the 4th Mountain Division.

On 11 August the commander of the 4th Mountain Division, Generalmajor Kress, died from a head wound during a frontal inspection. The division was taken over by Generalleutnant Braun.

BATTLE FOR KRYMSKAYA

Krymskaya, bulwark of the "Grossen Gotenkopfe" - The 56th Soviet Army breakthrough - The 97th Jäger Division holds - Marshal Zhukov's May Day gift to Generalissimo Stalin - Major Palaghita, the shepherd

Slavyanskaya was held by the northern flank of the 17th Army until 23 March 1943. The northern flank was withdrawn into the Kuban bridgehead in phases. The new course of the front ran from north to south: Kurka - Kuban rail sector point 17 (4 kilometers south of Troitskaya) - the Agudan and Vtoraya Rivers - west of Sheptalski - Novorossisk.

At this time the Soviets also did some rearranging. The "Black Sea Group" was disbanded and several formations were placed in reserve. The command was taken over by the "North Caucasus Group".

By this time the German crisis at Kharkov was developing. The Germans felt that they would be able to provide air support again to the Kuban bridgehead, in fact even increase it, so they could again attack out of the Kuban bridgehead into the Caucasus after Operation "Zitadelle" (the elimination of the Kursk salient) succeeded.

The new HKL proved to be very favorable, terrain-wise. In the north there were impassable reed moors on the edge of the Sea of Azov; to the south was the river sector, which was marshy. The southern front ran through the forested mountains and also offered good defensive possibilities. Only the middle sector on both sides of Krymskaya offered any large-scale attack possibilities, but a particularly strong and deeply echeloned German defensive system was constructed there.

The forward-most line near Krymskaya ran to the north along the Troitskaya - Krymskaya railroad embankment and through the hills running 3 kilometers east and southeast of Krymskaya. In the Neberdkhaevskaya area this line ran into the old front that was held in 1942.

At the end of March the staff of the North Caucasus Front worked out the attack plan against the core of the German bridgehead defense. Accordingly, the 56th Army was to break through on either side of the Krasnodar - Krymskaya rail line. The northern attack group had to capture the dominant Hill 30.7, 3 kilometers north of Krymskaya, and the 37th Army was to attack from the salient near rail sector point 17 and advance to the west with the 56th Army.

The tried and true 97th Jäger Division was located east of Krymskaya. Generalleutnant Rupp, the experienced divisional commander, knew that his division would soon stand at the focal point of the combat. However, he also knew that he could count on his Bavarians and Schwabians.

The 97th Jäger Division had a 10 kilometer wide sector in front of Krymskaya. On the left was Battlegroup Otte, in the center Battlegroup Höhne and on the right the Romanian Battlegroup Mosteoru, each with two battalions in the front line and one in reserve.

On 2 April the Soviets tested the new front with reconnaissance elements. By 3 April the Soviet 56th Army had assembled six divisions, several tank formations and 30 batteries for the attack. On this day elements of the 2nd Guards Rifle Division attacked Battlegroup Otte in the north in order to obtain more favorable departure positions for the main attack. The attack hit the seam between the II/207 Jg.Rgt. and the I/94 Rom.IR south of the Agudan bridge. A penetration was eliminated immediately by elements of the 94th Infantry Regiment under the command of Major Palaghita. Additional local attacks, which continued into the night, were repulsed.

On 4 April 1942 at 0800 hours the heavy mortars and artillery launched a fire-strike along the entire 97th Jäger Division sector. The major Soviet attack had begun! While the northern Battlegroup Otte was tied up by continuous attacks, which were, however, all repulsed, the enemy assault battalions attacked Battlegroups Höhne and Mosteoru with their main effort along the railroad and road. The Soviets achieved several penetrations between the railroad and road up to the adjacent 9th ID with the 55th Guards Rifle Division and the 383rd and 61st Rifle Divisions. The Bavarian jägers and the Romanians fought tenaciously until midday, but they were slowly being pushed back. Losses were high.

It looked as if the Soviets were going to achieve their breakthrough, but Generalleutnant Rupp did not give up. His staff worked feverishly. The telephones were ringing, the radio was squawking. Reserves were advancing on the threatened positions.

In the afternoon the German counterattack was launched against the already 1.5 kilometer wide penetration. With the support of the assault gun battery of the 5th Luftwaffe Field Division, the III/204 Jg.Rgt. threw the Soviets back and reoccupied the old HKL with the withdrawn companies of the I and II/204.

In the central sector, the reserve III/207 Jg.Rgt. advanced out of the northern portion of Krymskaya to the southeast and hit the Soviets penetrating into this sector in the flank. By evening the old HKL was also recaptured there. The first day of the battle for Krymskaya was successfully weathered by the 97th Jäger Division. The I and II/204 Jg.Rgt. had taken a high toll in casualties. Both battalions had to be relieved by the III/204 and the III/207. Therefore, the division had few reserves left.

The XXXXIV Jäger Corps and the 17th Army command both recognized the threat in the 97th Jäger Division sector. The army assembled Battlegroup Brux in the area southwest of Krymskaya from its reserve. The battlegroup, under the leadership of Oberstleutnant Brux, consisted of the 66th Panzergrenadier Regiment, a company each of heavy infantry guns, panzerjägers, tanks and artillery from the 13th Panzer Division.

On 5 April they had counted on the attack continuing, but the Soviet attack didn't materialize. The Soviets were forced to refit their exhausted formations and reinforce their artillery. In addition the Russian Caucasus work noted:

"The 56th Army was to advance in two attack groups on the right and left of the railroad and catch Krymskaya in its pincers. The breakthrough area of the two groups was 10 kilometers wide, that of the entire 56th Army 30 kilometers. On 4 April our troops attacked, but achieved no success. The attack was suspended."

After a ten day preparation the new Soviet offensive began on the night of 14 April with a particularly heavy air bombardment on Krymskaya. At 0500 hours a one hour artillery barrage was initiated and inflicted considerable damage on the defenders. Then the Soviet divisions attacked, this time supported by tanks.

The German positions were penetrated in the center and southern sectors and on the extreme right division flank. Three threatening attack wedges, led by tanks, materialized. With a two kilometer wide and deep penetration, victory seemed to be at hand for the Soviets. Krymskaya was the key to the German front in the Kuban bridgehead. From there led several roads to the Taman Peninsula and several more to Novorossisk. Again the 97th Jäger Division, along with its Romanian formations, was standing in the path of the rising flood. If the dam broke, then the 17th Army was lost.

At midday the defenders had been thrown back almost to the southern edge of Krymskaya. Hill 68.8 was in Soviet hands. Besides the available reserves, the neighboring III/228 Jg.Rgt. (101st Jäger Division) was also pushed into Krymskaya. In the afternoon the Germans launched a counterattack. On the right flank the Romanian II/95 threw back the 61st Rifle Division. The attack of Battlegroup Brux on the southeastern edge of Krymskaya stalled at the Soviet occupied Hill 68.8. The II/207, which was counterattacking from the northwest, had to go over to the defense in the area of the railroad station after occupying the dairy. The intended closing of the frontal gap by the flanking attack of Battlegroup Brux and the II/207 did not succeed. Would the Soviets pursue and expand their initial success into a decisive breakthrough?

The Soviet attack formations from the 83rd Mountain Rifle Division and the 383rd Rifle Division were also exhausted and were no longer in a position to continue the attack. Until new reinforcements arrived, the German side would also remain inactive.

During the night of 15 April all available German reserves were thrown into the penetration area. Battlegroup Otte, which had ironed out a penetration in its sector on 14 April, gave up the II/207. Knowingly weakening his northern flank, Generalleutnant Rupp threw everything he had onto the scale. Battlegroup Malter was formed from the II/204 and the II/207 and attacked to reach the old HKL together with Battlegroup Brux on 15 April. At 0945 hours Battlegroup Malter began the attack in conjunction with Battle Group Brux. The floodgates were opened! Soviet and German aircraft buzzed over the battlefield. Artillery participated. The bitter combat lasted all day. The focal point was Hill 68.8, which was still held by the Soviets after a heavy stuka attack. German companies drove up to the section of forest in front of the hill. The hard fought over dairy was recaptured south of the rail line and held against a counterattack supported by tanks.

In the evening the Soviets, after deploying reserves, repeated the attack on Hill 68.8 and again pushed the German companies back. As before, the

BATTLE OF KRYMSKAJA
April 1943

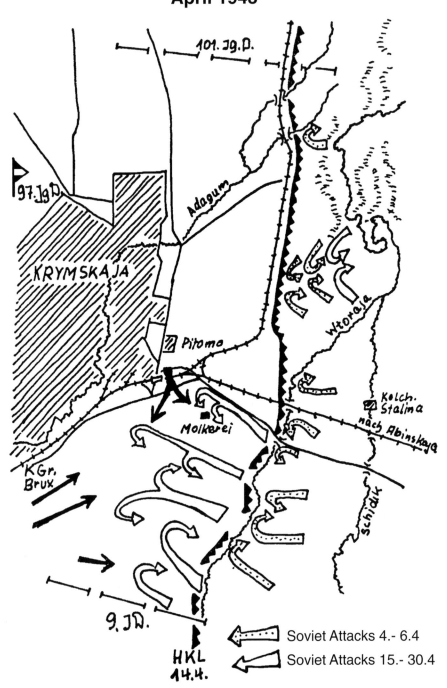

101. Jg.D.

97. Jg.D.

Adagum

KRYMSKAJA

Pitomo

Wtoraja

Molkerei

Kolch. Stalina

nach Abinskaja

K.Gr. Brux

Schidik

9. JD.

HKL
14.4.

Soviet Attacks 4.- 6.4

Soviet Attacks 15.- 30.4

344

threat of a Russian breakthrough was at hand. In view of the heavy casualties, Generalleutnant Rupp decided to suspend the counterattack and establish a new HKL further to the west. However, the corps and the army saw the prerequisite for holding the Kuban bridgehead as being the elimination of the Soviet penetration and deployed new reserves. During the night of 16 April, in addition to others, the II/13 Geb.Jg.Rgt. (4th Mountain Division) was transported by truck out of the Novorossisk area to Krymskaya.

In the morning hours of 16 April the Soviet infantry and tank forces again pushed Battlegroups Höhne and Malter from their occupied defensive positions. After the Soviet forces bogged down, the Germans launched their counterattack. The 3/249 Stu.Gesch.Brig. (tactical symbol was a wolf), which was subordinated to the V Army Corps during the battle for Novorossisk, lent momentum to the German counterattack. German stukas joined in the battle at midday. Hill 68.8 and the dairy were recaptured. Hand-to-hand combat ensued. There were attacks and counterattacks. By evening the old HKL was not regained, but the German front was again unified and the threat of a breakthrough was blocked. 38 Russian tanks were destroyed by ground troops, 10 by stukas.

On 17 April the anticipated Soviet attack did not materialize. On this day the German attack on the Myshako bridgehead began. The Soviets alleged that it was necessary to transfer their reserves and, in particular, all of the air sorties there.

On 17 April Generalleutnant Rupp thanked his troops in an order of the day: "In an indescribably difficult struggle the division, with the help of elements of a panzer division (13th), a Luftwaffe field division (5th) and a Romanian ID (19th), in cooperation with corps artillery and the Luftwaffe, which supported with strong artillery fire and numerous aircraft, frustrated the breakthrough attempt of five Russian divisions and two tank formations.

The leaders and troops have made superhuman efforts. The success was paid for with much sacrifice. However, it was decisive for the overall situation in the bridgehead."

The corps commander, as well as the commander of the 17th Army, praised the commitment of the 97th Jäger Division in a similar manner and a Wehrmacht report from 18 April added: "...The main effort of the defensive combat was borne by a Süddeutsche jäger division, which had been heavily tested for some time. However, thanks to its leadership and its combat spirit, it still knew how to master a serious situation..."

The following days remained quiet, but there was no doubt that the Soviets had not given up their intent to attack near Krymskaya. According to the statements of prisoners and defectors, Marshal Zhukov had taken command of the North Caucasus Front. By mobilizing all forces, Krymskaya was to be taken by 1 May. With the change in leadership new reserves became available; Zhukov's name carried weight in the STAVKA. His name would appear wherever great results were needed.

Soviet Air Force sorties increased both day and night. On 27 April the Soviets conducted smaller attacks at seven locations, which had to be considered reconnaissance forays. Zhukov was testing the front for a weak position. In the evening hours of 28 April artillery activity was heavy and air attacks were constant.

On the morning of 29 April a preparatory barrage was conducted with its main effort on the northern flank of the 97th Jäger Division. The following infantry attack was repulsed by the Bavarian jägers and the Romanians. Only a forward position in the Pyatiletka Sovkhoz, east of the railroad embankment, had to be given up. Sixty T-34s supported the attack. During the evening the German HKL was essentially still being held. During the night of 30 April Soviet aircraft bombarded Krymskaya with 3500 bombs and air mines in order to prevent the deployment of German reserves.

On the northern flank of the 97th Jäger Division lay Hill 30.1, dominating the field for some distance. On this hill, which was occupied by Battle Group Otte, the right attack flank of the Soviet 56th Army continuously failed. It was not possible to detour around this barrier. After careful preparation Lieutenant Masliev attacked the hill with a company from Major Shulga's regiment during the night of 30 April. Lieutenant Masliev and his Red Army soldiers crawled under the cover of darkness to the hill. In spite of all their caution, they were discovered. German machine-guns and mortars opened up. Masliev had issued strict orders not to open fire until a green light signal was flashed. Surprise was no longer possible. In spite of that the Soviets continued to crawl forward. When Lieutenant Masliev approached to within 150 meters of the German hill positions, he flashed the green light signal. The Soviet artillery fired on the German positions with a 10 minute fire-strike. Then the wall of fire moved back in order to prevent reserves from advancing. At this moment Lieutenant Masliev advanced with his men against the German hill positions.

This operation cannot be reconstructed from the German and Soviet war literature, even though both sides reference it. The Russians speak of destroying an infantry battalion along with 26 machine-guns, nine mortars, two light infantry guns and many hand weapons. The history of the 97th Jäger Division notes the defense against a heavy night attack on Battlegroup Otte.

On 30 April heavy combat again raged on the northern flank of the 97th Jäger Division, but all enemy attacks collapsed. Zhukov ordered the shifting of the main effort to the south. The Soviet formations were regrouped accordingly.

On 1 May at 0530 hours the enemy initiated a heavy artillery attack on the sector south of the Krasnodar - Krymskaya rail line. Then the Soviets crashed against the German positions in several waves. Penetrations in the Battlegroups Malter and Mosteoru areas were immediately eliminated by counterattack. On the evening of 1 May the German HKL was being held at all positions.

While heavy combat took place on the southern flank, two Soviet battalions penetrated through the weak front on the northern flank of the 97th Jäger Division up to Kesslerovo. The headquarters of the 97th Jäger Division was located in Kesslerovo, as well as great stores of weapons, ammunition and rations. Hauptmann Randelshofer from the divisional staff quickly organized the defense with members of the divisional staff, drivers and rear services personnel. In cooperation with a group consisting of elements of the 19th Romanian ID under Oberst Weber, the Soviets were thrown back.

The 97th Jäger Division had held out again for three days. On 1 May Krymskaya was not presented to Stalin. Therefore, Zhukov pursued his objective with extra tenacity.

In fierce combat the 97th Jäger Division under Generalleutnant Rupp held successfully east of Krymskaya from 25 March to 3 May 1943 and, therefore, played an important role in stabilizing the Kuban bridgehead. Under the common title of the "Battle for Krymskaya" were entered the names of the dairy, Hill 68.8, Alevra and Kotlyarevskiy. The 97th Jäger Division was sacrificed on a decisive position for the existence of the 17th Army; fighting to the end with exhausted battalions, which no longer had the combat strength of companies. One must take into consideration that the exceptional Army commander Marshal Zhukov had taken over the North Caucasus Front and could not achieve success with the troop reinforcements he obtained on the basis of his reputation. If one does, it puts the defensive success of the 97th Jäger Division in a whole new light.

On 3 May Zhukov ordered an attack south of Krymskaya. The main effort lay in the 9th ID area of operations and against elements of the 19th Romanian ID, which was located on the southern flank of the 97th Jäger Division. By evening the Soviet attack formations, led by 20 tanks, reached the Krymskaya - Neberdzhaevskaya road. It appeared that Krymskaya would be outflanked to the south.

During the night of 4 May Krymskaya was evacuated and the so-called D Line was given up. The D Line was practically an advance position of the "Grossen Gotenkopf", which was also called the "Blue Line"; "Blue Line" because of Hitler's use of a blue pencil on the large situation map when he established the course of the Kuban bridgehead.

The first days in the newly occupied "Grossen Gotenkopf" were relatively quiet. The Soviets had to regroup. On 6 May they tested the German positions. The "Blue Line" boasted a deeply echeloned, well constructed defensive system.

On 9 May the commander of the Romanian I/94 was killed during a counterattack. This battalion had displayed particular steadfastness under Major Palaghita. Generalleutnant Rupp dedicated the following obituary to the Romanian, whom his men affectionately referred to as Ciobanul (Shepherd):

"On 9 May 1943 the commander of the Romanian I/94 IR, Major Palaghita, met his soldier's death during a counterattack while he was leading his battalion. Since February 1943 he and his battalion had fought as a formation of the 97th Jäger Division. He had distinguished himself in combat near Abinskaya and Krymskaya as a leader and a soldier. On 10 April he was awarded the Knight's Cross because he had played a decisive role in eliminating an enemy penetration. He was a model leader and fighter for his own and our troops and a good comrade to us all..."

On 12 May the 97th Jäger Division had to take over a portion of the 9th Infantry Division's positions; this was adjacent to the south.

LAGOON COMBAT

Corduroy roads connect the strongpoints - Kampfgruppe Nagel beats the Soviets back across the Jäger Canal - Major Ivanov - Operation "Moorbad"

With the occupation of the Kuban bridgehead, the 50th ID was committed on the northern flank of the 17th Army. The men on the left flank did not look upon the Sea of Azov, but upon an endless forest of reeds instead. This reed moor loomed only a few centimeters above the sea. Because the moor region was difficult tank terrain the last eight kilometers to the Sea of Azov was defended in a series of strongpoints. The solid front of the 50th ID ran along the Kurka, a tributary of the Kuban, but this terrain was open and reasonable. South of the Kurchanskaya stretched a long chain of hills on which the 50th ID artillery was emplaced.

The construction of the positions was difficult. The wood had to be obtained from the Novorossisk mountains. Corduroy roads were laid to connect the individual strong points and shelters and combat bunkers were constructed in the higher positions, which had a good view of the terrain.

In May the lagoon region lost its winter colors. The ground dried up and made the land bridges between the marshes passable. Daily German reconnaissance elements advanced to the "Great Sea" and discovered that the Russians were also reconnoitering this region and establishing observation posts. On 5 May German Luftwaffe formations flew over the lagoon region and set the dried out reed forests on fire in order to deprive the enemy of cover. On this day Unteroffiziers Ippisch and Krüger, as well as Grenadier Rieger, captured an entire Russian company in front of the positions on the Kurka.

On the afternoon of 6 May Strongpoint 9 on the northern bank of the Kurchanskiy - Liman was suddenly attacked. The weak defenders gave it up and fought their way back to Strongpoint 10, a distance of 4 kilometers. The Soviets followed and attacked that strongpoint too. When reinforcements arrived, the Soviets withdrew. During the night, the III/121 (corps reserve) was brought up to Strongpoint 9 in order to recapture the lost strongpoint on the following morning. Attacking on a small, trafficable strip between the marsh and the sea was a problem. Attempts to outflank it bogged down in the marsh. Artillery forward observers were set up in boats across the Liman, but observation was limited. The punishing battle lasted all day. On the evening of 7 May 104 Russians surrendered along with Strongpoint 9.

In order to strengthen the northern flank, Battlegroup Brücker was formed from the 667th Grenadier Regiment, elements of the 122nd Grenadier Regiment, the 150th Reconnaissance Battalion and the 146th Construction Battalion. Oberst Brücker was named "Commander of the Northern Flank". This formation tightened the network of strongpoints. Reconnaissance elements monitored the marshes daily.

On 11 May a battle group under Oberleutnant Nagel was committed against a new Russian strongpoint established north of Strong- point 9. Artillery covered the enemy strongpoint with fire. When Battlegroup Nagel reached the Russian strongpoint all that was left were dead bodies and weapons. With difficulty, Battle- group Nagel tracked the enemy; it covered 500 meters in four hours. The Soviets were located south of the Jäger Canal. Because of fierce resistance and coming nightfall Battle Group Nagel suspended the battle and established a hasty defense. An enemy night attack was repulsed. In the early morning of 12 May Battlegroup Nagel threw the Soviets back across the Jäger Canal. 110 Russian dead were counted and 11 prisoners were taken. Battlegroup Nagel lost 10 killed, 24 wounded and 4 missing. At midday Battlegroup Nagel returned to Strong Point 9.

At the end of May "Operation Moorbad" was conducted with the following objective: Comb and clear the moors west of the duck ponds, in which elements of the 43rd Rifle Brigade infiltrated. The battle lasted all day in the marshes and moors. Several Soviet infantry positions were wiped out in a battle in which the legendary Major Ivanov, who led the Soviet action, was killed. The dead covered the moor.

On 26 June 1943, the beloved commander of the 50th ID, Generalleutnant Schmidt, was killed on his way to the III/121. His vehicle ran over a mine placed by Russian harassing troops. The commander and driver died immediately. On 3 July the 50th ID was taken over by Generalleutnant Sixt.

On 29 September, elements of the 667th Grenadier Regiment returned to the 370th ID with Oberst Brücker. The new commander of the "Northern Flank" was Oberst Grothe with the staff of the 122nd Grenadier Regiment and the III/122. As the lagoon region continued to dry up, Oberst Brücker and his battlegroup were again inserted between the 50th ID and the Sea of Azov.

COMBAT NEAR KIEVSKOE AND MOLDAVANSKOE

The 101st Jäger Division in the Gorishchiy inferno - Bataillon z.b.V. 500 is bloodied - Oberst Aulock and his young grenadiers - Leutnant Lumpp defends Borissovka with the I/226 Gren.Rgt.

As before, the land bridge west of Krymskaya offered the only possibility of a Soviet breakthrough to the Taman Peninsula. After the failure of the major Soviet attacks near Krymskaya, the Soviets wanted to try again further to the north. The North Caucasus Front worked out a new plan, according to which the 56th and 9th Armies were to force a breakthrough into the Kievskoe - Moldavanskoe sector. After the successful breakthrough the Soviet forces were to attack out of the Myshako bridgehead in the direction of Verkhne Bakanskaya and unhinge the defense of Novorossisk.

The German leadership was unaware of the Russian attack plan, but their enemy situation assessment came close. On 25 May 1943 the XXXXIV Jäger Corps assessed the situation as follows: "The enemy is preparing a new major attack against the `Grossen Gotenkopf'. He must first refit and regroup his exhausted formations. The time of the attack cannot be determined.

The objective of the operation still cannot be determined. Apparently he is striving to recapture Novorossisk. In addition, he will commit a strong group out of the area south of Krymskaya to open the mountain routes near Neberdzhaevskaya and Verkhne Adagum in order to then advance from the north into the Novorossisk area. It is possible that this attack will be supported by another attack out of the beachhead.

For the conduct of this operation, the occupation of the hills north of Nizhnaya Bakanskaya, around Gorno Vessely and east of Moldavanskoe is of decisive importance. Either as a prerequisite to the attack, or at the least at the very beginning of the operation, one must consider an attack of a second strong group against these hills. Moreover, the terrain favors the massive commitment of tanks.

There are no indications of a major attack on the Adugat and north of the Kuban, but if the enemy tried to come out of the lagoon region, the German forces would be split and the deep northern flank of the corps would be in danger. The focal point here would be Prikubanskiy. Landing operations against the northern and southern coast of the Taman Peninsula can only be considered as peripheral operations at this time."

The assessment of the 101st Jäger Division differed from that of the corps in that it did not fear the main strike coming south of Krymskaya, but to the north, in the Kievskoe area, to capture the only good east-west road, the Krymskaya - Taman Peninsula road.

In the meantime the front on the northern flank of the XXXXIV Jäger Corps was reinforced by the insertion of the newly arrived 79th ID. The original 79th ID was destroyed in Stalingrad; the new division was led by

Generalmajor Kreipe and had occupied the Adagum - Plavnenskiy sector. The young division was to become acclimatized in this sector.

There were changes in the leadership of the 17th Army; General der Pioniere Jänecke took command of the 17th Army from Generaloberst Ruoff. The Soviets also made some leadership changes; Marshal Zhukov went on to another command, the new commander of the North Caucasus Front was Colonel General I.W. Petrov.

The beginning of the new Soviet offensive was not placed well by the German situation assessments. On 25 May 1943 they still held: "...the time still cannot be determined...". A day later, the major Soviet attack was initiated.

The Soviet Savyalov/Kalyadin Caucasus work described the first day of the attack: "On 26 May 1943, a 100 minute-long artillery barrage fire and air bombardment opened the offensive to break through the `Blue Line'. After a six hour battle, our troops had captured several enemy strong points. The breakthrough was not achieved. A counterattack stopped our attack. At 1800 hours the battle was at its fiercest. In the sector of a guards unit four machine-gun bunkers were overcome, but the fifth held out. Then Sergeant Murtassov crawled up to the bunker and threw two hand-grenades into it, eliminating the defenders. Then he grabbed a German machine-gun and placed enemy infantry, who were coming to the aid of the bunker defenders, under fire. Sergeant Murtassov was awarded the Order of the Red Banner."

How did it look from the German side? On 26 May the major Soviet strike began in the Plavnenskiy - Hill 121.4 - Gorishchniy sector against the German HKL on both sides of the Varenikovskaya road. At 0500 hours after a murderous barrage fire from all calibers, supported by air attacks, the enemy forces, reinforced by tanks, attacked. At first they succeeded in throwing back Battlegroup Busche of the 101st Jäger Division, which was located between Hill 121.4 and Gorishchniy, and battering them. At almost the same time Battlegroup Schury, which was adjacent on the south, was hit and thrown back near Tambulovskiy and Hill 61. At 0600 hours Hill 121.4 and Gorishchniy were in Soviet hands. From out of this penetration rolled two T-34s with accompanying infantry against Hill 95 and, at the same time, approximately 30 to 40 tanks with accompanying infantry advanced out of Gorishchniy North in the direction of the rollbahn. The German artillery and anti-tank guns were blinded by the smoke grenades fired during the preceding fire-strike. At 0800 hours Oberst Busche was wounded; he died two days later in the hospital. Battlegroup Schury assembled and constructed a new defense in the area east of Gogolya - Podgorniy. Oberstleutnant Schury had to gather the many stragglers there. His II/229 was completely battered; the battalion commander, Oberleutnant Kiess, was taken prisoner; the commander of the 8/229 shot himself before being captured. Schury was able to recapture Hill 95 with his hastily thrown together group.

Battlegroup Busche, which was fighting in the north, faced difficult combat throughout. After reserves were committed, the penetration near Noviy was blocked.

There were similar developments north of the road to Kievskoe. There stood the 226th Grenadier Regiment of the 79th ID, which was led by Oberst Aulock. The main effort there was the village of Plavnenskiy and Hill 193. There was also a murderous barrage fire there. The young grenadiers of the newly formed regiments received some of the heaviest fire. Soon communications between the companies and the superior headquarters were lost. Smoke shells hindered visibility. In Plavnenskiy, the I/226 defended against a superior enemy force and had to withdraw when the Russian tanks rolled over them. Eight of these steel colossi were destroyed with close combat weapons. The I/226 withdrew to Borissovka with the enemy in pursuit. At 0855 hours the Soviets began the attack on Borissovka. Tanks rolled over the defenders. The Russian infantry attacked behind them, but the 226th repulsed them. The 4/85 AR (101st Jäger Division) fought in the village with four mountain guns. All four guns were overrun by tanks and destroyed. The emerging gap to the III/226 was closed by reserves and Borissov was held!

On 26 May the battle was extended to the northern flank of the 97th Jäger Division. After Generalleutnant Rupp had received the first reports of the penetration in the 101st Jäger Division area of operations, he alerted his reserves and advanced them. They were the 560th Special Purpose Battalion, the Romanian 94th IR, the Romanian II/95 IR, the III/381, the 97th Reconnaissance Battalion, the Special Purpose Regiment staff, the 2/249 Stu.Gesch.Brig. and the Assault Gun Battery of the 5th Luftwaffe Field Regiment.

At 0600 hours an enemy attack with tank support took place against the left flank of the 97th Jäger Division with its main effort near Hill 114.1. The 204th Jäger Regiment, which was located there, repulsed all attacks. Hill 114.1 lay about 4 kilometers from the northern edge of Krymskaya and dominated the area for some distance. In the meantime, the reserves came forward. They were committed to protect the northern flank of the 97th Jäger Division and block the enemy penetration.

The Soviet war literature remarks about 27 May 1943: "On the morning of 27 May at 0730 hours our attack was resumed, but the enemy also launched a counterattack, which received strong support from his air force. Neither side was successful."

The Germans were striving to close on the old HKL. In the early morning of 27 May three newly-formed battlegroups attacked Gorishchniy: from the northwest across Hill 121.4 was the battlegroup of Major Liebmann with the I/228 and II/226; in front against the east was Battlegroup Schury with the Rumanian II/95, the 46th Engineer Battalion and the 101st Engineer Battalion; from the south was the 208th Jäger Regiment (97th Jäger Division).

The German counterattack ran into the simultaneous Russian attack. The fiercely contested Hill 121.4 was lost to the Soviets. The 500th Battalion, which was inserted between the two battle groups of the 101st Jäger Division, slowly gained ground to the east. At 0615 hours, Hill 121.4 was again in German hands. At 0630 hours the 1 and 3/Btl. z.b.V. 500 penetrated into the northern portion of Gorishchniy; during the battle the battalion commander, Hauptmann Kachel, was severely wounded. A little later additional forces from Battlegroup Schury penetrated into the western portion of the town. The attack of the 208th Jäger Regiment from the southwest ran into the Russian attack.

Meanwhile the battle raged in Gorishchniy. Six officers in the 500th Battalion were killed. One company totaled five men, another seven, the Machine-gun Company still had 25 soldiers. The II/226, which was advancing from Hill 121.4 to the south, stalled in enemy blocking artillery fire and suffered 60% casualties. It was similar in the I/228 area of operations.

At 1000 hours the German forces were forced out of Gorishchniy. The Russians reinforced. Air reconnaissance discovered 60 enemy tanks.

Between 1400 and 1500 hours, after a strong artillery strike and air preparation, the second Soviet attack was initiated. The main attack direction was Hill 121.4 and the town of Noviy, as well as along the road to Varenikovskaya. Fierce combat developed around Hill 121.4, which was joined by eight Soviet tanks. The remnants of the 500th Special Purpose Battalion fought their way through to Noviy. A second attack supported by 15 tanks was blocked between Noviy and Hill 95. During the evening Hill 121.4 was recaptured by Battlegroup Liebmann.

The second emphasis on 27 May lay to the north of the road. The Soviet plan to gain freedom of mobility and the road to Varenikovskaya was indicated by the constant air attacks on Kievskoe. However, the way to Kievskoe led through Borissovka and Hill 193, which were steadfastly defended by Oberst Aulock's grenadiers.

At 0330 hours the first attack occurred against Borissovka and was repulsed. An hour later there was barrage fire from hundreds of tubes. Then there was a rolling air attack and strong enemy forces, supported by eight tanks, arrived in the Borissovka area and on the road to Kievskoe. Two enemy tanks were hit and stopped. Borissovka held! The 179th Reconnaissance Battalion, which was inserted near Hill 193, was pushed back to the eastern edge of Kievskoe. Shortly after that, Ju 87s buzzed over and attacked Plavnenskiy; their bombs brought a breather! The 179th Reconnaissance Battalion recaptured their old positions in a counterattack. Four more enemy tanks lay as wrecks on the battlefield.

At 1900 hours the Russians attacked again. Tanks with accompanying infantry, penetrated into Borissovka. There was a dramatic battle. Leutnant Ehmann, commander of the 2/226, was killed while attacking a tank with close combat weapons. Hauptmann Baumgartner, commander of the I/226 and combat commandant of Borissovka, was wounded. In his stead, the company commander of the 3/226, Leutnant Lumpp, continued the defensive combat in Borissovka. The I/226 had only three officers and 80 men left, but they were well entrenched.

During the following night, two heavy anti-tank guns and the 3/179 Pi.Btl.

were brought up. The attempt to destroy the enemy tanks, which had penetrated into Borissovka, failed. The Soviets reinforced their island of resistance.

On 28 May at 0430 hours the struggle for Borissovka intensified. Russian tanks suppressed the German grenadiers. A German outflanking attack against the penetration failed. The Soviets immediately counterattacked. The enemy counterattack was constantly provided fresh forces from Plavnenskiy. The fate of the German defenders appeared to be sealed. Oberst Aulock constructed a blocking position on the eastern edge of Kievskoe just in case.

In the meantime, a feat of arms was achieved in Borissovka. There, at the decisive moment, a Leutnant incited the highest bravery in his men. Forced into the last few houses of Borissovka, Leutnant Lumpp assembled his last 50 men and led them in a counterattack. Almost without ammunition, with empty weapons and spades, the small group attacked. They cleared house after house. A tank was destroyed in close combat, the others withdrew. At 1115 hours Leutnant Lumpp reported to the regiment: "Tanks have retreated. Borissovka again solidly in our hands. Leutnant Lumpp wounded." Within the space of two hours, Leutnant Lumpp was wounded a total of six times.

At 1210 hours German stukas again bombed Plavnenskiy. The Borissovka defense was reinforced by the deployment of a Rumanian squadron. The new combat commandant of Borissovka was Oberleutnant Mecke. Additional enemy attacks were repulsed.

How were things south of the road on 28 May? The hard-fought over Hill 121.4 changed hands several times. A counterattack on Gorishchniy and Hill 121.4, supported by assault guns, stalled. There was strong air commitment on both sides. Bombers and fighter-bombers buzzed incessantly over the battlefield. In the 97th Jäger Division sector, Hill 114.1 was held against heavy enemy attacks. From there the blocking front bent sharply to the west.

On 29 May combat around Borissovka and Hill 121.4 flared up again. At 0700 hours an enemy attack reached Noviy-North through Hill 121.4. A German counterattack was launched from Hill 103.3, which pushed the Soviets out of Noviy. The Soviets reinforced themselves on Hill 121.4, but the threatened attack on Noviy and Kievskoe did not occur. The Soviet formations were too exhausted.

In the Borissovka area all of the Soviet attacks collapsed in spite of the deluge of phosphorus, heavy artillery and air support. The Goriany Romanian Artillery Group played an important part in the defense. During the night the I/226 was relieved by the 179th Reconnaissance Battalion. The I/226 left their positions with only two officers and 80 non-commissioned officers and men.

On 30 May things were relatively quiet. Loudspeakers near Hill 121.4 sounded the enigmatic slogan: "We are waiting for your major attack!" The Germans were preparing a counterattack. Two battlegroups of the 13th Panzer Division were moved into their assembly areas from the army reserve.

BATTLE OF MOLDAWANSKOJE

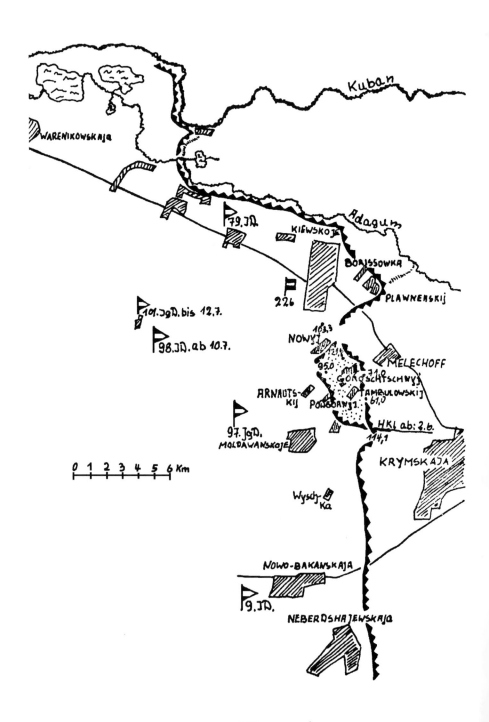

On the afternoon of 30 May 1943 a surprise air attack hit the 97th Jäger Division command post, which killed Generalleutnant Rupp. Along with the jägers of the 97th Jäger Division, the Romanian formations, which were under the command of the division, also had faith in this commander.

In the early morning of 31 May, Battlegroups Gaza and Polster counterattacked. The objective was Gorishchniy and Hill 71. First Battlegroup Gaza, consisting of a SPW battalion (100 men strong) and 12 Panzer IVs (long-barreled), was to pass to the south of Gorishchniy to Hill 71 and then penetrate to the north against the town. This attack was to include Battlegroup Polster and Gorishchniy-West was to be taken from the southwest. Hill 121.4 was to be recaptured in a subsequent attack to the north.

Both battlegroups attacked after a preparation by heavy weapons from the Arnautski - Podgorniy area. The Soviet observation posts on Hills 121.4 and 71 were blinded by smoke shells. Twelve Panzer IVs from the 4th Panzer Regiment rolled forward, followed by the SPW battalion. Attacking to the south of Gorishchniy, Battlegroup Gaza soon stood in front of Hill 71 and then turned toward the center of the village. An anti-tank blockade of 12 tubes and a light field battery stood in the way of the tanks. One tank and four armored vehicles were shot up but the enemy field battery was overcome, However, they could go no further. The German tanks rolled back toward the southern edge of Gorishchniy in order to await the closing of Battle- group Polster. In the meantime, it [Polster] was fighting its way to the southwestern edge of the village. It consisted of two battalions of the 93rd Panzergrenadier Regiment (600 men) and the 191st Assault Gun Brigade with 21 guns (Hauptmann Müller), as well as accompanying artillery from the II/13 Pz.AR. After destroying a T-34, the lead panzer group was forced to detour.

The 208th Jäger Regiment and the III/666 (370th ID) attacked Tambulovskiy from the southwest with the objective of taking Hill 71 and the northeastern portion of Gorishchniy in subsequent attack. Fierce combat see-sawed in Gorishchniy. Battlegroup Gaza was unable to make it through to Hill 121.4. The forces of the 97th Jäger Division stalled in front of Tambulovskiy. How victory and defeat hung by a thread was indicated by a Russian radio message, which was intercepted at 1245 hours: "Situation is difficult because the flanks and rear have been outflanked. Urgently request support!"

The Russian defensive fire from artillery and rocket launchers increased into a fire hurricane. Wave upon wave of Soviet aircraft probed over the battlefield. They dropped bombs and fired on-board weapons. At 1505 hours the German counterattack was suspended and the formations were pulled back somewhat.

In the Borissovka - Kievskoe sector the combat settled down noticeably. The young 226th Grenadier Regiment, which was led by Oberst Aulock, had successfully withstood the crashing enemy divisions and prevented them from opening the Kievskoe - Varenikovskaya road.

On 1 June the Soviets unsuccessfully attacked Hill 114.1 again because it allowed a good view into the enemy deployment area. Another attack against the same hill on 2 June quickly collapsed in the fire of the 97th Jäger Division. This was the last wave of the attack flood. The enemy's refitting and regrouping also gave the XXXXIV Jäger Corps the opportunity to pause for reorganization and fortifying its front.

Generalmajor Ludwig Müller took command of the 97th Jäger Division on 4 June. The offensive to gain the Kievskoe - Varenikovskoe road was at an end. Generalleutnant Vogel's Schwabians and Württemburgers had fought bravely. The front had changed very little.

COMBAT IN THE KUBAN BRIDGEHEAD
JULY - AUGUST 1943

The 98th Infantry Division arrives - The frontal salient near Hill 114.1 - "Then I can die peacefully" - The "Büffel" arrives - "Krähennest" holds - The I German Fliegerkorps

After the heavy combat near Gorishchniy, June and the beginning of July were relatively quiet. Both sides improved their positions and refitted their troops. On 10 July 1943 both sides conducted scouting operations in order to determine the enemy's plans.

On 15 July the Romanian 19th ID with the 94th and 95th IR, the 37th Artillery Regiment and the divisional units were withdrawn from the XXXXIV Jäger Corps.

At the beginning of June, as heavy combat in the XXXXIV Jäger Corps sector was coming to an end, the 98th ID was ordered transported by rail out of the Bryansk area to the Crimea and was unloaded near Feodosia. From there, the Franken and Sudeten Germans were marched to Kerch in 40 degree heat. From 15 to 26 June 1943 the division crossed the Kerch Strait and occupied shelters in the Gostagaevskaya - Gladkovskaya area. Some elements bivouacked in the brushy, forested valleys. 2500 men arrived as replacements.

At the end of June officers from the 98th ID conducted a frontal reconnaissance. On 1 July it was decided: The 98th ID would relieve the battered 101st Jäger Division.

On 7 July the 98th ID advanced into the Akermanka Forest. During the nights of 10 to 12 July the 101st Jäger Division was relieved as it pulled back into the 98th ID bivouac area.

16 July 1943 was the prelude to the fourth battle of Krymskaya. At 0400 hours barrage fire was placed on the German positions. The emphasis was placed on the frontal salient near Hill 114.1, the area around Hill 95 and Hill 121.4, which was occupied by the Russians. The main attack was directed against Hill 114.1. However, the tried and true 97th Jäger Division stood there and, adjacent on the north, the 282nd Grenadier Regiment (98th ID), which would give no quarter. The secondary emphasis lay near Hill 121.4 where the 290th Grenadier Regiment and a battalion from the 98th ID stood.

It was soon obvious that both hills were decisive terrain sectors. The Germans knew that they had to hold there and the Russians realized that a successful offensive to the Taman Peninsula could only advance over these hills. After the major combat in May the German positions were the best constructed. On this frontal sector the main battlefield boasted the greatest depth.

From 16 to 21 July the battle wavered around these hills. Again air commitments on both sides reached a climax. German stukas bombarded the Soviet assembly areas without pause. There were artillery duels every day.

Attacks and counterattacks alternated daily near Hill 114.1. The combat tested companies of the 97th Jäger Division would not give a meter of ground without exacting a price. Even the 98th ID fought its first major battle in the Kuban bridgehead successfully, with the 282nd Grenadier Regiment in the south and the 290th Grenadier Regiment in the north. The 98th ID battalion was the nucleus of the new 289th Grenadier Regiment, which would be organized a month later. The 98th ID, led by Generalmajor Gareis, held its HKL.

Representative of the defensive combat for the existence of the 17th Army was the death of a private soldier in this sector. Everyone knew that they must hold and that they would be called on for self-sacrifice. The Russians were able to dominate the German positions from Hill 121.4. The portion of the positions held by Battalion Maull south of this hill was repeatedly attacked by strong enemy assault groups. All penetrations were eliminated by counterattack. In this manner, Obergefreiter Bauer from the 3rd Company was severely wounded. His comrades carried him to a bunker. When Leutnant Kaiser visited the bunker after the enemy attack was repulsed, the severely wounded soldier called out to him and asked: "Is Ivan still in the trenches?" When the Leutnant said no, Bauer laid back and rasped: "Then I can die in peace!"

On 20 July three defectors brought new bad news into the 98th ID sector: The Russians were being relieved by fresh troops. They were preparing for a new attack. Generalmajor Gareis immediately passed on the report and requested stukas. Just before nightfall, German Ju 87's bombarded the Russian assembly areas.

On 22 July at 0530 hours strong barrage fire was unleashed. Stalin Organs fired without pause. All radio and voice communications were lost. Behind the wall of fire attacked two fresh Soviet divisions. The main effort of the battle lay in the 282nd Grenadier Regiment and Battalion Maull sector. Fifty Russian tanks supported the assaulting Russian infantry. Assault guns rolled against them. Sixteen enemy tanks were destroyed. Except for a penetration formed by 30 tanks, the front of the 98th ID held. German losses were high.

On 23 July it continued. At 0530 hours the enemy attack was resumed. This time it hit the I/282. By evening the front was essentially holding with the support of assault guns, only contact with the 97th Jäger Division had been severed. In the early morning of the following day a battlegroup from the 98th ID under Hauptmann Metz counterattacked through the "Valley of Death" southwest of Podgorniy and closed the gap to the 97th Jäger Division.

On 24 July there was also fierce combat around the frontal salient near Hill 114.1, but the 97th Jäger Division held its positions.

After three days the German HKL was not decisively broken. The first wave of the attack flood ebbed. On 25 July the start of the second wave was revealed by defectors. German batteries placed reconnoitered and assumed assembly areas under destructive fire, but that did not delay the beginning of the attack. On 26 July at 0930 hours the Soviets attacked again. Again the 282nd Grenadier Regiment and Battalion Maull stood at the focal point. At 1000 hours it had already degenerated into hand-to-hand combat. At 1400 hours the attack strength of the Soviets was temporarily paralyzed. However, at 1600 hours the enemy resumed his attack. 80 Russian tanks rolled onto the battlefield from the second echelon. Behind them were two fresh attack regiments. A penetration was achieved in the I/282 area of operations. Hauptmann Wahl led his battalion in a counterattack and threw the Soviets back. The old HKL was restored, but the victory was expensive, as Hauptmann Wahl was severely wounded. The winner of the Knight's Cross would not survive. Again the assault guns of the 191st Brigade mastered the enemy tanks.

On 27 July at 1600 hours, an unusual time, all hell broke loose again. There was a heavy armored duel and fierce infantry combat. The German stukas could not be committed because of the darkness. Is that why the attack was started so late?

On the German side the assault artillery of the 191st Assault Gun Brigade again supported the defensive combat of the 98th ID. This brigade, which had fought so successfully under Hauptmann Kapp as part of the LII Army Corps on the Terek, was reorganized after crossing into the Kuban bridgehead, while one combat battery, which was formed from all of the elements of the brigade, was already successfully participating in the battle for Krymskaya. Now the brigade under Hauptmann Alfred Müller faced its most crucial test. Wherever the "Büffel [Buffalo]" appeared they created breathing space. They were known as "Büffel" because of their tactical symbol, the jumping buffalo. In nine major Soviet attacks the 191st Assault Gun Brigade stood, in the literal sense of the words, "like boulders in the surf".

The brigade was later praised in a 17th Army daily report. It said: "The 191st Assault Gun Battalion, under the leadership of Hauptmann Müller, played a great part in the recent successful defense against the far superior enemy force. It joined in the defense and counterattacks with great elan. In the Kuban bridgehead it destroyed 95 enemy tanks, along with several 12 cm assault howitzers. It was mentioned in a Wehrmacht report."

The losses of the 98th ID from 16 to 27 July 1943 in dead and wounded totaled: 42 officers, 188 non-commissioned officers and 1537 men. The medical service of the division had to treat and transport wounded day and night at the Mikhailovskie and Varenikovskaya main first aid stations.

On 30 July the Soviets again made an attempt against the frontal salient near Hill 114.1. After strong artillery and air preparation 20 Soviet tanks rolled against the hill. Behind them were six fresh battalions. German assault guns and anti-tank guns shot up the first wave of eight tanks. The attack stalled! Then the stukas showed up. Bombs fell onto the groups of tanks and assembly areas. That was the end of the assault.

While the main attack was taking place in the XXXXIV Jäger Corps sector, Soviet formations were also attacking into the V Army Corps sector in the

Neberdzhaevskaya area. There the objective was to open the road to the Taman Peninsula from behind by attacking with a southern pincer into this area.

On 24 July, as the battle in the XXXXIV Jäger Corps sector reached its zenith, an attack also occurred against the 23rd Romanian Light Infantry Battalion. The objective was the capture of Hill 352.6 on the main road southwest of Neberdzhaevskaya. The Romanians were pushed back.

The remnants of the 7/213 and elements of the 173rd Reconnaissance Battalion under Oberleutnant Gollert-Hansen defended on Hill 352.6. The battle raged all day. Gollert-Hansen was wounded three times, but because of his example, Hill 352.6, nicknamed the "Krähennest [Crow's Nest]", was not taken. The way to Novorossisk remained blocked. By nightfall the reserves of the 73rd ID attempted to close the gap between the "Krähennest", that was now being held under Hauptmann Graber, and Point 62.1/Nabel. They did not succeed. As a precaution, the "Gunter Line" on both sides of Hill 223 was occupied by the 51st Construction Battalion.

On 25 July another heavy attack crashed against the "Krähennest". Two battalions of the 421st Grenadier Regiment (125th ID) were deployed to straighten things out. They were partially successful in reestablishing contact. The direct threat from Neberdzhaevskaya was diverted. During the night, two battalions of the 421st Grenadier Regiment advanced on the "Krähennest".

From 25 July to 10 August the Soviets tried to break through the "Krähennest" sector to the pass toward Novorossisk, but they did not succeed. After days of crisis the German front again stabilized.

During the first days of August all German observation posts in the XXXXIV Jäger Corps sector reported strong enemy movement. On 6 August there were reconnaissance operations, which were repulsed. From 7 to 12 August the Soviets attacked into the 98th ID sector and toward the northern flank of the 97th Jäger Division. The German front held! The main attack was launched at the seam between the 97th Jäger Division and the 9th ID with its main effort near Gorno Vessely and the Vyshka hill. A deep penetration caused a crisis, but it was mastered by reserves from the 9th ID and the 97th Jäger Division. From 8 to 11 August the Soviets were slowly driven back.

On 12 August the Soviets attacked with approximately two divisions, which were to penetrate to the Vyshka hill. On 13 August the penetration was eliminated. During this battle the XI Guards Rifle Corps was severely battered. On 19 August another Soviet attempt to make it to the Vyshka hill failed due to the steadfastness of the 97th Jäger Division.

In the next few days the Soviets made only half-hearted attempts to penetrate the German defense. On 3 September the 97th Jäger Division repulsed enemy attacks at several locations. On 14 September the 290th Grenadier Regiment (98th ID) defeated two tank-supported attacks. The 14./290 destroyed three enemy tanks and the Romanian Anti-Tank Battery Nr. 110

destroyed four. A day later, the 282nd Grenadier Regiment also repulsed a Soviet attack supported by 20 tanks.

The last Soviet attack on the Kuban bridgehead was more or less a probing attack. It proved that the Kuban bridgehead was stable, but there were already gloomy indications in von Manstein's army group sector that the 17th Army would also be forced to give up its hard won position in Asia. The Soviets suspended their major attack and took up ambush positions in order to be ready when the Germans withdrew.

In a comprehensive report, the 97th Jäger Division worked out the reasons for the failure of the Soviet offensive operations against the 17th Army:

1. By the end of January/beginning of February the Soviet equipment and personnel superiority was engaged to the south and southwest of Krasnodar. There was a lack of decisiveness on the part of the junior Soviet troop commanders. They were also inflexible. There was little support from heavy weapons because they could not be brought up due to weather conditions.

2. The battle near Abinskaya was foreseen in time by the German leadership and corresponding countermeasures were taken. For the first time artillery support laid down a barrage fire for one hour and air commitment was accurate. The Soviet attack formations set out from assembly areas that were set too far back after the end of the barrage fire, which resulted in the attack waves being destroyed by artillery and the Luftwaffe long before they reached the German HKL.

3. During the attack in front of Krymskaya, the enemy led his attack formations to the nearest penetration area while the barrage fire was still taking place. After penetrating, the unified command and control and, in particular, the artillery support, got out of hand. This increased the chances of success of the German counterattack.

4. During the major attack on 26 May a further increase of artillery, infantry, tank and air sorties was realized. Coordination was good. The massed commitment of tanks was new. There were no infantry attacks without tanks; there were no subsequent attacks without infantry.

The German defense continued to be able to separate the enemy infantry forces from the tanks and, therefore, splinter the attacking forces.

The assessment of the 97th Jäger Division showed that the Soviet leadership was gradually learning from its mistakes. On the other hand the Russians were constantly loosing experienced leaders who were being replaced with insufficiently trained replacements. This had a negative impact on the cohesion of the units.

In closing is presented a comparison of the air commitment on both sides. On 31 August 1943, the German Luftflotte 4's I Air Corps had 879 aircraft available, of which 514 were operational. The breakdown in numbers was as follows:

	Total	Operational
Close Recon	83	52
Long-rang Recon	62	37
Fighters	105	45
Night Fighters	21	13
Bombers	257	142
Stukas	193	112
Sea Planes	20	14
Transports	138	99
Total	879	514

On the other hand the North Caucasus Front had only about 750 Soviet aircraft.

The unqualified reader would think that the numerical difference was not that great, but the difference lay in the fact that the aircraft of the I Air Corps were allotted for the entire southern sector of the Eastern Front. These aircraft also had to fly sorties to Kharkov. From their airfields in the Crimea and in the interior of Army Group von Manstein the crews were committed without pause; first here, then there, wherever the crisis was hottest. The efforts of the men and the aircraft stretched the limits of endurance.

The German aircraft crews played an important part in the overall commitment. The German fighters constantly engaged Soviet bomber and fighter-bomber groups and participated in the ground battle. The German stuka pilots, however, deserve special praise. They consistently provided relief to the hard-pressed infantrymen. The shout: "Our stukas are coming!" always gave hope and new strength to persevere.

EVACUATION OF THE KUBAN BRIDGEHEAD

Soviet landing in Novorossisk harbor - Phased withdrawal - German naval forces secure the sea route - The "Kleinen Gotenkopf" - Long-range batteries cover the last spring-board from Kerch - In ferries across the Kerch Strait

The development of the situation on the southern flank of the German Eastern Front and the fall of Italy forced the surrender of the Kuban bridgehead. On 5 August Army Group A had to give up the 355th ID, which was committed to the defense of the Crimea, to Army Group South. The commander of Army Group A, Generalfeldmarschall von Kleist, ordered the remnants of the 13th Panzer Division to withdraw from the Kuban bridgehead. From 18 to 20 August the 13th Panzer Division made its way to the Crimea, but then it continued to march to the 6th Army, which was involved in heavy combat north of the Sea of Azov. The danger of the Crimea being cut off from the rest of the Eastern Front was great, and if the Crimea was lost, then the fall of Rumania would be close behind. On 3 September Army Group A received the evacuation order for the Kuban bridgehead from OKH; the first day of the evacuation was to be 7 September. Army Group A and the 17th Army worked out withdrawal plans, the "Krimhild" and "Brunhild" options.

"Krimhild" proposed a time period of from 10 to 12 weeks and foresaw the withdrawal of everything, important goods for the conduct of war, including a good part of the civilian population.

"Brunhild" proposed 38 days to withdraw Wehrmacht equipment and destroy the economic goods.

Both withdrawal plans included a phased withdrawal to the Kerch Strait, conducting defense at suitable terrain sectors. The "Kleinen Gotenkopf", which tied in with the Taman Peninsula at three locations, had special significance. Furthermore, the only good withdrawal route from Kievskoe to Varenikovskaya had to be utilized. The most important factor in the withdrawal was the coordination with the means of making the crossing. The plan foresaw a daily crossing of the Kerch Strait by one division.

The army drew up the general plan. The details had to be worked out by the corps, which were given 30 hours for the withdrawal of each division. Then each unit had to be told when and where!

13 engineer and 11 construction battalions were committed to establish obstacles and intercept positions. The need for timely monitoring of the Black Sea by air and naval reconnaissance against anticipated landing operations was recognized.

The German preparations could not be hidden from the Soviets. Both sides attempted to discover the intentions of the other through their intelligence sections, but the exact date of the withdrawal was kept from the Soviets.

In the meantime, the Soviets had already withdrawn their combat formations and threw them into the combat north of the Sea of Azov. At the same time, landing boats were brought into the southern Black Sea harbor of Gelendzhik. The assessment of the situation by the 17th Army did not foresee any large-scale combat operations within the near future.

During the night of 30 August a Russian naval Lieutenant, Vassilev, was captured in Novorossisk harbor. Vassilev had the mission of reconnoitering in a rubber boat the German defenses and the terrain between the western docks and Stanichka. His interrogation revealed a planned attack on the inner harbor, a simultaneous landing in the Anapa - Osereika area, a paradrop near Borissovka and a pinning attack near Temryuk. Was the Russian naval lieutenant telling the truth, or was it a bluff? Just in case, the I/228 Jg.Rgt. was transferred into Novorossisk harbor and additional regimental elements were placed in reserve. However, the Soviet strike did not materialize. The reserves were again dispersed. Vassilev's statements, it would turn out, were true! Because of unfavorable weather conditions, the landing operation was postponed twice.

On the evening of 9 September 1943 the landing formation under Vice Admiral Kholostyakov put to sea. It was a select formation: the 255th Naval Infantry Brigade under Colonel Potapov; the 393rd Independent Naval Infantry Battalion under Captain Botylen, which carried the honorific "Kunikov"; the 1339 Rifle Regiment under Lieutenant Colonel Kadanchik and some other smaller formations; in all there were 8935 men in 129 small craft.

At midnight the landing formation was in front of Novorossisk Bay. At the same time approximately 800 guns and heavy mortars, as well as numerous rocket batteries, opened fire on the harbor and the city. The long-range batteries on the Bay of Zemess fired far into the interior of the German troops.

On 10 September, at 0300 hours, a group of Soviet specialists advanced to the German harbor blockade and opened it. Shortly after that the first wave followed in three sub-groups, covered by 25 torpedo cutters under the command of Captain 2nd Rank Protsenko. The landing was not discovered until the "Kunikov" Battalion was already in the inner harbor.

Two marine companies under Kptlt. Hossfeld defended in the harbor. Protsenko committed a torpedo cutter into the battle. The torpedoes detonated on the wharves and piers. The German marine defenders were placed under fire by on-board weapons. The Soviets committed the second landing wave and established footholds at three locations within the inner harbor. The German marines defended desperately. However, after contact between the individual strongpoints was lost, the German harbor defense collapsed.

While the battle raged in the harbor basin, landing troops from the 18th Army also landed on the northern shore of the bay of Zemess in order to pin the German troops in their frontal positions.

In the meantime German reserves were deployed. Elements of the 73rd ID (Generalleutnant Böhme), the 101st Jäger Division and the 1st Romanian Mountain Division were committed in the Mefodievski-East quarter of the city. Elements of the 4th German and 4th Romanian Mountain Divisions were brought up into Novorossisk-West and Stanichka.

The advance of the landing forces on the western docks was repulsed by the

91st Gebirgsjäger Regiment, the 94th Battalion and the 3/94 Pi.Btl. under the command of Oberst Hörl. The enemy forces, which had established themselves at the seaside resort and the U-Boot dock, were thrown back into the sea. The counterattack against the cold-storage house and grain dock began at 1600 hours, but the enemy was not thrown back. Strong enemy artillery and rocket fire continued. The enemy landed new troops on 11 September at 0200 hours, under the cover of fire.

On 11 September the 13th Gebirgsjäger Regiment took over the right sector of the 91st Gebirgsjäger Regiment. At midday, on 12 September, the 94th Battalion, the III/13 and elements of the 91st Gebirgsjäger Regiment attacked the enemy occupied sector of the harbor and threw the enemy back from all sides. Loose contact was established with the 73rd ID.

The Soviet torpedo cutters TKA 124 and 125, as well as cutters SKA 025, 032 and 084, were lost in Novorossisk harbor.

An attack launched from the Myshako bridgehead to the north failed due to the defense of the 91st Gebirgsjäger Regiment. Oberst Hörl was awarded the Knight's Cross for combat around Novorossisk. If the landing operation could not shake the unity of the 17th Army, it did set back the planned destruction of the harbor for at least six months.

Plan "Krimhild" was no longer feasible. Plan "Brunhild" was initiated. During the night of 16 September the V Army Corps and the XXXXIV Jäger Corps began withdrawal operations. On 18 September the XXXXIX Mountain Corps joined in. The troops of the North Caucasus Front (Colonel General Petrov) immediately pursued; Lieutenant General Leselidse's formations from the 18th Army and XX Landing Corps, eight divisions and five brigades, were in the V Army Corps sector. Lieutenant General Grechko's seven divisions and two tank formations from the 56th Army were in the XXXXIV Jäger Corps sector, and the 9th Army, with five divisions and two marine brigades, as well as a tank formation, under Major General Grechin, were in the XXXXIX Mountain Corps area.

In the Novorossisk - Krymskaya area, forests and mountainous terrain favored the withdrawal. The western portion of the Taman Peninsula is a tree-less and shrub-less plain with scattered hills, numerous farmsteads, kolkhozes and spread-out villages. Many lakes could be utilized in the defense.

On 15 September the Soviets attacked with three regiments and 70 tanks in the Kievskoe area in order to interfere in the German withdrawal and to advance quickly on the main road to Varenikovskaya. The 79th ID held.

On the morning of 16 September the southern portion of the "Grossen Goten Positions" was occupied to the southern half of the "Siegfried Block" without problem. The 98th and 79th ID closed with the withdrawal and occupied the "Gernot Position".

On 16 September at 0830 hours the enemy pursued from evacuated Novorossisk on the road to the Volchi - Vorota Pass. The enemy columns were effectively engaged by the 94th Mountain Artillery Regiment. The northern flank of the 4th Mountain Division was withdrawn to the pass under enemy pressure. The enemy was temporarily halted at this dominant terrain sector. Because of technical problems, the blowing of the railroad tunnel was only partially successful.

Also, on 16 September, the 79th ID and the 98th ID were involved in heavy combat in the "Gernot Position". The Soviet 56th Army wanted to break through along the main road to the Taman Peninsula and pin the V Army Corps (General Allmendinger) and the XXXXIV Jäger Corps (General De Angelis), which were fighting west of Novorossisk. The 79th ID was forced to give up the "Gernot Position" a day earlier than scheduled, that is on 17 September due to enemy pressure. The 98th ID had to follow. In this situation the 97th Jäger Division was fighting with its northern flank between the "Siegfried" and "Volker Position" on 18 September while the southern flank was occupying unscheduled intermediate positions south of Gladovskaya in order to cover the planned withdrawal of the V Army Corps. The strong pressure on the 79th ID continued. In order to keep the Soviets in the dark about the early evacuation of the "Gernot Position", the 560th Special Purpose Battalion fought a delaying battle in the Gladovskaya area for the entire day.

On 18 September heavy combat developed around Mount Gudseva in the 4th Mountain Division sector. After defending against the enemy attack, the 4th Mountain Division withdrew into the "Volker Position" as part of the V Army Corps. This maneuver was copied by the southern elements of the XXXXIV Jäger Corps, while the northern elements remained in the "Siegfired Block". On this day, the XXXXIX Mountain Corps began the withdrawal into the "Harz Position". Therefore, the 17th Army reestablished a unified defensive front.

On 19 and 20 September the 4th Mountain Division defended against enemy attacks with tank support around Krasnaya Medvedovskaya. The 91st Gebirgsjäger Regiment destroyed six enemy tanks which had penetrated.

During the night of 21 September all three German corps withdrew to the "Hagen Position".

The Soviets pursued into the V Army Corps area with strong forces. On 21 September heavy attacks were launched against the southern flank with the objective of striking the German forces as they left the forest in the Anapa area, while simultaneously landing from the sea in the rear of the V Army Corps. In subsequent attacks, the two northern German corps were to be pinned before they reached the "Kleinen Gotenkopf".

On 21 September the 18th Soviet Army attacked. The heavy attack, supported by tanks, hit the companies of the 4th Mountain Division. While the I/13 Geb.Jg.Rgt. established a defense north of the Anapskaya, the main body of the division was located in the intermediate positions directly east of Gaikadsory and in heavy combat in the hills north of there. The superior enemy forces quickly pushed the Romanians, who were located on the coast, back and tried several times to overrun the front of the 4th Mountain Division to the north. The 94th Mountain Reconnaissance Battalion, under Rittmeister Thorey, could not fend off the heavy attack on the now open southern flank. Moreover, there was a simultaneous attack out of the forest north of Krasnaya Medvedovskaya. In spite of high enemy losses inflicted by the exceptional fire of the heavy field artillery battalions, the Russians continued to attack and achieved a penetration. In this situation, the divisional commander, Generalmajor Braun, subordinated elements of the 19th Romanian ID and the 6th Romanian Cavalry Division under his command in order to be able to exercise unified command over the combat on the coast. After the Romanian sector was taken over by the 13th Gebirgsjäger Regiment, the penetration near Politod was blocked by the 94th Gebirgsjäger Battalion and the III/13. In the afternoon (earlier than scheduled) the Romanians evacuated Anapa. Two hours later Russian troops disembarked in the harbor.

Soviet offensive activity revived in the XXXXIV Jäger Corps sector on 21 and 22 September. It climaxed with an armored strike at Pilenko. German assault guns and a stuka attack threw the Soviets back by destroying all eight tanks, but the 3rd Railroad Engineer Regiment could no longer evacuate the supply stores located in Pilenko because the railroad station was destroyed.

On the evening of 23 September the defenders in the "Hagen Position", which stuck out to the southeast, were withdrawn to the "Rüdiger Position", which, in conjunction with the "Rhön Block" adjacent to the north, essentially formed a small front. The relieved troop units either marched to Ilich to the Kerch crossing or were organized under the commander of the 50th ID, Generalmajor Sixt, into Gruppe Sixt, which had the mission of constructing a defense on the southern Taman Peninsula behind the present defensive line. The 370th and elements of the 50th ID were organized under the commander of the 370th ID, Generalleutnant Becker, into Gruppe Becker, which had the mission of taking over the defense in the Temryuk - Golubitskaya area.

On 24 September all three German corps repulsed enemy attacks at the "Rhön - Rüdiger Position". The 97th Jäger Division stood along the main axis on the central land bridge to the Taman Peninsula.

During the night of 25 September Russian forces landed 6 kilometers west of Blagovechenskaya. On the following morning the Soviets conducted a frontal attack with the support of 15 tanks. The forces of the 9th Romanian Cavalry Division under Oberst Grunau were thrown back and got into serious withdrawal difficulties. At midday the I/13 Geb.Jg.Rgt., which was resting in Utash, was alerted and deployed to the Romanians. Germans and Romanians fought their way free and withdrew to the next set of positions.

During the night of 25 September a landing was also conducted from the sea in Temryuk Bay in order to block the withdrawal route of Gruppe Becker. After fierce combat, the landing forces were wiped out and the following landing craft were forced to turn around. General Konrad praised the defeat of the enemy landing forces by the participating formations in an order of the day: "On 25 September 1943 enemy forces in the strength of 800 men (elements of the 389th Rifle Division and the 369th Marine Brigade), that had landed in the rear of the XXXXIX Mountain Corps near Temryuk and Golubitskaya, were destroyed and, therefore, a threatened blocking of the important supply route was removed. This combat achievement was due in great respect to the service of Oberst Biermann, commander of the 122nd Grenadier Regiment, and Babel, commander of the 666th Grenadier Regiment..."

At the same time, the XI Soviet Rifle Corps launched a heavy attack in the early morning on both sides of the Kurchanskaya - Temryuk road, which was repulsed by the 50th and 370th ID, as well as elements of the 101st Jäger Division. After being removed from Kievskoe area, the 101st Jäger Division had elements occupying security positions on the Azov coast and in the lagoons.

By evening of 25 September the V Army Corps had reached the "Kleinen Goten Positions". During the night of 26 September Gruppe Becker occupied the "Odenwald Block" in order to withdraw to the "Kleinen Gotenkopf" 24 hours later. The narroest point on the northern land bridge was blocked east of Golubitskaya, after Temryuk was evacuated and the Kuban bridgehead was destroyed.

The front was considerably shortened with the occupation of the "Kleinen Gotenkopf". The divisions freed-up were crossed to the Crimea; these were the V Army Corps command, XXXXIV Jäger Corps command, 125th ID (whose first formation began crossing on 7 September), 9th ID, 101st Jäger Division, 1st Romanian Mountain Division, 10th Romanian ID, 73rd ID, 79th ID and 9th Romanian Cavalry Division. The defense of the "Kleinen Gotenkopf" then lay in the hands of only the XXXXIX Mountain Corps with Gruppen Becker and Sixt. The corps command led the center itself. On the front from north to south stood: 50th and 370th ID (Becker), 98th ID and 97th Jäger Division (center), 4th Mountain Division and 19th Romanian ID (Sixt).

There was heavy activity on the Kerch road. The arriving formations were crossed according to plan. The overall burden lay in the hands of the "Black Sea" Admiralty (ASM), Vizeadmiral Kieseritzky, and the "Caucasus" Seekommandanten, Kapitaen zur See Grattauer. The 1st (Kptlt. Giele), 3rd (Freg.Kpt. Dtrempel), 5th (Korv.Kpt. Mehler) and 7th (Korv.Kpt. Stelzer) Landing Flotillas, as well as the 770th Heerespionier Landing Regiment under Oberst Henke, were committed.

Naval and engineer landing ferries (barges, 60 ton craft), engineer landing boats (30 ton), Siebelfaehren (two aircraft engines on a 10 ton craft) and lighter elements were utilized. The convoy routes were: Kerch - Temryuk (Toni and Theodor Convoys), Kerch - Taman (Bansin Convoy) and, at the beginning, Kerch - Anapa (Hagen Convoy).

The protection of the coast and the convoys was provided by naval forces consisting of small units. Often the small boats lay in the harbor for only a few hours to take on supplies, then they were off again. The crews of the small units were often without sufficient cooking and sleeping facilities.

The motor-torpedo boats, which served as outposts, were defenseless against air attack during the day. Thus, on 11 September, as the Soviet landing was taking place in Novorossisk, boats stationed in front of the Osereika

Estuary (based in Anapa and Ivan Baba) were attacked by Soviet fighter-bombers at 0430 hours. German fighter protection was immediately requested. The Soviets attacked to within ten meters and shot up the motor-torpedo boats. Anti-aircraft fire was ineffective because the 2 cm anti-aircraft shells bounced off of the armored fighter-bombers. All of the machinery went out of order on S-46; two torpedoes detonated in their tubes and the bow was completely destroyed. In spite of the continuing attack, the sister boat saved the partially wounded crew and two dead from the sinking S-46. At 0550 hours the requested fighter protection showed up and drove the Soviet fighter-bombers away.

On 27 September the boats of the 1st Motor-Torpedo Flotilla (Korv.Kpt. Büchting) were committed to the Anapa Harbor to harass Soviet transports. At 2300 hours the boats stood at the entrance to the harbor. After they acquired their targets on the docks they moved in closer and fired their torpedoes from a distance of 800 meters. Four craft of approximately 2200 BRT were sunk with eight torpedoes. During a repeat of the operation on the following night a close reconnaissance aircraft accompanied them, which illuminated the harbor with its incendiary bombs, but the harbor was empty.

The security of the northern Kerch Strait and the Bay of Temryuk was provided by the 3rd Mine-sweeper Flotilla (Kptlt. Klassmann) and artillery barges. The artillery barges were constructed from nine pontoons and equipped with two 8.8 cm anti-aircraft guns, one four-barreled anti-aircraft gun (2 cm) and a heavy machine-gun. Its shallow hull and low silhouette made the artillery barge an ideal coastal craft.

On 17, 20 and 24 September the German naval forces fought several battles with units of the Soviet Azov Flotilla (Vice Admiral Gorskov). In order to prevent new Soviet landing attempts in the Golubitskaya area the Krym Gruppe of the 3rd Räumboot Flotilla, under the leadership of Olt. z. See Schneider, was ordered to sow the entrance to the Primorsko - Akhtarskaya Sea of Azov harbor with mines on the night of 27 September. Schneider explains: "My plan was to navigate the Kerch Strait to Cape Khroni during the twilight. From there we would follow the Ukrainian coast in order to approach Primorsko from the west.

The trip went as planned. Weather was good. We covered the mines with tarpaulin for the trip through the Kerch Strait. I briefed the crew after we departed and, as we set course for the Sea of Azov, I had the feeling that all would go well in spite of the reconnaissance report that 18 artillery boats lay in the harbor at Primorsko.

We sailed in a `T' formation: R-35, R-203, R-197 and P-164. After initially sailing at top speed, I alternated speeds in the interest of navigation. The engines had underwater exhausts to reduce engine noise. Soon we were at the promontory at Kossa Achuevskaya. For security purposes we communicated by hand signals. I decided to set the fuses in 7 meter deep water. R-197 began sowing the mines. R-164 followed. After R-164 and R-197 used up all of their mines we sailed slowly to the west, while R-35 and R-203 provided the rear guard. We sailed off with the first rays of dawn."

Mines were laid at several locations to protect the Kerch Strait. The Soviets likewise tried to mine the German transport routes at night. The Soviets increasingly used aircraft to sow their mines.

German 250 ton U-boote were committed to harass enemy transports off the Caucasus coast. The boats, which were no longer needed for the Atlantic, did not have a large operational radius and were very slow under water. In spite of this, the small U-Boote in the Black Sea had a great success.

On 16 September, after a day in Constanza Harbor, U-18 went out again on operations. On 17 September the boat received a radio message to operate in the Gelendzhik - Tuapse area. A close reconnaissance aircraft was committed in support. On 18 September U-18, under Olt. z. See Fleige, sank a freighter from a Tuapse convoy. On 20 September at 0900 hours the boat sighted a large convoy and attacked it repeatedly. Five torpedoes were fired, but they were outmaneuvered by a tanker and a transport.

On 20 September U-20, under Olt. Z. See Schöler, was located near Poti with the mission of sowing the harbor entrance with mines. The mines were laid in water 17 to 24 meters deep 1.5 sea miles from the coast on the observed convoy route. The boat had 9 TBM/Torpedo Tube Mines, each 2.31 meters long weighing 800 kilograms, on board, three of them were in the torpedo tubes. After fulfilling the mission, U-20 returned to Sevastopol and by 30 September was patrolling in front of Anapa, where it sunk a light craft.

On 30 September, the Soviet destroyers "Sposobniy", "Boikiy" and "Besposadniy" conducted an unsuccessful attack on the German evacuation transports on the southern coast of the Crimea.

To protect the Kerch Strait, numerous long-ranged batteries were established on the coast of the Kerch Peninsula. On the northern tip in the Baksy area were 34 tubes, including 13 mortars (21 cm), and three heavy anti-aircraft batteries. In the Kerch sector there were 17 tubes, including two railroad guns of 28 cm caliber, and three heavy anti-aircraft batteries. In the Eltgen sector stood three captured 7.62 cm guns and one heavy anti-aircraft battery. In the Cape Takyl sector on the southern promontory of the Kerch Peninsula were 47 tubes; they were 15 to 17 cm caliber cannon with great range.

In all there were 101 tubes established to protect the Kerch Strait. They were mostly long-ranged cannon of German, French and Russian make. The Army and Navy manned the gun crews. The 28 [caliber] Railroad Gun fired over 30 kilometers and could cover three-fourths of the "Kleinen Gotenkopf". The 17 [caliber] cannon fired 25 kilometers. So could the 15 [caliber] cannon. The thirteen 21 [caliber] mortars could range Ilich and Kossa Chushka. It was a mighty artillery fist that covered the last phase of the withdrawal.

The 9th Air Defense Division under Generalmajor Pickert was committed with many light, medium and heavy air defense batteries. Besides air protection, the batteries were often used in ground combat, and they proved to be some of the best.

During the evacuation of the Kuban bridgehead, German transport formations were still committed from various airfields. From 7 September to 9 October 1943 transport aircraft brought back 15,661 soldiers and 1153.8 tons of equipment to the Crimea.

The evacuation of the "Kleinen Gotenkopf" was to be conducted according to the plan; speed, defense and transport capacity. Accordingly, a half division would be freed-up from one position to the next and then marched to the crossing.

Naturally, the Soviet main attack direction soon homed in on the central land bridge. The 98th ID and 97th Jäger Division held off all enemy attacks for over a week on the Dzhinginskoe - Starotitarovskaya road. German artillery engaged the assembly areas. A German stuka attack blasted a large Soviet tank concentration. The German defensive forces set up numerous mine obstacles.

On the morning of 26 September new enemy landing craft cruised into Temryuk Bay. The German security forces were on guard! Artillery fired on the Soviet ships, which had to sail bach out to the open sea. The Soviets launched a powerful attack against Golubitskaya. They attacked several times a day, every day. Gruppe Becker held!

On 28 September the commander of the 9th Soviet Army, Major General Grechin, assembled his commanders in Temryuk for a mccting. Grechin was dissatisfied with the previous attack against the German block near Golubitskaya. "It was a scandal", he thundered, "that the Germans concentrated in such a narrow area could not be wiped out! German losses were high, but not a single German was captured during the entire deployment!" The commanders cowered before the storming Grechin, who, after a short pause, continued: "We must now force a decision by a frontal attack on Golubitskaya and a simultaneous landing on the northern bank of the Akhtanisovsker - Liman!" Major General Grechin developed a plan from which he expected much. On 29 September at 2200 hours, while a night attack was being conducted against the German block at Golubitskaya, a Soviet penal battalion waded the Akhtanisovsker - Liman and penetrated two kilometers behind the German front. Another group of 70 men crossed to the northern bank of the Liman further to the west in boats. The Russians were discovered and the alert was given, but no countermeasures could be taken because of the darkness. By dawn the Germans initiated their countermeasures. Elements of the 666th Grenadier Regiment, a platoon from the 2/191 Stu.Gesch.Brig., as well as two platoons from the 2/86 Le.Flak-Abt., attacked the landing forces. First, the smaller enemy group southwest of Golubitskaya was to be destroyed, then the larger group south of the village.

By early morning the 2/86 Le.Flak-Abt. stood in the vicinity of the large beachhead. As it became light, the flak men realized that the enemy had worked their way up 50 meters. There was nothing else Hauptmann Bode, the battery chief, could do. He gave a short order. The engines were fired up and the self-propelled weapons rushed against the enemy in platoons. The two-centimeter guns fired on the move and hit the Soviets. At midday assault

EVACUATION OF THE KUBAN BRIDGEHEAD

SEA OF AZOV

Soviet Landings

BLACK SEA

Soviet Landings

Soviet Landings

Grossen Gotenstellung
15.9.43

0   10   20   30   40km

Wiener – Position
Bukarester –
Berliner –
Münchener –
Breslauer –
Ulmer –

Kuban
Protoka
Slawji-Kaja
REISSTR.
Kiewskoje
Krymskaja
Abins-Kaja
Neberd.-Kaja
Noworossisk
XX. Landungs-K.
Myshako
Oserejka
Siegfried
Volker-Riegel
Riegel-Gerno
Bakanski
Kr.-Med. Kaja
Anapa
Haagen
Gosta Kaja
Rüdiger Riegel
Warth. Kaja
Rhön
Temruk
Kurt.Kaja
Kurko
Golub-Kaja
Acht-Kaja
Sapor.
Wesselyj
Iljitsch
K.Chroni
Kertsch
Eltgen
K.Ta.kyl
Kossa Tusla
Kl.-Gotenkopf
Taman
Wysche-Kaja
Starot.t. Kaja
Wesselowka
Blago-Kaj.
Strait of Kertch

9.
56.
18.
98.
97.
9.
79.
107.
310.
50.
164.
137.
2.10.
949.
938.
149.

guns and elements of the 666th Grenadier Regiment joined in, then the last resistance collapsed.

On 26 September, at 0222 hours, a short fire fight occurred between German outpost boats and Soviet artillery boats in front of the southern Taman coast. After that the Soviets landed 1600 men south of Vesselovka in the early morning. They had orders to attack Vesselovka. The attack stalled in German defensive fire. During the following night German outpost boats were again in position. A naval barge made contact with a Russian boat. After that, the Soviets again landed a group and reinforced their withdrawn forces from the previous day. During the course of the day, additional battalions landed on the Bugaskaya Spit and waded through chest high water to attack the German positions near Vesselovka. Gradually, the Soviet strength increased to 8000 men. The German formations held until 29 September. At 2045 hours, the Soviets engaged Hill 36.4 with effective heavy weapons fire; artillery boats joined in from the sea. At 2200 hours four Soviet battalions penetrated the seam between the 94th Mountain Reconnaissance Battalion and the II/13 Geb.Jg.Rgt., but Hill 36.4 was held. A German counterattack failed. According to the withdrawal plan, Vesselovka was to be held until 2 October.

On the morning of 30 September the 94th Mountain Jäger Battalion narrowed the penetration area by attacking, but they were not able to throw the Soviets completely out of the German HKL. Supported by 20 tanks, which stayed out of the range of the German anti-tank guns, the Soviets held their combat island, which was to be reinforced by the deployment of reserves. An attempt to expand it with the support of tanks failed after two tanks were destroyed. Two German stuka attacks had a strong effect. After a third stuka attack, the 94th Mountain Jäger Battalion and the II/13 attacked the penetration area again without success. After committing all of their reserves, Gruppe Sixt was able to localize the Soviet penetration near Vesselovka until the German withdrawal could continue. The 17th Army had held the "Kleinen Gotenkopf" positions for a week. On the evening of 1 October the second phase of the evacuation of the Kuban bridgehead began.

First the extended middle section of the "Kleinen Gotenkopf" was evacuated. The 98th ID occupied the "Vienna Positions", the 97th Jäger Division marched even further and occupied the "Munich Positions". The previously withdrawn German artillery fired the usual wall of fire at their maximum ranges before the positions were evacuated. On the morning of 2 October the 98th ID was ready to defend in the "Vienna Positions". However, by afternoon the Soviets were already pressuring with strong forces. German radio reconnaissance intercepted a Soviet message. According to it, the Soviets were to attack with three divisions. Two stuka attacks and destructive fire from 15 concentrated batteries hit the Soviet assembly areas. For the first time the two 280 railroad guns participated on the Kerch Peninsula from Kolonka.

On 1 and 2 October bitter combat raged in the Gruppe Sixt sector. Stuka attacks held the Soviet artillery and tank concentrations in check on the Bugasska Spit. New landing attempts failed. The 4th Mountain Division knew it they must hold if the time table for the jump to Kerch was not to become unravelled. On 2 October the 98th ID was ready to defend in the "Vienna Positions". During the following night, Gruppe Sixt disengaged from the enemy. By morning of 3 October Soviet harassing fire was laid on the evacuated southern portion of the "Kleinen Gotenkopf". Gruppe Sixt, however, was already prepared to defend in the "Bucharest Positions".

After it was realized that the German positions were vacant, Soviet tanks with mounted infantry advanced toward Taman in the belief that they would catch the German troops loading onto ships there, but it turned out to be an attack into thin air! The German companies had turned to the north.

At 0800 hours eight Russian tanks rolled toward the outposts on Mount Komandantskaya; infantry forces followed. An additional 20 tanks blocked the route of the 19th Romanian ID along the coastal road. By 1400 hours the I/13 Geb.Jg.Rgt. under Major Schassner was holding in Mount Kommandantskaya. Then it withdrew to the "Bucharest Positions". The holding operation of the I/13 resulted in the fact that the Soviets could not conduct any large-scale attacks on the "Bucharest Positions" at that time. By the fall of darkness they concentrated approximately two divisions and 25 tanks in front of the western sector.

On 3 October the 98th ID was holding in the "Vienna Positions" in spite of heavy attacks from tanks and the air. The Germans successfully committed stukas and artillery.

The next maneuver took place during the night of 4 October. Elements of the 370th and the 50th ID occupied the "Berlin Positions". The remaining elements of the 50th ID occupied the weak "Pre-Berlin Positions". At the same time, Gruppe Sixt evacuated the "Bucharest" and the "Vienna Positions". The freed-up 98th ID, as well as the 19th Romanian ID, marched to load up in the Kerch Strait. The 4th Mountain Division occupied the southern sector of the "Breslau Positions" with the 13th Regiment and the Kossa Chushka Spit with the reinforced 91st Gebirgsjäger Regiment.

On 4 October the Soviets crashed against the "Pre-Berlin Positions". The grenadiers of the 50th ID held, effectively supported by elements of the 191st Assault Gun Brigade, which destroyed 12 Soviet tanks. An additional 18 tanks were destroyed by German artillery. During a Soviet air attack on the ferries in the Kerch Strait five aircraft were shot down by German fighters and another four by barge anti-aircraft guns. The enemy air attacks caused no damage because the landing craft were hidden from the enemy by smoke-screens.

On 4 October forces of Gruppe Becker were still located near Golubitskaya. After all of the attacks against the German blocking positions were repulsed, Major General Grechin grasped at his old plan again. At 2300 hours a Soviet landing group landed unnoticed northwest of Golubitskaya. At the same time a battlegroup of 550 men waded the Akhtanisovsker Liman and established itself southwest of Golubitskaya. During the same hour the Russians launched a frontal attack against the German defense. A confusing situation! The frontal penetration was eliminated in a counterattack. The beachhead on the Sea of Azov was pierced by elements of the 667th Grenadier Regiment, and the enemy group located southwest of Golubitskaya was defeated by the 2/191 Stu.Gesch.Brig. and III/666.

After this costly 4th of October Soviet attacks decreased noticeably. During the night of 5 October the German companies withdrew from the "Pre-Berlin" to the "Berlin Positions".

Up to this point in time the Soviet leadership had seen all of their plans wrecked. On 5 October a Soviet destroyer group under Captain 2nd Rank Negoda was committed against the German evacuation transports on the Crimean coast. The destroyers "Besposadniy" and "Sposobniy" ran into elements of the 1st Motor-Torpedo Boat Flotilla while deploying to Feodosia and conducted an inconclusive engagement. The flotilla leader "Kharkov" fired on Yalta and Alusta during the night. On the morning of 6 October 1943 the meeting of these formations was discovered by German air reconnaissance; Ju 87s from the 77th Stuka Squadron attacked. The "Kharkov" was hit during the first attack and was towed away by the "Sposobniy". The second attack hit all three ships. The "Sposobniy" then tried towing both of the other ships. The third attack sank the "Besposadniy" and "Kharkov". The "Sposobniy" was sent to the bottom of the sea during the fourth attack. After the loss of these three warships, Stalin forbid the commitment of large warships without his permission.

During the night of 6 October, the hotly contested positions near Golubitskaya were evacuated. The combat diary of the 17th Army noted: "...The 667th Grenadier Regiment and the III/666 Gren.Rgt. of the 370th ID have repulsed the attacks of three Soviet divisions at a decisively important position for ten days..."

And still more happened on that night! A Soviet landing group occupied the long island of Kossa Tusla in the Kerch Strait. On 5 October the I/282 Gren.Rgt. (98th ID) relieved the II/170 Gren.Rgt. (73rd ID) on the 7.6 kilometer long, 0.5 kilometer wide island, which was only 2 meters above sea level. The security forces noticed the landing, but they could not take any defensive measures due to the darkness. On 6 October the weak I/282 (Hauptmann Vockentanz) attacked the landing group without success. Even with the help of the old island defenders, the II/170 (Major Kremnitz), they could not throw the Soviets off. The commitment of the two German battalions did, however, prevent the threat to the crossing traffic from becoming serious.

On the evening of 6 October General Konrad transferred his command post to Ilich. At the same time he issued the order to evacuate the "Berlin Positions"; Gruppe Becker passed through the "Munich Positions", which were occupied by the 97th Jäger Division, to load directly at Ilich. An enemy group that landed on the coast was defeated by the rearguard of Gruppe Becker. The 370th ID and elements of the 50th ID crossed to Kerch on 7 October.

The 97th Jäger Division and the 4th Mountain Division were the only units involved in the final phase of the evacuation. Both divisions came under the command of Generalleutnant Müller (commander of the 97th Jäger Division). In the meantime, all of the artillery had crossed and taken positions with the long-ranged batteries on the Kerch Peninsula.

On 7 October three Soviet divisions attacked the "Munich Positions" with the support of 40 tanks. German stukas attacked the tanks, the artillery joined in and the enemy was repulsed with bloody losses.

On the morning of 8 October Soviet artillery again fired on the "Munich Positions", but they were already empty. During the night Gruppe Müller had already occupied the "Breslau Positions". At 1000 hours, 30 tanks with mounted infantry again attacked, but they didn't get far. They ran into the fire of 40 heavy rocket launchers near Zaporozhe, and 20 tanks were disabled. South of Zaporozhe enemy concentrations were blasted by stukas, rockets and artillery.

In the afternoon of 8 October General Konrad and Generalleutnant Müller established their command posts in Ilich. At 1800 hours the 13th Gebirgsjäger Regiment evacuated the southern portion of the "Breslau Positions". At the same time the northern portion was also being evacuated, and the defenders moved to the crossing at Ilich.

The landing positions were protected by the "Ulmer Positions" in front of Ilich and the "Stuttgart Positions" on Kossa Chushka. The defenders of this last line in the "Ulmer Positions" were provided by the 560th Special Purpose Battalion and the 97th Reconnaissance Battalion with ten mountain guns. The 13th Gebirgsjäger Regiment awaited crossing in the "Stuttgart Positions".

By the fall of darkness the first battalion withdrew and, at 1930 hours, was loaded onto two naval ferries and transferred to the northern docks at Kerch. German artillery created an impenetrable wall of fire. Soviet night bombers were committed; the Russian artillery blindly covered the terrain with fire, but the loading continued. Finally, Oberstleutnant Buchner's 13th Gebirgsjäger Regiment loaded onto the ferries.

At midnight the loading ramps were blown. On 9 October at 0100 hours the last boat drew away. The last formations arrived in Kerch at 0200 hours. On 9 October 1943 the 17th Army closed the report on the evacuation of the Kuban bridgehead:

Secret!
17th Army Command
Abt. Ia Nr. 14 674/43 geh   A Command Post, 9/10/1943
Morning Report 9/10/1943«)0»

1. The army has completed crossing the Kerch Strait. The last elements of the army, the 97th Jäger Division and the 13th and 91st Gebirgsjäger Regiments of the 4th Mountain Division, broke contact with the enemy, covered by concentrated fire from the heavy batteries established on the northeast of the Kerch and the destructive effectiveness of the heavy rocket launchers. With them crossed the commander of the 17th Army, General der

Pioniere Jänecke, and the commander of the XXXXIX Mountain Corps, General der Gebirgstruppen Konrad. The defenders of the island Kossa Tusla were also transferred to the Kerch coast.

Therefore, the evacuation of the Kuban bridgehead was completed as planned. Until the last company crossed, the army was able to insure that not one weapon was lost to the enemy that had not been damaged in action.

The majority of the craft used for the crossing of the Kerch Strait sailed off to the south into the Black Sea, unnoticed by the enemy, and are on their way to Sevastopol.

2. (Again treats the battles in the Kuban bridgehead.)

3. Evacuation of the Kuban bridgehead:

The original time frame delegated to the evacuation of the Kuban bridgehead of 8 to 10 weeks was shortened to 4 weeks due to the situation on other fronts and the necessity of quickly freeing-up forces for duty elsewhere. In spite of this, the majority of the winter equipment was successfully transported from the Kuban bridgehead to the Crimea, as was the majority of the population that was capable of working. All of the weapons, ammunition, trucks and equipment were also brought out. Equipment destroyed was limited mainly to railroad construction material, coal and raw materials. The roles played by the commander of the 700 Engineer Regiment Staff, Oberst Betz, in the Kuban bridgehead and the Kerch Strait Commander insured the smooth crossing. Transport craft of the Caucasus Seeko. and the 770th Engineer Landing Regiment, under the leadership of Oberst Henke, secured the crossing of the entire 17th Army with all of its men, vehicles, trucks and equipment over the Kerch Strait, in spite of strong enemy air attacks and, during the final phase, artillery fire from land.

During the course of the evacuation of the Kuban bridgehead the following was transported over the Kerch Strait:

177,355 German soldiers
50,139 Allied soldiers
28,486 Hiwis and workers
27,456 Evacuees, not including the 60,000 civilians that had already been withdrawn between February and August.
72,899 horses
27,741 towed vehicles
21,230 trucks
1,815 guns
115,477 tons of supplies, including:
27,670 tons of ammunition
29,500 tons of rations
13,940 tons of feed
74 assault guns and tanks

Destroyed were only:
82,300 tons, including:
    53,200 tons of railroad construction equipment
    10,150 tons of coal
    16,500 tons of feed

Flown out:
15,661 soldiers
1,153.8 tons of equipment.

The entire inventory of the field railroad was withdrawn with 109 locomotives and 1150 wagons, in addition to much of the construction equipment. 253 kilometers of track and 774 meters of railroad bridge were blown up. Anything the enemy could have used was destroyed.

18 land bridges with a total length of 1742 meters were constructed for the displacement on the western coast of the northern portion of the Taman Peninsula.

        For the Commander
        The Chief of Staff
        signed von Xylander
        9/10/1943 0730 hours

From 8 to 10 October 1943 240 craft withdrew the Kuban bridgehead in four large convoys from the Kerch Strait to Sevastopol. Engineer Assault Boat 229 was sunk by enemy air attack, Barge F-474 was sunk by a submarine attack.

Thus, the two year battle came to an end. It was initiated in 1942 by the drive for oil, so important for the war effort. Sufficient oil supplies had import of the first order during the Second World War. From the beginning to the end, land, sea and air forces relied on oil. The oil fields of the Caucasus would have supplied the German war effort with these necessary stocks.

At the beginning of the attack no one realized what dramatic course this campaign would take. It was a bitter struggle for military positions around passes, hills, mountains and harbors.

In spite of super-human effort and great sacrifice the objective was not achieved. The German war effort would have to make do without the Caucasus oil.

AFTERWORD AND THANKS TO CONTRIBUTORS

This work could not have been written without the help of a large group of former Caucasus fighters from all branches of the Wehrmacht, from the private soldiers to the Generals.

The author has been preoccupied with the Caucasus campaign for years, not only because he had participated in it, but also because he was fascinated with the cooperation of all of the branches of the Wehrmacht and the actions and reactions demonstrated by the German and Russian sides.

The unit designations used, that is the redesignation of infantry regiments in the infantry divisions and rifle regiments of the panzergrenadier and panzer divisions in October 1942 into grenadier and panzergrenadier regiments, were used throughout for simplicity's sake. This was also done to make a clear separation between the German and Soviet rifle regiments. This was also true for the designation jäger regiment for the army, jäger and mountain corps.

The author thanks the following men for their assistance and for providing maps, examples and excerpts: Oberst (Ret.) Auer, Oberstleutnant (Ret.) Brux, Generalleutnant (Ret.) Breith, Oberstleutnant (Ret.) Czech, the former SS Standartenführer Engelhardt, the former SS Hauptstrurmführer Ertel, Oberst (Ret.) Dr. Emsmann, Oberst (Ret.) Gollob, Oberst (Ret.) von Hake, W. Haupt, K. Joos, Dr. D. Jung, Generalmajor (Ret.) Dr. Kühn, Generalmajor (Ret.) von Liebenstein, the former SS Obersturmbannführer Lohmann, General der Gebirgstruppen (Ret.) Lanz, Oberst Lang, Oberstleutnant (Ret.) Musculus, the former SS Standartenführer Mühlenkamp, F. Memminger, J. Röge, Generalmajor (Ret.) Steets, J. Stigler, Generalleutnant J. Steinhoff, E. Stichnoth, M. Stöckle, H. Thraen, W. Weinmann, Oberst (Ret.) Dr. Westerburg, E. Werner, Oberst (Ret.) Zimmermann, D. Ziemssen, H. Flügel, R. Stock.

Special thanks go to the military History Research Department and the Bundesarchiv/Militärarchiv in Freiburg and the Bibliothek fuer Zeitgeschichte in Stuttgart and the Truppenkameradschaften for their assistance.

May this book clear up a dark portion of history for the young and, therefore, provide for a better future.

Gummersbach-Erbland, May 1970   Wilhelm Tieke